# CITIES
## and Suburbs
### an introduction to urban sociology

**Harvey M. Choldin**
Professor of Sociology
University of Illinois, Urbana-Champaign

**McGraw-Hill Book Company**
New York  St. Louis  San Francisco
Auckland  Bogotá  Hamburg
London  Madrid  Mexico  Montreal  New Delhi  Panama  Paris  São Paulo
Singapore  Sydney  Tokyo  Toronto

*To my parents, Dave and Hannah Choldin,
city people and good neighbors*

This book was set in Goudy Old Style by University Graphics, Inc. (ECU).
The editors were Eric M. Munson, Christina Mediate, David V. Serbun, and James R. Belser;
the designer was Jo Jones;
the production supervisor was Marietta Breitwieser.
The photo editor was Inge King.
The drawings were done by Wellington Studios Ltd.
Halliday Lithograph Corporation was printer and binder.

Cover Photograph Credit © by
J. Blank/H. Armstrong Roberts, Inc.

**CITIES AND SUBURBS: An Introduction to Urban Sociology**

Copyright © 1985 by McGraw-Hill, Inc. All rights reserved. Printed in the United States of America. Except as permitted under the United States Copyright Act of 1976, no part of this publication may be reproduced or distributed in any form or by any means, or stored in a data base or retrieval system, without the prior written permission of the publisher.
234567890HALHAL89

See Acknowledgments on page 495.
Copyrights included on this page by reference.

ISBN 0-07-010816-1

**Library of Congress Cataloging in Publication Data**

Choldin, Harvey M.
    Cities and suburbs.

    Includes bibliographies and indexes.
    1. Sociology, Urban.  I. Title.
HT151.C557   1985      307.7'6      83-25531
ISBN 0-07-010816-1

# CONTENTS

| | |
|---|---|
| *Preface* | vii |
| **CHAPTER 1  THE BEGINNINGS OF URBAN SOCIOLOGY** | 1 |
| The First Urban Researchers | 2 |
| The "Chicago School" | 13 |
| Emerging Theories | 24 |
| Summary | 29 |
| References | 30 |
| **CHAPTER 2  AN OVERVIEW OF THE FIELD** | 35 |
| Introduction | 36 |
| Human Ecology | 37 |
| Two Bridging Theories | 44 |
| Social Psychology | 53 |
| Summary | 58 |
| References | 59 |
| **CHAPTER 3  FROM NOMADISM TO THE MEDIEVAL TOWN** | 65 |
| Introduction | 66 |
| The Agricultural Revolution | 67 |
| The Urban Revolution | 73 |
| Cities of Classical Antiquity | 80 |

CONTENTS

| | |
|---|---|
| Medieval Towns | 83 |
| Summary | 90 |
| References | 93 |

**CHAPTER 4  THE RISE OF THE INDUSTRIAL CITY** — 97

| | |
|---|---|
| Beginnings of the Industrial Town | 99 |
| Manchester, England: The Prime Case | 105 |
| The Mature Industrial City: 1850–1920 | 112 |
| Community Problems of the New Cities | 121 |
| Summary | 130 |
| References | 133 |

**CHAPTER 5  UNITED STATES URBANIZATION** — 135

| | |
|---|---|
| The Census | 136 |
| Population Explosion | 145 |
| Urbanization | 150 |
| Systems and Types of Cities | 158 |
| Summary | 165 |
| References | 166 |

**CHAPTER 6  URBAN ECOLOGY: SPATIAL DIFFERENTIATION** — 169

| | |
|---|---|
| Principles of Differentiation | 171 |
| Nuclei and Districts in the Mature Industrial City | 177 |
| Nuclei and Districts in the Metropolis | 181 |
| Summary | 186 |
| References | 187 |

**CHAPTER 7  RESIDENTIAL DIFFERENTIATION** — 191

| | |
|---|---|
| Social Geography | 192 |
| Measuring Social Differentiation | 195 |
| Social Area Analysis and Factorial Ecology | 199 |
| Segregation Patterns | 206 |
| Differentiation Theories | 220 |
| Summary | 224 |
| References | 225 |

**CHAPTER 8  BLACKS IN THE METROPOLIS** — 229

| | |
|---|---|
| Introduction | 230 |
| Ghettos | 235 |
| Segregation Patterns | 244 |

| | |
|---|---|
| Changing Residential Patterns | 246 |
| Internal Differentiation of the Ghetto | 257 |
| Recent Developments | 260 |
| Summary | 265 |
| References | 266 |

## CHAPTER 9   THE LOCAL COMMUNITY — 271

| | |
|---|---|
| The Demise of "Perfect Little Neighborhoods" | 272 |
| The Community of Limited Liability | 273 |
| Use and Participation | 274 |
| Types of Neighborhoods | 287 |
| Summary | 295 |
| References | 296 |

## CHAPTER 10   COMMUNITY LIFE: RECENT CONCERNS — 301

| | |
|---|---|
| Public Opinion about Community Life | 302 |
| Two Critiques of the Metropolis | 316 |
| Summary | 326 |
| References | 326 |

## CHAPTER 11   NEIGHBORHOOD CHANGE — 331

| | |
|---|---|
| Stages of Neighborhood Growth and Decline | 332 |
| Residential Succession | 337 |
| Abandonment and Arson | 341 |
| "Gentrification" | 343 |
| Macrodevelopments | 347 |
| Summary | 349 |
| References | 350 |

## CHAPTER 12   SUBURBANIZATION AND THE NEW METROPOLITAN FORM — 353

| | |
|---|---|
| Introduction | 354 |
| History of Suburban Growth | 356 |
| People and Houses | 359 |
| The Suburbanization of Nearly Everything | 363 |
| Differentiation among Suburbs | 369 |
| Change and Stability | 371 |
| Emerging Metropolitan Structure | 373 |
| Summary | 382 |

# CONTENTS

**CHAPTER 13  SUBURBAN SOCIAL LIFE**  385
  The Suburban Myth  386
  First-Generation Sociological Studies  388
  Recent Suburban Research  393
  New Problems  400
  Summary  403
  References for Chapters 12 and 13  404

**CHAPTER 14  SOCIAL NETWORKS**  409
  Rediscovering Urban Social Life  410
  Two Case Studies  411
  Basic Concepts  416
  The Small-World Project  422
  Functions of Social Networks  424
  Summary  428
  References  429

**CHAPTER 15  SLUMS: CONDITIONS AND PROGRAMS**  431
  Basic Concepts  432
  The Residents' Point of View  435
  Immoral Landscapes  445
  Societal Responses  448
  Failures of Public Housing: Two Studies  454
  Beyond Public Housing  461
  Summary  464
  References  465

**CHAPTER 16  THIRD-WORLD URBANIZATION**  469
  Introduction  470
  Urbanization  472
  The Place of Cities in Rural Societies  478
  Dual Cities  480
  Urban Structure  487
  Summary  492
  References  494

*Acknowledgments*  495
*Indexes*  496
  *Name Index*  496
  *Subject Index*  499

# PREFACE

The scope of urban sociology in this textbook was determined by my view of what has concerned sociologists of the metropolis for a century. They have asked what we now call ecological questions, such as "How and why does the metropolis grow?" "What is its internal structure?" "To what extent and in what patterns are different subpopulations segregated?" At a more personal level, sociologists since Toennies (1887) and Simmel (1903/1957) have asked what effects the city has upon its residents' social relationships and psychological state. Urban sociologists also have long considered the qualities of subcommunities, such as racial and ethnic enclaves as well as poor, middle class, and wealthy districts, in cities and suburbs. Likewise, they have asked how such subcommunities change over time.

This view of the history of urban sociology has shaped my conception of the field and—consequently—it determines certain things which this textbook is not. It is not a course in introductory sociology with extensive discussion of each topic as it relates to the city. Thus, while family life and social stratification enter into certain areas in the book, neither has a special chapter of its own because neither has been isolated over the decades for major discussion by urban sociologists. On the other hand, neighborhoods and ghettos do receive extensive treatment. *Cities and Suburbs* is also not an urban-focused textbook for the social problems course. While the text should help the readers to understand several major problems, like racial segregation and slums, they are treated in the context of urban sociology. The book presupposes an exposure to introductory sociology and builds upon the concepts, such as primary group, bureaucracy, and stratification, which are usually taught in that course.

In recent decades urban sociologists have been divided into two camps, macro-ecological and microecological. There are now textbooks written for the students

vii

# PREFACE

of each camp. I am convinced that urban communities are better understood through a combination of perspectives and that students should not be denied one or the other point of view in the undergraduate urban sociology course. The student should study ecological aspects of the metropolis, its overall structure, segregation patterns, suburbanization processes, and the like. But the student also needs the microscopic perspective with its emphasis on neighborhoods, social relations, and networks in order to understand today's communities. It is still possible to introduce this material in a single semester and with a single textbook, as indicated by this volume.

Furthermore, the student should be helped to recognize connections between macro and micro phenomena. For example, by studying Firey's concepts of sentiment and symbolism at the local level as well as Suttles's discussion of the defensive community—both presented at the microlevel—students will be helped to understand processes which impact upon the macroscopic segregation patterns of cities and suburbs.

## ORGANIZATION OF SUBJECTS

The organization of chapters in *Cities and Suburbs* moves from past to present, although by far the greatest portion of the volume refers to the contemporary scene. Chapters 1 and 2 present the origins of urban sociology and its classical theoretical concerns. Chapters 3 through 5 are historical also, covering the origins of cities in the ancient near east and moving rapidly into the urbanization of the United States and the advent of the industrial city. By and large, Chapters 3 through 5 are written from an ecological perspective and emphasize social organization because the historical materials are not informative about urban social psychology. By Chapter 4 the student is reading about modern times, starting with the urban aspects of New England's industrial revolution, and then progressing to the type of American city which I have called "the mature industrial city," the predecessor of the contemporary metropolis.

The bulk of the book, in Chapters 6 through 15, is about the form and process of the contemporary metropolitan community. Chapters 6 and 8 form a group, referring to differentiation among the city's subareas. Chapter 6 introduces the concept of differentiation, functional and spatial. Chapter 7 deals exclusively with residential differentiation, including social-area analysis, factorial ecology, and the measurement of segregation. Chapter 8, about black ghettos, appears at this point to show differentiation and segregation in the extreme case.

The next group of chapters, 9 through 11, deals with local communities, or neighborhoods. Chapter 9 discusses the concept of neighborhood and summarizes a number of neighborhood studies. Chapter 10 deals with four current issues regarding neighborhood life: community satisfaction and dissatisfaction; fear of crime; and feminist and Marxist critiques of the metropolitan community. Chapter 11 presents processes of neighborhood change, particularly the neighborhood life

# PREFACE

cycle. This chapter also covers topical material on generification, abandonment, and arson.

The book's last section, comprising Chapters 12 through 14, deals in different ways with suburbs, although they have been mentioned at earlier points in the book. Chapter 12 presents the process of suburbanization, showing how it has transformed the metropolis. Shifting from macro to micro perspective, Chapter 13 deals essentially with suburbanism as a way of life, discussing the myth of suburbia and presenting the results of a number of suburban studies. Then, Chapter 14 attempts to resolve some problems in understanding city and suburban social life by means of social-network concepts which, incidentally, have been neglected in previous urban sociology textbooks.

Finally, Chapter 16 offers a brief overview of some major topics in the study of cities in the third world, indicating the universality of the process of urbanization.

Instructors may wish to assign two chapters at different points in the course. They may prefer to teach about the black ghetto (Chapter 8) after presenting the more conventional neighborhood material in Chapters 9 through 11. They may also choose to emphasize the idea of social networks (Chapter 16) at an earlier point in the course.

## ACKNOWLEDGMENTS

I am grateful to many individuals who helped me with this project. Colleagues at several universities served as readers and critics. Professor Ralph Thomlinson was extremely helpful, commenting on outlines and drafts. Likewise, Professors Daniel Koenigsberg, William Yancey, and Thomas Guterbock offered criticism and encouragement. Other helpful readers included Professors Alan Booth, Christen Jonassen, Ronald J. McAllister, Brian J. O'Connell, David Popenoe, and Aubrey Wendling. Thanks to all of them. Professor Leslie Moch helped me study urban history and Barry Wellman kindly advised on my plans for a chapter on networks.

I received a great deal of help from the University of Illinois's outstanding librarians, particularly from John Littlewood of the Documents Library. And my department's long-suffering typists, Margaret Quinn, Sheila Welch, and Bonnie Anderson, provided cheerful service through many chapters and drafts. I am grateful also to helpful colleagues and staff at the University of Illinois's Center for Advanced Study, where I began this book, and at Georgetown University's Center for Population Research, where I finished it.

Finally, a word of thanks to my family: Marianna, Kate, and Mary. While I don't think they particularly suffered through the writing process, like the families in so many prefaces, they supported me in many ways by not doubting that I had a book in me and by making life worth living.

Harvey M. Choldin

# CHAPTER · 1

# The Beginnings of Urban Sociology

**Chapter Outline**

THE FIRST URBAN RESEARCHERS
- Jacob Riis
- Adna F. Weber
- W. E. B. DuBois
- Charles Booth
- The Pittsburgh Survey

THE "CHICAGO SCHOOL"
- Robert Park and His Colleagues
- The Gold Coast and the Slum
- Juvenile Delinquency and Urban Areas

EMERGING THEORIES
- Gemeinschaft and Gesellschaft
- The Folk-Urban Continuum

SUMMARY

# CHAPTER · 1

The nineteenth century was a time of fabulous urban growth, with dozens of mushrooming cities. Old ones like New York and Philadelphia attracted millions of people, and newcomers like Chicago went from nothing to a million within a single life span. All sorts of new and transformed social institutions accompanied this growth. Factories, newspapers, and political parties grew bigger and became more influential; corporations arrived on the scene with a bang; and slums and tenements grew as well. Powerful technological changes preceded and accompanied this urban growth—inventions like the railroad, steam engine, telegraph, and trolley diffused rapidly across the urban landscape. The metropolis became a large, troubling, and puzzling feature on the social scene.

The emerging urban social situation inspired men and women to try to understand the new community and to ameliorate the living conditions of poor people in the cities. Two kinds of urban analysts began to study the city in the last decades of the nineteenth century. The first type, the reformers, included muckraking journalists and members of the new profession of social work who collected information in an attempt to solve problems right away. The second type included theorists and researchers who were more directly committed to studying the situation and less committed to solving the immediate problems. Both kinds of urban analysts made contributions which have lasting value for contemporary urban sociology.

Divided into three sections, this chapter opens on a historical viewpoint, summarizing four efforts in urban social research before the beginnings of contemporary urban sociology. With one exception, reformers conducted these early studies and collected valuable information about social life in the late-nineteenth-century and early-twentieth-century metropolis.

The second section summarizes the work of the Chicago school of urban sociology in the 1920s. We take this as the starting point of a more scientific approach to the subject. The kinds of questions the Chicago researchers asked about social life in the metropolis and the structure of this new sort of community are still being pursued by urban sociologists. The Chicago sociologists also introduced particular research methods which are being used and modified today.

The third section introduces two early theories in urban sociology, one from Germany and one from the United States. Both theories attempt to explain the differences between types of communities, with an eye toward understanding distinctive aspects about the city.

## THE FIRST URBAN RESEARCHERS

In order to understand the social life of the metropolis, some good, accurate information had to be collected. The first ones to gather the data were not sociologists, who, in the nineteenth century, were really social philosophers. The investigators who went into the community to collect firsthand information about the social

# THE BEGINNINGS OF URBAN SOCIOLOGY

situation were more likely to have been reformers. These reformer-researchers did their "fieldwork" in the great cities of England and the United States in the last decades of the nineteenth century and sought to improve the living conditions in the metropolis, particularly the situation of workers, immigrants, and their families, people living in a state of poverty. In the United States the period in which they worked has come to be known as the "progressive era" or the "age of reform" (Hofstadter, 1955), a time of numerous movements for social change, including muckraking journalism, exemplified by such urban books as Lincoln Steffens's *The Shame of the Cities* (1904) and Upton Sinclair's *The Jungle* (1906). The urban settlement house, which marked the beginning of the profession of social work, was developed at this time, as were several municipal regulations, such as building codes and zoning, which contributed to the birth of city planning as a profession. In this context, various individuals began to collect and publish information about social conditions in cities.

## Jacob Riis

One New York journalist who drew attention to slum conditions was Jacob Riis (Cordasco, 1968). Riis, an immigrant himself, wrote short vignettes on the ugly conditions in the slums and tenements where poor immigrant workers and their families lived. He published his newspaper columns in a series of books with titles such as *How the Other Half Lives* (1890); because he was a photographer as well as a writer, the books contain grim snapshots of barefoot children sleeping on the streets and large families living in single rooms. Basically an activist, Riis advocated new laws governing housing conditions and new kinds of apartment buildings built to higher standards, but he left vivid descriptive data on the urban life of his time to present-day sociologists. Thus Riis began the tradition of using descriptive fieldwork to gather information about social conditions and life in cities.

Note the tone of moral outrage in this example of Riis's writings about Italian immigrants:

> I have in mind one Italian "flat" among many, a half underground hole in a South Fifth Avenue yard, reached by odd passageways through a tumbledown tenement that was always full of bad smells and scooting rats. Across the foul and slippery yard, down three steps made of charred timbers from some worse wreck, was this "flat," where five children slept with their elders. How many of those there were I never knew. There were three big family beds, and they nearly filled the room, leaving only patches of the mud floor visible. The walls were absolutely black with age and smoke. The plaster had fallen off in patches and there was green mold on the ceiling. And yet, with it all, with the swarm of squirming youngsters that were as black as the floor they rolled upon, there was evidence of a desperate, if hopeless, groping after order, even neatness. The beds were made up as nicely as they could be with the old quilts and pieces of carpet that served for covering. (Riis, cited in Cordasco, 1968, pp. 134-135)

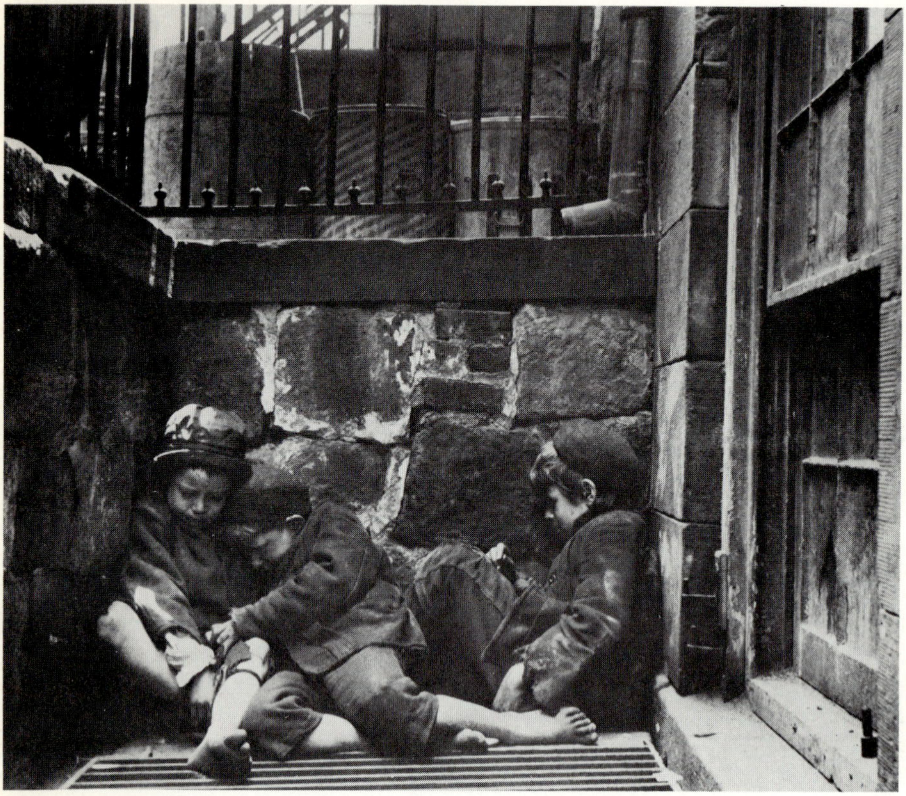

# CHAPTER · 1

The nineteenth-century city engendered a number of unsolved community problems, one of which was homeless children, or "street Arabs" as they were called at the time, shown here in a photograph by Jacob Riis. (Museum of the City of New York)

## Adna F. Weber

A contemporary of Riis in New York City was asking other urban questions and collecting information by radically different means. Adna F. Weber noted,[1] in a doctoral dissertation, that in Europe and the United States cities had grown rapidly during the nineteenth century: "The tendency towards concentration or agglomeration {of population} is all but universal in the Western world" (1899, p. 1). Using the published censuses of the United States and other countries, he documented the growth of cities and the "agglomeration of population." He looked for historical trends and compared countries and regions. Table 1-1 shows a typical product of

---

[1] Do not confuse A. F. Weber with Max Weber, the noted German sociologist-historian, whose work will be cited in Chapter 3.

# THE BEGINNINGS OF URBAN SOCIOLOGY

**TABLE 1-1**
**Proportions Living in Cities of 10,000+, by States and Territories, 1890***

| Area | Percentage | Area | Percentage |
|---|---|---|---|
| **Class I: More than One-Half Urban** | | **Class III: More than one-tenth Urban** | |
| 1. District of Columbia | 88.10 | 26. Maine | 17.16 |
| 2. Massachusetts | 65.88 | 27. Indiana | 16.68 |
| 3. Rhode Island | 57.91 | 28. Kentucky | 13.87 |
| 4. New York | 57.66 | 29. Iowa | 13.62 |
| 5. New Jersey | 50.91 | 30. Virginia | 12.85 |
| | | 31. Florida | 12.02 |
| **Class II: More than One-Quarter Urban** | | 32. Tennessee | 10.65 |
| 6. Maryland | 43.87 | **Class IV: Less than One-Tenth Urban** | |
| 7. Connecticut | 41.86 | | |
| 8. California | 40.98 | 33. Georgia | 9.91 |
| 9. Pennsylvania | 39.10 | 34. Kansas | 9.73 |
| 10. Illinois | 38.08 | 35. Texas | 9.71 |
| 11. Colorado | 37.07 | 36. Vermont | 7.93 |
| 12. Delaware | 36.46 | 37. South Carolina | 6.11 |
| 13. Ohio | 30.15 | 38. West Virginia | 5.85 |
| 14. Utah | 28.73 | 39. Alabama | 5.23 |
| 15. Washington | 28.27 | 40. North Carolina | 3.37 |
| 16. Minnesota | 27.69 | 41. Arkansas | 3.30 |
| — UNITED STATES | 27.59 | 42. South Dakota | 3.10 |
| 17. Missouri | 25.59 | 43. Mississippi | 2.64 |
| **Class III: More than One-Tenth Urban** | | **Class V: No Urban Population** | |
| 18. New Hampshire | 24.76 | 44. North Dakota. | |
| 19. Michigan | 23.90 | 45. Idaho. | |
| 20. Louisiana | 23.65 | 46. Nevada. | |
| 21. Wisconsin | 22.46 | 47. Arizona. | |
| 22. Nebraska | 22.15 | 48. New Mexico. | |
| 23. Wyoming | 19.26 | 49. Oklahoma. | |
| 24. Montana | 18.58 | 50. Indian Territory. | |
| 25. Oregon | 18.14 | | |

*Note the enormous range in levels of urbanization, from highly urbanized in the northeastern region to completely unurbanized in new rural states like the Dakotas and Oklahoma.
Source: Weber, 1899, pp. 31–32.

his analyses. Beyond describing the demographic situation and trends in the United States, he also asked what the causes and effects were of these urban developments.

Adna Weber did an impressive job of assembling and analyzing demographic information, reporting his results in a book entitled *The Growth of Cities in the Nineteenth Century: A Study in Statistics* (1899). Evidently, he was concerned that the United States was considered an undeveloped region of wide-open spaces, while

Europe was considered to be more civilized. He concluded his first section by showing that even though the United States appeared less urbanized than European countries, many states were really larger than small European nations and some states were as urban as the European nations. Attempting to account for the growth of cities, he considered migration and natural increase (the difference between the numbers of deaths and births). He discovered that for the first time in history, nineteenth-century cities had an excess of births over deaths, yielding more urban growth from natural increase than from internal migration from rural districts (1899). He also contributed to the understanding of migration processes, writing, "Migration is predominantly a short-distance movement, but the centers of attraction are the great cities.... The larger the city, the greater its power of attraction (i.e., the larger its proportion of outsiders, and the more distant the counties or districts which contribute to it)" (p. 283). Adna Weber also analyzed the composition of urban populations, arriving at some interesting generalizations. For example, he reported that cities tended to have female majorities and that, counter to common opinion, the proportion of foreign-born people was decreasing in U.S. cities in the second half of the nineteenth century, despite the large influx of immigrants. Most of the big cities hit their maximum proportion of foreign-born residents in 1860 (between 25 and 50 percent), and then the proportion began to decrease. The children of foreign-born people, of course, added to the native-born population. In addition to looking at these purely demographic concerns, Adna Weber also considered related processes.

He discussed the relationship between the economy and the urban community, stating that certain economic principles bring industry to the city—the availability of cheap labor, skilled labor, and local markets. He noted that technological and political conditions affect the relationship between city and countryside: "The cities have torn down their fortifications, which separated them from the open country; while the railways, the newspaper press, freedom of migration and settlement, etc., cause the spread of the ideas originating in the cities" (1899, p. 7).

Finally, Adna Weber consistently defended city people against their negative public image of being weaker, less productive, and more immoral than country people, and he always assembled numerical data on the subject. Typical of his conclusions is the following:

> It is commonly held that city life produces dwarfed, stunted men and degenerates; fortunately, statistics of physical infirmities exist which dispel such fears about the effects of city life.... Now recent statistics show that these infirmities (congenital blindness, deaf-mutism, imbecility or feeble-mindedness) are rather more prevalent in rural districts and small towns than in the cities, while insanity, which is rather a nervous than a bodily failing, prevails chiefly in the cities. (1899, p. 392)

Adna Weber, then, made several notable contributions to empirical urban analysis: the careful use of demographic information, from census and vital statistics; international comparative studies; analysis of changes over time; and the connections between economic, technological, and demographic processes. The connection between the aggregate statistics of urban populations and the way of life in cities obviously was no small contribution.

## W. E. B. DuBois

Another remarkable American urban study was published in 1899, *The Philadelphia Negro*, by W. E. B. DuBois. Himself the descendant of a slave, DuBois was the first black to earn a Ph.D. from Harvard University (in 1895). Soon thereafter he was appointed to the University of Pennsylvania to conduct a study of the condition of blacks in one district of the city. Some of the city's leaders defined the situation as a serious community problem and saw a need for additional information. DuBois was committed to developing a scientific approach to social problems, and his "inquiry ... sought to ascertain something of the geographical distribution of this race, their occupations and daily life, their homes, their organizations, and above all, their relation to their million white fellow-citizens" (1899, p. 1). He conducted a thorough house-to-house survey in "the central district of Negro settlement" (p. 2), supplemented by somewhat less systematic studies of other residential areas to see whether the situation was the same wherever blacks lived in the city.

Now looked upon as a sociological classic, *The Philadelphia Negro* can be considered a model for later community studies. This highly readable volume includes quantified information in maps, graphs, and tables, in addition to a good deal of description. The book begins with DuBois's summary of the blacks' problems and follows with the history of the blacks in Philadelphia. Then DuBois presents several chapters of sociodemographic information on age and sex composition, migration, literacy, occupations, and health, The next section covers social structure—family life, churches, and voluntary associations—and is followed by two chapters on social problems—"the Negro criminal" and "pauperism and alcoholism." DuBois's final chapters deal with race relations, suffrage, and city politics, plus his interpretation of the facts.

Noting that the rest of the city tended to see the blacks as a homogeneous mass, DuBois (1899) reported that they were highly differentiated into four social classes with different life styles and problems:

> The middle classes: "Families of undoubted respectability earning sufficient income to live well; not engaged in menial service" (pp. 310-311). Family living in a well-kept home, children in school.
> The respectable working-class: "In comfortable circumstances, with a good home, and having steady remunerative work. The younger children in school" (pp. 310-311).
> The poor: "Persons not earning enough to keep them at all times above want; honest, although not always energetic or thrifty, and with no touch of gross immorality or crime" (pp. 310-311).

The vicious and criminal classes: "The lowest class of criminals, prostitutes and loafers; the 'submerged tenth'" (pp. 310–311).

DuBois's research is thoroughly sociological and is well-grounded in the history of the black experience in America and its effects on culture and personality. Like urban researchers decades later, DuBois looked at geographical patterns and demographic composition as well as at the blacks' occupational distribution in order to discover their place in the city's social structure. By documenting the patterns of institutional development in the form of churches, schools, and clubs, he set the pattern for later ghetto studies. Unlike more "modern" social researchers, though, DuBois did not hesitate to conclude his report with a set of prescriptions to blacks and whites separately as to the reforms that would be needed to remedy the situation.

## Charles Booth

Across the Atlantic, another intrepid researcher was empirically examining urban social conditions. Charles Booth, a wealthy businessman, became convinced that something had to be done about the problem of poverty. There was considerable controversy in England late in the nineteenth century about the causes and cure of urban poverty, with solutions varying from ordinary charity to socialism. But the advocates of different solutions could not even agree on the extent of the problem because no one knew how many poor people lived in London (Pfautz, 1967). Booth resolved to collect the information needed to understand the problem, and he embarked upon an inquiry which took seventeen years and was finally published in a seventeen-volume report (Booth, 1902–1903). He mixed a number of research methods, including analysis of the censuses of 1801 through 1881; records collected by the municipal schools; personal observation; and maps. Box 1-1 shows the kinds of facts he collected. Although he began as an educated layman, he found it necessary to use statistics to analyze the information and became such an expert that he became president of the Royal Statistical Society. An acquaintance said of Booth, "He himself intended to make, at his own expense, an elaborate inquiry into the condition of the workers of London: the wages they received and the amount of subsistence they could obtain for the money remuneration they were being paid" (Pfautz, 1967, p. 22). In stating the aims of his research, Booth said that one of his objectives was "to describe the industrial peculiarities of London (and of modern towns generally) both as to character of work, character of workers, and of the influences which act upon both" (p. 23).

Like modern urban sociologists, he was interested in neighborhoods, social class, social institutions, and the urban environment. He collected and reported information by street and described each one vividly, and in minute detail, presenting not only the characteristics of the street itself but also specific information about each household. He also examined occupations very closely and divided them into

## THE BEGINNINGS OF URBAN SOCIOLOGY

classes. Having done this, he was able to classify streets (neighborhoods) into seven levels, color-coded for mapping. He expressed his interest in the urban environment mainly in terms of housing conditions, as well as in detailed descriptions of the streets and shops of poor neighborhoods, and expressed his interest in social institutions mainly in discussions of work and of religion in the city.

In an admiring assessment of Booth's contribution, Pfautz (1967) commends him for focusing upon the problems of an urban community in an industrial society, for using statistical data and methods to describe and study the changes in social structure, and for assembling and assessing social information with impressive techniques. Pfautz commends him as well for emphasizing social class as central to social organization. All these concerns recur in the development of twentieth-century urban sociology.

### The Pittsburgh Survey

In 1907 a charitable foundation provided support for a monumental research effort to collect information on the social conditions of a modern metropolis. Selecting Pittsburgh, the sponsors said, "The plan of the survey proposed a careful and fairly comprehensive study of the conditions under which working people live and labor in a great industrial city" (Butler, 1909). They had two broad areas of inquiry—working conditions and community—and surveyed factories and households on such topics as pay, working conditions (including the dangers of factory conditions), hours of work, and the situation of immigrants. The titles of the six (thick) published volumes that resulted from the survey indicate the range of topics studied: *Women and the Trades* (Butler, 1909); *Wage-Earning Pittsburgh* (Kellogg, 1914b); *Work-Accidents and the Law* (Eastman, 1910); *The Steel Workers* (Fitch, 1910); *Homestead; The Households of a Mill Town* (Byington, 1910); and *The Pittsburgh District: Civic Frontage* (Kellogg, 1914a). At that time the term "survey"—rather than having the restricted meaning it has now as a set of public opinion interviews from a scientific sample of a population—meant a survey of the situation, a collection of various pertinent facts by various means. Thus the Pittsburgh survey included interviews with workers and with influential persons, as well as reports on visits to factories, inspections of wage and accident reports, laws, and all sorts of other documents about the work system, the households, and the community. The reports included explicit descriptions of cases of poverty and of the hard times of the workers.

A variety of educated workers, including Pittsburgh locals and experts imported from around the nation, collected the information; housing inspectors, "sanitarians," lawyers, engineers, labor experts, and others participated (Butler, 1909, p. 492). The "field work was done in railroad yards and mill towns, sweatshops and great manufacturing plants; in courts, hospitals, and settlements. The investigators talked with priests and labor leaders, superintendents, claim agents and labor bosses, landlords, housewives, butchers and bakers—the workers themselves and those who

# CHAPTER · 1

## BOX 1-1
## Three "Reports" from Charles Booth's *Life and Labour of the People in London* (1892)

### A. A Single Household Case Report: Number 32 Shelton Street*

At *No.* 32, in the lower rooms, were the usual shifting class of people. At the top, on the third floor, Mrs. Makin, a widow, lived for two years. She gained her living by shelling peas, &c., in Covent Garden. A tidy person, very industrious and wretchedly poor, frequently without food or fire; would try to do her washing, and not know how to dry the things in winter. In the other room on this floor lived a market porter with a woman who sold oranges. About ten years they had lived so when, by the visitor's influence, they were married. The man, a pensioner, spends nearly all his pension in drink when he takes the money, and then is cruel to the woman, who does most to support the home.

### B. A One-Street Neighborhood Reportt

**Specimen Block with Over 45 Per Cent of Poverty, East Lambeth**

| Houses Character | No. of children, 3–13 | Description of street |
|---|---|---|
| Very dilapidated large double houses, 15s; 2 families 8s each tenement | 75 | Clerks, mechanics, &c.: built for a better class |
| Vary; large to very small cottages, all in very disgraceful state | 66 | Very mixed; some very poor hawkers, &c.; several gone hopping |
| Fairly good | 119 | Mixed; comfortable to poor |
| 2 rooms and 4 rms., 5s and 7s 6d, fair condition | 86 | Decidedly poor, mechanics and labourers |
| Top decent, others very poor | 160 | Poor labouring class; many in gasworks |
| Tenements, 3s 6d to 5s | 10 | Wretchedly poor |
| Poor style | 32 | Very poor; 17 empty houses as well |
| Small, 5s 6d to 7s | 35 | All labouring class |
| 8s to 10s, fair | 102 | Mixed; nearly all Irish |
| New and good | 10 | New road, not yet finished; villa style |

## C. Scheme of Social Classes and the All-London City Summary‡

The classes into which the population of each of these blocks and districts is divided are the same as were used in describing East London, only somewhat simplified. They may be stated thus:

- **A.** The lowest class—occasional labourers, loafers and semi-criminals.
- **B.** The very poor—casual labour, hand-to-mouth existence, chronic want.
- **C and D.** The poor—including alike those whose earnings are small, because of irregularity of employment, and those whose work, though regular, is ill-paid.
- **E and F.** The regularly employed and fairly paid working class of all grades.
- **G and H.** Lower and upper middle class and all above this level.

The proportions of the different classes shown for all London are as follows:

| | | | | |
|---|---|---|---|---|
| A (lowest) | 37,610 | or | 9 per cent. | In poverty, |
| B (very poor) | 316,834 | " | 7.5 per cent. | 30.7% |
| C and D (poor) | 938,293 | " | 23.3 per cent. | |
| E and F (working class, comfortable) | 2,166,503 | " | 51.5 per cent. | In comfort, |
| G and H (middle class and above) | 749,930 | " | 17.8 per cent. | 69.3% |
| | 4,209,170 | | 100 per cent. | |
| Inmates of Institutions | 99,830 | | | |
| | 4,309,000 | | | |

Graphically, the proportions may be shown thus:

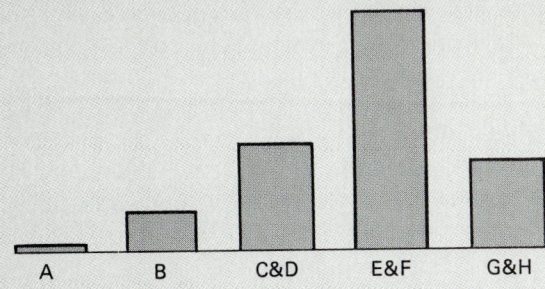

*The volumes contain thousands of reports like this; "Number 32" is one of the shorter reports.
†Notice that the table describes the conditions of the houses and of the people.
‡Notice that Booth estimates that more than 30 percent of the people are living in poverty.
*Source:* Booth, 1892, vol. 2. A is from p. 59; B is from Chapter 1; C is from pp. 20–21.

live close to them" (p. 492). They conducted case investigations and statistical studies and presented their information in graphs, maps, charts, diagrams, photographs, and drawings.

The reports conveyed a sense of outrage at what the investigators found. For example, in the summary of one investigation (Kellogg, 1914a) they reported that they found "an altogether incredible amount of overwork by everybody, reaching its extreme in the twelve-hour shift for seven days in the week in the steel mills and the railway switchyards" (p. 3). They criticize absentee capitalists, absentee landlords, and "archaic social institutions" such as the aldermanic courts, the garbage disposal system, and the charities. They are concerned about the way overwork destroys family life, and they angrily contrast the prosperity of the community with the neglect of life and health. In sum, the authors of these reports made a brave attack upon "the establishment"; on the other hand, their views may have been distorted by overenthusiastic reformism, or what Short (1971) referred to as "highly partisan purposes of immediate social reform" (p. xvi).

Modern sociologists admire these early researchers because they collected and analyzed data from the "real world." Nonetheless their studies, particularly those by Riis, Booth, and the Pittsburgh survey team, have been severely criticized for being moralistic and diffuse. Although Riis and Booth used different methods to collect information, they were both dedicated reformers who saw problems in the community and were committed to solving them. This, unfortunately, put a "filter" on their perceptions. Booth, for example, brought a strong middle-class bias to his observation of poor folks, as may be seen most clearly in his abhorrence of alcoholic beverages.

The reform impulse evidently prevented these great researchers from seeing the situation from the participant's point of view. One objective of the modern social researcher, particularly the ethnographer, is to get the "inside view," to see the situation from the participant's perspective. Thus from today's viewpoint, for example, when Barbara Heyl (1979), a sociologist, studied the process of becoming a prostitute, she did not push the information through a moralistic filter, and when anthropologist Elliot Liebow (1967) studied poor young men in one of Washington's slums, he did not impose a middle-class bias upon their behaviors. To do that would prevent understanding the social reality.

The survey movement has been criticized on other grounds—for being unsystematic and atheoretical. While the early surveys assembled great quantities of information, there was a random quality to the selection of topics—women's work, parks, city administrations. What connected these spheres of social life? What was the objective of knowing all these facts? There was no hypothesis or theory to hold them together. While no social scientists can fully overcome these problems, the sociologists of the Chicago school became more scientific and theoretical than their predecessors had been. Contemporary sociologists, such as Madge and Whyte, while admiring the quantity and quality of Booth's data, have criticized him for his moralistic approach. Whyte quotes the following paragraph, describing the treatment of the poor by the rich in a London parish, as an example of Booth's moralizing:

> their poverty has met with compassion and those who visit in the name of Christianity seek to relieve the distress they find.... The heart is softened, gratitude is felt, and in this mood the poor are pointed to God. Sin is rebuked, virtue extolled, and warning words are spoken against drunkenness, extravagance, and folley. Advice, assistance, and rebuke are all accepted. (Booth, cited in Whyte, 1964, p. 256)

Whyte, who conducted a more modern study of social life in the slums (*Street Corner Society*, 1943, a sociological classic), said that Booth's point of view was "quaint and naive." Whyte argued that good sociology would have to achieve an objective, nonjudgmental approach.

## THE "CHICAGO SCHOOL"

### Robert Park and His Colleagues

Urban sociology as we know it today began at the University of Chicago in the 1920s. That university had established the first department of sociology in 1892, and in 1914 Robert E. Park came there to teach, staying until he retired from the faculty in 1933 (Faris, 1967). Others on the growing faculty, including William I. Thomas and William F. Ogburn, were leading scholars of the time and contributed to the study of the city. A number of talented students came to the department, and some, like Ernest W. Burgess and Louis Wirth, later joined the faculty, contributing to the "Chicago school." The school refers to the faculty and students plus their numerous studies of Chicago and other cities, done with a particular set of research methods, in the context of an emerging theory of the urban community.

Park strongly advocated getting out of the "ivory tower" and studying the city, and he encouraged the students to do so. He had a personal fascination with cities, having been a newspaper reporter in Minneapolis, and once boasted:

> I wrote about all sorts of things and became in this way intimately acquainted with many different aspects of the city. I expect that I have actually covered more ground, tramping about in cities in different parts of the world, than any other living man. Out of all this I gained, among other things, a conception of the city, the community, and the region, not as geographical phenomena merely, but as a kind of social organism. (Park, cited in Hughes, 1952, p. 5)

Park argued that researchers should study the city empirically, by observation, and said they should emulate the methods of anthropologists who went into the field to study the way of life of the North American Indians (Park, 1916/1969). He said that people could come to understand the "customs, beliefs, practices, and general conception of life" in a Chicago immigrant slum or even in New York's sophisticated Greenwich Village; both were subject to social science investigation, just as if they were on an island in the South Seas.

Just as the other scientists at the university had laboratories, the sociologists had theirs—Chicago itself, a social laboratory. It was out there just waiting to be studied. Furthermore, Park and the other members of the Chicago school treated the city as a natural phenomenon, subject to a set of natural processes. For example, segregation is a natural process, and areas within the city differentiate by natural processes; likewise, growth is a natural process.

> The metropolis is, it seems, a great sifting and sorting mechanism, which, in ways that are not yet wholly understood, infallibly selects out of the population as a whole the individuals best suited to live in a particular region and a particular milieu.... The city grows by expansion, but it gets its character by the selection and segregation of its population, so that every individual finds, eventually, either the place where he can, or the place where he must, live. (Park, 1916/1969, p. 79)

In addition to treating the city as a laboratory in which natural processes took place, Park and his colleagues subjected the city to another regular scientific approach—natural history. (Just as a geologist or an ornithologist could study the natural history of a site, the sociologist could study the natural history of the city, or more typically, of one of its sections.) They saw the city as having a characteristic organization, a typical life history, and generalizable features. Furthermore, they saw cities as a category, so that what a person learned about one city could, within limits, be generalized to others (Park, 1916/1969).

Park (1916/1969) had many questions about the city:

> What part [of the city's growth] is due to migration?
>   What are the outstanding "natural" areas, i.e., areas of population segregation?
>     How is distribution of population within the city area affected by (a) economic interest, i.e., land values? (b) by sentimental interest, race, vocation, etc.?
>   How many people live in hotels, apartments, and tenements?
>   What proportion of population consists of nomads, hobos, gypsies? (pp. 18–19)

These and other questions appeared in a 1916 essay entitled "The City: Suggestions for the Investigation of Human Behavior in the Urban Environment." Many of the questions became the subjects of master's theses or doctoral dissertations over the next two decades.

According to Short (1971), Park and his colleagues were aware of the previous urban research but they aspired to greater "objectivity and disinterested investigation" (p. xiv). The very title of Park and Burgess's widely used textbook, *Introduction to the Science of Sociology* (1921), showed their commitment to the development of the field as a science. They wanted to move sociology away from social

## THE BEGINNINGS OF URBAN SOCIOLOGY

philosophy and said the field was going into a period of "investigation and research" (Park & Burgess, cited in Short, 1971, p. xii).

Park and Burgess encouraged their students to research the city, which they did, producing scores of studies, many of which became the cornerstones of urban sociology. A very brief list of books by faculty and students includes: *The Polish Peasant in Europe and America* (Thomas & Znaniecki, 1918-1920); *Vice in Chicago* (Reckless, 1933); *The Hobo: The Sociology of the Homeless Man* (Anderson, 1923); *Suicide* (Cavan, 1928); *The Gang: A Study of 1,313 Gangs in Chicago* (Thrasher, 1927); *The Ghetto* (Wirth, 1928); *Mental Disorders in Urban Areas: An Ecological Study of Schizophrenia and Other Psychoses* (Faris & Dunham, 1939).

The research projects generally fell into two types, both of which have continued in urban sociology: "ecological analyses" of the metropolis as a whole and "ethnographic studies" of individual districts or neighborhoods. There were other types of studies as well, such as examinations of particular occupations and kinds of institutions, but the ecological analyses and ethnographic studies looked more consistently at the community itself. Students who did ecological analyses typically focused on some social phenomenon and how it was distributed over space—which parts of the city had more of it and which had less. They usually plotted data on a map of Chicago to see whether a pattern arose. Most of these studies were grounded in Professor Burgess's conception of the social pattern of the city, known as the "concentric circles model" (see Chapter 4). Ecological analyses were often concerned with patterns of social segregation by race, nationality, and social class. In the second type of study, describing and analyzing a particular locality, the students set forth, like anthropologists, to study the natives in that area. They studied Jewish, Chinese, and black areas (but never ordinary, middle-class white ones). These ethnographic studies explored the "social worlds" of the different locales. They were grounded in the theory that the city was divided into a set of "natural areas," that is, the city's physical features, such as rivers, railway embankments, and industrial districts, divided the city into subareas. Each subarea had its own type of residents, segregated by nationality, race, and social class, and tended to develop its own social world, based on language, traditions, and a whole way of life. Natural areas were tempting sites for social research—a student could go to one to document and interpret its unique characteristics.

### The Gold Coast and the Slum

*The Gold Coast and the Slum* (Zorbaugh, 1929) is an enduring study in the ethnographic tradition that describes the social life of one of Chicago's natural areas in the mid-1920s. The area, adjacent to the "Loop," covered about 1½ square miles and housed and about 90,000 residents. Zorbaugh, interested in the natural history of the subcommunity and the way of life of city people, used the actual area as a social laboratory and went to explore. The near north side provided fertile ground for exploration because it contained radically different subareas. Along Lake Michigan, at the eastern edge of the district, were the mansions and fancy apartment buildings of the wealthy. Just inland there was a strip of deteriorated dwellings used as rooming houses, occupied by urban newcomers, bohemians, prostitutes, and others. Also within the district was a slum, which, at the time of the research, housed Sicilian immigrants. As Madge (1962) wrote, "In a very small area it was possible to study a microcosm of the whole city, with the added advantage that 'all the phenomena characteristic of the city are clearly segregated and appear in exaggerated form'" (p. 95).

Zorbaugh used several research methods. He collected personal documents, life histories, explaining individuals' experiences in the city. Box 1-2 quotes brief excerpts from one of the longest personal documents he included in his book. It tells the sad story of a young woman who migrated to the city to become a musician, and it illustrates why *The Gold Coast and the Slum* (1929) and so many other urban ethnographic studies make fascinating reading. In addition to collecting personal documents, Zorbaugh collected hundreds of school essays, conducted a house-to-house survey which provided information on the people living in rooming houses, and used numerous files of existing records, including the "Illinois Lodging House Register," a school census, records of the Juvenile Protective Association, and case histories of the United Charities (Madge, 1962). His book contains 15 maps, several of which show particular types of events, such as suicides, which are plotted on the base map of the near north side. It is this combination of methods which makes *The Gold Coast and the Slum* a powerful study.

Zorbaugh devotes much of the book to a detailed history: which groups lived in the area at different times, when different sorts of buildings were constructed, and what they have been used for. He then connects these changing uses of the area with the social life he observes. He calls this connection the "natural history" of the area, showing that as the city grows, various activities shift around within it, and one kind of shift affects other kinds. One of the city's main dynamics, emphasized in various Chicago school studies, is the expansion of the central business district. Since the near north side was adjacent to this district, it was affected by its growth. Thus, in recounting the natural history of the area, Zorbaugh (1929) reported that it once was a "wealthy and fashionable residential area" (p. 69), but then businesses moved in and it became less desirable. "Gradually, the fashionable families moved out of their own homes. Less well-to-do, transient, and alien groups came in ... the large old residences have been turned into rooming houses—another chapter in the natural history of the city" (p. 70). In this instance, the natural history of an area involves a shift in land use (business expands into the district); a shift in population (upper class leaves, transients and immigrants enter); and a shift in environmental uses (old mansions are converted into rooming houses).

Zorbaugh presents minute descriptions of the way of life in each section. The gold coast, which houses the city's elite, has tight social connections among the households and individuals, but, he says, the connections and traditions are not based upon living near each other. He describes the bohemian part of the transient, rooming-house area, calling it "Towertown." Although some of the residents are students and artists, he emphasizes the social uses of the area. It provides opportunities for unconventional behavior and anonymity, and it offers "escape from the conventions and repressions of the small town or the outlying amd more stable communities of the city" (1929, p. 91).

Discussing the rooming-house area, which he calls "the world of furnished rooms," he elaborates one of his principal themes, that the social life of the city tends to make people isolated, lonely, and personally disorganized. This theme is well-illustrated by the sad story recounted in "Document 15" (Box 1-2). Transiency is one of the enemies of community and personal stability, in Zorbaugh's view. He writes that the world of furnished rooms is the direct antithesis of "all we are accustomed to think of as normal in society" (1929, p. 82).

> The exaggerated mobility and astonishing anonymity of this world have significant implications for the life of the community. Where people are constantly coming and going; where they live at best but a few months in a given place; where no one knows anyone else in his own house ... where there are no groups of any sort—it is obvious that there can be no community tradition or common definition of situations, no public opinion, no informal social control. As a result, the rooming-house world is a world of political indifference, of laxity of conventional standards, of personal and social disorganization. (1929, p. 82)

The world of furnished rooms shows the potential of urban life at its worst. It is a world of "constant restlessness." People there are atomized individuals, without stable social relationships; they have no roots in the community.

Overall, Zorbaugh's conclusions are quite negative; he emphasizes the lack of community in the metropolis. In his theoretical summary (1929), he says that local life in the city lacks local sentiment and tradition. Elsewhere, he says that the social contacts among city people are superficial and external, marked by social distances; city people are absorbed in their own affairs. He blames this way of life on the economic differentiation of the city, which takes commerce and industry out of the local area. Many of the activities that once gave rise to a common body of experience among the members of a community are gone. People become more involved in their occupations than in their localities. He also blames mobility for much of the breakdown of community, "a rate of movement that makes strangers of neighbors" (1929, p. 251).

Zorbaugh occasionally compares the city with villages or small towns, always suggesting that these smaller communities had a more complete social life. At one point he writes, "The community, represented by the town or peasant village where everyone knows everyone else clear down to the ground, is gone" (1929, p. 16). The city lacks informal social control based upon a moral commonality. He notes that in traditional communities, people's behavior is held in line by informal means such as gossip. (Curiously, he implies that stable middle-class neighborhoods on

# CHAPTER·1

### BOX 1-2
### Document 15: The Life Story of a "Charity Girl"

Emporia, Kansas, was my home until I was twenty-two. . . .

We were a large family but father managed to save enough to send me, the oldest, to a small college in the state. And from the time I was a little girl I had music lessons. It is about these music lessons that the story of my life revolves. . . .

. . . the day I got my diploma I wrote home that instead of going back to Emporia to marry a "Babbitt" and live on "Main Street," I was going to Chicago to study music. . . .

Never shall I forget the time of the night that I arrived at the Northwestern Station, my purse clutched tightly in one hand, and my bag in the other, shaking my head at redcaps, confused and dazzled by the glare of the lights—but my heart singing, my ambition aflame, it was the gate to the promised land. I went to the Travelers' Aid Bureau and inquired how to get to the Y.W.C.A. I walked uptown, carrying my bag, too excited to be tired. . . .

The first few weeks went by like magic. It was all so strange and maddeningly stimulating to my small-town soul. The "Y" was a pleasant enough place to live—not at all the institutional sort of place I had expected it to be. But even in these first weeks I began to know what loneliness is. Most of my evenings were spent sitting in corners of the sitting-room, watching the old girls playing the piano and victrola, or entertaining their beaux. I got acquainted with a few other newcomers—a girl from Indiana who came to study, like myself, a girl who came from Alabama to get work as stenographer, and four or five others, from small towns in Illinois. All but myself seemed to have acquaintances or connections of some sort in Chicago. And sometimes, when I felt too unbearably lonely, I would go back to the big station in the evening, at the time when the train I came on would be coming in, and watch the faces in the crowd for a face from Emporia. . . .

After six weeks at the "Y" I moved to the Near North Side, to be nearer my music school. And during the next few months I lived at a dozen rooming-houses and homes for girls. . . .

The days were long and exhausting—up at six, a bath, a cup of coffee on a "sterno" stove, tidy my room a bit, and in the Loop by seven-thirty or eight. Then a long steady grind until five; a mile walk out to my rooming-house; supper in a nearby restaurant—and a

## THE BEGINNINGS OF URBAN SOCIOLOGY

plain supper at that; the evening devoted to my lesson or practicing; back to my room at ten-thirty or eleven, often too tired to undress until I had slept an hour or so.

I had come to the city in June. By Christmas my loneliness amounted almost to desperation. . . .

(A year of this had gone by, when one day her music teacher told her there was no hope of her ever realizing her ambitions.) I turned dazedly from the piano. . . . I scarcely heard him. I picked up my music and tossed it into a waste-basket in the corner; and then I walked out of the room.

It was late afternoon, and I walked the streets, neither noticing nor caring where, until late that night I ended up along the embankment in Lincoln Park, and sat down exhausted, on the stone wall by the lake. My head was a bit clearer by now, and I began to take stock of myself. . . .

The ambition for which I had sacrificed, which had kept me alive and going, was dead. . . .

I never went back to music school. I had been working as a waitress of late, . . . and I kept on with it. But the days and nights were empty now—and at last I knew to the full what loneliness could be. One night a nice boy came into the restaurant—it was one of the larger downtown restaurants—and sat down at my table. He talked to me, as they all did; told me he was from a small town in Oklahoma, that he'd made money, and had come to see the big city. He was friendly, and ended by asking me to a show. I accepted, and we went to a cabaret afterward. In a spirit of reckless bravado, to show the small-town boy I was a city-wise woman, I smoked my first cigarette and took my first drink. . . .

There's no use in making a story of it. He had an engaging smile, and was in search of adventure. I was unutterably lonely—and tired. He said that he loved me, and I was willing not to question too closely. I left the rooming-house, and we took a little flat out near Rogers Park. . . . Then, one day, B. came home and told me he was going back to Oklahoma, and that I wasn't going with him. I said little; I had known it must come, of course, though I had hoped it wouldn't come so soon. There was a generous check. And I moved back into the rooming-house.

*Source:* Zorbaugh, 1929, pp. 76–81.

the periphery of the city maintain such a moral community.) Later, he comments of the city, "There arises an extreme individuation of personal behavior that makes of the local area within the city something vastly different from the town or village community. There is within it no common body of experience and tradition, no unanimity of interest, sentiment, and attitude which can serve as a basis of collective action" (p. 251). Madge (1962) and others have criticized Zorbaugh and the Chicago school in general for this backward-looking perspective—who knows if the small town was ever as ideal as Zorbaugh implies?

### Juvenile Delinquency and Urban Areas: An Ecological Analysis

In 1929 four sociologists published a report entitled *Delinquency Areas* (Shaw et al.), an ecological analysis of the distribution of juvenile delinquency among Chicago's residential areas. They concluded that considerable differences existed among the city's residential areas in their levels of truancy, delinquency, and criminality (Shaw & McKay, 1942/1969). They demonstrated that the low-income communities near commercial areas and heavy industrial districts had the highest rates and the outlying residential areas of higher economic status had low rates. Two of the researchers, Clifford R. Shaw and Henry D. McKay, conducted follow-up research and published their findings in a volume first published in 1942, *Juvenile Delinquency and Urban Areas: A Study of Rates of Delinquency in Relation to Differential Characteristics of Local Communities in American Cities*. Like *The Gold Coast and the Slum*, this book became a sociological classic, exemplifying the ecological studies of the Chicago school.

Going beyond the conclusions of the 1929 study, Shaw and McKay wanted to discover whether differences among residential areas persist over time and whether this persistence occurs even if the groups in the areas change. (They also got several colleagues around the country to study delinquency rates to see whether the conclusions of the earlier study could be generalized to different types of cities, but the discussion which follows applies mainly to the Chicago research.) Introducing the second study, Shaw and McKay ask: (1) How much correlation is there between neighborhood characteristics—economic, social, and cultural—and rates of delinquency, and (2) do the changes in nativity and nationality in neighborhoods affect their delinquency rates? Clearly then, these analysts, like Zorbaugh, are working within the school's framework, which emphasizes social differences among local communities within the metropolis. They, too, viewed the city as a natural phenomenon, and even the differences among neighborhoods in their delinquency levels arise out of natural processes. "Areas acquire high delinquency rates neither by chance nor by design," they wrote "but rather, it is assumed, as an end-product of processes in American city life over which, as yet, man has been able to exercise little control" (1942/1969, p. 18). The reader might assume, though, that scientific research could penetrate and explain these processes.

## THE BEGINNINGS OF URBAN SOCIOLOGY

Shaw and McKay's research methods were statistical and geographical. They collected statistics from numerous municipal agencies, including the courts, school board, and health commission, but they could use only records which had geographical identifiers, such as street addresses of delinquents' residences, so that the researchers could plot them on maps and assign them to neighborhood units for analysis. Figure 7-1 represents a typical research operation in which they located on a Chicago base map the residences of 8,141 male delinquents brought before the county court during the years 1917-1923. From such raw data, they computed delinquency rates, having divided the city into different kinds of areas, for square-mile blocks of territory as well as for irregularly shaped community areas (natural areas). They also divided the city into concentric zones. In addition, they computed demographic and socioeconomic statistics for the areas—showing the racial and nationality groups that lived in the units, income levels, kinds of occupations of the residents, levels of homeownership and rentership, and the like.

First they searched for patterns over space, as illustrated in Figures 7-1 and 1-1. Figure 7-1 shows discernible differences among the residential areas of the city according to zone. (They analyzed the city within the concentric zones model which is explained in Chapter 4.) The graphs in Figure 1-2 show this same result. Just as they examined delinquency by zone, they also looked at neighborhood social characteristics. Table 1-2 shows that the central zone (I) has the most family dependency and the most foreign born. The peripheral zone (V), on the other hand, has the highest proportion of homeowners. Next, the researchers looked to see whether the delinquency patterns persisted over time, using statistical methods of correlation and regression. They also looked for relationships between different deviant phenomena—the correlation between truancy and delinquency, for example. They used these same methods, correlation and regression, to see whether social conditions, such as being on welfare, were connected with delinquency rates. Shaw and McKay were well ahead of their time in applying these statistical tools, since more than a quarter-century passed before many sociologists began to use correlation and regression, and then only with the aid of powerful computers. Shaw and McKay had to do the calculations the hard way, by hand.

The results of the research confirmed the community differences found in the earlier project and enabled the researchers to go forward with new findings. They found, for example, that many of the juvenile delinquents were later apprehended as adult lawbreakers. Furthermore, the likelihood of this occurring varied among neighborhoods: "A striking variation is seen among types of areas, 70.7 per cent of the delinquents from high-rate areas, on the average, being arrested as adults, in comparison with 53.9 per cent from areas where the rates were low" (1942/1969, p. 134). They concluded that community conditions directly affected delinquency and criminality; in particular, income levels varied inversely with delinquency.

They discovered that high-delinquency communities tended to maintain these deviancy rates over long periods of time. The delinquency rates followed the social pattern of the city, being highest in the areas adjacent to commercial centers and heavy industry; regardless of which nationality groups lived in these poverty areas,

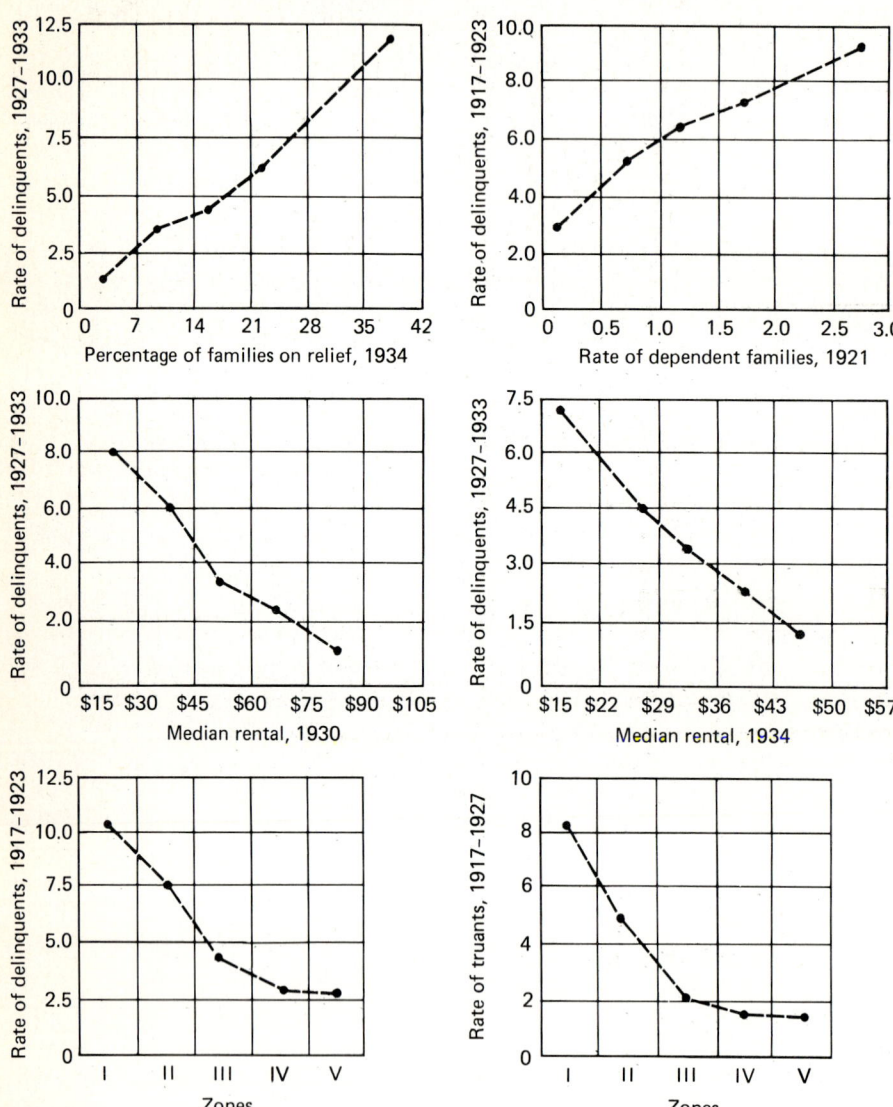

**FIGURE 1-1**
Selected graphs from *Juvenile Delinquency and Urban Areas*. These four graphs show the relationship between neighborhood socioeconomic status and delinquency rates. Poverty areas had more delinquency; high-rent areas had less. Comparing older and newer data shows that these relationships did not change over time. Zone I was at the city center and Zone V was at the periphery. The further a neighborhood was from the center, the less likely it was to have delinquency and the more likely it was to have higher socioeconomic status. (Source: Shaw & McKay, 1942/1969.)

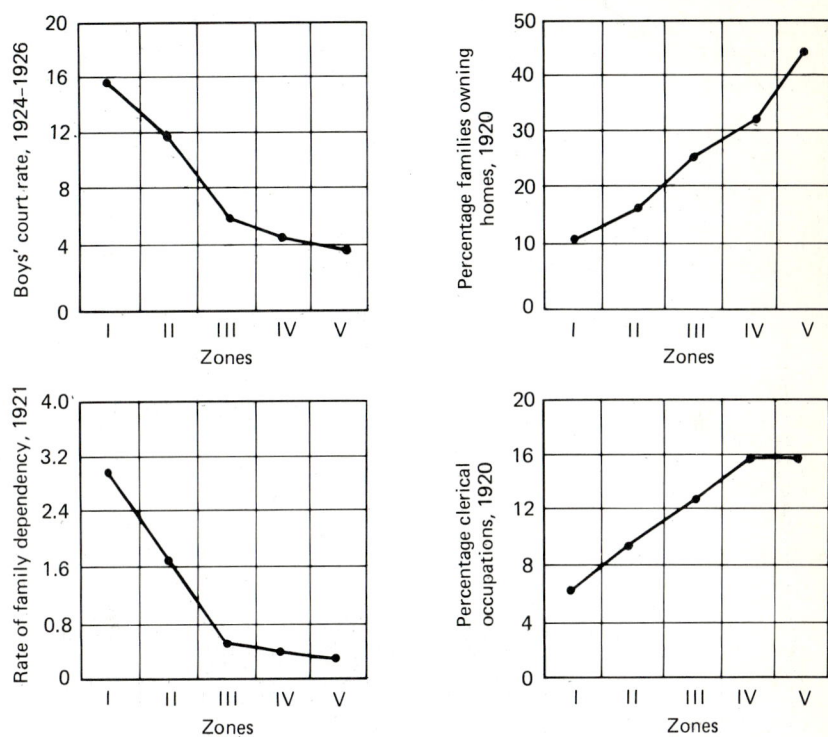

their delinquency rates stayed even. Therefore, Shaw and McKay (1942/1969) concluded that delinquency-producing factors are inherent in the community.

They argued that lower-status communities tended not to have coherent value systems which could be imparted to young people. (This argument is similar to Zorbaugh's (1929) interpretation of the world of furnished rooms.) To the extent that the communities have cultural traditions, they foster delinquent behavior. The traditions manifest themselves in ways a boy can appreciate and pass on through the "conduct, speech, gestures, and attitudes of persons with whom he has contact" (Shaw & McKay, 1942/1969, p. 315.) Perhaps the most harmful link in this chain of criminal tradition is the child's association with predatory gangs and other forms of delinquent and criminal organization.

In sum, working within the theory that the metropolis is socially differentiated into local communities with different social conditions and different local cultures, Shaw and McKay conducted a study which assembled and analyzed an enormous quantity of data. They used relatively advanced statistical methods, decades before other sociologists mastered them. They discovered consistent ecological patterns which conformed with their colleagues' model of the city. While their specific con-

**TABLE 1-2**
Rate of Delinquents, Percentage Increase or Decrease of Population, Economic Segregation, Segregation by Race and Nativity, and Employment by Type of Industry, for 2-Mile Zones, 1917–1923 Juvenile Court Series

| Community characteristics | Zones |  |  |  |  |
|---|---|---|---|---|---|
|  | I | II | III | IV | V |
| Rate of delinquents, 1917–23 | 10.3 | 7.3 | 4.4 | 3.3 | 3.0 |
| Percentage increase or decrease of population, 1910–20 | −22.8 | −2.2 | 35.3 | 71.0 | 124.4 |
| Economic segregation: |  |  |  |  |  |
| Rate of family dependency, 1921 | 3.0 | 1.7 | 0.6 | 0.4 | 0.3 |
| Juvenile court dependency cases, 1917–23 | 1.7 | 1.2 | 0.7 | 0.5 | 0.4 |
| Juvenile court mothers' pension cases, 1917–23 | 1.7 | 1.2 | 0.7 | 0.4 | 0.3 |
| Percentage of families owning homes, 1920 | 11.9 | 17.5 | 25.6 | 31.9 | 43.6 |
| Segregation by race and nativity: |  |  |  |  |  |
| Percentage of foreign-born and Negro heads of families, 1920 | 72.3 | 69.7 | 55.1 | 42.6 | 40.6 |
| Percentage of Negroes in total population, 1920 | 2.5 | 8.3 | 4.3 | 1.6 | 0.4 |
| Percentage of foreign-born in white population, 1920 | 41.0 | 37.5 | 30.1 | 23.6 | 22.6 |
| Percentage of aliens in foreign-born population 21 and over, 1920 | 41.9 | 33.1 | 22.5 | 16.6 | 16.2 |
| Percentage of aliens in white population 21 and over, 1920 | 24.0 | 19.0 | 9.9 | 5.7 | 5.6 |
| Employment by type of industry, 1920: |  |  |  |  |  |
| Percentage manufacturing and mechanical | 46.6 | 50.2 | 43.3 | 39.3 | 40.3 |
| Percentage clerical | 6.7 | 9.5 | 13.0 | 15.8 | 15.5 |
| Percentage professional services | 3.4 | 3.2 | 4.4 | 5.7 | 6.4 |
| Percentage domestic and personal services | 10.3 | 7.2 | 5.3 | 4.1 | 3.3 |

Source: Shaw and McKay, 1942/1969.

clusions have been questioned, their general approach continues to be used and modified by criminologists.

## EMERGING THEORIES

Concerned and puzzled by the amazing growth and troubled social situations of cities in the late nineteenth century, social thinkers tried to interpret and explain the metropolis. Sociologists in Europe and the United States developed several relevant new theories in the last decades of the nineteenth century and the first decades of the twentieth, most of which attempted to explain modern industrial society and its social relationships. Although not necessarily focused on city life, their ideas were still directly applicable. Several of the European theorists are now counted among the patriarchs of modern sociology—Tönnies, Durkheim, Simmel, and Weber. This book includes ideas from all of them, but this chapter draws upon Tönnies and, in particular, his theory of "gemeinschaft and gesellschaft." This chapter also includes one theory originating in the Chicago school: the "folk-urban continuum." These two theories offer ways in which the city can be compared with other, more familiar types of communities.

Both theories are based upon "ideal types" of societies or communities. These types represent polar extremes, constructed opposites, and are used to differentiate between traditional, small-scale societies and modern, large-scale societies. The authors of the theories defined the different types to highlight the particular characteristics which they considered to be important. The term ideal types does not mean that the types have some moral perfection but that they represent the extreme form of an idea; they are intellectual devices, heuristic tools designed to help us see the relevant characteristics and variables which make a difference. Fortunately or unfortunately, these types, as defined, are never seen in the real world; actual cities may have some traditional elements in their way of life, just as actual small towns may have some urban features. But the theories are put forward hopefully to help people perceive differences and understand real situations.

## Gemeinschaft and Gesellschaft

In 1887 Ferdinand Tönnies published a theoretical volume, entitled *Gemeinschaft and Gesellschaft*, which attempted to explain the difference between traditional and modern societies. Gemeinschaft and gesellschaft, which are usually translated as "community" and "society," suggest basically different ways in which human aggregates are held together.

Gemeinschaft is the kind of social bond in small, traditional societies—villages, tribes, and other small communities. The word cannot be translated simply and directly, but it refers to a "community of feeling" (Miner, 1968, p. 175). It is a sort of primitive connection based on feelings, seen most directly among members of the same family, between mother and child, between brothers, etc. Tönnies (1887/1957) suggests that in a stable, small community where people are very much like one another, this sort of primordial tie holds them together; the community is like a big family. (Indeed, in primitive human communities, membership was by kinship only.) In the village, and even in the town, "original kinship and inherited status remain an essential, or at least the most important, condition of participating fully in common property and other rights" (p. 228). Gemeinschaft, according to Tönnies, "represents the special social force and sympathy which keeps human beings together as members of a totality" (p. 47).

Gemeinschaft is not only a property of families but can also be the basis of social relations in a broader setting. Tönnies (1887/1957) specifically related it to one kind of community life:

> Neighborhood describes the general character of living together in the rural village. The proximity of dwellings, the communal fields, and even the mere contiguity of holdings necessitate many contacts of human beings and cause inurement to and intimate knowledge of one another. They also necessitate cooperation in labor, order, and management, and lead to common supplication for grace and mercy to the gods and spirits of land and water. (p. 43)

Tönnies argues that beyond kinship, physical proximity can be the basis for gemeinschaft, and beyond that, even intellectual proximity may suffice. No wonder, then, that in "pop sociology" the term gemeinschaft has come to connote a kind of warm, happy friendliness about a group or situation.

Unfortunately, gesellschaft goes along with the movement to city life. Tönnies says the historical trend has been to move from a life based on gemeinschaft to one based on gesellschaft. Gemeinschaft may survive, partially, in towns, but social relations in cities have a new basis. There is no underlying unity in the city; thus people are basically separated from each other. Even the family, so essential to gemeinschaft, is undermined in the city, according to Tönnies. Individuals are drawn away from tight involvement with the family by alternative attractions, such as business and other personal influences. The question, then, is, What is the basis for ongoing social life in cities, once gemeinschaft has been lost?

"The theory of the Gesellschaft deals with the artificial construction of an aggregate of human beings which superficially resembles the Gemeinschaft in so far as the individuals live and dwell together peacefully" (Tönnies, 1887/1957, p. 64).

Tönnies portrays an extreme form of individuation in the urban milieu. Each person is an independent individual, essentially separated. "Here everybody is by himself and isolated, and there exists a condition of tension against all others" (1887/1957, p. 65). People get involved in their own interests and develop rules of privacy; they resist the attempts of others who may get involved with them or "invade" their privacy. Furthermore, they become selfish, not wanting to do anything for others without something in exchange. The key word for the new urban person is "individualism."

Social relations in the city are formed on a new basis; urban people don't have the familial attachment, the natural common will, of gemeinschaft, so their relationships are not based upon the cooperation which arises naturally out of that common will. The new system is gesellschaft, based on exchange. Individuals may have many social relationships in the city, but each party to a relationship expects to get from the other an amount equivalent to what he or she puts in. Contract is an essential of this system; contracts validate the exchanges and state the terms. In the city, each actor is an individual, operating on the basis of personal needs, interests, desires, and decisions.

There is a capitalistic flavor to Tönnies's formulation of urban social relations based upon exchanges and contracts. He emphasizes that the city is the true home of gesellschaft, particularly the commercial-industrial city. Furthermore, he emphasizes that the city creates a set of hostilities between social classes and that the new sort of social relationships has to mediate these antagonisms. "This is especially true," he writes, "of the antagonism between the rich or the so-called cultured class and the poor of the servant class, which try to obstruct and destroy each other" (1887/1957, p. 227). Consistent with the theories of Karl Marx, cited at other points in the book, he argues that in the capitalist city, workers are exploited as their products are appropriated. He writes that an upper class dominates the city.

There is nothing pretty about Tönnies's depiction of gesellschaft, urban social life. The gemeinschaft-gesellschaft contrast is a theory of loss. What was valuable—the natural, familial, satisfying basis of social life in the small community—is lost to humanity in a process of social evolution toward gesellschaft. The new basis of social life appears to be selfish and nasty—a large aggregation of individualists out for their own interests and able to get along with others only when they can arrange an exchange and formalize it with a contract. Instead of having cooperation based on commonality and good feeling, the city has an exploitative elite always living in potential conflict with everyone else.

## The Folk-Urban Continuum

Returning to the Chicago school, we find another theoretical framework which contrasts social life in little communities with that of cities. Robert Redfield, a social anthropologist educated at the University of Chicago, defined the characteristics of folk societies. He acknowledged that he had used some of Tönnies's ideas, as well as those of some of the other social theorists who had contrasted traditional and modern societies: Maine, Durkheim, and Becker (Leslie, 1968). Unlike his predecessors, however, he was an empirical researcher and could build his theories upon data. He and his students conducted a series of studies of Mexican peasants and of other types of communities as well, including a city and a tribal settlement of Indians (Miner, 1968). He defined the folk society as follows:

> Such a society is small, isolated, nonliterate, and homogeneous, with a strong sense of group solidarity. The ways of living are conventionalized into that coherent system which we call "a culture." Behavior is traditional, spontaneous, uncritical, and personal; there is no legislation or habit of experiment and reflection for intellectual ends. Kinship, its relationships and institutions, are the type categories of experience and the familial group is the unit of action. The sacred prevails over the secular; the economy is one of status rather than of the market. (Redfield, cited in Miner, 1952, p. 529.)

> **BOX 1-3**
> **Folk-Urban Contrasts in Redfield's Definition**
>
> | Folk | Urban |
> | --- | --- |
> | Small | Large |
> | Isolated | Integrated with larger society, world |
> | Nonliterate (oral tradition) | Literate (based on print media) |
> | Sense of group solidarity | Lack of group solidarity |
> | Way of life = a culture | No unifying agreed-upon culture |
> | Kinship and family are basic | Kinship and family are not basic |
> | Sacred emphasis | Secular emphasis |
> | Status-based economy | Market-based economy |
> | Behavior: traditional, spontaneous, uncritical, personal | More formalized rules and systems governing behavior: laws, experiments, calculations |

Redfield never exactly defined the characteristics of the urban way of life, but it is implicit that they represent the opposite of the folk. Thus while the folk is small, isolated, and homogeneous, the city is large, integrated with the rest of society, and heterogeneous. While the folk has group solidarity and a coherent culture, the city lacks solidarity and a coherent culture, perhaps having numerous conflicting subcultures. The folk definition may be dissected to produce a list of folk-urban contrasts, as in Box 1-3.

Redfield hypothesized that smaller communities differed significantly from cities. He suggested that as a little community became less isolated, by gaining new attachments to the larger society—roads, trading connections, etc.—and more heterogeneous, it would lose the folk characteristics. In particular, the loss of isolation and the increase of heterogeneity would produce social disorganization, secularization, and individualization (Miner, 1968). He conducted a comparative study of communities in Yucatan and confirmed this central hypothesis. Over the years, however, other anthropologists have continued to test this theory and have modified and challenged some of Redfield's ideas. Like *The Gold Coast and the Slum* (Zorbaugh, 1929) and the gemeinschaft-gesellschaft formulations, the folk-urban continuum features the attractive qualities of little communities and the unattractive qualities of social life in the city.

## SUMMARY

Before urban sociology began, social reformers such as journalists and social workers were describing the wretched living conditions of poor people in the cities. These reformers were active in the last decades of the nineteenth century and the first decades of the twentieth. The enormous growth of cities in the nineteenth century created an impetus for urban sociology; the newly expanded metropolis encompassed a new and puzzling way of life and a set of social problems which inspired sociological analysis.

Urban sociology began with the Chicago school in the 1920s. Professors and students in this group sought to develop a scientific sociology, which meant that they would not be directly involved with social reform. Heavily committed to empirical research, the Chicago sociologists used the city as their laboratory.

Several of their projects were ethnographic studies of individual districts or neighborhoods. To do this kind of research, the sociologist approached the neighborhood as an anthropologist approaches a village on a distant island, observing and collecting information to write a detailed description of the way of life. *The Gold Coast and the Slum* (Zorbaugh, 1929) is a classic of this genre. A second type of Chicago study was the ecological analysis of the social life of the city. Heavily based on mapping social data, this kind of study looked for spatial patterns in the metropolis, such as concentration and segregation. *Juvenile Delinquency and Urban Areas* (Shaw & McKay, 1942/1969) typifies this approach.

*Gemeinschaft and Gesellschaft,* written in 1887 by the German sociologist Ferdinand Tönnies, put forth one of the leading theories which helped to understand social differences between small communities and cities. This theory stated that social relationships in the small, traditional community were cemented together by a natural common will shared by all the members. City people lack this common will; they are isolated and potentially opposed to each other. Urban relationships tend to be businesslike, based on exchange and contract. This theory is not necessarily true, but it establishes the terms of future debates about urban life.

The folk-urban continuum, developed by the Chicago school anthropologist Robert Redfield, expressed a similar contrast between the ways of life in small and large communities. It emphasized five key variables: isolation of the folk community and heterogeneity, secularization, individualization, and social disorganization of the urban community.

From this beginning period of urban sociology, several themes and questions continue to the present:

1. An emphasis on the metropolis as a natural phenomenon
2. An emphasis on high-quality data and scientific analysis
3. A continued search for the distinctiveness of urban ways of life and social relations in the metropolis

4. A continuation of both kinds of research: looking for the way of life and looking for the ecological pattern (although both approaches have incorporated new research techniques over the years)

## REFERENCES

Anderson, Nels. 1923. *The Hobo: the Sociology of the Homeless Man.* Chicago: University of Chicago Press.

Booth, Charles. 1982. *Life and Labour of the People in London,* vol. 2. "Streets and Population Classified," 2d ed. London: Macmillan.

Booth, Charles. 1902–1903. *Life and Labour of the People in London* (First Series: "Poverty"; Second Series: "Industry"; Third Series: "Religious Influences"; final volume: "Notes on Social Influences and Conclusions"; 3d ed., 17 vols.). London: Macmillan.

Butler, Elizabeth B. 1909. *Women and the Trades,* Pittsburgh, 1907–1908. New York: Charities Publication Committee.

Byington, Margaret F. 1910. *Homestead; The Households of a Mill Town.* New York: Charities Publication Committee.

Carey, James T. 1975. *Sociology and Public Affairs: the Chicago School.* Beverly Hills: Sage.

Cavan, Ruth S. 1928. *Suicide.* Chicago: University of Chicago Press.

Cordasco, Francesco. 1968. *Jacob Riis Revisited: Poverty and the Slum in another Era.* New York: Anchor. (Includes long excerpts from Riis's *How the Other Half Lives: Studies among the Tenements of New York, Children of the Poor,* and *A Ten Years' War: An Account of the Battle with the Slum in New York.*)

DuBois, W. E. B. 1899. *The Philadelphia Negro.* Philadelphia: University of Pennsylvania.

Eastman, Crystal. 1910. *Work-Accidents and the Law.* New York: Charities Publication Committee.

Faris, Robert E. L. 1967. *Chicago Sociology, 1920–1932.* San Francisco: Chandler.

Faris, Robert, E. L., and H. Dunham. 1939. *Mental Disorders in Urban Areas: An Ecological Study of Schizophrenia and other Psychoses.* Chicago: University of Chicago Press.

Fitch, John A. 1910. *The Steel Workers.* New York: Charities Publications Committee.

Heyl, Barbara. 1979. *The Madam as Entrepreneur.* New Brunswick, N.J.: Transaction Books.

Hofstadter, Richard. 1955. *The Age of Reform: from Bryan to F.D.R.* New York: Knopf.

Hughes, Everett C. 1952. "Preface," pp. 5–7 in Park, 1952.

Kellogg, Paul U. (ed.). 1914. *The Pittsburgh District: Civic Frontage.* New York: Charities Publication Committee, 1914.

Kellogg, Paul U. (ed.). 1914b. *Wage-Earning Pittsburgh*. New York: Charities Publication Committee.
Leslie, Charles M. 1968. "Robert Redfield," pp. 350–353 in *International Encyclopedia of the Social Sciences* (vol. 13). New York: Macmillan and Free Press.
Liebow, Elliot. 1967. *Tally's Corner: A Study of Negro Streetcorner Men*. Boston: Little, Brown.
Madge, John. 1962. *The Origins of Scientific Sociology*. New York: Free Press.
McKenzie, Roderick. 1923. *The Neighborhood, a Study of Local Life in the City of Columbus, Ohio*. Chicago: University of Chicago Press.
McKenzie, Roderick. 1968. *On Human Ecology*. Chicago: University of Chicago Press.
Miner, Horace M. 1952. "The Folk-Urban Continuum." *American Sociological Review*. 17:529–537.
Miner, Horace M. 1968. "Community-Society Continua," pp. 174–180 in *International Encyclopedia of the Social Sciences* (vol. 3). New York: Macmillan and Free Press.
Park, Robert E. 1916/1969. "The City: Suggestions for the Investigation of Human Behavior in the Urban Environment." *American Journal of Sociology*. 20: Reprinted in Sennett, 1969.
Park, Robert E. 1929/1952. "The City as a Social Laboratory," pp. 1–19 in T. V. Smith and L. White (eds.), *Chicago: An Experiment in Social Science Research*. Chicago: University of Chicago Press. Reprinted in Park, 1952.
Park, Robert E. 1952. The Collected Papers of Robert Ezra Park: *Human Communities: The City and Human Ecology*, vol. 2, Everett C. Hughes et. al. (eds.). Glencoe: Free Press.
Park, Robert E. 1936/1952. "Human Ecology." *American Journal of Sociology*. 42:1–15. Reprinted in Park, 1952.
Park, Robert E., and Ernest W. Burgess. 1921. *Introduction to the Science of Sociology*. Chicago: University of Chicago Press.
Pfautz, Harold W. 1967. "Charles Booth: Sociologist of the City," pp. 3–168 in *On the City: Physical Pattern and Social Structure*, (ed.) Charles Booth. Chicago: University of Chicago Press.
Reckless, Walter. 1933. *Vice in Chicago*. Chicago: University of Chicago Press.
Redfield, Robert. 1947. "The Folk Society." *American Journal of Sociology*. 52:293–308.
Riis, Jacob. 1890. *How the Other Half Lives: Studies among the Tenements of New York*. New York: Scribner's.
Riis, Jacob. 1892. *Children of the Poor*. New York: Scribner's.
Schnore, Leo F. 1967. "Community," pp. 79–150 in *Sociology*, (ed.) Neil J. Smelser. New York: Wiley.
Shaw, Clifford R., and Henry D. McKay. 1942/1969. *Juvenile Delinquency and Urban Areas: A Study of Rates of Delinquency in Relation to Differential Characteristics of*

*Local Communities in American Cities* (rev. ed.). Chicago: University of Chicago Press.

Shaw, Clifford R., Frederick M. Zorbaugh, Henry D. McKay, and Leonard S. Cottrell. 1929. *Delinquency Areas*. Chicago: University of Chicago Press.

Short, James F., Jr. (ed.). 1971. *The Social Fabric of the Metropolis: Contributions of the Chicago School of Urban Sociology*. Chicago: University of Chicago Press.

Sinclair, Upton. 1927. *The Jungle*. New York: Vanguard.

Steffens, Lincoln. 1904. *The Shame of the Cities*. New York: McClure, Phillips.

Thomas, William I., and Florian Znaniecki. 1918–1920. *The Polish Peasant in Europe and America*. Boston: R. G. Badger.

Thrasher, Frederick. 1927. *The Gang: A Study of 1,313 Gangs in Chicago*. Chicago: University of Chicago Press.

Tönnies, Ferdinand. 1887/1957. *Community and Society (Gemeinschaft and Geselle-*

*chaft*). East Lansing, Mich.: Michigan State University Press. (Translated and edited by Charles P. Loomis.)

Weber, Adna F. 1899. *The Growth of Cities in the Nineteenth Century: A Study in Statistics*. New York: Macmillan.

Whyte, William F. 1964. "On *Street Corner Society*," pp. 256–268 in *Contributions to Urban Sociology*, (eds.) Ernest W. Burgess and Donald J. Bogue. Chicago: University of Chicago Press.

Whyte, William F. 1943. *Street Corner Society: The Social Structure of an Italian Slum*. Chicago: University of Chicago Press.

Wirth, Louis. 1928. *The Ghetto*. Chicago: University of Chicago Press.

Zorbaugh, Harvey. 1929. *The Gold Coast and the Slum*. Chicago: University of Chicago Press.

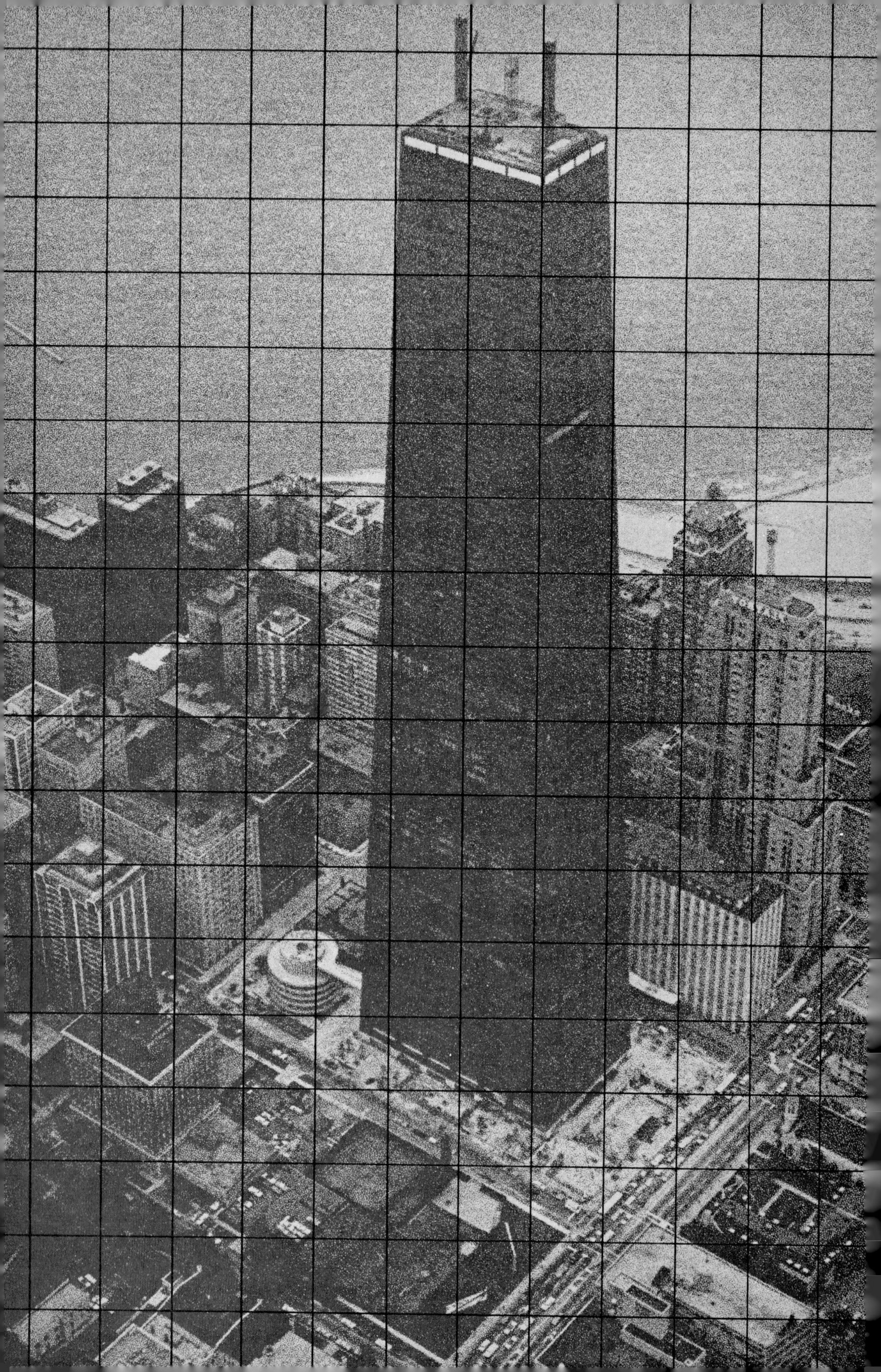

# CHAPTER · 2

## An Overview of the Field

## Chapter Outline

INTRODUCTION
  Microscales and Macroscales
  Three Aspects of Sociology

HUMAN ECOLOGY
  Origins of Human Ecology
  Criticisms of Early Human Ecology
  Postwar Human Ecology
- Broader scope
- The ecosystem

TWO BRIDGING THEORIES
  "Urbanism as a Way of Life"
- Basic concepts
- Effects of the main variables
- Deterministic reasoning

Responses to Wirth's Theory
- Gideon Sjoberg
- Herbert Gans

Subcultural Theory of Urbanism
- "Critical masses" and subcultures
- Unconventional behavior
- Propositions about subcultures

SOCIAL PSYCHOLOGY
  Effects of the Community
- The density-pathology hypothesis
- Mental health in the metropolis
- Tolerance and diffusion of innovations

  Social Relations
  Effects on Human Ecology

SUMMARY

## INTRODUCTION

This chapter has two purposes: to show the central concerns of urban sociology and to introduce the rest of the book. It presents two major approaches to metropolitan communities—human ecology and social psychology—with some of their questions and concepts. It also summarizes a central theoretical debate in the field about the nature of urban social life, beginning with an older theory known as "urbanism as a way of life" and culminating with a contemporary response known as the "subcultural theory of urbanism." These theoretical perspectives and issues are intended to show the scope of urban sociology and some of its central concerns.

The chapter also serves as a guide to the text. The presentation of human ecology shows the approach which will be used in the early chapters in urban history. Other sections of the chapter introduce issues which will receive more thorough coverage in later parts of the book.

## Microscales and Macroscales

Urban studies are usually either microsociological or macrosociological; the distinction refers to the number of individuals and the amount of area involved. Microstudies operate at the individual and group level—looking at such phenomena as interaction, networks, attitudes, and the like—and their geographical scope is likely to be the neighborhood, the residential area, or, at the largest, the suburb, but never a whole metropolis. The only exception to this is the study of interaction—kinship or friendship patterns, for example—in which patterns are scattered at large distances, but in such cases it is the interaction and relationships which are of interest, not the territory per se.

Macrosociological studies, on the other hand, look at large aggregates or large pieces of territory. A macrosociological study might well take an entire metropolitan area or even a number of metropolitan areas as units of analysis. Within a community, macrosociological units might be large units of the social structure such as racial and ethnic groups, social classes, corporations, or large governmental bureaucracies.

## Three Aspects of Sociology

Sociologists have often divided their field into three parts: human ecology, social organization, and social psychology, to distinguish different levels of analysis and general theoretical approaches. Although the dividing lines between the parts are not always perfect, the three labels do designate definable sections of the discipline. Figure 2-1 shows several subjects in urban sociology, cross-classified by the micromacro distinction and by the part of sociology into which they fall. The outline

| "Branch" | Scale Macro | Scale Micro |
|---|---|---|
| Human ecology | Urbanization; growth of cities; metropolitan development; suburbanization; spatial patterns; racial and ethnic segregation; differentiation among residential areas | The built environment; behavior settings (This is almost a null cell.) |
| Social organization | Social stratification; community power structure; race relations | Neighborhood organization; suburban social life; voluntary associations; Ghettos and urban villages; slums |
| Social psychology | Urban imagery (This is almost a null cell.) | Urban and suburban social relations; lifestyles; social networks |

**FIGURE 2-1**
Some subjects studied in uban sociology.

should become clearer after an introduction to some theoretical approaches and concerns, starting with human ecology.

## HUMAN ECOLOGY

Human ecologists have always been concerned about the spatial pattern and structure of the community. Questioning how different groups were distributed in the metropolis, why the distribution took a particular shape, and where households and neighborhoods of different socioeconomic levels and racial and ethnic groups were located has led them to concerns about residential segregation. Concerned also about mobility and change, migration, growth and decline of communities, and suburbanization, they have attempted to understand the structure of the metropolis and its relationship to its hinterland. These macro questions about population aggregates are ecological questions, referring to whole communities or their parts, not to individuals and their attitudes and values.

Human ecology starts with space, time, and population. Thus it may look at the pattern of population in a metropolitan area or at the growth or decline of a community over time.

## Origins of Human Ecology

Human ecologists argue that social life rests upon demographic foundations, an idea originated by the great French sociologist, Emile Durkheim, in his theory of social morphology (Halbwachs, 1938/1960; Schnore, 1958). As explicated by Durkheim's student Halbwachs, the theory shows that many social processes, from economics to politics and religion, are influenced by demographic processes in spatial context. Industrial growth is tied to the migration of workers; political systems which work for small, sparsely settled populations may be inappropriate for large, dense collectivities; and growing religious bodies are likely to behave differently from groups which are losing members. Halbwachs elaborates on such items in *Population and Society* (1938/1960), which is the fullest theoretical statement of social morphology.

Durkheim's contribution to this theory appears in his book *The Division of Labor in Society* (1933), in which he explained that the rise of modern society was based upon increasing "dynamic density" which, in turn, had a demographic element, increasing population density. This, in combination with increasing interpersonal communication, generated dynamic density.

Leo Schnore (1958) summarizes Durkheim's theory of the division of labor as follows: Population growth in societies tends to change their social structure; the social structural change to be explained is the integration and interdependence of the parts of a society by means of the division of labor. In other words, in small simple societies, everyone can do the same work—say, hunting or gathering food—and there is not much division of labor. In complex societies, individuals do specialized work and the members of the population are interdependent, unable to survive on their own. Large aggregates allow for greater differentiation. Population growth and increasing density are necessary but not sufficient causes of change; physical density makes a difference, but "moral" or "dynamic density" is crucial. "In contrast to physical density—the numbers of people per unit of space—'dynamic density' refers to the density of social intercourse or contact or, more simply, to the rate of interaction.... According to Durkheim: 'The division of labor develops ... as there are more individuals sufficiently in contact to be able to act and react upon one another'" (Schnore, 1958, p. 623). Modern cities, of course, have a very high division of labor.

In the United States, Robert Park pursued a similar line of thought in developing sociological human ecology. Park (1967) argued that a community operates at two levels, the subsocial and the social. The subsocial level, in which a population engages in competition for space (environment) and other amenities, was considered to be ecological. One effect of this competition is to develop the community's spatial pattern, with business at the center and different social and ethnic groups distributed in a regular pattern. (This pattern is presented in Chapter 4 as the concentric zones model of the industrial city.) The social level, which involved higher social processes like cooperation, organization, and culture, was considered to be more human and civilized.

Contemporary human ecologists no longer see communities in terms of levels, nor do they see ecological processes as subsocial, and they do not necessarily emphasize competition as a central process. But they argue that ecological processes should be studied on their own terms. Ecologists look at aggregate phenomena, like growth of cities, migration flows, and segregation patterns, and deliberately avoid considering social psychological phenomena like motivations, attitudes, and values.

Using the ecological framework, Park's students and colleagues studied social processes and patterns in Chicago and produced analyses of neighborhoods and of the social geography of the city. Perhaps the most notable product of the latter category is the concentric zones model, which not only sets forth a regular spatial pattern of social groups in cities but also posits a regular urban growth pattern (Burgess, 1925).

Roderick McKenzie of the University of Michigan also contributed major ideas to human ecology, including the theory of ecological expansion (Kasarda, 1972; McKenzie, 1933a, 1933b). His theory explains urban communities' transformation as they grow spatially, demographically, and functionally. A half-century ago McKenzie was one of the first to recognize that the industrial city was giving way to the metropolitan community because cities were expanding, swallowing nearby communities and adding new suburbs. McKenzie's theory attempted to explain how great metropolitan areas could have internal coordination despite their size. (This is like explaining the size of brain and nervous system which would have been necessary to make dinosaurs viable and adaptive.) Urban expansion "connotes movement outward from a spatially determined center of settlement without loss of contact with that center" (McKenzie, cited in Kasarda, 1972, p. 165). The point of the theory of ecological expansion is that as the suburban periphery grows, the central city's organizations—banks, newspapers, courts, etc.—must expand in order to provide "integration and coordination of activities and relations throughout the expanded system" (Berry & Kasarda, 1977, p. 195). Chapters 12 and 13 discuss related materials on urbanization and suburban growth.

## Criticisms of Early Human Ecology

Starting in the late 1930s, several sociologists severely criticized the Chicago school's human ecology. One critic, Milla Alihan (1938), stated that while the urban sociologists claimed to be studying spatial competitive (subsocial ecological) processes, many were actually looking at cultural phenomena and using ordinary sociological explanations. She said, for example, that *The Gold Coast and the Slum* incorporated space and environment merely as a setting but explained the situation sociologically. She also accused the Chicagoans of using the biologist's ecological concepts as analogies, even if they did not apply accurately to human groups.

Another critic, Walter Firey (1945), also rejected the ecological theory of urban form, asserting that forces other than economic competition for central location may produce the city's land uses. Firey's argument, which is presented more fully in Chapter 7, states that the nonecological forces of sentiment and symbolism can determine land uses. A third critic of urban ecology, Maurice Davie (1938/1961), was less concerned with theoretical validity than with the generalizability of research findings. Studying rates of juvenile delinquency in New Haven, he found that the ecological pattern did not apply. Davie argued that other factors were more important than concentric zones for determining high-delinquency areas in individual cities. Despite such criticisms as those of Alihan, Firey, and Davie, interest in sociological human ecology revived after World War II.

## Postwar Human Ecology

### Broader scope

Contemporary human ecology has maintained certain themes since its origins. Within sociology, ecology is distinctive for the way it looks at the interplay of technology, environment, and population, with social organization as an outcome.

Sociologists have recently applied ecological thinking to phenomena other than cities. The first ecological theorists were building a theory of communities, and later writers made broader claims, asserting that all macrosociology is ecological (Duncan & Schnore, 1959). Like biological ecologists, they start with a population and ask how it adapts to its environment. Humans adapt by means of organization and technology; the dependent variable (that which is to be explained) is adaptation by means of social organization (Berry & Kasarda, 1977; Hawley, 1968; Micklin, 1973). Division of labor is one form of social organization. Two contemporary ecological studies use this broader, noncommunity expansion of human ecology; one examines the birth and death of corporations (Hannan & Freeman, 1977), and the other, the growth and change of school systems (Kasarda & Bidwell, 1983). Both studies show that ecological analysis need not be restricted to communities. However, the bulk of the literature in human ecology applies to cities and suburbs, and this text will be restricted to these community-based materials (for examples of urban ecology, see Berry & Kasarda, 1977; Hawley, 1950; 1981; Schwirian, 1974; Theodorson, 1982).

### The ecosystem

Human ecology differs from much of sociology by excluding people's attitudes and values and emphasizing the interplay of **p**opulation, social **o**rganization, environment, and technology (represented by the mnemonic device "p-o-e-t"). Duncan's (1959) outline of human ecology states that the basic unit of analysis is an ecosystem which can be understood by an examination of variables in these four clusters.

**Population** Studied by social scientists known as demographers, population is the basic material of an ecosystem. A population's size is one of its important properties; changing size—growth or contraction—has a major impact upon community life. Growing communities encounter different problems from those of "shrinking" cities; for example, imagine the differences between contemporary Houston, a boomtown, and Detroit, with its contracting automobile industry and widespread unemployment. Three processes generate population changes: fertility (birth rates), mortality (death rates), and migration. Some places have high birth rates, others low. Overall, death rates and infant mortality rates vary—there are differences between cities and even between different sections of the same metropolitan area. Migration, both international and internal, is also important. Detroit loses people when they move to areas with greater employment opportunities, while Houston gains to the point where it may not be able to accommodate all the newcomers.

Another property of a population is its composition, that is, such variables as age, sex, and race. Growing suburbs have a large proportion of infants and children, for example, while southwestern retirement communities have none. Racial and ethnic compositions vary: California's cities have a rich mix of whites and blacks, Hispanic- and Oriental-Americans; Minnesota's cities, in contrast, have mostly whites of European ancestry. Other compositional variables include proportion of male and female (known as the sex ratio), educational levels, and rural-urban background, to name a few.

The fascinating discipline of demography contributes a great deal to urban sociology. This text incorporates many demographic facts from such sources as the United States Census of Population, which is conducted every ten years, and the many periodic surveys carried out by the Census Bureau, like the Current Population Survey and the Annual Housing Survey. Every library contains a one-volume summary of demographic facts called the *Statistical Abstract of the United States*. The *County and City Data Book* and the *State and Metropolitan Area Date Book* contain numerous facts about cities and suburbs.

**Environment** Sociologists tend to ignore the environmental variables which form a backdrop to urban life. For example, when studying urban growth patterns, sociologists implicitly assume that the environment consists of flat land surrounding an existing city. The one central ecological variable which explicitly incorporates the environment is population density, which is the ratio between population and land area.

Urbanites occupy a "built environment," which is defined as the constructed features of the urban settlement: streets, buildings, parks, etc. Since building forms change in response to inventions—the elevator and the steel frame, for example, made the skyscraper possible—the built environment reflects technology, another major ecological concern. To some extent, urban sociologists have recognized the built environment for decades, since the beginnings of research in slums, but the discipline has always emphasized social facts before environmental ones. Chapter 15 summarizes a number of studies of the effects of slum housing versus modern housing. Likewise, Chapter 13 presents studies of the social effects of suburban environments. Sociologists who work with architects and city planners provide more general theories about the built environment as an element of the social scene (Gans, 1968; Gutman, 1972; Michelson, 1976; Zeisel, 1975). Architects and environmental psychologists also study this subject (Rapoport, 1976; Wicker, 1979).

**Social Organization**  Social organization, sometimes called social structure, refers to the way in which a population is organized. At the urban level this means the system of stratification, the organization of work and the economy, and the political system. It refers to the way community decisions are made and municipal systems like education and policing are organized. Urban sociology has not devoted equal attention to all these subjects.

Segregation and residential patterns of racial and ethnic groups and different socioeconomic statuses have long been central research concerns in urban sociology. Human ecologists and social geographers, aided in recent years by computers, have developed sophisticated methods of measuring spatial patterns, including segregation. Theoretically, segregation reflects social distance—subpopulations that do not live together are considered distant in other ways as well. But residential segregation may have additional consequences, in terms of educational integration and access to employment opportunities and other amenities in the metropolis (Harvey, 1973; Orfield, 1982).

For the most part, urban sociologists have left the political system to their colleagues in political science. In regard to contemporary cities, one structural characteristic has been taken for granted: Major municipal services (such as police, firefighting, school, and welfare systems) are organized into highly centralized bureaucracies which make rules and decisions (figuratively, in "city hall"). Such organizations deal with the public at the neighborhood level only through branch offices and local operatives. Even churches and charities—the United Way—may take the same centralized bureaucratic form. (In ordinary usage, the word "bureaucracy" has nasty connotations, but sociologists use it to denote a particular form of organization which is used to organize large numbers of individuals for specified purposes according to prescribed rules.) As it has been taken for granted, bureaucratic structure has rarely been studied by ecologists. Indeed, with few exceptions (Hawley, 1963; Hawley & Zimmer, 1961; Lincoln, 1976, 1978), ecologists tend to ignore political processes (Form, 1954). An emerging group of Marxist urban sociologists severely criticize the ecologists for this omission (Castells, 1977).

Ecological sociologists, pursuing Durkheim and McKenzie's studies, have conducted numerous studies of work and the metropolitan division of labor. These studies show the intensive division of labor within cities and, to some extent, among cities (Eberstein & Frisbie, 1982). With a precisely defined occupation, each resident of a metropolis is totally dependent upon the overall system for survival—thus the population is completely interdependent. Recent studies of the metropolitan labor force have looked particularly at the loss of jobs in older central cities and the creation of jobs in suburbs (Kasarda, 1976). Related studies point to the isolation of poor black and Hispanic workers in central cities, essentially cut off from the growth sector of the suburbanized economy.

**Technology**   Technology has been neglected somewhat in ecological research, although it has been considered in a historical context, (Lenski & Lenski, 1978). The history of cities shows numerous instances in which social changes followed particular inventions (Hawley, 1981). Sometimes, the effects of inventions on cities are indirect; for example, the development of certain navigational devices permitted long-distance ocean trade, fostering industrial growth that contributed to the development of factory towns. In other instances, though, technological change has direct effects upon urban growth and form; for example, the electric trolley contributed to the emergence of one sort of city in the late nineteenth century, and the automobile and freeway contributed to another in the midtwentieth. Ecological analysis of cities needs to take into account energy flows (Cottrell, 1955), communication devices, transportation, medicine and sanitation, and manufacturing technology.

**Combinations**   These four elements may have reciprocal effects on each other or may operate in combination. For example, Sly (1972) studied the migration of blacks from the rural south to the urban north, and his ecological explanation showed the effects of technology on population. Agriculture in the south was being mechanized in a way which required the consolidation of small fields and the use of less labor—a technological change. The blacks, who had formerly worked on small, labor-intensive farms, were forced out, so they moved to areas where opportunities were better at the time—a demographic effect from a technological cause. Another combination of variables: The recent "aging" of suburban populations and their low birth rates cause a shortage of young children. In consequence school boards have to decide which schools to close, often in a context of strong feelings among competing neighborhoods—a demographic change requiring an organizational response. Urban renewal projects illustrate a combination of three elements—social organization, environment, and population. A civic decision to redevelop a certain area may result in the demolition of residential buildings, causing their residents to relocate. There are innumerable other examples of interconnections among ecological elements.

Chapters 3 through 5 illustrate the application of the ecological perspective to urban history and urbanization by tracing the growth and development of cities from prehistoric time. The chapters emphasize how major technological changes triggered or permitted new types of cities. For example, the mechanization of manufacturing and the rise of factories were key elements in the beginnings of industrial towns; later, railroads and trolley lines affected urban form. The chapters also show how population made a difference at certain times. For example, heterogeneous groupings were the basis for the first cities; thousands of years later, the decimation of populations by plagues contributed to the decline of European cities. These historical chapters also highlight the urban social organization and stratification of each period. Consistent with the ecological mode of analysis, these chapters neglect the social psychology of urban life because there is no systematic record of people's attitudes and opinions in history—survey research is a contemporary social invention. The social psychology of urban life is reserved for the chapters about modern communities, starting with Chapter 4.

## TWO BRIDGING THEORIES

The two theories emphasized in this section build theoretical bridges in urban sociology, from macro to micro and from human ecology to social psychology.

### "Urbanism as a Way of Life"

In 1938, Louis Wirth, who had been both a student and a professor in the Chicago school, published an essay entitled "Urbanism as a Way of Life," which became one of the most influential theoretical statements in urban sociology. It has been widely cited for decades, inspiring countless theoretical responses and empirical research projects which test its hypotheses. Although the original essay, a sort of outline of urban sociology, covered a mere 24 pages in the *American Journal of Sociology*, one author filled an entire book explaining its ideas (Morris, 1968). Later empirical studies have disproven some of Wirth's assertions, but his theory still deserves study because it defines the scope of a major portion of urban sociology and can be seen as a paradigm for the field.

### Basic concepts

Wirth asks what the social life of the metropolis is and what causes it. He defines urbanism as "that complex of traits which makes up the characteristic mode of life in cities" (1938, p. 7). The main part of his essay sets forth a theory of urbanism.

Wirth built upon the theory presented by Georg Simmel in an essay entitled "The Metropolis and Mental Life" (1903/1957). Simmel, a great German social theorist, had a particular interest in the effects of numbers upon social relationships. In this essay he argued that certain of the city's features affect social relationships, behaviors, and personality. The fast pace of the city and the large numbers of persons and contacts produce an intensification of nervous stimulation for the individual, who is bombarded by swift and uninterrupted stimuli. Essentially, the human creature is not naturally built to receive so much stimulation, so it responds adaptively. Urban individuals develop a special personality type: They react with the head rather than the heart; thus they calculate the costs and payoffs of particular actions, including interpersonal relations. They develop an intellectuality and a heightened awareness of situations. Urban individuals become impersonal, with a blasé attitude which protects them from overstimulation of the nervous system; in social relations they are reserved. Perhaps the only good thing Simmel saw in the metropolis is that it offers the individual greater personal freedom than smaller communities offer.

In "Urbanism as a Way of Life," Wirth defines cities ecologically and argues that the defining qualities generate specific social organizational and social psychological outcomes. "For sociological purposes," according to Wirth, "a city may be defined as a relatively *large, dense,* and permanent settlement of socially *heterogeneous* individuals" (1938, p. 8, italics added). This means that the student body of an enormous campus like the University of Illinois, with more than 35,000 members, cannot be considered a city. Its population is large and dense, but since most of the students fall within a narrow age range (say, 17 to 28), it is too homogeneous to be a city within Wirth's definition. Each key term in Wirth's definition—large size, high density, and social heterogeneity—refers to the community's population. (Actually, density—the ratio of population to land area—incorporates environment too.) Wirth's definition must be considered ecological because it is based on properties of population and environment, two elements of human ecology. While this definition may appear simple and obvious, there are other, very different ways to define cities, such as in terms of their political or economic structures. Wirth's theory goes on to deduce a number of social consequences of the city's three ecological properties (see Figure 2-2).

## Effects of the main variables

**Large size** Large numbers yield individual variation and potential differentiation. This principle applies to all sorts of objects—a thousand apples will vary more than a dozen in weight, color, sweetness, and skin texture, for example. Likewise, large numbers of persons will vary in size, talents, interests, etc. Starting with this statistical reasoning, Wirth (1938) wrote:

> Large numbers involve ... a greater range of individual variation. Furthermore, the greater the number of individuals participating in a process of interaction, the greater is the *potential* differentiation between them. The personal traits, the occupations, the cultural life, and the ideas of the members of an urban community may, therefore, be expected to range between more widely separated poles than those of rural inhabitants. (p. 11)

Largeness of population yields segmental role relations and secondary relationships. Because it is impossible for an individual to have primary relationships with large numbers of people, most interpersonal contacts must be "impersonal, superficial, transitory, and segmental." In consequence of the multitudes, the city person becomes sophisticated and rational in relating to others, according to the theory.

The prevalence of secondary role relationships coupled with urban sophistication and rationality is one of Wirth's most frequently cited ideas. This portion of the theory has an ecological variable (large numbers) causing social psychological effects (secondary role relationships, managed rationally).

Wirth's reasoning always has the small traditional community's social life as an implicit background, standard, or contrast. Like others in the Chicago school, he used the logic of the folk-urban contrast. Implicit in the idea of the city's secondary segmental role relationships is that people enjoy a rich abundance of primary relationships in small communities.

In Wirth's theory urbanism also has social organizational qualities which are produced by the city's ecological properties. When there is a large population, people must communicate through indirect media and they must govern themselves by delegated authority. Implicit again is the small community where face-to-face communications would suffice. Wirth's metropolis needed a newspaper plus radio broadcasting; in contrast, the small community could govern itself directly with a participatory town meeting. A city has too many individuals for such a meeting; a large community in a democratic society requires elections and representatives.

**High density**  Urban population densities mean that there are large numbers of "others" in many urban settings: streets, apartment buildings, department stores, parks, etc. High density has social psychological effects, according to Wirth's theory. Physical contacts are close, but social contacts must be distant. Urbanites become sensitive to surface cues in others, such as their style of dress and personal grooming, not to others as individuals. This assertion is one of the two most widely cited propositions in the theory (secondary role relations and rationality, discussed above, is the other one). High density inspires some of Wirth's most negative assertions:

> The close living together of individuals who have no sentimental and emotional ties fosters a spirit of competition, aggrandizement, and mutual exploitation.... Frequent close physical contact, coupled with great social distance, accentuates the reserve of unattached individuals toward one another, and gives rise to loneliness. The necessary frequent movement of great numbers of individuals in a congested habitat gives occasion to friction and irritation." (1938, p. 14)

In combination, density and size affect urban social organization. A large population leads to proliferation of specialized tasks; similarly, high density yields differentiation. These ideas come from Darwin, who showed that densely settled habitats had different species in ecological niches which allowed them to coexist, and from Durkheim (1933), who showed that the division of labor is in part a function of density. In a small population everyone can do the same work, say, fishing, but

*Size*

An increase in the number of inhabitants of a settlement beyond a certain limit brings about changes in the relations of people and changes in the character of the community

- The greater the number of people interacting, the greater the potential differentiation
- Dependence upon a greater number of people, lesser dependence on particular persons
- Association with more people, knowledge of a smaller proportion, and of these, less intimate knowledge
- More secondary rather than primary contacts; that is, increase in contacts which are face to face, yet impersonal, superficial, transitory, and segmental
- More freedom from the personal and emotional control of intimate groups
- Association in a large number of groups, no individual allegiance to a single group

*Density*

Reinforces the effect of size in diversifying individuals and their activities, and in increasing the structural complexity of the society

- Tendency to differentiation and specialization
- Separation of residence from work place
- Functional specialization of areas—segregation of functions
- Segregation of people: city becomes a mosaic of social worlds

*Heterogeneity*

Cities products of migration of peoples of diverse origin

Heterogeneity of origin matched by heterogeneity of occupations

Differentiation and specialization reinforces heterogeneity

- Without common background and common activities, a premium is placed on visual recognition; the uniform becomes symbolic of the role
- No common set of values, no common ethical system to sustain them; money tends to become measure of all things for which there are no common standards
- Formal controls as opposed to informal controls; necessity for adhering to predictable routines; clock and the traffic signal symbolic of the basis of the social order
- Economic basis: mass production of goods, possible only with the standardization of process and products
- Standardization of goods and facilities in terms of the average
- Adjustments of educational, recreational, and cultural services to mass requirements
- In politics, success of mass appeals—growth of mass movements

**FIGURE 2-2**
Schematic outline of Wirth's theory. (Source: Shevky & Bell, 1955.)

this is impossible in a large population. Wirth asserts that a community can support a large population only through differentiation. Competition is another process in Wirth's city, having the effect of efficient allocation of activities to places.

**Heterogeneity**  The variety of peoples in the city tends to produce a relativistic perspective and a sense of tolerance of differences (these are social psychological effects). While residents of a small community may live among others who share their ancestry and outlook on life, urban individuals live with diversity. They may not be able to support an ethnocentric outlook as easily as people in a small community can. Wirth suggests that the relativistic perspective and sense of tolerance of differences are prerequisites to the urbanite's rationality and secularity.

Heterogeneity also breaks down rigid caste and class boundaries, according to the theory (this is a social organizational effect). Every urban individual is involved in multiple groups and has divided loyalties. The extensive division of labor requires rational allocation of persons to occupations; thus there must be social mobility. In addition, heterogeneity, combined with density, spatially sorts the population into homogeneous small areas (but does not "freeze" individuals in place—to do so would eliminate social mobility).

## Deterministic reasoning

The theory's direction of causality is clear: Given a settlement with certain demographic and environmental properties, that settlement will generate particular social psychological traits and certain forms of social organization known as urbanism. In other words, human ecology influences or causes social psychology and social organization. Interpreting Wirth's theory, Fischer (1976) calls it deterministic, alleging that it says a settlement's size, density, and heterogeneity *determine* its social life. At least, "Urbanism as a Way of Life" says there are some forms of social life which cannot survive in the metropolis and others which are likely to arise there.

## Responses to Wirth's Theory

The tone or flavor of Wirth's legacy to urban sociology is somewhat negative; current writers emphasize Wirth's remarks about the more unpleasant aspects of urbanism—impersonality, loss of primary ties, and superficiality. But this interpretation neglects the more positive elements of Wirth's urbanism, such as tolerance, as well as his treatment of the city's social organization.

"Urbanism as a Way of Life" inspired numerous responses, ranging from rejection to modification (as well as acceptance). Some sociologists wrote theoretical counterarguments, while others conducted full-scale research projects to test or challenge Wirth's hypotheses.

## Gideon Sjoberg

In a broad-ranging book, *The Preindustrial City* (1960), Sjoberg asserted that Wirth had neglected industrialism as a key variable affecting modern urbanism. After conducting historical research on city life prior to the industrial revolution and comparative research on twentieth-century cities without industry (which might now be called "third-world cities"), Sjoberg concluded that large, dense, heterogeneous settlements existed *without* what Wirth called urbanism. Sjoberg criticized Wirth and Redfield for neglecting the social system of the overall societies in which cities are located; he said the social life of a community is affected not only by its demography but also by its sociopolitical context. In his historical and comparative survey, Sjoberg found highly religious cities—Wirth had said urbanism is secular. Sjoberg also found cities with powerful elites and rigid caste and class systems, despite Wirth's assertion that heterogeneity and the division of labor yield social mobility. These findings did not necessarily disprove "Urbanism as a Way of Life," but they implied that before the theory could be applicable to any given community, certain underlying conditions must be present, namely, national democracy based upon a literate public; capitalistic economy, including the urban real estate market; and industrial technology.

## Herbert Gans

A 1962 essay entitled "Urbanism *and Suburbanism* as Ways of Life" [italics added] by Herbert J. Gans presented a very different challenge to Wirth's theory. Having already studied city neighborhoods, Gans was one of the first sociologists to examine the emerging suburbs. He said in the essay that Wirth's theory assumed the metropolis harbored a single way of life; according to Gans, the metropolis has several types of subcommunities and several types of individuals with different ways of life. Gans acknowledged that a couple of the city's types, the deprived and the trapped, might practice the sort of urbanism described in Wirth's theory. In contrast, though, another type, the urban villagers in first- and second-generation ethnic neighborhoods, were still locked into primary groups and were highly traditional, religious, and personalistic, quite unurban in Wirth's terms. Gans implied that Wirth was looking backward and that his theory missed an enormous section of the contemporary metropolis, the suburbs. While suburbs are urban, according to Gans, they foster a new "quasi-primary" relationship, neither primary nor secondary. Neighbors in the suburbs may have close relationships with each other which could also be circumscribed, so they would not have the fullness of primary ties. "Whatever the intensity or frequency of these [quasi-primary] relationships, the interaction is more intimate than a secondary contact, but more guarded than a primary one" (1962, p. 634). Like Sjoberg, Gans said that a large, dense, heterogeneous population does not necessarily produce Wirth's urbanism. Gans argued that there are several urban ways of life.

## A Subcultural Theory of Urbanism

The most recent response to Wirth's theory is Claude Fischer's subcultural theory of urbanism (1975). Like other critics of Wirth, Fischer contends urban ecology does not necessarily produce social disorganization and personal alienation. He says size and density have social effects, and his central point is that the congregation of large numbers of individuals, by virtue of their variability, yields "critical masses" which permit or foster "unconventional behavior" in subcultures.

## "Critical masses" and subcultures

As noted earlier, large numbers of individuals always include more variability than do small numbers. Most traits are normally distributed in populations, as shown in the bell-shaped curve in Figure 2-3. This graph could represent the distribution of such disparate traits as height, weight, or intelligence. If it represented the body weight of a population of adult males, the graph would show that most are near an average but they range toward two extremes, very light and very heavy. Height would be distributed similarly, from very short through average to exceptionally tall, and would fit the same graph. Now if 5 percent of the adult males are extremely heavy, then a town with 1,000 men would have about 50 who were extremely heavy. In a large city with a quarter-million adult males, 5 percent would equal 12,500 extremely heavy ones. In the small community, no single clothing retailer could afford to stock special clothes for the 50 men; they would have to order from a catalog or travel to a city to shop. But with several thousand potential customers,

**FIGURE 2-3**
A normal distribution of a trait within a population. If the population is small, a few individuals are at each of the extremes, but if it is large, as in a city, many are at the extremes.

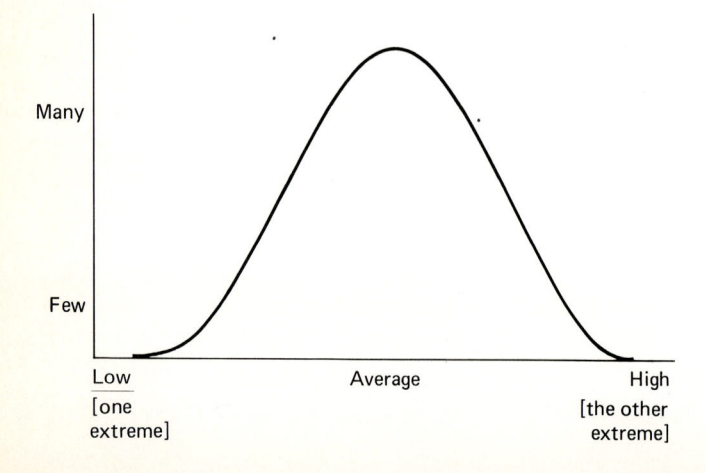

a city retailer could open a special shop for the "large-sized" man. This is the marketing equivalent of Fischer's critical mass; however, Fischer's analysis refers to subcultures rather than shops.

Imagine now that the horizontal axis of the graph in Figure 2-3 represents some other variable, perhaps musical talent. The graph could range from zero musical talent all the way to genius; the majority of people would fall in the middle, with moderate, or average, ability. As with very overweight men, a small population might have a few very musical individuals; but through simple variability, a large population would have thousands of them. Using the same principles, we could explain the presence of thousands of homosexuals in cities; in this case, the graph's horizontal axis would represent sexual preferences, ranging perhaps from homophilia through homosexuality. Again, even if only a small percentage of the population were homosexuals, a very large population could yield thousands. In general, these thousands who share rare characteristics or preferences are what Fischer means by a critical mass.

The metropolis also *attracts* persons with special interests or talents; their migration from smaller places contributes to the critical mass. Certain talents need cities for their development—musicians and dancers need special teachers and shops, for example. Certain behaviors are not tolerated in small communities—thus homosexuals have strong incentives to migrate to cities. Critical masses, therefore, develop as a result of variability in large populations and migration from smaller communities.

Subcultures grow within critical masses. "A 'subculture' is a set of modal beliefs, values, norms, and customs associated with a relatively distinct social subsystem (a set of interpersonal networks and institutions) existing within a larger social system and culture," according to Fisher (1975, p. 132). A city might well have a musical subculture, for example, which would have special shops and service personnel for instruments and sheet music, studios for practicing and recording, recital halls, teachers, classes, seminars, workshops, and the like. Musicians could communicate through special newspapers, bulletin boards, newsletters, etc., and could organize into unions, clubs, and orchestras. In a big enough city like New York they might even diversify internally into groups who prefer ancient and groups who prefer contemporary compositions. Members of the subculture would be likely to live in the same neighborhoods, frequent the same bars, see each other at parties, and foster their common interests in other ways. They could set styles and inspire each other by mutual listening and criticism. (Two recent sociological studies have looked into these subcultural processes among graphic artists: Hudson, 1982; Simpson, 1981.)

Similarly, a large city is likely to have male homosexual and lesbian subcultures, whose members may cluster in particular residential areas, such as Los Angeles's West Hollywood, which has come to be called "Boys Town." Like other subcultures, male homosexuals and lesbians develop networks and business enterprises, so in large cities members (and others) may call upon homosexual lawyers, carpenters, clergy, and other specialists.

Touching an imaginary wall, a pantomimist entertains pedestrians along New York's Fifth Avenue. The metropolis attracts individuals with special interests and talents. (Timothy Eagan, Woodfin Camp & Associates)

In addition to subcultures which emerge because of variability and large numbers, metropolitan areas contain ethnic subcultures that emerge because of the population's heterogeneity, which may be a function of migration patterns. No large city is homogeneous by race or national origin; each one accommodates a mix of peoples via international and internal migration. Sufficient numbers of an identifiable subpopulation become a critical mass for a subculture—Cincinnati's Appalachian whites, Miami Beach's elderly Jews, Houston's "urban cowboys," San Francisco's native Americans (American Indians).

## Unconventional behavior

According to Fischer, urban communities differ from rural ones by harboring much unconventional behavior. People of the metropolis are "more likely than rural residents to behave in ways that diverge from the central and/or traditional norms of their common society" (1975, p. 1321). Some urban unconventional behaviors are socially approved—cities have more inventing, writing, performing, and painting. Others are severely disapproved—cities also have more crime, drug use, and homosexuality.

## Propositions about subcultures

In developing the subcultural theory, Fischer sets forth several propositions, including the following:

> The bigger and denser a place, the greater its subcultural variety.
>
> The bigger and denser a place, the more intense its subcultures. This means that as a critical mass grows, the subculture can develop elaborate institutions and communicative devices. (Chapter 8 describes the institutions of large black ghettos as an example.)
>
> The bigger and denser a place, the higher the rates of unconventionality. "A small town may have a few delinquent youths, but only in a large city will there be sufficient numbers (i.e., a critical mass) sufficiently distinctive to establish a viable delinquent subculture. The same holds true for political dissidents, splinter religious sects, and criminals.... With size comes 'community'—even if it is a community of thieves, counterculture experimenters, avant-garde intellectuals, or other unconventional persons" (Fischer, 1975, pp. 1328-1329).

## SOCIAL PSYCHOLOGY

"Urbanism as a Way of Life" and the subcultural theory of urbanism showed that the metropolis has another dimension beyond the ecological. Urban social psychology refers to the social relationships of urban residents as well as to their attitudes, values, and personalities. The central questions in urban social psychology are the following, including a third one that sociologists and social geographers have added in recent years:

1. What effects does metropolitan residence have on individuals—their behavior, attitudes, and personalities?
2. What sorts of social relationships, if any, do people have in metropolitan communities; how do they develop and maintain them?
3. What effects do people's mental processes and social relationships have on the community's ecology?

## Effects of the Community

Conventional thinking has almost always held that the city has negative effects on individuals. Sociological theories like Simmel's and Wirth's highlight this sort of allegation, saying, in effect, that the urban community's size and complexity overwhelm the individual's capacity to handle it and that the city, therefore, makes the individual defensive, calculating, hard, lonely, and neurotic. In recent years, three lines of research have questioned this argument: studies on the effects of urban density, on urban mental health, and on tolerance and diffusion.

## The density-pathology hypothesis

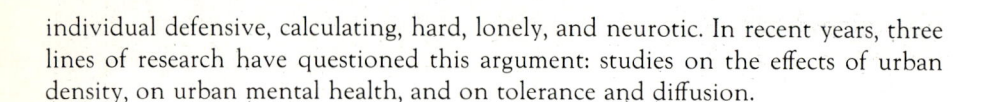

In the 1960s, several writers picked up the idea of the "behavioral sink" as a model for urban life. This concept was introduced by a biological psychologist, John Calhoun (1962a, 1962b), who conducted a series of experiments on crowded rats to determine the effects of high density. Calhoun built an environment in which rats would be confined to a limited amount of space, four pens, arranged in order with little passageways. He used different feeding devices in different versions of the experiments—some allowed the rats to eat separately, others forced them to crowd together to get food; there was always plenty of food, though. He inserted a number of rats in the pens and allowed them to multiply; soon there were so many that they far exceeded the number which would normally live in this amount of space—they had achieved a very high density. Then they began to deviate sharply from normal behavior patterns. Some became quite passive, allowing others to dominate them; many became quite aggressive, biting at each other's tails when they ate. Under ordinary conditions mother rats maintain nests and carry their offspring from place to place by the scruff of the neck. Under crowded conditions the mother rats stopped nurturing the babies; they failed to keep proper nests; and if they dropped a pup while carrying it, they just left it to die. Adult male rats became pansexual, attempting to mount males or females indiscriminately. Altogether, this breakdown of normal behaviors is called a behavioral sink.

Calhoun and others said cities were becoming behavioral sinks; excessive density was generating urban riots and escalating crime rates. Such writers were unaware, evidently, of the fact that density had been falling in most American metropolitan areas just as crime rates were rising. These writers also neglected the historical fact that when urban density was much higher (in immigrant slums after the turn of the century, for example), crime rates were lower.

Psychologists and sociologists tested the density-pathology hypothesis among human populations. Psychological small-group experiments did not confirm the hypothesis—crowding experiments yielded mixed results, sometimes even showing that increased density produced nonpathological behavior: quiet, nonagressive play among children, for example (Freedman, 1975; Loo, 1972). Baldassare and Fischer (1977) then challenged the validity of the psychological small-group experiments, asserting that they could not possibly illuminate the effects of the urban environment. They and other sociologists contended that the rat model was simply a misapplied analogy which should not have been applied to the human situation. Because they have culture, humans can use and handle physical environments in ways which lower mammals cannot (Gans, 1968; Suttles, 1972). Choldin and Roncek (1976; Choldin, 1978) tested the density-pathology hypothesis ecologically in the context of the fact that many individuals who live in high-density environments are poor. They concluded that neighborhood density did not have an independent harmful effect, apart from the effects of slum life, poverty, and discrimination. These researchers emphasized the effects of income and other socioeconomic variables in metropolitan neighborhoods. While dense poor neighborhoods often have high illness and high crime rates, dense prosperous neighborhoods may not. Other sociological researchers (Booth, 1976) reached the same conclusion. At the micro level, though, two studies concluded that physical household crowding has some negative effects. (These studies looked at the effects of crowding within individual apartments or houses, rather than at overall neighborhood density.) Gove et al. (1979) found negative mental health consequences of household crowding and Baldassare (1981) found that certain categories of households and individuals were adversely affected. Household crowding is especially irritating in low-income households and to mothers with young children. In combination, the macro and micro studies suggest that while neighborhood density per se does not have the hypothesized effects, crowded housing units are a problem.

## Mental health in the metropolis

While it is almost an article of faith among Americans that the country is more wholesome than the city and that rural folk have better mental health than their neurotic city cousins, the little research that has been done on the subject fails to confirm this myth. The mental health sections of two national health surveys do not show superior mental health in rural areas and small towns (see Table 2-1 for 1960–1962 research). In fact, the data in Table 2-1 show that rural and small-town residents had more negative psychological symptoms than residents in metropolitan areas had. A second survey, taken ten years later, also failed to show better

**TABLE 2-1**
**Mean Age-Adjusted Psychological-Symptom Scores by Sex and Type of Community (Whites Only), 1960–1962**

| (Number of cases = 6,678) | Males | Females |
|---|---|---|
| Largest metropolitan areas (at least 3 million population) | 1.53 | 2.73 |
| Intermediate metropolitan areas (500,000–3 million) | 1.65 | 2.77 |
| Smaller metropolitan areas (50,000–500,000) | 1.63 | 2.70 |
| Other urban (2,500–50,000) | 1.98 | 3.26 |
| Rural nonfarm | 1.90 | 3.14 |
| Rural farm | 1.81 | 3.25 |

*Source:* National Center for Health Statistics, cited in Srole, 1980, p. 18.

mental health in the countryside. Other surveys of general happiness show no difference between urban and rural areas, according to Srole (1980). Strole's own study of mental health in central Manhattan, America's densest district, tested two hypotheses: (1) The longer people lived in the metropolis, the worse their mental health became, and (2) over the decades, urban mental health is deteriorating. His careful psychiatric research failed to confirm either hypothesis.

## Tolerance and diffusion of innovations

Another aspect of metropolitan social psychology is tolerance of subcultures and ways of life other than one's own. Fischer's subcultural theory (1975) states that residents of large communities are more tolerant of differences than their small-town counterparts. This has been shown in studies of tolerance of various sorts of nonconforming behavior, from the political to the sexual (Fischer, 1971). Diffusion of innovations is a related metropolitan phenomenon; ideas and items diffuse between subcultures in cities and from there to smaller places. The mass media—broadcasters, publishers, film makers and other style setters like clothing manufacturers and advertising agencies—are centered in cities.

## Social Relations

Current writing in urban sociology tends to refute the determinist hypothesis that urban settlements destroy social relationships. Perhaps the most powerful research to this effect is on urban and suburban "social networks," demonstrating that metropolitan residents have extensive primary ties (Fischer, 1982; Wellman, 1979). This text presents social network concepts and research findings in Chapter 14.

People may have misunderstood urban life because they failed to distinguish between public and private social worlds (Fischer, 1981). By definition, the public world of the metropolis is visible and the private world is not. Wirth's propositions about the effects of size, density, and heterogeneity must hold true in public; no one can know personally all the people on the street or in a department store. This fact gave rise to many stereotyped notions of the impersonality of city life. But each person has close ties to others who comprise a private world, and this network of intimate contacts is likely to be equally satisfying in the city, suburb, or countryside.

Another aspect of metropolitan life is the potential disconnection of location from relationship. Contemporary metropolitan residents do not ncessarily depend upon their neighborhoods for their private relationships. The suburbanized metropolis, with widespread automobile ownership and access to telephones, facilitates "community without propinquity" (Craven & Wellman, 1974; Webber,

1963). Each individual's close friends and kinfolk may be scattered through a large metropolis, yet they can maintain close relationships and contacts (Wellman, 1979).

## Effects on Human Ecology

Up to this point, theories have shown how ecology affects social psychology, but social psychological processes also affect urban ecology. Common "preferences," which are expressions of culture or subcultural themes, affect certain demographic and environmental processes such as suburbanization and suburban form. Americans value privacy and "wide-open spaces," so most people will choose detached houses with yards rather than apartments. Furthermore, our long-standing antiurbanism leans toward the pastoral imagery of the suburb as a pseudo small town, whether or not the reality fits the image (Riesman, 1957; White & White, 1962).

The housing industry and the government respond to such preferences; certainly, both combined to provide a plethora of low-density suburban housing in the decades of the 1950s and 1960s (Downs, 1974). Other preferences are accommodated too. In the 1970s and beyond, the market provided special housing developments for "singles," elderly, and other categories of persons. Thus, to some extent, the built environment expresses cultural preferences.

Sociologist Gerald Suttles argues that social psychological processes can produce ecological effects inadvertently or deliberately. In a study of a Chicago lower-class neighborhood, Suttles (1968) showed that four different ethnic groups used certain meaningful communicative devices to maintain group identity, to distance themselves from the other groups, and to mark their own turf. The communicative devices included distinctive ways of speaking, dressing, and even walking. Social geographers have shown other ways of defining and marking urban and suburban spaces. One study in Philadelphia showed how adolescent gangs claimed particular streets or blocks by marking them with graffiti (see Figure 2-4). Another study in an East Coast suburb showed that two different status groups expressed their affiliations and lifestyles by using different landscaping and exterior decorations on their houses (Duncan, 1973). Hunter (1975) argues that a set of "community area" maps prepared by sociologists has affected official concepts of the city's ecology and policies toward particular districts for over a half-century.

More consciously, residents or developers may try to influence the development of built environments; community "boosters"—bankers, shopkeepers, builders, and the like—have long promoted their towns or areas (Strauss, 1961). Nowadays, such individuals, in league with residents' associations, may promote the reputation and development of their areas to build what Suttles (1982) calls a "contrived community." Suttles proposes a new concept, "the social construction of community," which means that people impart meaning to their social and environmental situations, sometimes deliberately.

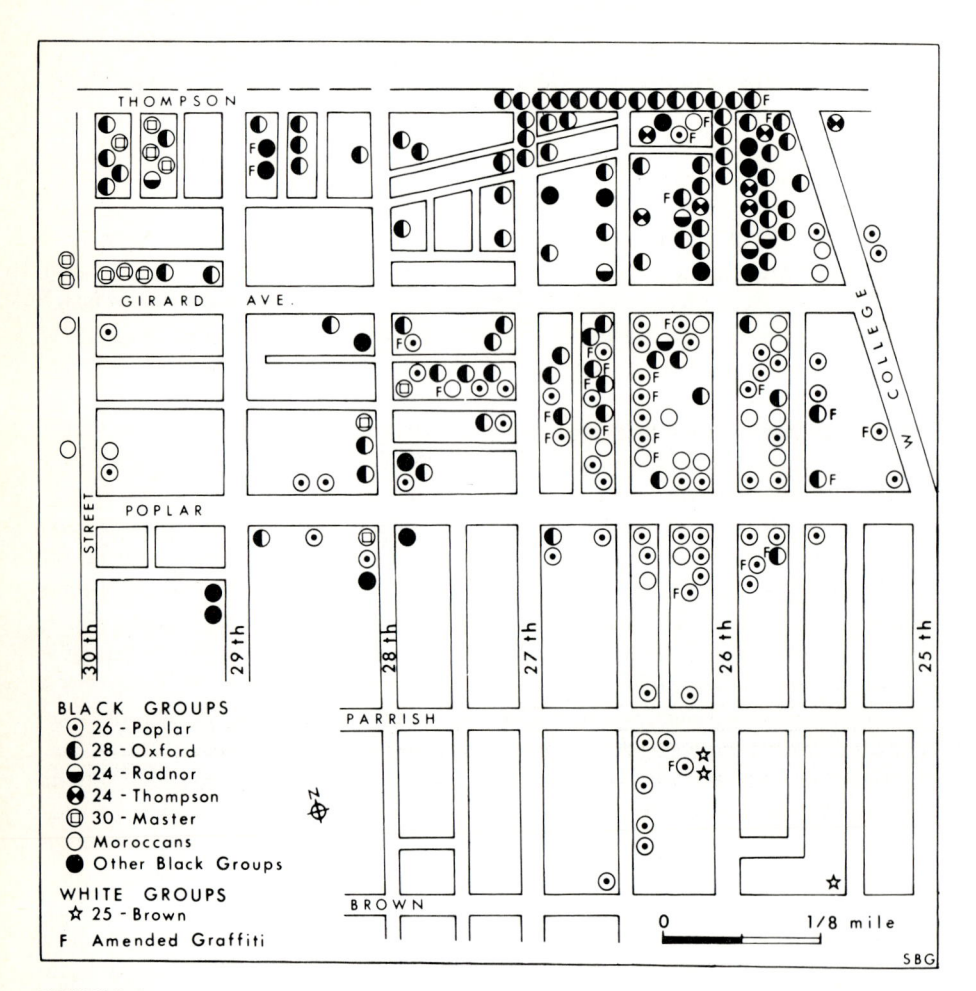

**FIGURE 2-4**
Urban graffiti as territorial markers. Gang graffiti in the northwestern portion of Fairmount, a section of Philadelphia. Each boys' gang marks the walls of structures in its claimed "turf." A team of urban geographers carefully recorded all the graffiti in this district. (Source: Ley & Cybriwski, 1978.)

## SUMMARY

Urban researchers typically focus on questions at either the microsociological or macrosociological scale. Micro questions refer to social relationships, networks, and geographical segments no larger than neighborhoods, whereas macro questions refer to the metropolis as a whole or to its major segments, including racial and ethnic subpopulations, overall spatial patterns, demographic growth, etc.

Human ecology is one of urban sociology's major theoretical perspectives; typically applied at the macro level, it combines four major clusters of variables referring to population, environment, social organization, and technology. Ecological theory eliminates most psychological and cultural concerns, such as people's attitudes and values, and attempts to explain community structure and change in terms of such phenomena as technological inventions and demographic developments. Human ecology draws attention to fundamentally important community phenomena such as whether the community is growing or shrinking, whether the population is young or old, whether different segments are integrated or segregated, how densely the population lives, and what sort of transportation and communications systems are used.

Urban social psychology asks very different questions. Typically applied at the micro level, it asks what effect the metropolis has upon its residents; how does it affect their behavior, attitudes, personalities; and relationships?

Two central theories in urban sociology build bridges between human ecology and social psychology. Louis Wirth's urbanism as a way of life suggests that three urban ecological properties—large size, high density, and heterogeneity of population—have powerful effects on social organization and psychology. They tend to make people distant and calculating in dealing with each other, unconnected, atomistic, and lonely. Claude Fischer's more contemporary subcultural theory also states that the ecological properties have effects, but they are not necessarily negative ones. A larger population, by virtue of human variability and migration, contains critical masses of people with different talents and preferences, thus giving rise to many subcultures. Subcultures, ranging from the artistic to the criminal, make urban individuals more tolerant of differences among groups.

Another recent theory by Gerald Suttles, the social construction of community, suggests that social psychological processes may affect urban ecology. Individuals desiring a particular sort of environment or community life may group together in one section and may foster a particular lifestyle (see, for example, Hunter, 1975).

One of the goals of this book is to show that the best understanding of urban and suburban communities comes as the observer-analyst moves between levels or combines theories and perspectives. Some of the literature of urban sociology is strictly macro or micro; some, definitely ecological or social psychological. Two central theories, urbanism as a way of life and the subcultural theory, move from ecology to social psychology; some recent work proceeds in the opposite direction. Writings by Suttles and several other sociologists cited heavily in the text, including Gans, Michelson, Fischer, and Hunter, exemplify the payoff from moving between levels and among theories.

## REFERENCES

Alihan, Milla. 1938. *Social Ecology: A Critical Analysis.* New York: Columbia University Press.

Baldassare, Mark. 1981. "The Effects of Household Density on Subgroups." *American Sociological Review.* 46:110-118.

Baldassare, Mark, and Claude S. Fischer. 1977. "The Relevance of Crowding Experiments to Urban Studies," pp. 273-285 in *Perspectives on Environment and Behavior,* (ed.) Daniel Stokols. New York; Plenum.

Berry, Brian J. L., and John D. Kasarda. 1977. *Contemporary Urban Ecology.* New York: Macmillan.

Booth, Alan. 1976. *Urban Crowding and Its Consequences.* New York: Praeger.

Burgess, Ernest W. 1925. "The Growth of the City: An Introduction to a Research Project," pp. 47-62 in *The City,* (eds.) Robert E. Park et al. Chicago: University of Chicago Press.

Calhoun, John B. 1962a. "A Behavioral Sink," pp. 295-315 in *Roots of Behavior,* (ed.) E. L. Bliss. New York: Harper.

Calhoun, John B. 1962b. "Population Density and Social Pathology." *Scientific American.* 206:139-148.

Castells, Manuel. 1977. *The Urban Question.* Cambridge, Mass.: MIT Press.

Choldin, Harvey M. 1978. "Urban Density and Pathology." *Annual Review of Sociology.* 4:91-113.

Choldin, Harvey M., and Dennis W. Roncek. 1976. "Density, Population Potential and Pathology: A Block-Level Analysis." *Review of Public Data Use.* 4:19-30.

Cottrell, Fred. 1955. *Energy and Society.* New York: McGraw-Hill.

Craven, Paul, and Barry Wellman. 1974. "The Network City," pp. 57-88 in *The Community: Approaches and Applications,* (ed.) M. P. Effrat. New York: Free Press.

Davie, Maurice R. 1938/1961. "The Pattern of Urban Growth," pp. 77-92 in *Studies in Human Ecology,* (ed.) George A. Theodorson. Evanston, Ill.: Row, Peterson.

Downs, Anthony. 1974. "Successes and Failures of Federal Housing Policy." *Public Interest.* 34:124-145.

Duncan, James S., Jr. 1973. "Landscape Tastes as a Symbol of Group Identity: A Westchester County Village." *The Geographical Review.* 63:334-355.

Duncan, James S., Jr. 1976. "Landscape and the Communication of Social Identity," pp. 391-404 in *The Mutual Interaction of People and Their Built Environment,* (ed.) Amos Rapoport. The Hague: Mouton.

Duncan, Otis D. 1959. "Human Ecology and Population Studies," pp. 678-716 in *The Study of Population,* (eds.) P. M. Hauser, and O. D. Duncan. Chicago: University of Chicago Press.

Duncan, Otis D., and Leo F. Schnore. 1959. "Cultural, Behavioral, and Ecological Perspectives in the Study of Social Organization." *American Journal of Sociology.* 65:132-146.

Durkheim, Emile. 1933. *The Division of Labor in Society.* New York: Macmillan.

Eberstein, Isaac, and W. Parker Frisbie. 1982. "Metropolitan Function and Interdependence in the U.S. Urban System." *Social Forces.* 60:676-700.

Firey, Walter. 1945. "Sentiment and Symbolism as Ecological Variables." *American Sociological Review.* 10:140-148.

Fischer, Claude S. 1971. "A Research Note on Urbanism and Tolerance." *American Journal of Sociology.* 76:847-856.

Fischer, Claude S. 1975. "Toward a Subcultural Theory of Urbanism." *American Journal of Sociology.* 80:1319–1341.
Fischer, Claude S. 1976. *The Urban Experience.* New York: Harcourt Brace Jovanovich.
Fischer, Claude S. 1981. "The Public and Private Worlds of City Life." *American Sociological Review.* 46:306–316.
Fischer, Claude S. 1982. *To Dwell among Friends: Personal Networks in Town and City.* Chicago: University of Chicago Press.
Form, William H. 1954. "The Place of Social Structure in the Determination of Land Use." *Social Forces.* 32:317–322.
Freedman, J. L. 1975. *Crowding and Behavior.* San Francisco: Freedman.
Gans, Herbert J. 1962. "Urbanism and Suburbanism as Ways of Life," pp. 625–648 in *Human Behavior and Social Processes; an Interactionist Approach,* (ed.) Arnold M. Rose. Boston: Houghton Mifflin.
Gans, Herbert J. 1968. "The Potential Environment and the Effective Environment," pp. 4–11 in *People and Plans, Essays on Urban Problems and Solutions,* (ed.) H. J. Gans. New York: Basic Books.
Gove, Walter R., Michael Hughes, and Omer R. Galle. 1979. "Overcrowding in the Home: An Empirical Investigation of Its Possible Consequences." *American Sociological Review.* 44:59–80.
Gutman, Robert (ed.). 1972. *People and Buildings.* New York: Basic Books.
Halbwachs, Maurice. 1938/1960. *Population and Society: Introduction to Social Morphology.* Glencoe, Ill.: Free Press.
Hannan, Michael T., and John Freeman. 1977. "The Population Ecology of Organizations." *American Journal of Sociology.* 82:929–964.
Harvey, David. 1973. *Social Justice and the City.* Baltimore: Johns Hopkins University Press.
Hawley, Amos H. 1950. *Human Ecology.* New York: Ronald Press.
Hawley, Amos H. 1963. "Community Power and Urban Renewal Success." *American Journal of Sociology.* 68:422–431.
Hawley, Amos H. 1968. "Human Ecology," pp. 329–337 in *International Encyclopedia of the Social Sciences* (vol. 4). New York: Macmillan and Free Press.
Hawley, Amos H. 1981. *Urban Society* (2d ed.). New York: Wiley.
Hawley, Amos H., and Basil Zimmer. 1961. "Resistance to Unification in a Metropolitan Community," in *Community Political Systems,* (ed.) Morris Janowitz. New York: Free Press.
Hudson, James R. 1982. "Changing Land-Use Patterns in SoHo: Residential Invasion of an Industrial Area," pp. 241–248 in *Urban Patterns: Studies in Human Ecology* (rev. ed.), (ed.) George A. Theodorson. University Park, Pa.: Pennsylvania State University Press.
Hunter, Albert. 1975. "The Loss of Community: An Empirical Test through Replication." *American Sociological Review.* 40:537–553.
Kasarda, John D. 1972. "The Theory of Ecological Expansion: An Empirical Test." *Social Forces.* 51:165–175.
Kasarda, John D. 1976. "The Changing Occupational Structure of the American

Metropolis: Apropos the Urban Problem," pp. 113–135 in *The Changing Face of the Suburbs,* (ed.) Barry Schwartz. Chicago: University of Chicago Press.
Kasarda, John D., and Charles E. Bidwell. 1983. "A Human Ecological Theory of Organization Structuring," chap. 5 in *Sociological Human Ecology,* (eds.) Michael Micklin and Harvey Choldin. Boulder, Colo.: Westview Press.
Lenski, Gerhard E., and Jean Lenski. 1978. *Human Societies: An Introduction to Macrosociology* (3d ed.). New York: McGraw-Hill.
Ley, David, and Roman Cybriwski. 1978. "Urban Graffiti as Territorial Markers," chap. 3 in *An Invitation to Geography,* (eds.) David A. Lanegran and Risa Palm. New York: McGraw-Hill.
Lincoln, James R. 1976. "Power Mobilization in the Urban Community: Reconsidering the Ecological Approach." *American Sociological Review.* 41:1–15.
Lincoln, James R. 1978. "Community Structure and Industrial Conflict: An Analysis of Strike Activity in SMSAs." *American Sociological Review.* 43:199–220.
Loo, Chalsa. 1972. "The Effects of Spatial Density on the Social Behavior of Children." *Journal of Applied Social Psychology.* 2:372–381.
McKenzie, Roderick. 1933a. "Industrial Expansion and the Interrelations of Peoples," pp. 19–33 in *Race and Cultural Contacts.* (ed.) E. B. Reuter. New York: McGraw-Hill.
McKenzie, Roderick. 1933b. *The Metropolitan Community.* New York: McGraw-Hill.
Michelson, William. 1976. *Man and His Urban Environment: A Sociological Approach* (2d ed.). Reading, Mass.: Addison-Wesley.
Micklin, Michael (ed.). 1973. *Population, Environment, and Social Organization: Current Issues in Human Ecology.* Hinsdale, Ill.: Dryden Press.
Morris, R. N. 1968. *Urban Sociology.* New York: Praeger.
Orfield, Gary. 1982. *Toward a Strategy for Urban Integration: Lessons in School and Housing from Twelve Cities.* New York: Ford Foundation.
Park, Robert E. 1967. "The Urban Community as a Spatial Pattern and a Moral Order," pp. 55–68 in *Robert Park on Social Control and Collective Behavior,* (ed.) Ralph H. Turner. Chicago: University of Chicago Press.
Rapoport, Amos (ed.). 1976. *The Mutual Interaction of People and Their Built Environment.* The Hague: Mouton.
Riesman, David. 1957. "The Suburban Dislocation." *Annals of the American Academy of Political and Social Science.* 314:123–146.
Schnore, Leo F. 1958. "Social Morphology and Human Ecology." *American Journal of Sociology.* 63:620–634.
Schwirian, Kent P. (ed.). 1974. *Comparative Urban Structure: Studies in the Ecology of Cities.* Lexington, Mass.: D. C. Heath.
Shevky, Eshrev, and Wendell Bell. 1955. *Social Area Analysis: Theory, Illustrative Application and Computational Procedure.* Stanford, Cal.: Stanford University Press.
Simmel, Georg. 1903/1957. "The Metropolis and Mental Life," pp. 635–646 in *Cities and Society: The Revised Reader in Urban Sociology,* (eds.) Paul K. Hatt and Albert J. Reiss, Jr. Glencoe, Ill.: Free Press.

Simpson, Charles R. 1981. *SoHo: The Artist in the City.* Chicago: University of Chicago Press.
Sjoberg, Gideon. 1960. *The Preindustrial City.* Glencoe, Ill.: Free Press.
Sly, David. 1972. "Migration and the Ecological Complex." *American Sociological Review.* 37:615-628.
Srole, Leo. 1980. "Mental Health in New York." *The Sciences.* 20 (10):16-29.
Strauss, Anselm. 1961. *Images of the American City.* New York: Free Press.
Suttles, Gerald D. 1968. *The Social Order of the Slum.* Chicago: University of Chicago Press.
Suttles, Gerald D. 1972. *The Social Construction of Communities.* Chicago: University of Chicago Press.
Suttles, Gerald D. 1982. "The Contrived Community: 1970-1980," pp. 224-229 in Theodorson.
Theodorson, George A. (ed.). 1982. *Urban Patterns: Studies in Human Ecology* (2d ed.). University Park, Pa.: Pennsylvania State University Press.
U.S. Bureau of the Census. 1978. *County and City Data Book, 1977.* Washington, D.C.: Government Printing Office.
U.S. Bureau of the Census. 1981. *Statistical Abstract on the United States: 1981.* Washington, D.C.: Government Printing Office.
U.S. Bureau of the Census. 1982. *State and Metropolitan Area Data Book, 1982.* Washington, D.C.: Government Printing Office.
Webber, Melvin M. 1963. "Order in Diversity: Community without Propinquity," in *Cities and Space: The Future Use of Urban Land.* (ed.) L. Wingo. Baltimore: Johns Hopkins University Press.
Wellman, Barry. 1979. "The Community Question: The Intimate Networks of East Yorkers." *American Journal of Sociology.* 84:1201-1231.
White, Morton, and Lucia White. 1962. *The Intellectual versus the City.* New York: Mentor.
Wicker, Allan W. 1979. *An Introduction to Ecological Psychology.* Monterey, Cal.: Brooks/Cole.
Wirth, Louis. 1938. "Urbanism as a Way of Life." *American Journal of Sociology.* 44:1-24.
Zeisel, John. 1975. *Sociology and Architectural Design.* New York: Russell Sage Foundation.
Zorbaugh, Harvey. 1929. *The Gold Coast and the Slum.* Chicago: University of Chicago Press.

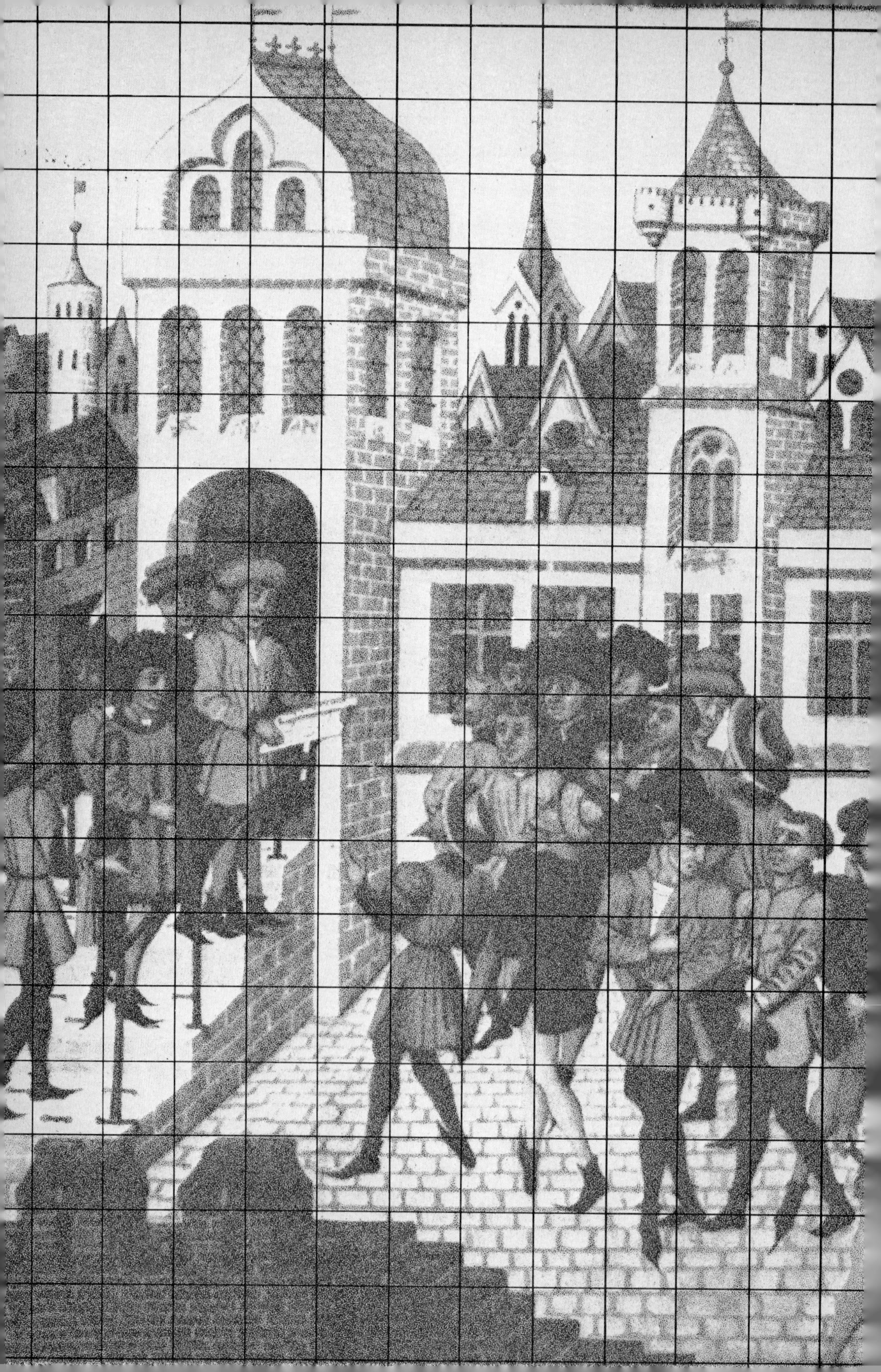

# CHAPTER · 3

# From Nomadism to the Medieval Town

## Chapter Outline

INTRODUCTION

THE AGRICULTURAL REVOLUTION
 Before Agriculture: Nomads
 The First Communities
 The Transition from Villages to Cities

THE URBAN REVOLUTION
 Ecology
 Social Organization
 Cultural Developments
 Childe's Fundamental Features
 Cities on Four Continents

CITIES OF CLASSICAL ANTIQUITY
 Ecology
 Social Organization

MEDIEVAL TOWNS
 Background
 Urban Growth
 - Ecology
 - Social organization
 - Mumford's appreciation of the medieval town

SUMMARY
 Why did People Build Cities?
 - For defense
 - For worship
 - For production and exchange
 Why do People Live in Cities?
 - For opportunity
 - For freedom
 General Points

## INTRODUCTION

Every day, in our own communities, we see the descendants of buildings and institutions which were present in the earliest cities. Churches, synagogues, and mosques; city hall; warehouses; and shopping malls all had their equivalents in the first cities. And any contemporary city on a river or other navigable body of water has docks, just as its predecessors in the distant past had elementary mooring facilities for boats.

North American cities are young, so they have only recent versions of these ancient facilities, but travelers to Europe can see older ones, including some urban structures which are no longer built. One such obsolete structure is the city wall with its gates—the great stone wall and its narrow opening, perhaps wide enough for a cart or two, with a guardhouse and heavy wooden gates ready to be closed at night. Many old European cities retain some of the basic institutions in historical forms—cathedrals, far larger in proportion to the other buildings than churches of our times; medieval town halls, far smaller in proportion than the government buildings of today's cities.

These artifacts of the past imply questions about the social life of their times. Why was there a wall? What was the place of the religious structure, of religion, in the first communities? How were people organized to support the church, the palace, the army? How big were the communities; who lived in them?

These are sociological questions, but in this portion of the text we answer them not with sociological research but with the materials of history and anthropology. As the story of cities begins before history, evidence of the beginning stage is taken from two branches of anthropology: archaeology and ethnography. During the relevant prehistoric period, starting about 50,000 years ago, humankind lived as nomads, hunting and gathering to survive. Not being literate, they left no written record, but archaeologists have studied what they did leave—their caves, tools, burials, etc.—to reconstruct their way of life. Ethnographers have studied those nomadic and hunting peoples who have survived into modern times. Sometimes it is reasonable to extrapolate backward from the ethnographic evidence and to infer that some features of the demography, technology, and way of life of the prehistoric peoples were like those of the contemporary nomads and hunters. (The modern world has impinged on the contemporary tribes to such an extent that soon there may be none left.) After writing was invented in the first cities, people began to leave written records, so we rely upon historians for information once we reach the urban part of the chapter.

In a historical context, this chapter follows the theme set forth in Chapter 2. That is, in order to understand urban communities, one must use various sociological perspectives in combination. In this case, studying the emergence and evolution of cities, it is important to look at the interplay between ecology and social organization to see the effects of technological inventions in a particular environment in the rise of agriculture, which made cities possible. We see the emergence of urban-built environment in the first cities; changing forms of social organization in different urban historical epochs; and, running through the history, cultural themes as well, particularly the centrality of religion, in historical cities.

This chapter starts with humanity before there were any cities and goes through a series of historical episodes, ending with the medieval town and city. Chapter 4 picks up the history with the beginnings of industrial towns, and Chapter 5 arrives at the modern metropolis. This chapter does not give a continuous history of urban development, which would be far too lengthy for an urban sociology course, but it moves discontinuously through four key episodes:

1. *The agricultural revolution* deals with humankind before there were any cities, or even villages, presenting the nomadic way of life and the development of agriculture, which made urban settlements possible.
2. *The urban revolution* shows the emergence in Mesopotamia of the first cities and their social organization.
3. *The cities of classical antiquity* present the changes in urban form in ancient Greece and Rome.
4. *The medieval town* shows the revival of urban communities several hundred years after the fall of the Roman Empire.

Each of these periods highlights some key social or environmental feature of urban communities, with some relevance to the understanding of the contemporary scene.

In this chapter each period and region is treated as though it had a single, typical urban community. Strictly speaking, this is not true, since variation occurred over time and space in each of these periods and regions. This sociological approach is used, though, to permit certain abstractions and generalizations by highlighting major common features and trends. The method, called the "constructed type," was developed by Sjoberg (1960) in his global survey of cities. Sjoberg introduced the concept of the preindustrial city, a single constructed type, to represent cities in agricultural societies prior to industrial development. The constructed type allows the sociologist to emphasize major features and processes which would be obscured by considering the details of variation among places.

## THE AGRICULTURAL REVOLUTION

### Before Agriculture: Nomads

In the long sweep of human history and prehistory, cities are a recent innovation—most of the human experience was spent before the erection of any sort of fixed communities. Our species, *Homo sapiens,* has been on earth in something like our modern version for perhaps 50,000 to 100,000 years, and closely related variants, including *Homo erectus,* were present for much longer. For all of this time, with the exception of the last 10,000 years (or so), people lived without communities. The first fixed communities were settled as agriculture developed in the Neolithic period of prehistory, and the first true cities emerged only about 5,500 years ago.

Before there were settled communities, people lived as nomads, wandering about in pursuit of sustenance. They lived in small bands of fewer than 50 members, all of whom were related as family and kin. Undoubtedly, only kinfolk could be part of the band, and all outsiders would be rejected. Much of their daily life was devoted to getting food—hunting for game and collecting roots, seeds, fruit—whatever was edible, nourishing, and available in the environment. Their food had to generate and regenerate itself in a state of nature with no artificial assistance. For these reasons they are known as hunters and gatherers.

They lived at low population densities which were limited by the carrying capacity of the land and their feeble technology for getting food. Based upon the densities of modern-day hunters and gatherers, one authority estimates densities of populated regions between 0.11 per square mile and 0.026 per square mile, with one exceptional area as high as 1.7 (Kroeber, cited in Childe, 1954, p. 45). Another writer, using similar kinds of data, found that in the most favorable environments, modern hunting and gathering societies have rarely reached 10 persons per square mile in settled areas (Birdsell, cited in Lenski & Lenski, 1978, p. 117). In sum, bands of hunters and gatherers were small, and they lived at low densities.

The clan, the basic unit of social organization in the nomadic band, is "a kin group whose members claim descent from a common ancestor" (Lenski & Lenski, 1978, p. 438). Although the social organization of the prehistoric bands cannot be known, Childe generalizes about the observed groups of hunting tribes, noting that there is some variety in their organization and beliefs. He writes that the members of the clan are believed to be descended from a totem ancestor; furthermore, "The totem is generally an edible animal, insect, or plant, important in the tribal economy" (1954, p. 45). There is a set of rules as to the mutual rights and duties of members, who may marry whom, etc. "Hunting and fishing grounds, and the food obtained therefrom, are generally owned and enjoyed in common. But something like personal property in weapons, vessels, and finery and even in spells or dances may be recognized" (p. 46). Inequality exists within the system, at least to the extent that old men have authority and prestige entitling them to have women and other sorts of wealth. The band has a sacred religious life, a set of rituals, and beliefs—initiations and other ceremonies.

Exhausting the food supply of a given local area and lacking the technology to replenish it, they frequently have to pack their scanty belongings and move. Some contemporary groups stay as little as a week in a single stop (Lenski & Lenski, 1978). They might have to move after the local fruits have been collected and the game has been killed or scared away.

A band is likely to have a fixed circuit of places to which it moves; by the time the group completes the circuit, the food and game will have regenerated since the last visit. Lenski and Lenski (1978) sum up the migration as follows:

Despite their nomadism, hunters and gatherers usually restrict their movements to fairly well-defined territories. When they move, they usually settle in or near some former camp site. There may even be a regular circuit of sites that the groups use year after year ... they normally have a strong attachment to their own historic lands, which have often acquired a sacred or semisacred character through song and legend. (p. 118)

Hunters and gatherers must know their territory, and the migratory circuit must be based upon knowledge of water holes, locations of plants, and the habits of game.

Lewis Mumford, a great student of urban history, picks up upon the fact that nomads made repeated visits to certain places, adding that the places were invested with sacred significance. Mumford (1961) lists four types of places to which nomadic bands returned on a regular basis: the campsite, cave, cache, and cairn. Each had a sacred dimension, particularly the cave and the cairn. The cache was a place where a band might store heavy possessions—tent poles, perhaps. The cairn is a heap of stones, placed as a memorial or landmark, marking where the group had buried its dead. Mumford marvels at the aesthetics of the artwork found in prehistoric caves, noting that they must have been used as ritual centers (see picture). He argues that these sacred places were the nuclei for the settled communities, even the cities which followed after the nomadic period of prehistory. "In these paleolithic sanctuaries," he writes, "as in the first grave mounds and tombs, we have, if anywhere, the first hints of civic life, probably well before any permanent village settlement can even be suspected" (1961, p. 9). Mumford says that the city begins, even before people live in a fixed place, as a meeting place to which people periodically return.

"Little Horses" painted roughly 17,000 years ago deep in a cave at Lascaux, France where daylight could not reach it. Seasonally scheduled hunters and gatherers used the cave for part of each year and lived near its entrance. (Mazonowicz, Monkmeyer)

## The First Communities

While hunters and gatherers lived in many places around the world, the first cities and the developments which preceded them originated in the Middle East, in a region known as the "Fertile Crescent" (see Figure 3-1). This region stretches in a curved shape from the Mediterranean Sea to the Persian Gulf in what appears on

**FIGURE 3-1**
The Fertile Crescent. The first cities developed in this region, near the Tigris and Euphrates rivers. Inset shows this area of the Middle East as it is today.

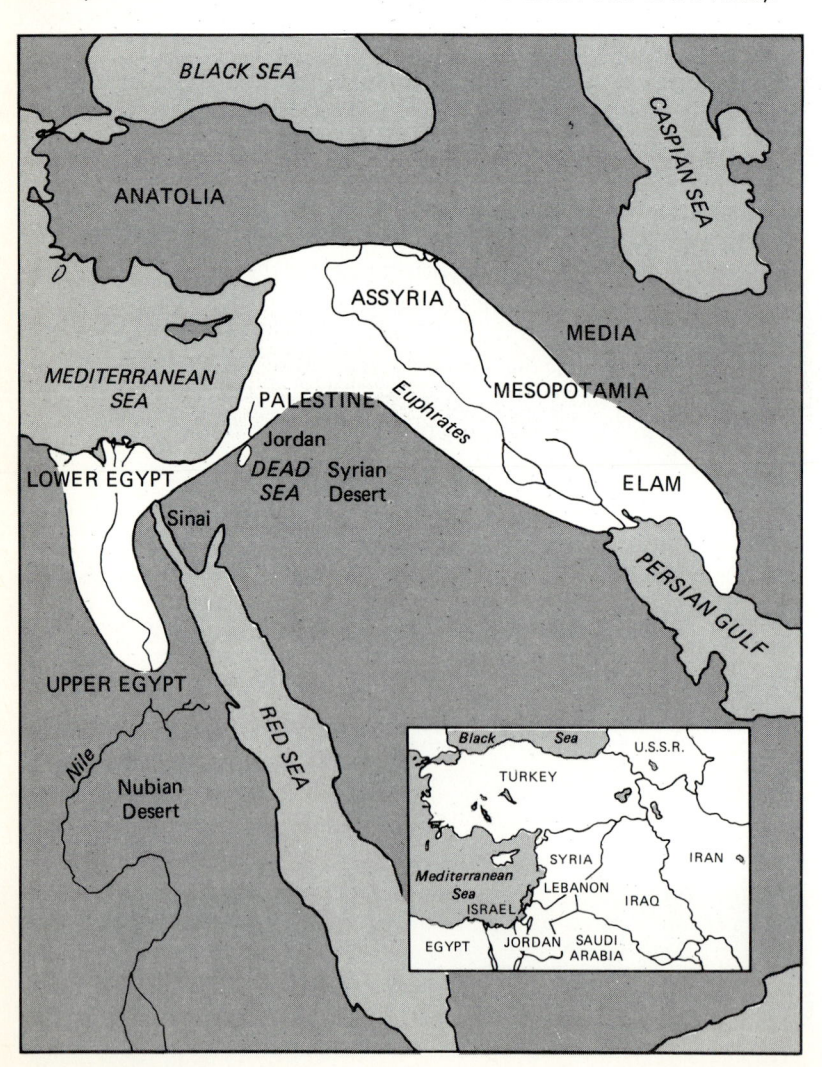

a map as a crescent shape; it includes the contemporary nations of Jordan, Israel, Lebanon, Syria, and parts of Turkey. The region has a semitropical climate, but conditions vary considerably between desert and nondesert sections. The Tigris and Euphrates rivers flow through the parts of the region which figure most prominently in the history of the rise of agriculture and, later, of urbanism. Hills and valleys adjacent to these rivers provided the environmental setting for the first villages and cities; the grassy and forested hills of the northern section of the Fertile Crescent provided a favorable locale for agricultural developments, having a climate with generous winter and spring rainfall.

Robert Braidwood (1960), an archaeologist, outlines a transitional period, lasting about 40,000 years, starting with nomadic hunting and gathering and ending with settled agriculture. Technological developments based upon increased knowledge and the invention of new tools, including blade tools, lamps, and hammers, occurred at increasing rates during this long period (Lenski & Lenski, 1978). As the people began moving less, they became what Braidwood calls "intensified food collectors," accumulating a "rich lore of experience" with the natural products of their area: wild wheat and barley as well as wild dogs, sheep, pigs, cattle, and horses (1960, pp. 19-20). Eventually, around 8,000 B.C., these people came to know their habitat so well that they could domesticate the plants and animals they had been collecting and hunting. Thus began agriculture.

By then there were villages—fixed communities of agriculturalists. In the next preurban period, the Neolithic, communities continued to develop and agriculturalists cultivated two types of wheat. In the Neolithic period people continued to gather some of their food in addition to growing crops on farms. The inventions of the time included fish hooks and arrows as well as tools and weapons with handles, such as flint sickles, chisels, axes, and spears. According to one historian (Hammond, 1972), "Handmade pottery, spinning, and weaving on looms began.... But such industry was still practiced in the separate homes; each man made his own tools or weapons and each woman produced her pots or cloth" (p. 22). Village communities grew during the Neolithic period, reaching populations of between 200 and 500 (Adams, 1960). By the end of the period the villagers still lived off the produce of their immediate countryside and had only rudimentary contacts of trade and communication with their neighbors (Hammond, 1972). However, social organizational complexity among the agriculturalists probably increased to coordinate the new kind of farming. They must have needed to plan and cooperate to some extent "to determine the best use of land, to allocate it to cultivators, to regulate seed time and harvest, and to provide for the storage of surpluses" (1972, p. 21). Hammond summarizes the neolithic changes as follows:

> In short, the neolithic revolution, by making possible the growth of sedentary communities, the accumulation of surpluses of food, the improvement of tools and techniques, the specialization of occupations, and organized community effort, prepared the way for [the] second revolution, the urban, that is, for the emergence of the city in the ancient world. (p. 23)

## The Transition from Villages to Cities

Archaeologist Robert M. Adams (1960) offers an explanation of the transition from late Neolithic villages to the first cities over a period of about 1,000 years, from 5,500 to 4,500 B.C. This transition took place further south along the same two rivers, in the valleys, rather than the hilly areas of early agriculture. Living in the lowlands required a somewhat more complex type of agriculture, which entailed new problems of managing farm animals and herds and introducing irrigation, albeit on a small scale. Both these processes required more complex forms of social organization that impelled people eventually to build cities, according to Adams (1960). For example, although irrigation stimulated organizational development through the challenging task of constructing channels, providing workers, and allocating water, on the other hand, "by engendering inequalities in access to productive land, irrigation contributed to the formation of a stratified society. And by furnishing a reason for border disputes between neighboring communities, it surely promoted a war-like atmosphere that drew people together in offensive and defensive concentrations" (Adams, 1960, p. 6). The farming and herding operations in the valleys may have created other social problems as well. How "to mediate between herdsman and cultivator; between fisherman and sailor; between plowmaker and plowman?" (p. 7). A city might help resolve both categories of problems—by building walls for defense and maintaining an army, the people of a microregion could defend themselves against potential enemies. And by having a governing system and market, a city could mediate between different groups within the emerging division of labor. The city would also provide "a logical and necessary setting for storage, exchange and redistribution" (p. 7).

The greatest transitional achievement of this period was the first accumulation of a food surplus, which had enormous ramifications for potential urban emergence. Agriculture with irrigation was more productive of food than any preceding technology. "In spite of chronic water shortage ... and period floods ... farming yielded a clear and dependable surplus of food" (Adams, 1960, p. 157). The surplus was small, of course, as the agricultural productivity was low and each farmer could produce only slightly more than the household required. But the surpluses from numerous farmers could be accumulated, making enough to support some nonproducers. This potentiality represented a radical change; for the first time a population could include some members who did not get or grow their own food. At first there were a few nonproductive individuals living among the growers, but later there would be entire communities of people who did not grow their own food.

Why, though, were the farmers willing to part with their surplus to support "freeloaders"? There are at least three possible explanations. One is trade: Some persons who didn't grow food developed skills and began to make special things—tools, pottery, cloth—which the farmer wanted. Another explanation is religion: The *priest* appears to have been the first nonagricultural occupation. The priest was able to specialize in ritual observation, blessings, and the like, and the farmers, living in a deeply religious culture, were obligated to support him. The third explanation is that the nonproducers forced the producers to support them; the urban residents organized armies and tax collectors and extracted the surplus from producers, in exchange for some degree of military security. In this system, if enemies from nearby regions posed a threat, the new "army" could defend the countryfolk, who could gather within the fortified walls of the settlement.

## THE URBAN REVOLUTION

### Ecology

The first cities arose in Mesopotamia, mostly in Sumer, its southern region, about 3,500 B.C. Some of their names, such as Babylon and Baghdad, are commonly known, whereas others, like Ur, Eridu, Lagach, and Kish, are not. Before these "true cities" arose, large communities had been established in the Fertile Crescent, such as Jericho, but they appear to have been wholly agricultural and are not considered cities (Hammond, 1972). The Sumerian cities are considered true cities because, in addition to having relatively large and heterogeneous populations plus large structures such as walls, they had *writing*, which implies the existence of highly specialized nonagricultural workers, according to Sjoberg (1960) and Davis (1955). Sumer provided a relatively hospitable physical environment for settlement along its river

**FIGURE 3-2**
Some cities of ancient western Asia. (Source: *Random House Encyclopedia.*)

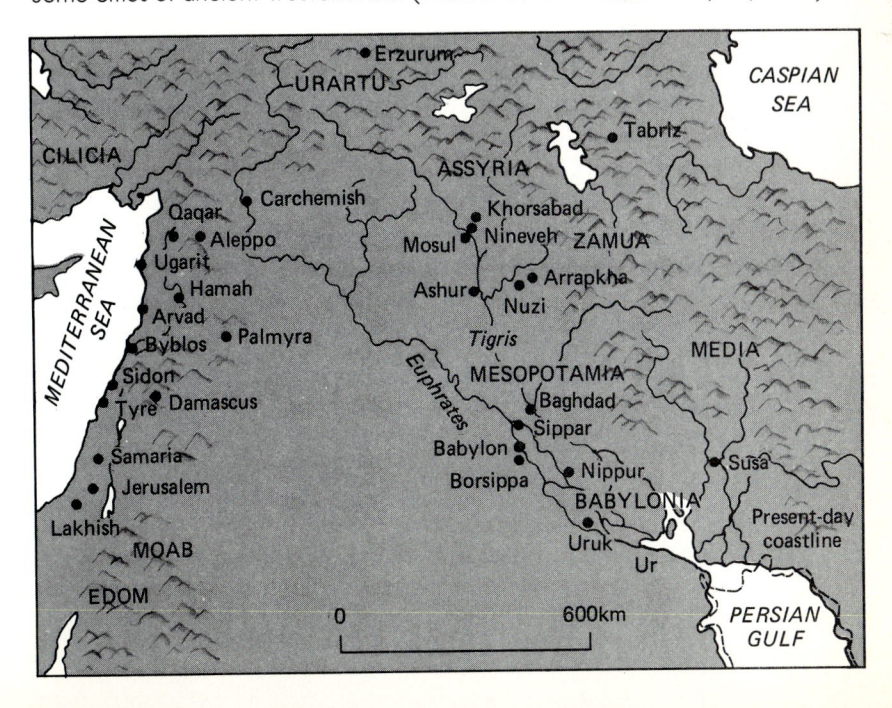

deltas, an environment of wet, rich, productive land (Davis, 1973) that could support the nonproductive segment of the population. The rivers themselves facilitated transportation and trade between places by boat. Here a number of cities arose, more than a dozen of them (Hammond, 1972).

Many of the sites of these early cities have been excavated and measured by archaeologists, and by modern standards, the urban settlements in Mesopotamia were tiny. The walls of Ur, for example, surrounded only about 220 acres, and Babylon, one of the biggest communities, had about 3.2 square miles. City populations ranged between 5,000 and 10,000 for the larger places in the Sumerian-Mesopotamian period before the year 3,000 B.C. (Sjoberg, 1960). Sjoberg, who wrote *The Preindustrial City* (1960), notes that agriculturalists lived in and adjacent to the cities, but he excludes full-time farmers from these population estimates.

The Sumerian city was surrounded by a wall and divided into three main districts. A brick wall fortified the community, providing defense against attack by outsiders, and farmers living nearby could gather inside the wall in times of conflict. It may also have provided some protection against flooding from the rivers. A second wall surrounded the central district, or inner city, which contained "the temples of the city's gods, the palace of the ruler, and private houses" (Hammond, 1972, pp. 37–38). The palace developed later than the temple; political leaders and kings came to dominate the cities after the priestly domination. The second district was residential and "contained houses and gardens and cattle pens, for the immediate support of the population" (pp. 37–38). It had narrow, crooked streets between the low buildings. The third part of the city, the harbor, was sometimes located outside the main wall, on a river; it was a commercial area which handled trade and sometimes housed foreign and native merchants. In sum, ecologically, these walled cities were divided into three sections: the center, with temple and palace; the residential area; and the commercial harbor.

## Social Organization

Unlike the members of a band or a village in earlier periods, the residents of the cities were not all related to each other through kinship, for there were simply too many people. They came from too many different places, as in-migrants from different agricultural villages of the city's hinterland, as wanderers, and even as prisoners of war from near and distant regions. In this we first see a demographic property of all cities, including those of the present. The homogeneity of the band and village vanished; the city now had a mixture of peoples. For this and other reasons social organization in the early cities was unlike anything seen before.

Membership in the community became based upon residence—simply living there—rather than upon kinship. But kinship affiliation was still relevant to the social organization of the Sumerian city, and each person's place in the community was based upon his or her original kinship group, the clan. Each person was first and foremost a member of a clan, and the city was a confederation of clans. Furthermore, each clan had its fixed place in the social order, so that the city had a priestly clan, a kingly dynasty, "middle-class" clans of farmers and artisans, and even clans of slaves who had entered the city as prisoners. Social mobility did not exist, so each child could expect to spend a lifetime in the clan of birth.

Religion held the different groups together, in the form of a city cult. The king himself might have been considered the embodiment of a god. Religion justified the collection of the farmers' surpluses, in the form of tribute, tithe, and sacrifice, to support the temple, the priests, and the court. Even before the first cities, the first class of nonproductive specialists, individuals who did not grow their own food, was the priests. In the cities, priests had several key functions in the social organization, as reflected by the number of activities clustered in and about the temple.

The temple, as an artifact, reveals several points about urban social organization of the times. It was the city's largest and most prominent building, built upon an artificial hill or a platform; eventually, the form evolved into a type known as a "ziggurat," such as the Bible's Tower of Babel (see Figure 3-3). In addition to being a sacred place for rituals and worship, the temple was also "a place for meditation and research, a warehouse, an accounting and distributing agency.... There, writing was invented to keep records of crop yields, of heads of cattle, and of services rendered. Grain and other merchandise were stored, treasure was kept, loans were granted," according to Comhaire and Cahnman (1959, p. 2). Evidently, priests served also as economic administrators (Adams, 1960); the concentration of so many critical community functions in the temple suggests the importance of the priests in the social organization. More generally, "The construction and maintenance of such elaborate structures, with their surrounding complexes of buildings, and the organized cult which they imply must reflect a complex and specialized social and political community in which religion was central" (Hammond, 1972, p. 39). This represents a continuity of the theme emphasized by Mumford (1938), when he discussed the sacredness of places to the nomadic hunters and gatherers, that religion represented a focus for the origins of community life.

The division of labor in the early cities far surpassed that of earlier human collectivities. There were priests and kings, farmers and artisans, slaves and traders, and numerous sorts of specialized workers, such as carpenters, bricklayers, and boatmakers. Priests and kings coordinated the work and commerce, having "soldiers watching on the ramparts, privileged tillers of the soil who spent their nights behind the protecting city walls, boatmen and fisherfolk, building and maintenance workers, and craftsmen of all sorts" (Comhaire & Cahnman, 1959, p. 2-3).

Great differences in wealth and rank emerged in the cities of Sumer. "Oppression of the poor by the rich seems to have been common, and there are traces of occasional attempts on the part of the rulers to restore justice" (Comhaire & Cahnman, 1959, p. 44). The lower classes were even exploited by the temple administrators. Based upon their connection with the gods, priests had "pervasive power," so much so that finally a rule had to be enacted to prevent them from going into the garden of a lower-class farmer to take away his fruit, for example. Comhaire and

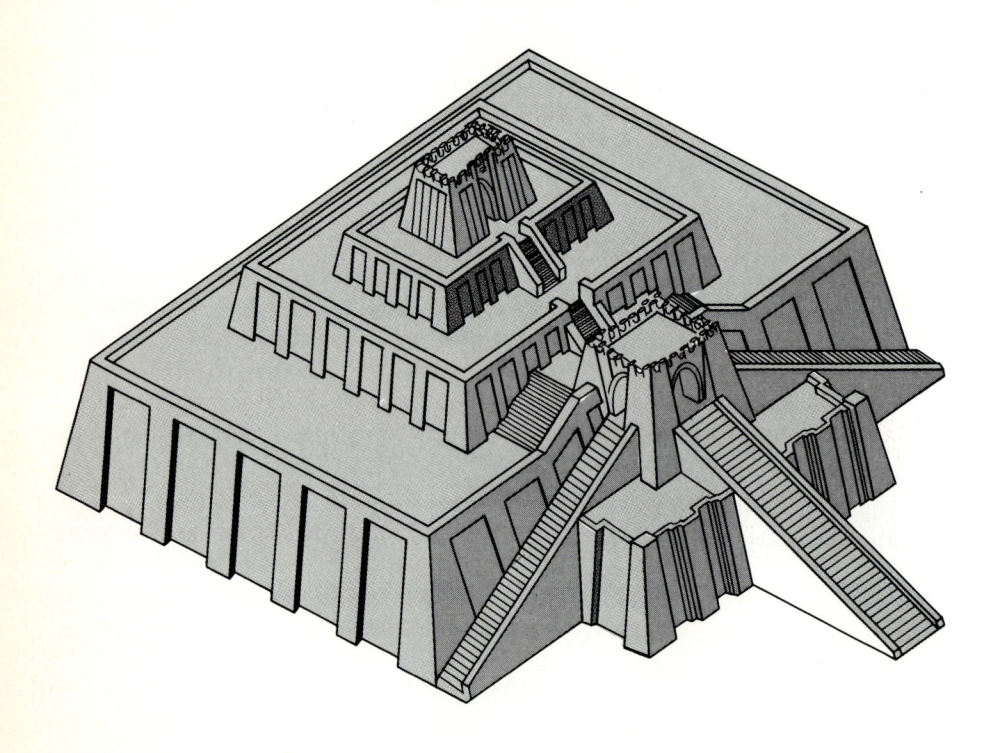

**FIGURE 3-3**
A Babylonian ziggurat. Example of an urban religious center in the city of Ur, begun perhaps as early as 2,100 B.C. Indeed, this ziggurat, dedicated to a moon god, may have been built on the site of an earlier shrine.

Cahnman continue, "Slavery ... became a formal and widespread institution" in these cities, and they note also that "commoners {not slaves} sometimes acquired considerable wealth by means of farming, crafts, and trade" (pp. 45-46).

There were also *social inventions*, that is, inventions of ways to organize activities, during this period. The Sumerians developed systems of law, particularly written legal codes and commercial practices. Extensive trade developed between the countryside and the city—although it did not work through a simple free market since products could be sold or exchanged only at established prices. Sumerians had schools, in which scribes were taught to write; invented the army; and elaborated on religion, including mythology and ruler worship (Hammond, 1972).

## Cultural Developments

Fabulous cultural developments coincided with the rise of the Mesopotamian cities. Some of the innovations have already been mentioned above, such as the architectural and engineering, as well as aesthetic, developments reflected in the ability to construct large and elaborate structures. (Remember that the previous period had people practicing primitive agriculture and shepherding and living in village huts.) Writing was invented, as written expression shifted from simple pictographs to ideographs with grammar. The Sumerians also developed a system of weights and measures with standards of length, area, capacity, and weight. "Careful astronomical observation served to establish fixed measures of time" (Hammond, 1972, p. 36). Although they did not invent coins, they created a rudimentary form of money with units of value based on weights of metal. All these important cultural advances facilitated the complex social and economic life of a large community.

Technology developed as well. This period saw the emergence of bronze metalwork, including processes of smelting and metalwork which required a high degree of specialization among workers. "Other technological improvements appear at about the same time as writing and bronze. For instance, the plow replaced the hoe as the major implement for planting, and the wheel provided easier mobility than the sledge or the roller and also made possible pulleys, cogs, and the potter's wheel" (Hammond, 1972, p. 30).

## Childe's Fundamental Features

V. Gordon Childe, a great archaeologist, in an essay entitled "The Urban Revolution" (1950) argued that the first true cities arose in Mesopotamia. He said that the presence of 10 features distinguished these communities as a new form of human community. (Childe's criteria, which are widely accepted by urbanists, appear in Box 3-1.)

In sum, then, Mesopotamia, toward the end of the fourth millenium B.C., was the site of the development of the first true cities, what Childe called the "urban revolution." Many of the characteristics of this new type of community have persisted throughout history, although some have dropped by the wayside. The small cities in Mesopotamia had a complex social organization with an elaborate division of labor and new coordinative organizations, centered about the priests and kings. There was structured social inequality, by property and privilege, a set of social classes which included slavery. As membership in the community was based upon residence rather than kinship, the city, from its onset, was a population of strangers—but not complete strangers, as each person's place in the social order was based upon affiliation with a clan. The city included a market, a place for trade with the countryside as well as with distant places. And the city was a fortress, walled for the purpose of defense.

## Cities on Four Continents

Although the very first cities arose in Mesopotamia, early cities also grew elsewhere in the world, in some places by diffusion and in others by going through the agri-

**BOX 3-1
Childe's Fundamental Features of the "Urban Revolution"**

1. *Size.* "The first cities must have been more extensive and more densely populated than any previous settlements."
2. *Nonagricultural members.* "All cities must have accommodated ... classes who did not themselves procure their own food by agriculture, stockbreeding, fishing or collecting—full-time specialist craftsmen, transport workers, merchants, officials and priests."
3. *Collection of the agricultural surplus.* "Each primary producer paid over the tiny surplus he could wring from the soil ... as tithe or tax to an imaginary deity or a divine king."
4. *Monumental public buildings.* "Every Sumerian city was from the first dominated by one or more stately temples, centrally situated on a brick platform raised above the surrounding dwellings."
5. *Division of mental and manual labor.* Priests and civil and military leaders form a "ruling class." They were "exempt from all manual tasks." Lower classes were guaranteed peace and security and were "relieved from intellectual tasks," such as organizing and planning.
6. *Writing and recording.* Invented systems of writing and numerical notation; useful to administer the revenues of a temple or a kingdom.
7. *Practical sciences.* Arithmetic, geometry, astronomy, and calendars enabled the rulers to regulate successfully the cycle of agricultural operations.
8. *Plastic arts.* Specialists—artist-craftsmen—began to depict persons and things "according to conceptualized and sophisticated styles."
9. *Long-distance trade.* "Importation of raw materials, needed for industry or cult and not available locally."
10. *Residence-based membership.* Membership in the community based upon residence rather than kinship.

*Source:* Childe, 1950/1970, pp. 116–118 passim.

## FROM NOMADISM TO THE MEDIEVAL TOWN

**Mesopotamia** — Eridu | Ur | Babylon

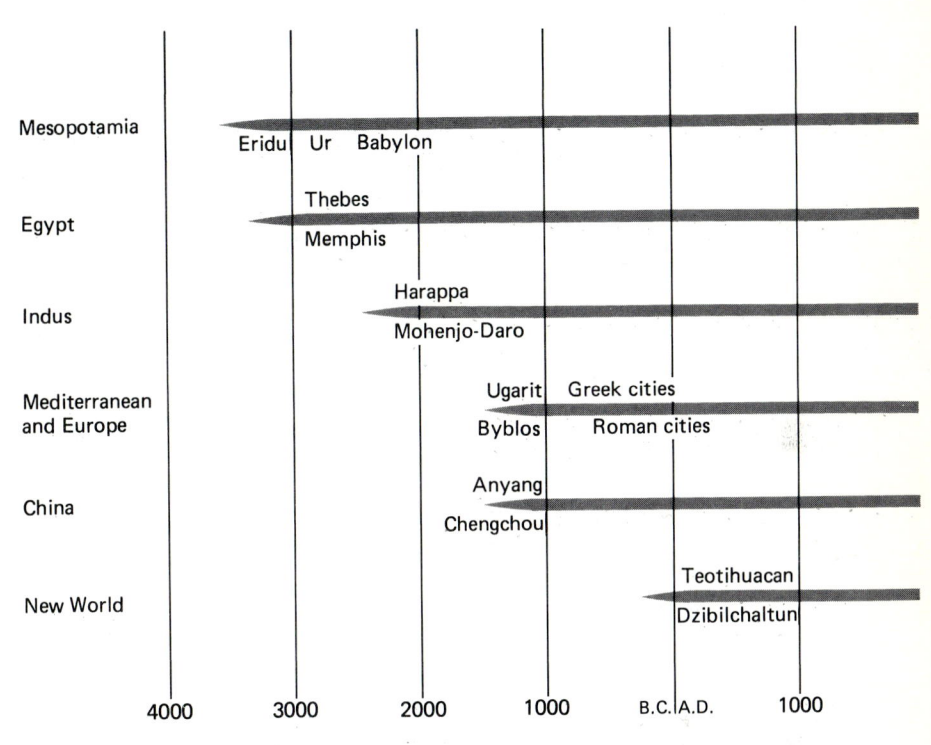

**Egypt** — Thebes | Memphis

**Indus** — Harappa | Mohenjo-Daro

**Mediterranean and Europe** — Ugarit | Greek cities | Byblos | Roman cities

**China** — Anyang | Chengchou

**New World** — Teotihuacan | Dzibilchaltun

Time axis: 4000 | 3000 | 2000 | 1000 B.C. | A.D. | 1000

**FIGURE 3-4**
Time-lines showing the sequence of cities arising in six regions of the world. (Source: Sjoberg, 1965.)

cultural and urban revolutions independently. Their environmental situations were similar: "The first urban settlements arose where the advanced Neolithic arts ... were most productive—that is, where abundant water was available for irrigation by gravity flow, and where at the same time the climate was dry, sunshine plentiful, winter mild, soil renewal possible, and transport relatively unimpeded" (Davis, 1973, p. 12). Cities arose near the Nile in Egypt well before the year 3,000 B.C. Less than 1,000 years later, cities were built in the Indus Valley in what is now Pakistan and India. Around 1,500 B.C., there were also Greek and Roman cities, as well as cities along the Yellow River in China. Sjoberg (1965/1973) leans toward the argument that the concept of urban living diffused to these areas from Mesopotamia, but he notes as well, though, that "the indigenous population contributed uniquely to the development of the cities in its own area" (p. 21). On the other hand, pre-Columbian peoples of Mesoamerica (Mexico and Guatemala) evidently developed cities quite independently. Sjoberg states that in the first millenium A.D. there were numerous genuine cities in Mesoamerica.

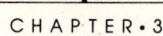

## CITIES OF CLASSICAL ANTIQUITY

### Ecology

Skipping perhaps 2,000 years from the urban revolution in Mesopotamia toward the present, we see the emergence of much larger cities in Greece and Rome. Around the year 430 B.C., in Greece, Athens had a population estimated at 155,000, Sparta 40,000 (Chandler & Fox, 1974). Although the Greek and Roman cities differed in political structure, they shared some major features of the built environment.

Like the earlier cities in Mesopotamia, Greek cities were walled and contained religious temples, governmental buildings, and markets. The temples and governmental buildings were dominant monumental structures, far overshadowing other structures like houses and shops. The city center, often located upon a rocky hill guarded by cliffs, contained the great religious and defensive structures of the community (Vance, 1977). The center, more generally, became an area known as the "agora," and by about 400 B.C. the fully developed version of the agora was visible, with three major functions. The first was as the location of the holy buildings. The second was as a gathering place for public events, which Vance refers to as the theatrical activities of urban life. "Theatrical undertakings," Vance writes, "were not merely drama as we know it but included all manner of public spectacles and activities which could be observed by large crowds" (p. 48). The third function was for trade, as an area for artisans and sellers of goods. Not only were the artisans and sellers located in this district, but they were clustered by product so that the sellers of food would be together, but potters, armorers, sellers of wine, of oil, etc., would each have their special area in this "downtown" section. Housing surrounded the agora, mostly single-story dwellings separated by little alleyways collectively known as a "residential maze." The city was cut through by very few proper streets. Vance notes that this identifiable segregation of different activities and different sorts of buildings in different parts of the area represents an ongoing urban phenomenon. As he writes, "The process of land-use separation was already at work" (p. 50).

Like the earlier cities, the Greek ones had great defensive walls—with one notable exception: Sparta, but it, too, was defensible; according to Weber (1921/1958), it was organized like a "permanent open military camp" (p. 75). Cities near deep water had their harbors outside the walls. As in Mesopotamia, some of the people who lived within the walled area were farmers who left the city daily to work their fields.

Rome was an exceptional case among the cities of classical antiquity, growing far larger than any of the others. As the center of an empire, Rome depended upon a far greater hinterland than any preceding city (greater than all but a few later cities as well). At its greatest, the city itself had a population of 650,000 (Chandler & Fox, 1974; estimate ca. A.D. 275). By building roads all over the continent and cultivating colonial towns, the imperial authorities, through their armies and bureaucratic structures, collected food and other resources from what was, in effect, an enormous hinterland. Rome's buildings, like its population, were far larger than any before them. The city had dozens of monumental temples, such as the Temple of Venus and Roma and the Temple of Augustus. In addition, the Romans built enormous multipurpose structures such as the Thermae of Caracalla which contained shops, baths, gymnasiums, libraries, and lecture halls. The city also had large buildings like the Colosseum for public gatherings.

## Social Organization

Family and kinship groupings continued to decline in importance in Greek and Roman cities. At first, evidently, they were very important as different clans lived in their own quarters, intermarried only within their own group, and worshipped only their own gods. One theory of the development of the ancient city emphasizes the fusion of these worship groups (Fustel de Coulanges, cited in Weber, 1921/1958). This theory says the political city coalesced as the noble families fraternized in a "cultic community," overcoming the division of the population into a number of cults (Weber, 1921/1958). Furthermore, "The critical element in the formation of the ancient city was found to be the invention of a new more comprehensive religious structure permitting and confirming the confederation of existing social elements in to the new unity of the city" (Weber, 1921/1958, p. 144n). Thus the sacred dimension of community life was still central to the social organization of the Hellenic city, as it was in all prior historical periods. The Greek and Roman cities developed democratic political structures, although without universal suffrage; however, according to Weber, "the individual could be a citizen ... only as a member of his clan" (1921/1958, p. 101).

The military dimension of the ancient city was important. Each city was, in effect, also a garrison, housing military command headquarters in the form of the government; also, many of the citizens were soldiers, based in the city. Eventually, in Rome, following the fall of the patricians, the soldiers (whom Weber calls "burgher-hoplites") "formed the decisive class of full citizens" (1921/1958, p. 220). Greek and Roman cities dominated their hinterlands. The countryside and city were united into a city-state, which in the case of Rome had become the center of a vast empire. Political decisions were made in the city and were imposed upon those outside. "The citizens commanded superior armor and exploited the countryside" (Comhaire & Cahnman, 1959, p. 3). Furthermore, wealthy merchants of the city owned the agricultural land itself (Weber, 1921/1958). One of the important functions of the city was to provide food for the poorer classes who lived there to prevent them from becoming disruptive; thus public policy was directed toward grain imports and the prohibition of grain exports (Weber, 1921/1958). Obviously, this policy was not likely to be beneficial to the farmers and herdsmen.

The division of social classes in the Greek and Roman cities was far more elaborate than it had been in the earlier urban communities, and there was also social mobility—downward as well as upward—in the Hellenic cities, which had been unknown in earlier communities. Athenian democracy, often cited as the original model of that venerated political system, included only the free citizens, but ancient Athens had another category of residents as well, the slaves, who were excluded from the political process. Another class of residents in Hellenic cities included foreigners, or "metics," who "formed a middle class interposed between the 'old citizens' and the slaves" (Comhaire & Cahnman, 1959, p. 22). Metics were not citizens, but they could participate in commerce. On the other hand, many slaves were captives of war, working as laborers, servants, or policemen. Among the free men there was another division, between creditors and debtors (Comhaire & Cahnman, 1959). Rome also had a clearly structured stratification of inequality: At the top there were patricians, members of families descended from warrior clans. Below them were plebians, a mixed multitude of small farmers, laborers, poor craftsmen, and petty traders. In addition, foreigners and merchants lived in the city (Comhaire & Cahnman, 1959). Incidentally, urban poverty and public welfare are not new phenomena, having been well known in Augustan Rome, 43 B.C.–A.D. 18. According to one authority, "We may picture the population of Rome as consisting chiefly of a few patrician families ministered to by a very large number of slaves, and a populace of needy citizens" (Loch, 1910, p. 866), plus their wives and children. Not counting slaves, the needy may have numbered as many as 960,000, of a total population of perhaps 1,500,000. Patricians had property and slaves had regular patrons, but the majority depended for its livelihood upon the provision of "public corn."

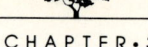

Ancient cities had other classes as well: bondsmen, debt slaves, clients, and enfranchised individuals (Weber, 1958). The rights and privileges of these classes were very precisely defined. For example, "enfranchised persons" owed allegiance to the lordly family for whom they had worked. They could hold some jobs but could not become civic officers or priests; they could serve in the army but could not become knights.

Although the class divisions were clear at early points in cities in Greece and Rome, social mobility eventually developed. In Greece, by the fifth century B.C., metics were sufficiently successful at commercial pursuits and skilled crafts that they "had crowded the citizens out of the majority of lucrative occupations" (Comhaire & Cahnman, 1959, p. 22). In Rome, social mobility came about in a similar way. At first, persons were members of the upper class only by birth, but eventually wealth was sufficient for entry into that level. Wealthy landholders were on top, and it was possible for merchants and plebians to acquire land; at some point it became possible for nonpatricians even to intermarry with members of the upper class. On the other hand, downward mobility existed, and a person unfortunate enough to fall from being a property holder to a debtor was then in a lowly stratum. According to Weber (1958), members of this category presented a serious threat to the community: "The opposition of the lower strata to others was very sharp and the ancient city recognized the economic differentiation causing it as a paramount danger" (p. 198). The potential negativism arising from declassed freemen who descended to the bottom of indebtedness presented a particular problem. In general, the beginning of social mobility should be noted as a distinctive change in social organization which occurred first in the Roman city. As Weber noted, "In Antiquity ... the city was already a place where the ascent from bondage to freedom by means of monetary acquisition was possible" (1958, p. 93).

## MEDIEVAL TOWNS

### Background

The 500 years after the fall of Rome and the collapse of the Roman Empire in the fifth century were a period of urban decline in Europe. Most of the existing cities contracted in this period. The population of Rome itself fell spectacularly to 50,000 by the year 622 and down to an estimated 17,000 by the year 1377! (Chandler & Fox, 1974). Without the military order imposed by the central imperial authority, long-distance trade disintegrated and food collection from larger hinterlands to feed substantial urban populations became impossible. Furthermore, epidemics of bubonic plague, smallpox, and dysentery in the sixth and seventh centuries severely cut the sizes of European cities (Russell, 1968).

Unlike the widespread political and economic integration of Europe under the Roman Empire, social and economic life became highly localized in medieval times before the renewal of trade and urbanism. The overall social system of the medieval era, which lasted roughly from the tenth century to the sixteenth, is known as "feudalism." Large areas, which much later became unified nation-states such as France and Germany, were divided into hundreds of independent fiefdoms. Each fief had its own lord who had at least one castle and a court plus a small army. There were no long-distance highways, and the traveler who went by land or river ran the risk of being victimized by bandits or by local armies.

Each feudal lord had extraordinarily pervasive power over the peasants, known as "serfs," the poor primitive farmers and herdsmen living on his villages in his territory. Like sharecroppers of a later era, they were obliged to give him a percentage of their agricultural produce (known as a "tithe") and a certain number of days of work each year. Furthermore, the lord made the laws for the area and enforced them—being, in effect, the chief magistrate and commander of the local army. In addition to ordinary manor-based fiefdoms, there were also churchly ones, large estates controlled by monasteries rather than by ordinary lords; in such cases the serfs paid their obligations to the religious landlords. Obviously, this was a two-tiered stratification system, with lords at the top and peasants far below at the bottom. Thus it lacked a middle class, which became a basic feature of medieval and later cities (Vance, 1977).

The manor or barony was the basic geopolitical, economic, and social unit. In the absence of interregional trading, each manor became self-sufficient in the production of essential goods; thus there was no dependence upon cities for trade and no provision for the needs of cities. Certain central-place villages became trading areas, but the system did not foster urban communities (Vance, 1977). "The ninth century is the golden age of what we have called the closed domestic economy and which we might call with more exactitude, the economy of no markets" (Pirenne, cited in Vance, 1977, pp. 81–82). In effect, the local self-sufficiency of the feudal economy was highly antiurban.

Typically, the manor house was a fortress usually built on a defensible site, such as a hilltop. Many were built as castles, with moats, drawbridges, turrets, and the other paraphernalia of fairy tales. They housed the knights and provided a place for the peasants to gather in times of war.

## Urban Growth

Despite these unpromising circumstances, urban growth revived in the eleventh century (Mumford, 1938), largely impelled by the rise of trade between regions and even between continents.

There were three kinds of potential nuclei in Europe around which cities could grow. First, the Roman cities did not all crumble to dust in the dark ages, for although they shrank in population, many survived as small cities, operated in effect by the Christian church. "Tours, Lyon, Narbonne, Cologne, Trier, and a number of Roman towns became the seats of powerful bishops, who wielded influence within the church but also served on occasion, or commonly, as lay lords of the cities themselves" (Vance, 1977, p. 83). Second, there were central-place villages, sites of occasional markets where villagers could buy and sell; traders who traveled bravely across the continent visited these villages. Third, there was the "burg," a defensible settlement, built as a fortress (Pirenne, 1952/1956; Vance, 1977). The burg, a walled enclosure surrounded by a moat, included a home for the lord, a chapel, a granary, and cellars for provisions. Although military and administrative centers from which to dominate the people of an area, burgs were not urban places, but some of them provided the locale for urban settlements. Traders and artisans began to settle outside the burgs, near the wall or at the foot of the hills, and markets developed at such places; these settlements grew into towns and cities.

Urban development, though, was incompatible with absolute control by the local lord. The traders and artisans, who sought economic opportunities and growth, were frustrated by the prevailing system. In many cases these permanent settlers demanded independence from the feudal control of the lord and, eventually, were able to gain independence for the emerging community. Evidently, a higher-level lord would permit the growth of a market-based town in his territory because of the consequent benefits. He would have to make certain concessions for a town to grow, and he might have to guarantee its protection. But by having a town, the lord could get a regular supply of foreign articles and trade products as well as collect tolls for the passage of roads and rivers through his territory. He might also collect taxes and tariffs on the market and on proceedings in the law courts of the town. Furthermore, the lord or prince might hope to collect taxes from the tradesmen and merchants settling at the market (Weber, 1958). When the town's freedom was won, the lord granted a charter of self-government to the community. The town became a free place; its residents enjoyed freedom from the system which governed the village serfs so tightly.

## Ecology

The dominant features of a medieval town's built environment were the wall, cathedral, and town hall. Each town was surrounded by a large wall, which was punctured by a few gateways; people could enter and leave the community only through the gates, which were closed tightly at night. A definite boundary existed between town and countryside—a person was either in or out of town. In case of war or threat, though, people from the surrounding countryside could gather within the town for protection. Beyond the walls, there were no highways and river travel could be dangerous, so each town was quite isolated. Modern-day travelers in Europe may see whole medieval walls, or at least fragments and gates, in many places.

Like castles, towns tended to be located at defensible places such as on river islands and hilltops where the inhabitants could fight off attackers from elsewhere; Paris, for example, began on an island in the Seine River. A second locational principle is trade—throughout history towns have been built at the junctions of trade routes. Here shippers or traders may buy and sell, or they may use warehouses and divide large shipments for distribution. Early in the development of medieval towns the defense principle must have predominated, and later, as larger national areas became politically and economically integrated, the trade principle became more important than it had been.

Like cities of earlier periods, the medieval town was also a fortress. Within such a fortress there would be a garrison of mercenaries, vassals, or servants (Weber, 1958). The folk who lived in areas adjoining the castle were bound to "the performance of certain military duties such as building and repairs of the walls, guard duty, and the like" (Weber, p. 77). In later medieval towns, Weber notes, townsmen—"burghers"—had the duty of maintaining the wall, the fortification; furthermore, "The entrepreneurs of the major guilds were often extraordinarily militaristic" (p. 223).

After the wall, the second physical feature of the medieval town was the cathedral. This enormous structure required immense investments of work and material; building one often took well over a century. Such a construction project took a great deal of organizational, as well as building, skill and necessitated the assembly of capital from the rich and poor. Thousands of workers performed highly differentiated tasks, from stonemasonry to cutting and glazing stained-glass windows. When completed, the cathedral towered over the low buildings of the community, and its magnificence stood in sharp contrast to the filth of much of the rest of the environment. Medieval towns had none of the excellent water and sewerage systems which had been developed in ancient Rome.

CHAPTER·3

England's Canterbury Cathedral. Here a contemporary community continues to use and adapt the small crooked streets and tightly packed structures of a medieval environment. (Bernard Silberstein, Monkmeyer)

Each town also had a town hall, a central building usually far humbler than the cathedral. This structure was used by the elite merchants' guild for meetings as well as for parties and dances.

As the only free places on the late medieval scene, the towns were attractive for settlement by men who were not the firstborn of their families and, consequently, had no inheritance rights under the laws and traditions of the times. Thus they had reason to seek the opportunities that the town offered. Similarly, a serf seeking the freedom that he could not have in the village might flee to the town. The charters provided that after a year of residence, a serf gained his freedom from the lord and his wife and children would also be free. As a German maxim of the times said, "City air makes men free." The demographic existence of these towns depended upon the in-migration of such persons. The communities did not provide particularly healthy environments; their density fostered deadly epidemics, and their lack of sanitation facilities also promoted high death rates. Thus the only basis for population stability or growth had to be the addition of new migrants.

Although the late medieval period was a time of substantial growth, new intercontinental contacts through trade and migration brought new diseases to Europe that severely cut into the urban populations (McNeill, 1976). While populations may develop immunities over time to particular diseases, new arrivals tend to have powerful effects. The pandemic spread of plague, known as the "Black Death," killed enormous numbers of city people between 1348 and 1350; for example, Florence went from 90,000 to 45,000 people; Siena went from 42,000 to 15,000; Hamburg lost two-thirds of its population (Langer, 1964); and other large cities across the continent suffered losses on the same scale. A series of these epidemics occurred between 1350 and 1450 (Vance, 1977). Other new diseases, against which the Europeans had no immunities, swept the continent during the same period. In addition, periodic famines in the fourteenth and fifteenth centuries devastated urban populations (Vance, 1977).

## Social Organization

Social organization of the medieval town differed considerably from that of previous cities. Kin and clan groupings were no longer as significant as they had been in the previous types of cities. An individual was a member of the community on his own. "The oath of citizenship was taken by the individual. Personal membership, not that of kin groups or tribe, in the local association of the city supplied the guarantee of the individual's personal legal position as a burgher" (Weber, 1958, p. 102). Furthermore, the medieval city did not have slaves; this does not mean that there was great equality among the city people but simply that each person was a member of the city as a citizen.

The social organization was based upon the division of labor in a new way, through a set of guilds, which were specialized associations to which all the mem-

Members of the shoemakers' guild in their shop as depicted in the sixteenth century *Book of Trades.* (The Metropolitan Museum of Art, Rogers Fund, 1913)

bers of a given occupation belonged. For example, a town might have a stonecutters' guild, a glassblowers' guild, as well as one each for weavers, goldsmiths, cobblers, carpenters, and many others. Birth and apprenticeship determined entry into the guild, so that a carpenter, for example, would bring his son into the occupation and the association. By enjoying a complete monopoly of its trade—for example, no one but a member of the goldsmiths' guild could deal in gold—the guild could control the entire market of its product. A merchants' guild might control trade with a particular foreign country; in consequence, the guild could control the prices of labor and commodities. Thus while the city incorporated a market, and the market was a basic part of the community, it was anything but a free market. The guilds themselves were stratified, with the merchants' guild at the top. It was, in effect, the governing body of the community.

Florence had two basic levels of guilds. The upper-level, senior guilds included those of the physicians, jurists, bankers, jewelers, dealers in furs, and others. The lower guilds consisted of butchers, bakers, tailors, cobblers, carpenters, stonemasons, blacksmiths, swordmakers, metalworkers, and the like (Comhaire & Cahnman, 1959). In Italy consistent opposition arose between these two levels of guildsmen, while in Germany the merchant guild stayed firmly in control.

There were social class distinctions as well as potential class conflict within the cities. Weber notes that "the typical medieval needy person was the poor artisan, the craftsman without work" (1958, p. 199). Other low-level workers who were potentially part of a proletariat consisted of sweepers, draymen, and the like. The relationship between debtors and creditors was antagonistic, as it had been in Rome. Furthermore occasional bread riots occurred in the medieval towns (Comhaire & Cahnman, 1959). Some sociologists note that the ranking of the guilds by occupation marked the beginning of what later became the modern urban stratification system.

The town's basis as a market gave rise to a set of legal and commercial innovations which facilitated the growth of commerce and industry. The charter was a new device, guaranteeing the town's independence from the rules of the local nobleman. As Comhaire and Cahnman (1959) note, "The independent status enjoyed by [the medieval towns] also enabled them to give Western business life a peculiar character through the creation of commercial law and courts which recognized letters of exchange, banks and stock companies, and other new institutions" (p. 83). The growth of business would have been impossible, of course, under the arbitrary and personal legal system where all power rested in a single lord.

## Mumford's Appreciation of the Medieval Town

For Mumford (1938), the medieval town was the best type of city; surely, he prefers it to the contemporary modern metropolis. This is ironic in that by current housing standards, the people were highly crowded. Small in area and high in population density, the towns had, as noted above, primitive sanitation. Why, then, would Mumford idealize these communities? Because they were small, manageable, and integrated. Work was either done at home or someplace within walking distance; people also walked to the market to shop or to the cathedral to pray. The marketplace was by the cathedral, and people met there for mystery plays, miracle plays, and other public ceremonies. As the streets were narrow and the houses close together, friends and strangers enjoyed a great deal of contact. Each guild, in addition to economic functions, also bore sociopolitical responsibilities, serving as a health and old-age insurance society as well as a dramatic and educational association. And aside from the cathedral, the buildings were not overwhelmingly large. Saying the medieval city promoted social unity, Mumford (1938) speculated that the wall itself had this effect: "One was either in or out of the city; one belonged or one did not belong. When the town gates were locked at sundown, and the portcullis was drawn, the city was insulated from the outside world. As in a ship, the wall helped create a feeling of unity between the inhabitants: in a siege or a famine the morality of the shipwreck—share and share alike—developed easily" (p. 54). The other side of the coin, unfortunately, was a sense of insularity. In sum, the community existed at a *human scale* and worked as an integrated whole.

This is not to say that the entire social scene was harmonious; it never is. A certain degree of public disorder existed as there was no municipal police force (this social invention would not appear for another 400 years). Thus the streets could be dangerous after dark, and one was well advised to travel only with some trusted kinsmen in case of meeting strangers. Another source of potential conflict was between the laborers, the proletariat, who stood at the bottom of the social order, and those above them (Hawley, 1971). Nonetheless, despite these sources of conflict, Mumford appreciates the interpersonal contact and the wholeness of the medieval town.

## SUMMARY

### Why Did People Build Cities?

Having studied urban history from the beginning of cities, we can start to answer this question.

### For defense

In Mesopotomia and again in the medieval period disorder might occur among the peoples of large areas; they might raid each other or make war in other ways. People built cities with walls, and in times of trouble, countryfolk gathered within the walls for safety. Furthermore, in all three periods studied, one function of the urban community was to organize an army and to provide protection to the rural population. A primary function of the city, according to Weber and others, was to serve as a fortress.

### For worship
Mumford argues that the core of the first settled communities was religion. Architecturally, at least, this is confirmed in all periods studied: In the biblical period, the tallest and largest structure was the ziggurat, or temple, at the city center; in the ancient cities, temples to the gods were prominent among the monumental buildings of the center; and in the medieval town the cathedral towered above all. Furthermore, at the beginning of urbanity, as agriculture came to the point of supporting nonfood producers for the first time, the first specialist supported by the community was the priest.

### For production and exchange
Clearly, people began to make and trade things at the beginning of settled community life, and the city facilitates these activities. Bringing together large numbers of artisans and laborers facilitates the production of goods for urban and rural people and permits the emergence of ancillary services: banking, shipping, etc. The city also facilitates exchange by providing a place for markets and for traders to operate. Weber's urban theory emphasizes that a city is a fusion of a market and a fortress.

## Why Do People Live in Cities?
We can't interview any of the early urbanites, so we must surmise their reasons for living in cities. In retrospect we can see some disadvantages to urban life, perhaps the greatest being the presence of unknown, possibly dangerous, nonkin in near proximity. Why, then, did people live in cities?

### For opportunity
Perhaps if a rural father had too little capital—land, animals—to divide among his children, he might send one or more of them to try to make a living in the town. Or if a young rural person aspired to wealth or power in some way which could not be satisfied in the countryside, he might try his luck in the city. Or some people may have had talents—in anything from music to warfare—which could be better expressed in town. One of the special opportunities of urban life which developed in the Greek and Roman cities was that of social mobility; unfortunately for some, though, the system allowed people to fall as well as to rise in social class.

### For freedom

This principle is seen most clearly in the medieval period when the town offered much more political and economic freedom than the village. Thus a man who sought to escape the oppression of life as a serf could attempt to escape to the town.

### General Points

The history of cities is a background to urban sociology which is mostly about twentieth-century communities. We should retain several general points from the historical survey, though.

The very existence of the urban community depended upon technological inventions. The first cities could begin only after the development of agriculture led to the production of food surpluses to feed the urban people who were non-producers of food. Urban populations have always been dependent upon the countryside for food.

Other technologies have also influenced the development and changing forms of cities. In particular, technologies of communication and transportation such as road building and shipping have affected cities, permitting connections with larger hinterlands and with distant places and facilitating urban growth. The technologies of war and defense, of building construction, of sanitation, and of food storage all influenced the development of cities.

From the outset cities have been communities of strangers, populations of individuals who were not related to each other. Lofland (1973), a contemporary sociologist, emphasizes this as a feature of modern cities, which it is, but it derives from the earliest places that were too large to be tied by the bonds of kinship. A city brings people together; it makes contact.

As Durkheim's (1933) theory shows, the division of labor has been an ongoing process throughout the history of cities. The first communities had specialists, non-farmers, such as priests and artisans; ever since, the process of specialization and division of occupations and roles has continued steadily. Furthermore, all cities have had inequalities among social classes—kings and commoners, creditors and debtors, citizens and slaves. The problem of social organization has been to integrate strangers and to hold together and coordinate the differentiated groups of the community.

Cities of the past may provide models or attractive features for cities of the present or the future. For example, throughout the ages people have admired the monumental dominant centers of ancient cities, such as Athens' Parthenon. Another attractive quality of a historic type is the high-contract walkability of the medieval town, much praised by urbanist Lewis Mumford.

Finally, lest the student get the impression that urban history simply records an unending progression of growth and development, we should note that many cities have died. Although some great cities, such as Athens, Rome, Paris, and London, have survived the ages, numerous Mesopotamian, Roman, and medieval cities eventually shrunk into insignificance or ended in rubble.

## REFERENCES

Adams, Robert M. 1960. "The Origin of Cities." *Scientific American*. 203(3):153–168.
Adams, Robert M. 1966. *The Evolution of Urban Society: Early Mesopotamia and Prehistoric Mexico*. Chicago: Aldine.
Braidwood, Robert J. 1960. "The Agricultural Revolution." *Scientific American*. 203(3):130–148.
Chandler, Tertius, and Gerald Fox. 1974. *3000 Years of Urban Growth*. New York: Academic.
Childe, V. Gordon. 1950. "The Urban Revolution." *Town Planning Review*. 21:9–16. Reprinted in Gutman and Popenoe, 1970.
Childe, V. Gordon. 1954. *What Happened in History* (rev. ed.). Harmondsworth, Middlesex: Penguin.
Comhaire, Jean, and Werner J. Cahnman. 1959. *How Cities Grew: The Historical Sociology of Cities*. Madison, N.J.: Florham Park Press.
Davis, Kingsley. 1955. "The Origin and Growth of Urbanization in the World." *American Journal of Sociology*. 60:429–437. Reprinted in Gutman and Popenoe.
Davis, Kingsley. 1973. "The First Cities, How and Why Did They Arise?" pp. 9–18 in *Cities: Their Origin, Growth, and Human Impact*, Kingsley Davis. (ed.) San Francisco: Freeman.
Durkheim, Emile. 1933. *The Division of Labor in Society*. New York: Macmillan.
Fustel de Coulanges, Numa Denis. 1864/1956. *The Ancient City: A Study on the Religion, Laws, and Institutions of Greece and Rome*, (trans.) Willard Small. Garden City, N.Y.: Doubleday Anchor. Originally published in French in 1864.
Gutman, Robert, and David Popenoe (eds.). 1970. *Neighborhood, City, and Metropolis: An Integrated Reader in Urban Sociology*. New York: Random House.
Hammond, Mason. 1972. *The City in the Ancient World*. Cambridge, Mass.: Harvard.
Hawley, Amos H. 1971. *Urban Society: An Ecological Approach*. New York: Ronald.
Langer, William L. 1971. "The Black Death," pp. 32–37 in *Man and the Ecosphere*. San Francisco: Freeman.
Lenski, Gerhard E., and Jean Lenski. 1978. *Human Societies: An Introduction to Macrosociology* (3d ed.). New York: McGraw-Hill.
Loch, Charles Stewart. 1910. "Charity and Charities," in *Encyclopedia Britannica* (11th ed., vol. 5). Cambridge, England: Cambridge.
Lofland, Lyn. 1973. *A World of Strangers*. New York: Basic Books.
McNeill, William H. 1976. *Plagues and Peoples*, Garden City, N.Y.: Anchor Doubleday.
Mumford, Lewis. 1938. *The Culture of Cities*. New York: Harcourt, Brace.
Mumford, Lewis. 1961. *The City in History*. New York: Harcourt, Brace & World.

Pirenne, Henri. 1934. "Commune, Medieval," pp. 61–63 in *Encyclopedia of the Social Sciences*. New York: Macmillan.

Pirenne, Henri. 1934. "Guilds, European," pp. 208–214 in *Encyclopedia of the Social Sciences*. New York: Macmillan.

Pirenne, Henri. 1925/1956. *Medieval Cities*. Garden City, N.Y.: Doubleday Anchor. Originally published in 1925.

Platt, Colin. 1976. *The English Medieval Town*, New York: David McKay.

Russell, Josiah C. 1968. "That Earlier Plague." *Demography*. 5:174–184.

Sjoberg, Gideon. 1960. *The Preindustrial City: Past and Present*. New York: Free Press.

Sjoberg, Gideon. 1965. "The Origin and Evolution of Cities." *Scientific American.* 213(3):54–63). Reprinted in Davis, 1973.

Vance, James E., Jr. 1977. *This Scene of Man: The Role and Structure of the City in the Geography of Western Civilization.* New York: Harper & Row.

Weber, Max. 1921/1958. *The City.* (trans.) Don Martindale and Gertrud Neuwirth. New York: Free Press. Original German edition published in 1921.

Weber, Max. 1927. "Citizenship," chap. 28 in his *General Economic History.* (trans.) Frank H. Knight. Glencoe, Ill.: Free Press.

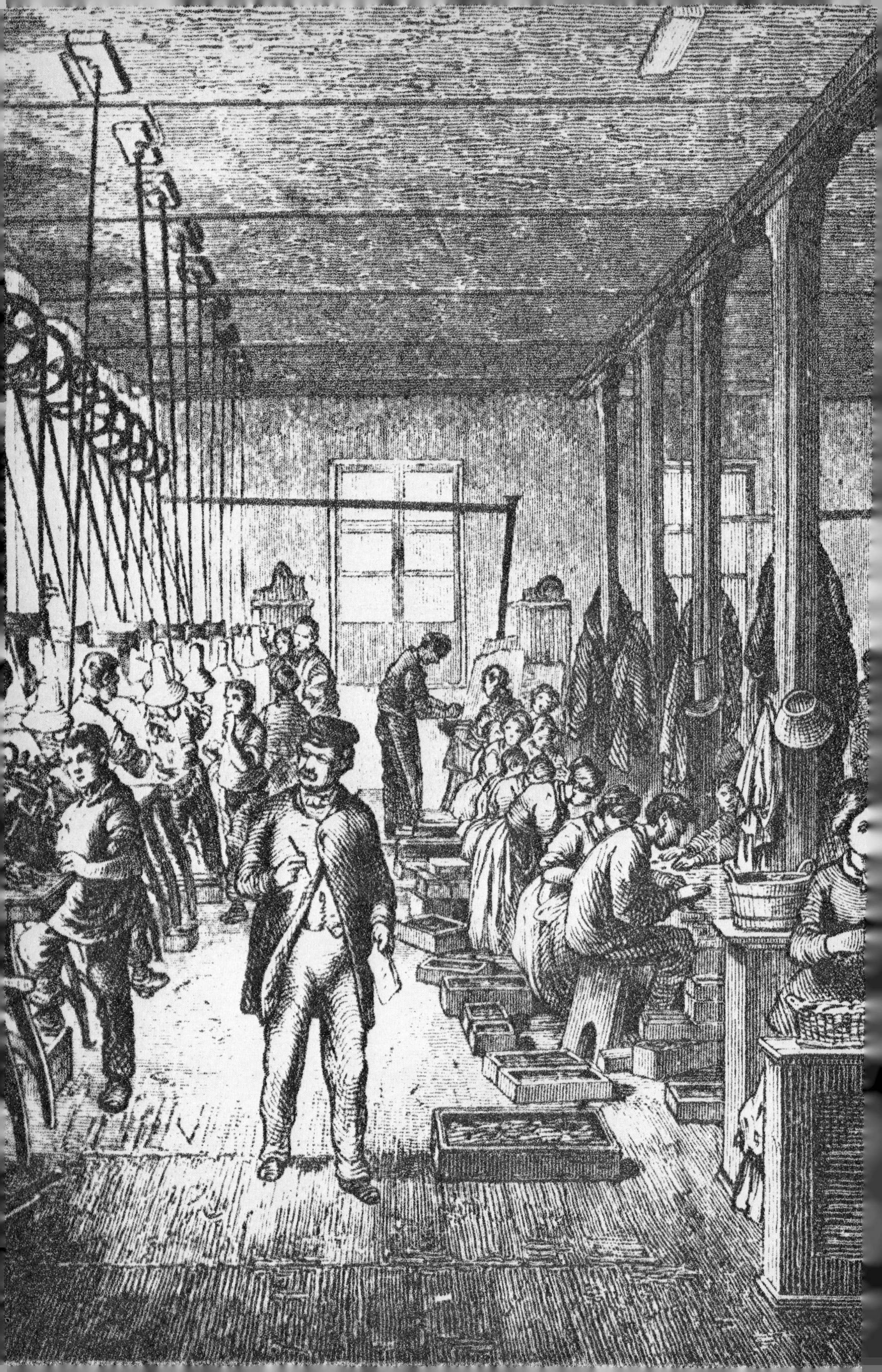

# CHAPTER · 4

# The Rise of the Industrial City

## Chapter Outline

BEGINNINGS OF THE INDUSTRIAL TOWN

The Factory System
Populating the New Industrial Towns
- Depopulating the countryside
- Beginnings of the demographic transition

MANCHESTER, ENGLAND: THE PRIME CASE

Differential Urban Growth
Social Structure
Spatial Structure
- The cellular city
- Differentiation

THE MATURE INDUSTRIAL CITY: 1850–1920

Centralization
- Technological changes
- The central business district
- The Concentric Model of Urban Growth and Form
Occupational Structure

COMMUNITY PROBLEMS OF THE NEW CITIES

Riots
- New York's draft riots
- Chicago's race riot

Poverty and Slums
Attempted Solutions to Community Problems
- Institution building
- Time and prosperity

SUMMARY

This chapter deals with the rise and development of industry in conjunction with the emergence of industrial cities. It takes us from the remote past of the medieval town to the brink of the present, covering a period from about 1770 to about 1920. Urban history during this period is divided into two parts: the industrial town (1770 to 1850) and the industrial city (1850 to 1920). By the twentieth century we have what I have called the "mature industrial city." To present the first period, I deal mostly with England, where the first effects of factories and their industrial processes were seen. The fledgling United States also had mills and factories, not long after England had them, but the impact of industry can be seen dramatically where it originated, particularly through a case study of Manchester as an industrial town. To present the second period, the emergence and development of the industrial city, I shift to the United States, where the focus remains throughout the rest of the book.

The mature industrial city is particularly important in this text because urban sociological research and theories looked first at this type of community. Human ecology, the theory of urbanism as a way of life, and the concentric model of urban growth and form (presented in this chapter) were all based on this type of city. Furthermore, mature industrial cities contain many of the elements of the contemporary metropolis: large size and high density, industrial production, mechanized transport, high-rise construction (then called "skyscrapers"), bureaucratic organizations, etc. Physical vestiges of those cities remain now, except in the newest metropolitan areas. Older metropolitan areas still have streets, subways, rail depots, city halls, downtown skyscrapers, and other elements of infrastructure which were developed in the period of industrialization. (Some of the oldest cities, like Philadelphia, Boston, and Charleston, have old sections with street patterns laid out *before* the industrial period, but even they have major districts from the industrial era.) Many of the contemporary community's social problems surfaced in that period—race and ethnic relations, public education and municipal administration, for example—and people are still attempting to solve them.

This chapter is mostly macroscopic and ecological. Reflecting a materialistic viewpoint, it emphasizes the impact of inventions and technology on spatial patterns and social structure. Thus, regarding the first period, the chapter suggests that the rise of the factory affected the organization of a new type of community, the industrial town. Regarding the second period, the chapter suggests that additional technological changes, particularly in transportation and communications, affected community structure in the rise of the industrial city. In taking this emphasis, the chapter is not meant to imply that technology determines or causes these social results but that societies and communities develop within the realm of the possible in a particular time and place. Given a particular environment and technology, certain developments are impossible and others may occur. (Given its climate, Houston probably would not have developed into a great city without air conditioning; on the other hand, the invention and diffusion of air conditioning did not cause Houston to grow.)

# THE RISE OF THE INDUSTRIAL CITY

There are other fundamental social theories about the rise of capitalism and industrial production which emphasize the importance of changing religious beliefs, concepts of citizenship, and social-class relationships in regard to social change over the past two centuries; these theories tend not to be materialistic. Some of the deepest controversies in social science surround these issues of economic, political, and social change in the development of modern society. Fortunately for students, though, this chapter is restricted to an ecological examination of the emergent industrial towns and cities.

Unlike most urban sociology textbooks, this chapter contains extended descriptions of social problems which arose in industrial communities. It describes slums in early industrial towns, using Manchester as an example, and it reports on slums, poverty, and riots in industrial cities on this side of the Atlantic. These descriptions indicate that the industrial city generated the great irony of producing wealth and misery simultaneously. A similar irony appears in the process of immigration, in which poor people left desperate situations to travel to burgeoning American cities where they found opportunities but also new miseries.

## BEGINNINGS OF THE INDUSTRIAL TOWN

Medieval towns were fully urban, but their economies were small and localized and all manufactured goods—from hats to hinges—were handmade in little shops. Furthermore, the towns' social and economic systems were tightly controlled by the guilds, whose rights and privileges determined who could do what sorts of work, what the prices would be, etc. This system was well suited to the small-scale localized economy, but it was unable to grow to any extent or to adapt to new technologies or opportunities. When the industrial revolution began in the eighteenth century, the existing urban communities with medieval structures confronted major challenges.

After the end of feudalism several developments—technological, economic, and political—formed a backdrop to the rise of a new type of city. The medieval period in Europe drew to a close by the year 1500 (or 1600, depending upon which historian you prefer) and, increasingly, areas which had been fiefdoms consolidated into nations, like France, ruled by kings. Trading and marketing areas expanded on the continent and into the oceanic transcontinental realm. Scientific developments and inventions of the fifteenth and sixteenth centuries, particularly Mercator's new world map and improved navigational instruments such as the astrolabe, cross-staff, and backstaff, allowed sailors (like Columbus) to go far beyond their previous limits. This "age of exploration" put Europeans into contact with India, the New World, and other places; soon thereafter, the Europeans began militarily to conquer and colonize such areas. Eventually, the colonies—India, Indonesia, Belgian Congo, Brazil, and scores of others—were economically tied to the European powers, forced to supply raw materials to the Europeans and to purchase their manufactured goods. Thus markets expanded tremendously, first within Europe in the emerging nation-states and soon thereafter in the colonial international orbit.

## The Factory System

The medieval system of production was insufficient to deal with these expanding market opportunities. In medieval times things were made in people's homes; spinning and weaving, for example, were done in individual rural households, under a system known as "cottage industry." Country people could do this work during the winter and at other times when they were not farming. The unit of production was the family, each having some spinning wheels or a hand-operated loom where individuals, particularly women and children, would work. Spinners turned the wheel by hand and weavers used their feet and hands to work the loom, there being no source of inanimate power; this was a labor-intensive technology, meaning that the work was done with a great deal of labor. The opposite is a capital-intensive technology like that of a contemporary factory in which machines, even robots, perform many of the operations formerly done by people.

Cottage industry was organized into the "putting-out system," which meant that there were individual contractors, known as "factors," who dealt with individual households. For spinning, the factor would buy raw material, say sheep's wool or flax; distribute it to the individual households, who would comb, card, and spin it into thread; and then buy the thread back from them. Similarly, other factors would buy thread yarn in bulk, parcel it out to individual weavers' households, and then buy back their cloth. But, in the sixteenth century, London exporters wanted to operate on a larger scale in the emerging markets; factors appreciated this and saw that machinery was going to be a good investment (Vance, 1977).

Factories appeared first in the making of textiles, transforming production technologically and organizationally. They brought together newly invented machines and large numbers of workers to produce more goods at lower cost.

A series of eighteenth-century inventions which revolutionized the cotton industry gave rise to the factory. According to Hammond (1931), England had a silk factory as early as 1718 but most factory development started fifty years later. "The application of power to the making of yarns ushered in what we think of as the Industrial Revolution" (Vance, 1977, p. 281). Spinning was mechanized first (a spinning device was invented in 1738, and Richard Arkwright patented a successful machine for automatic spinning in 1769), and automatic weaving came soon afterward. Vance continued, "If any date deserved to be counted as the first year of the Industrial Revolution, it was 1771," when a mill was set up to use Arkwright's spinning machine (p. 284).

The first factories did not have an urbanizing effect. Their machines were waterwheels, so the buildings required riverside locations, at or near waterfalls. (Waterwheels captured power from rushing water, turning shafts which, via gears and belts, moved machinery.) Thus the woolen industry developed in the valleys of Yorkshire in the eighteenth century; this was a sort of rural industrialization.

The steam engine existed in a usable form by 1712 but was not used in factories until the 1780s. Making the waterwheel obsolete as a power source, the steam engine liberated the factory from the riverside. According to Mumford (1938):

> Steam worked most efficiently in big concentrated units, with the parts of the plant no more than a quarter of a mile from the power-center: every spinning machine or loom had to tap power from the belts and shafts worked by the central steam engine. The more units within a given area, the more efficient was the source of power: hence the tendency toward giantism in textile factories, which covered a large area and were usually five stories high. (p. 157)

After the 1820s a typical large English factory employed 250 "hands," as the workers were called.

At first a factory accomplished only one part of the textile process, but soon entrepreneurs concentrated all processes, including all the steps of spinning, weaving, dying, printing, and finishing, under one roof. The first fully integrated textile factory was opened in Waltham, Massachusetts, in 1814. Soon afterward, makers of other items, including leather goods, machinery, and furniture, began developing factories, also integrating different manufacturing processes into single buildings.

The factory gave the owner more control over the manufacturing process than he had had in cottage industry. Now he controlled the cost of labor as workers became completely dependent upon the factory for work and subsistence. No longer did they own their looms, and having left their homesteads, they could not even produce food with a garden and a few animals, as they had done in the past. Mumford (1938) goes so far as to compare the factory to a prison, with "enforced silence, the repetitive routine, the lockstep, the constant surveillance of the foreman..." (p. 180). Marshall's (1940) remark also emphasizes how tight the discipline was:

> Factory overseers ... with elaborate codes assessed fines for lateness, leaving before the machinery stopped, waste of light and water, and breakage of materials, machinery and fixtures ... factory owners declared that they employed women and children not because they were cheaper but because they were more submissive to factory discipline than men. (p. 147)

Working conditions were severe, to say the least. In the 1830s a worker had to put in a thirteen-hour day, seven days a week; an eighteenth-century invention, artificial illuminating gas, fueled the factory's lamps, facilitating such long work sessions. So much for progress. With unguarded machines, belts, shafts, stairwells, and openings, conditions were dangerous and industrial accidents were frequent; factories were overheated, dimly lit, and filled with fiber dust. Neither the state nor the employer provided any insurance or other benefits or protections for the workers. Worst of all was the widespread employment of children; for example, Arkwright's mill at Cromford, opened in 1774, was staffed by the orphan's ward of the county of Derby (Vance, 1977)! From the age of 9 or 10, children did routine jobs like sweeping, carrying, and setting bobbins. Like adults, the children worked from sunrise into the night, and they, too, were the victims of industrial accidents as well as damage to their lungs, eyesight, education, and bodily development (United Kingdom, 1832).

## Populating the New Industrial Towns

Manufacturing towns grew as the factories multiplied; but before looking at these burgeoning communities, we shall look at the population movements that supported their expansion.

Why did people come to live by these wretched factories with their inhuman working conditions? A major migration from rural England supplied people to the growing urban communities; in addition, an international migration stream brought rural folk from Ireland to England's growing industrial towns.

Populations may grow from either of two sources, natural increase or net in-migration. "Natural increase" is growth based upon an excess of births over deaths. Subjected to high death rates from epidemics and poor sanitation, urban places almost never grew by natural increase before the twentieth century. In 1780, at the outset of industrial development, crude death rates in urban England, at 38.8 per 1,000, almost equalled crude birth rates, 40.1 per 1,000 (Loschky, cited in Daunton, 1978). A recent study (Sharlin, 1978), though, argues that the appearance of very high urban death rates before the industrial revolution is somewhat deceptive, saying that among permanent city people, births outnumbered deaths, at least at a modest level. But there were also many temporary migrants in the towns and cities; most of them were artisan journeymen and servants who could not marry. Thus they did not contribute births, at least not legitimate ones, but under the high mortality conditions of the time, they added to the number of deaths.

## Depopulating the countryside

When towns and cities grew during the industrial revolution, the additional people came from migration. In 1851, 3,336,000 persons over the age of 20 were counted in 62 towns and cities in England and Wales; of those counted, only 1,337,000 had been born in the place where they resided (Mumford, 1938). Almost two-thirds of these urbanites were migrants. Similarly, Marshall (1940) mentions that in 1851 only 28 percent of Manchester's male adults were natives.

Sociologists and demographers often commonly refer to push and pull factors in migration. A "push" is something in the home situation—economic, political, personal—which impels an individual or group to move; a "pull" is some attraction of a particular place which draws migrants to it. Pushes and pulls were involved in the large-scale migration into the industrializing towns.

The main pull of the towns, of course, was jobs. Artisans and mechanics were needed to build and supervise machines. "Every improvement of a machine which enabled a child, a woman, or an unskilled laborer to operate it created a demand for this type of worker" (Marshall, 1940, p. 146). Furthermore, the growing population itself required builders, tailors, tradesmen, messengers and porters, and commercial clerks (Marshall). Such opportunities were similar to those in contemporary boomtowns like Houston and in the energy towns of Wyoming and Alberta, Canada. In addition, the early factories offered better wages than those available in the countryside; this drew rural workers who were under- or unemployed, as well as those who sought financial improvement (Vance, 1977). Relying on Engels, Vance says, though, that wages were soon cut, falling rapidly to the point where former handworkers might earn less in towns than they had in the villages. Vance argues that "the oversupply of the labor answering the call to the city created, at least in considerable measure, the deterioration of social and economic conditions there" (p. 299). This point is disputed by some economic historians who contend that workers' real income increased during the industrial revolution.

Major pushes were also at work. Rural handworkers could not compete with the more efficient factories; thus, forced out of business, many looked to the town for new work. New poor laws were enacted which encouraged some places to send their poor to Manchester (Marshall, 1940).

But perhaps the most powerful push was the reorganization of land in the countryside, called the "enclosure movement," under an emerging set of rights and regulations governing the use of open meadows and woods known as "commons." Enclosure had been under way for centuries, but it accelerated considerably during the period 1750–1860. Commons had been available to landless families and those with small homesteads, but enclosure permitted the fencing of common lands, either dividing them among various landholders or assigning them to manorial lords. Thus they became inaccessible to the landless, and the rural poor, unable to graze their animals, could no longer subsist. Where else could they go but to the towns? By the thousands they migrated to growing industrial towns for work.

Another push came from rural population growth itself. Major changes were underway in the agriculture which, indirectly, caused populations to grow; as the countryside did not offer increasing opportunities, many rural people had to leave. This population growth was the beginning of what demographers call the "demographic transition."

## Beginnings of the demographic transition

Throughout history, until the industrial revolution, human populations usually had high birth rates and high death rates. Birth rates stayed high because each healthy woman gave birth to several children throughout her childbearing years. Females married young, became mothers in their early teen years, and continued a long series of pregnancies unless they died or became debilitated. On the other hand, death rates were also high. Food supplies were far from perfectly dependable as the agricultural technology was not highly productive and farmers could not control insect pests. Farming could be temporarily wiped out by bad weather, such as a drought, and there was no way to move food from an agricultural area with a surplus to another in distress. Medical and sanitary knowledge was primitive. The standard of housing and clothing was low, offering people scant protection against the winter's cold. So, nutrition was marginally adequate in good times, but people were subject to temporary food shortages as well as to diseases, both ordinary infections and epidemics. Childbirth was risky to infant and mother; childbirth fever, an infection associated with delivery, was a common cause of death among young women. High rates of infant mortality also prevailed.

The net effect was fluctuating, but high, overall death rates. Death rates might fall when crops were bountiful and rise in time of drought or epidemic; on average, before the industrial revolution, they were generally high. The net effect of high death rates was to cancel out the potential effects of high birth rates, resulting in a very low population growth rate. But European death rates began to fall more than a century before the erection of the first factories in England.

The lowly potato made a big difference. Introduced into Europe in the second half of the sixteenth century, the potato became a major crop in Ireland by the end of the seventeenth; one hundred years later it was widely grown in Germany and quickly diffused throughout the rest of Europe. This crop increased the amount of usable food a farmer could grow on his land. Potato cultivation was one element in a wider transformation of European agriculture in the eighteenth and early nineteenth centuries; other agricultural developments also helped increase the volume and dependability of food production and improved the common diet (Wrigley, 1969). "The introduction of roots and clovers enabled larger numbers of livestock to be maintained and kept through the winter" (p. 168). Other productive practices were introduced, including more use of manure, better drainage, improved animal breeds, better storage, and new tools, especially seed drills. Long-distance trade also increased Europe's food supply: wheat from the new world, plus maize and cane sugar (Mumford, 1958).

More dependable food production tended to lower the death rate. People increased their caloric intake, and fewer died of starvation; since birth rates were still high, the population explosion was on. This section makes reference to the theory of the demographic transition, which shows how national populations have changed over a period of about three centuries in the now-industrialized countries. In earlier centuries there had been very little population growth, due to a "high balance": high death rates canceled the potential effects of high birth rates. In the period described here, death rates fell while birth rates remained high, so populations grew rapidly. Throughout the nineteenth and twentieth centuries, birth rates fell steadily as women had fewer and fewer children. This trend brought populations into the third stage of the transition, in which there is a small growth rate due to a balance of low birth rates and low death rates (Thomlinson, 1965).

Returning to the beginnings of the demographic transition, we see that rural population growth impelled people to migrate from the land. Agriculture could accommodate some of the additional population, but not nearly all of it. Now more people were living in the rural areas with no work for them. The cultivable land was soon fully occupied, and the existing farms needed no additional laborers. Thus some individuals had to leave the land: second sons, sons of landless laborers, and others with no opportunities in the countryside. They, too, migrated to the new factory towns looking for work.

## MANCHESTER, ENGLAND: THE PRIME CASE
### Differential Urban Growth

When steam became the dominant power source, industry moved out of the countryside into the towns and cities, but not all of England's existing towns and cities grew equally in the late eighteenth and early nineteenth centuries. Many of the older, established cities declined during the early period of industrial development; for example, Bristol, Norwich, and Newcastle, which were the second-, third-, and fourth-ranking cities in 1750, grew very little or lost, and by 1800 Manchester, Liverpool, and Birmingham surpassed them in size (Daunton, 1978). In the nongrowing cities, the guilds were strong and well-entrenched. Guild rules prohibited nonmembers from doing their sorts of work in factories; for example, the weavers' guild would not tolerate the use of laborers to operate mechanical looms in factories. Therefore, factory investors built elsewhere, and the existing city industries declined. Daunton relates the following example of the decline of an existing urban place:

> Exeter in 1700 was the finishing and marketing centre for the local serge industry ... concentrated upon the finishing, dyeing and exporting of goods manufactured in its hinterland. These processes were closely regulated by the {guild} of Weavers, Fullers and Shearmen which had been incorporated in 1490 and which continued to enforce apprenticeship, to limit entry to freemen, to fix rates and prices.... By 1800 the industry was insignificant.... The town experienced severe relative decline ... {and} became a centre for shopkeeping and services.... The town which had once extended its entrepot trade from Holland to Newfoundland, and from Norway to the Canaries, was now a small market town collecting and distributing for only twenty miles around. (pp. 269-270)

Thus a particular form of social organization, the guild, was incompatible with the emerging technology and the new social organization; guilds were inflexible, and the community failed to adapt to the new situation. Daunton suggests that by the eighteenth century the established towns had become a conservative influence which had to be bypassed. There was, however, a category of smaller towns which were hospitable to factory development, and these grew rapidly. Manchester fell into this category.

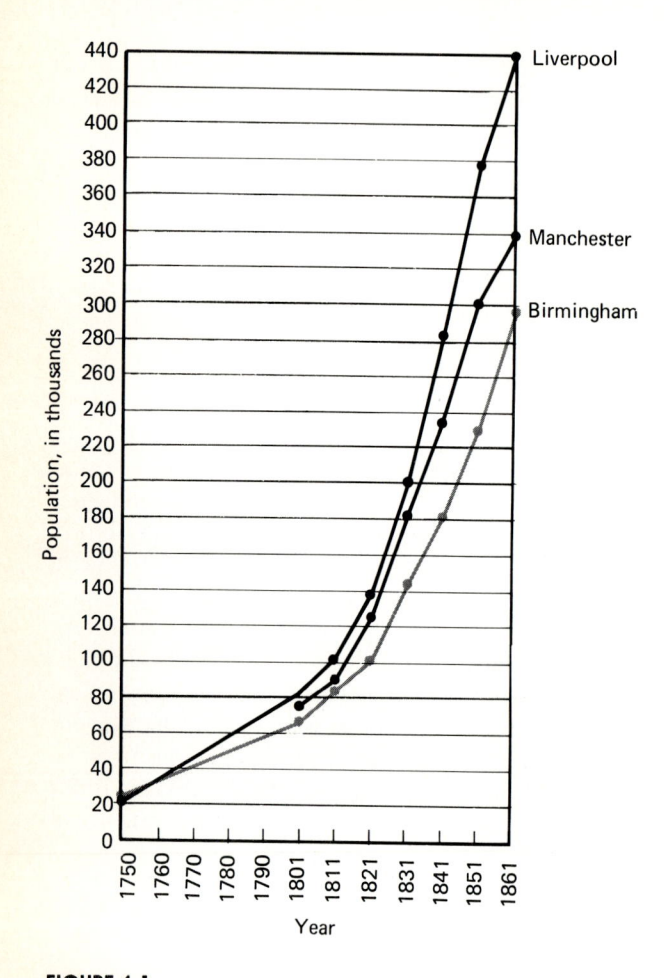

**FIGURE 4-1**
Populations of three English cities during the industrial revolution. These places grew extremely rapidly, from small towns to large cities. Liverpool gained 80,000 people within a decade! (Source: Data for 1750 are from Daunton, 1978; data for 1801–1861 are from Mitchell, 1962.)

## Social Structure

Manchester provides a vivid example of urban development during the industrial revolution, expanding rapidly in the late eighteenth and nineteenth centuries. Manchester—a typical provincial market town until Arkwright built a factory there in 1780—and its nearby satellite town, Salford, grew rapidly in population from 25,000 in 1772 to 367,000 in 1851 (Marshall, 1940). After 1785 other merchant manufacturers built factories in the vicinity; by 1820 they had erected 66 cotton-, 6 silk-, and 6 wool-spinning mills. Then, integrating spinning and weaving,

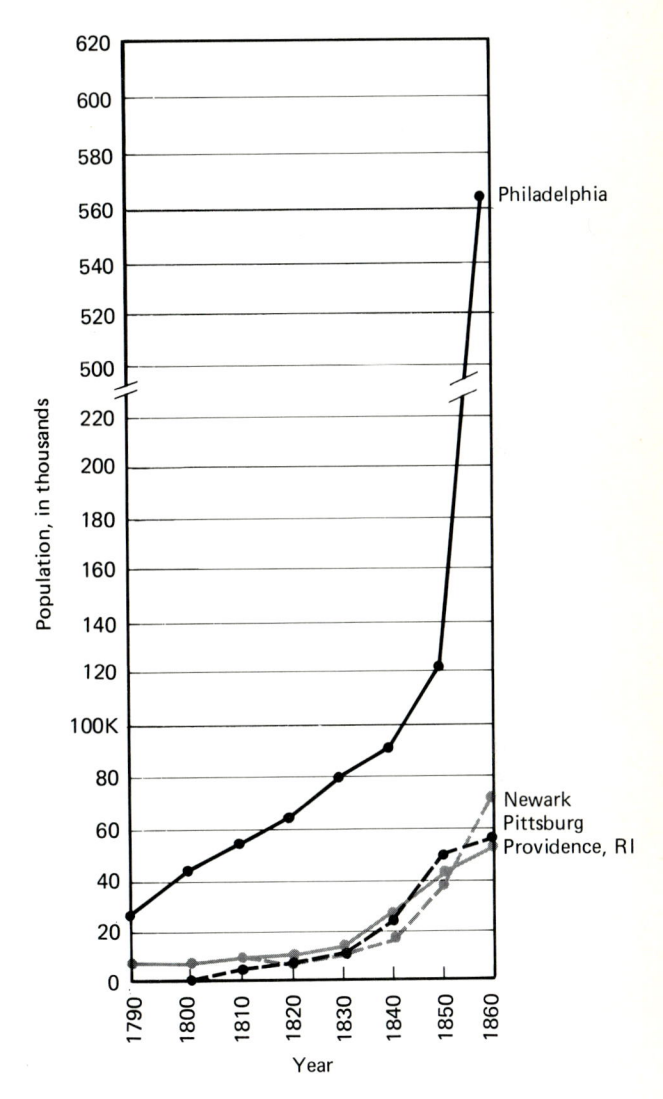

**FIGURE 4-2**
Populations of four American cities during the early industrial revolution. The American cities sometimes doubled within a decade; Pittsburg and Newark between 1840 and 1850, for example. (Source: *U.S. Bureau of the Census,* 1900, vol. 1, pp. 432–433.)

they built larger factories, with 300 to 1,000 hands; by 1845 Manchester and Salford had 100 such establishments.

Historians disagree about using Manchester as a typical case. Marshall (1940) said it was typical of towns based upon woolens, silk, tools, brewing, and other factory products. Engels (1887/1900) in his history-making book, *The Condition of the Working Class in England in 1844*, used Manchester as a typical example. Following Dickens, whose novels describe the harsh conditions of life then, Mumford (1938) calls Manchester "Coketown"; he vehemently insists that the early industrial towns, like Manchester, hit one of the low points in urban history. But, more recently, Briggs (1965), in his *Victorian Cities*, contends that social structure was quite different in other places such as Leeds and Liverpool and that one should not generalize from Manchester which was an isolated, and perhaps worst, case. Regardless of its typicality, though, Manchester around 1840 shows many urban consequences of the industrial revolution.

The factory system created a new social class, the proletariat, composed of workers and unemployed workers, whom Marx (1867/1977) called the "Industrial Reserve Army." In Manchester, as in other industrial towns, the factory working class was far larger than the artisan class had been before the introduction of factories.

Manchester's social structure changed dramatically after the rise of the factories (Marshall, 1940). There used to be a small number of gentlemen and wealthy merchants, an elite which dominated the town, along with a group of clergymen, lawyers, and physicians. Below them were artisans, the largest occupational stratum: tailors, wool combers, worsted weavers, shoemakers, dyers, joiners, silk weavers, and hatters. "At the bottom of the social scale were porters, unskilled laborers, and a growing number of cotton weavers and shopkeepers" (p. 145). This three-level configuration shifted in the first half of the century. In the new social structure factory owners, bankers, merchants, and wealthy shopkeepers comprised a new elite; they controlled the city government, chambers of commerce, and the philanthropic and intellectual institutions. There was also a new professional class—newspaper editors, teachers, commercial clerks, overseers, and engineers—in addition to the old one. Both were subservient to the new business elite, administering their enterprises and propagating their views (Marshall, 1940).

Hawley (1971) argues, in effect, that domination by the business elite was inevitable: In a social system, "the unit that mediates the relations between the external world and the internal system sets the conditions under which the other units must operate" (pp. 129-130). The external world consisted of the suppliers of cotton, near and far; the buyers of cloth, the government; and the main banks in London—all impinging upon the survival and prosperity of Manchester's industry. This principle suggests that owners and bankers controlled the flow of resources and income to the community. Ultimately, service units—truckers, printers, lawyers—plus the proletariat at large, depended upon the factory. Thus power resided with the business elite.

Utilitarianism, the dominant philosophy of the times, supported and justified the factory owners' interests; it sought to break through the restrictive and outmoded institutions of feudalism. Utilitarians, according to Mumford (1938), "wished to have a free hand in making investments, in building up industries, in buying land, in hiring workers" (p. 153). They reasoned that the marketplace would determine a balance and harmony in the economy and, hence, in the society; this justified a system of free capitalism in which capitalists had great freedom to pursue economic advantage. Mumford notes that this philosophy implied the community government should be weak: "The location of factories for the workers, even the supply of water and the collection of garbage, should be done exclusively by private enterprise..." (p. 154). But Mumford deemed the result to be a failure: "There was no limit to congestion, no limit to rent-raising: there was no standard of order or decency or beauty... Only one controlling agent remained: profit" (p. 155).

In addition to the potent mechanical inventions already mentioned, the industrial revolution brought forth a number of social inventions, that is, new ways of organizing social relations to accomplish some goal. The social inventions of the time promoted the ability to do business on a large scale, and they included new forms of corporate organization and administration; delegation of administrative authority under divided ownership; and control of the enterprise via budget and audit (Mumford, 1938). Overall, the bureaucratic organization of work in large factories was a social invention. And while Mumford bitterly decries the lack of civilization in the growing industrial towns, he notes that they had the beginnings of some "new organs for social co-operation and social thought, the trade union, scientific society, co-operative society, and public library" (p. 222).

## Spatial Structure

The three main features of Manchester's built environment were a spread of factory-slum complexes, a commercial center, and a high pollution level.

### The cellular city

As Manchester spread to include Salford and other nearby places, the bulk of the town comprised numerous subareas, each containing a factory surrounded by a residential slum for its workers. Some of the residential areas consisted of little old houses or shacks, others of newer one-story tenements. Some factory proprietors owned housing for their workers, kept shops for them, and provided apprentice houses for the pauper children who worked in the mill (Hammond, 1931). But, eventually, most of the housing became part of an open market (Vance, 1977). The residential slums also included other local facilities, such as shops, taverns, and perhaps a brothel (Mumford, 1938).

Hawley (1971) refers to the pattern formed by an undifferentiated spread of these factory-slum complexes as the "cellular city," which implies a biological metaphor, like tissue composed of identical cells. In early industrial towns, subareas or neighborhoods are cells, more or less equivalent to each other, each nucleated by a factory and engaged in the same activity, making a product (usually cotton cloth) and providing housing for workers. The town grew by adding cells: "As mills were

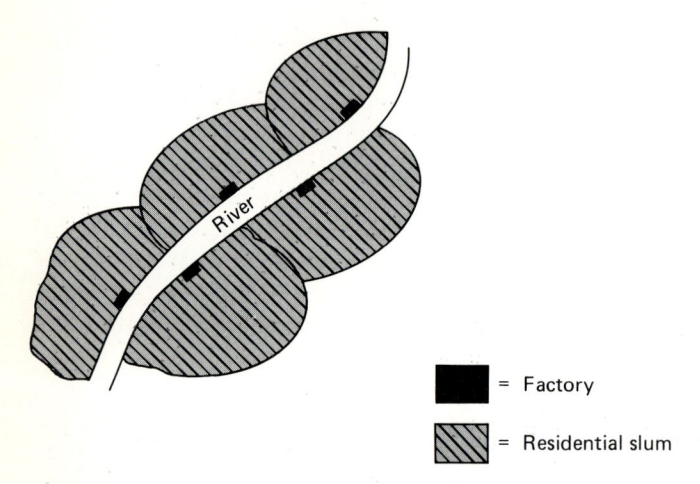

**FIGURE 4-3**
A cellular city with five cells. At least from the workers' point of view, the city center was unimportant in this type of community.

erected along the rivers and canals, the new population burst through the limits of the old town and settled in slums around the factories" (Marshall, 1940). Subareas had to be compact because the only mode of commuting was on foot; given the long hours of work, workers had to live near their places of employment. (The cellular concept also implies segmental structure, in which the units are in no way interdependent. Thus the loss of a cell would have little effect upon the city as a whole.)

Manchester's slums, as described by Engels (1845/1958) offered very little as human environments.[1] Engels wrote about several slums, all dreadful at best. For example: "In the houses one seldom sees a wooden or a stone floor, while the doors and windows are nearly always broken and badly fitting.... Everywhere one sees heaps of refuse, garbage and filth. There are stagnant pools instead of gutters and the stench alone is so overpowering that no human being ... would find it bearable to live in such a district" (p. 61). Another area had pigs in the street and so few privies "that they are either filled up every day, or are too far away for those who need to use them" (p. 62) and no access to water for washing except the polluted river. This pollution promoted endemic typhoid among the population.

The neighborhoods were densely built, and the standard of housing was remarkably low; Engels refers to an estimate that in 1833, 20,000 persons (amounting to

---

[1]Vance gives Engels high marks as a geographical reporter. "No one, it seems to me, looked upon Manchester as an Industrial Era city with the perceptive morphogenetic eye that Engels seems to have possessed," wrote Vance (1977, p. 298).

an eighth of the working class) lived in cellars. Even the new housing was poor; row houses were built as two-room units, back to back. Only the room facing the street had windows or doors; the interior rooms had no ventilation or daylight. Each family with several children had one room; even the beds were overcrowded, with "three to eight people of different ages sleeping on the same pallet," according to Mumford (1938, p. 164), who said that this standard of housing was worse than the lowest serf's cottage in medieval Europe. Although economic historians debate this point, Mumford states unequivocally that the workers' standard of living was declining during the early industrial period.

The housing market was a new feature of the industrial towns. Traditionally, a master was responsible for his helpers and apprentices, who became part of his household. At the beginning of the factory system, owners provided housing for their workers, and some continued to do so, particularly in one-industry "company towns"; in effect, housing was a supplement to cash wages. But in nineteenth-century Manchester this pattern became uncommon as owners stopped using capital to develop housing. "Essentially, they threw their workers onto the general 'market' for housing," according to Vance (1977, p. 306). Under the new arrangements, employees had to use some of their wages to acquire shelter; this transition also provided new capital opportunities for individuals who would invest in rental housing.

Poor environmental and work conditions promoted poor health, as reflected in high mortality levels. Throughout the nineteenth century urban mechanics had a lower expectation of years of life than poor farm laborers had (Mumford, 1938). Infant mortality was also high. Manchester municipality was unable to deal with the public's health, although the board of health published reports on sanitary conditions and in 1801 promoted the erection of a hospital. The board recommended preventive measures for families and owners in the event of epidemics, but this was an ineffectual gesture. Sanitary conditions reached their nadir during the cholera epidemics of 1831 to 1933 (Marshall, 1940).

## Differentiation

English society was so sharply divided by social class that Benjamin Disraeli, statesman and author, referred to "two nations." Factory workers, displaced poor folk from the countryside, and unurbanized Irish peasants lived in slums while the middle and upper classes lived elsewhere. Wealthy manufacturers lived in two districts far from the factories and the city center; located on high ground, these districts were situated so that the prevailing wind patterns took the factories' smoke elsewhere. Middle-class suburbs were located closer to the city center (Marshall, 1940).

The city had a clearly demarcated functional center, the crossroads for heavy traffic; it contained offices and warehouses and, according to Engels (1845/1958), was unpopulated at night. The central area contained bankers', solicitors', and other financial offices; stores for the well-to-do, such as jewelers, tailors, and dressmakers; and governmental and ecclesiastical offices. It had nothing for workers except "stews," back-alley clusters of tiny deteriorating buildings which housed the very poor who provided menial and casual labor for central activities (Vance, 1977).

Vance argues that Manchester epitomized some major features of industrial cities. Residential stratification graduated toward the center: "The pattern emerging in Manchester by 1840 was very strikingly that of the modern city, with separation of one function from another and the separation of one social class from all others" (p. 303). Vance also contends that the spatial division exacerbated the social distance between classes by cutting off contact.

Manchester's environment was deeply polluted. The river had dyes and wastes from the mills, animal refuse from tanneries, and additional human wastes. "The atmosphere is polluted by the stench and is darkened by the thick smoke of a dozen factory chimneys" (Engels, 1845/1958, p. 71), and foul smells arose from the tanneries and from the neighborhoods themselves, with their insufficient privies, open drains, roving pigs, and uncontrolled garbage.

## THE MATURE INDUSTRIAL CITY: 1850–1920

At this point we shift our attention to the United States. As English weaving and manufacturing was switching to the factory system, so was the United States. Dozens of industrial towns and cities were growing here: Pawtucket, Paterson, Worcester, Waltham, Lowell, and Providence, as well as Newark, Pittsburg, and Youngstown; by the time of the Civil War some of these places were emerging as large industrial cities. The war spurred industrial development while energetic railroad building continued; both supported the growth of great cities.

### Centralization

### Technological changes

Once again in the nineteenth century major changes in transportation technology precipitated major changes in urban form. Railroads spanned North America by 1869, culminating more than two decades of energetic railroad building, particularly east of the Mississippi. Rails linked regions as well as cities; able to move far more freight than any previous inland transport system except rivers and canals, they vastly increased the potential "hinterland" of any city. Thus the railroad multiplied the potential population size of a city as a function of the agricultural surplus which could move there.

Within the cities, the trolley exerted a powerful influence toward centralization. Previously, in the early industrial town where employees walked to work, it was efficient to have workplaces scattered near the workers' residences—generating the cellular pattern. But the horse-drawn trolley, introduced in numerous cities after 1850, changed that situation (Muller, 1981); given the same travel time from home to work, the trolley could move a person further. Tracks typically followed radial patterns, converging at the city center. This means of transportation, moving passengers about 5 miles per hour, extended the range of the built-up area to about 3 miles from the center.

Lasting only about thirty years, the horse-drawn trolley was soon supplanted by the electric trolley ("streetcar") and by intraurban railways in three forms: street level, elevated, and subway. These new transportation devices again stretched the journey to work, thereby multiplying the area which could be developed. Local transportation companies tended to lay out trolley lines and electric railway routes radially from the center, like the spokes of a wheel from the hub (see Figure 4-4). Trolley speeds averaging 15 to 18 miles per hour facilitated residential development as far as 10 miles from the city core. "At least five times the area of the horsecar city now potentially came within 30 minutes' travel time of the CBD [central business district} (Muller, 1981, p. 31).

Radial trolley lines gave rise to a "starfish pattern" of urban development (see Figure 4-5). Investors built shops, often with apartments above them, along streets with trolley lines, many of which were major radials. The first buildings were toward the city center, but eventually the developments extended to the end of the line. Then, at least in the more central areas, residential development filled in the interstitial areas. But the geometry of the situation was such that far out, distances to the trolleys were too great for walking, so they remained undeveloped.

The skyscraper was another technological innovation which permitted accentuated development of the city center. This new type of building became possible after two late-nineteenth-century inventions: the steel-frame structure and the elevator. Prior to the development of the steel frame, builders could go up only about ten stories; beyond that, the stone or brick load-bearing walls would have to be too thick. But the new type of frame allowed builders to go almost indefinitely. Once this was possible, builders could use the safety elevator, invented by Elisha Otis in 1852, to move people and objects vertically. William L. Jenney, an engineer, built the first practical steel-frame building in Chicago in 1884, a 10-story structure which may be considered a "proto-skyscraper"; true skyscrapers soon followed (Condit, 1964). Several additional skyscrapers were built in Chicago in the decade of the nineties, but the new type of building caught on most rapidly in New York City. Soon all sorts of business activities, including commercial offices, department stores, and small factories, were housed in these multistory buildings with elevators. By carrying human activities upward into space, builders increased the *intensity of land use* in central areas; more people and activities could be accommodated on a given amount of land. The new commuting patterns and clustering of commercial activities in the central business district required a higher intensity of land use; the technology of the skyscraper thus facilitated the development of the city center.

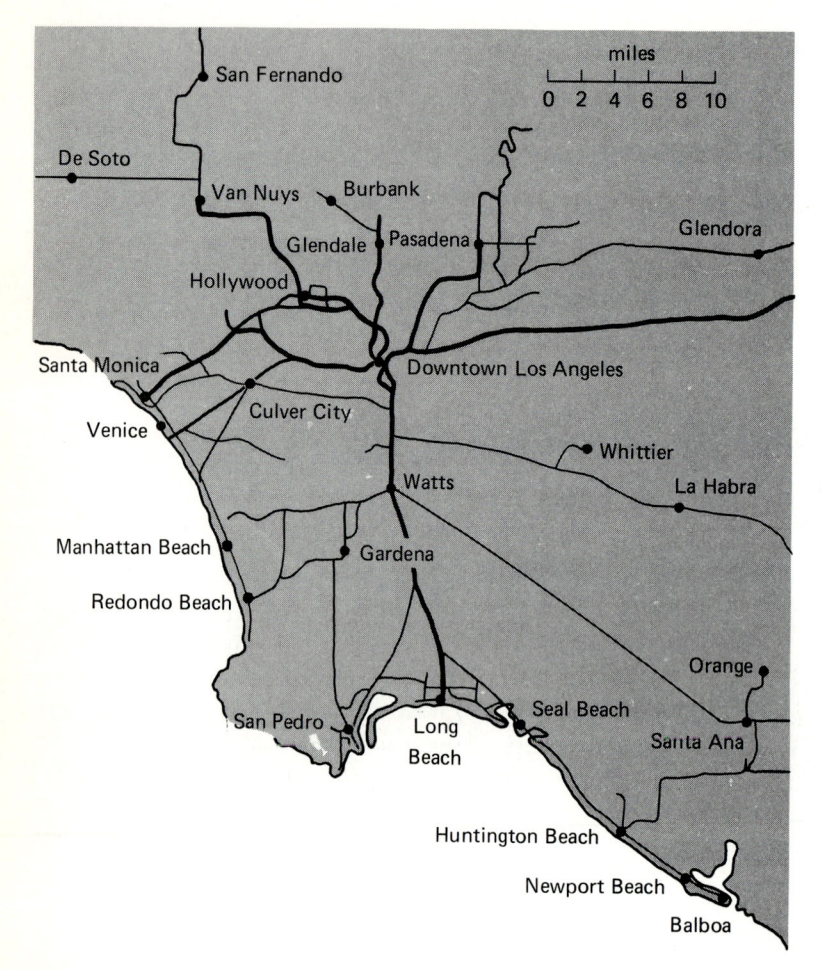

**FIGURE 4-4**
Route map of the Pacific Electric Railroad, Los Angeles, 1923. Despite Los Angeles's reputation as the original decentralized metropolis, it actually had a well-developed street railway which converged on the CBD before the advent of the expressway. This trolley system was completely junked after World War II. (Source: Banham, 1971, p. 80.)

## The central business district

The radial pattern on transport lines made the center into the most accessible point in the urban area for work, shopping, and other activities. Furthermore, the rapid growth of the economy in general, including agriculture, manufacturing, railroads, land development, wholesaling, retailing, banking, etc., generated innumerable activities which were best conducted in a central area. Office-based activities grew rapidly: banking, insurance, commodity and stock exchanges, advertising, account-

# THE RISE OF THE INDUSTRIAL CITY

**Central business district**

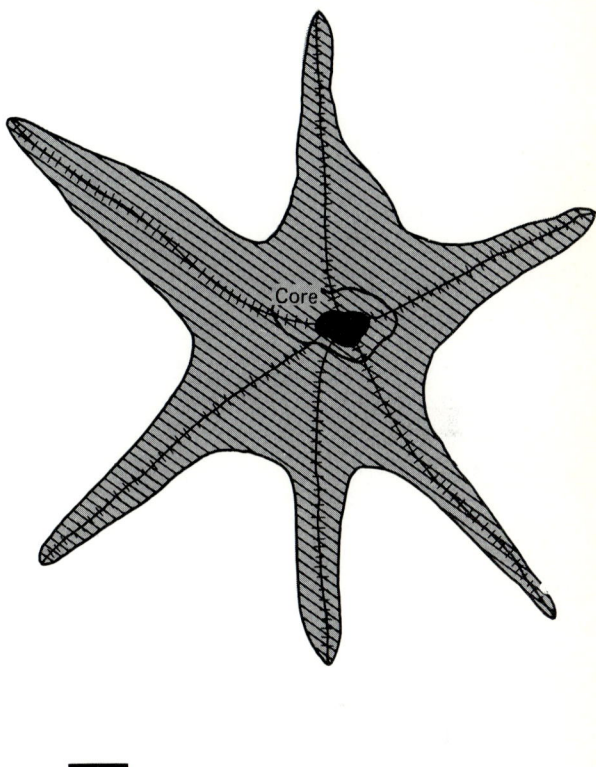

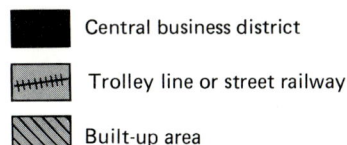

**Trolley line or street railway**

**Built-up area**

**FIGURE 4-5**
Starfish development pattern. Builders tended to stay close to the trolley and rail lines, filling in the gaps later. Even so, all the developed areas had to be within walking distance of the arterial lines, which left open areas at the periphery.

ing, and law. This type of coordinative work required locational proximity among the units for frequent and rapid communication; lawyers needed to be near bankers, stock brokers near accountants. Furthermore, large business offices which employed thousands of clerks, secretaries, and managers required accessible locations to which these workers could commute daily; this also fostered centralization. Although heavy manufacturing, such as steel or railway cars, had to avoid expensive downtown locations, light manufacturing, such as printing and jewelry making, clustered in the city center.

**New York's garment district** Making "ready-to-wear" clothing in New York City offers an ideal example of the advantages of centralization. Traditionally, women bought cloth by the yard and made clothes at home; wealthier individuals bought clothes from tailors and seamstresses. The production system changed during the Civil War, though, when uniforms were mass-produced, and thereafter men's civilian clothing was mass-produced. Later in the nineteenth century, factory production of women's ready-to-wear skirts, blouses, and coats began; the "needle trades" grew rapidly in New York, concentrated on several blocks in Manhattan. The division of labor was extreme; numerous small, highly specialized factories performed parts of the manufacturing process. The industry was divided by product: One company made expensive coats for women, another midpriced coats, and another cheap coats; other factories made skirts, similarly divided by price, etc. Furthermore, for a given garment, the manufacturing process might be divided by steps: One factory might do linings, collars, pockets, buttonholes, cutting or embroidery, or "finishing." Since many independent little establishments were in close proximity, sometimes even in the same building, the unfinished coats could be moved from factory to factory to add each step to the manufacturing process. In addition, the garment district housed the industry's ancillary suppliers and tradespeople; dealers in cloth, lace, ribbon, linings, buttons, and thread all had their shops there, as did the people who sold and repaired sewing machines. Proximity had other advantages: As popular styles changed, they diffused rapidly through the industry. Also, retail and wholesale buyers could examine the offerings of all the competitors in a circumscribed area. In the garment district, we see the division of labor carried to its extreme and also the locational process of proximity facilitating interpersonal contact.

## The Concentric Model of Urban Growth and Form

Rapidly expanding industrial cities followed a fairly predictable growth pattern which was encapsulated in Ernest Burgess's growth model. In 1925, in a paper entitled "The Growth of the City: An Introduction to a Research Project," Burgess, who was then a young sociologist at the University of Chicago, introduced his now-famous circular pattern. Taking the city of Chicago as a case in point, he noted that the growing city had a central business district (CBD), called the "Loop," which was surrounded by more-or-less circular social zones, as illustrated in Figure 4-6. (The Loop took its name from the elevated intraurban railroad tracks which formed a loop around the CBD.) Surrounding the CBD was the "zone in transition," which had the city's oldest structures, in deteriorated condition. This zone included some buildings used for warehousing and light manufacturing, but it also had immigrant slums—"The Ghetto," "Little Sicily," "Chinatown," and others—as well as red-light districts and skid row. Since the CBD was growing, land in the area presumably awaited the time when it would be reused for some central function, hence this zone's name. The next ring was called the "zone of workingmen's homes." Housing and shops in this area were newer than those in the zone of transition and were occupied by workmen and their families, many being second-generation Americans. The next ring, filled with newer homes and apartment buildings, was the "middle-class zone." It was surrounded by the lower-density residential areas of the "commuter zone," the furthest from the center. To some extent each zone's social class was a function of the residents' ability to afford the cost of commuting to the CBD.

The concentric zones pattern, even in Chicago, was far from perfect. Industry was segregated into particular districts, sometimes crosscutting zones. There were

**FIGURE 4-6**
Burgess's concentric model of the growth of the city. This diagram represents the concentric model in its most general form, assuming rapid growth over flat terrain. Because they will be affected by history and site conditions, no real cities will look exactly like this. An abstract model is supposed to highlight basic tendencies. (Source: Burgess, 1925, p. 51.)

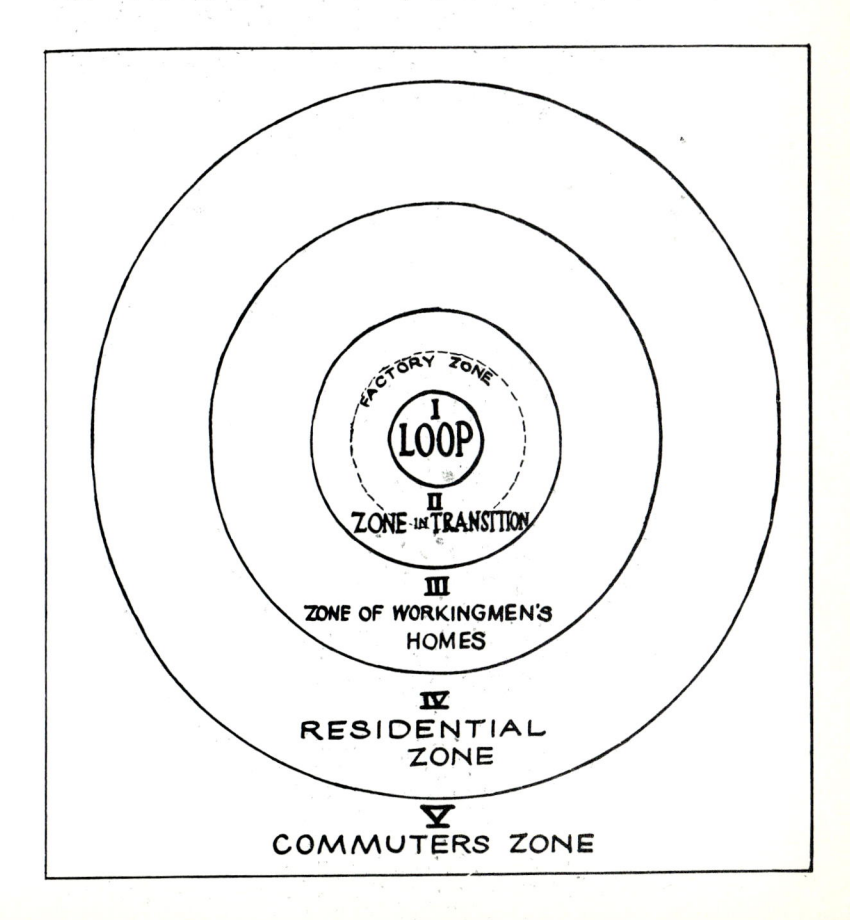

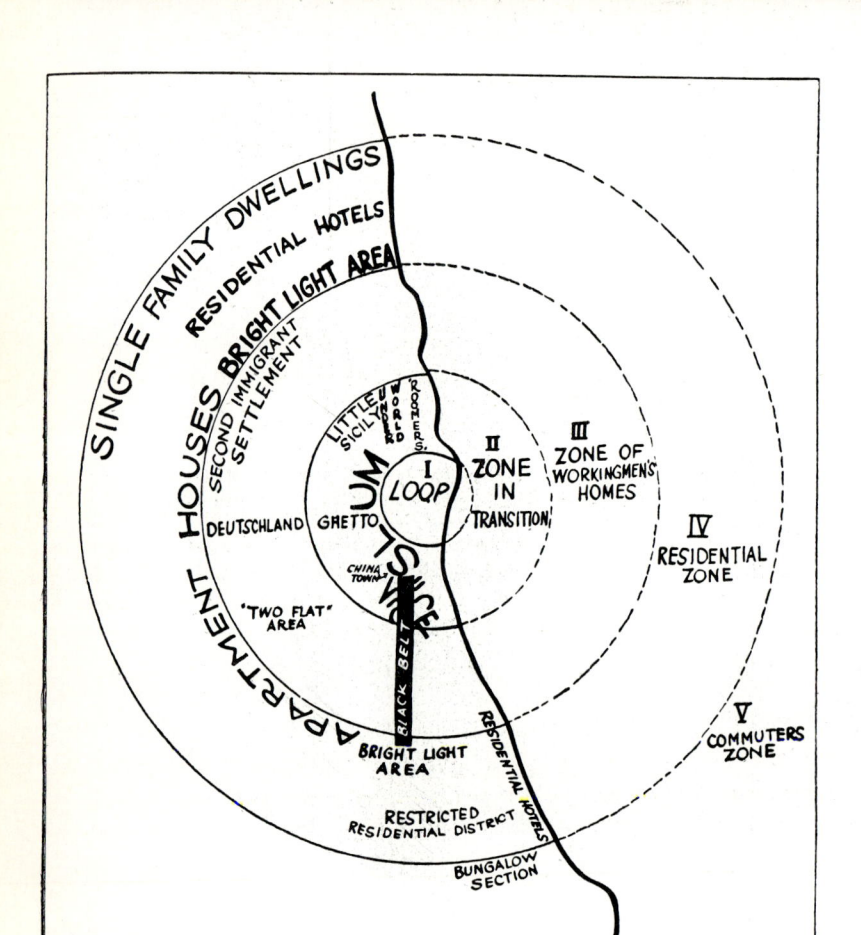

**FIGURE 4-7**
The concentric model applied to Chicago. Burgess applied the model to Chicago in the 1920s, the real city he knew best. Obviously, the insertion of Lake Michigan's shoreline distorts the model. The "black belt" ghetto, which cuts through three zones, also fails to conform to the general pattern. (Source: Burgess, 1925, p. 55.)

also some anomalies, such as the lower-class black district, which took the shape of a rectangle, cutting through two zones. And there was an upper-income residential sector which followed the northern lake shore, also cutting through at least two zones. These anomalies were tolerable because Burgess posited the scheme as a *generalized* growth model for a rapidly expanding city on an open terrain.

The city grew in two ways in Burgess's scheme. First, commercial growth occurred at the center; old businesses and shops expanded, and new enterprises wanted downtown space for offices, retail shops, etc. Other core activities—wholesaling and light manufacturing, for example—while not requiring prime downtown space, also needed to be in the urban core. Assuming rapid economic growth, this meant that the CBD was expanding; it had a powerful need for adjacent land. Thus it would nibble or gobble buildings and lots of the city, like moving ripples in a pond after a pebble hits the surface. Poor households in the zone in transition would encroach upon the nearest housing in the zone of workingmen's homes; its residents, in turn, would look to the housing in the middle-class for new space, etc. Thus the expanding center exerted a particular growth dynamic which was felt in the entire urban system. Second, residential growth took place at the city's periphery, where open land was available for development. To erect new subdivisions, investors bought farms; plotted lots; laid streets, sidewalks, and sewer connections; and built single-family dwellings or better-quality apartments. Thus new housing was added to the outermost zone, for the middle and upper classes; the metropolis was spreading at the periphery.

In sum, the mature industrial city had three major sociospatial features: a dominant center, division of residence and work, and division among social areas. The emergence of the dominant center, the CBD, made the new type of city different from its predecessor, the early industrial city, which had a cellular (segmental) structure and lacked a center. In the mature industrial city, the center contained the coordinative and distributive functions of the large community. Coordinative functions included communications, in the form of newspapers, publishers, advertisers, telegraph offices, shipping offices. and the like, as well as markets such as the stock and commodity exchanges. The government, which also serves coordinative functions, was there: city hall, the courts, and the jail. The CBD also contained visitors' facilities—stations, hotels, restaurants, and convention halls—plus large retail establishments and highly specialized ones. The CBD had all but one of the major functions which were in the center of the ancient city; the modern version of the palace was still there, as was the market, but the sacred function was missing. Even if there were large churches downtown, as there sometimes were, by no means did they dominate the scene; the commercial skyscrapers overshadowed them. Religion, dispersed to neighborhood churches, was no longer a function for the community center.

Work and residence were further divided in the mature industrial city. In rural cottage industry and in the medieval town, the home was often a workshop as well as a place to live; in the medieval town and in the early industrial city, a person could walk to work. This ceased to be the case in the mature industrial city where mass transit systems could move thousands of workers relatively long distances. Neighborhoods still had some jobs in "mom-and-pop stores" and small factories, but more and more blue- and white-collar workers commuted to their places of employment. The "journey to work" was born. The city was developing single-purpose districts: heavy industry in one area, the CBD in another, and residences in others.

Residential areas themselves were differentiated according to the social characteristics of their occupants; high-class areas, working-class areas, immigrant slums, and other types of neighborhoods developed. Within a purely capitalistic housing market, the price of housing determined the social class of the occupants of each residential area. Then, within social-class labels, neighborhoods were further differentiated by ethnicity; this was true both in the immigrant slums and in the working-class neighborhoods to which the second-generation Americans were moving. This ethnic differentiation gave rise to an image of the mature industrial city as a patchwork quilt of national areas. New York City at the turn of the century was the prime example, with such neighborhoods as "Hell's Kitchen" (Sicilian) and the Lower East Side (Jewish). Nonetheless, this image was somewhat overdrawn: All these areas had mixtures of immigrant nationalities living side by side.

## Occupational Structure

Every urban community has structured social inequality, sometimes known as a class system. Social classes are difficult to measure, but the distribution of occupations is one good way to represent them because jobs can be roughly ordered from the top ones, with prestige and financial rewards, to those at the bottom, with not much of either.

The occupational structure of one mature industrial city, Boston, appears in Figure 4-8; social historians carefully analyzed the city's occupational structure at three points over a forty-year period. Taking Boston as an emerging example of the

**FIGURE 4-8**
Occupational distribution in a mature industrial city; Boston, 1880–1920. Note the consistently large proportions in the two white-collar categories. Over time, the proportion of skilled manual workers declines along with the unskilled, while the proportion of service and "semiskilled" (factory) workers grows. (Source: Drawn from data in Thernstrom, 1973, p. 50.)

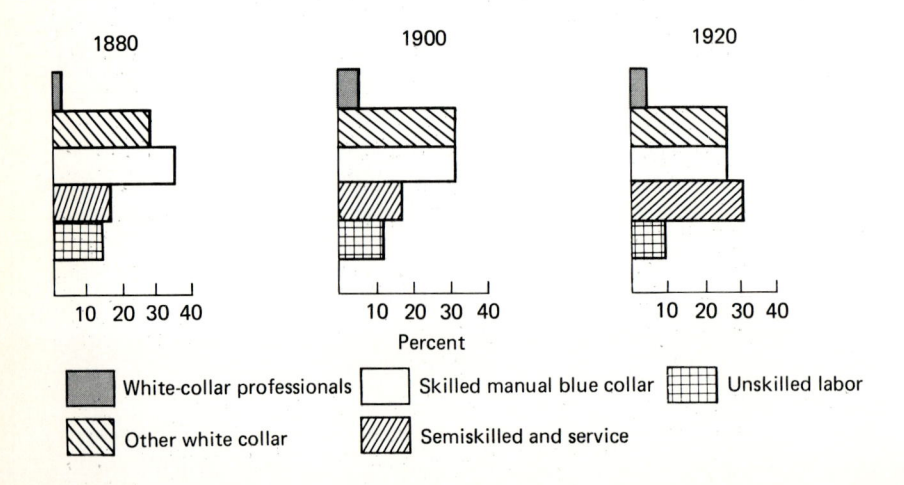

mature industrial city, we can see the occupational distribution and how it shifts over time. The upper-class elite, shown as the white-collar professionals at the top of the graph, was small throughout the period. Most workers were in blue-collar categories, meaning that they worked with their hands; at each time point about two-thirds of the male labor force consisted of blue-collar workers. The graphs represent only the employed labor force, so they omit an important part of the poorer classes, the unemployed, who would have appeared at the bottom. The data also omit females, introducing another distortion; working as servants, washerwomen, semiskilled laborers, and the like, most of them would also have appeared at the bottom of the display.

Two trends are evident in the graph's forty-year period: The proportion of professional workers increases between 1880 and 1900. (It drops slightly thereafter but is still substantially higher in 1900, at 5 percent, than it was in 1880, at 3 percent.) The blue-collar occupations change as there are fewer skilled craftsmen and unskilled workers; they are replaced by increasing numbers of semi-skilled and service workers. These important trends continue in the twentieth century.

Boston's substantial proportion of clerical workers shows that a big city had special functions that a simple manufacturing town would not have had at that time. The manufacturing town would have had a preponderance of blue-collar workers and very few white-collar ones—just clerks in the company and the banks. But a big city had regional coordinative and distributive functions, such as insurance companies, brokerages, wholesalers, publishers, associations, etc., which swelled the ranks of the white-collar occupations.

## COMMUNITY PROBLEMS OF THE NEW CITIES

Not surprisingly, big cities engendered a number of severe social problems. Some were due to rapid growth; some to the mix of different unacculturated peoples who lacked even a common language; some to the inequalities of the capitalist industrial system; and some to poorly formed municipal institutions, unable to handle city problems. Riots and public disorder as well as poverty and slums are examples of major urban problems during the late nineteenth and early twentieth centuries.

### Riots

### New York's draft riots

Many cities had severe destructive riots in the midnineteenth century; New York City's notorious 1864 draft riots exemplify this problem at its worst. The draft riots occurred in July, after President Lincoln ordered conscription of men for the Union Army. The rules of the draft stated that names would be drawn by lot but that for $300 a man could buy his way out to support a substitute. Thus the poor had to serve while the more prosperous did not.

Irish immigrants, concentrated in the poorer classes, composed a large part of the city's population. Tens of thousands left their homeland, particularly after the potato famines of the 1840s, and by 1860, almost a quarter of New York City's population was Irish or of Irish descent. The immigrants were rural folk, poor and illiterate; many lived in a slum district known as the "Bloody Ould Sixth" (ward), which also housed some free blacks.

In those days discrimination and prejudice were open and unvarnished. "Citizens who thought of themselves as native Americans despised the poor Paddy; his rough, alien ways; his papist religion; and his uncouth, barbaric brogue, with a bitter prejudice that is difficult to comprehend today" (McCague, 1963, p. 23). Some political parties were openly anti-immigrant and anti-Catholic. Poor whites, in turn, including the Irish, were antiblack, opposing abolitionism for fear that the city would be flooded with freed slaves who would compete for jobs.

Urban disorder was endemic. New York had several violent Irish gangs, including the "Dead Rabbits" and the "Plug Uglies." In addition, the municipality was ill-equipped to deal with its problems. The civil government was known to be corrupt, and the city had a rather new police department which had gone through a very rowdy period of disorganization in the late 1850s.

Riots began after the implementation of the draft. The first day of forced recruitment went peacefully enough, but on the second day, a Monday, the situation deteriorated. Early in the morning thousands, mostly lower-class Irish, gathered in the streets with crude placards bearing the slogan "No Draft." People moved through the streets, breaking windows and entering factories and shops to bring out workers to join their parade. Eventually, they gathered at a draft office and set fire to it, which also drove out the residents of apartments above. The rioters cut telegraph lines, cutting off police communications. A contingent of soldiers came to drive off the crowd, but even though the military fired, the mob beat them and drove them away. Later, the rioters captured the armory and its weapons until the buiding was set afire and the rioters were expelled or killed.

The riot took on an antiblack aspect. Rioters set fire to the Colored Orphan Asylum and lynched blacks on the street, burned them, or drove them into the East River to drown.

Rioters also fought against militiamen, firemen, policemen, and civic officials; the mob looted shops and burned buildings. Eventually, city officials appealed to the War Department in Washington for troops, which arrived late in the week after the riot; it had lasted more than three days before coming to an end.

Although a definitive tally of the damages does not exist, there are estimates (McCague, 1968). The police commissioner estimated that the total number of dead was approximately 1200, including rioters and innocent victims. Other official records show that rioters killed 18 people, including 11 blacks, and that 70 persons were reported missing. Three policemen were killed, and many others severely injured; there must have been many additional casualties among the militia.

THE RISE OF THE INDUSTRIAL CITY

Depicted here is one scene of the notorious draft riots of 1863 entitled "The Riot in Lexington Avenue." (Culver Pictures)

Between 50 and 100 buildings were burned, and at least 200 more were badly damaged or completely wrecked.

Against a background of considerable civic disorder, hard conditions of life within the working class, and flagrant and blatant prejudice and discrimination against the Irish and the blacks, the main social elements of the event were the following:

1. Interethnic or interracial conflict—immigrant vs. native, white vs. black, Irish vs. everybody
2. Lower class vs. upper class, a fight against the establishment and the inequity of the draft
3. The inability of the agencies of formal control, particularly the underdeveloped police force, to impose order

## Chicago's race riot

Chicago's 1919 race riot had most of the same elements as the New York draft riots. When a black youth at a Chicago beach swam beyond the conventional boundary into a "whites only" area, whites began to throw stones at him; unable to reach a safe place, he drowned. Later, bloody riots erupted around the borders of the black ghetto in Chciago's South Side; carloads of whites made forays into the black territory and shot at the blacks. The underlying conditions were quite the same as in New York. During World War I several thousand southern blacks came to Chicago, as the city's industries needed additional laborers. Racism was blatant; whites did not hesitate to stereotype blacks, to make jokes about them, to demean them, and to discriminate against them. Working-class whites feared that blacks would take their jobs or be used against them as scab labor during strikes, and whites also feared that blacks would take up needed housing (Chicago Commission on Race Relations, 1922).

## Poverty and Slums

Although the national economy was growing and providing more and more jobs for the immigrant lower classes, short-term fluctuations occurred. The economy was cyclical as periods of growth and prosperity alternated with periods of contraction and depression. Obviously, the latter worked hardships upon the immigrant labor force, putting many out of work and leaving others to subsist upon lower wages. Most immigrants entered the labor force at the bottom, working as construction laborers, helpers, sweepers, and the like; some individuals who brought skills from the old country got jobs as tailors, carpenters, and stonemasons. The needle trades again illustrate the poor working conditions. Many sweatshops were located in tenement buildings. Around 1911 such shops had "leaky illuminating glass tubes, high temperatures, and bad light and ventilation. Shop walls and floors were grimy, separate washrooms an exception, lunch areas either nonexistent or 'in a dark and dirty corner'" (Howe, 1976, p. 156). Very few women earned over $10 a week in 1911; males earned more, but fewer than one-third received over $12.50 (Howe, 1976). Workers had no fringe benefits, such as vacations and insurance, which contemporary employees take for granted. The infamous fire in the Triangle Shirtwaist Company's factory in 1911—in which 146 workers, mostly young Jewish and Italian women, perished—brought the dangers and inhumanity of the sweatshop system to public attention. The conditions of work in male occupations, such as construction, were no better. Wages were so low that families needed to have more than one member working, so it was not uncommon to have a father plus one or more of his grown unmarried children contributing to the household's income. Unfortunately, many employers at that time could not afford to provide better wages or conditions to their employees; many of them operated small factories with very little capital within a highly competitive environment.

Immigrants' residential situations were no better than their working conditions. They lived in dilapidated housing in older parts of the cities; many of these slum districts were adjacent to the central business districts, and others were near docks, railroad stations, and factories. Population density in many immigrant neighborhoods was extremely high. To cite the extreme case, in 1905 New York's lower Manhattan district reached what must be a record level of population density, housing 742,135 persons on 2,415 acres (New York City, 1911). This averages to more than 195,000 people per square mile, and the local population was still increasing. A housing expert at the time wrote that "the conditions in New York are without parallel in the civilized world" (New York City, 1911, p. 85). As in immigrant slums in other large cities, this density was the result of high-intensity land use plus extraordinarily high occupancy of houses, rooms, and apartments. In many immigrant districts, residential lots were used twice, with regular houses at the street plus additional, smaller houses built behind at the alley. In New York, five- and six-story tenement apartment buildings were built as workers' housing; with cold-water plumbing at best, and lacking sunshine or fresh air, these buildings had few amenities. Occupants had to walk up to their apartments, even if they were located on the sixth floor; what little air the tenements had was stale with a constant odor of cooking.

Meager as these quarters were, they were severely overoccupied. Many families with five or more children could afford to rent only a single room; they shared a toilet and possibly a kitchen with several other families. When newcomers arrived, many families took in kinsfolk to provide temporary housing.

Neighborhood environments were no better than the tenements themselves. Alleyways and areas between buildings were deeply littered with trash; their air spaces were festooned with laundry; and the streets were dense with people and peddlers.

Immigrants created a special sort of neighborhood in the slums, the "port of entry." Despite poor living conditions, each nationality built a network of organizations which made life bearable by meeting poor people's minimal needs: for example, in burial societies, individuals made small deposits regularly so that the society would provide funerals. Some schools taught English and citizenship for accommodation to the new country. Churches and synagogues were prominent nodes within the immigrant social system, performing communication and social welfare functions in addition to their rituals. Many of the immigrant groups published newspapers in their native languages, such as the *Polish Daily Zgoda* and the *Svenska Amerikanaren Tribunen* in Chicago, circulated to immigrants regionally and nationally. Some achieved large circulation, like New York's *Progresso Italo-Americano,* exceeding 120,000 in 1920 (Park, 1922). Furthermore, many immigrants became entrepreneurs, providing jobs for their compatriots; some opened shops providing specific ethnic foods. Also, through family and friendship networks, earlier immigrants helped newcomers, passing along information about job openings and other useful tips about urban survival (Choldin, 1972).

The net effect of these activities—supporting the ethnic church, forming voluntary associations, opening ethnic shops—was to create a localized network of ethnic institutions in the port-of-entry neighborhood. The immigrants were creating a supportive community within the city to help them survive.

The immigrant experience shows that there are different types of slums. Although the port-of-entry area was environmentally a slum, for most of its inhabitants it was a "slum of hope" rather than a "slum of despair." There was certainly plenty of despair among the immigrants. Jacob Riis (reprinted in Cordasco, 1968) described half-starving ragpickers who lived beneath tenement stairways and mothers who were so poor they had to give away their babies, but most of the immigrants were employed, and they or their children were occupationally mobile. Their stay in the slum proved to be temporary; at least their offspring could get out. In Seeley's (1959) terms, they were temporary necessitarians, living temporarily in the slum because they had to. In later chapters we will encounter slums of despair and slum dwellers who are not there temporarily.

## Attempted Solutions to Community Problems

### Institution building

The growing cities responded to many of these problems by attempting to build effective institutions, including school systems and police forces. Through a sort of experimental and political process, the cities tried one solution and then another, beginning in the middle of the nineteenth century. For example, between 1859 and 1910, Cincinnati fundamentally reorganized its police system 10 times, shifting control from mayor to board of commissioners to director of public safety (Fosdick, 1920). Three major themes appear in the emerging systems:

1 The shift of control of official community functions from the periphery to the center—from the wards to city hall (Silver, 1967)

2 The emergence of citywide bureaucratic structures, implying citywide systems, standards, and procedures
3 The rise of professionalism—teaching, police work, city planning, social work, etc.

**Public schools** One of the institutions which promoted community life despite the heterogeneity of peoples and cultures was the public school. But at midcentury, when massive immigration began, the cities lacked unified school systems; schools were controlled at the ward level by numerous local school boards. Late in the century, a controversy arose over organization; elites promoted the idea of consolidation, putting all the schools under a single, citywide board.

Local boards were probably more responsive to the cultural demands of immigrants than were the later unified boards. "Defenders of the ward system argued that grass-roots interest in the schools and widespread participation in school politics was healthy, indeed necessary, in large cities, but centralizers saw in decentralization only corruption, parochialism, and vestiges of an outmoded village mentality" (Tyack, 1974, p. 127). Eventually, the reformers were victorious, and cities throughout the nation developed consolidated school systems.

Opponents of consolidation perceived that the reformers were attempting to destroy parts of their culture. "This was particularly true of Catholics, many of whom bitterly resented the Protestant character of public education in nineteenth century America" (Tyack, 1974, p. 84). Immigrant groups used several strategies to deal with the schools for cultural preservation. In cities with large numbers of Catholics, they entered politics effectively and also expanded their parochial school systems rapidly. In Cincinnati, which had many immigrants from Germany, they succeeded in gaining a bilingual program in the public schools. By 1899 over 13,000 children in the first four elementary grades were splitting their school week evenly between a German teacher and an English teacher. This program also produced positions for almost two hundred teachers. This sort of assertion by the immigrants met with considerable resistance. In 1888, for example, the school board voted to discontinue use of an anti-Catholic textbook, thereby arousing the anger of some Protestants. Bilingual and bicultural education was controversial in the late 1880s (as it is today), and some cities had movements to eliminate or curb foreign languages in elementary schools (Tyack).

By the end of the century universal public education was a fact in American society. In 1898, 71 percent of youngsters between the ages of 5 and 18 were in school, up from 61 percent in 1870 (Tyack, 1974). Most of them were in elementary schools, because the teenagers left to go to work; the typical youngster of 1898 could expect to receive five years of schooling. The city schools were filled with the children of immigrants. A 1908 investigation for the Senate's Immigration Commission covered 37 cities, including most of the largest and those with the largest concentrations of immigrants. The study found that 58 percent of all students had fathers who had been born abroad, ranging as high as 72 percent in New York, 67 in Chicago, 64 in Boston, 60 in Cleveland, and 58 in San Francisco (Tyack).

City schools taught these children to read and write, of course, but in a broader sense they socialized the children to American urban culture. The schools taught reading, computation, some history, and geography, and standard spoken English. In addition, children were supposed to learn "order, regularity, industry and temperance," as well as "to obey and respect" their superiors (Rothman, cited in Tyack, p. 72). Schools enforced norms of punctuality and standardized performance, which socialize a child to life in industrial urban society.

Americanization classes for adults and children also taught certain elements of the way of life and introduced American economic and political institutions. But some teachers and schools went beyond the curriculum, emphasizing the middle-class way of life—stressing cleanliness, for example—and demanding total assimilation. Some educators assaulted all forms of cultural difference and attempted to make the immigrants ashamed of being "foreign" (Tyack).

Despite the conflicts and what may have been its excesses, the urban public school effectively introduced millions of immigrant children to American customs and mores and created a common culture within the city for the disparate groups within the population.

**Police** Following English tradition, early American towns had very little policing. At first, citizens' night watches were a rotating responsibility; later, towns began to employ night watchmen. In the bigger cities the individual wards handled this separately; a unified city force did not exist. These watch corps tended to be undisciplined groups; the men were politically appointed, not required to wear uniforms or badges, sometimes paupers, and often caught sleeping on the job. Once civic disorder, from rioting to street assaults, was recognized as a problem in the early nineteenth century, the "system" of the night watch was clearly seen as unsatisfactory. Between 1845 and 1855, several communities introduced what are recognizable as modern police forces by consolidating ward watch forces (Fosdick, 1920). Some of these citywide systems were controlled by a board, others by the mayor; many consolidated responsibility to an overall chief of police. Despite resistance from the employees, uniforms and badges were introduced. To some extent, the appointment of policemen was taken out of the hands of politicians, but the systems still retained a good deal of corruption, including political involvement. Overall, experts on police systems do not award high grades to American cities in the history of municipal development and wish that most of its sordid story could be blotted out (Fosdick).

Two more sociological points should be mentioned. First, this history of urban police suggests that the neighborhoods (wards) lost control of the system as it moved downtown, from periphery to center. Like education, most urban institutions were bureaucratically centralized in the industrial city. Second, the whole basis of social control shifted. The addition of the police force at least served as a supplement to the traditional forms of social control, known as informal social control. This represented a major shift in the social life of cities.

**Other laws and institutions** Churches and settlement houses also socialized immigrants to the host community. Even though many churches were oriented toward immigrant parishes, offering services in the language of the old country, the churches were still tied into extralocal networks and tended to bring their parishioners into city life. Settlement houses had specific activities to introduce the immigrant to American society, teaching English and "Americanization" classes for citizenship. Furthermore, the youth programs taught American games and customs.

Local government attempted specifically to address community problems. A history of attempts to improve the built environment is presented in Chapter 15.

The growth and enrichment of the economy also helped to solve community problems by providing more substantial jobs and opportunities for small business development. The rising level of prosperity eliminated the level of utter destitution, and the spread of trade unionism tended to improve workers' wages and benefits, allowing them to afford better housing.

Philanthropists and charity workers also served the poor immigrants during this period. Social work began with the establishment of settlement houses in the slums, where educated, prosperous young women ministered to the needs of the poor, distributing food and clothing, teaching English, and performing other services. Philanthropists provided free medical clinics, playgrounds, and the like. Undoubtedly, many immigrants and their children benefited individually from these efforts, but I doubt that they had a major impact upon the process of community integration. I suspect that the self-help efforts within the immigrant community were more important on the local level and that the development of citywide institutions, such as the police and the schools, and the macroscopic growth of the economy were much more important processes toward community integration.

### Time and prosperity

Time itself tended to amalgamate the disparate nationality groups and their neighborhoods into a viable city. Acculturation, the process of adopting some or all of the elements of another culture, occurred over time. Immigrants, and particularly their children, began to acculturate by adopting the American English language and abandoning the old country's language and by adopting popular consumer items and symbols such as clothing and personal grooming. The acculturation of the immigrants is a twice-told tale and does not need to be repeated here. The net effect over time was to bring the divided ethnic groups into membership in the nation and to help them coexist relatively peaceably in a single city.

The growing economy, offering a considerable degree of opportunity and openness, involved social mobility for most of the immigrants' children. Some groups, such as the Greeks and the Jews, moved rapidly into the middle class by opening small businesses; others remained in the working class. But in both cases the rising prosperity of the cities enabled most of the immigrants to leave the grinding poverty of the slums; as their incomes rose, they moved into newer and more comfortable housing in less crowded neighborhoods.

## SUMMARY

Starting in England, the development of factories for production gave rise to a new type of community, the industrial town, which emerged during the period 1770-1850. Although England had towns and cities before this period, not all of them grew during the industrial revolution; those that were tightly controlled by medieval guilds resisted the emergence of factories. However, factories came to dominate others, like Manchester. A new elite, consisting of factory owners, bankers, merchants, and wealthy shopkeepers, controlled the social structure of these industrial towns.

Although the industrial town may have had a central area, with city hall, banks, and cathedral, the community was not highly centralized and many of its members did not use the central area. The town had a cellular structure; it comprised several equivalent subcommunities, each nucleated by a factory and surrounded by residential slums for its workers and, perhaps, by some local shops as well.

Profound social and demographic changes supported population growth in the new industrial towns. Poor folk migrated from England's countryside in the wake of accelerated enclosure of common lands; others migrated from rural Ireland due to a potato famine and a general lack of opportunities in the agricultural sector. They thronged to the English factory towns. In addition, England had entered into the demographic transition—death rates, falling somewhat due to increased agricultural productivity, were no longer in balance with the country's high birth rates. Therefore, for a short time, births exceeded deaths, yielding population growth. Especially in the countryside, no opportunities existed for additional people, so they moved to the towns and cities.

The mature industrial city (1850-1920) developed along with continued economic growth in the United States—associated with industrialization and the development of the railroad. The new city was larger than the industrial town and, unlike the cellular structure of the industrial town, was highly centralized. The central business district was based upon the principles of accessibility and intensity of land use. The use of the electric trolley as a system of intraurban transportation maximized the accessibility of the CBD. Trolley lines, laid out in radial lines converging on the CBD, allowed workers as well as shopkeepers to travel to and from the center. The CBD facilitated contact within the business world among the highly specialized units of the economy. The skyscraper epitomized the intense land use in the CBD, showing that there were so many activities that they had to be stacked vertically.

The highly centralized industrial city gave rise to the concentric model of urban growth and form, a theory which states that the sociospatial pattern of the metropolis starts at the CBD and that a set of predictably arranged zones with increasing social status surrounds the CBD. The closest zone contains warehouses, slums, and areas of commercialized vice; more distant zones contain working-class residences, middle-class residences, and, finally, a commuters' area. This theory posits two sources of growth: central expansion as the CBD needs more land and peripheral expansion as new residential subdivisions are erected on the open land beyond the city's built-up area.

Rapidly growing industrial cities generated a number of serious internal social problems. Immigrants, who were the poorest workers, lived in squalid slum tenements and suffered from their poverty. The cities had considerable social disorder, manifested in street gangs and major riots, sometimes exhibiting interethnic or interracial conflict. The city's institutions were weak and decentralized and were unable to handle these serious problems of social order. As the cities grew and matured, though, they consolidated and bureaucratized these institutions, such as police forces and public schools, attempting to handle large-scale community problems. Inadvertently, the growth of the American economy in the twentieth century solved some of the problems of poverty, as most of the minority groups (with some notable exceptions) achieved better incomes and situations through increased workers' pay or through social mobility.

## REFERENCES

Banham, Reyner. 1971. *Los Angeles: The Architecture of Four Ecologies.* New York: Harper & Row.

Briggs, Asa. 1965. *Victorian Cities.* New York: Harper & Row.

Burgess, Ernest W. 1925. "The Growth of the City: An Introduction to a Research Project," Chap. 2 in *The City,* (eds.) Robert E. Park and Ernest W. Burgess. Chicago: University of Chicago Press.

Chicago Commission on Race Relations, 1922. *The Negro in Chicago: A Study of Race Relations and a Race Riot.* Chicago: University of Chicago Press.

Choldin, Harvey M. 1973. "Kinship Networks in the Migration Process." *International Migration Review* 7:163–176.

Condit, Carl W. 1964. *The Chicago School of Architecture: A History of Commercial and Public Building in the Chicago Area, 1875–1925.* Chicago: University of Chicago Press.

Cordasco, Francesco. 1968. *Jacob Riis Revisited: Poverty and the Slum in another Era.* New York: Anchor.

Daunton, M. J. 1978. "Towns and Economic Growth in Eighteenth-Century England," Chap. 10 in *Towns in Societies: Essays in Economic History and Historical Sociology,* (eds.) P. Abrams and E. A. Wrigley. Cambridge, Mass.: Cambridge.

Duis, Perry. 1976. *Chicago: Creating New Traditions.* Chicago: Chicago Historical Society.

Engels, Frederick. 1845/1958. *The Condition of the Working Class in England in 1844.* Oxford: Basil Blackwell. Original German edition published in 1845.

Fosdick, Raymond B. 1920. *American Police Systems.* New York: Century.

Hammond, John L. 1931. "The Factory System," pp. 51–55 in *Encyclopaedia of the Social Sciences,* vol. 6. New York: Macmillan.

Hawley, Amos H. 1971. *Urban Society: An Ecological Approach.* New York: Ronald.

Heady, Joel T. 1873/1970. *The Great Riots of New York: 1712–1873.* New York: E. B. Treat. Reprinted by Bobbs-Merrill.

Howe, Irving. 1976. *World of Our Fathers.* New York: Harcourt Brace Jovanovich.

Marshall, Leon S. 1940. "The Emergence of the First Industrial City: Manchester, 1780–1850," pp. 140–161 in *The Cultural Approach to History,* (ed.) Caroline F. Ware. New York: Columbia.

Marx, Karl. 1867/1977. *Capital: A Critique of Political Economy.* Volume 1. New York: Vintage. Original London edition published in 1867.

McCague, James. 1968. *The Second Rebellion: The Story of the New York City Draft Riots of 1863.* New York: Dial.

Muller, Peter O. 1981. *Contemporary Suburban America.* Englewood Cliffs, N.J.: Prentice-Hall.

Mumford, Lewis. 1938. *The Culture of Cities.* New York: Harcourt Brace. See, in particular, Chapter 3, "The Insensate Industrial Town," pp. 143–222.

New York City. 1911. *Report of the Commission on Congestion of Population.* New York: Lecouver.

Park, Robert E. 1922. *The Immigrant Press and Its Control.* New York: Harper.
Seeley, John R. 1959. "The Slum: Its Nature, Use, and Users." *Journal of the American Institute of Planners* 25:7–14.
Sharlin, Allan. 1978. "Natural Decrease in Early Modern Cities: A Reconsideration." *Past and Present* 79:126–138.
Silver, Allan. 1967. "The Demand for Order in Civil Society: A Review of Some Themes in the History of Urban Crime, Police, and Riot," Chap. 1 in *The Police: Six Sociological Essays,* (ed.) David J. Bordua. New York: Wiley.
Thernstrom, Stephan. 1973. *The Other Bostonians: Poverty and Progress in the American Metropolis.* Cambridge, Mass.: Harvard.
Thomlinson, Ralph. 1965. *Population Dynamics: Causes and Consequences of World Demographic Change.* New York: Random House.
Tyack, David B. 1974. *The One Best System: A History of American Urban Education.* Cambridge, Mass.: Harvard.
United Kingdom. 1832. *Parliamentary Papers,* vol. 15. London. (Evidence before the Sadler Committee to Investigate the Conditions of Factory Children.)
Vance, James E., Jr. 1977. *This Scene of Man: The Role and Structure of the City in the Geography of Western Civilization.* New York: Harper.
Wrigley, E. A. 1969. *Population and History.* New York: McGraw-Hill.

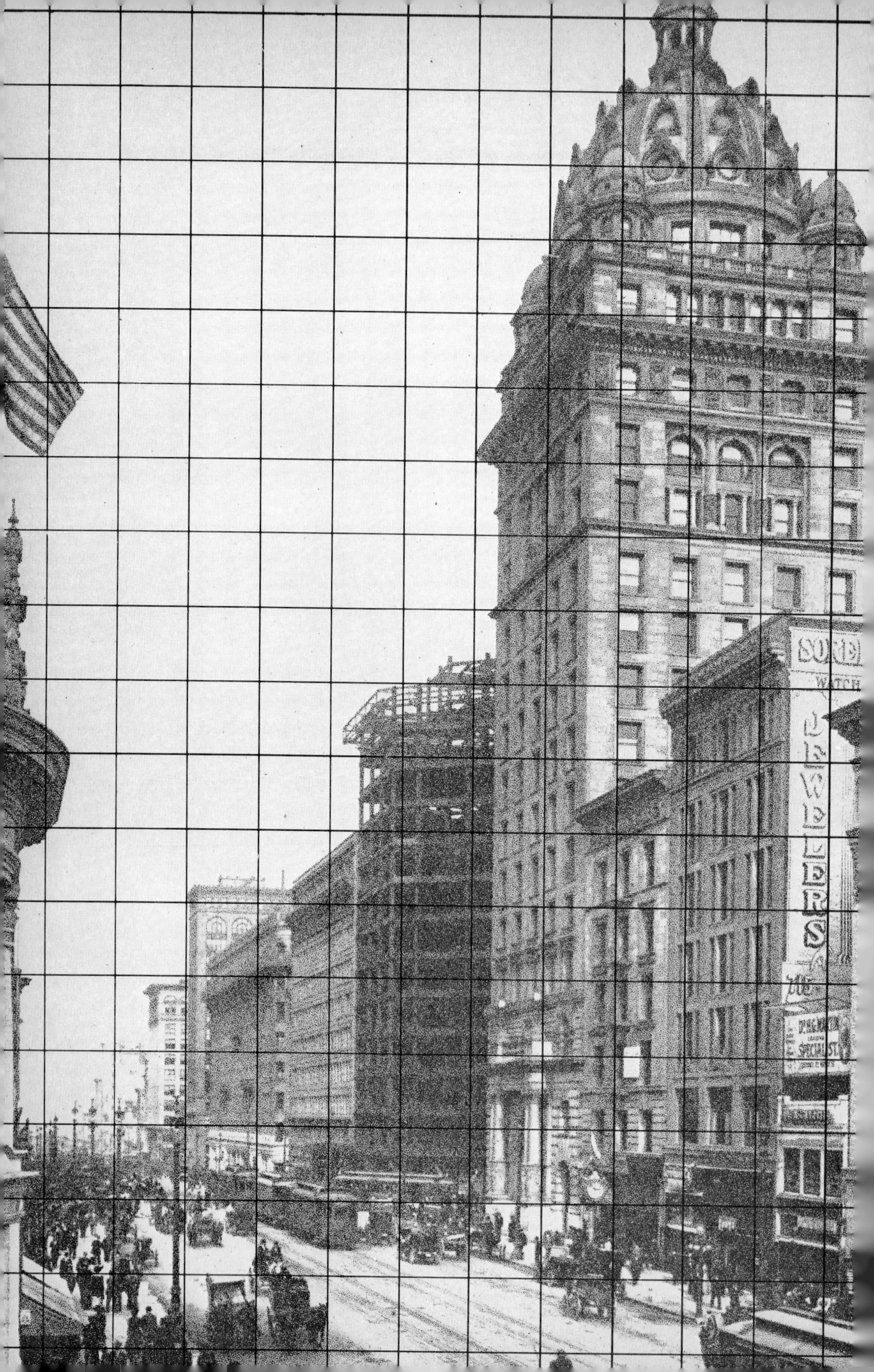
WATCH
JEWELERS

# CHAPTER • 5

## United States Urbanization

### Chapter Outline

THE CENSUS

   History
   Geographical Units
- Defining rural and urban
- Metropolitan concepts

POPULATION EXPLOSION

   Natural Increase: Births and Deaths
   Immigration

URBANIZATION

   The Demographic Concept
   United States Urbanization
- Growth of big cities
- Regional differences

   Social and Economic Context

SYSTEMS AND TYPES OF CITIES

   Systems of Cities
- Central places in the Pacific Northwest
- The structure of the metropolitan community

   Types of Cities
- Typologies
- Dimensions

SUMMARY

Chapter 4 was macroscopic, and this chapter is even more so. By the end of Chapter Four we had looked at the industrial city and had asked what sort of structure it had and what sorts of social problems it contained—the focus was on the city. In Chapter 5 we look at the whole nation and ask how it became urbanized. What demographic processes contributed to this process of urbanization? Then, knowing that many towns and cities exist, we ask what relationships exist among them; what different types of cities are there; what kind of system do they make together?

In the history of the United States, urbanization represents a continuing process —part of a larger demographic process—over the nation's two centuries. The whole national population was growing rapidly during these 200 years; in the nineteenth century, the U.S. population was growing even faster than the multiplying European populations. Eventually, demographers came to refer to a "population explosion." Within that great growth process, urban communities were growing disproportionately; basic demographic processes contributed to urbanization— migration to the cities and, eventually, natural increase within the urban places themselves. When the North American colonies gained their independence, the new nation was almost completely rural; now the society is highly urbanized.

Initially, as towns and cities developed, they also differentiated in function—for example, ports, mill towns, and marketing centers. With the rise of large cities and metropolitan areas, communities differentiated even further. Some places specialized in manufacturing certain kinds of goods, others in financial offices, education, shipping, etc.; the biggest places were likely to combine a number of these activities. Furthermore, large and small places developed particular relationships with each other—in trading, government, communications, etc.—which give rise to the idea that the nation has a *system of cities*.

The chapter begins with a methodological section about the U.S. census. The nation had its first census over two centuries ago, and the series of censuses provides the basic information documenting the nation's urbanization. For macroscopic urban sociology, therefore, it is essential to know something about this immense data source to understand urbanization as well as a number of other subjects which appear in later chapters—residential segregation, suburban growth, and many others. (The census can be used for micro research too—neighborhood growth and decline, for example.)

## THE CENSUS

### History

The Constitution specifies that the people must be counted every 10 years in order to apportion the seats of the House of Representatives. There has been a national census every 10 years since 1790. The first census did not go into much detail, calling only for the name of the head of the family and the number of persons in each household of the following descriptions: "free white males 16 years old and

UNITED STATES URBANIZATION

upward; free white males under 16 years; free white females; all other persons; and slaves" (Kaplan et al., 1980, p. 10). The facts, including individuals' names, were public information and had to be posted locally in places such as inns or taverns. (If someone was left off the list, that person could add his or her name.) Now the census collects many more facts from each person, and the information is confidential.

The organization and administration of the census has grown and changed over the centuries. At first, the data collection was a temporary chore for U.S. marshals, who hired temporary enumerators. Only Massachusetts had printed forms; enumerators in other states and territories had to supply their own, even though paper was expensive. Before the 1840 enumeration, the government opened a centralized census office for the first time, but it was in operation just until the job was finished. By the 1870s a number of problems were apparent: (1) The volume of data to be

**FIGURE 5-1**
One page from the report of the second census. Notice the crude biosocial categorization by sex with five age groupings. Slaves appear in a separate column toward the right.

## WHOLE NUMBER OF PERSONS

WITHIN

### The Eastern District of Pennsylvania.

| NAMES OF THE TOWNSHIPS AND BOROUGHS. | FREE WHITE MALES. |  |  |  |  | FREE WHITE FEMALES. |  |  |  |  | All other Free Persons except Indians, not taxed. | Slaves. | Total in each County. | TOTAL |
|---|---|---|---|---|---|---|---|---|---|---|---|---|---|---|
|  | Under 10 Years of Age. | Of 10 and under 16. | Of 16 and under 26, including Heads of Families. | Of 26 and under 45, including Heads of Families. | Of 45 and upwards, including Heads of Families. | Under 10 Years of Age. | Of 10 and under 16. | Of 16 and under 26, including Heads of Families. | Of 26 and under 45, including Heads of Families. | Of 45 and upwards, including Heads of Families. |  |  |  |  |
| City of Philadelphia, | 4485 | 2256 | 4518 | 5247 | 2118 | 4736 | 2424 | 4626 | 4233 | 2312 | 4210 | 55 |  | 41,220 |
| County of Ditto, | 5915 | 2480 | 3204 | 4198 | 2635 | 5877 | 2439 | 3713 | 4114 | 2599 | 2585 | 30 |  | 39,789 |
| Montgomery, - | 3887 | 1869 | 2269 | 2349 | 1744 | 3699 | 1797 | 2196 | 2144 | 1636 | 527 | 33 |  | 24,150 |
| Bucks, - - | 4753 | 2243 | 2296 | 2755 | 1853 | 4220 | 2205 | 2326 | 2567 | 1609 | 610 | 59 |  | 27,496 |
| Delaware, - | 1958 | 1217 | 1221 | 1108 | 796 | 1808 | 1140 | 1055 | 1022 | 832 | 645 | 7 |  | 12,809 |
| Chester, - - | 5117 | 2407 | 2852 | 3224 | 2323 | 4865 | 2201 | 2868 | 2963 | 2082 | 1145 | 46 |  | 32,093 |
| Lancaster, - - | 7080 | 3235 | 4110 | 4277 | 2970 | 6853 | 3154 | 4263 | 3928 | 2569 | 786 | 178 |  | 43,403 |
| Berks, - - | 5934 | 2659 | 2598 | 3271 | 2002 | 5783 | 2425 | 2776 | 3056 | 1719 | 165 | 19 |  | 32,407 |
| Northampton, - | 5333 | 2288 | 2686 | 2821 | 1919 | 5447 | 2098 | 2588 | 2741 | 1892 | 241 | 8 |  | 30,062 |
| Luzerne, - - | 2450 | 1029 | 1125 | 1256 | 787 | 2439 | 940 | 1016 | 1104 | 597 | 78 | 18 |  | 12,839 |
| Dauphin, - - | 4082 | 1955 | 1730 | 2465 | 1057 | 3804 | 1891 | 1783 | 2233 | 1011 | 166 | 93 |  | 22,270 |
| Northumberland, (part) | 1293 | 570 | 542 | 624 | 447 | 1243 | 538 | 465 | 567 | 359 | 41 | 10 |  | 6699 |
| Wayne, - - | 480 | 230 | 242 | 269 | 174 | 402 | 175 | 204 | 220 | 112 | 54 | 1 |  | 2562 |
|  | 52,767 | 24,438 | 29,393 | 33,864 | 20,824 | 51,176 | 23,427 | 29,879 | 30,892 | 19,329 | 11,253 | 557 | 327,799 | 327,799 |

collected swamped the marshals (by then the census included hundreds of items); (2) there was no check of the data for accuracy; (3) the figures were processed and published too slowly; and (4) there was no planning for future censuses (Kaplan et al., 1980). The Census Act for 1880 attempted to solve some of these problems, placing a census office in the Department of the Interior, appointing supervisors and enumerators instead of marshals, and checking on the quality of work. The act also, for the first time, prohibited enumerators from disclosing any information collected, thus ensuring confidentiality more dependably than in the past. In 1902 Congress established a permanent Census Bureau, moving it three years later to the Department of Commerce.

Confidentiality did not reach its current level until 1929, though, when tight restrictions were enacted. Earlier laws required enumerators and supervisors to take an oath not to disclose any personal information from the census. Another law prohibited the director from disclosing personal information, stating that census publications should be prepared in such a way that the identity of an individual—person or business—would not be revealed. Current law states: "(1) The information gathered by the Census Bureau may be used only for statistical purposes; (2) the publication of the data must be such that neither establishments nor individuals may be identified; and (3) only sworn officers and employees of the Department of Commerce or the Census Bureau may examine individual reports" (Kaplan et al., 1980, p. 71). The bureau may not even release individual information to another governmental agency.

Many technological advances are associated with the history of the census. The punch card and tabulating machine were invented for the census by H. Hollerith; patented in 1889, they were used to prepare the results of the 1890 census. (Hollerith soon formed a company which became the International Business Machines, IBM, Corporation.) In the late 1940s the Census Bureau sponsored the development of UNIVAC1, the first computer used for mass data processing, and in the late 1950s an electronic device to "read" the millions of questionnaires was developed (similar to the machines which score large-scale examinations). All these devices helped the Census Bureau to process and digest massive volumes of data from a growing nation.

## Geographical Units

From the beginning, census information has been organized into geographical units which form the building blocks of the study of organization. The first censuses were compiled and reported by state, district, and town; for example, Pennsylvania's results were published for the eastern and western divisions, and New York State was similarly divided. These delineations have long since been abandoned for statistical purposes. Within states and divisions, people were counted by county, town, and township.

Table 5-1, copied directly from the report of the second census, presents tallies for the eastern district of Pennsylvania, including Philadelphia. The geographical breakdown in Table 5-1 is by counties, plus the single city. Another table in the 1801 volume has Philadelphia's population divided into fourteen named wards. The biosocial categorization of persons in the table is quite primitive: First, it distinguishes between free white persons and slaves, about whom there is no information beyond number. Second, it divides the free whites by sex and then into broad age groupings.

Over the years, the census has come to include much more information; it still has age, sex, and race, but now it includes detailed occupational data, income sources, education, possessions, and many other sorts of facts which may be useful for governmental and economic analysis. The census also contains information about housing units, for example, rent levels; number of rooms; amenities such as central heating, air conditioning, and plumbing; and level of occupancy. These are only a fraction of the items in the decennial census, and all the information included is useful in urban analysis. Figure 5-2 displays a few of the actual questions asked in 1980. Consistent with the separation of church and state, the census, which is administered by a federal agency, deliberately avoids the topic of religion; this is frustrating to researchers who would like enumerations of different religions. Ethnicity is included in the census, but it is sometimes difficult to measure; in recent decades, the census has frequently changed its methods of enumerating Hispanics.

## Defining rural and urban

The census has defined urban places several ways over the years. Its first definition used 8,000 as the cutoff—all communities with that many inhabitants were called urban, and the rest of the population was defined as rural. In 1880 a new cutoff defined urban at 4,000 persons; finally, in 1906 the current cutoff of 2,500 was established (Petersen, 1975). The current definition says that urban population lives in *urbanized areas* (defined below) plus all places outside urbanized areas with 2,500 or more inhabitants; everything else is classified as rural (Kaplan et al., 1980). In other countries census officials employ widely varying definitions of urban places, from areas with fewer than 1,000 to 20,000 or more inhabitants. The most common cutoffs are between 2,000 and 2,999, as in the United States, and between 5,000 and 7,499, as in several other nations (Davis, 1969).

The growth of large cities and metropolitan communities played havoc with simple urban and city definitions like these. One problem was with the concept of "city limits." Geographers Simmons and Bourne wrote, "The building block of every empirical concept of an urban area is the political municipality, that is, the city, town, or township" (1978, p. 30). But then they tell why this legal definition of the city is inadequate, especially after the onset of suburbanization. First, the central city of a metropolis usually does not correspond to the city as a social, economic, or spatial unit. Cities may be *underbounded* or *overbounded*. "Most often they

CHAPTER·5

| Here are the QUESTIONS ↓ | These are the columns for ANSWERS → Please fill one column for each person listed in Question 1. | PERSON in column 1<br>Last name<br>First name / Middle initial | PERSON in column 2<br>Last name<br>First name / Middle initial |
|---|---|---|---|
| 2. How is this person related to the person in column 1?<br><br>Fill one circle.<br><br>If "Other relative" of person in column 1, give exact relationship, such as mother-in-law, niece, grandson, etc. | | START in this column with the household member (or one of the members) in whose name the home is owned or rented. If there is no such person, start in this column with any adult household member. | If relative of person in column 1:<br>○ Husband/wife ○ Father/mother<br>○ Son/daughter ○ Other relative _____<br>○ Brother/sister<br>If not related to person in column 1:<br>○ Roomer, boarder ○ Other nonrelative _____<br>○ Partner, roommate<br>○ Paid employee |
| 3. Sex  Fill one circle. | | ○ Male  ■ Female | ○ Male  ■ Female |
| 4. Is this person —<br><br>Fill one circle. | | White / Asian Indian<br>Black or Negro / Hawaiian<br>Japanese / Guamanian<br>Chinese / Samoan<br>Filipino / Eskimo<br>Korean / Aleut<br>Vietnamese / Other — Specify<br>Indian (Amer.)<br>Print tribe → | White / Asian Indian<br>Black or Negro / Hawaiian<br>Japanese / Guamanian<br>Chinese / Samoan<br>Filipino / Eskimo<br>Korean / Aleut<br>Vietnamese / Other — Specify<br>Indian (Amer.)<br>Print tribe → |
| 5. Age, and month and year of birth<br><br>a. Print age at last birthday.<br>b. Print month and fill one circle.<br>c. Print year in the spaces, and fill one circle below each number. | | a. Age at last birthday  c. Year of birth<br>[  1  ]   1  8  0  0<br>               ●  9  1  1<br>b. Month of     2  2<br>birth           3  3<br>               4  4<br>○ Jan.–Mar.    5  5<br>○ Apr.–June    6  6<br>○ July–Sept.   7  7<br>○ Oct.–Dec.    8  8<br>               9  9 | a. Age at last birthday  c. Year of birth<br>[  1  ]   1  8  0  0<br>               ●  9  1  1<br>b. Month of     2  2<br>birth           3  3<br>               4  4<br>○ Jan.–Mar.    5  5<br>○ Apr.–June    6  6<br>○ July–Sept.   7  7<br>○ Oct.–Dec.    8  8<br>               9  9 |
| 6. Marital status<br><br>Fill one circle. | | ○ Now married   ○ Separated<br>○ Widowed       ○ Never married<br>○ Divorced | ○ Now married   ○ Separated<br>○ Widowed       ○ Never married<br>○ Divorced |
| 7. Is this person of Spanish/Hispanic origin or descent?<br><br>Fill one circle. | | ○ No (not Spanish/Hispanic)<br>○ Yes, Mexican, Mexican-Amer., Chicano<br>○ Yes, Puerto Rican<br>○ Yes, Cuban<br>○ Yes, other Spanish/Hispanic | ○ No (not Spanish/Hispanic)<br>○ Yes, Mexican, Mexican-Amer., Chicano<br>○ Yes, Puerto Rican<br>○ Yes, Cuban<br>○ Yes, other Spanish/Hispanic |
| 8. Since February 1, 1980, has this person attended regular school or college at any time?  Fill one circle. Count nursery school, kindergarten, elementary school, and schooling which leads to a high school diploma or college degree. | | ○ No, has not attended since February 1<br>○ Yes, public school, public college<br>○ Yes, private, church-related<br>○ Yes, private, not church-related | ○ No, has not attended since February 1<br>○ Yes, public school, public college<br>○ Yes, private, church-related<br>○ Yes, private, not church-related |
| 9. What is the highest grade (or year) of regular school this person has ever attended?<br><br>Fill one circle.<br><br>If now attending school, mark grade person is in. If high school was finished by equivalency test (GED), mark "12." | | Highest grade attended:<br>○ Nursery school   ○ Kindergarten<br>Elementary through high school (grade or year)<br>1 2 3 4 5 6  7 8  9 10 11 12<br>College (academic year)<br>1 2 3 4 5 6 7 8 or more<br>○ Never attended school – Skip question 10 | Highest grade attended:<br>○ Nursery school   ○ Kindergarten<br>Elementary through high school (grade or year)<br>1 2 3 4 5 6  7 8  9 10 11 12<br>College (academic year)<br>1 2 3 4 5 6 7 8 or more<br>○ Never attended school – Skip question 10 |
| 10. Did this person finish the highest grade (or year) attended?<br><br>Fill one circle. | | ○ Now attending this grade (or year)<br>○ Finished this grade (or year)<br>○ Did not finish this grade (or year) | ○ Now attending this grade (or year)<br>○ Finished this grade (or year)<br>○ Did not finish this grade (or year) |
| | | CENSUS USE ONLY  A. | N | CENSUS USE ONLY  A. | N |

**FIGURE 5-2**

Some questions from the 1980 census. This is a copy of one page of the actual forms which were mailed to households across the nation. Every household received questions 1 through 7, but only a sample had to answer the more detailed questions beginning with number 8.

are spatially underbounded, excluding suburban and exurban areas which are closely integrated with the central city" (p. 30). A recent discussion of the census notes that city boundaries established for administrative purposes rarely delimit the actual extent of urban settlement and that this problem arose as early as the 1850 census (Kaplan et al., 1980)! On the other hand, though, some cities (for example, Santa Fe and Phoenix) are overbounded, including vast tracts of undeveloped land within the city limits. Second, state and local governments occasionally alter political boundaries by annexation or metro consolidation; while this may be helpful to the community, it confounds the analyst who is attempting to develop consistent statistics over time.

On the other hand, looking at suburbs as separate statistical units can also yield distortions. For some purposes, including local planning and analysis, suburbs are individually interesting, but they must also be seen as part of a metropolitan aggregate. Individually, single suburbs may have extreme characteristics. An industrial suburb may show millions of dollars per resident in industrial assets if only a handful of persons lives there, or another suburb may have one physician for every 60 persons (Simmons & Bourne, 1978). Each of these places serves a wider segment of the metropolis and can be understood only in that context.

## Metropolitan concepts

**Metropolitan districts** For several decades it has been necessary to develop statistics which conform with the trend to metropolitan development. If the census had continued to report discrete information for individual towns only, people who use it would have no statistical image of the metropolitan aggregates, unless they added them up themselves. Recognizing the metropolitan trend as early as 1910, the Census Bureau began to develop expanded urban units. In 1910 and 1920, the bureau created expansions of large cities simply by taking the big cities (those with populations of at least 100,000) and adding a zone of 10 miles beyond the city limits. For the largest cities, those with 200,000 or more, the bureau refined this procedure by including all adjacent minor civil divisions (mcd's) with densities of at least 150 persons per square mile (McKenzie, 1933). Ninety-six such "metropolitan districts" appeared in the 1930 census (McKenzie, 1933; Queen & Thomas, 1939), as shown in Figure 5-3.

**Standard metropolitan statistical areas** The metropolitan concept has been used ever since, modified and refined into the current "Standard Metropolitan Statistical Areas" (SMSAs). The current system, though, is built of entire counties (not minor civil divisions). "An SMSA consists of one or more entire counties economically and socially integrated that have a large population nucleus" (Kaplan et al., 1980, pp. 139-140). The central city must have at least 50,000 inhabitants. If the central city has 25,000 inhabitants, an SMSA may be designated if the city plus contiguous places total at least 50,000; they constitute a single community for economic and social purposes; and the county has at least 75,000 persons. An SMSA may include

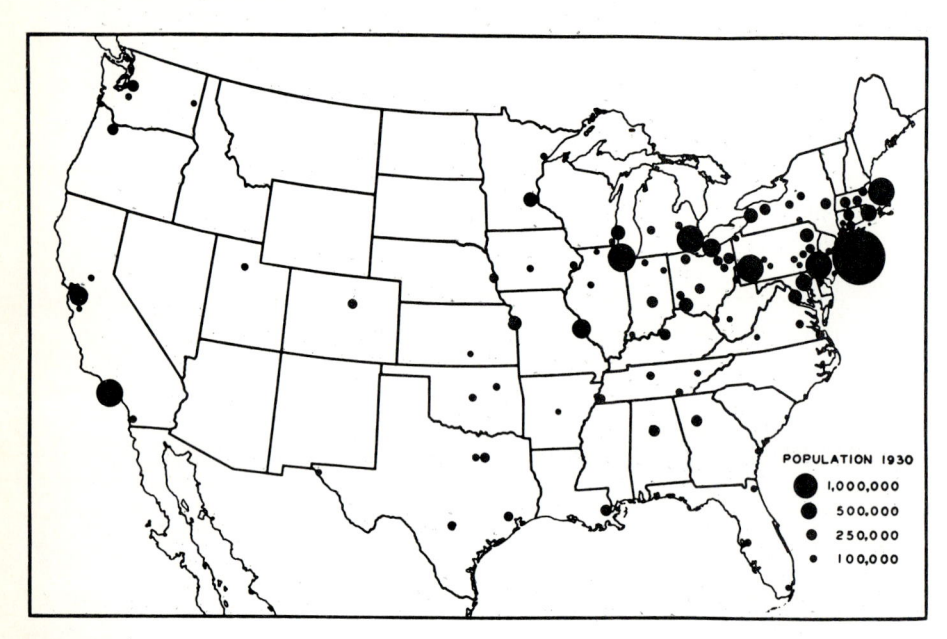

**FIGURE 5-3**
Metropolitan districts, 1930.

counties in more than one state; Memphis, Tennessee's SMSA, for example, includes counties in Arkansas and Mississippi.

How does the bureau decide which counties near a city are part of its SMSA? Its home county is always included, and an adjacent county is included if 75 percent of its labor force is nonagricultural; a specified proportion of the county's workers commute to the central county (or vice versa); and at least 50 percent of the residents live in built-up areas of a specified density (Kaplan et al., 1980). (There are additional technical criteria, but this presents the main idea.)

The number of metropolitan areas has increased rapidly in the twentieth century; from the original 96 areas in 1930, the total rose to 288 by 1980 (See maps in Figure 5-3 and inside front cover). Counties that comprise an SMSA are called "metropolitan counties"; other counties are called "nonmetropolitan." In 1980, 74.8 percent of the U.S. population lived in metropolitan counties.

While the SMSA framework has provided a good statistical base for analysis, there are some problems with using counties as basic units. A county, particularly a large one, *may* include a good deal of rural land and population that is not involved with the city and suburbs; it can be a "crude and unwieldy unit" (Simmons & Bourne, 1978, p. 31). To cite an extreme case, California's Riverside–San Bernadino–Ontario SMSA consists of two counties with some urban places and thousands of square miles of unpopulated desert land, and it is larger than the states of Connecticut and Massachusetts together. Some New England states are not divided into counties, so cities and towns are used instead. In spite of these problems, the SMSA has generated a useful statistical series, fairly stable over time, and each SMSA includes a metropolitan labor force.

**Urbanized areas**   Since 1950 the Census Bureau has defined another metropolitan unit to represent a central city together with its suburbs; known as the "urbanized area," this unit excludes the rural, out-county area which falls into an SMSA. "Urbanized Areas are defined by population density. Each urbanized area includes a central city and the surrounding closely settled urban fringe (suburbs) which together have a population of 50,000 or more" (Kaplan et al., 1980, p. 138). The urbanized area embraces the bulk of urban activity, but its boundaries change at each census, as the built-up area expands (Simmons & Bourne, 1978, p. 31). Although the urbanized area is useful for some sorts of research, the SMSA is a far more popular statistical unit.

**Standard consolidated statistical areas**   Another designation used in the analysis of urban data is the "Standard Consolidated Statistical Area" (SCSA). See Box 5-1 for an explanation of this metropolitan unit.

Some metropolitan areas have spread so far as to adjoin each other, giving rise to the concept of *megalopolis* (Gottman, 1961). The heavily urbanized East Coast region, from metropolitan Boston to metropolitan Washington, sometimes called the Boswash corridor, serves as North America's primary example of a megalopolis. Other oft-noted examples of megalopolises include the area from Milwaukee through Chicago to northern Indiana and the area from San Francisco south to San Diego. Intuitively, to envision megalopolis, imagine driving on interstate highways through any of these areas, continuing in highly populated areas all the way. On such a drive one might never see a truly rural area. Nonetheless, despite the intuitive attraction of the concept of megalopolis, it has yet to find scientific validity. After studying the Boswash corridor, Weller (1967) found few signs of interdependence or fusion among the constituent SMSAs. He concluded that the region was, in effect, a set of discrete metropolitan communities which have no overall form of organization or integration.

**Refinements to the current system**   New standards were introduced in 1980 to refine the definitions of SMSAs and SCSAs. Although the "S" for Standard is dropped in the new terminology, the basic definition does not deviate far from the previous one. "A metropolitan area is generally defined as a large population nucleus together with the adjacent communities which have a high degree of economic and social integration with it" (*Data User News*, 1980, p. 2). The new system, like the previous one, is based upon counties, except in New England, where it is based upon cities and towns. The new standards specify exact levels of commuting, population sizes, etc., determining metropolitan inclusion.

> **BOX 5-1**
> **Standard Consolidated Statistical Areas (SCSAs)**
>
> An SCSA is an area used to facilitate the presentation and analysis of data for concentrations of metropolitan population. It includes two or more contiguous standard metropolitan statistical areas that meet specific criteria of size, urban character, integration, and contiguity of urbanized area. In 1972 the two in existence were called standard consolidated areas.
>
> The two standard consolidated areas recognized in the 1970 census, metropolitan complexes around New York and Chicago, were retitled and, in the case of New York, redefined to become SCSA's. In addition, 11 new SCSA's were established in 1976, each comprising an SMSA of at least one million population plus one or more adjoining SMSA's related to it by continuously developed high density population corridors and/or metropolitan commuting of workers.
>
> The SCSA's as now defined are:
>
> 1. Boston-Lawrence-Lowell, MA-NH
> 2. Chicago-Gary, IL-IN
> 3. Cincinnati-Hamilton, OH-KY-IN
> 4. Cleveland-Akron-Lorain, OH
> 5. Detroit-Ann Arbor, MI
> 6. Houston-Galveston, TX
> 7. Los Angeles-Long Beach-Anaheim, CA
> 8. Miami-Fort Lauderdale, FL
> 9. Milwaukee-Racine, WI
> 10. New York-Newark-Jersey City, NY-NJ-CT
> 11. Philadelphia-Wilmington-Trenton, PA-DE-NJ-MD
> 12. San Francisco-Oakland-San Jose, CA
> 13. Seattle-Tacoma, WA
>
> *Source:* Kaplan et al., 1980, p. 142.

This system defines three sets of areas:

1. Metropolitan Statistical Areas (MSAs), equivalent to SMSAs
2. Primary Metropolitan Statistical Areas (PMSAs)
3. Consolidated Metropolitan Statistical Areas (CMSAs), equivalent to SCSAs

Introduction of the second concept, PMSA, makes it possible to designate additional cities as central cities within a large, multicounty metropolitan area. The new standards also differentiate Metropolitan Statistical Areas by total population size:

UNITED STATES URBANIZATION

Level A—1,000,000 or more
Level B—250,000 to 1,000,000
Level C—100,000 to 250,000
Level D—less than 100,000

With this differentiation an MSA like Greeley, Colorado, with 123,000 people, falls into a different category from Atlanta, Georgia, with its 2 million, as intuition says it should.

When the new standards were proposed, it was projected that they would have several effects, including the possible addition of up to 40 new metropolitan areas centered on smaller cities; an increase in the number of consolidated areas; and increasing difficulty for cities and counties to be designated as metropolitan in the future (*Data User News*, 1980).

## POPULATION EXPLOSION

Perhaps the simplest and most dramatic phenomenon that every U.S. census has shown is the continuous growth of the population since colonial times. While this book and chapter are about cities and suburbs, it must be recognized that their

**FIGURE 5-4**
U.S. population, colonial times to 1980. (Source: Data to 1970 are from Thomlinson, 1976; 1980 data are from U.S. Bureau of the Census, 1981 b.)

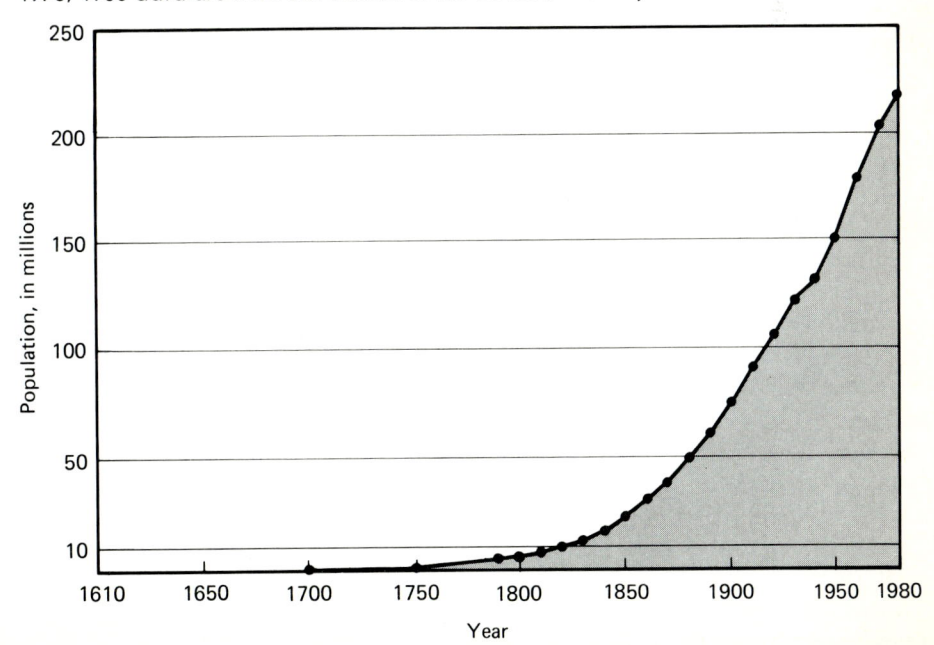

growth has taken place in the context of the growth of the nation and its population. Therefore, this section summarizes the U.S. population explosion.

The first census, in 1790, found 3.9 million inhabitants, not counting Native Americans (Indians). Population grew rapidly in the nineteenth century, doubling between 1800 and 1823, again by 1847, and again by 1873; by the end of the century, the nation had 76 million inhabitants. The graph in Figure 5-4 portrays the population explosion in the United States, from colonial times through the twentieth century, reaching 226 million by 1980. The growth rates, particularly in the eighteenth and nineteenth centuries, were fabulously high; typically, the population grew by at least 30 percent in each decade, missing that level only twice during the two centuries (Thomlimson, 1976). The growth rate, with some fluctuations, decelerated in the twentieth century, reaching its lowest levels in the 1930s (7.3 percent growth in ten years) and the 1970s (11.4 percent).

## Natural Increase: Births and Deaths

A population can grow in only two ways, through *natural increase*, an excess of births over deaths in a given period of time, and through *in-migration*. Actually, most populations simultaneously have in- and out-migration, and the difference is called "net migration." A population gains when net migration favors arrivals over departures. During its centuries of rapid growth, the United States gained from both natural increase and net migration, but natural increase contributed more (Matras, 1973). Throughout the nineteenth century, the population grew and, despite the increasing immigration, the gain from natural increase exceeded net migration in each decade. Birth rates were high during that century because most women married and became mothers, giving birth to six children on the average (Petersen, 1975). This fertility level represented a decline from eight children in the previous century; by the end of the nineteenth century, the average was down again, to five and a half. Obviously, such high birth rates contributed a great deal to population growth.

Nineteenth-century death rates were also high, but not high enough to negate the growth contribution of high fertility. Because the United States lacks a long historical series of dependable mortality statistics, having completed the national system of uniform death registration in 1933, much of the history must be pieced together from separate local studies. Death rates in the late eighteenth and early nineteenth centuries were high in normal times, but they fluctuated. One local study of Boston late in the eighteenth century estimated the death rate at 33 per 1,000, although rural rates were undoubtedly lower. At the same time, during epidemic years in New York City, death rates hit 45 to 50 per 1,000 (Taeuber & Taeuber, 1958). One demographic tool for summarizing mortality rates is the expectation of life at birth. One study shows an expectation of life equaling thirty-five years in parts of New England in 1789. By 1900, for whites, both sexes combined, this figure rises to 47.6 (Taeuber & Taeuber). (The estimate for 1900 is based upon better statistical sources than the eighteenth-century data.) One national historical study shows that expectation of life, "improved slowly from 1850 to 1900, much more rapidly from 1900 to 1950, and again more slowly since 1950" (Rao, cited in Petersen, 1975, p. 580).

By 1980, the American population had reached a new balance between birth and death rates, which had declined deeply from their high levels in colonial times. The decline in fertility, though, was not constant. One exceptional episode, which contributed mightily to population growth, was the "baby boom" after World War II, when birth rates rose. But the boom was temporary, and after 1960 the long-term fertility decline resumed. The birth rate rose slightly in 1969 and 1970, then continued to fall even lower. In the 1960s and 1970s fertility fell in all sectors of the population—white and black, rural and urban—and in all regions (Petersen, 1975). More and more women entered the paid labor force, which provided a disincentive to having large families. Also, improvements in contraception, particularly the widespread diffusion of the birth control pill, gave women increased ability to limit fertility. Mortality also stabilized at a low level, with a crude death rate of 8.9 deaths per 1,000 population. The net effect of low birth and death rates was the smallest natural increase in U.S. history, well under 1 percent per year. These rates imply zero population growth by the year 2050, given certain assumptions about longevity and migration (U.S. Bureau of the Census, 1982). That is, if these same birth and death rates continue, the population will stop growing in that year.

## Immigration

Immigration also contributed enormously to American population growth. The migration from Europe to North America, known as the "Atlantic migration" (Hansen, 1940), was one of the largest population shifts in human history. Taeuber and Taeuber (1958) estimate that from 1810 to 1900 the United States gained more than 18 million individuals through immigration—more than one-fourth of the total growth during that period. Furthermore, most of the immigrants were young and went on to produce large families, so much of the natural increase of the time can also be attributed to them.

The history of U.S. immigration may be divided roughly into three periods, differing by volume and by national origin of the newcomers. The first period, called the "old immigration," lasted until the Civil War; Germany, England, and Scotland were its largest contributors, but great numbers from Ireland arrived toward the end of the period. The volume of immigration rose markedly in the 1880s, which began the "new immigration." This second period saw continued Irish and German immigration, supplemented by large numbers of southern and eastern Europeans, most of them from Italy and Poland, as well as East European Jews, Greeks, Slavs, and others. There were also significant numbers of Chinese immigrants during this period. (See Figure 5-5 for national origins of immigrants.) Politically, this enormous immigration inspired a nativist reaction, culminating in the

**FIGURE 5-5**

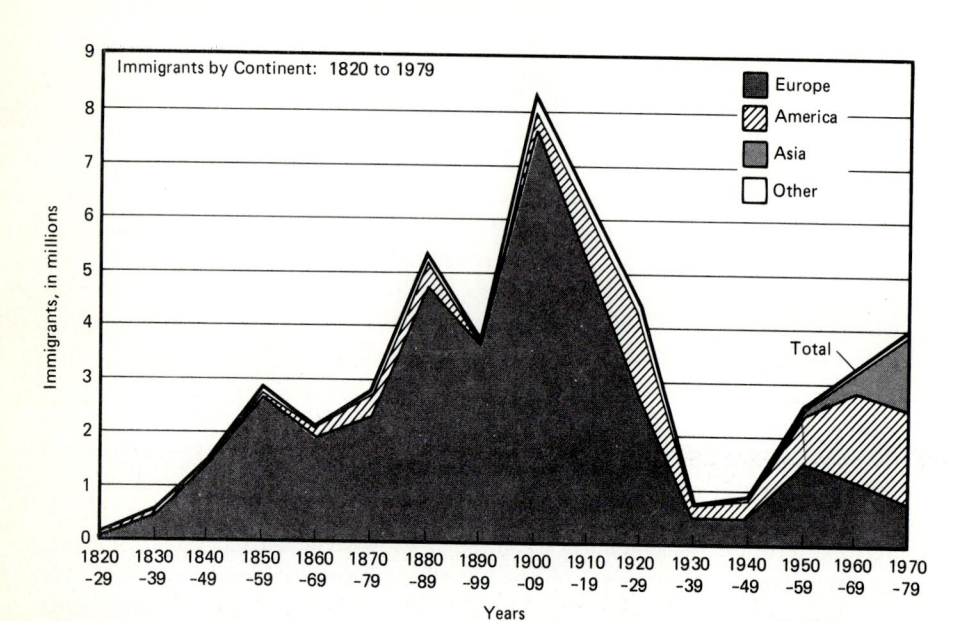

Immigrants by continent, 1820–1979. Notice the enormous volume of immigration between about 1880 and 1920. Immigration has been increasing since 1950, but the origins of the newcomers are different from those of the previous migrants. (Source: U.S. Bureau of the Census, 1981, p. 85.)

immigration restriction acts of 1921, 1924, and 1929 that established quotas and thereby concluded this period of massive immigration. The purpose of the laws was to admit fewer immigrants, especially from eastern and southern Europe (Thomlinson, 1976); Asians had already been excluded by the act of 1917, which defined an "Asian barred zone." The quota system, in its 1929 form, allowed a maximum of 153,174 immigrants per year, a drastic cut from the boom years between 1900 and 1910, which brought an average of more than 810,000 net arrivals annually. The law was designed to perpetuate the ethnic composition of the American people as it used to be, eventually making the quotas proportionate to the nationalities of 1920. But Petersen (1964) contends that by then it was almost impossible to discover our genetic origins, so the national quotas were "fudged" to some extent. Ninety-eight percent of the quota was designated for Europeans, leaving the rest for Asians and Africans. The biggest allocations went to Great Britain (65,721), Germany (25,957), and Ireland (17,853), but these countries did not all use their full quotas (Bogue, 1959). The quota system worked as planned so that in 1952, for example, there were about 126,000 immigrants from northwest Europe, 24,000 from southern and eastern Europe, and 9,000 from everywhere else (Petersen, 1975).

## UNITED STATES URBANIZATION

European immigrants with their possessions arriving at Ellis Island, the government's reception and processing center, at the turn of the century during the height of the "new immigration." (The Library of Congress)

Although the third period, beginning with the restrictive laws of the 1920s and continuing to the present, has been characterized by far less immigration, there has still been enough to contribute substantially to national population growth. Migration has been selective as well as episodic in this era. The national quotas were dropped by the Immigration and Nationality Act of 1965, and the current rules exclude communists and criminals and favor kinfolk of U.S. citizens and individuals with specific desired occupations.

The 1965 act, in effect since 1968, employs a first-come first-admitted policy. The law allows up to 170,000 immigrant visas per year to nations outside the western hemisphere, with no more than 20,000 to any one country. In addition, 120,000 immigrants are allowed from within the western hemisphere. Between 1970 and 1980 legal immigrants, including refugees, were arriving at a rate of approximately 400,000 per year. Their national origins were radically different from the origins of those who had come under the quota system: From 1971 to 1977, 45 percent came from the Americas, 32 percent from Asia, and 20 percent from Europe (U.S. Bureau of the Census, 1980, p. 126). Mexico, the Philippines, and Korea sent far more immigrants in the seventies than any other country. Since the 1940s immigration has been episodic, responding to wars and international political situations; after World War II, and the Korean and Vietnam wars, the nation accepted various refugees.

In recent decades there have also been immigrations to the United States of people from various communist countries, including thousands of Cubans in 1960 and again in 1980 and Jews from the Soviet Union in the 1970s. A massive migration from Puerto Rico began in the 1940s. Since this is not an international movement, federal immigration statistics do not cover it, but the 1960 census showed 617,056 first-generation Puerto Ricans living on the mainland (Sandis, 1970). By 1970 this number had risen to 810,087, with more than half living in New York City (Fitzpatrick, 1980). Throughout this period, there has been a good deal of two-way migration between the mainland and the island, but in recent years the balance has shifted toward Puerto Rico. In five out of six years between 1969 and 1974, net migration was away from the U.S. mainland (U.S. Commission on Civil Rights, 1976). Mexicans have also migrated to the United States, some legally and others surreptitiously. Between 1900 and 1969, 441,800 Mexicans immigrated; an additional 364,100 immigrated during the next five years (Cortes, 1980).

A recent review of immigration concluded as follows:

> The overall pattern of immigration to the United States has undergone a major shift. Western Europe and Canada, once the leaders in exporting people, have been replaced by Asia, Mexico, and the Caribbean.... From 1968 to 1977, about one-third of all immigrants have been Hispanic.... In August 1980, the federal government reported that there were about 380,000 Indochina refugees in the United States and more were coming. Moreover, another Third World Hispanic group, the 1980 flotilla of over 120,000 Cubans, will also appear in the later figures, as will some Haitians. (Reimers, 1981, p. 11)

In sum, the history of U.S. population growth shows explosive expansion from fewer than 4 million in 1790 to more than 225 million in 1980. High rates of natural increase combined with high rates of immigration produced this growth, although both diminished in the twentieth century. Philip Hauser (1969), a sociologist-demographer, has noted that throughout the world, population explosions have been accompanied by rapid urban growth, which he calls a population "implosion." His metaphor suggests that as national populations have grown, towns and cities have grown even faster as rural individuals have moved to urban places. In this sense, U.S. population history is typical—rapid population growth has been accompanied by rapid urbanization.

## URBANIZATION

When the first U.S. census was taken in 1790, the country had 3.9 million people, but there were only 24 urban communities housing a mere 5 percent of the population. The remaining 95 percent—in other words, almost everyone—lived and worked on farms (Kaplan et al., 1980). Five percent urban is an extremely low level of urbanization by current standards; Bangladesh, one of the world's least urban countries, was about 9 percent urban in 1974. Among the 24 urban places in the United States in 1790, Manhattan was the largest with 33,000 inhabitants—hardly a great metropolis, even then.

## The Demographic Concept

Demographers define "urbanization" as the proportion of a population which resides in urban places; a population is urbanized to the extent that its members live in urban places, given some definition of an urban place. Urbanization, defined this way, should not be confused with urbanism as discussed in Chapter 2.

Table 5-2 shows the wide variance in urbanization levels among countries. Some

**TABLE 5-2**
**Urbanization Levels in Selected Nations**

| Nation* | Percent urban |
|---|---|
| Australia (1976) | 86.0 |
| Bangladesh (1974) | 8.8 |
| Belgium (1976E) | 94.6 |
| Brazil (1977E) | 61.2 |
| Canada (1976) | 75.5 |
| Egypt (1977E) | 44.1 |
| France (1975) | 73.0 |
| Guatemala (1975E) | 35.5 |
| India (1977E) | 21.2 |
| Iran (1976) | 46.8 |
| Israel (1977E) | 87.2 |
| Japan (1975) | 75.9 |
| Libya (1974E) | 29.8 |
| Mexico (1978E) | 65.2 |
| Nepal (1971) | 4.0 |
| Poland (1977E) | 57.0 |
| Rwanda (1974E) | 3.5 |
| Sweden (1975) | 82.7 |
| Uganda (1972E) | 7.1 |
| United Kingdom: England and Wales (1973E) | 77.7 |
| United States (1980) | 73.7 |
| U.S.S.R. (1977) | 62.2 |

*The letter "E" after a year means that the urbanization level for that year was estimated; absence of an "E" usually signified a census in the year listed. Countries use their own definitions of "urban," so the definitions vary.

Source: United Nations, 1979, table 8, for all nations but the United States; U.S. data from U.S. Bureau of the Census, 1981, table 10.

African and Asian countries like Rwanda and Nepal are almost completely rural; at the other extreme, small industrialized nations like Belgium and Israel are almost completely urbanized. Australia and Brazil are unusual cases; both nations have vast expanses of open land as well as high levels of urbanization, meaning that most of the population resides in towns and cities. Within the spectrum suggested by the table, the United States is clearly among the highly urbanized populations of the world.

Urbanization may also be used as a temporal concept, referring to change. In this usage urbanization is seen as an increase in the extent to which a population lives in urban places.

## United States Urbanization

The nineteenth century was a period of rapid urbanization. Starting at 5 percent, the urban proportion rose steadily to 11 percent by 1840 and continued to rise in every decade thereafter, with one exception; by 1920 the population was 51 percent urban.

The growth rate of the urban population has exceeded that of the rural population in every decade since 1800, with the exceptions of 1810 to 1820 and 1930 to 1940. During the 1810–1820 decade, both sectors grew rapidly, but more growth took place in the rural areas. During the Great Depression of the 1930s general diminution of population growth occurred and some of the urban populations returned to farms and smaller rural communities. The national population became predominantly urban in 1920 when the census first showed more than half the people living in urban areas. This trend, which had started more than a century earlier, continued for several decades and, by 1970, reached 75 percent. Particularly in the 1950–1970 period, population growth was heavily urban; the rural population stayed constant at about 54 million, while the urban sector gained more than 50 million, rising to 149.3 million.

## Growth of big cities

In the nineteenth century the number of urban places grew rapidly from the two dozen recorded in the first census to 1,732 urban communities by 1900, as shown in Figure 5-7. Big cities as well as small towns multiplied during the century, and by the turn of the century 3 cities had at least 1 million persons, another 35 cities had more than 100,000 residents (see Table 5-3), and 122 communities had between 25,000 and 99,999 persons. Most of these large communities continued to grow for several additional decades and became substantial cities.

Seventy years later, six cities had more than 1 million residents and 156 cities had more than 100,000; 760 communities comprised populations between 25,000 and 99,999 inhabitants.

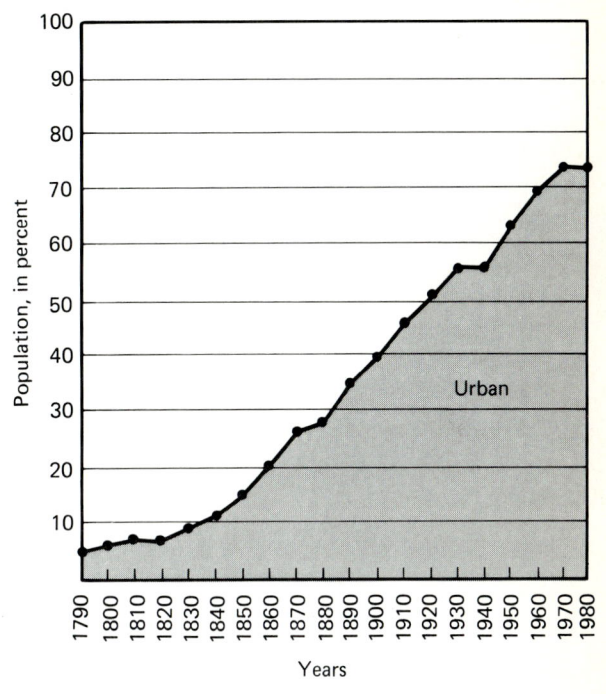

**FIGURE 5-6**
Rural and urban population, 1790–1980. In any given year, the percent rural equals 100 minus the percent urban. Thus in 1830, for example, when urban was about 10 percent, rural was about 90; in 1960, when urban was about 70 percent, rural was about 30. (Source: Data for 1790–1970 are from U.S. Bureau of the Census, 1975; data for 1980 are from DeAre & Long, 1982, p. 8.)

Industrial cities were growing extremely rapidly during the second half of the nineteenth century—more rapidly, in fact, than cities had ever grown in world history. The population of Manhattan tripled from half a million between 1850 and 1890. Chicago, which was a frontier fort at a lakeside swamp in 1830, grew to a city of a million by 1890. Both cities were well served with rail connections (New York was a major seaport as well), and they enjoyed substantial economic growth during the Civil War.

## Regional differences

Major geographical regions urbanized at different times, starting with the Atlantic coastal regions of the original colonies and then moving toward the west and the south. The series of regional maps in Figure 5-8 shows these shifts from 1790 to

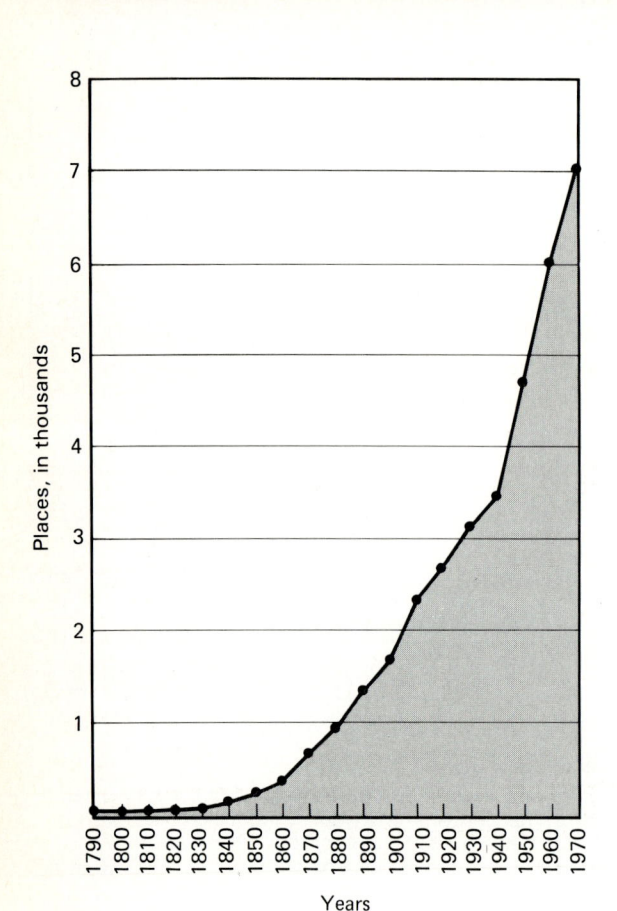

**FIGURE 5-7**
Number of places in urban territory, 1790–1970. (Source: Data from U.S. Bureau of the Census, 1975.)

1980. In the first half of the nineteenth century, the urban populations of the northeast and the south multiplied 14 times and almost 18 times, respectively. Proportionately, this was their era of most rapid growth, although they continued to add large numbers of urban individuals in decades to come. In the next fifty-year period the north central and western regions began to urbanize, rapidly multiplying their city populations. In the twentieth century, regional urbanization rates diminished, with the west showing more growth than the other regions in the first fifty years; urban population in the south also exceeded the rates in the east and north central regions. After 1950, urban growth in the west and south continued to outstrip the northeast and north central regions. To summarize, urbanization began in the northeastern region and shifted to the north central region and, in the twentieth century, to the west and south.

**TABLE 5-3**
**Emergence of Big Cities in the Nineteenth Century**

| Name of city | Census year when it first had 100,000 population* |
|---|---|
| New York | 1810 |
| New Orleans | 1840 |
| Baltimore | 1840 |
| Boston | 1850 |
| Cincinnati | 1850 |
| Philadelphia | 1850 |
| Chicago | 1860 |
| St. Louis | 1860 |
| Buffalo | 1870 |
| San Francisco | 1870 |
| Washington | 1870 |
| Milwaukee | 1870 |
| Pittsburgh | 1870 |
| Newark | 1870 |
| Providence | 1880 |
| Cleveland | 1880 |
| Jersey City | 1880 |
| Detroit | 1880 |
| Denver | 1890 |
| Indianapolis | 1890 |
| Kansas City, MO | 1890 |
| Rochester | 1890 |
| Minneapolis | 1890 |
| St. Paul | 1890 |
| Fall River | 1900 |
| Los Angeles | 1900 |
| Paterson | 1900 |
| Scranton | 1900 |
| Syracuse | 1900 |
| Toledo | 1900 |
| Worcester | 1900 |
| New Haven | 1900 |
| Omaha | 1900 |
| Memphis | 1900 |

*The year in which a city hit 100,000 population may be considered its "birthday" as a big city. Notice that Los Angeles, which may be considered the nation's "number two" metropolis, is almost a century younger than New York City. Notice also that some places which were once among the largest cities in the country, such as Fall River, Mass., and Paterson, N.J., are no longer considered major cities.

Source: Thirteenth Census of the United States: 1910, volume 1, Population: General Report and Analysis, Washington, 1913. table 56, page 82.

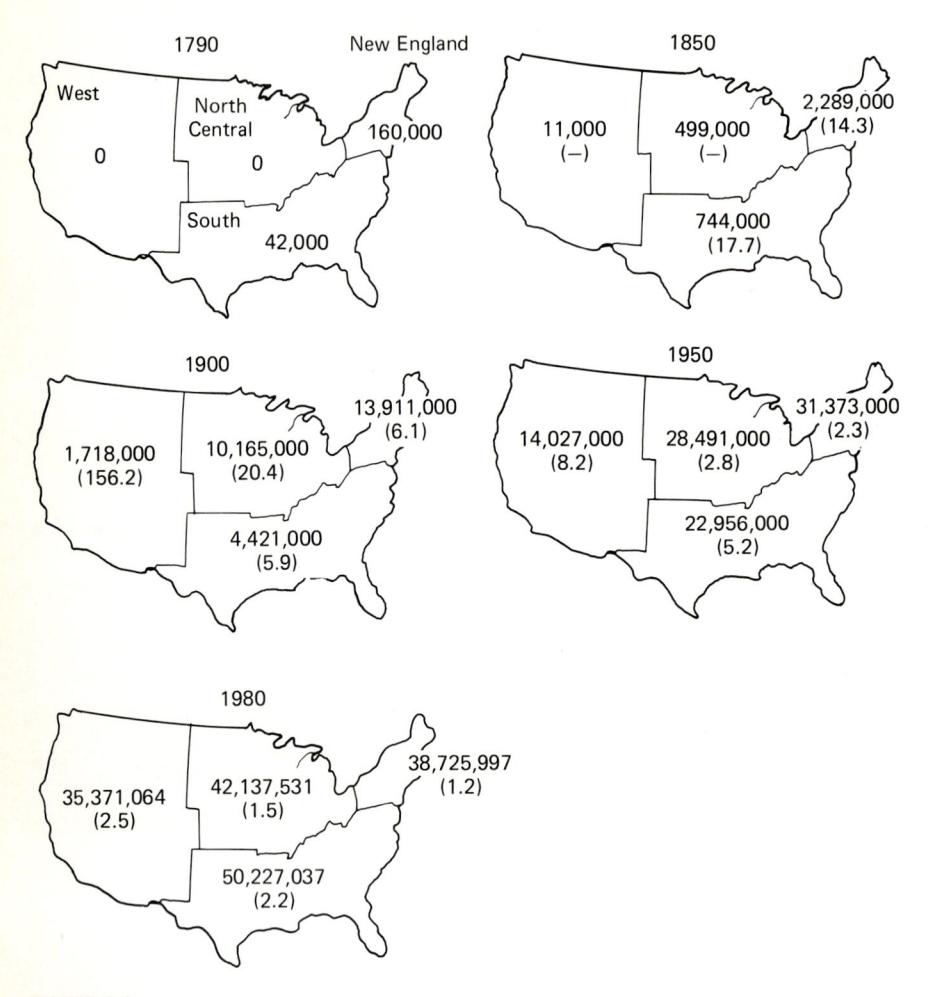

**FIGURE 5-8**
Urban population by regions, 1790–1980. First number represents total urban population in the region. Number in parentheses represents multiple of that number over the number for the previous year mapped. (Source: Basic data for 1790–1950 are from U.S. Bureau of the Census, 1975; 1980 data are from U.S. Bureau of the Census, 1981a.)

## Social and Economic Context

Certain features of the economy provided a context for urban development and influenced the ways in which the cities grew. These features included a capitalist economy, reinforced by the practices and philosophy of the national government; rapid economic growth and industrialization; and rapid agricultural development; they were all situated in an environment rich in natural resources.

In the nineteenth century the United States had a strong commitment to unrestrained capitalism; the government's philosophy was to interfere as little as possible with the rights of property holders to do business. The federal government promoted development of transportation infrastructure, aiding in the development of harbors and canals and later, especially, making grants of public lands to promote the construction of railroads. The scale of economic enterprises expanded during the century, starting with small, locally owned businesses and by 1900 adding large firms such as the railroads, U.S. Steel, and the Pullman Seating Car Company. Entrepreneurs took advantage of social inventions, particularly the limited liability corporation, which facilitated the assembly of large amounts of capital. Initially, family firms with few employees conducted businesses to serve local markets, but with the growth of corporations some firms expanded to serve regional and national markets. Growing industries required many laborers; the companies provided numerous jobs.

Rapid agricultural change also supported urbanization. Starting with the introduction of McCormick's reaper, agriculture was mechanizing and rising in productivity. The midwest's fertile prairie lands were coming under cultivation, thus there was ample food to support growing urban industrial populations. Note that we are dealing here with the same question we encountered when the first communities were built at the beginning of history: the production of agricultural surplus to sustain urban populations. By the end of the century the produce of a single agricultural worker could feed more than seven individuals. Simultaneously, with the advent of farm machinery, there was a decreasing need for agricultural workers. In 1820, 83 percent of American males worked in agriculture; in 1870, 53 percent; and by 1920 the number in manufacturing equalled the number in farming (Taeuber & Taeuber, 1958). The absolute number of farm workers grew until 1910, when even it began to decline. These work force shifts contributed to a trend of rural-urban migration, as the surplus agricultural population migrated toward towns and cities.

The continent's abundant unexploited resources supported rapid development in the nineteenth century. Vast stands of virgin timber throughout New England, the upper midwest, and beyond represented an apparently unlimited supply of wood for urban construction projects and probably contributed to Americans' proclivity toward single-family dwellings. Undeveloped land everywhere made it possible for most cities to expand peripherally; exceptions were cities on constrained sites—those on islands, like Manhattan; in valleys, like Harrisburg and Birmingham; and on peninsulas, like St. Petersburg. In addition to wood and land, potential industrial inputs were abundant: coal, iron ore, petroleum. Thus the environment had everything to support rapid growth of cities, and city builders took advantage of it.

Migration provided the "people power" for urban and industrial growth. In addition to the people arriving from domestic rural areas, a flood of immigrants was arriving from Europe. Although many immigrants came to this continent dreaming of getting their own farmland, they arrived in port cities and often, taking "temporary" urban jobs out of necessity, never left the cities. However reluctantly they settled, they and their children contributed to urban growth (Handlin, 1951).

## SYSTEMS AND TYPES OF CITIES

The simple fact of urbanization masks some greater complexities among the communities of a nation. Differences exist among the cities, towns, and smaller communities, not only in size but also in function. Further, the communities are interrelated, forming systems of cities. Communities compete with each other—some grow large, while others remain small. Once these differences and relationships emerge among small and large places, they considerably constrain the future development of individual places.

Communities differ by size, and within a nation or state a regular pattern emerges in the distribution of sizes. The larger the size category, the fewer the number of places; thus there are many small towns but not so many great metropolises. A pyramidal graph, such as Figure 5-9, shows the distribution of places by size (Golden, 1981). Places grow differentially, but the shape of the distribution tends to remain the same. Between 1860 and 1920, the number of urban places increased from 392 to 2,722. During this period the number of big cities with populations exceeding 100,000 increased from 9 to 65, the number between 50,000 to 100,000 from 7 to 76, and the number between 25,000 and 50,000 from 19 to 143. "Despite the selectivity of the growth of particular places, the pyramid of American cities tended to retain a constant shape, though it developed a broader base and a higher narrow top" (Golden, 1981, p. 194).

These different-sized places were interrelated; they exchanged different sorts of goods and services and were connected by communications lines—in short, they developed into systems of cities. "Industrialization and economic development produced a full-scale system of cities: small service and trading centers and mining

**FIGURE 5-9**
Number of municipalities by population-size class, 1976.
(Source: Kaplan et al., 1980: p. 108; data regrouped and redrawn.)

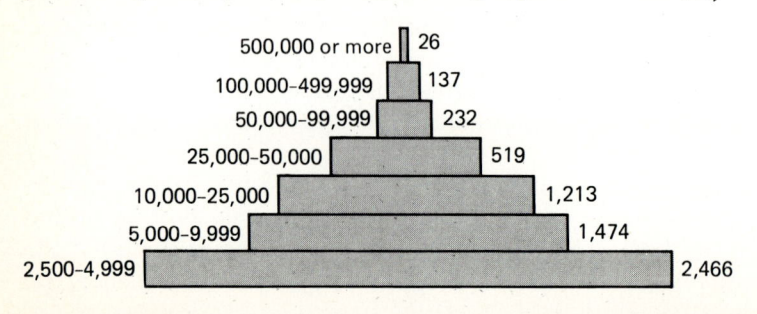

| Population | Number |
|---|---|
| 500,000 or more | 26 |
| 100,000–499,999 | 137 |
| 50,000–99,999 | 232 |
| 25,000–50,000 | 519 |
| 10,000–25,000 | 1,213 |
| 5,000–9,999 | 1,474 |
| 2,500–4,999 | 2,466 |

towns, large factory towns, larger manufacturing centers, and huge multifunction cities" (Golden, 1981, p. 202).

The larger the place, the wider the range of market functions it performs, serving larger hinterlands as well as other communities. Small places serve very general market functions for small hinterlands. Smaller places serve fewer functions, while larger places serve more and provide for increasingly specialized needs. Thus all small places would provide ordinary automobile repairs. but only a large place would provide specialized parts and service for a particular unusual car. There is a very regular gradation in the functions offered by places according to their size. An intensive geographical analysis of all the communities in southwestern Iowa revealed the hierarchical array of market functions shown in Table 5-4 (Berry, Barnum, & Tennant, 1962).

## Systems of Cities

In the system concept, the community is considered an urban node, a spatial concentration of people and activities within a region or nation (Simmons, 1978). To understand such a system, the analyst asks what the relationship of a node is to its surrounding area and what the linkages are among nodes. The system concept implies that there are patterns of connections and flows among cities, large and small, and that communities within a system are interdependent.

The idea of a system of urban places assumes a hierarchical pattern of functions and interrelationships, with large communities dominating smaller ones (Hawley, 1981). There are hierarchies at different geographical scales—within a state or region, for example—as well as a hierarchy of metropolitan areas in the nation. Every city has relations with both higher-order and lower-order centers (Bourne & Simmons, 1978).

## Central places in the Pacific Northwest

A single regional study will serve to present and illustrate several key concepts. Preston (1971) studied the system of cities in the Pacific northwest region, consisting of Washington, Oregon, Idaho, and part of Montana. For analytical purposes, he treated it as a self-contained system, but in fact, cities of the northwest are also linked to cities in other regions. They are closely tied to nearby cities in Utah and Montana and also to more distant cities.

The 4-state region had 164 places with populations of 2,500 or more. Preston, looking for patterns of functional interdependence and linkages, measured patterns of spatial interaction. He looked at banking relationships, daily and Sunday newspaper circulation, commuting patterns, and branch-firm distribution. One example of interdependence and linkage would be in banking. Very small places might not have banks; the banks of small towns might borrow from banks in larger towns, which, in turn, depend upon metropolitan banks for loans as well as for

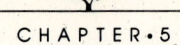

**TABLE 5-4**
**Central Functions Typical of Levels in the Hierarchy of Central Places, Southwestern Iowa, 1960**

| The village-level functions | |
|---|---|
| Gas and service station | Meeting hall |
| Automobile repair | Hardware |
| Bars | Farm materials |
| Restaurants | Farm sales |
| Grocery | Farm implements |
| Post office | Oil fuel bulk station |
| Local government facility | Barber |
| Church | Beaty shops |

| The town-level functions | |
|---|---|
| Furniture | Doctors |
| Appliances | Dentists |
| Variety | Building services |
| General clothing | Building materials |
| Drugstores | Radio-TV sales and service |
| Banks | Movers and haulers |
| Insurance agents | Funeral home |
| Real estate | Veterinarian |
| Telephone exchange | Automobile accessories |
| Cleaners | Farmers' cooperatives |

| The city-level functions | |
|---|---|
| Women's clothing | Newspaper publisher |
| Men's clothing | Office of labor union |
| Shoes | Sales of new automobiles |
| Jewelry | Sales of used automobiles |
| Florist | Specialized automobile repairs |
| Supermarket | Automobile wrecking |
| Bakery | Cleaners and laundry (operator) |
| Liquor store | Self-service laundry |
| Other medical practices (optometrists, etc.) | Shoe repairs |
| Lawyer | Plumbing |
| Hotel | Fixit |
| Motel | Movies |
| County government | Indoor amusements (billiards, etc.) |
| | Drive-in eating places |

*Source:* Berry, Barnum, and Tennant, 1962, tables IV–VI.

check-clearing functions, computer services, connections with international banks, etc.

Hierarchy within a system of cities implies that places are arrayed on different levels by the sorts of functions they perform. In the northwest region, Preston found the typical pattern, identifying five distinct levels, or orders, of centers. Fifth-

UNITED STATES URBANIZATION

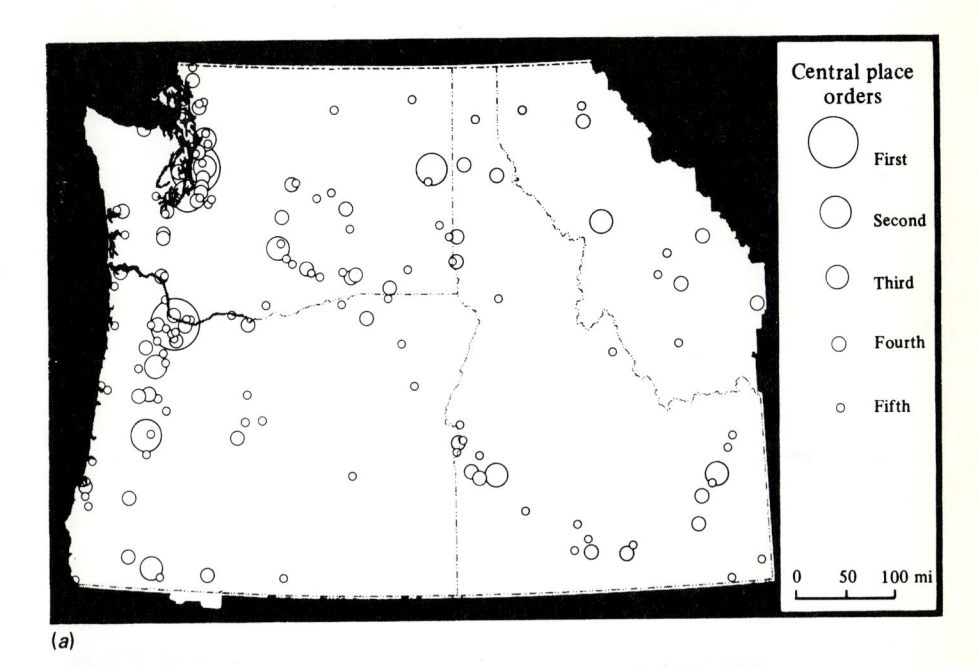

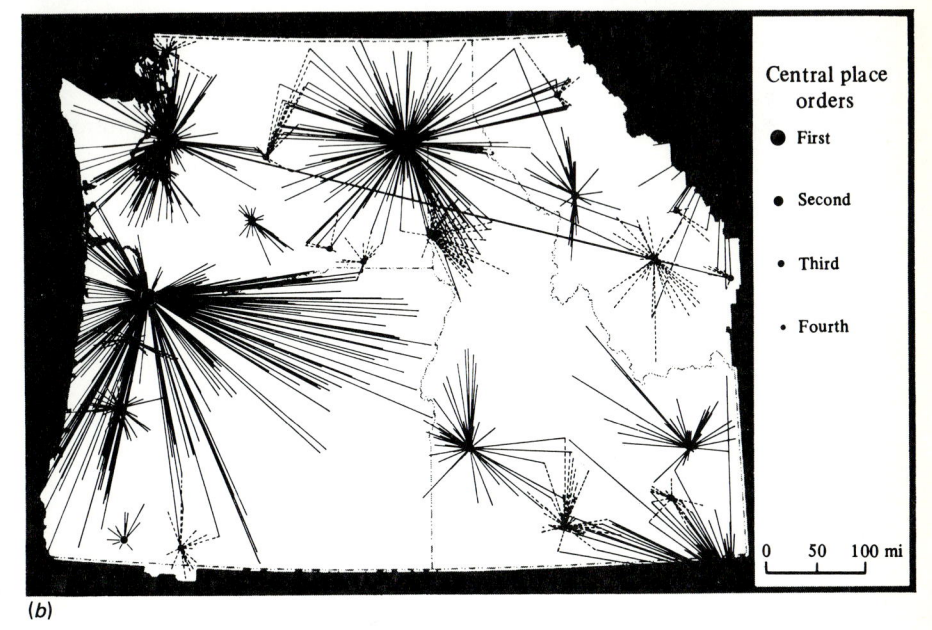

161

**FIGURE 5-10**
Central-place heirarchy in the Pacific Northwest. (*a*) Central-place heirarchy. (*b*) Patterns of Sunday newspaper dominance. (Source: Preston, 1971.)

order places, the most numerous, are little communities that function as central places for the people of the countryside. Fourth-order places, fewer in number, serve the fifth-order places with services such as banking and weekly newspapers. Third-order places, in turn, serve their own residents plus the lower-order communities.

Preston concluded that the region had a "clear-cut central place hierarchy through five orders" (1971, p. 153). Within it, he found two nested hierarchies branching down from the two first-order cities, Seattle and Portland. See Figure 5-11 for the nested hierarchy connecting the four lower levels of places with Seattle.

Preston summarized three main principles of central-place theory:

1 Larger centers are functionally more complex than small centers.
2 Increasing functional complexity is accompanied by increasing size of the urban complementary region.
3 Because of the differential provision of central functions, interdependence exists between urban centers in the distribution of central goods and services.

Systems of cities need not be seen within the restricted scope of single regions. On a larger scale, the United States also has a system of cities. The map in Figure 5-12 shows the banking relationships among larger and smaller cities of the coun-

**FIGURE 5-11**
Nesting relationships of higher-order central places tied to Seattle. (Source: Preston, 1971.)

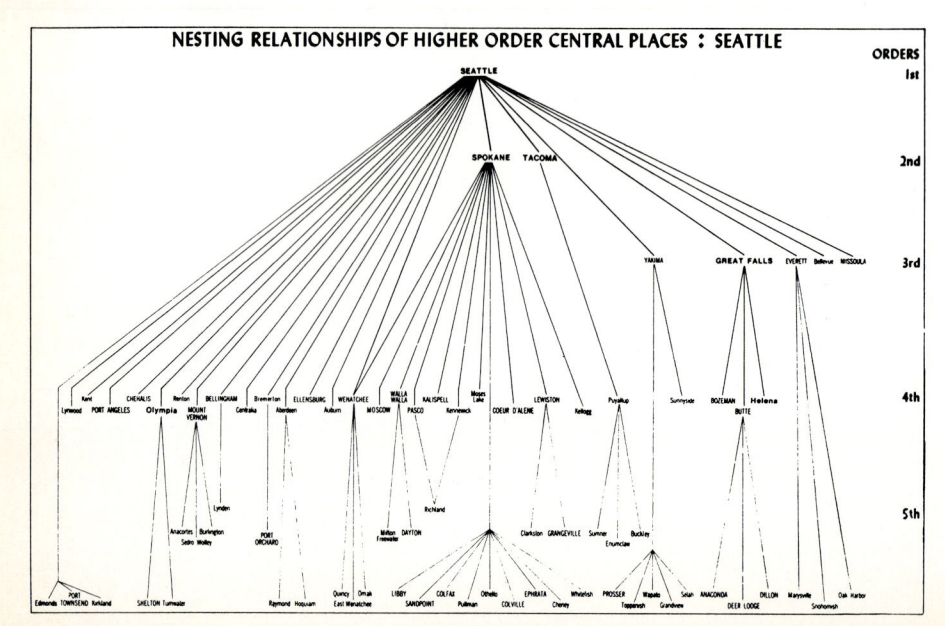

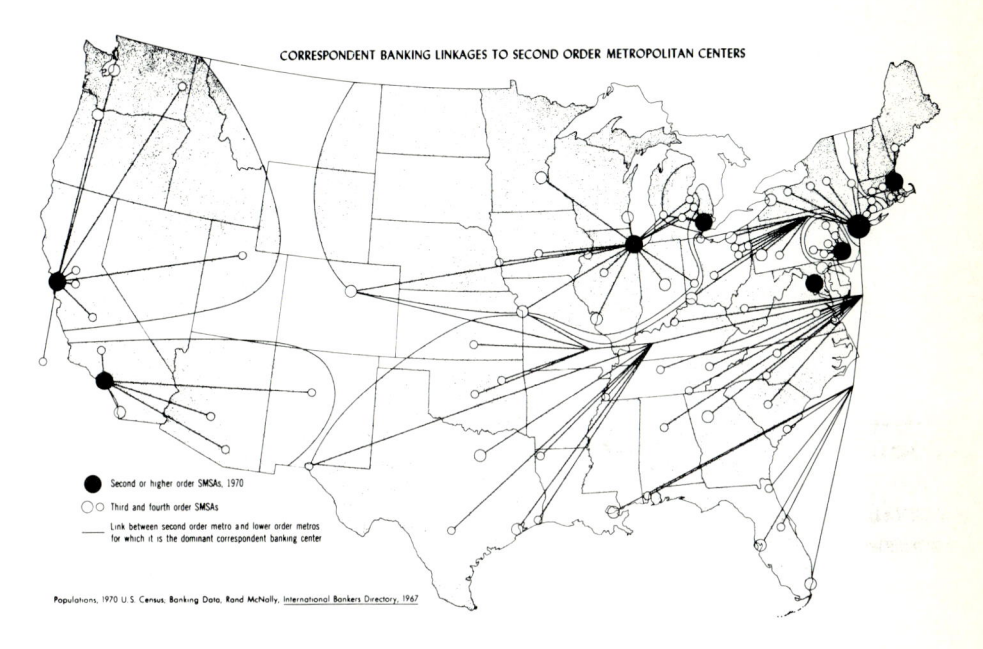

**FIGURE 5-12**
Correspondent banking linkages between major and lower-order centers. (Source: Borchert, 1972; reproduced in Getis et al.)

try; it does not include the even higher-level set of relationships among the largest banks of the big metropolises.

## The structure of the metropolitan community

Donald Bogue (1949) approached the same question as Preston but used the entire nation as a field of inquiry. Bogue introduced a slightly different vocabulary. He divided the nation into regions, each having one metropolitan area, which he referred to as metropolitan communities. Then he looked at the sizes and functions of all the cities and towns in a metropolitan community and divided them into types according to their functions. He focused on the levels of manufacturing and volume of sales in wholesale, retail, and service establishments among the cities and towns of each metropolitan community.

The largest city dominates the metropolitan community and is called a "dominant." "A dominant city is a city which controls many of the conditions of life of all the communities lying within a broad area surrounding it" (Bogue, 1949, p. 61). Its control arises from its high level of specialization in such functions as services and wholesaling, which it provides to the lower-order cities. The dominant is also able to provide favorable combinations of the factors of production to the smaller places. The other cities and towns must specialize in other activities, and they become dependent upon the bigger city for goods and services which their residents require but which they cannot provide locally. The dominant also retains its position of control because it integrates exchanges among the other communities by means of housing markets, means of communication, banks, etc.

In Bogue's terminology, the lower-order places are called "subdominants," "influents," and "subinfluents," in order of size and degree of control over those below them. "A subdominant city is a city which adapts to the condition of general dependence upon the center and which functions, through specialization in one or more of the sustenance activities, as an intermediary between the metropolis and the outlying areas" (p. 61). It has a trade territory comparable to the hinterland of the metropolis, but smaller. Influents and subinfluents are simply smaller places, similar to third- and fourth-order central places.

A metropolitan community is far larger than a single SMSA; it is a metropolis *plus* its hinterland. In sum, according to Bogue,

> A metropolitan community is an organization of many subdominant, influent, and subinfluent communities, distributed in a definite pattern about a dominant city, and bound together in a territorial division of labor through a dependence upon the activities of the dominant city. (p. 61)

## Types of Cities

The cities of the nation are differentiated not only by size and dominance but also by type. Researchers have divided cities by type in a number of ways, but each attempts to find the basic function or the main function(s) of the cities.

### Typologies

One report (cited in Getis, Getis, & Fellman, 1981) divided the metropolitan areas of the United States into 11 functional types, based upon proportions of workers in various industries. Here is a list of the functional types, plus two examples of each:

| | |
|---|---|
| Agriculture | Fresno, Calif.; Orlando, Fla. |
| Construction | Fort Lauderdale, Fla.; Honolulu, Hawaii |
| Durable manufacturing | Flint, Mich.; Youngstown, Ohio |
| Entertainment | Los Angeles, Calif.; Miami, Fla. |
| Finance | Hartford, Conn.; Des Moines, Iowa |
| Minerals | Duluth, N. Mex.; Tulsa, Okla. |
| Nondurable manufacturing | Akron, Ohio; Wilmington, Del. |
| Public administration | Washington, D.C.; Harrisburg, Pa. |
| Retailing | Tampa-St. Petersburg, Fla.; El Paso, Tex. |
| Transportation | Omaha, Neb.; New Orleans, La. |
| Wholesaling | Charlotte, N.C.; Spokane, Wash. |

This list indicates the range of diversity of functions among cities; it does not imply, though, that any of these places is devoted entirely to a single economic specialty, as every large urban place has a diversity of economic activities. Another study, classifying places by their basic economic functions, arrived at a similar list of types: manufacturing, wholesale trade, retail trade, education, public administration, transportation, military, and entertainment and recreation (Duncan & Reiss, cited in Hawley, 1981).

The largest places tend to be the most diversified. "The concentration of many basic functions in them prevents any one activity from attaining absolute dominance" (Getis et al., 1981). Thus some of the biggest cities—Los Angeles, New York, Philadelphia, San Francisco, Chicago, Boston, and St. Louis—are so highly diversified that they cannot be forced into a single type.

## Dimensions

Another approach to the question of differences among cities and metropolitan areas does not try to force them into types but asks what the basic dimensions are along which they differ. Berry (1978) performed a statistical analysis of the characteristics of more than 200 SMSAs and discovered 11 major dimensions. Each dimension, in turn, was indicated by certain specific characteristics of the city. For example, SMSAs differed in *socioeconomic status,* indicated by family incomes, rent levels, and proportion of white-collar workers in the area, and by *age and size,* indicated by total population, age of the central city, level of manufacturing, and rail and air connections. (These items may seem quite disparate, but the factor analysis showed them to be highly intercorrelated.) Other dimensions which differentiated metropolitan areas included their density levels, foreign-born proportions, presence of institutional or military population, and commercial versus manufacturing orientation (Berry, 1978). These last two factors highlight cities with large university or military populations and places with particularly heavy concentrations of commercial or manufacturing facilities.

## SUMMARY

The U.S. census, taken every ten years since 1790, provides a rich source of accurate data for the study of urbanization. The census defines the urban population as that which lives in urbanized areas and all places outside urbanized areas with 2,500 or more inhabitants. The most commonly used unit to denote a metropolis is the Standard Metropolitan Statistical Area, which consists of one or more entire counties economically and socially integrated that have a central city with at least 50,000 persons.

The nation has undergone a population explosion for two centuries, growing from fewer than 4 million in 1790 to 226 million in 1980. Although birth rates were falling throughout this period, large families were the rule in the nineteenth century, contributing to growth. Immigration also contributed greatly to the explosion, but natural increases contributed more. Immigration peaked between 1900 and 1910, was cut legally in the 1920s, and rose again in the 1970s, though not nearly to the levels of the Great Migration. Immigrants, whether by intention or not, settled disproportionately in cities.

Urbanization, viewed demographically, is the proportion of a population living in urban places or a rise in this proportion. The United States has experienced urbanization throughout its history. It began in New England and spread to the midwest and the south and, most recently, to the western region. The nineteenth century witnessed spectacular growth of large cities; the twentieth century has seen the spread of metropolitan areas—there were 288 SMSAs by 1980.

The nation's thousands of towns and cities are not simply scattered about and unrelated but have systematic relations to each other, especially within regions. The relationships tend to be hierarchical; small places offer common general services to the people of the countryside, and metropolitan cities provide specialized services and functions—including communications and coordination—to smaller cities and towns. There are differences among communities in functions as well as in size. Thus cities may be sorted into functional types—from heavy manufacturing to recreation—but the largest metropolitan areas are so diversified that they do not fall into single-function types.

## REFERENCES

Berry, Brian J. L. 1978. "Latent Structure of Urban Systems: Research Methods and Findings," Chap. 3.4 in Bourne and Simmons.

Berry, Brian J. L., H. G. Barnum, and R. J. Tennant. 1962. "Retail Location and Consumer Behavior." *Papers and Proceedings of the Regional Science Association.* 9:65–106.

Bogue, Donald J. 1949. *The Structure of the Metropolitan Community.* Ann Arbor: University of Michigan.

Bogue, Donald J. 1959. *The Population of the United States,* Glencoe, Ill.: Free Press.

Bourne, Larry S. and James W. Simmons (eds.). 1978. *Systems of Cities.* New York, Oxford.

Cortes, Carlos E. 1980. "Mexicans," in *Harvard Encyclopedia of American Ethnic Groups.* Cambridge, Mass.: Harvard.

Data User News. "New Standards for Metropolitan Statistical Areas," vol. 15, no. 6, 1980.

Davis, Kingsley. 1969. *World Urbanization 1950–1970. Volume I: Basic Data for Cities, Countries, and Regions.* Berkeley: University of California.

Fitzpatrick, Joseph P. 1980. "Puerto Ricans," in *Harvard Encyclopedia of American Ethnic Groups.* Cambridge, Mass.: Harvard.

Getis, Arthur, Judith Getis, and Jerome Fellman. 1981. *Geography.* New York: Macmillan.

Golden, Hilda H. 1981. *Urbanization and Cities.* Lexington, Mass.: Heath.
Gottmann, Jean. 1962. *Megalopolis: The Urbanized Northeast Seaboard of the United States.* New York: Twentieth Century Fund.
Handlin, Oscar. 1951. *The Uprooted.* New York: Grosset & Dunlap.
Hansen, Marcus L. 1940. *The Atlantic Migration.* Cambridge, Mass.: Harvard.
Hauser, Philip M. 1969. "The Chaotic Society: Product of the Social Morphological Revolution." *American Sociological Review.* 34:118.
Hawley, Amos. 1981. *Urban Society: An Ecological Approach,* 2d ed. New York: Wiley.
Kaplan, Charles P., Thomas Van Valey, and associates. 1980. *Census '80: Continuing the Factfinder Tradition.* Washington, D.C.: U.S. Bureau of the Census.
Matras, Judah. 1973. *Populations and Societies.* Englewood Cliffs, N.J.: Prentice-Hall.
McKenzie, Roderick D. 1933. *The Metropolitan Community.* New York: McGraw-Hill.
Petersen, William. 1964. *The Politics of Population.* Garden City, N.Y.: Doubleday.
Petersen, William. 1975. *Population,* 3d ed. New York: Macmillan.
Preston, Richard E. 1971. "The Structure of Central Place Systems." *Economic Geography.* 47:136-155.
Queen, Stuart, and Lewis F. Thomas. 1939. *The City.* New York: McGraw-Hill.
Reimers, David M. 1981. "The Post-World War II Immigration to the United States: America's Latest Newcomers." *Annals of the American Academy of Political and Social Science.* 454:1-12.
Sandis, Eva E. 1970. "Characteristics of Puerto Rican Migrants to and from the United States." *International Migration Review.* 4:22-42.
Simmons, James W. "The Organization of the Urban System," Chap. 1.4 in Bourne and Simmons.
Simmons, James W. and Marry S. Bourne. "Defining Urban Places: Differing Concepts of the Urban System," Chap. 1.1 in Bourne and Simmons.
Taeuber, Conrad, and Irene Taeuber. 1958. *The Changing Population of the United States.* New York: Wiley.
Thomlinson, Ralph. 1976. *Population Dynamics: Causes and Consequences of World Demographic Change,* 2d ed. New York: Random House.
United Nations. 1979. *Demographic Yearbook 1978.* New York.
U.S. Bureau of the Census. 1975. *Historical Statistics of the United States. Colonial Times to 1970.* bicentennial edition, parts 1 and 2. Washington, D.C.
U.S. Bureau of the Census. 1982. *Current Population Reports,* series P-25, no. 922, "Populations Estimates and Projections; Projections of the United States: 1982 to 2050 (Advance Report)." Washington, D.C.
U.S. Bureau of the Census. 1981b. *Statistical Abstract of the United States, 1981.* Washington, D.C.
U.S. Commission on Civil Rights. 1976. *Puerto Ricans in the United States: An Uncertain Future,* Washington, D.C.
Weller, Robert H. 1967. "An Empirical Examination of Megalopolitan Structure." *Demography* 4:734-743.

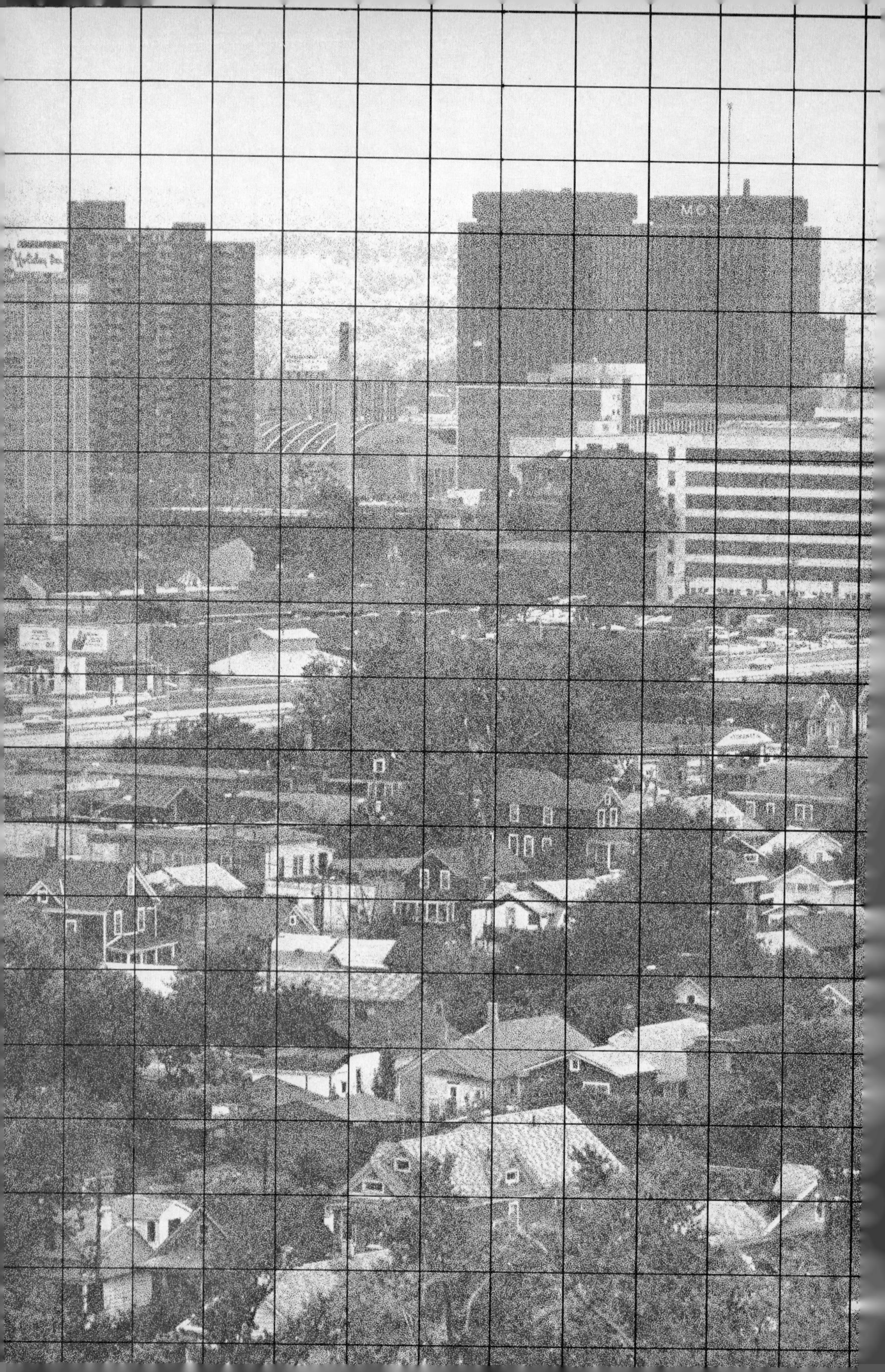

# CHAPTER · 6

# Urban Ecology: Spatial Differentiation

**Chapter Outline**

PRINCIPLES OF DIFFERENTIATION
   Friction of Space
   Division of Residence and Work
     • Work leaves the neighborhood
     • Contemporary commuting
   Zoning
NUCLEI AND DISTRICTS IN THE MATURE INDUSTRIAL CITY
   Central Business District
   Heavy Industrial District
   Suburbs and Satellites
   Minor Nuclei
NUCLEI AND DISTRICTS IN THE METROPOLIS
   Central City
     • Changes in the central business district
     • The rise of institutional districts
   Differentiation in the Suburban Zone
SUMMARY

Imagine a drive through a metropolitan area. Entering, you notice oil refineries, large factories, and tall smokestacks; perhaps they are making tires or steel. Then you go through an area of low warehouses, and you see terminal lots with dozens of parked trucks and semitrailers. You pass through a slummy area with empty lots; some houses in use and others boarded up; abandoned cars, weeds, broken glass, and cans on the street; and kids playing basketball on a paved court. Next, you see a university with tennis courts, ivy-covered pseudo-gothic buildings, parking garages for the hospital, and campus police in marked cars. Then you are downtown, with its new, large hotels, fancy shopwindows, banks, tall office buildings, paved malls with sculptures and fountains, cops with whistles, street vendors selling ice cream and hot dogs, and crowds waiting to cross the street at the light. You enter an area where the stores have signs in Spanish offering special foods and products. In the next area some of the people on the street look like artists, others like students, others like Oriental immigrants. You enter another district where the streets are densely built-up with brick apartment buildings and elderly people are on the streets conversing. Finally, you look out and see long, high hedges; occasionally, you can see beyond the rustic mailboxes and up the driveways to notice large, bright-green lawns and enormous tudor-style homes.

On this tour you have observed the spatial differentiation of the urban community, functional and social. There are different activities, facilities, and groups in different districts of the larger community, and this differentiation has fascinated urban sociologists and geographers for generations.

The idea of spatial differentiation of residential areas is familiar in everyday thought. Many popular movies have depicted big-city boys' gangs defending their "turf" against the incursions of other gangs. *West Side Story* is a musical in which a Puerto Rican gang vies with an Italian gang over turf. More recently, the movie *Saturday Night Fever* showed a fight in Brooklyn between groups representing these same nationalities. In older novels and reminiscences of immigrant childhoods, authors often wrote that they were afraid to walk through a certain neighborhood because the local boys of one or another group would annoy them for being in their territory. Perhaps the most contemporary expression of the delineation and claiming of turf is by means of a modern invention, the aerosol spray can of enamel paint, with which gangs can declare their domination of a particular district by inscribing graffiti on the walls: "Latin Kings Rule;" "White Power;" or "Do Not Enter," at a turf boundary.

In general, inhabitants of each community recognize the social differentiation of residential areas; thus people of smaller towns know which is the good side and which is "the other side of the tracks." Sometimes, though, contradictions exist within urban districts. For example, a sociological book about Chicago was called *The Gold Coast and the Slum* (Zorbaugh, 1929); the title refers to a single district in which the buildings near the lake shore housed an elite class, while the adjacent area comprised of rooming houses and a nearby slum housed poor Sicilian immigrants. Similarly, there are points along the western boundary of Central Park in New York City where upper-middle-class households live in fine apartment buildings within blocks of deteriorated buildings which house families in poverty.

# URBAN ECOLOGY: SPATIAL DIFFERENTIATION

Over the course of history, cities have tended to become larger and more spatially differentiated. Recall that the focal points of the biblical city were the temple, the palace, and the market, with the entire community surrounded by a wall. In some cases, these facilities occupied the same part of the city; later, as in ancient Athens, the market was separated from the religious-administrative center. But, often, functions were mixed in the same area, so a temple might have been surrounded by a market or cheek by jowl with residential structures. In the medieval town a great mixture of functions—work, government, trade, and residence—occurred in the same district. Indeed, in the more compact towns it is not clear that there was a division into districts. Historically, though, like the progressive division of labor, functional differentiation has existed among the areas of urban communities.

## PRINCIPLES OF DIFFERENTIATION

In an essay which became a geographical classic, Harris and Ullman (1945) stated that separate nuclei and differentiated districts arise because of a combination of four principles of differentiation.

1. Certain activities require special locations and specialized facilities. For example, the optimum location for a retail outlet, especially a large or highly specialized one, is at the point of greatest intraurban accessibility—thus large department stores and shops catering to the entire population should be at the convergence of roads and mass transit lines—the central business district must be central. Similarly, manufacturing tends to cluster into specialized districts because of its needs: large blocks of land plus water or rail connections.
2. "Certain like activities group together because they profit from cohesion" (p.14). Retail districts benefit from grouping. The presence of a number of similar shops in a retail district permits comparison shopping, which attracts more customers. Likewise, the clustering of banks, brokers, law offices, and the like, within financial and office-building districts facilitates communication among offices. The garment district, described in Chapter 4, illustrates this principle, extended one step further to include the clustering of symbiotic units. Not only do the tailors locate together but also the cloth and button wholesalers and sewing machine repair services.
3. On the negative side, "certain unlike activities are detrimental to each other" (p. 14). Obviously, developers of high-class residential areas avoid factory areas. Retailing and wholesaling are also incompatible activities; retail areas generate heavy concentrations of pedestrians and automobiles (and streetcars, when Harris and Ullman wrote), whereas wholesale areas require extensive frontage for truck-loading and railroad facilities. Trucks and pedestrians just don't mix well on the same sidewalk.
4. Certain activities cannot afford the high rents of the most desirable sites. Bulk

wholesaling and storage, for example, require a great deal of cheap floor space and must therefore avoid high-rent areas.

## Friction of Space

Another ecological principle governing the location of activities is explained by Hawley in his *Human Ecology* (1950). In order to have human relationships, it is necessary to overcome a number of resistances, known as the "friction of space." People must expend time and energy to traverse space; thus friction of space is a function of distance as well as of the obstacles along the path. On the other hand, the friction of space may be reduced by improvements in transportation technology; at any given time, the efficiency of the current means of transportation and communication devices mediates the friction of space. This friction, in human terms, is not measured in linear units, such as miles and blocks, but in units of time and cost. Thus, in the metropolitan context, it is much more meaningful to say that it takes 40 minutes to get from one place to another (and perhaps that the trip costs $3) than to say that the places are 7 miles apart.

The consequence of this, according to Hawley, is that "the territorial pattern of collective life is largely a result of the friction of space as manifested in time-cost distance" (p. 237). Improvements in transportation and communication reduce the friction of space and permit a wider scatter of an interrelated population without loss of contact. When the cost of travel is high, differentiation of function is limited, "but, when the friction of space is overcome by improved systems of transportation and communications, then and then only can an area develop fully its various use potentialities" (p. 238).

In the single-centered, mature industrial city, the friction of space tended to cluster certain kinds of like units within the CBD; it was one of the main principles governing the distribution of activities within the community. Units housing specialized activities were not able to contend with the friction of space and, therefore, sought central locations. Other units "arrange themselves at distances from the center in keeping with different abilities for bearing the time and cost to the center" (p.264). Overall, the operation of this principle tended to produce the pattern of concentric zonation.

Later in this chapter, a contemporary theory of suburban development is discussed which states that the emerging metropolis has largely overcome the friction of space.

## Division of Residence and Work

### Work leaves the neighborhood

Very few people live and work in the same place, and this separation, multiplied by large numbers of individuals, contributes strongly to the spatial differentiation of the metropolis. By 1949, for example, in a survey of local activities in Rochester, New York, Foley (1952) found that only 17 percent of the people worked in their own neighborhoods; a quarter-century later only 11 percent worked in their home neighborhoods (Hunter, 1975). Other contemporary neighborhood studies have consistently found the same result, but this was not always the case. According to Schnore (1968), "Commutation is essentially a modern development, dating from the rise of the factory system in the course of the industrial revolution. Earlier periods were characterized by a virtual identity between residence and workplace" (p. 140). Even in nineteenth-century New York City, the division between residence and work was limited; in 1899 the average "commuting" distance in that city was a quarter-mile, indicating many home workers (Hawley, 1981). Hawley writes that New York City at that time was composed of self-contained districts incorporating their own industries, shops, and other institutions.

Large-scale industrial development provided an impetus to the division between residence and employment. "The industrial revolution brought about massive changes in land use, especially within cities. Centrally located workplaces, powered by inanimate forms of energy, came to employ dozens and even hundreds of workers" (Schnore, 1968, p. 140), yielding a sharp division between home and work.

Each new development in the technology of intraurban transportation lengthened the distance a worker could travel from home to job (assuming that the worker could afford to pay the fare). A series of transportation innovations took place in the nineteenth and twentieth centuries, starting with horse-drawn vehicles and progressing to electric trolleys, steam and electric railways, and the automobile. "The work trip lengthened substantially and it became common for the worker to reside at a considerable distance from his job" (Schnore, 1968, p. 140). The horse-drawn trolley, which was used in many cities from 1850 to 1890, made it possible for people to live as far as 4 miles from the city center, and the electric-powered streetcar, which was installed in hundreds of communities by 1895, extended the range of commuting much further. According to Hawley (1981), ... "The effective radius of daily commutation was extended to as much as 12 miles from central business districts" (pp. 89–90).

Hawley's (1950) rule of thumb is that the distance which can be traveled in one hour's time defines the radius of the zone of daily interchanges which is the effective community limit. He says that during the pedestrian period the one-hour trip was 2-1/2 to 3 miles; during the period of the horsecar it was 4 to 5 miles; during the period of electric traction it was 7 to 8 miles; and with rapid transit electric lines—trolley, "el," and subway—it lengthened to 17 to 28 miles.

## Contemporary commuting

In the current period, most commuting is done by car. A large national survey of commuters found that 75 percent of all home-to-work trips were made by automobile, with another 8 percent by truck (U.S. Dept. of Transportation, 1973). Well under a tenth of the commuters used mass transportation.

CHAPTER·6

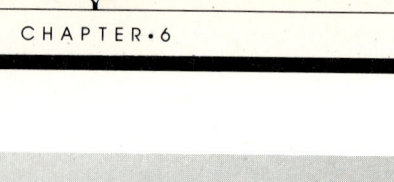

Fourteen lanes of morning commuter traffic merge onto the San Francisco–Oakland Bay bridge. (Joe Munroe, Photo Researchers, Inc.)

This survey and another, which was conducted by the U.S. Bureau of the Census (1978) and studied only residents of metropolitan areas, found that the average journey to work is shorter than might be expected. The Department of Transportation survey showed that the average trip, by all modes of transportation, is 9.9

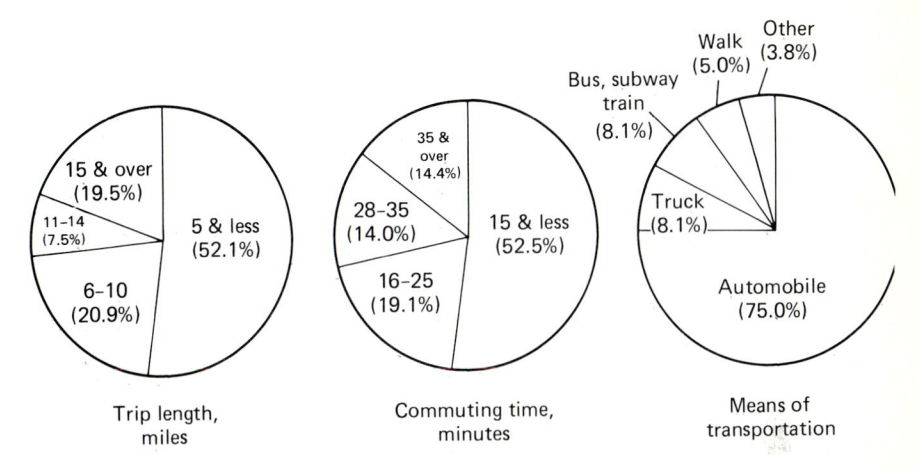

**FIGURE 6-1**
Characteristics of home-to-work trips. (Source: U.S. Dept. of Transportation, 1973, p. 14)

miles. See Figure 6-1 for other results of that survey. The metropolitan survey, sampling 20 SMSAs, showed that the median travel time to work was 21.8 minutes. The longest trips, in time, were made by New York City's commuters, who had a median travel time of 28.7 minutes. Residents of small and medium-sized metropolitan areas like Grand Rapids, Allentown-Bethlehem-Easton (Pennsylvania), and Las Vegas had much shorter commutes, with a median of approximately 16 minutes. Car and truck commuters spent far less time traveling (a median of 20.2 minutes) than did mass transit commuters (a median of 39.5 minutes). Median distances traveled in the 20 metropolitan areas are shown in Table 6-1. Comparing the travel times in the areas, the second survey shows that the larger the metropolitan area, the longer the trip to work (U.S. Bureau of the Census, 1978).

At present the division of work and residence is almost complete—the home worker is certainly the exception. The figures discussed above conceal the commuters who are not average, though. More than half of all workers live 5 miles or less from work and arrive in 15 minutes or less (U.S. Dept. of Transportation, 1973); on the other hand, some workers commute long distances and their mileage and clock times far exceed the average.

## Zoning

Zoning is a municipal legal process that has tended to reinforce the ecological processes which are producing differentiation among subareas. Implicit in the ecological theory—considering Harris and Ullman's four principles, for example—is that these are natural processes which operate and yield a predictable result. Thus, in the normal course of events, "certain unlike activities are detrimental to each other" (Harris & Ullman, 1945, p. 14), as stated in Principle 3, and we would expect them

**TABLE 6-1**
**Median Distance from Home to Work for 20 SMSAs and SMSA Transportation Groups, 1976**

| SMSAs and SMSA groups* | Total workers (in 1,000s)† | Median distance (miles) |
|---|---|---|
| Total, 20 SMSAs | 10,734 | 7.6 |
| Group A | | |
| New York | 3,323 | 7.9 |
| Group B | 2,138 | 8.3 |
| Baltimore | 773 | 8.8 |
| Cleveland | 614 | 7.8 |
| St. Louis | 751 | 8.4 |
| Group C—north | 1,369 | 6.0 |
| Buffalo | 417 | 5.5 |
| Indianapolis | 420 | 7.3 |
| Omaha | 205 | 5.4 |
| Providence | 327 | 5.2 |
| Group C—south and west | 2,689 | 8.3 |
| Birmingham | 250 | 8.4 |
| Denver | 545 | 7.4 |
| Honolulu | 276 | 6.5 |
| Houston | 858 | 9.2 |
| Louisville | 260 | 7.7 |
| Seattle-Everett | 501 | 8.9 |
| Group D | 1,215 | 6.4 |
| Allentown | 210 | 4.8 |
| Grand Rapids | 207 | 6.1 |
| Las Vegas | 135 | 5.8 |
| Oklahoma City | 255 | 7.0 |
| Raleigh | 98 | 6.8 |
| Sacramento | 310 | 7.3 |

*SMSAs as of 1970 census.
†Workers not working at home who reported distance traveled to work.
*Source:* U.S. Bureau of the Census, 1978, p. 8.

to segregate from each other. But in the completely free and unregulated urban land market of the nineteenth century, enough exceptions existed to cause some property owners to seek the protection of law to be sure that unlike activities were kept apart from each other. In particular, inhabitants of middle- and upper-class residential areas in fast-growing cities were sometimes annoyed to find their neighborhoods invaded by offensive land uses, particularly such "nuisances" as commercial laundries and brickyards. These, of course, threatened the property values in the residential areas. Other consequences of unregulated real estate development became apparent toward the end of the century. Skyscraper construction was capable of depriving neighboring lots of light and air; building intensity was generating congestion in many areas. These problems gave rise to a demand for regulations backed with the force of law.

As defined in the *Encyclopedia Britannica,* zoning is "the regulation of the use of land and buildings, the density of population, and the height, bulk, and spacing of structures.... It is accomplished by dividing the land area into zoning districts, each having specific conditions under which land and buildings may be legally developed and used." Thus one district may be zoned for industry, another for commerce, and another for residences. Different residential areas are designated for single-family houses, low-density apartments, and high-density apartments.

Zoning eventually became one of the city planner's most powerful tools for the regulation of land use and for the implementation of large-scale plans. While there were some European precursors, the beginning of zoning is generally dated from New York City's comprehensive ordinance of 1916. The objectives of the first ordinances were to protect existing property values and to preserve light and air, but the objectives widened to incorporate other goals, including controlling congestion, consolidating commercial districts, and protecting the environment of the home. One leading objective was to prevent mixed and incongruous building development, "which leads to obsolescence of existing structures and to such uncertainty as to the future that a condition of depreciated value and general blight often sets in, resulting in social and economic loss," as one advocate wrote (Whitten, 1931, p. 538). Overall, one effect (perhaps a latent function, perhaps not) was to objectify the tendency of urban districts to differentiate into areas of homogeneous use.

## NUCLEI AND DISTRICTS IN THE MATURE INDUSTRIAL CITY

The big city of the 1920s and its metropolitan area were highly differentiated; although the city had a single dominant center, the CBD, it had other nodal points as well. Harris and Ullman (1945) list the following types of areas:

1  Central business district (CBD)
2  Outlying business district
3  Wholesaling and light manufacturing
4  Heavy manufacturing
5  Industrial suburb
6  Low-class residential
7  Medium-class residential
8  High-class residential

Harris and Ullman put forth the "multinuclear model" of the metropolis which incorporates these types of areas. (See Figure 6-2, which diagrams an imaginary

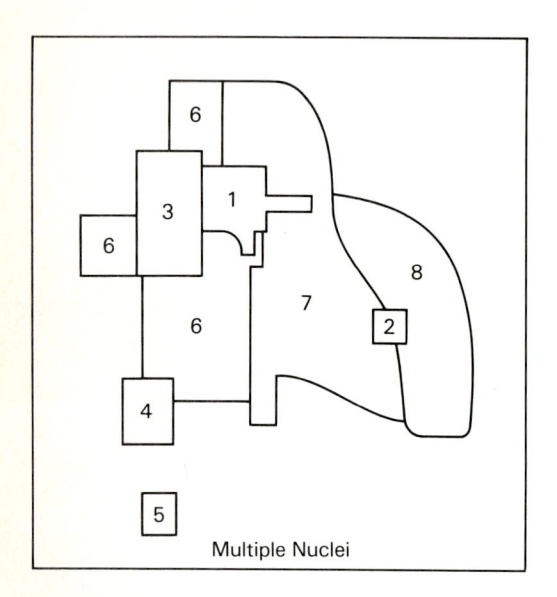

**FIGURE 6-2**
The multinuclear model of the metropolis.
(Source: Harris and Ullman, 1945, p. 13)

metropolitan area.) This section discusses the differentiated areas of the mature industrial city, and the next section tells how some of them changed and new ones arose in the period of suburbanization. Differences among residential areas (types 6,7, and 8 in the list) are discussed in the next chapter. The multinuclear model fits the suburbanized metropolis particularly well, so it is discussed further in Chapter 12 which is about suburbanization.

Already in 1945 American cities were sufficiently suburbanized and decentralized for Harris and Ullman to perceive their multinuclear structure. What is a nucleus? The list of types of areas (above) actually includes two sorts of places; the first five types are commercial-industrial and the last three are residential. Strictly speaking, only the first five should be considered nuclei and the residential areas should not. A nucleus is a place which sets the conditions for places around it. It attracts people from beyond its own locality, for work, shopping, or other activities (hospital service, museum viewing, dining, etc.). If it provides shops or services, these must not be merely of the first or second order. Thus not every shopping center is a nucleus. Except in the cases of vast megalopolitan areas, the nuclei of a metropolis are to be counted in the single digits. Harris and Ullman's scheme accounted for two urban ecological phenomena which didn't fit into the earlier concentric zones model. Strangely enough for metropolitan Chicago had a great deal of it, there was no place in the circular model for heavy industry. The multinuclear model shows a separate district for it, as far as possible from high- and "medium-class" residential areas. (Chicago had at least two heavy industrial districts, one running south along Lake Michigan's shoreline to Gary, Indiana, and the other running southwest from the CBD along major rail lines.) Burgess's omission was peculiar, but it shows his concentration on the sociological questions of stratification and ethnicity. The second phenomenon which was missing from the concentric model but which is included in the multinuclear model is the outlying business district. Even in the highly centralized mature industrial city not all the major retailing was downtown. Each city also had secondary shopping districts, usually at intersections of major arterial streets with trolley lines, which included department stores, other specialty shops such as shoes and furniture, banks and offices, and the like. This means that beyond being residential, each zone also contained nodal points.

## Central Business District

"This," wrote Harris and Ullman (1945) "is the focus of commercial, social, and civic life, and of transportation. It is the downtown retail district with its department stores, smart shops, office buildings, clubs, banks, hotels, theaters, museums, and organization headquarters" (p. 12).

Physically, the district is highly compact. As the geographers Horwood and Boyce (1959) note, walking distances have traditionally been a critical factor in restricting the spread of the CBD. Therefore, real estate developers have exploited the vertical dimension, using the airspace above the district. Skyscrapers abound in the CBD, and interaction is promoted by use of the elevator.

The highest *intensity of land use* occurs in the CBD. A city planner's concept, "intensity" represents the amount of use and activity on the land. A piece of land with a single use by a few individuals, like a single-family home on a large lot, represents a low level of intensity of land use. In contrast, a lot covered by a multi-story building, heavily used, occupied by different users—perhaps stores at ground level and offices above—represents high intensity. Traffic flows, vehicular and pedestrian, are heavy in high-intensity districts. High intensity, or the potential thereof, is a determinant of land values, which are highest by far in the CBD.

The CBD itself is differentiated into two parts, the "core" and the surrounding "frame" (Horwood & Boyce, 1959). The core has the highest intensity of land use, with its multistoried buildings, and has the densest daytime population. It accommodates three major groups of activities (Berry & Kasarda, 1977):

1 Financial functions, including banks, lending institutions, insurance companies, and brokers
2 Specialized retail functions, including department stores, which require large population support at a point of conflux, and firms supplying high-quality and rare goods
3 Social and professional functions, including the headquarters and main-office function

The surrounding frame has activities which cannot support the high rents of the core. Land use is intensive in the frame, but not nearly as high as in the core; buildings are not nearly as tall in the frame. Typical activities in the frame are wholesaling with stocks, warehousing, light manufacturing, and service industries. There are also transportation facilities such as trucking and intercity transportation terminals.

Accessibility and the potential for contact are the key features of the CBD. Located at the junction of the city's major roads and mass transit lines, it is the most accessible place on the map. With a high intensity of land use and a large daytime population, the downtown creates innumerable opportunities for face-to-face contact and for maximizing linkages among activities and markets (Manners, 1974). To employers, the CBD offers accessibility to the large urban labor pool, particularly skilled office workers. It also offers individuals and organizations the ability to exploit the information and ideas available from other centrally located activities such as law offices, advertising agencies, trade associations, clubs, and financial institutions (Manners, 1974). In addition, there has always been a prestige value to certain downtown addresses.

## Heavy Industrial District

This area was originally located far from the city center, near the edge of the city, or where the edge once was. Because of its special locational needs, heavy industry is incompatible with most of the activities of the CBD. "The noise of boiler works, the odors of stockyards, the waste disposal problems of smelters and iron and steel mills, the fire hazards of petroleum refineries, and the space and transportation needs which interrupt streets and accessibility—all these favor the growth of heavy industry away from the main center of the large city" (Harris & Ullman, 1945, p. 16).

## Suburbs and Satellites

The mature industrial city had at least a few suburbs and was likely to have one or more satellite cities. "Satellites differ from suburbs in that they are separated from the central city by many miles and in general have little daily commuting to or from the central cities, although economic activities of the satellite are closely geared to those of the central city" (Harris & Ullman, 1945 p.16). The satellite is basically subordinate to the larger city, but it retains a high degree of independence stemming from its importance as a production and employment center (Douglass, cited in Schnore, 1968, p.137). The satellite has one or more major factories and offers employment to its own residents and, in some cases, to commuters as well, unlike the surburban "bedroom community."

## Minor Nuclei

In addition to major nodes, the urban community has minor nuclei as well (Harris & Ullman, 1945, including "cultural centers, parks, outlying business districts, and small industrial centers" (p. 16). A university campus may serve as a nucleus for its surrounding neighborhood and for some local supporting commercial activities such as shops and taverns.

Together, the nuclei and districts mentioned above, plus different sorts of residential areas, represent a composite sketch of the mature industrial city.

## NUCLEI AND DISTRICTS IN THE METROPOLIS

While all eight types of areas in Harris and Ullman's list still exist in the contemporary metropolis, some were transformed in the period of suburbanization and new types of nuclei and districts have arisen. Two new types are the institutional district (within the central city) and the suburban minicity; variants of the latter type include the airport complex and the suburban freeway corridor.

## Central City

### Changes in the central business district

While the old CBD retains its advantage of centrality, it has nonetheless lost its dominance over many functions and thus been reduced to being only one nucleus among several in the overall metropolitan map. In most large metropolitan areas, however, it continues as the largest district in terms of daily visitors, floor space, and even retail dollar volume. It is the greatest single focus of aggregate daily vehicular and pedestrian traffic, and it has the highest intensity of land use and the highest land values (Yeates & Garner, 1980).

The downtown area has lost its retail dominance relatively but not absolutely. In the post-World War II era, suburban retail sales grew rapidly while the CBD stayed constant, thus commanding a shrinking share of the market. This is shown in Tables 6-2 and 6-3, which reflect a period of rapid suburbanization. Table 6-2 shows that in the smaller metropolitan areas, retail sales in the CBD were declining, even on an absolute basis, while suburban sales grew rapidly. Even in the largest SMSAs, downtown retail sales were growing less than 1 percent per year, while suburban sales were increasing more than 10 times as fast (Berry & Kasarda, 1977).

The nature of downtown retailing has changed during the suburbanization period. To some extent, this shift reflects the changing social class and racial composition of central city versus suburb. The middle class, having moved to the suburbs, also shops there at the large regional shopping centers. The CBD remains then, as "the main shopping center for the less mobile, less wealthy, inner-city population" (Yeates & Garner, 1980, p.337). Nonetheless, the large department stores,

**TABLE 6-2**
Retail Change, by City Size Class, 1954–1967

|  | Population of metropolitan area (in thousands) | | | |
|---|---|---|---|---|
|  | 3,000+ | 1,000–3,000 | 500–1,000 | 250–500 |
| Percentage change in sales: current dollars | | | | |
| CBD | 12.1 | 8.3 | −3.7 | −6.7 |
| Central city | 34.3 | 26.8 | 58.4 | 61.4 |
| Suburbs | 132.2 | 175.0 | 209.0 | 193.1 |
| Percentage change in numbers of establishments | | | | |
| CBD | −26.0 | −26.9 | −38.2 | −37.6 |
| Central city | −26.3 | −23.7 | −8.4 | −8.4 |
| Suburbs | 29.9 | 30.3 | 51.3 | 48.0 |

Source: Berry and Kasarda, 1977, table 13.3.

in most cities, continue to operate their old, large CBD stores and to survive. In addition, the CBD has elite retail outlets, often located on selected streets.

> The distinctive feature of downtown retailing today is its concentration on high-quality and rare goods, including rare books, chic and expensive clothing and home furnishings, jewelry, tapestries, original paintings and works of art, antiques, and major department stores. Other features include a range of cultural activities, such as theaters, opera, art galleries, and museums; specialized medical and personal services for which a prestigious downtown address is essential; and more recently, convention centers and sports complexes, all of which can satisfy their large thresholds only at the point of maximum accessibility to the entire metropolitan market. (Yeates & Garner, 1980 p.337)

These retail shops, large and small, in the CBD are supported by the visitors to the city as well as by its residents. The CBD attracts tourists, conventioneers, people coming for medical treatment or for legal and banking services, all of whom are potential shoppers.

Beginning in the mid-1960s—at the same time, surprisingly, that office functions were being suburbanized—a boom in the construction of downtown office buildings occurred in many city centers. Undoubtedly, the most dramatic case was Manhattan, which had 140 million square feet of office space in 1950 and added 104 million square feet by 1970. Many other downtowns increased office space by over 75 percent between 1960 and 1970, and some, such as San Francisco and Minneapolis-St. Paul, increased it by more than 100 percent (Yeates & Garner, 1980). This growth in office space paralleled the growth in office employment; white-collar jobs grew from 35.5 percent of the national labor force in 1950 to 50 percent in 1970.

**TABLE 6-3**
**Percentage Increase in Retail Sales Deflated by General Price Increase, 1958–1967, for Selected Metropolitan Areas**

| Area | Central city | Suburbs |
| --- | --- | --- |
| Washington, D.C. | 10.5 | 134.8 |
| Baltimore, Maryland | 4.9 | 128.2 |
| Boston, Massachusetts | −1.4 | 79.2 |
| Newark, New Jersey | −14.1 | 37.1 |
| Paterson-Clifton-Passaic, New Jersey | 0.9 | 74.5 |
| Buffalo, New York | −9.9 | 54.7 |
| New York, New York | 9.7 | 60.2 |
| Rochester, New York | 18.1 | 91.3 |
| Philadelphia, Pennsylvania–New Jersey | 6.2 | 65.4 |
| Pittsburgh, Pennsylvania | 7.8 | 28.7 |
| Providence, Rhode Island | −36.3 | 73.1 |
| Chicago, Illinois | 5.3 | 86.6 |
| Indianapolis, Indiana | 20.0 | 160.8 |
| Detroit, Michigan | 0.7 | 86.4 |
| Minneapolis–St. Paul, Minnesota | 7.9 | 149.7 |
| Kansas City, Missouri-Kansas | 55.2 | 64.3 |
| St. Louis, Missouri-Illinois | −7.6 | 76.2 |
| Cincinnati, Ohio-Kentucky-Indiana | 4.6 | 129.4 |
| Cleveland, Ohio | −15.2 | 269.1 |
| Columbus, Ohio | 22.8 | 141.9 |
| Dayton, Ohio | 3.6 | 125.5 |
| Milwaukee, Wisconsin | 7.5 | 108.3 |
| Miami, Florida | −2.5 | 98.2 |
| Tampa–St. Petersburg, Florida | 30.9 | 108.9 |
| Atlanta, Georgia | 37.7 | 153.9 |
| Louisville, Kentucky-Indiana | 14.0 | 101.8 |
| New Orleans, Louisiana | 21.0 | 141.9 |
| Dallas, Texas | 33.6 | 119.2 |
| Houston, Texas | 55.9 | 63.3 |
| San Antonio, Texas | 36.4 | 79.9 |
| Los Angeles–Long Beach, California | 22.2 | 75.4 |
| San Diego, California | 25.6 | 91.8 |
| San Francisco–Oakland, California | 16.3 | 81.6 |
| Denver, Colorado | 11.1 | 132.4 |
| Portland, Oregon-Washington | 28.1 | 180.3 |
| Seattle, Washington | 18.0 | 152.5 |

Source: Berry and Kasarda, 1977, table 13.2.

## The rise of institutional districts

A new type of specialized area is the "institutional district"; the most common is the multihospital medical center, but university, museum, and fine arts areas have also arisen. The medical center comprises more than one hospital, plus a medical

CHAPTER·6

college and schools for nurses and other health professionals. This type of area may also have laboratories, medical bookshops, pharmacies, suppliers of specialized equipment, restaurants for medical personnel, facilities for visitors, geriatric residential facilities, and the like. In addition, dormitories and apartment complexes for nurses, interns, students, and other members of the medical network are located at the medical center.

A university district is likely to include one or more universities, public and private, along with their professional schools such as law and medicine, and it may also have one or more theological seminaries. Like the medical center, it will have a variety of units in symbiotic relationships with the educational institutions: bookshops, bars, restaurants, suppliers of office and laboratory materials, etc. In addition, various institutes and foundations related to the academic and scientific strengths of the university may be found in this district. Manufacturing and con-

Factories, offices, and cars in California's "Silicon Valley," located in the San Francisco metropolitan area, a suburban minicity based on high-technology industries. (See Chapter 12.) (Robert Isaacs, Photo Researchers, Inc.)

## BOX 6-1
## Residential Sectors

Chapter 5 presented criticisms of Burgess's concentric circles model of urban spatial patterns which posits a series of circular *zones* around the city center. One major alternative to that model suggests that the residential areas of a city or metropolitan area tend to fall into *sectors*.

Proposed by urban analyst Homer Hoyt in 1939, this model suggests that each city or metropolitan area is divided into a number of sectors. A sector is a wedge-shaped subarea of the larger community, with its point toward the city center (see the schematic map below). Hoyt came to this conclusion by intensively studying the real estate patterns in dozens of American cities. After constructing maps which showed rent levels and prices of houses, he discovered that low-cost housing typically created a sector, expensive housing created a sector, etc. He looked at the patterns in individual cities over time and inferred a growth pattern.

His sector theory states that growth along a particular transportation line—a trolley, rail, riverside, etc.—is likely to consist of similar types of land use. The residential land uses are likely to provide for particular segments of the housing market and additional housing for that segment is likely to follow that line outward from the city center. Thus, if the most expensive housing in a city is in its eastern quadrant, additional housing for that segment of the market is likely to be built toward the east. Likewise, working-class housing will be adjacent to working-class areas and in the same direction. Residential sectors are likely to reflect a community's social stratification. As geographers Harris and Ullman (1945) wrote in a summary of the sector scheme, "The migration of high-class residential areas along established lines of travel is particularly pronounced on hig ground, toward open country, to homes of community leaders, along lines of fastest transportation, and to existing nuclei of buldings or trading centers."

In current usage, the concepts sector and zones are sometimes used in an abstract geometrical sense (apart from socioeconomic content). Thus, sector refers to any characteristic which is distributed in a wedge shape and zone refers to any characteristic which is in a circular band.

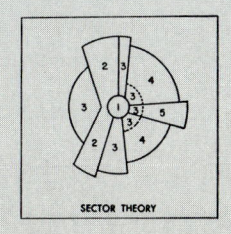

SECTOR THEORY

sulting companies, and laboratories formed by faculty and graduates that benefit by continued contact with the campus, are also located in this type of district.

Many private universities with large endowments, such as Columbia and Chicago, own an appreciable fraction of the housing stock in the university district. This property interest, plus a concern for the safety of students and staff as well as for the institution's reputation, often leads such universities into urban renewal and neighborhood redevelopment projects. The university also influences local social life in other ways. For example, its police force is likely to discourage lower-class strangers from frequenting the area, and the college calendar will influence the timing of public events, when shopkeepers have sales, and the like.

### Differentiation in the Suburban Zone

Suburbs are much more highly differentiated than they were once expected to be; there are business suburbs and residential ones, new and old, large and small, black and white. They vary by socioeconomic status as well. This chapter presents emerging concepts of suburban functional differentiation and leaves residential status differences for Chapters 7 and 12.

## SUMMARY

Ecology, social organization, and social psychology interplay in the functional spatial differentiation of the areas of the metropolis, just as they do in urban community phenomena. This chapter has been about an ecological phenomenon, the differentiation of areas. We have seen that it is caused to a large extent by processes which are themselves ecological, for example, the gravitation of heavy industry toward waterfronts, rail connections, and open land or the location of large department stores at points of passenger conflux—downtown at an earlier period, at the intersection between two freeways today.

Initially, we see spatial differentiation as a consequence of demographic and economic growth. Differentiation becomes necessary because of the increasing scale of economic activity—units such as factories, warehouses, and office buildings that are too large to scatter about within the community. Thus the system works more efficiently when such units are segregated into specialized districts. At this point, the explanation is entirely on an ecological level—population and economic growth, facilitated by technological change, influence the spatial layout of the community, the arrangement of social units.

Differentiation has a social organizational aspect to it as well. The factory and, later, the corporation are social inventions, new forms of social organization, that contribute to the increasing economic and social scale which is driving the ecological differentiation. Furthermore, increasing division of labor, another organizational process, is also contributing to the economic growth, and the spatial differentiation is, in a sense, a reflection of the division of labor.

Also at the ecological level, technological change—particularly transportation and communication—affects spatial differentiation. Nineteenth-century transportation systems, rail-based technologies between and within cities, dealt with the friction of space in such a way that the easiest place to go was the center, and the inventions leading to the skyscraper—the elevator and the steel building frame—contributed further to the center's capacities. These technologies increased the center's value, both for organizing acitivites, through coordination of the many units which could exist in proximity, and through selling things, due to the potential availability of numerous customers. By bringing together into the downtown area so many individuals and social units, the ecology is facilitating a particular sort of social organization.

The ecological patterning also affects social organization and social psychology—as shown in the ecological concentration of units in the CBD, which has the social effect of facilitating frequent contact. This permits a great deal of coordination in those industries which require it—investment deals involving bankers, lawyers, investors, and insurance companies working together, for example. It also permits the operation of rapidly shifting industries based upon fashions and styles—clothing, advertising, and television broadcasting, for example.

This discussion has neglected social psychological processes, seen more prominently in residential differentiation, which is covered in the next chapter. Nonetheless, social psychology, coupled with social organization, can be seen operating in the rise of zoning. Here we see the emergence of certain preferences on the part of middle- and upper-class residents for clean, homogeneous neighborhoods for protected property values, and these preferences are embodied in the zoning laws, a social organization device to regulate officially the functional division of space.

## REFERENCES

Berry, Brian J.L., and John D. Kasarda. 1977. *Contemporary Urban Ecology*. New York: Macmillan.

Foley, Donald L. 1952. *Neighbors or Urbanites? A Study of a Rochester Residential District*. Rochester, N.Y.: University of Rochester.

Harris, Chauncy D., and Edward L. Ullman. 1945. "The Nature of Cities," Annals of the American Academy of Political and Social Science. 242:7–17.

Hawley, Amos H. 1950. *Human Ecology: A Theory of Community Structure*. New York: Ronald.

Hawley, Amos H. 1981. *Urban Society: An Ecological Approach*, 2d ed. New York: Wiley.

Horwood, Edgar M., and Ronald R. Boyce. 1959. *Studies of the Central Business District and Urban Freeway Development*. Seattle: University of Washington Press.

Hunter, Albert. 1975. "Loss of Community: An Empirical Test through Replication." *American Sociological Review.* 40:537–553.

Manners, G. 1974. "The Office in Metropolis: An Opportunity for Shaping Metropolitan America." *Economic Geography.* 50:93–110.

Schnore, Leo. 1957/1965. "Satellites and Suburbs," chap. 7 in *The Urban Scene: Human Ecology and Demography.* New York: Free Press.

Schnore, Leo. 1968. "Commutation," in *International Encyclopedia of the Social Sciences* 16:140–44. New York: Macmillan.

U.S. Bureau of the Census. 1978. *Current Population Reports,* series P-23, no. 72, "Selected Characteristics of Travel to Work in 20 Metropolitan Areas: 1976," Washington, D.C.

U.S. Department of Transportation, Federal Highway Administration. 1973. *National Personal Transportation Study*, Report no. 8, "Home-to-Work Trips and Travels." Washington, D.C.

Whitten, Robert. 1931. "Zoning," pp. 538–539 in *Encyclopaedia of the Social Sciences*, vol. 15. New York: Macmillan.

Yeates, Maurice, and Barry Garner. 1980. *The North American City*, 3d ed.. New York: Harper & Row.

Zorbaugh, Harvey. 1929. *The Gold Coast and the Slum*. Chicago: University of Chicago Press.

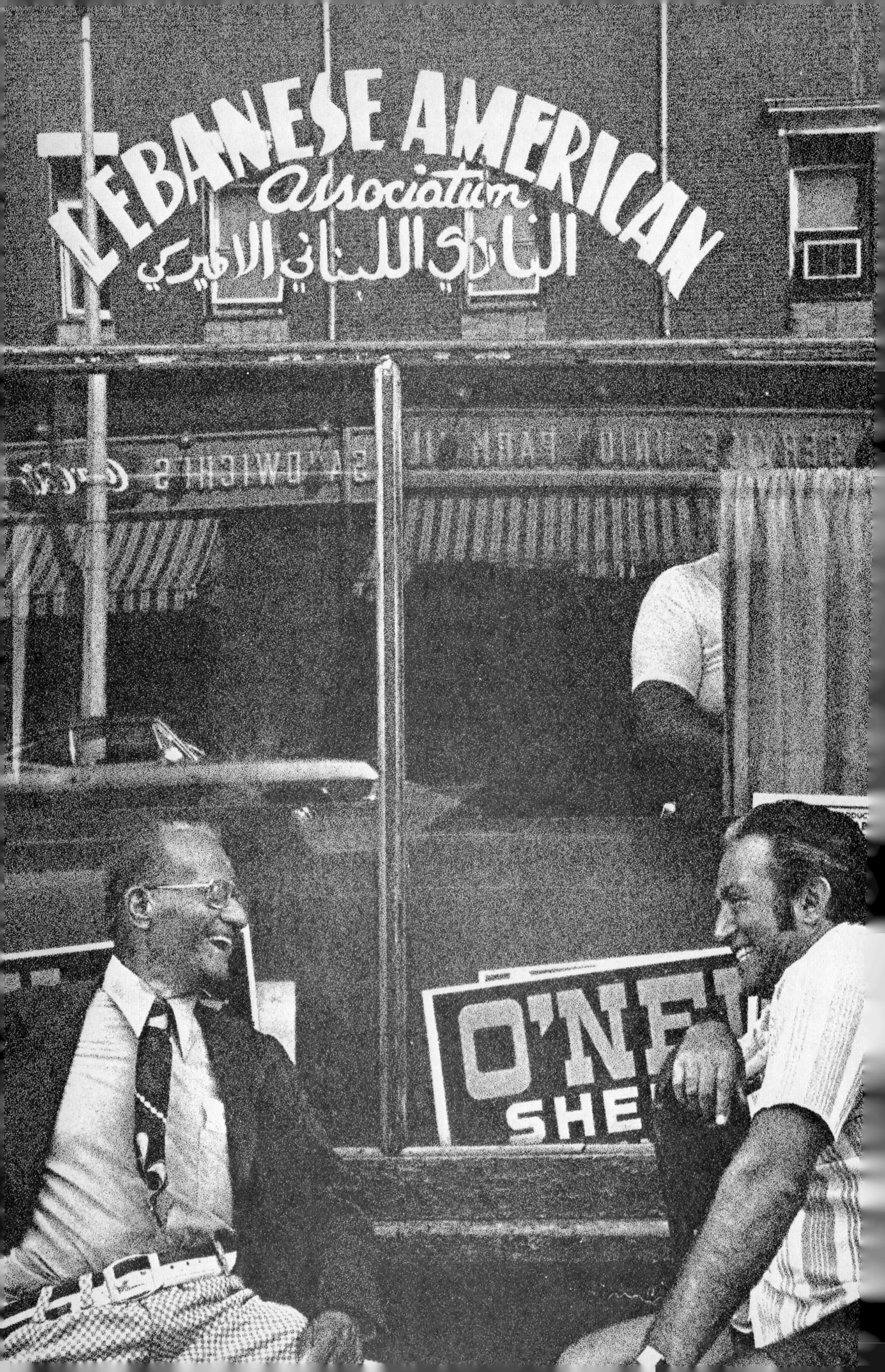
LEBANESE AMERICAN
Association
النادي اللبناني الاميركي

# CHAPTER · 7

# Residential Differentiation

## Chapter Outline

SOCIAL GEOGRAPHY
   Chicago School Maps
   The Prevalence of Social
     Differences
MEASURING SOCIAL DIFFERENTIATION
   Individual Cases
   Distributions
SOCIAL AREA ANALYSIS AND FACTORIAL ECOLOGY
   Social Area Analysis
   Factorial Ecology
SEGREGATION PATTERNS
   Stratification and Segregation

Ethnic Segregation
- Recent studies
- Hypotheses

Segregation by Family Status and Age
- Types of households
- Segregation of the elderly

DIFFERENTIATION THEORIES
   Economic Competition
   The Privileges of High Status
   Overcoming Density and
     Heterogeneity
   Sentiment and Symbolism
   Looking for Trust
SUMMARY

## SOCIAL GEOGRAPHY

### Chicago School Maps

Within the broader field of sociology, one special feature of urban sociology is its ongoing concern with spatial patterns. Since they began studying cities, sociologists have focused on spatial differentiation. Particularly in the University of Chicago group, they were addicted to mapping—plotting the distribution of all sorts of urban phenomena. E.W. Burgess, one of the leading professors of the Chicago school, wrote of the research beginnings:

> In every course I gave I am sure there were one or two students who made maps. I think the maps of juvenile delinquency were the first ones undertaken. They were followed by maps showing the distribution of motion picture houses. Then came maps showing the distribution of the patrons of the public dance halls. The students made maps of any data we could find in the city that could be plotted. (Burgess & Bogue, 1964, p. 6.)

Eventually, they mapped the locations of immigrant groups, status groups, mental illness cases, and many other phenomena. Figures 7-1 and 7-2 present typical social maps from studies of juvenile delinquency and neighborhoods.

Why were they so committed to mapping, a method usually tied to the discipline of geography? Certainly no other subfield of sociology has been particularly interested in the spatial dimensions of social phenomena. Burgess partially answers this question:

> [We were] discovering the Physical Pattern of the City. We were very impressed with the great differences between the various neighborhoods in the city, and one of our earliest goals was to try to find a pattern to this patchwork of differences and to "make sense of it." (Burgess & Bogue, 1964, p. 6.)

Robert E. Park, Burgess's senior colleague, asserted that a fundamental connection exists between spatial relations and social relationships. Park (1926) said that social relations are frequently and inevitably correlated with spatial relations and that physical distances frequently are, or seem to be, the indexes of social distances. Many empirical studies have verified these assertions over the years. Studies of racial and ethnic segregation have shown spatial divisions that correspond to social divisions. Timms (1971) makes this point trenchantly, saying, "Residential dissimilarity correlates highly with social distance: the less desirable a given group is as intimate role-partners for another, the greater will be their residential dissimilarity" (p. 3). Likewise, studies of social status have shown the separation of households with different ranks in the occupational hierarchy.

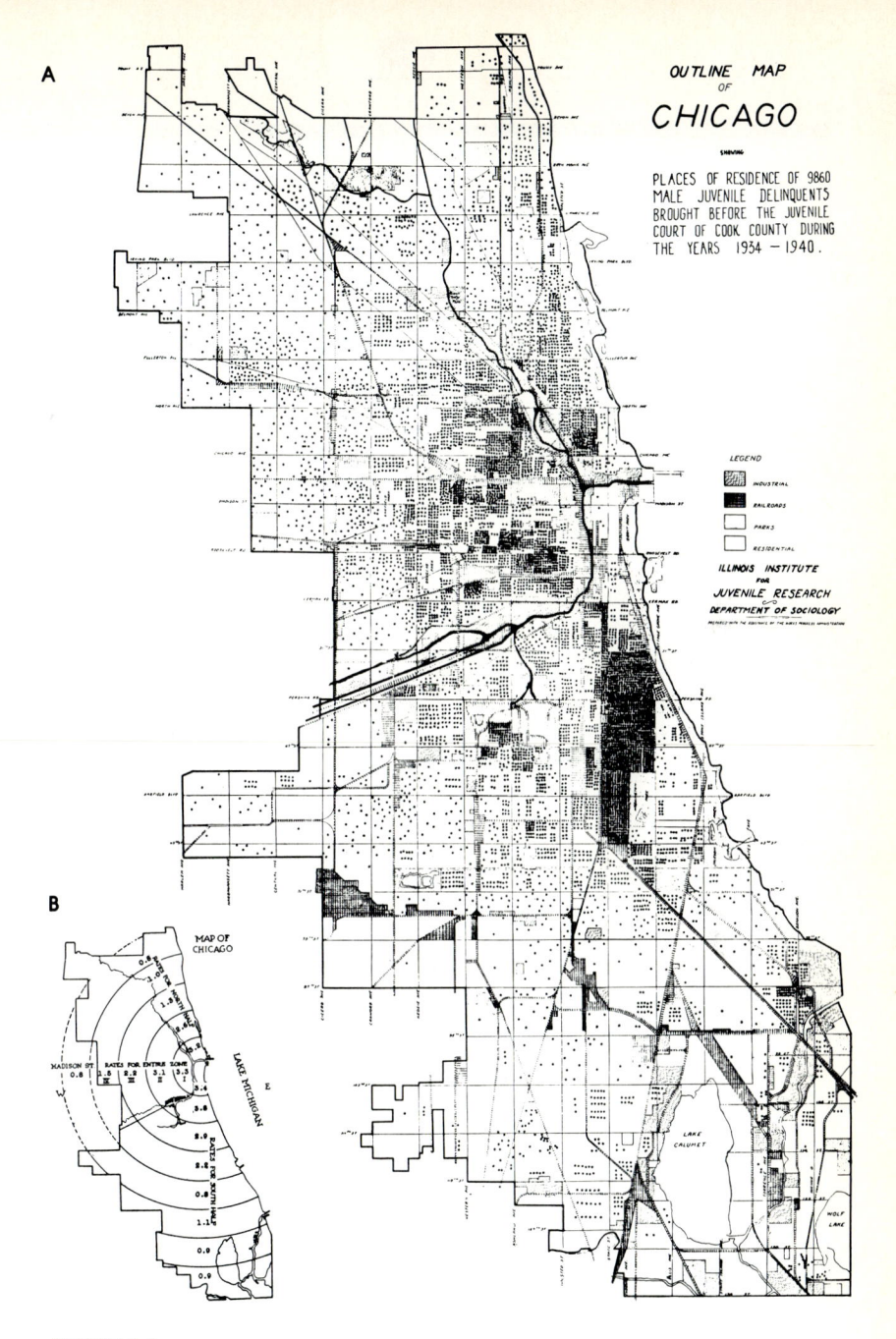

**FIGURE 7-1**
Two Chicago school maps. (A) This map plots data from a study of juvenile delinquency at the neighborhood level. Each dot represents the home address of a delinquent brought to court. (B) This more abstract map represents a search for a pattern, showing the offense rate in each concentric zone. (Source: Shaw & McKay, 1942.)

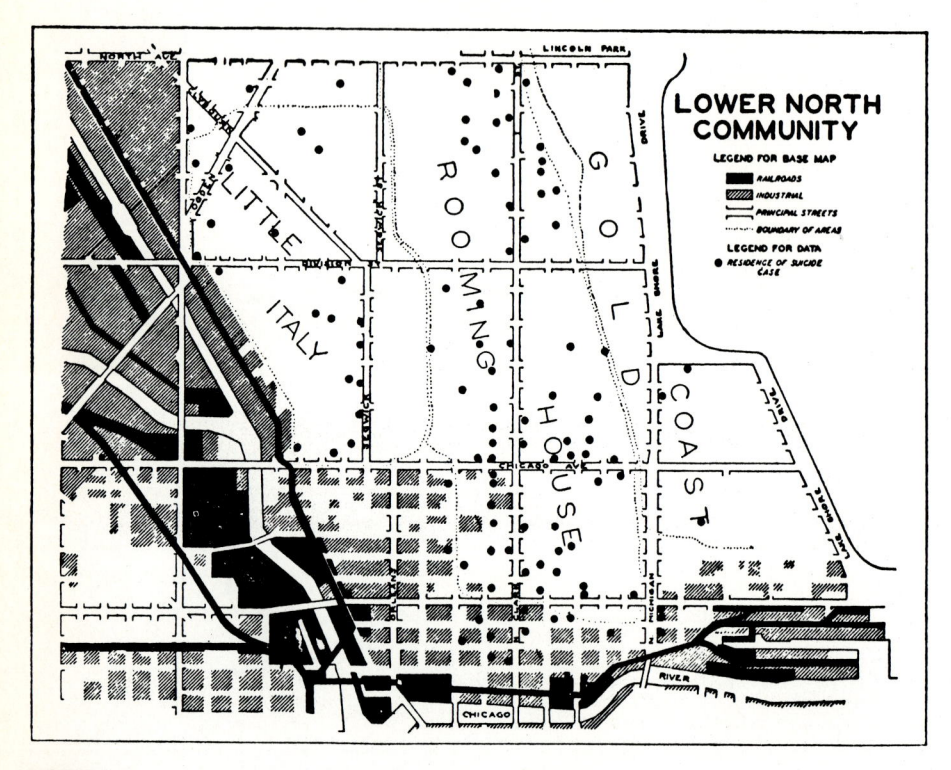

**FIGURE 7-2**
Suicide map from *The Gold Coast and the Slum.* After excluding industrial and railroad areas, the author divided the area into three parts: the Gold Coast, to the east; the roominghouse district, in the center; and "Little Italy," to the west. Each dot represents the address of a suicide between 1919 and 1922. As the author noted, "Suicide tends to concentrate in roominghouse areas." (Source: Zorbaugh, 1929.)

## Prevalence of Social Differences

Large cities everywhere are internally differentiated along social dimensions, particularly by social status; that is, neighborhoods or districts differ—some house the middle class, others are lower-class slums, etc. The community's households are sorted into different residential areas, as sociological and geographical research throughout the world has shown. (For examples from widely different cities, see Abu-Lughod, 1971, on Cairo; McElrath, 1962, on Rome; and Weinstein, 1974, on Madras.) In some cities in the past, differences among urban quarters were objectified by the erection of walls within the city. An individual could pass from one quarter to another only through a door which was likely to be locked at night.

## MEASURING SOCIAL DIFFERENTIATION

### Individual Cases

Information from just a small number of census tracts will show some of the measurable differences among urban residential areas. Figure 7-3 presents social statistics about three census tracts in the greater Los Angeles metropolitan area in 1970. A very few facts about these tracts will indicate that they are quite unlike each other. The statistics should also demonstrate that the "dry and dusty numbers" of the census can provide lively insights into communities.

The three graphs are "age-sex pyramids." Each is essentially two bar graphs, or histograms, set back to back. The one toward the left of the vertical center line represents males in the population, and the one toward the right represents females. Each bar represents the percentage of the total tract population in that age-sex category; thus, for example, the longest bar on the left side of the graph of Anaheim's tract 0219.01, toward the bottom, shows that more than 12 percent of the people there are boys between the ages of 5 and 14. The shapes of the three age-sex pyramids are quite different. The first two have broad bases and small tops; the third, in contrast, has a broad top and a small base. This shows that the first two are youthful, growing populations consisting of many children and young adults but very few older people. (They are by no means perfectly alike, though.) The third is a very elderly population, representing an area having many more old folks than children or young adults. In addition to showing the age compositions, the graphs also show the proportions male and female in the tract populations. In the Anaheim tract the bars are roughly equal on both sides, showing equal numbers of males and females in most age categories. This is reflected in the sex ratio of 101.1, which means that the population there has 101 males for every 100 females. The sex ratio in the elderly Los Angeles tract is radically different, though, with many more females than males in all the older age categories, starting at 45. This reflects the differential mortality of males and females at the older ages and the preponderance of widows in an elderly community such as this one. The sex ratio (78.6) shows that there are about 79 males for every 100 females in the area. If we were to recompute the sex ratio for the older age categories alone, it would show a greater imbalance yet. The age-sex pyramid is a simple but effective tool for showing basic demographic facts about a population. These comments have not exploited all the information contained in these three examples. The smallness of the bars representing ages 0 to 4 shows the declining birth rates in the years preceding the 1970 census. The proportions in different age categories can be used to understand the economic dependence of working and nonworking groups, and with additional censuses, the analyst can discover the direction of change in the individual community.

Five other numbers for each tract show that they differ in other ways as well. In terms of racial and ethnic composition, none of the areas is highly integrated; two

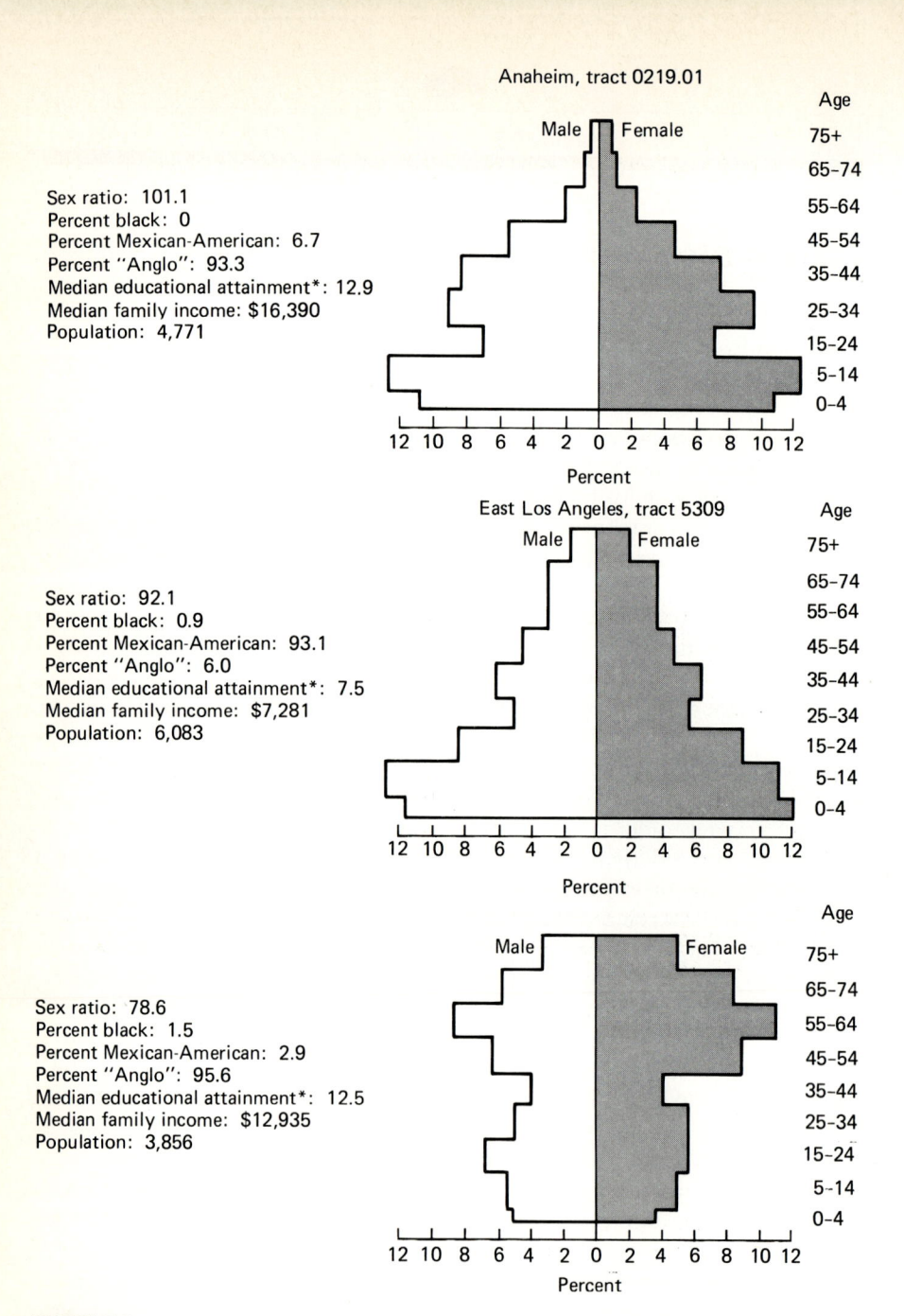

**Anaheim, tract 0219.01**

Sex ratio: 101.1
Percent black: 0
Percent Mexican-American: 6.7
Percent "Anglo": 93.3
Median educational attainment*: 12.9
Median family income: $16,390
Population: 4,771

**East Los Angeles, tract 5309**

Sex ratio: 92.1
Percent black: 0.9
Percent Mexican-American: 93.1
Percent "Anglo": 6.0
Median educational attainment*: 7.5
Median family income: $7,281
Population: 6,083

Sex ratio: 78.6
Percent black: 1.5
Percent Mexican-American: 2.9
Percent "Anglo": 95.6
Median educational attainment*: 12.5
Median family income: $12,935
Population: 3,856

**FIGURE 7-3**
Social statistics of three census tracts in metropolitan Los Angeles. Notice the gross difference in age composition among these residential areas. They differ also in sex ratio, ethnicity, and socioeconomic status. *Anglo represents 100 percent minus percent Hispanic. **Educational attainments represents median school years completed by persons 25 years of age and older. (Source: U.S. Bureau of the Census, 1970.)

are predominantly "Anglo" with very few blacks or Latinos, and one is composed predominantly of persons with Spanish surnames or who speak Spanish, which was the Census Bureau's way of identifying Latino populations—in east Los Angeles these are, presumably, mostly Mexican-Americans. Major disparities also exist in socioeconomic status among the three tracts, with east Los Angeles far poorer than the others, showing far less educational attainment as well as lower incomes. The adults of the Anaheim and Los Angeles tracts are not far apart in educational attainment, but the family income levels are higher in the Anaheim area. Further analysis, though, might reveal equal incomes per capita in these two areas, as the Anaheim tract has families with children while the Los Angeles tract, by and large, does not.

The facts in Figure 7-3 illustrate ways in which residential areas differ. These particular items were chosen from among hundreds which might have been presented to describe the populations and their environments. The census also reports on the amount of area; the population density; the kinds, costs, and conditions of the houses and apartments; the national origins of the foreign-born residents; and many other pieces of information about every metropolitan census tract in the nation—all 32,773 of them as of 1970—every ten years.

## Distributions

Urban social scientists, such as sociologists, economists, and geographers, usually examine statistical patterns among numerous areas rather than looking at individual cases. Figure 7-4 shows all the census tracts in one large city, Houston, and allows the analyst to see how residential areas vary overall. The city has 337 tracts, and each little bar graph shows how they vary along one dimension, or variable. Consider variation in age composition, for example. The fifth graph shows what proportion of elderly persons (over age 64) lives in each tract. The tallest bar, toward the left of the graph, shows that more than 40 tracts have only 3 percent elderly persons; the other two very tall bars show that about 38 tracts have 4 percent elderly and 40 tracts have 5 percent elderly. All the tall bars represent tracts with less than 10 percent elderly; thus, the distribution is skewed in one direction, toward nonelderly populations. On the other hand, the right-hand edge of the graph shows a few exceptional tracts with more than 20 percent of the people over age 64. The other graphs may be interpreted similarly; the third shows that most tracts have households of between three and four persons, although a handful of tracts have very small households. Most tracts are composed of single-family detached houses; reading from right to left in the first graph, one sees the number of tracts with increasing proportions of multifamily housing—apartments, duplexes, and the like. Again, it should be noted that these eight bar graphs represent a tiny sample of the ways in which residential areas vary, and other variations could be graphed and interpreted following the same procedure as that

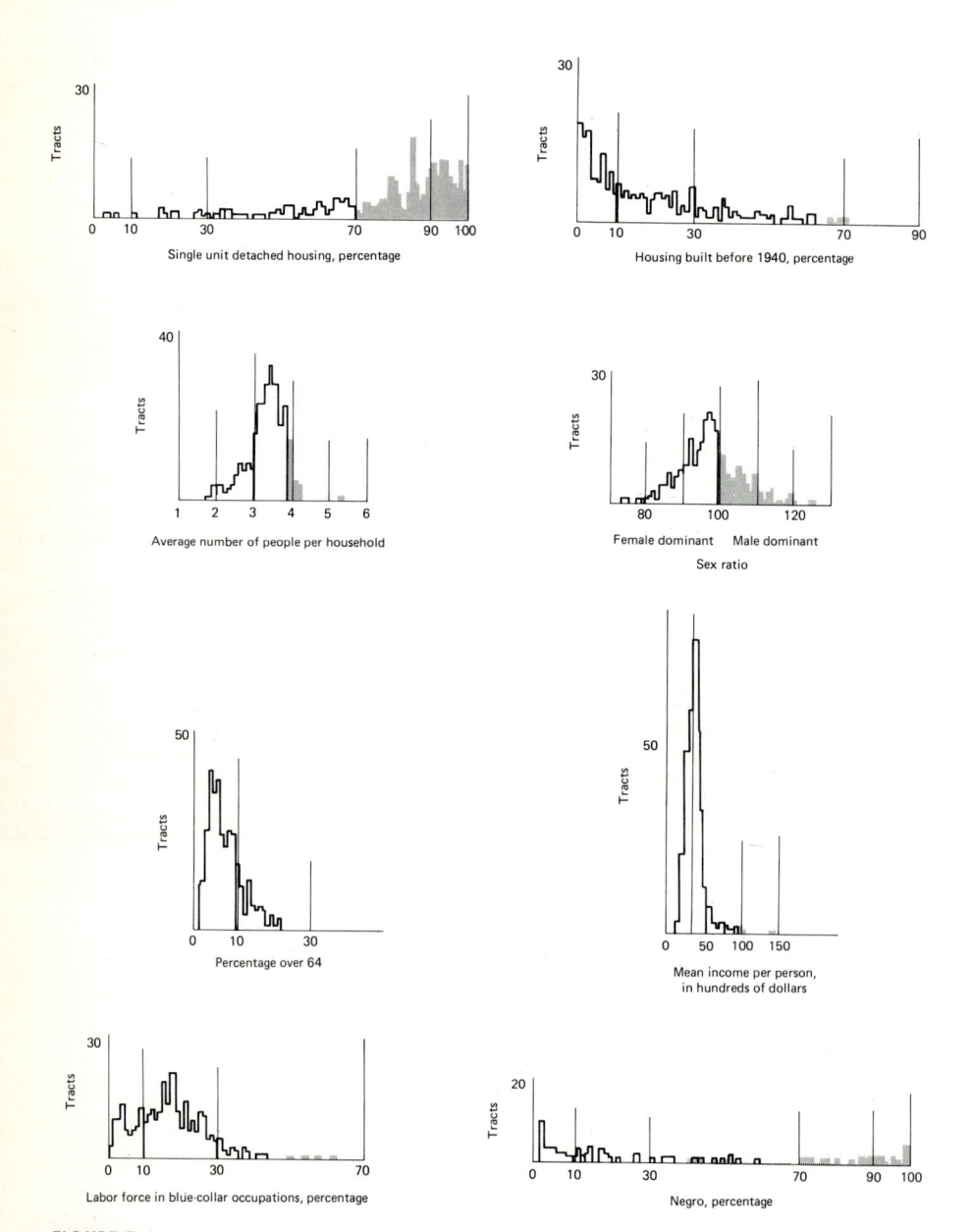

**FIGURE 7-4**
Variability among census tracts in the Houston SMSA, 1970. Total number of tracts equals 337. (Source: Abler & Adams, 1976, Chap. 21.)

employed here. In sum, the lesson of Figures 7-3 and 7-4 is that the residential areas of each metropolis vary considerably along several social dimensions and that this variance is revealed in census tract statistics.

## SOCIAL AREA ANALYSIS AND FACTORIAL ECOLOGY

Chapter 4 introduced the concentric circles model of the city's social patterns, with different social classes and immigrant generations arranged in zones surrounding a single center. The beginning of this chapter presented the statistical elements that may be used to analyze neighborhood differentiation employing other approaches. In the late 1940s, social scientists on the West Coast began to develop a new way to examine this differentiation and to look for spatial patterns. They introduced an approach known as "social area analysis," which later evolved into "factorial ecology."

### Social Area Analysis

The researchers who introduced social area analysis (Shevky & Bell, 1955; Shevky & Williams, 1949) posited three principal dimensions differentiating residential areas: social rank, urbanization, and segregation. "Social rank" was their name for socioeconomic status, the wealth and prestige of the residents of an area. "Urbanization" was a concept representing whether the area embodied traditional family types and detached housing structures. And "segregation" represented the extent to which some particular racial or immigrant group (excluding native-born nonethnic whites) predominated in an area. These researchers assumed that social rank, urbanization, and segregation were the "factors necessary to account for the observed social differentiation between urban subpopulations" (Shevky & Bell, 1955, p. 18).

In the censuses of 1940 and 1950 for Los Angeles and San Francisco, they found tract-level variables that could be used to represent the three principal dimensions. Accordingly, they measured the social rank of each tract by determining the occupations of adult workers, particularly what proportion were craftspersons, operatives, and laborers, and the educational level of the adults, specifically what proportion had only a grade school education or less. (For 1940 they also looked at the rental levels of each area.) Shevky and Williams wrote that an area with many craftspersons, operatives, and laborers, many persons who had completed grade school only, and low rent indicated low social rank. The second index, urbanization, was computed from three other variables: the fertility of the women in the area, the proportion of women who were in the labor force, and the proportion of dwelling units that were single-family detached houses. "A high index shows low fertility, many women in the labor force, and few single-family dwelling units" (Shevky & Williams, 1949, p. 35). In other words, their concept of a highly urbanized residential area was one where people lived in apartment buildings, they had small families and few children, and the women worked outside the home. In developing their third index, they noted that certain areas of every city are populated largely by a single nationality or racial group. They considered such groups to be isolated, and they developed an index of segregation to represent this phenomenon. In their study of the social areas of Los Angeles, they looked specifically at the segregation of five subpopulations: blacks, Mexicans and Mexican-Americans, Orientals, persons born in Russia (mostly Jewish), and persons born in Italy. These tract-level variables are like the ones depicted in Figures 7-3 and 7-4 except that these new ones are *composite* variables constructed by combining two or more of the elementary variables.

One goal of the originators of social area analysis was to develop a "typology" of residential areas. A typology is a set of categories, kinds, or types of objects, and its development is a common and powerful tool in science. In this case, the objective was to see whether identifiable types of neighborhoods existed in contemporary metropolitan areas. In order to develop types by means of the three indexes, the investigators had to assume that the three varied independently of each other. This implied that if a residential area had high social rank, it might be high or low on urbanization, for example. Shevky and Williams suggested that there were 18 types of social areas (see Table 7-1). They divided social rank into "high," "average," and "low," did the same to urbanization, and crossclassified them to establish a set of nine types of areas. Thus there were nine types of unsegregated areas and an additional nine types of segregated areas.

**TABLE 7-1**
**Los Angeles Census Tracts by Social Area Types**

|  | Social rank |  |  |
|---|---|---|---|
|  | Low | Average | High |
| **Low index of segregation (unsegregated tracts)** | | | |
| Urbanization | | | |
| High | ... | 60 | 15 |
| Average | 28 | 205 | 62 |
| Low | 5 | 26 | 23 |
| **High index of segregation (segregated tracts)** | | | |
| Urbanization | | | |
| High | 8 | 19 | |
| Average | 53 | 45 | |
| Low | 8 | 10 | 2 |

*Source:* Adapted from Shevky and Williams, 1949.

After measuring each of Los Angeles's tracts for the 1940 census, Shevky and Williams assigned each of them to a type, as shown in Table 7-1. Lending further detail to their report, the authors even presented the names of some areas which fell into each type. The names given in Table 7-2 are just a small sample, showing only places with low segregation scores. Similarly the authors published the names of some highly segregated areas—including Little Tokyo, Boyle Heights, and Watts—divided into types. Following the Los Angeles study, Shevky and Bell (1955) examined the residential areas of the San Francisco Bay region at two points in time, 1940 and 1950. Basically, they followed the logic and procedures established in the first research project, although they made some modifications. Bell (1955) introduced the statistical method known as "factor analysis" to determine that the variables in the indexes were closely enough related to be combined. Shevky and Bell also refined the typology to generate 16 types under each condition of segregation by dividing the two main variables into quarters instead of thirds. (This suggests, of course, that the typology could be divided arbitrarily into any number of cells depending upon the judgment of the analyst.) One advantage of the San Francisco study was that Shevky and Bell were able to look at change over a ten-year period.

After the publication of the California studies, other sociologists (Anderson & Bean, 1961; Van Arsdol, Camilleri, & Schmid, 1958) tested and modified social area analysis. One early modification was that the term "urbanization" was quickly replaced by "family status" (Bell, 1955) or, occasionally, "familism." The variables representing this dimension shifted over time and tended increasingly to measure whether or not a residential area housed families with children. Another modification which stuck was the wedding of factor analysis to social area analysis. This combined approach became quite popular, particularly among urban geographers, and literally dozens of cities around the world were analyzed in this mode in the

**TABLE 7-2**
**Names of Selected Social Areas in Metropolitan Los Angeles**

|  | Social Rank | | |
| --- | --- | --- | --- |
| | Low | Average | High |
| **Urbanization** | | | |
| High | | Echo Park<br>Exposition Park | Wilshire<br>Hollywood |
| Average | Bell Gardens<br>Firestone Park | Alhambra<br>Highland Park<br>North Hollywood | Beverly Hills<br>Glendale-North<br>Pacific Palisades |
| Low | Hawthorne<br>Roscoe | Garvey<br>Reseda<br>Temple City | Flintridge<br>San Marino<br>Santa Anita Oaks |

*Source:* Adapted from Shevky and Williams, 1949.

late 1950s and throughout the 1960s. (See the review essays and bibliographies by Rees, 1972, and Timms, 1971, to appreciate the range of this analysis.) As this research proceeded, it quickly shed the limitations of two socioeconomic variables and three family status variables, as well as the objective of developing a typology, and moved toward a search for broad spatial patterns. In this new form the research also took a new name.

## Factorial Ecology

Perhaps the greatest difference between social area analysis and factorial ecology is that the newer approach rejected the assumption that there are necessarily only three dimensions differentiating residential areas and that they can be specified a priori. Using factor analysis, researchers could search inductively among many tract-level variables to discover which ones were closely interrelated. Social scientists had increasing access to high-speed computers in the 1960s and 1970s, and this liberated them to a large extent from the laborious calculations that had previously been necessary to conduct statistical analyses. This facilitated the sorts of searches that were possible with factor analysis plus many pieces of information about many census tracts. Studies in factorial ecology incorporated increasing numbers of primary variables—for example, a study of Canada's largest metropolitan areas began with no less than 113 variables, which the analysts later trimmed to 63 (Foggin & Polese, cited in Yeates & Garner, 1980). Another study of a Canadian city, Toronto, employed 83 primary census variables (Murdie, 1969). A large study of 13 U.S. metropolitan areas (Rees, 1979) was based upon a total of 61 variables, 41 referring to characteristics of the tract population and 20 to housing. The third column of Table 7-3 lists many of the primary variables and certainly represents an expansion of the 11 variables of the first Los Angeles study.

Factorial-ecology studies of dozens of North American cities (reviewed by Rees, 1979) reveal that three basic factors always emerge—socioeconomic status, family status, and a minority group, or ethnic, factor. Different analysts may give different names to the factors, but they emerge nonetheless. The socioeconomic factor usually contains some or all of the following primary variables: educational attainment, the occupational mix, income, house value or rent paid, and possessions. (The U.S. Census collects information on automobiles, televisions, and other possessions.) The family-status factor usually contains some or all of the following primary variables: median age, size and type of household, fertility, and age and type of housing. The minority group, or ethnic, dimension may generate more than one factor, depending upon the number of nationalities living in the metropolitan area studied (Rees, 1979).

Rees discovered that all 13 of the areas studied had a factor representing socioeconomic-status and that the variables fell together in remarkably similar patterns to create these factors. Table 7-4 presents the socioeconomic-status (SES) factor from Minneapolis-St. Paul, one of the metropolitan areas he analyzed, and shows

**TABLE 7-3**
**Variables in a Factorial Ecology Study of American Cities**

| Main concept | Variable subset | Primary variable |
|---|---|---|
| \multicolumn{3}{c}{**Population variables**} | | |
| Socioeconomic status | Education | Median school years<br>% Grade school<br>% College |
|  | Occupation (1) | % White collar<br>% Blue collar |
|  | Income | Median income of families<br>% Under $4,000<br>% $10,000 or more |
|  | Occupation (2) | % in each of eight occupations.<br>% Unemployed |
| Family status | Age | Median age (male):<br>% Under 15<br>% 65 and Over |
|  | Women in the labor force | % Women in the labor force |
| Ethnic status | Racial status | % Black<br>% Other nonwhite |
|  | Nativity | % Foreign born |
|  | National origin | % from Sweden, Norway, Poland, and 10 other countries. |
| \multicolumn{3}{c}{**Housing variables**} | | |
| Housing worth | Housing value | Median home value<br>Less than $10,000<br>$20,000 or more |
|  | Housing rent | Median rent<br>Under $40<br>$100 or more |
| Housing type | Structure type | % 1 unit<br>% 3 or more units |
|  | Age of structure | % Built before 1940<br>% Built 1950–1960 |
|  | Tenure | % Owner occupied<br>% Renter occupied |

*Source:* adapted from Rees, 1979, tables 5 and 6.

that the SES factor, as usual, is composed of variables representing education, occupation, and income. Some of the variables have "plus" marks, indicating they are positively related to the factor. Thus the higher the proportion white collar, the higher the SES score; the higher the median family income, the higher the SES score. Other variables have "minus" marks, indicating they are negatively related to the factor. Thus the lower the proportion of individuals with a low level of

**TABLE 7-4**
**Example of a Basic Socioeconomic Status Factor, Minneapolis–St. Paul, 1960**

| Factor loading | Variable |
|---|---|
| +.97 | Occupation: percent white collar |
| +.94 | Education: percent ever attending college |
| +.87 | Income: percent $10,000 or more, families |
| +.85 | Education: median years completed, adults |
| +.85 | Occupations: percent professional* |
| +.85 | Occupations: percent managerial |
| +.80 | Income: family median |
| +.76 | Occupations: percent sales workers |
| +.41 | National origin: United Kingdom |
| −.97 | Occupation: percent blue collar |
| −.86 | Education: percent attending grade school or less |
| −.85 | Occupations: percent operatives |
| −.68 | Occupations: percent laborers |
| −.60 | Percent unemployed |
| −.58 | Income: percent $4,000 or less, families |
| −.56 | Occupations: percent service workers |
| −.46 | Occupations: percent craftspersons |

*Occupational data in Rees's study refer to males and females in the labor force. Most studies referred to males only.
Source: Rees, 1979, table 8.

education, the higher the SES score; the lower the percent unemployed, the higher the SES score. Noting the consistency of the SES factors across all 13 areas studied, Rees (1979) commented:

> This consistency implies that socioeconomic status is a universal sorting principle in American cities. People of like social rank tend to live together and apart from those of unlike rank. Residential areas in American cities are clearly arranged in a consistent fashion along a common and unidimensional scale of socioeconomic status. (p. 47)

Unlike the social area analysts, Rees contends that race is not independent of socioeconomic status in most cities. He discovered a factor that he called "race and resources" in an earlier study of Chicago and again in several studies of other cities. This factor shows the close association between percent black and poverty indicators at the tract level in 7 of the 10 cities that did not have large Hispanic populations. Table 7-5 shows a race-and-resources factor for Richmond, Virginia, revealing the high degree of correspondence between the proportion black and low-status occupations (such as laborer), families in the lowest income category, and crowded households. Rees notes that in some southwestern cities such as El Paso, Texas and Riverside, California, which have large Hispanic populations, a similar factor emerges with percent Mexican-American substituted for percent black.

**TABLE 7-5**
**Example of a Race-and-Resources Factor: Richmond, Virginia, 1960**

| Factor loading | Variable |
|---|---|
| +.80 | Percent black |
| +.81 | Occupations: percent service workers |
| +.69 | Occupations: percent laborers |
| +.67 | Income: percent $4,000 or less, families |
| +.53 | Percent unemployed |
| +.51 | Percent households with 6 or more persons |
| +.43 | Occupations: percent blue collar |
| −.83 | Occupations: percent craftspersons |
| −.73 | Occupations: percent clerical |
| −.60 | National origin: Czechoslovakia |
| −.42 | Occupations: percent white collar |
| −.41 | Occupations: percent sales workers |

Source: Rees, 1979, table 10.

Family status, like SES, emerged as a factor in each metropolitan area, and the constituent variables were quite consistent (Rees, 1979). Table 7-6, representing the family-status factor for Des Moines, Iowa, is typical.... The results show that the variables representing small households and high proportion of elderly population are included in the factor and, negatively, that high proportions of children and many large households are also tied to the factor. A tract with a high score on this family-status factor tends *not* to have families with children. Thus, mentally, the reader must reverse the pluses and minuses in order to appreciate the results in Table 4 intuitively. Rees's summary of the family-status factor says that tracts with high scores have elderly populations and small size (although some tracts with high scores have concentrations of young, single persons). Tracts with negative scores

**TABLE 7-6**
**Example of a Family-Status Factor: Des Moines, Iowa, 1960***

| Factor loading | Variable |
|---|---|
| +.96 | Percent households with 1 or 2 persons |
| +.87 | Percent age 65 and over |
| +.84 | Median age, male |
| −.96 | Percent under age 15 |
| −.88 | Persons per household |
| −.82 | Percent households with 6 or more persons |

*List does not report associated ethnic and socioeconomic variables.
Source: Rees, 1979, table 14.

tend to have young populations with larger-than-average households. One major departure from social area analysis in this study is that in many cities women's labor force participation was not necessarily associated with the family-status variables.

Research in factorial ecology has shown that the socioeconomic and family-status factors are independent of each other but SES and race-ethnicity usually are not. Rees (1979) noted, "Most studies of cities located in the northern and western portions of the United States and in Canada have found that social status and family status emerged as independent dimensions" (p. 18). His results from 13 metropolitan areas were consistent with this generalization. On the other hand, cities vary considerably as to the strength of association between race and ethnic status; in the extreme cases race may be very closely associated with socioeconomic status, negatively.

Factorial ecology, then, is a widely used method for analyzing the residential areas of metropolitan areas, using detailed census data. While it is not used to build typologies of tracts, it does disclose the major dimensions which differentiate residential areas and it reveals the associations between the factors. As shown later in this chapter, the results of factorial-ecology studies can also contribute to the development of large-scale sociospatial patterns of metropolitan areas.

## SEGREGATION PATTERNS

Another approach to analyzing sociospatial differentiation is to study the segregation patterns of the metropolis—asking, "Who doesn't live with whom?" There have been numerous studies of U.S. urban communities using this approach, examining segregation along several dimensions, including race, nationality, occupation, family status, and age. There have been more studies of segregation by *race* than by the other dimensions, and these are presented separately in Chapter 8.

The sociologist is interested in spatial differentiation as an objectification of social relations. Park (1926), who may be called the father of the Chicago school, put forth this idea in a somewhat exaggerated manner, stating, "It is because social relations are so frequently and inevitably correlated with spatial relations; because physical distances so frequently are, or seem to be, the indexes of social distances, that statistics have any significance whatever for sociology" (p. 18).

### Stratification and Segregation

Social stratification, also known as structured social inequality or social class, has long been of interest to sociologists. In modern societies, occupations are rewarded differentially, in wealth and income as well as in prestige. The ranking of occupations is one good indicator of the stratification system, and sociologists have measured the rankings of occupations and developed standardized ways of ordering them. For example, Table 7-7 presents the rankings of occupations according to

**TABLE 7-7**
Rankings of Urban Occupations and Occupational Groups

| Occupation* | Prestige | Socioeconomic |
|---|---|---|
| Professional, technical | 59 | 68.6 |
|     Accountants | 62 | 70.2 |
|     Civil engineers | 70 | 75.3 |
|     Drafters | 55 | 46.3 |
| Managers and administrators | 53 | 51.1 |
|     Construction and inspectors | 61 | 38.9 |
|     Postmasters and mail superintendents | 58 | 45.2 |
| Sales workers | 39 | 42.3 |
|     Sales representatives, wholesale trade | 47 | 47.3 |
| Clerical | 42 | 32.0 |
|     Bank tellers | 48 | 33.5 |
|     Insurance adjusters, examiners, and investigators | 49 | 58.5 |
|     Keypunch operators | 45 | 32.2 |
| Craftspersons and kindred workers | 39 | 25.6 |
|     Bakers | 33 | 18.5 |
|     Compositors and typesetters | 42 | 28.1 |
|     Motion picture projectionists | 34 | 30.0 |
| Operatives, except transport | 32 | 18.2 |
|     Meatcutters and butchers, manufacturing | 18 | 18.5 |
|     Welders and flame cutters | 39 | 19.8 |
| Transport-equipment operatives | 30 | 20.4 |
|     Bus drivers | 32 | 21.2 |
|     Parking attendants | 24 | 19.2 |
| Laborers | 21 | 16.0 |
|     Garbage collectors | 13 | 15.0 |
|     Longshoremen and stevedores | 21 | 21.8 |
| Service workers, except private household | 29 | 20.8 |
|     Chambermaids and maids, except private household | 14 | 15.7 |
|     Barbers | 30 | 18.2 |
|     Firefighters, fire protection | 35 | 32.7 |
| Private household workers | 20 | 14.0 |

*Group titles are the broad occupational groups of the U.S. census, and their scores are averages for all occupations in these groups. The specific occupations indented and listed under the group titles are illustrative examples chosen from among the dozens of positions that are rated in the full reports.

Source: Prestige rankings are from Treiman, 1977, Appendix C.4. Socioeconomic rankings are from Stevens and Featherman, 1981, their MSE 12 index.

two different ranking systems: average rankings for broad occupational categories, such as professional and technical, craftspersons, and the like, and rankings for a very small selection of specific occupations. The scores were produced by two systems, the first based upon prestige, as determined by public opinion surveys, and the second based upon the income and educational levels of the workers in that occupation. While the two scores are not equal for most occupations, both systems tend to rank the occupations similarly, from high to low. This ordering and the index scores imply that more social distance exists between civil engineers and bus drivers than between postmasters and drafters, to use Park's terminology. Research on occupational segregation attempts to discover the extent to which different occupational groups occupy exclusive residential areas. By extension, studying the segregation of occupational groups should give some insight into the spatial patterning of social classes, if occupations are taken as surrogate indicators of the stratification system. Furthermore, exclusive residential areas may be taken as one of the differential rewards of status, with higher-status groups getting neighborhoods with newer houses, better location, and more open space and lower-status groups getting less of all the residential amenities. Differential location by occupation and class was suggested in the concentric circles model and was further elaborated upon and measured as part of the social rank indicator of social area analysis, but the relationship between residence and occupation was more explicitly and thoroughly examined by Duncan and Duncan (1955).

These two sociologists studied the residential patterns of occupational groups, by census tract, in metropolitan Chicago. First, they examined the extent to which each general occupational category had its "own" residential areas. The results of this analysis are shown in the first numerical column of Table 7-8. The higher the score, the more likely the area is to house only people of the named occupational group; a perfectly segregated occupation would have a score of 100, but none approaches that level. The indexes of residential segregation show a U-shaped pattern, with the highest-and-lowest-ranked occupations most likely to live in segregated residential areas and the midrange occupations—clerical workers, craftspersons, and foremen—more likely to live in mixed areas. According to Duncan and

**TABLE 7-8**
**Indexes of Residential Segregation and Low-Rent Concentration of Each Major Occupation Group, for Employed Males in the Chicago Metropolitan District, 1950**

| Major occupation group* | By census tracts | Index of low-rent concentration (total employed persons) |
|---|---|---|
| Professional, technical, and kindred workers | 30 | −32 |
| Managers, officials, and proprietors, except farm | 29 | −30 |
| Sales workers | 29 | −25 |
| Clerical and kindred workers | 13 | −9 |
| Craftspersons, foremen, and kindred workers | 19 | 11 |
| Operatives and kindred workers | 22 | 29 |
| Service workers, except private household | 24 | 7 |
| Laborers, except farm and mine | 35 | 32 |

*Does not include farmers and farm managers, farm laborers, private household workers, and occupation not reported.
Source: Duncan and Duncan, 1955, tables 2 and 4.

Duncan (1955), "This finding suggests that residential segregation is greater for those occupational groups with clearly defined status than for those groups whose status is ambiguous" (p. 497). And, as might be expected, the analysis showed that the lower the status of an occupational group, the more likely it was to live in a low-rent census tract. This is reported in the last column of Table 7-8.

The main result of the study is that status differences correspond with spatial distances. As Table 7-9 shows, the greater the difference in rank between two occupational groups, the less likely they are to live in the same residential areas. Thus, reading across the top row, not much segregation (index of dissimilarity equals 13) exists between professionals and managers, much more segregation (35) occurs between professionals and upper-level blue-collar workers; and the highest level of segregation is between professionals and laborers (54). In most cases, not much segregation exists between one occupational group and the next-ranked group, moving upward or downward in the rank order. One anomalous finding in this table is that the clerical workers, despite their white-collar occupations, are more segregated from the higher white-collar occupations than they are from the blue-collar workers. Duncan and Duncan (1955) noted, "Clerical and kindred workers have substantially more education than craftsmen, foremen, and kindred workers, and the clerical occupations are usually considered of greater prestige" (p. 502). But craftsmen and foremen, on the average, have higher incomes. The fact, as revealed in Table 7-8, that clerical workers are not likely to live in low-rent districts means that they are paying high proportions of their incomes for housing. Duncan and Duncan refer to this discrepancy in the prestige, education, and residential pattern of the clerical workers as a case of status inconsistency.

Other researchers have replicated the original Chicago study in other places and with more recent data and have consistently confirmed the same pattern of segregation by occupation. Wheeler (1968) analyzed Pittsburgh for 1958 and found that its occupational groups were segregated like Chicago's. Rees (1979), in his exploration of 13 metropolitan areas, expanded the framework of analysis, asking what the pattern of segregation was, not only for occupational groups, but also for educational and income strata. Regarding occupations, in all the cities Rees found a strong and consistent pattern of residential segregation like the one reported in the first Chicago study. The division between the locations of white-collar and blue-collar groups was particularly striking. He commented, "The transition [in the tables] between clerical workers and craftspersons is always marked by a fairly substantial jump in the dissimilarity index value, a jump larger than that between any two other adjacent occupational groups" (p. 216). Rees found that educational and income segregation was even more perfectly patterned than occupational segregation. Table 7-10 shows one example of residential segregation, Honolulu, 1960, which is typical of his 13 cases. In summary, Rees wrote: "The relationship between social distance and spatial distance proves to be very strong when social distance is measured in terms of family income. The wider the gap separating the income of two families, the less likely they are to live together in the same neighborhood" (p. 223). Households were more severely segregated by income than by occupation or

> **BOX 7-1**
> **The Index of Dissimilarity**
>
> Many of the studies summarized in this chapter are based on an ecological statistic known as the "index of dissimilarity," or the "segregation index." Understanding the index will help the reader to understand the results of the studies. A researcher examines the segregation of any two categories of people—whites from blacks, people over age 65 from people under age 65, etc.—and computes the statistic over small geographical areas, usually census areas or blocks. The index score represents how segregated an entire large community is by considering the composition of its small component areas. A completely segregated community gets a score of 100, a completely integrated community gets a score of 0, and all intermediate scores are possible, indicating degrees of segregation or integration.
>
> The map illustrates a black-white segregation index for a hypothetical community that has 3,050 residents living in "10 areas." If it were completely integrated, each area would have 72 percent whites and 28 percent blacks, equal to the citywide proportions, but this is not the case. In order to compute the index, we compute the percentage of each race in each area; then we calculate the absolute difference between the percent white and the percent black, sum these differences, and divide by the number of tracts. In this case, as the map shows, the community is highly segregated, with an index score of 84.
>
> Fortunately, as Guest (1977) notes, "the index values have a substantive interpretation, indicating the percentage of one group that would have to change neighborhoods in order to be equally distributed with another group" (p. 329). In this case, in order to integrate our hypothetical community, almost 86 percent of the blacks would have to move out of their current tracts in order

education in all the areas he studied. Duncan and Duncan (1955) concluded that Park's basic idea was correct.

> The ecological analysis has provided strong support for the proposition that spatial distances between occupational groups are closely related to their social distances... that the most segregated groups are those at the extremes of the socioeconomic scale; that the concentration of residence in low-rent areas is inversely related to socioeconomic status. (p. 502)

## Hypothetical community

Black majority areas

50-50 integrated areas

Tract 1: 200 whites, 0 blacks
Tract 10: 200 whites, 0 blacks
Tract 9: 150 whites, 0 blacks
Tract 2: 500 whites, 0 blacks
Tract 3: 360 whites, 40 blacks
Tract 8: 270 whites, 30 blacks
Tract 4: 30 whites, 270 blacks
Tract 7: 100 whites, 100 blacks
Tract 5: 0 whites, 400 blacks
Tract 6: 400 whites, 0 blacks

Total population = 3,050
Whites = 2,210 or 72%
Blacks = 840 or 28%

| Tract | % white | % black | Absolute difference between col. (2) and col. (3) |
|---|---|---|---|
| 1 | 100 | 0 | 100 |
| 2 | 100 | 0 | 100 |
| 3 | 90 | 10 | 80 |
| 4 | 10 | 90 | 80 |
| 5 | 0 | 100 | 100 |
| 6 | 100 | 0 | 100 |
| 7 | 50 | 50 | 0 |
| 8 | 90 | 10 | 80 |
| 9 | 100 | 0 | 100 |
| 10 | 100 | 0 | 100 |

Sum = 840
(Divided by number of tracts, 10 = 84)

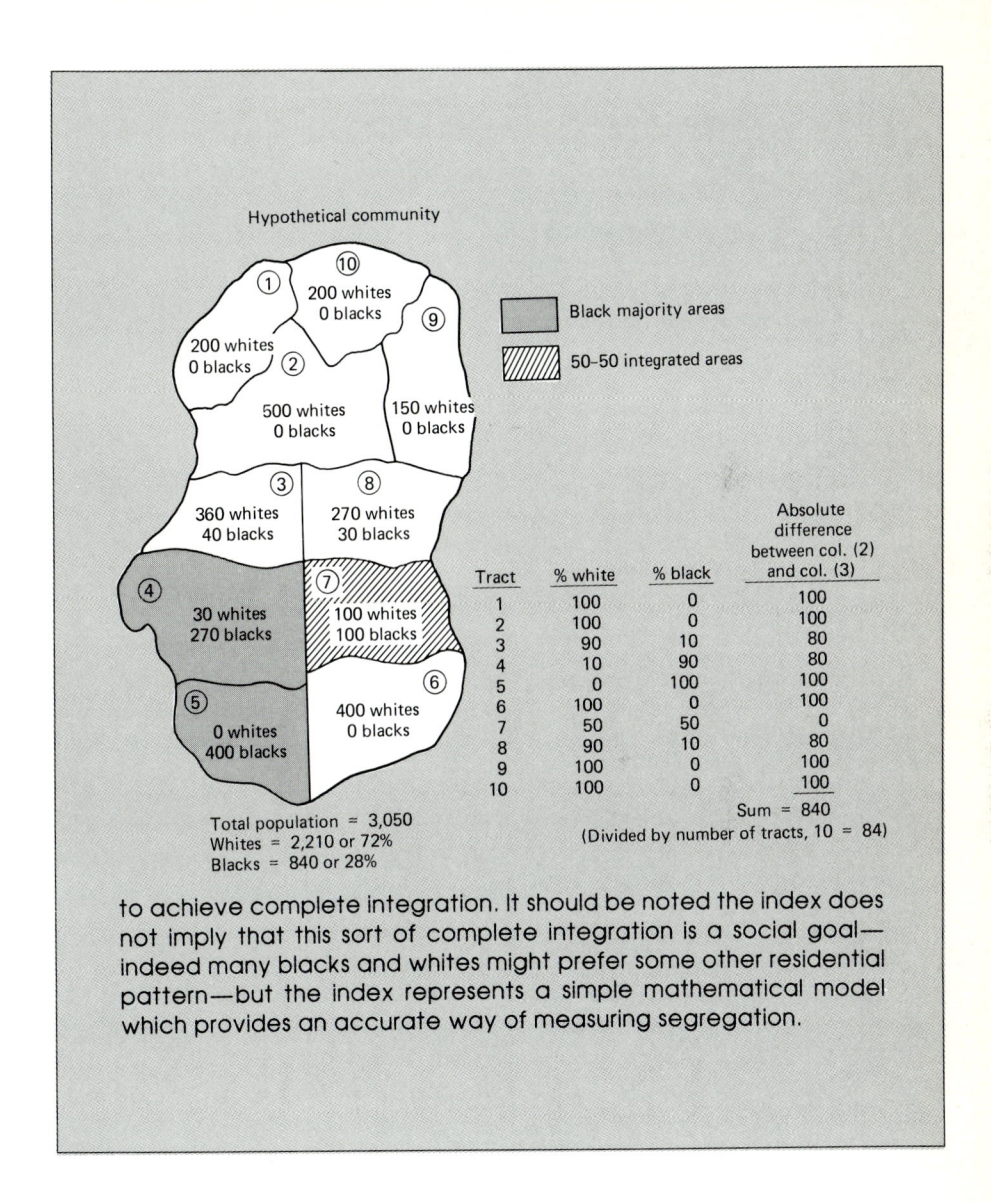

to achieve complete integration. It should be noted the index does not imply that this sort of complete integration is a social goal—indeed many blacks and whites might prefer some other residential pattern—but the index represents a simple mathematical model which provides an accurate way of measuring segregation.

## Ethnic Segregation

Urban sociologists have also been fascinated since the beginnings of their field by ethnic relations. Studying the burgeoning cities of the early twentieth century how could they fail to notice the European immigrants and their settlements? "Ethnicity" refers to differences by national origin of identifiable subpopulations. Ethnic groups usually have distinctive cultural patterns, especially language, but also including some or all of the following: clothing, food preferences, music, patterns

TABLE 7-9
Indexes of Dissimilarity in Residential Distribution among Major Occupation Groups, for Employed Males in the Chicago Metropolitan District, 1950

| Major occupation group[a] | Professional, technical, kindred workers | Managers, officials, and proprietors, except farm | Sales workers | Clerical and kindred workers | Craftspersons, foremen, kindred workers | Operatives, kindred workers | Service workers, except private household | Laborers, except farm and mine |
|---|---|---|---|---|---|---|---|---|
| Professional, technical, kindred workers | .... | 13 | 15 | 28 | 35 | 44 | 41 | 54 |
| Managers, officials, and proprietors, except farm | .... | .... | 13 | 28 | 33 | 41 | 40 | 52 |
| Sales workers | .... | .... | .... | 27 | 35 | 42 | 38 | 54 |
| Clerical and kindred workers | .... | .... | .... | 16 | 21 | 24 | 38 | .... |
| Craftspersons, foremen, kindred workers | .... | .... | .... | .... | .... | 17 | 35 | 35 |
| Operatives, kindred workers | .... | .... | .... | .... | .... | .... | 26 | 25 |
| Service workers, except private household | .... | .... | .... | .... | .... | .... | .... | 28 |
| Laborers, except farm and mine | | | | | | | | |

[a] Does not include farmers and farm managers, farm laborers, private household workers, and occupation not reported.
Source: Duncan and Duncan, 1955, table 3.

212

TABLE 7-10
Index of Dissimilarity for Educational Attainment Levels, Honolulu Urbanized Area, 1960

| Educational Category | Percent* | S† | 2 | 3 | 4 | 5 | 6 | 7 | 8 |
|---|---|---|---|---|---|---|---|---|---|
| 1. Number of school years completed | 5.01 | 36 | 24 | 25 | 30 | 34 | 40 | 54 | 57 |
| 2. Elementary: 1 to 4 years | 6.55 | 28 | .... | 14 | 20 | 25 | 33 | 49 | 52 |
| 3. Elementary: 5 to 7 years | 10.20 | 23 | .... | .... | 13 | 19 | 26 | 45 | 47 |
| 4. Elementary: 8 years | 10.21 | 16 | .... | .... | .... | 14 | 20 | 39 | 42 |
| 5. High school: 1 to 3 years | 16.13 | 13 | .... | .... | .... | .... | 15 | 32 | 37 |
| 6. High school: 4 years | 33.15 | 13 | .... | .... | .... | .... | .... | 24 | 28 |
| 7. College: 1 to 3 years | 8.22 | 29 | .... | .... | .... | .... | .... | .... | 15 |
| 8. College: 4 years or more | 10.53 | 34 | | | | | | | |

*Percent of urbanized area total in each category.
†S = index of dissimilarity.
Source: Rees, 1979, table 53.

of childrearing, and the like. Sometimes, as in the cases of Oriental immigrant groups, racial differences coincide with ethnic differences.

When the Chicago school was in its heyday, the leading theory of immigration and ethnic relations predicted that eventually immigrant groups would be absorbed into the broader American society and culture. This theory of assimilation underlies the central questions in the study of ethnic segregation.

Lieberson (1963) set forth the basic idea relating ethnic segregation and assimilation. He said that residential segregation tends to inhibit the assimilation of the group into the social structure; if it does not have this negative effect, at least it shows how unassimilated a particular group is if it is segregated. "Residential segregation maintains visibility and awareness of the status of the ethnic group both for its own members and for other segments of a city's population," he wrote (p. 6). Residential assimilation may have an effect on other aspects of ethnic assimilation, inhibiting individuals from obtaining education or employment, for example. He justified studying the segregation patterns of ethnic groups by saying that these patterns may be seen as a significant element in the assimilation of the ethnic groups.

More recent sociological discussions of the question do not necessarily agree that assimilation is a natural and necessary course for an ethnic group—contemporary analysts ask whether some degree of ethnic segregation will not persist in the social arrangements of cities and suburbs (Bleda, 1979; Kantrowitz, 1973).

In addition to weighing the question of assimilation versus persistence, segregation researchers have asked what accounts for the residential differentiation of ethnic groups. Is it simply a function of socioeconomic status and resources—are ethnic groups ranked and segregated because they have differential income levels and therefore acquire housing in different areas? Or is segregation a function of the length of time since the group immigrated?

An alternative point of view suggests that segregation is a function of ethnic status itself, not just a secondary consequence of SES. This argument, delineated by Darroch and Marston (1971), states that members of an ethnic group may desire to maintain their ethnic identity and may therefore prefer to live among others with similar backgrounds. They may find that they can better maintain their ethnic institutions when they live in an area with others of their subpopulation. This argument, then, posits a process of self-selection into ethnic neighborhoods.

These arguments may be distilled into three hypotheses:

1 *Assimilation:* Ethnic segregation tends to diminish over time and eventually will approach zero.
2 *Status effects:* Ethnic segregation, to the extent it exists, is a function of SES differences among ethnic groups.
3 *Ethnic status:* Ethnic segregation, to the extent it exists, is a function of ethnicity itself, not just of SES.

It should be noted that in American society ethnic groups are not ranked as occupations are. That is, ordinarily, one would not say people whose ancestors came from Hungary have more or less prestige than people whose ancestors came from Germany. At the turn of the century, a broad nativist political movement was aimed at limiting the inflow of foreigners. This movement came in the midst of, and partly as a reaction to, the enormous influx of immigrants from Europe. Between 1871 and 1900 there were 11.7 million immigrants, representing more than a quarter of what the total U.S. population had been in 1870 (39.8 million). A massive congressional report by the Immigration Commission of 1907 distinguished between the "old" immigration and the "new" immigration. The old immigration referred to groups arriving before 1850 who were from northwestern Europe and Germany; the new immigration was from southern and eastern Europe. Clearly, the commission made invidious comparisons between the two categories, with the old groups deemed to be superior. Furthermore, another implicit ranking was that native-born individuals whose parents were also native-born were superior to immigrants or the children of immigrants. This ordering underlies part of Lieberson's (1963) study, published in a book entitled *Ethnic Patterns in American Cities*.

Lieberson studied these patterns during a period, 1910 to 1950, when there were large numbers of immigrants and their children in the cities. Analyzing 10 cities, he found measurable levels of segregation. Immigrants were segregated from native whites, and groups of the "new immigration" were more segregated from native whites than groups of the "old immigration." (Incidentally, he found that immigrants were more segregated from blacks than they were from native whites.)

The results showed clearly that ethnic groups were becoming less segregated over time and across generations. "The segregation of foreign-born groups from each other and from native whites declined through the forty year period" (Lieberson, 1963, p. 14). The second-generation members of the groups were less segregated from each other and from native whites than were members of the immigrant generation. On the other hand, ethnic segregation did not disappear by 1950, and a degree of stability characterized the patterns regarding particular groups. "The relative positions of ethnic groups with respect to segregation from native whites and from each other were very similar in the years measured," according to Lieberson (p. 14).

### Recent studies

While the previous study examined the situation up to 1950, newer publications reported on the following two censuses. This research concludes that ethnic groups continue to be measurably segregated in the metropolitan areas. The New York SMSA, which had not previously been studied due to the vast amount of data generated in such a large population, had clear segregation patterns. The "segregation of European ethnic populations remains strong" in 1960, according to Kantrowitz (1973, p. 11). New York is an interesting case because such a large fraction of its population is of foreign stock—71 percent of the city and 64 percent of the metropolitan population. ("Foreign stock" is defined as foreign-born or native-born persons with at least one foreign-born parent.) Kantrowitz, impressed with the extent of ethnic differentiation, wrote:

> In effect, nearly forty years after the end of large-scale European migration, a segregation index number encompassing both the migrants and their children (but primarily the children) in a highly suburbanized metropolis indicates that, on the average, 51.6 percent of the population of southern European origin would have to be redistributed in order to achieve full integration with the northern European population. (p. 24)

He also reported the extremely high segregation of blacks and Puerto Ricans at the time, far exceeding that of the new and old European groups.

Reports of two other more recent studies tended to emphasize declining segregation levels for European nationalities, but the spatial differentiation was still clearly discernible. Studying a dozen national groups in 15 large SMSAs, Bleda (1978, 1979) analyzed the situation as of 1970. She chose cities with substantial foreign-stock subpopulations, but examining 1970 levels, she did not find any as high as reported for New York ten years earlier. Ranging in foreign stock from 13 percent in the Washington, D.C., metropolitan area to a high of 39 percent in New York, all the metropolitan areas had large native-born majorities. She also noted the growth of the second generation and the diminution of the immigrant generation; the second generation was 2 to 4 times larger than the first in the different metropolitan areas.

Bleda (1978) concluded that the various nationality groups are "moderately" segregated from native white parents and that within the ethnic groups the second generation is less segregated than the first. The segregation index scores ranged between 30 and 70. The least segregated subpopulations were descendants of the old immigrants, people with ancestors in Germany and the United Kingdom (plus Canada). The most segregated groups were those who came from Sweden, U.S.S.R. (including Jews in several of the cities), and Czechoslovakia. Bleda discovered that within each nationality the second generation was at least 10 points less segregated than the first.

The results of a third recent study also show persistent measurable ethnic residential differentiation, although not nearly as pronounced as it was in 1930. This study, by Guest and Weed (1976), probed three metropolitan areas, emphasizing a comparison of 1960 and 1970 patterns. The authors concluded that in the thirty years prior to 1970, the new European groups decreased their segregation from each other and from the old northern European groups. Some of these declines were fairly substantial. Guest and Weed also found that Asian Americans were becoming less segregated and that the European groups were much more segregated from blacks than they were from each other.

The authors of all these studies agreed that segregation by ethnic group is an enduring feature of the American metropolitan community. Having found very little diminution in the 1970s, Guest and Weed concluded, "The continued existence of ethnic segregation in American cities is clear from these results. There is no evidence that it will disappear in the near future" (p. 1109). Likewise, Kantrowitz (1973) implies that segregation is a deep-seated trait and finds it noteworthy that seemingly similar subpopulations like Swedes and Norwegians are segregated from each other as are different groups which share the Catholic religion.

## Hypotheses

The researchers do not agree on all points regarding the meaning and causes of the studies results. Kantrowitz, Guest and Weed, and Bleda all reject the assimilation hypothesis. All the studies have found lowered levels of ethnic segregation (not including black-white), but they find sufficient indications that members of ethnic subpopulations are not randomly scattered among the residential areas. They endorse the idea of persistence, predicting that urban areas will continue to display ethnic differentiation.

While they are unanimous about persistence, they disagree about the causes of ethnic segregation. Guest and Weed endorse Hypothesis 2, which states that ethnic differentiation is a function of SES. They found that income, education, and occupation accounted for most of the variation in segregation with income the strongest predictive variable. They admit there is some residual element that is strictly ethnic, but they conclude SES is most important. Bleda (1979), on the other hand, concluded that Hypothesis 3, emphasizing ethnicity itself, was supported by her analysis. She discovered SES accounted for much of the variation in segregation but an ethnic variable—language—was more important. She wrote that mother tongue, representing "a cultural aspect of ethnic identity," accounted for a much greater proportion of ethnic segregation than did SES. The research literature, then, is not entirely conclusive as to the relative importance of SES versus ethnicity; both causes appear to be operating, but the exact amount of influence exerted by each has yet to be ascertained.

## Segregation by Family Status and Age

### Types of households

There have been far fewer studies of differentiation by family status and age than of SES and ethnicity, but some spatial patterns have been disclosed. Family structure and household formation have changed greatly in American society. At one time an extended family with grandparents, children, and sometimes even grown children who had not yet married might occupy the same house. This is no longer the case; increasingly, young people establish their own residences, even if they are not forming a family, and many elderly persons maintain their own households rather than living with others in their family. This leads to a differentiation among household types which are not distributed randomly throughout the metropolitan area (Guest, 1977).

In the most thorough study of the subject, Guest (1972) found different locational patterns of different types of households. He divided all households into six types:

Young couples—husband under age 45, no children
Young families—husband under age 45, children under age 18
Old families—husband over 45, children under age 18
Old couples—husband over 45, no children at home
Single heads—relatives, perhaps children, living together
Primary individuals—one to three unrelated individuals

Then he plotted the locations of these types across Cleveland's census tracts.

He found that residential areas were different with regard to concentrations of different family types and that a clear locational pattern over space existed. Young families were more likely to live at the metropolitan periphery and unlikely to concentrate at the city center. As the gradient in Figure 7-5 indicates, the increasing proportion of young families corresponds to distance from the CBD. Exactly the opposite gradient shows households of primary individuals have higher concentrations nearer the CBD and lower concentrations in suburbia.

More generally, all types of families, young and old, tended to be decentralized, while primary individuals, single heads, and young couples tended to be centralized.

After analyzing the causes of these patterns, Guest concluded that increasing distance from the CBD is associated with particular site and space features. Further from the center are lower density and bigger houses, both of which attract families. All kinds of families locate where more rooms per dwelling are available, and old couples remain in such areas after their children have gone because they own their

**FIGURE 7-5**
Two types of households by distance from city center. (Source: Drawn from data in Guest, 1977.)

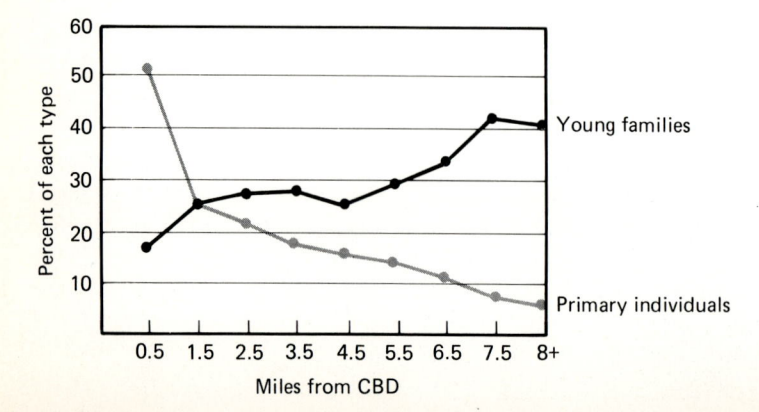

houses. In general, then, the location of family types is determined by the location of particular kinds of housing.

Two other studies, in the social areas and factorial-ecology research traditions, revealed the same family-status pattern as the one in Cleveland. A study of family status in four cities—Akron, Dayton, Indianapolis, and Syracuse—showed that family status was arranged zonally, with families with children located in the outermost zone (Anderson & Egeland, 1961). Toronto exhibited the same pattern of family status (Murdie, 1969).

A study of a smaller city, Peoria, Illinois, showed the segregation of certain kinds of households, focusing on the situation of divorced and separated families (Choldin & Roncek, 1975). Peoria resembled the other cities in having households with children located away from the city center, but a special category of households, those headed by females, showed a different pattern. A high degree of segregation existed between female-headed households, headed by divorced and separated women, and young and old families, to use Guest's terminology. That is, female-headed households, even though they contained children, were not located in the peripheral familistic areas and tended not to be on blocks with single-family detached houses. As many of these female-headed households were black, they were also unlikely to be located in high-income areas.

## Segregation of the elderly

The research literature yields an unclear picture of the residential distribution of elderly people. Unsupported by empirical evidence, some popular commentaries

While elderly individuals are not as segregated as racial or ethnic minorities, they are more likely to reside together in certain areas. Such locations are likely to be in central cities and to have multiple-unit residential structures. (Richard Kalvar, Magnum)

have suggested the elderly are so isolated in the central cities that they live in "geriatric ghettos." But ecological analyses have not found a high degree of segregation. A study of Toledo, Ohio (Hiltner & Smith, 1974), consistently showed a segregation index of only 13 over a thirty-year period, which means that only 13 percent of the people over age 65 would have to be redistributed to have no "segregation" at all. Pampel and Choldin (1978), studying San Diego and Cleveland, were unable to account for much of the variation in the distribution of the elderly, which meant that they were scattered among various neighborhoods. A larger-scale study, though, by LaGory, Ward, and Juravich (1981) found discernible levels of age segregation in some metropolitan areas. They computed segregation indexes for populations aged 65 and over in 70 metropolitan areas; the range for the indexes was between 11.9 and 46.4 with a mean of 24.2 and a standard deviation of 7.5. This means that while the level of segregation is moderate in most metropolitan areas, it is substantial in several and therefore communities vary considerably in this respect.

## DIFFERENTIATION THEORIES

Sharp theoretical disagreements have taken place about why residential areas are differentiated. Timms (1971), an Australian urbanist, says:

> The process of separation may be accomplished through force, through a variety of sanctions, through a voluntary aggregation designed as a defense against unfamiliar ideas or customs or as an escape from persecution and discrimination, and through a selection of market forces. (p. 1)

Sociologists have tended to disagree about which of these processes is most important.

### Economic Competition

Robert E. Park, founder of the Chicago school, argued that the land use of the city is determined by the user's ability to pay for a location; that is, a market process determines land uses. For businesses, centrality was the main advantage of location; thus the biggest, richest establishments could afford to locate at the city center, the most desirable place in the community. Park's main principle for the allocation of the city's spaces was competition, the ability to pay in a free market.

Among residential users a sifting and sorting process tends to bring categories of people together in their own residential areas, which Park called "natural areas." As the city grows, he says, there is a "social selection and segregation of the population and the creation, on the one hand, of social groups, and on the other, of natural areas" (1926, p. 8). Park continues "The physical or ecological organization of the community, in the long run, responds to and reflects the occupational and the cultural. Social selection and segregation, which create the natural groups, determine at the same time the natural areas of the city" (p. 9). Nonetheless, in addition to this sorting which brought like individuals together, Park always assumed the operation of a capitalistic real estate market, which sorted households by ability to pay for accommodation.

This meant that households and neighborhoods were allocated by the value of the housing itself and by its location. Housing values were determined by the size and quality of the accommodations and by the attractiveness and desirability of the neighborhood environment. Quality of accommodation was likely to be closely correlated with the age of the housing; poorer classes got housing in the old residential areas of the central city, and more prosperous classes occupied newer residential areas. Location determined the cost of travel to work, so poorer workers were constrained to live nearer their workplaces to minimize commuting costs, while more prosperous workers could afford to spend more on daily transportation. Middle-class neighborhoods tended to be located farther from the central business district and from industrial areas. All of this, in Park's theory, reflected competition in an economic market which in effect, allocated neighborhoods to different social classes.

## The Privileges of High Status

David Harvey (1973), a geographer, also employs an economic point of view, but he emphasizes the unequal benefits of different residential areas. Good location itself is one of the benefits of high position in the stratification system, according to Harvey. A stratification system, by definition, is a system of inequalities in which various tangibles and intangibles are awarded unequally. People at the top get more of the attractive tangibles such as possessions, vacations, medical care, etc., as well as more prestige, a social intangible. Spatial location may confer both tangible and intangible benefits. Harvey states differential accessibility is a dimension of urban location. Consider, for example, accessibility to community amenities—an attractive hilltop, a park, a shoreline, or the like—and to community facilities and services—the best schools, the fire station, a good shopping center, etc. Obviously, accessibility to these attractive places and services is desirable, and inaccessibility is not. Furthermore, Harvey notes, location has a negative side: "A household may [thus] find itself proximate to a source of pollution, to a source of noise, or to a run-down environment. This proximity tends to impose certain costs upon the household" (pp. 56-57). The sociological point here is that accessibility to attractions and proximity to undesirable environmental features are not distributed randomly within the population but, rather, systematically to different neighborhoods within the community. This unequal distribution is a basic feature of the stratification system. Location, like income, is one of the perquisites of status.

## Overcoming Density and Heterogeneity

Louis Wirth, who belonged to the Chicago school, suggested that force and necessity tend to bring socially similar individuals into identifiable neighborhoods. He said, "Persons become segregated more by virtue of differences in race, language, income, and social status, than through choice or positive attraction to people like themselves" (1938. p. 17). As noted in Chapter 2, his essay on urbanism as a way of life attempted to explain social relations in the metropolis. Another aspect of Wirth's theory states that large size, high population density, and heterogeneity tend to produce segregation among the peoples of the city. Wirth noted that large numbers give rise to individual variation; when there are large numbers of persons, there must be differences among them.

> That such variations should give rise to the spatial segregation of individuals according to color, ethnic heritage, economic and social status, tastes and preferences, may readily be inferred. The bonds of kinship, of neighborliness, and the sentiments arising out of living together for generations under a common folk tradition are likely to be absent or, at best, relatively weak in an aggregate the members of which have such diverse origins and backgrounds. (Wirth, 1938, p. 11).

Lacking such a unifying culture, the different sorts of individuals in the city can at least form homogeneous neighborhoods in which to support their distinct subcultures.

Wirth also said density and heterogeneity tend to promote residential differentiation. High population density means numerous individuals are living close together; heterogeneity means they have different styles of life, some of which may be incompatible at close contact. The social solution: to have different neighborhoods for different subcultures. As Wirth put it:

> Diverse population elements inhabiting a compact settlement [thus] tend to become segregated from one another in the degree in which their requirements and modes of life are incompatible with one another and in the measure in which they are antagonistic to one another. Similarly, persons of homogeneous status and needs unwittingly drift into, consciously select, or are forced by circumstances into, the same area. (1938, p. 15).

## Sentiment and Symbolism

Walter Firey, when a sociologist at Harvard University, severely criticized Park's theory, calling it "rationalist determinism." He challenged the idea that individuals in the city were "economic men" making single-minded rational decisions about their residential locations. Firey conducted an original study, published in a volume entitled *Land Use in Central Boston* (1947), in which he argued that people's values and sentiments affect the ways in which they use urban land. Reporting on Beacon Hill (an elite residential district), Boston Commons (a large park in the middle of the city), and the North End (a lower-class immigrant area), he asserted that rational economic allocation would have used the land differently in all three places.

In each case, Firey emphasized sentiment and symbolism as affecting land use. If the wealthy residents of Beacon Hill were simply rational, they would abandon the old houses of densely settled Beacon Hill for more spacious dwellings. But they remain in the older neighborhood because it symbolizes their traditions and allows them to perpetuate their cherished family connections and customs, such as Christmas carolling, based upon residential proximity. Likewise, the Italian immigrants of the North End, who did not necessarily have the means to leave the area, used the neighborhood for social and cultural purposes; for example, they established food shops to supply the special ingredients for their traditional cuisine. Like the elite residents of Beacon Hill, they used their area and their proximity to each other for interpersonal contact to maintain their kinship networks and churches. Thus they enjoyed the continuation of Italian culture in their city district. In a similar vein, Firey said that it was economically irrational for the city of Boston to devote 48.5 acres of precious central land to a park, the Commons, but the community's traditions and values—the memory of historic events there, plus patriotism—dictate that the Commons be maintained.

## Looking for Trust

Gerald Suttles (1972, p. 242) says three different processes tend to support the differentiation of residential areas. Perhaps the simplest is civic administration: The residential area is served or administered by the city and its agencies. Thus city planners, school superintendents, and others divide the map of the city into residential areas, using them as service districts.

In addition to being an object of administration, the residential area is an identity distinguished from other areas and groups. The most effective and frequent definitions of local communities are "enacted boundary lines," which are formally or informally recognized over the history of a city. They are "a historical debris left over from the previous proclamations of developers, planners, boosters, mapmakers, sociologists, newspapers and businesses (Suttles, 1972, p. 242). Thus, if a builder-developer assigns a name to a tract or subdivision, it may survive for decades, long after the area has been engulfed by the growth of the metropolis and after new generations of residents have come and gone. When suburban towns are annexed and absorbed by growing cities, as were Chicago's nineteenth-century suburbs of Hyde Park and Lake View, they may retain their names and thus their identities indefinitely.

The last basis for differentiation is associational selection. Suttles, too, observes that residential areas are differentiated by socioeconomic level, ethnicity, and lifestyle. He observes, as well, that the price of housing in different neighborhoods tends to segregate households by socioeconomic status.

Underlying this third basis of differentiation is the matter of trust. Urban people desire to be able to trust their neighbors, according to Suttles; this is the basis for personal safety. "People want to live in a 'good area' where they feel reasonably safe and are a known distance from those people they distrust. They also want to know something about how far the 'good area' extends" (1972, pp. 233-234). Many everyday activities require that people break the city into "more or less trustworthy areas." After carefully studying social organization within a Chicago slum, Suttles (1968) showed that even among people at the poverty level, bonds of trust are forged, usually within single ethnic groups.

## SUMMARY

Cities and suburbs always exhibit social differences among their residential areas. This phenomenon appears to reflect a connection between social differences and spatial distances. A considerable research literature in urban sociology and social geography documents the extent and variables involved in spatial differentiation. The chapter begins with ways of showing the characteristics of individual residential areas from census data and then the text moves on to differences and patterns when many areas are considered.

Social area analysis and factorial ecology are closely related approaches to the study of differentiation among residential areas. (Social area analysis was developed first but was supplanted by factorial ecology.) Based upon a statistical technique called "factor analysis," both have been used by sociologists and geographers to examine numerous urban areas. Applied to North American metropolitan areas, these approaches always show that residential areas are differentiated along three dimensions: socioeconomic status, familism, and race and ethnicity. The studies have shown that these dimensions may be independent of each other, giving rise to a typology of residential areas, such as middle-class, familistic, white; middle-class, familistic, black; etc. By conducting a factorial ecology of a metropolitan area and mapping the results, a social scientist may reveal its overall sociospatial pattern.

Sociologists have also explored sociospatial patterns by studying the residential segregation of people by occupation. (In such cases, occupation is used to represent socioeconomic status.) This type of research relies upon a statistical technique known as "the index of dissimilarity." These studies have revealed clear spatial differentiation between the residences of blue-collar and white-collar occupations.

Likewise, there have been studies of the residential patterns of ethnic and nationality groups, also using the index of dissimilarity. These studies have shown that ethnic groups have become less segregated over time and across generations. Ethnic segregation is still discernible, but it is diminishing, being replaced by socioeconomic segregation.

Five theories deal with causes and effects of sociospatial differentiation. Park and Wirth recognized a sorting process within the urban population, distributing households into residential areas. From his ecological point of view, Park saw competition within the real estate market as sorting people by ability to pay for housing and location, and this process created residential areas which were differentiated by socioeconomic status. Thus, the city's stratification system was reflected in its housing pattern. Wirth's explanation of segregation was consistent with Park's, although Wirth was concerned with more than ability to pay. He said that within the heterogeneous urban population people tended to be repelled from others very different from themselves, so they sorted themselves into residential areas with like individuals. This would tend to produce relatively homogeneous places by ethnicity as well as class.

Walter Firey rejected these ecological premises and said that land use in cities is heavily influenced by people's values and sentiments. Traditions may determine the way a group maintains the character of a particular area of the city. Firey rejected the supremacy of competitive processes in the housing market, postulated by Park. Community symbols, people's sentiments about particular places are important; therefore, the owners and residents of a particular area may use it for purposes which are not necessarily the most profitable. As Firey portrays them, city people are not simply pushed or sorted into places, they may choose places and then continue their traditions.

Gerald Suttles's writings may be seen as a bridge between Park and Wirth, on the one side, and Firey, on the other. Suttles emphasizes the importance of trust within the urban dweller's concerns. Like Wirth, Suttles suggests that within the metropolitan housing market, an individual seeks to live among the kinds of people he or she can trust. Thus, individuals are likely to avoid areas with others very different from themselves and to seek areas with the kinds of persons who can be understood and trusted. Living in a chosen residential area, the urban individual establishes a set of boundaries which describes the local trustable area. Suttles assumes a sorting process, but he also describes a social-psychological and cultural process akin to local sentiment and tradition, like Firey's.

David Harvey, however, views sociospatial differentiation from a different vantage point. Taking differentiation for granted, he emphasizes its effect as one of society's implicit mechanisms of distributing benefits unequally among groups. He points out the different locational amenities of residential areas, so that upper-status areas typically have the best locations in terms of natural attractions, the best accessibility to other desiderata, whether they are jobs, shops, parks, or other features, as well as receiving the best community services.

**REFERENCES**

Abler, Ronald, and John S. Adams. 1976. *A Comparative Atlas of America's Great Cities: Twenty Metropolitan Regions.* Minneapolis: University of Minnesota Press and Association of American Geographers.

Abu-Lughod, Janet. 1971. *Cairo: 1001 Years of the City Victorious.* Princeton, N.J.: Princeton.

Anderson, Theodore R., and Lee L. Bean. 1961. "The Shevky-Bell Social Areas: Confirmation of Results and a Reinterpretation." *Social Forces.* 40:119–124.

Anderson, Theodore R., and Janice A. Egeland. 1961. "Spatial Aspects of Social Area Analysis." *American Sociological Review.* 26:393–399.

Bell, Wendell. 1955. "Economic, Family, and Ethnic Status: An Empirical Test." *American Sociological Review.* 20:45–52.

Bleda, Sharon E. 1978. "Intergenerational Differences in Patterns and Bases of Ethnic Residential Dissimilarity." *Ethnicity.* 5:91–107.

Bleda, Sharon E. 1979. "Socioeconomic, Demographic, and Cultural Bases of Ethnic Residential Segregation." *Ethnicity.* 6:147–167.

Burgess, Ernest W., and Donald J. Bogue. 1964. "Research in Urban Society: A Long View," pp. 1–14 in *Contributions to Urban Sociology,* (eds.) Ernest W. Burgess and Donald J. Bogue. Chicago: University of Chicago Press.

Choldin, Harvey M., and Dennis W. Roncek. 1975. "Urban Density and the Family." Paper presented at the meeting of the American Sociological Association.

Darroch, A.G., and W.G. Marston. 1971. "The Social Class Basis of Ethnic Residential Segregation: The Canadian Case." *American Journal of Sociology.* 77:491–510.

Duncan, Otis D., and Beverly Duncan. 1955. "Residential Distribution and Occupational Stratification." *American Journal of Sociology.* 60:493–503.

Firey, Walter. 1947. *Land Use in Central Boston.* Cambridge, Mass.: Harvard.

Guest, Avery M. 1972. "Patterns of Family Location." *Demography.* 9:159–171.

Guest, Avery M. 1977. "Residential Segregation in Urban Areas," p. 268–337 in *Contemporary Topics in Urban Sociology,* (ed.) Kent Schwirian, Morristown, N.J.: General Learning Press.

Guest, Avery M., and James A. Weed. 1976. "Ethnic Residential Segregation: Patterns of Change." *American Journal of Sociology.* 81:1088–1111.

Harvey, David. 1973. *Social Justice and the City.* London: E. Arnold.

Hiltner, J., and B. Smith. 1974. "Intraurban Residential Location of the Elderly." *Journal of Geography.* 73(4):23–33.

Kantrowitz, Nathan. 1973. *Ethnic and Racial Segregation in the New York Metropolis.* New York: Praeger.

LaGory, Mark, Russell Ward, and Thomas Juravich. 1981. "The Age Segregation Process: Explanation for American Cities." *Urban Affairs Quarterly.* 16:59–80.

Lieberson, Stanley. 1963. *Ethnic Patterns in American Cities.* New York: Free Press.

McElrath, Dennis. 1962. "The Social Areas of Rome." *American Sociological Review.* 27:376–391.

Murdie, Robert A. 1969. *Factorial Ecology of Metropolitan Toronto: 1951–1961: An Essay in the Social Geography of the City.* Chicago: Department of Geography, University of Chicago.

Pampel, Fred and Harvey M. Choldin. 1978. "Urban Location and Segregation of the Aged." *Social Forces.* 56:1121–1139.

Park, Robert E. 1926. "The Urban Community as a Spatial Pattern and a Moral Order," in *The Urban Community,* (ed.). Ernest W. Burgess. Chicago: University of Chicago Press.

Rees, Philip H. 1972., "Problems of Classifying Subareas within Cities," p. 265-330 in *City Classification Handbook: Methods and Applications*, (ed.) Brian J. L. Berry, New York: Wiley.

Rees, Philip H. 1979. *Residential Patterns in American Cities: 1960*. Chicago: Department of Geography, University of Chicago.

Shaw, Clifford R., and Henry D. McKay, 1942. *Juvenile Delinquency and Urban Areas*. Chicago: University of Chicago Press.

Shevky, Eshrev, and Wendell Bell. 1955. *Social Area Analysis: Theory, Illustration, Application and Computational Procedures*. Stanford, Calif.: Stanford University Press.

Shevky, Eshrev, and Marilyn Williams. 1949. *The Social Areas of Los Angeles*. Berkeley: University of California Press.

Stevens, Gillian, and David Featherman. 1981. "A Revised Socioeconomic Index of Occupational Status." *Social Science Research*. 10:364-392.

Suttles, Gerald. 1968. *The Social Order of the Slum*. Chicago: University of Chicago Press.

Suttles, Gerald D. 1972. *The Social Construction of Communities*. Chicago: University of Chicago Press.

Timms, Duncan. 1971. *The Urban Mosaic: Towards a Theory of Residential Differentiation*. Cambridge: Cambridge.

Treiman, Donald J. 1977. *Occupational Prestige in Comparative Perspective*. New York: Academic.

U.S. Bureau of the Census. 1970. *Census of Population and Housing, 1970, Census Tracts*, PHC (1)-117 and PHC (1)-9. Washington, D.C.

Van Arsdol, Maurice D., Jr., Santo F. Camilleri, and Calvin F. Schmid. 1958. "The Generality of Urban Social Area Indexes." *American Sociological Review*. 23:277-284.

Weinstein, Jay A. 1974. *Madras: An Analysis of Urban Ecological Structure in India*. Beverly Hills, Calif.: Sage.

Wheeler, James O. 1968. "Residential Location by Occupational Status." *Urban Studies*. 5:24-32.

Wirth, Louis, 1938. "Urbanism as a Way of Life." *American Journal of Sociology*. 44:1-24.

Yeates, Maurice, and Barry Garner. 1980. *The North American City*. 3d ed. New York: Harper & Row.

Zorbaugh, Harvey, 1929. *The Gold Coast and the Slum*. Chicago: University of Chicago Press.

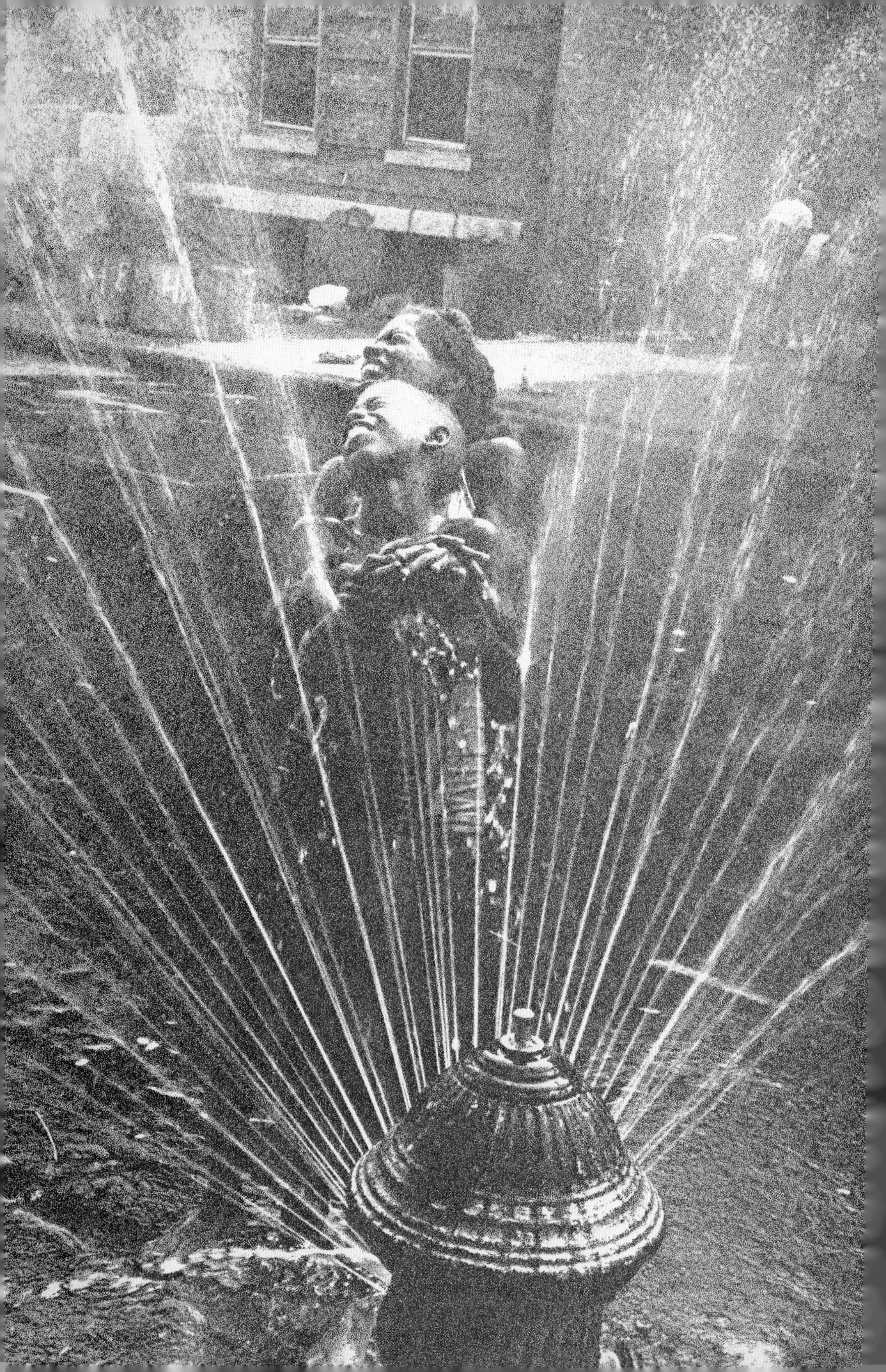

# CHAPTER • 8

## *Blacks in the Metropolis*

## Chapter Outline

**INTRODUCTION**
  Two Models of Blacks in Cities
- Immigrant-assimilation model
- Ghetto-colony models

  Is the Situation Changing?
- The progress perspective
- The stasis perspective

**GHETTOS**
  Concept of the Ghetto
  Creation of Two Black Ghettos
- Harlem
- Chicago's south side

  Blacks in the Urban Economy
- Failure of black business
- Dual housing market

**SEGREGATION PATTERNS**
  Segregation Index
  Levels of Segregation
  Trends since 1940

**CHANGING RESIDENTIAL PATTERNS**
  Background: Migration to the Cities
  Racial Transitions in Residential Areas
- Housing turnover
- "Tipping point" theory

  Institutional Transition
- Businesses
- Schools

**INTERNAL DIFFERENTIATION OF THE GHETTO**
  Socioeconomic Status Gradient
  Types of Black Neighborhoods

**RECENT DEVELOPMENTS**
  School Desegregation and "White Flight"
  Black Suburbanization

**SUMMARY**

## INTRODUCTION

Why have an entire chapter on blacks in metropolitan America? There are other minorities, some larger, like Catholics, others smaller, like Puerto Ricans. Blacks constitute 11.7 percent of the American population, but the situations and problems of blacks are particularly prominent in the national consciousness.

At worst, the black situation has been explosive. The notorious urban riots which took place between 1965 and 1968 all occurred in black slums: Watts, Los Angeles; central Detroit; Chicago's West Side, and in dozens of other cities. See Box 8-1 for a typical case from that period, Newark, New Jersey. Sometimes, when national leaders wish to make a particular point on behalf of employment or social welfare programs, they say the potential exists for another "long, hot summer," like that of 1967. Indeed, Miami had major violent disturbances in its black districts in 1980 and 1982, showing that the potential is real.

Urban imagery, as presented on television programs, often depicts the uneasy state of race relations. Many police programs show white officers attempting to deal with black offenders of one sort or another and often portray uneasy relationships between black and white police officers. Many movies and TV series present images of black situations, whether in housing projects, slums, or other settings. To some extent, the fear of crime among whites represents fear of black criminals, although blacks themselves are more likely to be victims.

Social scientists have devoted an enormous amount of attention to race relations in America. Some of the greatest works in social science have explored race relations and the black experience. A very short list includes W. E. B. DuBois, *The Philadelphia Negro* (1899); E. Franklin Frazier, *The Negro Family in the United States* (1939); Gunnar Myrdal, *An American Dilemma* (1944); John Dollard, *Caste and Class in a Southern Town* (1937); Elliot Liebow, *Talley's Corner* (1937); Karl and Alma Taeuber, *Negroes in Cities* (1965). This list is highly selective and a full bibliography would include thousands of entries. The fact that so much research has been done on a still-unsolved problem does not represent a failure of social science, though; it shows that the problem is deep and not simply understood.

### Two Models of Blacks in Cities

Two models dominate the literature concerning minority groups in American cities: the immigrant-assimilation model and the ghetto-colony model. Each offers a way of looking at the situation of blacks and how it has been changing and at race relations in metropolitan American. The black experience has differed from the immigrant experience, so this chapter will emphasize the ghetto-colony.

### Immigrant-assimilation model

One may suggest that blacks are not the first minority group to live in American cities. In this context one is tempted to say that there has been a typical pattern for such groups—involving a certain amount of acculturation or assimilation, along with residential dispersion and, most important, upward mobility in occupational status. The immigrant model usually refers to European groups and shows them adopting "American" cultural patterns while they get better jobs and rise in socioeconomic status over a course of perhaps two or three generations. Within the city, the immigrants and their descendants pass through a series of neighborhoods in the process of succession, which is a part of the immigrant-assimilation model. The process of ethnic succession through neighborhoods and suburbs is presented in Chapter 11.

But this model does not explain the black experience very well. Blacks lived in American cities before many of the European immigrant groups, yet they were not assimilated. If anything, blacks appear to be the exception to the assimilation model.

### Ghetto-colony models

Another way of looking at the black experience suggests that blacks were not the free agents the immigrants were in the cities, that blacks were held back or otherwise treated differently. The black subcommunity may be seen as a *ghetto* or even as an *internal colony* from this point of view. The ghetto concept is explained in the next section. The internal-colony concept develops an analogy of the relationship between black and white city areas and the relationship between a colony and the country which dominates it. In the colonial relationship the dominant nation keeps an army and other officials in the colony; the home country takes raw materials from the colony and sells manufactured goods to it. The relationship is clearly unequal, with the lion's share of the benefits going to the dominant nation. The urban model suggests that the rest of the city uses the black section as a colony. The city puts its "army" (the police) into the colony to subdue it and exploits the blacks in various ways. Welfare workers, politicians, and other municipal employees may also be seen as colonial agents. Both the ghetto and colony models assume that blacks are in their situation against their wills. These models may go even further to assert that federal policies of the part quarter-century have had the effect of perpetuating the ghettoization of urban blacks. This argument would state that the erection of massive, concentrated housing projects in black districts has continued the segregation of poor blacks and that welfare policies have made the poor dependent upon the government.

### Is the Situation Changing?

Observers disagree as to the current direction of change. Some argue that the situation has changed considerably in recent years, generally for the better; others argue that it has worsened or just stayed the same. To some extent one's choice in this debate depends upon whether one emphasizes the situation of the middle or lower classes.

## BOX 8-1
## Two Black Ghetto Riots

**Newark, New Jersey, 1967***

**Precipitating incident**

*July 12, approximately 9:30 p.m.:* A Negro cab driver was injured during or after a traffic arrest in the heart of the central ward. Word spread quickly, and a crowd gathered in front of the Fourth Precinct stationhouse across the street from a large public housing project.

**Initial violence**

*Same day, approximately 11:30 p.m.:* The crowd continued to grow until it reached 300 to 500 people. One or two Molotov cocktails were thrown at the stationhouse. Shortly after midnight the police dispersed the crowd, and window-breaking and looting began a few minutes later. By about 1 a.m., the peak level of violence for the first night was reached.

**Escalation**

On Thursday . . . a picket line was formed to march in front of the police station. (Other people assembled nearby. A black city official made a speech with an offer from the mayor.)

The response from the loosely milling mass of people was derisive. One youngster shouted "Black Power!" Rocks were thrown. . . . The barrage of missiles that followed placed the police station under siege.

After the barrage had continued for some minutes, police came out to disperse the crowd. . . . A number of police officers and Negroes were injured.

As on the night before, once the people had been dispersed, reports of looting began to come in. Soon the glow of the first fire was seen.

Without enough men to establish control, the police set up a perimeter around a 2-mile stretch of Springfield Avenue, one of the principal business districts, where bands of youths roamed up and down smashing windows. Grocery and liquor stores, clothing and furniture stores, drugstores and cleaners, appliance stores and pawnshops were the principal targets. Periodically, police officers would appear and fire their weapons over the heads of looters and rioters. Laden with stolen goods, people began returning to the housing projects.

Near midnight, activity appeared to taper off. The mayor told reporters the city had turned the corner.

As news of the disturbances had spread, however, people had flocked into the streets. As they saw stores being broken into with impunity, many bowed to temptation and joined the looting.

Without the necessary personnel to make mass arrests, police were shooting into the air to clear stores. Guns were reported stolen from a Sears, Roebuck store. Looting, fires, and gunshots were reported from a widening area. Between 2 and 2:30 a.m. on Friday, July 14, the mayor decided to request Gov. Richard J. Hughes to dispatch the state police and National Guard troops. The first elements of the state police arrived with a sizeable contingent before dawn.

During the morning the Governor and the mayor, together with the police and National Guard officers, made a reconnaissance of the area. The police escort guarding the officials arrested looters as they went. By early afternoon the National Guard had set up 137 roadblocks, and state police and riot teams were beginning to achieve control. Command of antiriot operations was taken over by the Governor, who decreed a "hard line" in putting down the riot.

### Counterviolence and confusion

Although, by nightfall, most of the looting and burning had ended, reports of sniper fire increased. The fire was, according to New Jersey National Guard reports, "deliberately or otherwise inaccurate." Maj. Gen. James F. Cantwell, Chief of Staff of the New Jersey National Guard, testified before an Armed Services Subcommittee of the House of Representatives that "there was too much firing initially against snipers" because of "confusion when we were finally called on for help and our thinking of it as a military action."

"As a matter of fact," Director of Police Spina told the Commission, "down in the Springfield Avenue area it was so bad that, in my opinion, Guardsmen were firing upon police and police were firing back at them...."

A number of eye witnesses, at varying times and places, reported seeing bottles thrown from upper story windows. As these would land at the feet of an officer he would turn and fire. Thereupon, other officers and Guardsmen up and down the street would join in....

Nevertheless, at six o'clock that evening two columns of National Guardsmen and state troopers were directing mass fire at the Hayes Housing project in response to what they believed were snipers.

### Conclusion

By Monday afternoon, July 17, state police and National Guard forces were withdrawn.

Of the 250 fire alarms, many had been false, and 13 were considered by the city to have been "serious." Of the $10,251,000 damage total, four-fifths was due to stock loss. Damage to buildings and fixtures was less than $2 million.

Twenty-three persons were killed—a white detective, a white fireman, and 21 Negroes. One was 73-year-old Isaac Harrison. Six were women. Two were children.

### Miami, 1980

More than a decade later, Miami's black districts erupted with events very much like those of the earlier disturbances. In May 1980, there was a riot in a predominantly black, low-income area known as Liberty City. It occurred after the conclusion of a trial in which four white policemen were acquitted of having killed a black man. Among the underlying conditions was the common perception that Cuban immigrants were moving up far more effectively in socioeconomic status while the blacks were stagnated in the lower class. The Liberty City riot was violent and destructive like its predecessors, but it had one major difference, being clearly antiwhite. "Violence against people was cold-blooded. . . . Rioters deliberately sought out white victims for the first night of the explosion" (Harrigan & Stevens, 1980, p. 1). Newspaper reports stated that blacks beat and killed whites in the area. "Many rioters carefully picked out white-owned businesses to burn and left black stores and neighborhoods mostly intact" (Harrigan & Stevens, 1980, p. 1). By the end of the episode there were six whites and nine blacks dead and almost 400 injured. Arson and looting produced damages estimated as high as $100 million. Again in 1982, Miami had a similar but smaller riot in another black area.

*Excerpts from the *Report of the National Advisory Commission on Civil Disorders*, 1968, pp. 30–38, 68–69.

## The progress perspective

Since 1950 large numbers of blacks have entered the middle- and upper-middle classes. In 1950, about 5 percent of adult blacks had attended college; by 1980, this number had quadrupled to 20.4 percent.[1] In 1950, 9.6 percent of employed blacks had white-collar jobs; by 1980 this figure had risen to 37.9 percent.[2] Other indicators of middle-class status would show the same trend toward the development of a substantial black middle class. (On the other hand, in 1950 median black income

---

[1] 1950 data are from *Historical Statistics of the United States*; 1980 data are from *Statistical Abstract of the United States*, 1981, Table 232.
[2] 1950 data are computed from *Census of Population, 1950, Special Report: Occupational Characteristics*, 1956, Table 3; 1980 data are from *Statistical Abstract of the United States*, 1980, Table 698. Figure is somewhat overestimated as table reports on blacks and other races together.

was 54.3 percent of white, whereas in 1980 it was 60.2 percent,[3] thus showing that black equality of reward was not occurring overnight.)

## The stasis perspective

While some observers are looking at the middle classes and perceiving progress, others are looking at the poor and seeing no progress. A large number of blacks are still on welfare, with about 1.5 million families receiving Aid to Families of Dependent Children (AFDC) in 1977 out of more than 8 million black households.[4] Large all-black housing projects still exist, where people live in fear of violence. Nonwhite unemployment still exceeds white unemployment by a ratio of 2 to 1.[5] Black central-city schools still carry poor reputations, etc. Many black slum areas were burnt and destroyed in the 1960s, never to be rebuilt. Indeed some observers in the 1970s came to see the poor blacks as a permanent element of the urban scene, coining a new name for them, the "underclass."

The purpose of this chapter is to examine blacks in metropolitan America. The chapter covers the history of black ghettos, including recent statistical analyses of residential segregation, and looks at changing residential patterns—expansion of black districts, neighborhood transitions, and suburbanization. The different models and perspectives should be used to see how they illuminate the situation. The chapter should also reveal which of them are most useful and credible.

## GHETTOS

### Concept of the Ghetto

A ghetto is a section of a community in which a specified category of people *must* reside; the exclusion of this category of people from the rest of the community is enforced. The ghetto is defined by enforced boundaries; the specification of a certain category; and exclusion of members of this category from the rest of the community. The external force which maintains the boundaries may be legal or quasi-legal. The first official permanent ghetto was established in Venice in 1516 as a district where Jews had to live. The institution spread to other Italian cities during the course of the next century. The ghetto was surrounded with gates which were closed at night and on all important Christian festivals. These boundaries were enforced by law, and no Jew could reasonably think about living elsewhere. As the histories (summarized below) of black districts in two cities show, twentieth-century Americans also deliberately created ghettos. In this case, a quasi-legal device was created to enforce the urban black ghettos. A clause called a "restrictive covenant"

---

[3]Computed from *Statistical Abstract of the United States*, 1980, Table 745.
[4]Computed from *Statistical Abstract of the United States*, 1980, Table 577.
[5]Computed from *Statistical Abstract of the United States*, 1981, Table 639.

was attached to each deed requiring the owner of a lot or building never to sell it to anyone but a white. (In 1948 the Supreme Court ruled that restrictive covenants are unenforceable, so they have been useless since then.)

Black ghetto boundaries have also been enforced in the United States by violent extralegal methods. Many incidents have been documented in which blacks who have attempted to move into all-white neighborhoods had their houses burned, garbage dumped on their property, and crosses burned on their lawns. Often, vigilante groups were formed to carry out such acts of boundary enforcement.

An important analytical distinction exists between a *ghetto* and a *slum*. Nowadays, in common parlance and in journalistic usage, ghetto means black central-city slum, but this casual usage combines two distinct concepts which are separable in more precise sociological terminology. In this text, we define a ghetto as a bounded residential area in which a defined racial or ethnic group is forced to live. A residential area may be a slum without being a ghetto, and another area may be a ghetto without being a slum. Thus any lower-class run-down area which houses a mixture of racial groups is not a ghetto, even if it has all the characteristics of a slum (see Chapter 15). It is also possible that an area to which a certain group is confined—if they are not permitted to live elsewhere—is a livable residential neighborhood, a ghetto but not a slum.

## Creation of Two Black Ghettos

The segregation of blacks into ghettos in U.S. cities did not just happen; these districts were created by a combination of social processes which were intended to keep blacks out of white residential areas.

The story of urban racial segregation begins in the midnineteenth century. At that point in history very few blacks lived in northern cities: 16,785 (1.5 percent) in New York (including Brooklyn) and 22,185 (3.9 percent) in Philadelphia, for example.[6] These northern blacks tended to live in dispersed residential locations. Then, and well into the early twentieth century, racial prejudice was widespread and blatant among whites. No white had to apologize for talking about "niggers" or "coons," for expressing any number of stereotypes depicting blacks as inferior, or for ridiculing their way of life. In this context, whites did not hesitate to insist that blacks had to live apart from whites.

### Harlem

New York City's Harlem was for many decades the most famous black ghetto—the home of many nationally known black celebrities and style-setter for the national black subculture. It was also notorious for its tenements, poverty, prostitution,

---

[6]Computed from 1860 Census.

drugs, and despair. The history of the development of Harlem as a black district is well presented in a book by Gilbert Osofsky (1968), *Harlem: The Making of a Ghetto, Negro New York, 1890–1930*.

Osofsky explains that the "choice" of Harlem as the site of the great ghetto was inadvertent at first. Harlem, which was farmland north of the built-up part of the city, was developed as a fairly expensive new suburb between 1880 and 1910. It was ripe for development because new trolley and subway lines were extended out there. A building boom occurred in the decades of the 1880s and 1890s when numerous high-quality apartment buildings were erected along with a great deal of real estate speculation. By 1904–1905 the area was overbuilt; there was a surplus of expensive apartments with many vacancies. Some landlords, in order to fill these vacancies and collect some income, began to rent to blacks. This was a profitable decision: "Rather than face 'financial destruction' some landlords and corporations opened their houses to Negroes *and collected the traditionally high rents that colored people paid*" (Osofsky, 1968, p. 92, italics added). Some of the owners and real estate brokers schemed to buy property from white owners by scaring them into thinking that blacks were moving into the neighborhood. A black entrepreneur organized a corporation, the Afro-American Realty Company, to buy and manage Harlem properties for black occupants, but after four years of acquiring numerous buildings, this company failed in 1908. Nonetheless, the black population, which had been growing elsewhere in the city and suffering from a housing shortage, for the first time had accommodations in a high-quality residential environment. "Harlem was originally not a slum, but an ideal place in which to live. For the first and generally last time in the history of New York City, Negroes were able to live in decent homes in a respectable neighborhood, 'the best houses that they have ever had to live in'" (Osofsky, 1968, p. 111). This situation was soon to change for the worse.

"The Harlem slum of today was created in the 1920s," according to Osofsky (1968, p. 136); "Largely within the space of a single decade Harlem was transformed from a potentially ideal community to a neighborhood with manifold social and economic problems called 'deplorable,' 'unspeakable,' 'incredible'" (p. 134). Osofsky explains that the neighborhood deteriorated rapidly because the housing was heavily overoccupied. There was a serious shortage of housing for blacks in the city in general, and then, during the 1920s, there was a tremendous in-migration of blacks from the south and from the West Indies, all of whom needed housing. Since housing was available for blacks in Harlem, the newcomers swarmed in, and owners could continue to raise the rents. Entire families were crowded into single rooms. Neither the buildings nor the public services were adequate to accommodate the great density and overcrowding. "Some landlords, after opening houses to Negro tenants, lost interest in caring for their property and permitted it to run down—halls were left dark and dirty, broken pipes were permitted to rot, steam heat was cut off as heating apparatus wore out—homes became vermin-infested [with rats and roaches]" (Osofsky, 1968, p. 141). Health conditions in the area were poor, and there were high rates of infectious and epidemic diseases, as well as infant mortality.

CHAPTER·8

A photograph of Harlem taken in the 1920s shows major commercial and entertainment establishments. (The Bettmann Archive)

Furthermore, from having started as New York's most respectable residential area, the situation changed to where there was considerable gambling, drinking, and juvenile delinquency. Needless to say, the blacks were severely discriminated against in the city's occupational system. Those who were employed had low-paying service jobs as porters and dishwashers; females also had household jobs as maids. Thus the Harlem residents were both overcrowded and very poor.

This deteriorating situation should not obscure another aspect of ghetto development—the growth and proliferation of exclusive institutions. Foremost among these in the black case was the church. Certain churches were active in buying and selling real estate to promote Harlem as a new area for black settlement in the early years. Numerous churches moved to Harlem as the people moved there, and additional congregations formed in the early decades of the twentieth century. The churches were stratified, with some serving the more prosperous upper classes and others catering to the poorer blacks. As they had during slavery, the churches furnished much of the leadership of the black community. There were also newspapers, such as *The Amsterdam News,* and self-help voluntary associations, such as the Committee for Improving the Industrial Condition of the Negro in New York, the National Urban League, the National Association for the Advancement of Colored People, and many others. Blacks in Harlem also promoted their subculture in the form of jazz and black theater. In sum, although Harlem was a ghetto and a slum, it also organized and promoted a network of black institutions.

## Chicago's south side

The story in Chicago is much like the New York case, although it did not begin in an attractive new residential environment. The history which follows is based largely on *Black Chicago: The Making of a Negro Ghetto, 1890–1920,* by Allen H. Spear (1967).

At the turn of the century Chicago blacks were even more dispersed than were their counterparts in New York. A study by S. Lieberson (1963) shows that in 1910 blacks were less segregated from native-born whites than Italian immigrants were. Not many blacks lived in the rapidly growing city, and they were scattered in different areas. As in New York, whites in Chicago were blatantly prejudiced against blacks. For example, when a Black teenager swam into the "whites-only" waters off a Chicago beach in 1919, whites threw stones at him, he was unable to swim to a safe place, and he drowned (Chicago Commission on Race Relations, 1922, p. 4). After this there was a race riot in which groups of whites pursued and attacked blacks at the perimeter of the black ghetto and stoned some of them to death. Blacks were routinely called "niggers." Race relations deteriorated around the time of World War I when a migration of 50,000 blacks into Chicago precipitated competition for jobs and for space.

Many whites favored racial segregation, and the Chicago Real Estate Board recommended a residential segregation ordinance. In the city council in 1917 a resolution was introduced "to consider the question of segregating the races within certain established zones" (Spear, 1967, p. 217). In one mostly white area of the city which housed a few pockets of blacks, the citizens mobilized to prevent any expansion of these areas and, indeed, to buy houses occupied by blacks to be reoccupied by whites. The "neighborhood improvement club" decreed that the blacks must be confined to certain designed areas, that "real estate agents must refuse to sell property in white blocks to Negroes, and landlords must hire only white janitors," and the club's president decreed, "The districts which are now white must remain white. There will be no compromise" (Spear, 1967, p. 22). Throughout the city, the Chicago Real Estate Board and numerous neighborhood business groups endorsed the idea of having confined black districts and preventing blacks from moving into white areas. Not infrequently, vigilante groups took violent action—fires and stonings—against whites who went against this policy.

Real estate operators and brokers as well as civil officials took action in black residential areas which adversely affected their community life:

> White real estate agents, insensitive to class differences among Negroes, made no attempt to uphold standards in middle-class Negro neighborhoods as they did in comparable white districts. They persistently rented flats in "respectable" Negro neighborhoods to members of the "sporting element," thus forcing middle-class Negroes to move continually in search of decent areas to live and rear families. As a result, neighborhood stability was at best temporary. (Spear, 1967, pp. 24–25)

Furthermore, city authorities attempted to move the red-light district away from commercial and white residential districts. Thus it was located in or near the black area, even though it catered primarily to whites. This, too, tended to undermine black neighborhood stability.

In Chicago the problem was that the white leadership had determined blacks should live exclusively among their own people. It determined that of the two areas of black settlement, on the South and West sides, only the South was to grow. The black district was near the center of the city with relatively old housing, and was bounded by Lake Michigan, by a warehouse district, and by white residential areas. Yet the black population of the city was growing rapidly, creating a massive demand for additional housing. The terms of Chicago's spatial racial conflict were then set for generations to come: A series of lines of demarcation was to be established between black and white neighborhoods. The blacks would continue to need housing and to push into the next adjacent neighborhood. The main tools of enforcement of the boundaries were the restrictive convenant and informal social pressure on both whites and blacks and—where these failed—violence.

The South Side black district did continue to grow in population and area, particularly after the Supreme Court invalidated the restrictive covenant as a useful instrument of segregation. The black South Side grew to such an extent that two sociologists, studying it in the late 1930s, called it "Black Metropolis" (Drake & Cayton, 1962). Like Harlem's blacks the Chicagoans used their ghetto to develop their subculture and to generate an elaborate network of institutions: churches, voluntary associations, newspapers, clubs, and the like.

One type of institution that did not prosper in the black ghetto was capitalist business. Neither in Harlem nor in Chicago did the blacks develop a growing and viable private economy.

In summary, these two histories epitomize much of the urban situation of blacks. The two ghettos show relationships that persist to the present, expanded into the metropolitan context. Both cities segregated the blacks into definite districts, or ghettos, setting a pattern of highly segregated residential areas. In both cases this was a consequence of white rejection, and the residential environment deteriorated to slum conditions, with substandard overcrowded housing, high levels of crime and delinquency, and poor public health. On the other hand, ghettoization also brought about internal social organization: churches, voluntary associations for self-help, and the evolution of black culture into distinctive urban forms.

On the current scene, we see ghettoization continued, not quite as severely as in the past, as reflected in high levels of racial residential segregation. The segregation is enforced through the operation of the dual housing market.

## Blacks in the Urban Economy

### Failure of black business

Despite the proliferation of institutions in the ghetto, small business failed to develop (Light, 1972). Whereas most other nationality neighborhoods in the city developed their own small retail stores for local trade—indeed, in the extreme case, nobody but Chinese operated retail shops in San Francisco's Chinatown—very few blacks became small-scale capitalists. The majority of retail outlets serving blacks were owned and operated by whites. Ivan Light, who studied this situation historically, concluded that the reason for this black pattern was that blacks did not develop family-based mutual credit associations. He discovered these associations had existed in African tribes and were probably stamped out by the institution of slavery. Without a number of small businesses in their own sections of American cities, blacks lacked one effective route to upward social mobility.

### Dual housing market

The histories of Harlem and the South Side illustrate the phenomenon of the dual housing market. This concept assumes that a community has a housing stock and a system which allocates it to individuals or groups. The housing stock is like any other stock: For example, an automobile dealer has an inventory of vehicles: some new, others used; some station wagons, others subcompacts; and so on. Likewise, a community has a housing stock of dwelling units: some new, others old; some are in apartment buildings, others are single-family houses, mobile homes, and so on. The system which allocates these units to individual households consists of numerous agencies of which banks and savings and loan associations plus real estate brokers are the most important. Newspaper advertising departments, insurance companies, builders, municipal building inspectors, building and project managers, and others round out the system.

Within urban areas, one housing market exists for whites and another for blacks. The markets are territorially based, with certain districts for whites and others for dark-skinned peoples. To some extent, the institutional structure of urban real estate is differentiated, with one sector serving the white population and handling the white housing stock and the other serving the black. Thus real estate brokers, bankers, developers, and others have buildings and customers that are localized in some particular section of the metropolitan area; each firm is likely to have a black or a white clientele. A few large metropolitan firms may deal routinely with black and white customers, but most would deal only with one racial group.

The basis of the dual market is the white rejection of black neighbors.[7] From the outset of northward black migration this has created an artificial shortage of housing for black households. The peak shortage was in the late 1940s after hundreds of thousands of blacks had moved to northern cities to work in the industries that needed workers during World War II. There was a general housing shortage then, but during the following decades builders erected large numbers of new houses and apartments which alleviated crowded conditions for whites. Restricted in their choices and confined to certain areas, blacks benefited far less from the expanded supply.

For many years one major effect of the dual housing market was to cause blacks to pay more for housing than whites paid for equivalent accommodations. This was because despite population growth in the ghetto, the supply of housing there grew very little, given the tight boundaries. Thus demand for housing grew while supply did not, and the effect was rising costs for blacks and considerable overcrowding. This dynamic also created considerable pressure for new housing at the borders of the ghettos. While the black districts were expanding, beginning in the early 1950s, "housing on the market [was] worth more to blacks than to whites" (Molotch, 1972, p. 20).

However, since the fifties, housing supply has expanded and better accommodations have become available to blacks, at least to some blacks (Downs, 1981). Now, despite agreement on the existence of the dual market, some economists disagree as to whether blacks pay a premium for housing. Kain says, "Most researchers have concluded that blacks do pay more than whites for housing of comparable size and quality, but this view is by no means unanimous" (1975, p. 140). He explains that the dispute is over the question of whether blacks and whites are getting the same bundle of amenities and services with the housing they rent or buy. After reviewing the studies and conducting his own research, Kain concludes that "a premium is required to shift units to the black submarket" (p. 140), meaning that blacks do pay more.

Downs, another urban expert, reaches the opposite conclusion. Citing a study of 39 metropolitan areas in the mid-1970s, he says that in most of them "for housing of comparable quality, blacks paid an average of 15 percent less to buy and 6 percent less to rent than whites paid" (1981, p. 92). In 6 metropolitan areas among the 39, blacks paid more than whites. Downs draws two implications from these findings: "First, the relative housing situation of blacks has improved since the early 1950s. Second, many whites are willing to pay premiums to live in segregated neighborhoods, even though they could reduce their housing costs by moving into mainly black neighborhoods" (1981, p. 93). Downs, though, is not negating the existing dual market, nor is he denying that blacks traditionally occupied inferior housing.

---

[7] See "Racial Violence in Boston Forcing Blacks to Move," *New York Times*, June 2, 1982, p. 10, for a contemporary incident.

"Steering" is the current term for the process of leading blacks into certain neighborhoods and whites into others. Real estate brokers who employ this practice tend to show houses in certain neighborhoods to whites and in other neighborhoods to blacks. If a certain neighborhood has begun to "go black," brokers are likely to stop taking white customers there. If houses are offered for sale there, brokers bring only blacks to see them. The brokers also have more subtle techniques of suggesting to people which neighborhoods they will like, particularly by what they say about the quality and safety of the schools (Pearce, 1979).

"Redlining" is another technique used to maintain the dual housing market. This is a banker's practice which took its name from the routine of drawing red lines on city street maps around neighborhoods that usually had older houses and mixed racial populations. Even the Federal Housing Authority, a governmental mortgage-insuring agency, once practiced redlining, although it no longer does so. The red line meant the bank would not loan money for mortagages or for home improvements on properties located in the designated zone. Similarly, insurance companies redlined neighborhoods and either refused to insure their buildings or charged higher premiums (Squires et al., 1979). This practice had severe negative consequences for the neighborhoods. It meant ordinary families could not get normal mortgage loans at good interest rates to buy or improve houses in these areas. The net effect was to promote the deterioration of the buildings and of the redlined neighborhoods.

**The institutional web**  Several components together, which Foley (1973) calls an "institutional web," support the dual housing market and include "the services of realtors, mortgage lenders, appraisers, and developers; the administrative and political behavior of government officials" (p. 96), as well as the behaviors of white residents and homeowners. Foley quotes an analyst who refers to a "web of urban racism," including all these elements plus "subtle conscious and unconscious actions." While any one of these elements might be weak or temporary, *in sum* they produce enduring residential segregation.

The private housing market has numerous mechanisms which block access to white areas. One mechanism is to make it difficult for blacks to rent in certain buildings. Foley (1973) quotes from a study of the San Francisco area housing market:

> Almost all [apartment owners] believe that their white tenants will leave if they rent any of their apartments to minority families. Their usual tactics for avoiding integration are delay and red tape, i.e., the minority prospect gets delay and red tape and the white gets the apartment.
>
> Time is bought in all kinds of ways by setting requirements almost no one can meet: by forms, by demanding references, by myriad uncertainties, even by failing to call back.... Actually, most minority prospects are easily turned away. They are too proud to force the issue, and also very worried about the amount of time it takes to follow through a complaint. (p. 98)

This same study also concluded that real estate brokers attempt to prevent minority households from buying property in all-white residential areas. In this realm, also, a variety of small and subtle techniques may be used to prevent a sale. Furthermore, real estate boards are crucially important in this process. Only if a broker is a member of the board does she or he have access to the listings in an area. Thus even if a minority broker is a member of a central-city board, she or he cannot show suburban houses to clients. Foley says suburban boards have typically resisted having minority-group individuals as members. Other mechanisms as well enter into the institutional web. While restrictive covenants are not legally enforceable, Foley says they are still prevalent on individual house deeds, and he suspects that many white homeowners may feel they represent a personal obligation to the neighborhood. Foley also notes that there are probably no black certified real estate appraisers and that certain procedures in the mortgage finance business make it difficult for minority-group members to borrow money to purchase houses outside their old areas. Ironically, the attempts to provide financial resources for minority areas may be preventing people from dispersing. "Earmarking 'minority mortgage money' for loans on so-called ghetto property means that minority applicants are more likely than ever to find it hard to get loans for purchase in suburban areas" (Foley, 1973, p. 106). In addition to this list of obstacles in the private sector, Foley has an equally long list of governmental policies and practices that are part of the institutional web which maintains the dual housing market.

## SEGREGATION PATTERNS

### Segregation Index

In 1965, a husband-wife team of sociological demographers, Karl and Alma Taeuber, published *Negroes in Cities,* which showed a way to analyze segregation patterns. Using a statistical technique known as a "segregation index," they measured the residential locations of blacks and whites in 207 cities in the United States in 1960. The segregation index is calculated from data census reports on city blocks. Among other facts, these show the number of white and black inhabitants of every block in every city in the nation. (They also show the ages of the people, the number of houses and apartments on each block, and a few other selected pieces of information.) Theoretically, the Taeubers said, a city could have two opposite sorts of racial patterns. In a perfectly segregated city, all blocks would be either all white or all black, whereas in a perfectly integrated city, all blocks would be racially mixed such that the proportion of each race was equal to the city average. Thus a perfectly integrated city with 70 percent whites and 30 percent blacks, would have all blocks also at a 7:3 ratio. This model has a certain artificial quality, and alternatives to it do exist, but it permits accurate measurement of segregation levels, and given the situation of the cities, the others would undoubtedly generate the same results. The segregation index produces a single score for the whole city (or metropolitan area, depending upon which is being studied). The highest possible score is 100, which represents perfect segregation, and the lowest possible score is 0, which represents perfect integration.

## Levels of Segregation

The simple conclusion of the Taeubers' analysis was that U.S. cities are extremely highly segregated. Among all cities, the average segregation index was 86.2. As the Taeubers said, the broad generalizations were clear:

> In the urban United States, there is a very high degree of segregation of the residences of whites and Negroes. This is true for cities in all regions of the country and for all types of cities—large and small, industrial and commercial, metropolitan and suburban. It is true whether there are hundreds of thousands of Negro residents, or only a few thousand. Residential segregation prevails regardless of the relative economic status of the white and Negro residents. It occurs regardless of the character of local laws and policies, and regardless of the extent of other forms of segregation or discrimination. (1965, pp. 35–36)

**FIGURE 8-1**
Frequency distribution of indexes of residential segregation for 109 cities, 1980. (Source: data provided by K. Taeuber).

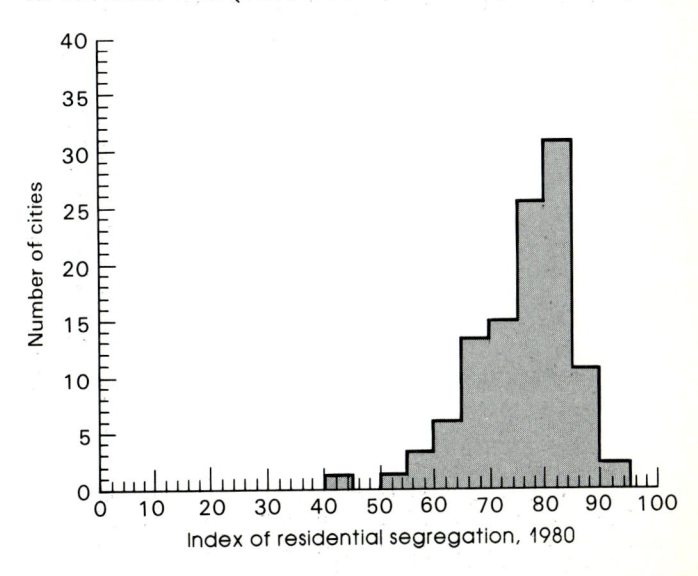

## Trends since 1940

After the 1970 census, Karl Taeuber and two colleagues computed segregation indexes for 109 of the original cities and were able to assemble a time series of measurements for each of them from 1940. They discovered that the level of segregation was rather stable, that it remained at the high levels measured earlier. It might have been anticipated that patterns would have changed in the decade of the 1960s. Federal and local governments had enacted antidiscrimination laws; some desegregation of public schools took place; programs such as urban renewal, model cities, and the Economic Opportunity Act (the "war on poverty") focused on urban neighborhoods and the problems of the poor. The civil rights movement had affected cities across the nation. Thus it was surprising to find the high levels of residential segregation undisturbed almost everywhere.

Some regional differences were found among the city patterns. Cities in the western region are somewhat less segregated than cities elsewhere in the nation. Northern cities are more segregated than southern cities, but the latter have had *increasing* segregation levels in recent decades. Notice in Table 8-1, for example, that Charleston, South Carolina, went from 60.1 in 1940 to 86.5 in 1970 and Montgomery, Alabama, went from 86.8 to 93.2 during the same period. This was a time of industrial and economic development in the south, and evidently, the cities of the region began to adopt residential segregation patterns resembling those of the north.

Traditionally, southern cities had more of a scattering of black households throughout white areas. They had all-black areas too, but the scattered households elsewhere in the city made for more spatial integration than was present in the northern cities with uniform ghetto patterns. In the southern cities there were little houses for blacks behind white residences and small pockets of servants' quarters in white neighborhoods. In the current era, though, this arrangement has given way to exclusively white and exclusively black districts, like those found in the north.

In sum, the segregation studies show that levels of segregation are high in almost all cities. Segregation is persistent, falling slightly over the decades and actually rising in some cities. Evidently, it was unaffected by the civil rights movement of the 1960s and by federal urban programs such as urban renewal, model cities, and the so-called war on poverty.

## CHANGING RESIDENTIAL PATTERNS

### Background: Migration to the Cities

During the 1940s and particularly during the 1950s and 1960s, millions of blacks moved from the rural south to the industrial cities of the other regions, particularly of the northeastern and midwestern regions. "Pushes" and "pulls" impelled this migration. The pushes moved blacks from the rural south where they had worked in agriculture, often as sharecroppers—tenant farmers who paid part of their crops

**TABLE 8-1**
**Housing Segregation, 109 U.S. Cities, 1940–1980**

| | Segregation indexes | | | | | |
|---|---|---|---|---|---|---|
| City | 1940 | 1950 | 1960 | 1970 | 1980 | Rank |
| Akron, Ohio | 82.2 | 87.6 | 88.1 | 81.2 | 76.8 | 51 |
| Asheville, N.C. | 88.6 | 89.2 | 92.3 | 88.5 | 77.0 | 53 |
| Atlanta, Ga. | 87.4 | 91.5 | 93.6 | 91.5 | 85.8 | 101 |
| Atlantic City, N.J. | 94.6 | 94.0 | 89.2 | 86.9 | 85.1 | 97 |
| Augusta, Ga. | 86.9 | 88.9 | 93.0 | 93.3 | 84.9 | 96 |
| Austin, Tex. | 84.8 | 92.0 | 93.1 | 84.6 | 69.1 | 21 |
| Baltimore, Md. | 90.1 | 91.3 | 89.6 | 88.3 | 85.6 | 99 |
| Beaumont, Tex. | 81.0 | 89.6 | 92.3 | 89.7 | 80.2 | 66 |
| Berkeley, Cal. | 81.2 | 80.3 | 69.4 | 62.9 | 71.6 | 27 |
| Birmingham, Ala. | 86.4 | 88.7 | 92.8 | 91.5 | 84.8 | 94 |
| Boston, Mass. | 86.3 | 86.5 | 83.9 | 79.9 | 79.8 | 64 |
| Bridgeport, Conn. | 78.8 | 74.4 | 69.7 | 71.7 | 64.5 | 11 |
| Buffalo, N.Y. | 87.9 | 89.5 | 86.5 | 84.2 | 82.0 | 78 |
| Cambridge, Mass. | 74.3 | 75.6 | 65.5 | 52.6 | 56.3 | 3 |
| Camden, N.J. | 87.6 | 89.6 | 76.5 | 67.4 | 54.4 | 2 |
| Canton, Ohio | 89.9 | 89.3 | 81.5 | 82.4 | 74.9 | 37 |
| Charleston, S.C. | 60.1 | 68.4 | 79.5 | 86.5 | 81.3 | 73 |
| Charleston, W. Va. | 80.3 | 79.6 | 79.0 | 74.3 | 63.7 | 9 |
| Charlotte, N.C. | 90.1 | 92.8 | 94.3 | 92.7 | 82.1 | 79 |
| Chattanooga, Tenn. | 86.5 | 88.5 | 91.5 | 89.9 | 81.8 | 77 |
| Chester, Penn. | 85.1 | 88.1 | 87.4 | 82.2 | 72.8 | 32 |
| Chicago, Ill. | 95.0 | 92.1 | 92.6 | 88.8 | 91.9 | 109 |
| Cincinnati, Ohio | 90.6 | 91.2 | 89.0 | 83.1 | 79.3 | 61 |
| Cleveland, Ohio | 92.0 | 91.5 | 91.3 | 89.0 | 91.0 | 108 |
| Columbia, S.C. | 83.0 | 88.1 | 94.1 | 86.7 | 66.3 | 15 |
| Columbus, Ohio | 87.1 | 88.9 | 85.3 | 84.1 | 75.1 | 40 |
| Covington, Ken. | 80.6 | 85.0 | 87.8 | 86.9 | 78.5 | 58 |
| Dallas, Tex. | 80.2 | 88.4 | 94.6 | 92.7 | 83.2 | 86 |
| Dayton, Ohio | 91.5 | 93.3 | 91.3 | 90.1 | 84.6 | 91 |
| Denver, Col. | 87.9 | 88.9 | 85.5 | 77.6 | 74.9 | 37 |
| Des Moines, Iowa | 87.8 | 89.3 | 87.9 | 79.2 | 74.1 | 36 |
| Detroit, Mich. | 89.9 | 88.8 | 84.5 | 80.9 | 73.4 | 34 |
| Durham, N.C. | 88.2 | 88.8 | 92.7 | 87.5 | 76.7 | 50 |
| East Chicago, Ind. | 74.5 | 79.6 | 82.8 | 79.0 | 75.3 | 42 |
| East Orange, N.J. | 85.3 | 83.7 | 71.2 | 60.8 | 44.4 | 1 |
| East St. Louis, Ill. | 93.8 | 94.2 | 92.0 | 76.8 | 60.5 | 6 |
| Elizabeth, N.J. | 75.9 | 76.1 | 75.2 | 75.5 | 72.1 | 29 |
| Evanston, Ill. | 91.5 | 92.1 | 87.2 | 78.3 | 69.9 | 23 |
| Evansville, Ind. | 86.2 | 92.4 | 91.2 | 88.6 | 77.6 | 55 |
| Flint, Mich. | 92.5 | 95.3 | 94.4 | 81.7 | 81.7 | 76 |
| Fort Worth, Tex. | 81.3 | 90.4 | 94.3 | 92.6 | 85.8 | 101 |
| Galveston, Tex. | 72.2 | 78.3 | 82.9 | 77.4 | 72.3 | 31 |
| Gary, Ind. | 88.3 | 93.8 | 92.8 | 82.9 | 68.2 | 16 |
| Greensboro, N.C. | 93.1 | 93.5 | 93.3 | 91.4 | 79.9 | 65 |
| Harrisburg, Penn. | 87.2 | 89.8 | 85.7 | 76.2 | 63.1 | 8 |

**TABLE 8-1** *(continued)*
**Housing Segregation, 109 U.S. Cities, 1940–1970**

| City | Segregation Indexes | | | | | Rank |
|---|---|---|---|---|---|---|
| | 1940 | 1950 | 1960 | 1970 | 1980 | |
| Hartford, Conn. | 84.8 | 84.4 | 82.1 | 77.4 | 72.0 | 28 |
| Houston, Tex. | 84.5 | 91.5 | 93.7 | 90.0 | 81.2 | 72 |
| Huntington, W. Va. | 81.6 | 85.8 | 88.8 | 85.9 | 78.8 | 59 |
| Indianapolis, Ind. | 90.4 | 91.4 | 91.6 | 88.3 | 83.2 | 86 |
| Jacksonville, Fla. | 94.3 | 94.9 | 96.9 | 92.5 | 82.1 | 79 |
| Jersey City, N.J. | 79.5 | 80.5 | 77.9 | 75.6 | 80.2 | 66 |
| Kansas City, Kan. | 90.5 | 92.0 | 91.5 | 84.7 | 76.9 | 52 |
| Kansas City, Mo. | 88.0 | 91.3 | 90.8 | 88.0 | 85.5 | 98 |
| Knoxville, Tenn. | 88.6 | 89.6 | 90.7 | 89.6 | 76.0 | 47 |
| Little Rock, Ark. | 78.2 | 84.5 | 89.4 | 89.7 | 80.6 | 70 |
| Los Angeles, Cal. | 84.2 | 84.6 | 81.8 | 78.4 | 80.9 | 71 |
| Louisville, Ken. | 81.7 | 86.0 | 89.2 | 88.9 | 86.2 | 103 |
| Macon, Ga. | 74.9 | 77.1 | 83.7 | 90.2 | 79.5 | 63 |
| Memphis, Tenn. | 79.9 | 86.4 | 92.0 | 91.8 | 84.6 | 91 |
| Miami, Fla. | 97.9 | 97.8 | 97.9 | 89.4 | 84.7 | 93 |
| Milwaukee, Wis. | 92.9 | 91.6 | 88.1 | 83.7 | 80.3 | 69 |
| Minneapolis, Minn. | 88.0 | 86.0 | 79.3 | 67.9 | 69.9 | 23 |
| Mobile, Ala. | 86.6 | 89.4 | 91.9 | 91.0 | 85.7 | 100 |
| Montgomery, Ala. | 86.8 | 90.5 | 94.7 | 93.2 | 86.4 | 104 |
| Mt. Vernon, N.Y. | 78.9 | 78.0 | 73.2 | 78.4 | 74.9 | 37 |
| Nashville, Tenn. | 86.5 | 88.7 | 91.7 | 89.0 | 80.2 | 66 |
| Newark, N.J. | 77.4 | 76.9 | 71.6 | 74.9 | 76.4 | 49 |
| New Bedford, Mass. | 83.4 | 86.8 | 81.6 | 72.7 | 70.5 | 25 |
| New Haven, Conn. | 80.1 | 79.9 | 70.9 | 69.1 | 68.8 | 20 |
| New Orleans, La. | 81.0 | 84.9 | 86.3 | 83.1 | 76.2 | 48 |
| New Rochelle, N.Y. | 80.6 | 78.9 | 79.5 | 70.7 | 68.6 | 19 |
| New York, N.Y. | 86.8 | 87.3 | 79.3 | 73.0 | 75.3 | 42 |
| Norfolk, Va. | 96.0 | 95.0 | 94.6 | 90.8 | 75.8 | 46 |
| Oakland, Cal. | 78.4 | 81.2 | 73.1 | 63.4 | 58.6 | 4 |
| Oklahoma City, Okla. | 84.3 | 88.6 | 87.1 | 81.8 | 81.6 | 74 |
| Omaha, Neb. | 89.5 | 92.4 | 92.0 | 85.6 | 82.9 | 82 |
| Pasadena, Cal. | 84.2 | 85.9 | 83.4 | 75.0 | 66.0 | 14 |
| Paterson, N.J. | 79.8 | 80.0 | 75.9 | 70.3 | 65.1 | 12 |
| Philadelphia, Penn. | 88.0 | 89.0 | 87.1 | 83.2 | 87.6 | 105 |
| Pittsburgh, Penn. | 82.0 | 84.0 | 84.6 | 83.9 | 83.4 | 89 |
| Port Arthur, Tex. | 81.7 | 91.3 | 90.4 | 87.0 | 82.9 | 82 |
| Portland, Ore. | 83.8 | 84.3 | 76.7 | 69.0 | 77.3 | 54 |
| Providence, R.I. | 85.8 | 85.5 | 77.0 | 72.0 | 69.2 | 22 |
| Richmond, Va. | 92.7 | 92.2 | 94.8 | 90.8 | 78.8 | 59 |
| Roanoke, Va. | 94.8 | 96.0 | 93.9 | 91.8 | 83.2 | 86 |
| Rochester, N.Y. | 85.5 | 86.9 | 82.4 | 73.8 | 65.1 | 12 |
| Sacramento, Cal. | 77.8 | 77.6 | 63.9 | 56.3 | 59.6 | 5 |
| St. Louis, Mo. | 92.6 | 92.9 | 90.5 | 89.3 | 89.9 | 107 |
| St. Paul, Minn. | 88.6 | 90.0 | 87.3 | 76.8 | 75.1 | 40 |
| San Antonio, Tex. | 79.6 | 88.3 | 90.1 | 81.8 | 75.3 | 42 |

**TABLE 8-1** *(continued)*
**Housing Segregation, 109 U.S. Cities, 1940–1970**

|  | Segregation Indexes | | | | | |
|---|---|---|---|---|---|---|
| City | 1940 | 1950 | 1960 | 1970 | 1980 | Rank |
| San Diego, Cal. | 84.4 | 83.6 | 81.3 | 71.6 | 61.9 | 7 |
| San Francisco, Cal. | 82.9 | 79.8 | 69.3 | 55.5 | 68.2 | 16 |
| Savannah, Ga. | 84.2 | 88.8 | 92.3 | 91.2 | 82.9 | 82 |
| Seattle, Wash. | 82.2 | 83.3 | 79.7 | 69.2 | 72.2 | 30 |
| Shreveport, La. | 90.3 | 93.2 | 95.9 | 97.4 | 89.1 | 106 |
| Springfield, Ohio | 80.9 | 81.6 | 84.7 | 81.1 | 75.6 | 45 |
| Tampa, Fla. | 90.2 | 92.5 | 94.5 | 90.7 | 83.1 | 85 |
| Terre Haute, Ind. | 86.6 | 89.8 | 90.1 | 82.5 | 70.8 | 26 |
| Toledo, Ohio | 91.0 | 91.5 | 91.8 | 86.7 | 82.7 | 81 |
| Topeka, Kan. | 80.8 | 80.7 | 83.5 | 74.1 | 64.3 | 10 |
| Trenton, N.J. | 81.9 | 83.0 | 79.6 | 77.2 | 77.8 | 56 |
| Tulsa, Okla. | 84.6 | 91.2 | 86.3 | 76.4 | 84.8 | 94 |
| Waco, Tex. | 80.1 | 87.0 | 90.7 | 86.8 | 78.4 | 57 |
| Washington, D.C. | 81.0 | 80.1 | 79.7 | 77.7 | 79.4 | 62 |
| Wichita, Kan. | 92.0 | 93.3 | 91.9 | 85.0 | 81.6 | 74 |
| Wilmington, Del. | 83.0 | 86.2 | 79.8 | 69.8 | 68.3 | 18 |
| Winston Salem, N.C. | 92.9 | 93.8 | 95.0 | 94.0 | 84.3 | 90 |
| Yonkers, N.Y. | 82.0 | 81.7 | 78.1 | 68.0 | 73.2 | 33 |
| Youngstown, Ohio | 80.0 | 83.5 | 78.5 | 74.9 | 73.4 | 34 |

*Note:* 1940–1970 indexes refer to white-nonwhite segregation; 1980 index refers to black-nonblack segregation.

*Source:* 1940–1970 statistics from Taeuber, Sorenson, and Hollingsworth, 1975; 1980 statistics supplied to author by K. Taeuber.

as rent. By the middle of the current century, tractors and other machines were replacing animal and human labor in southern agriculture. The system of land tenure changed to accommodate this new technology; the small holdings of the past were incompatible with mechanization. Larger-farm operations could better handle the new technology. Thus smallholders, sharecroppers, black and white, were forced from the land. They migrated to places of economic opportunity. The industrial cities pulled them; a demand for labor existed during the war years and continued during the period of massive economic growth of the following decades. In the decade of the 1940s, 1.45 million blacks migrated into 13 states plus the District of Columbia. They were followed by 1.36 million in the 1950s and another 1.37 million in the 1960s (see Table 8-2 for details). Most went to New York, New Jersey, Pennsylvania, Ohio, Illinois, Michigan, Maryland, California, and the District of Columbia. They came from about 11 southern states. This was an enormous migration—over 4 million people in thirty years.

The black populations of numerous cities grew rapidly. Table 8-3 shows that New York City gained 895,000 blacks in the twenty-year period from 1950 to 1970. Chicago gained almost 600,000, and Detroit gained well over 300,000 blacks. Some

**TABLE 8-2**
Net Migration of Blacks by States, 1940–1970 (in Thousands)*

|  | 1940–1950 | 1950–1960 | 1960–1970 |
|---|---|---|---|
| *Receiving* | | | |
| New England | | | |
| Connecticut | 15 | 37 | 38 |
| Massachusetts | 12 | 20 | 33 |
| Middle Atlantic | | | |
| New York | 266 | 255 | 296 |
| New Jersey | 61 | 107 | 120 |
| Pennsylvania | 107 | 75 | 25 |
| East north central | | | |
| Ohio | 131 | 129 | 45 |
| Indiana | 39 | 42 | 32 |
| Illinois | 203 | 182 | 127 |
| Michigan | 186 | 122 | 124 |
| Wisconsin | 14 | 29 | 27 |
| West north central | | | |
| Missouri | 31 | 24 | 14 |
| South Atlantic | | | |
| Maryland | 37 | 31 | 79 |
| District of Columbia | 61 | 51 | 36 |
| Pacific | | | |
| California | 289 | 255 | 272 |
| *Sending* | | | |
| South Atlantic | | | |
| Virginia | −29 | −74 | −79 |
| West Virginia | −17 | −41 | −20 |
| North Carolina | −164 | −204 | −175 |
| South Carolina | −208 | −218 | −197 |
| Georgia | −243 | −205 | −154 |
| East south central | | | |
| Tennessee | −48 | −59 | −51 |
| Alabama | −204 | −224 | −231 |
| Mississippi | −326 | −323 | −279 |
| West south central | | | |
| Arkansas | −158 | −150 | −112 |
| Louisiana | −147 | −93 | −163 |
| Oklahoma | −47 | −21 | −3 |
| Texas | −107 | −33 | −4 |

*This is the estimated net intercensal migration of black population, by states, 1940–1970. Computed by the Bureau of the Census components-of-change method.
Source: *Historical Statistics of the United States*, part 1, 1975, table series C25-75.

**TABLE 8-3**
**The 25 Cities with Largest Black Populations in 1980***

| Rank in 1980 | | Black pop. 1910† | % black 1910 | Black pop. 1950† | % black 1950 | Black pop. 1980† | % black 1980 | Gain 1950–1980† |
|---|---|---|---|---|---|---|---|---|
| 1 | New York | 92 | 1.9 | 773 | 9.8 | 1784 | 25.2 | 1011 |
| 2 | Chicago | 44 | 2.0 | 511 | 14.1 | 1197 | 39.8 | 686 |
| 3 | Detroit | 6 | 1.2 | 303 | 16.4 | 759 | 63.1 | 456 |
| 4 | Philadelphia | 84 | 5.5 | 379 | 18.3 | 639 | 37.8 | 260 |
| 5 | Los Angeles | 8 | 2.3 | 211 | 10.7 | 505 | 17.0 | 294 |
| 6 | Washington | 94 | 28.5 | 284 | 35.4 | 448 | 70.3 | 164 |
| 7 | Houston | 24 | 30.4 | 126 | 21.1 | 440 | 27.6 | 314 |
| 8 | Baltimore | 85 | 15.2 | 226 | 23.8 | 431 | 54.8 | 205 |
| 9 | New Orleans | 89 | 26.3 | 183 | 32.0 | 308 | 55.3 | 125 |
| 10 | Memphis | 52 | 40.0 | 147 | 37.2 | 308 | 47.6 | 161 |
| 11 | Atlanta | 52 | 33.5 | 121 | 36.6 | 283 | 66.6 | 162 |
| 12 | Dallas | 18 | 19.6 | 57 | 13.2 | 266 | 29.4 | 169 |
| 13 | Cleveland | 8 | 1.5 | 149 | 16.3 | 251 | 43.8 | 102 |
| 14 | St. Louis | 44 | 6.4 | 154 | 18.0 | 206 | 45.6 | 52 |
| 15 | Newark | 9 | 2.7 | 75 | 17.2 | 192 | 58.2 | 117 |
| 16 | Oakland | 3 | 2.0 | 56 | 14.5 | 159 | 46.9 | 103 |
| 17 | Birmingham | 52 | 34.9 | 130 | 39.9 | 158 | 55.6 | 28 |
| 18 | Indianapolis | 22 | 9.3 | 64 | 15.0 | 153 | 21.8 | 89 |
| 19 | Milwaukee | 1 | 0.3 | 23 | 3.6 | 147 | 23.1 | 124 |
| 20 | Jacksonville | 29 | 50.8 | 73 | 35.5 | 137 | 25.4 | 64 |
| 21 | Cincinnati | 20 | 5.4 | 79 | 15.6 | 130 | 33.8 | 51 |
| 22 | Boston | 14 | 2.0 | 42 | 5.3 | 126 | 22.4 | 84 |
| 23 | Columbus, Ohio | 13 | 7.0 | 47 | 12.5 | 125 | 22.1 | 78 |
| 24 | Kansas City, Mo. | 24 | 9.5 | 56 | 12.3 | 123 | 27.4 | 67 |
| 25 | Richmond | 47 | 36.6 | 73 | 31.7 | 112 | 51.3 | 39 |

*Figures for 1910 and 1980 refer to blacks; figures for 1950 refer to "nonwhites."
†In thousands.
Source: For 1910, Davis, 1966, p. 119, and U.S. census; for 1950, U.S. census; for 1980, *Statistical Abstract of the United States, 1981.*

of these gains were attributable to natural increase, but most were produced by the migration from the south. Another aspect of this shift and growth was the dramatic shift in majority-minority proportions. At the beginning of the century, the northern cities had small black minorities, all well under 10 percent. The southern cities and ones in the border states, like Memphis and Washington, D.C., had large black minorities early in the century, but none of the northeastern and midwestern cities had. By 1970 almost all the northern cities had large black minorities. (The only ones that did not were places in the upper midwest, like Minneapolis and St. Paul, which had 6.5 percent blacks in 1980, and cities in the Pacific northwest, like Seattle, with 3.9 percent. By comparison, 43.8 percent of Cleveland's population and 45.6 percent of St. Louis's population were black in the same year.[8] The size of the minority was so large as to give them political control of some of these cities, as in Detroit, where more than 40 percent of the people were blacks in 1970. (Some cities, like Newark, Washington, D.C., and Atlanta, had black majorities in 1970.)

In the 1940s and 1950s these newcomers and their families were confined within the boundaries of the traditional ghetto. They created an enormous demand for new houses and new neighborhoods, which quickly caused the ghettos to grow. Two other developments permitted ghetto expansion: After the Supreme Court invalidated restrictive covenants in 1948, they could no longer be used to bolster black-white boundary lines. And as suburban residential construction accelerated in the 1950s, the white housing market loosened in the cities.

As the housing supply grew in the 1950s, neighborhood space became more plentiful. By the end of the 1940s the existing apartments and neighborhoods, white and black, were densely occupied. For more than fifteen years there had been almost no residential construction. During the depression there had been very little residential construction—banks were unable to make mortgage loans and unemployed people could not buy houses. Then during World War II the nation's economic resources were diverted to military purposes, so, again, no new houses or apartments were built. After the war, with demobilization, men returned home and new families were formed, creating a great housing shortage. Under those circumstances the whites living in neighborhoods surrounding black ghettos were unlikely to move for any reason—there was no place to go. But as new suburbs were built along with additional housing in cities, the shortage eased and some flexibility and movement entered into the urban systems. Traditional ghetto walls cracked and the black districts grew enormously.

### Racial Transitions in Residential Areas

Thousands of city blocks have shifted from white to black residences since the late 1940s; these transitions follow a fairly general process (Molotch, 1972). Usually, the changing blocks are adjacent to the expanding black ghetto. Since a housing short-

---

[8]Calculated from 1980 Census, Advance Reports.

age existed in the ghetto—and since blacks were always looking for standard-quality housing—the houses and apartments in nearby neighborhoods were attractive to them.

In any big-city neighborhood a good deal of moving always takes place, for many reasons. Renters may be leaving their apartments for better ones, or people may be selling their houses and moving. Thus some vacancies are usually available in the housing stock, and transfers occur, with new individuals entering. The crucial matter in racial transition, of course, is the color of the new buyers and renters. In the transition process, all the new buyers and renters are black. Even if housing turnover is occurring at the normal rate, that is, even if there is no particular panic or flight of the current residents, the fact that all the new residents are black means the transition is in progress. Molotch concludes that as long as a dual market exists with a shortage of standard housing for blacks, the transition process is usually inexorable: "Racial change patterns are determined by ecological forces beyond the local community" (1972, p. 172).

## Housing turnover

Racial transition of a neighborhood must begin with the turnover of one house or apartment from white to black occupancy. The transition may be handled directly between a white homeowner and a black buyer, but it is more likely to be mediated by some middle person, usually a real estate broker. The overall transition involves the progressive turnover of more and more housing units to the entering group.

Real estate brokers have often been accused of unscrupulous actions and practices promoting rapid racial transition. One such practice is to instigate panic selling among white homeowners by exploiting their fear of living in a black area and their fear of losing the value of their housing investment. In this situation, brokers may spread rumors to the effect that the neighborhood is "going black" and that people should quickly sell their houses. This process generates a vicious circle: As more white homeowners put their houses on the market, others are further frightened and are also encouraged to sell. One technique in this process is for the broker to advise the owner to take a chance on the market by putting a "for sale" sign on their lawn. Once a few residents do this, it gives the appearance that a large-scale exodus is underway. For this reason, some cities have outlawed the use of such signs. After some white homeowners have offered their properties for sale, brokers and speculators can purchase them cheaply, because the sellers are in a rush to leave the area. The new owners hold the properties temporarily until they can be sold to blacks. Taking advantage of the dual market, the brokers and speculators then sell the houses to black families at high prices. Obviously, this is a highly profitable business.

## "Tipping point" theory

At one time, sociologists and economists suggested that there was a tipping point for the maximum proportion of blacks, which was usually estimated at about 30 or

40 percent. The idea was that if the whites maintained a substantial majority, integration would work. Once the black proportion exceeded the tipping point, the rest of the whites would leave.

After his study of racial transition in one part of Chicago, though, Molotch vigorously disputed the tipping point theory and said the so-called tipping point was illusory. Racial transition is caused by the blacks' long-unsatisfied need for additional housing. Given high black demand, each time a housing unit becomes available in a neighborhood, some black household will take it as long as the area is not closed. This argument implies that an integrated neighborhood just exists during the time between when a place is all white and when it is finally all black.

Anthony Downs (1968) explains this process of neighborhood racial transition with "the law of cultural dominance." Like other urban analysts, such as Gans (1968) and Suttles (1972), he says that individuals prefer to live in residential areas with individuals like themselves. The area need not be perfectly homogeneous, but they must be able to see that people like themselves are in the majority. They "want to be sure that the social, cultural, and economic milieu and values of their own group dominate their own residential environment and the educational environment of their children" (Downs, 1968, p. 1338). Thus when whites perceive that a neighborhood is undergoing racial transition, they do not shop for housing there on the assumption that it will soon have a very large black majority. Presumably, they would be willing to live in an area with blacks of their own socioeconomic status and lifestyle if they could be sure that it would retain a white majority—to ensure their cultural dominance.

## Institutional Transition

### Businesses

As the succession of white-to-black residents takes place, there is also a succession of the shops and other businesses in the area. Aldrich and Reiss (1977) carefully studied this process in changing areas of several cities. Their basic research approach was to select a number of business locations (sites) in areas which were undergoing racial change or were likely to undergo racial change. At the outset, each of the sites was occupied by an active business owned and run by whites. The researchers kept track of each of these business sites for a period of four years. Some turnover of small businesses always occurs—they have a high mortality rate for various reasons including lack of capital and lack of access to the best sources of financing. The businesses may also fail due to poor management, inability to compete, changing market conditions, and for other reasons. Thus under ordinary circumstances a certain proportion of store properties is likely to become vacant every year, perhaps as many as 1 in 10. But, ordinarily, in an all-white area with no racial change, the vacant sites will be taken by new white business operators. Aldrich and Reiss approached the succession question, just as Molotch had looked at the process of residential succession, to see whether there was an accelerated departure of white business operators due to the influx of blacks into the area.

Aldrich and Reiss found that businesses did not exit particularly rapidly from the racially changing areas but that the business population did change from white to black or Puerto Rican. This happened because once racial change began in the areas, no new white business operators moved in. As vacancies occurred, if they were taken over by new businesses, the operators were all black or Puerto Rican. As Aldrich and Reiss note, "The withdrawal of white-owned businesses opens up opportunities heretofore closed to minorities" (1977, p. 855). Numerous new small businesses do emerge, particularly in the fields of personal services, such as cleaners, beauty shops, and barbers; business services; retail food; and restaurants and bars. There tends to be a decline in the numbers of all businesses, particularly in the areas of consumer goods, restaurants and bars, and nonretail establishments. But evidently the blacks do not have the sort of shortage of business locations that they have of houses and apartments. A large proportion of the business sites abandoned by the departing whites are not taken by businesses at all. Many are left vacant, and the rest are used for noncommercial establishments: "Some former business sites are converted to nonprofit uses, especially by government-sponsored organizations and black community-oriented organizations" (Aldrich & Reiss, 1977, p. 855). These locations would be occupied by numerous governmental social welfare programs such as job-training centers, drug-rehabilitation clinics, neighborhood health centers, and the like.

During the racial transition, after blacks or Puerto Ricans occupy some of the business locations, there is some turnover and attrition. Minority-owned small businesses are at least as fragile as white-owned ones. Most of the minority businesses also operate with insufficient capital, based on personal savings and borrowings from relatives and friends. Many of the operators are inexperienced managers as well. Furthermore, bankers, suppliers, insurance companies, and potential financial backers may discriminate against minority entrepreneurs. Therefore, many of the businesses fail, and the sites are again occupied by new minority businesspersons. Eventually, after the complete racial transition, there are fewer retail businesses in the area than there were formerly. This means residents must travel farther, usually to newer, larger retail establishments, for many things they buy.

Just as the pattern of business ownership changes, the color composition of the shoppers themselves also shifts. Molotch, while studying white-to-black succession in one of Chicago's residential areas, tried to discover who was shopping where. At the time he examined the situation, the housing in the area farthest from the ghetto was still occupied exclusively by whites, while the section closest to the ghetto was almost entirely occupied by blacks. This spatial pattern was reflected almost perfectly in the usage of the stores on the two main shopping streets. Looking at shoppers in stores on one street during the day on a weekday, he found that almost 90 percent of the shoppers were white in the stores near the white residential area. As he moved down the shopping street toward the all-black area, the next two blocks had 66 percent white shoppers; the next two blocks had 35 percent white shoppers; and the next two blocks, by the predominantly black housing, had only 15 percent white shoppers. Thus the whites still living in the area had stopped shopping in those stores, and they effectively belonged to the new residents.

During this transition period, Molotch found three types of stores, classified by the racial composition of their customers: white, black, and integrated. On the street closer to the ghetto, most of the stores were integrated, whereas on the street closer to the all-white section, most of the stores were white. On Saturday night, though, the pattern changed radically, and there were many fewer integrated places. Fewer kinds of places were open on Saturday night, and people tended to be involved in sociable group activities. The places included bars and restaurants, movie theaters, bowling alleys, plus a few late-hour grocery stores and supermarkets. Molotch reported that whereas during the daytime 70 percent of the stores were integrated on one street, on Saturday night this proportion fell to 42 percent. On the other, less integrated, street, the daytime proportion of 22 percent integrated stores fell to 9 percent on Saturday night. Molotch implies that the whites had hard feelings about "losing" a particular tavern to a new black clientele, saying that "the colored took the place over" or "the colored forced everybody out." Molotch noted that in some cases white bartenders made the newcomers feel welcome but that in other cases blacks began to frequent certain bars nonetheless. A bar is a special sort of social environment which usually has a particular network of friends and acquaintances who are the regular customers. If newcomers arrive with a different style, with special "mannerisms, clothing tastes, musical preferences, and other tavern-specific behavior habits at variance with white cultural counterparts" (Molotch, 1969, p. 884), they are likely to discourage an informal group of old-timers from feeling their usual sense of comfort and intimacy at the tavern. Thus the whites abandon it to the new users.

## Schools

Public schools in the neighborhood are quite crucial in the transition process because many white parents are fearful of sending their children to school with black students, especially in situations where the whites may be in a small minority. This fear reflects a complex mix of fact and imagination: Lower-class black adolescents have high delinquency rates and whites have certain racial fantasies. Thus one of the developments which encourages whites to leave the neighborhood is the perception that the numbers of black children are increasing in the local schools. The proportion of black children is likely to rise faster than the proportion of black households because low-income black families tend to have relatively large numbers of children. Furthermore, in some cases they replace older white households who had no children in school. Some of the white parents may withdraw their children from the newly integrated neighborhood public schools and enroll them in parochial schools, but eventually, no new white families with children move into the area.

In his study of the South Shore, a changing residential area in Chicago, Molotch documented the racial composition of elementary and high schools over a four-

TABLE 8-4
Racial Composition of South Shore Public Schools, 1963 to 1966

|  | \multicolumn{4}{c}{Proportion of student body black} |
|---|---|---|---|---|
|  | 1963 | 1964 | 1965 | 1966 |
| Elementary schools* |  |  |  |  |
| Parkside | 90.3 | 96.6 | 97.8 | 99.1 |
| O'Keeffe | 39.8 | 67.3 | 85.4 | 93.9 |
| Bryn Mawr | 16.3 | 37.2 | 55.2 | 66.1 |
| Mann | 7.0 | 26.6 | 43.0 | 55.1 |
| Bradwell | 0.1 | 0.2 | 0.7 | 3.7 |
| Sullivan | 0.0 | 0.0 | 0.0 | 2.3 |
| High school |  |  |  |  |
| South Shore High | 1.5 | 7.0 | 24.8 | 41.8 |

*The list of elementary schools is ordered roughly by distance from the point of black migration from the old ghetto. Thus Parkside School is nearest the old ghetto and Sullivan is farthest from it.
Source: Molotch, 1969, p. 885.

year period. Table 8-4 shows that by 1963, his earliest time point, 90 percent of the children were black in the school nearest the old ghetto, and three years later there were almost no white children in the school. Three other schools were also undergoing rapid racial transition, depending upon their distance from the racial frontier. One school went from 40 to 94 percent black in three years, another from 16 to 66, and another from 7 to 55. What is most impressive in these numbers is the great speed of the transition. Clearly, a complete transition from all white to all black took far less than ten years.

## INTERNAL DIFFERENTIATION OF THE GHETTO

### Socioeconomic Status Gradient

The very growth of the postwar black district generated sociospatial differentiation internally. The new distribution of blacks began to differ from the old ghetto because some differentiation between middle-class and poverty areas was emerging. If one thinks of the urban black population as having a poverty class, a working class, and a set of middle classes, it was the working and middle classes which had the resources as well as the motivation to seek housing outside the older ghetto areas. They wanted to leave the old ghetto to get better neighborhoods in which to raise their children. They wanted to leave the social and physical dangers of the slums, to get better schools for their children, to avoid the youth gangs, and for other obvious reasons. Thus these households, with one or more stable incomes, were the first to seek housing outside the traditional black territory. Certainly, only a brave few were willing to be the first to buy or rent in an all-white area, but needing the housing, others were quick to follow. This process was the basis for the emerging differentiation among black residential areas.

The pattern of differentiation is that the older, poorer, slummier areas are nearest the central business district and the upper-middle-class black areas are farthest from the center, with intermediate areas in between. The highest-status, most expensive neighborhoods are at the greatest distance from the old ghetto. Another way of expressing this pattern is to say that there is a status gradient from the old lower-class slum increasing toward the most recently settled upper-middle-class residential area. Indeed E. Franklin Frazier (1937/1982), a black sociologist, discovered this gradient in New York as early as 1937.

Two ecological studies of the distributions of black households demonstrate these points. An examination of the location of households of differing income levels in Milwaukee distinguished between the inner-core areas, which were heavily nonwhite and "changing areas," which housed blacks and whites (Edwards, 1974). The inner core began about a mile from the downtown area, while the changing areas were farther out. Within the inner core there was some income differentiation by census tract, although not as much as is found in white areas of the city. But the higher a black family's income was, the more likely it was to live outside the core area altogether, farther from the city center. Another study of Chicago's black residential areas showed the pattern more explicitly (Duncan & Duncan, 1957, Table 68). An ecological analysis of two large black districts, revealed that (1) the farther from the city center a given census tract was, the higher its income and educational levels and the higher the level of homeownership and (2) the closer a tract was to the city center, the higher the proportion of substandard dwelling units and the higher the level of crowding in housing. These findings within the ghetto conform exactly to the status pattern described by Burgess's (1925) concentric circle model of the city.

## Types of Black Neighborhoods

In addition to being differentiated by socioeconomic status, black areas are also differentiated into types. D. I. Warren (1975) conducted a large survey in metropolitan Detroit, sampling from 28 neighborhoods, 12 white and 16 black. This sample permitted a comparison between white and black communities and then a comparison of black areas, among themselves. There were major differences in the ways blacks and whites used their local areas: The "neighborhood was more likely to play a significant role in the lives of black individuals than in the lives of whites" (Warren, 1975, p. 61). Blacks were more likely to use the neighborhood as a social context, or reference group, and as an interactional arena. This means that blacks were more likely to concentrate their social life in the residential area and that they were concerned about how others in the area felt about them—the neighborhood was an important area in their lives. (Black and white communities were no different in the level of mutual aid or organizational activity.)

As explained in Chapter 9, the residential areas were divided, regardless of race, into six types: integral, parochial, diffuse, stepping stone, transitory, and anomic (Warren & Warren, 1977). There were white and black neighborhoods of every type.

Comparing black neighborhoods with white ones, he found, "Black neighborhoods are more likely to be among those types reflecting a strong reference group tie to the local area as opposed to those which are reflective of weak orientations to the neighborhood" (Warren, 1975, p. 154). The black neighborhoods were more likely than the white to be those where people "feel they belong to a neighborhood" and have a "sense of consciousness about what their neighborhood is and where it is spatially and symbolically" (Warren & Warren, 1977, pp. 94–95). Black neighborhoods were also more likely than white ones to have interaction among the residents, but Warren also found several neighborhoods of the stepping-stone, transitory, and anomic types where people were less likely to be so involved with their local communities. Indeed, in these three types, blacks were likely to have negative attitudes toward their neighborhoods.

Two factors affecting the form of black neighborhoods are how transitory the population is and how heterogeneous it is. Areas with high population turnover tended to fall into the three types in which people had negative orientations toward the area.

Warren notes a moderate degree of mixture by socioeconomic status in most white residential areas; within a specified white district, some variation in status will occur. Among black residential areas, on the other hand, two conditions are found: either no mixture—as in the case of large public-housing projects in which people are uniformly poor—or polarization—as in the case of two very different classes living in the same residential area. Warren argues that in either case this sort of composition undermines the possibility of positive community development. In the case of the all-poor residential area, Warren quotes Suttles, as follows: "One consequence of public housing life may be the way in which it restricts most opportunities to achieve a stake in the prospects of the local community and to develop the kind of leadership and social differentiation that is so critical in forming a stable, moral community" (1975, p. 66). This is the effect of homogeneity at the poverty level. The effect of having a polarized population of widely different socioeconomic levels in the same neighborhood is that they cannot find a meeting ground and have different educational levels, styles of public and private behavior, consumption patterns, and, in short, different lifestyles. "This heterogeneity produces a type of neighborhood which forms a weak structure for effective social and group action" (Warren, p. 67).

Warren's Detroit findings are closely related to processes which became apparent in the historical development of the forced ghettoization of the South Side of Chicago, indifferent mixture of social classes, and blockage between majority and minority segments of the community. Beginning in the 1920s, real estate operators forced middle- and lower-class blacks to share the same neighborhoods, even the same buildings. This process continued for decades—in the dual market blacks did not have free choices of neighborhoods. By the time Warren studied the situation, in a different city which operated by the same principles, he found that middle- and lower-class blacks shared neighborhoods and that they were unable to transcend the lifestyle differences of social classes to forge neighborhood unification. White neighborhoods do not have this bifurcated class structure and are more able to organize internally.

Finally, Warren developed a theory of "social compression" to explain continuing ghettoization. Historically, the black community experience in large cities has differed from that of the European immigrant groups. The immigrants, such as the Italians and Jews, were confined to their own areas for a relatively brief period of time—one or two generations at most—whereas the urban blacks have been ghettoized for three generations or more. Furthermore, the immigrants brought well-developed institutions, such as church and business structures, from their European communities and simply transplanted and modified them in the United States. Some of these structures helped them achieve social mobility and to enter the wider society; the institutions built bridges outside the ethnic group. The blacks, on the other hand, emerging from centuries of adaptation to plantation slavery, lacked such urban institutions and had to build new ones which, fortunately or unfortunately, were appropriate to life inside a ghetto. These local institutions have been continued up to the present and, as the ghetto shows no signs of breaking up, serve to perpetuate the internal structure of the black community. The mass media covers black events from the outside, and the black press covers the ghetto from the inside, but the stories do not effectively cross racial boundaries. Warren's theory of social compression emphasizes the *isolation* of the ghetto from the rest of the metropolitan community.

## RECENT DEVELOPMENTS

### School Desegregation and "White Flight"

Racial change in city schools has entered into local and national politics with a vengeance. The political question is whether the federal courts should force local school districts to integrate their schools, particularly by means of "busing" children from one part of the city to another. When a judge issues a court order to that effect, the objective is to eliminate the traditional pattern of having all-white schools in white neighborhoods and all-black schools in the ghetto. Desegregating the schools is based upon court precedents that assert it is impossible to have schools which are "separate but equal." Court orders may also be based upon social research which demonstrated that black children are likely to learn better in integrated schools than in all-black ones. But busing became highly unpopular among white parents who do not want to have their children transported to ghetto schools to achieve racial balance. Some whites also do not want to have black children brought into their neighborhoods for schooling. This issue of school integration has become entangled with the question of white flight from the cities.

The "white flight" controversy surrounds two questions: First, were whites relocating to the suburbs in order to avoid living in the same cities with blacks, or was white migration to the suburbs simply a response to better housing and other attractions and a way of leaving old housing and physically deteriorating city environments? The white-flight hypothesis said they were leaving to avoid blacks: Second, if a judge ordered mandatory busing of school children, would that accelerate white migration out of the city—inducing more white flight?

Research on intrametropolitan migration patterns is not perfectly clear on the relative importance of black avoidance. A series of studies demonstrated that in the peak years of suburbanization, families were positively choosing to buy houses in the suburbs in order to pursue a familistic lifestyle. An aggregate demographic study by Guterbock (1976) demonstrated that the pull of suburbia was more important than the avoidance of urban conditions. A newer study, though, of migration patterns between 1965 and 1970 in 39 metropolitan areas, reaches a more equivocal conclusion. Its author, Frey (1979) shows that several nonracial factors—such as differences between city and suburban tax rates, differences between educational expenditure, and the newness of the suburban housing stock—strongly affect whites' propensity to migrate toward suburbs. He also found that racial factors, particularly the proportion black of the central city's population, made a difference. He noted, however, that racial factors were less powerful predictors of suburban migration than were factors related to population structure and central-city decline.

Apart from the general question of white movement to the suburbs, the white-flight controversy now centers on the question of racial integration in city schools. Many big cities have large black and Hispanic minorities; as they tend to be young with relatively large families, they contribute numerous children to the school systems. By 1979 many big-city school systems had large *majorities* of black and Hispanic children. The loss of white children need not be attributed to their parents' fleeing the new city residents. White public school enrollment in cities began to decline early in the postwar suburbanization. Furthermore, the birth rate of white women had declined rapidly during the 1970s, contributing fewer and fewer children to the school systems. And the white population of the central cities tends to be rather old, which means these people do not have children in school. (Many of the white children are in the suburbs.) Integration became increasingly difficult in the cities' public schools because there were few whites with whom to integrate, particularly as parents and educators were unwilling to create white-minority schools. The net effect of the migration and fertility patterns has been that many of the largest cities have black majorities in their school-aged populations. By 1974 Chicago's school district had 58 percent black students; Philadelphia, 62; Detroit, 72; Cleveland, 57; and St. Louis, 70 (Farley, 1978, Table 2.1). The average for 76 northern and western big-city school districts was 31 percent. In the southern region a number of school districts also had black majorities, led by Washington, D.C., with 96 percent; Baltimore, 72; Memphis, 70; New Orleans, 79; Atlanta, 85; and Louisville, 54.

The main conclusion of a review of the available studies of cities which had court-ordered busing was that the introduction of desegregation would speed up the loss of white children by about one year (Rossell, 1978). In other words, the enrollment shift is well advanced already in many cities, and mandatory desegregation only boosts it slightly and temporarily. Referring to white enrollments, Rossell, who reviewed the available studies, concluded; "Any school district which implements a city-wide two-way reassignment can expect, in the year of implementation, at least a doubling of its normal loss rate" (1978, p. 46). Over the long run, though, this effect is minimal because the main trend in many cities' public school systems is toward increasing proportions of children from minority groups (Farley, Richards, and Wurdock, 1980).

Rossell arrived at several general propositions about the process of racial transition in school populations. The whites who leave the school system during the first year of a court-ordered plan do not necessarily move out of the city; they are much more likely to transfer into private and parochial schools and remain in the city. Those parents who withdraw their children from the public schools tend to have higher-income levels than those who leave their children in the system. Rossell concluded that different kinds of desegregation plans produce different effects. Greater white flight follows desegregation of elementary schools than desegregation of high schools. "Plans which encompass metropolitan areas have fewer white enrollment losses with desegregation than city school district plans" (Rossell, 1978, p. 48). This would be because a much larger pool of white children exists with whom to integrate and because parents lose the alternative of fleeing to the suburbs to escape the process. Furthermore, a metropolitan desegregation plan tends to send minority children out to the suburban schools more than to send white children into the formerly black schools.

The overall size of an urban community also affects its ability to integrate the schools. According to Farley (1976) it is easier to achieve racial integration in schools of smaller cities. Presumably, this is because the distances between social districts and between schools are shorter; children would not have long bus rides to go from one part of the city to another. Perhaps such cities are characterized by less fear or by greater confidence in social control of minority areas or of the schools in general.

## Black Suburbanization

Two contradictory trends are occurring in the movement of blacks to the suburbs. On the one hand, as the black middle-class grows, increasing numbers move out of the city into the suburbs. On the other, the suburbs remain disproportionately white, and the blacks in suburbia are highly segregated for the most part.

Black suburbs have existed for decades, mostly near heavy industrial districts. For many years, suburbs like Robbins, Illinois, and Kinlock, Missouri, were rundown towns with industrial railroad yards and heavy pollution from nearby fac-

Like others of equivalent occupational and income levels, middle-class blacks are likely to choose suburban areas in which to raise their families. (Ray Ellis, Rapho/Photo Researchers, Inc.)

tories, power plants, breweries, tanneries, and the like. Housing was cheap, if primitive, and poor people could afford to live there. Such communities also housed black working-class households, including factory workers.

During the decades of mass northward black migration, most of the movers settled in central cities; very few went to the suburbs. In the mid-1960s, though, as the interregional migration "wound down," numerous blacks relocated from cities into the suburban zone. For the nation it has been estimated that "black movement to the suburbs averaged less than 20,000 per year during the period 1960–66, but in 1967 and 1968, the volume increased more than ten fold" (Rose, 1976, p. 26). Some moved into the older black suburbs, but others moved into previously all-white communities. Old black suburbs responded in two different ways to the potential of population growth. Some had open land and added new subdivisions. These new housing developments followed the conventional design patterns of the time—i.e., their streets, houses, and schools looked like other suburbs—providing desirable housing for the families leaving the city. Other towns were either fully built or were so unattractive that none of the new suburban households would have chosen them.

More recently, more attractive black suburbs and subdivisions have emerged. "First-tier" suburbs, directly in the line of ghetto expansion, were the most likely to undergo racial succession. These are the older suburbs directly abutting the central city.

Some of these suburbs are undergoing rapid racial transition and are becoming all black. Residents in other suburbs have organized to attempt to become racially integrated. This objective requires them to develop strategies to continue to attract white newcomers along with the blacks. Rose (1976) notes that within each metropolitan area there is likely to be an area of black residence. Often this sector is located on a line with the direction in which the old ghetto had expanded within the central city.

Social class is another aspect of the shift in black suburbanization. Rose notes that until 1970, suburban blacks, on average, had *lower* social status than city blacks. In 1970, for the first time, the census showed that suburban blacks had superior status. On the other hand, suburbanizing blacks were less likely than whites to buy homes. A move to the suburbs has typically included buying a home. Nonetheless, blacks with equivalent status characteristics are less likely to buy homes in the suburbs; they are more likely than whites to continue renting (Lake, 1979). Furthermore, even at upper-middle-class levels, they are likely to remain segregated, located in heavily black or all-black suburbs (Muller, 1981).

Black migration appears to have turned a corner in the mid-1970s. "The black population of central cities was reported to have stabilized between 1974 and 1977, rather than to have grown as significantly as it had in previous years.... Second, the number of blacks living in the suburbs was reported to have increased by 34 percent between 1970 and 1977" (Spain & Long, 1981, p. 1). This represented a higher rate of black suburbanization than in the previous decade. Indeed, in the 1970s black suburbanization was proceeding at a faster rate than white suburbanization (49 percent as compared with 21 percent). This comparison is somewhat misleading, though, since the blacks started with such a small number of suburban households. By 1976 the total of 1.4 million represented 5 percent of all suburban households (Lake, 1979).

Perhaps the most noteworthy development in this accelerated suburbanization was that the black households may not have been ghettoized in their new communities. Research by two sociologist-demographers at the Census Bureau showed that some of the movers were settling in mostly white residential areas. "Approximately 40 percent of blacks who moved to or within the suburbs in the mid-1970s went to census tracts that were at least 90 percent white in 1970; another 27 percent went to census tracts that were 60 to 90 percent white in 1970" (Spain & Long, 1981, p. v). Others moved into predominantly black suburban tracts.

One may speculate that black suburbanization is a continuing trend but that it does not necessarily lead toward a high degree of residential integration. Blacks with sufficient incomes prefer to leave the city ghettos, in pursuit of better housing and schools, and like whites, they move to suburbs. However, either because of real estate steering or following the "law of cultural dominance," they are likely to move to particular suburbs or particular subdivisions with other blacks, sometimes with large majorities. Although a segregation index would not show this as integration, it does represent a greater scatteration of the black population throughout a metropolitan area which might promote more interracial contact than was possible in the age of the single large ghetto.

## SUMMARY

A look at the historical development of black districts in two large cities revealed that earlier in the twentieth century, whites deliberately excluded blacks from residential areas; the blacks were confined to specified ghetto areas. Since the late 1940s original boundary lines of the black areas were broken and the ghettos expanded to accommodate the large numbers of blacks who had migrated from the rural south. Some dispersion of blacks has also occurred outside of ghetto areas, to other residential areas of the city and to suburbs. But statistical ecological analysis, by means of segregation indexes, has revealed that the metropolian areas remain highly segregated. Since 1940 the segregation indexes have declined very slightly. (In southern cities the level of segregation rose to resemble the northern pattern.)

Around 1920, the Chicago realtors' association could advocate ghettoization openly. Violence was frequently applied to blacks who attempted to occupy housing in white areas. After World War II, the mechanisms of ghetto development and enforcement have become more subtle. Federal laws attempt to prevent banks, insurance companies, and governmental agencies from redlining particular residential areas. Laws have also been designed to prevent racial discrimination in the sale and renting of housing. However, individuals in the real estate business still practice racial steering, which is harder to detect.

By and large, metropolitan areas now fit the image of "chocolate city and vanilla suburbs." Central cities have high concentrations of blacks and other minorities; some industrial cities have black majorities; and several have public school systems in which black, Hispanic, and other minority-group children heavily outnumber the whites. Each census shows the black suburban population growing, particularly with members of the middle and upper-middle classes. Nonetheless, in 1980 blacks constituted 6.1 percent of the total suburban population, while they were 11.7 percent of the national population. Whites, on the other hand, constituted 89.7 percent of the suburban population. Outside the south, blacks represented 4 percent of the suburban population. And suburban blacks were not scattered and integrated among the population at large; they were concentrated in particular suburbs and in particular subdivisions, perhaps representing a contemporary extension of black ghettoization, this time in ghettos which are not slums.

Most students of black residential patterns reject the hypothesis which suggests that blacks are concentrated in particular locations because of their low incomes. This hypothesis is rejected because low-income whites are not similarly concentrated and segregated. Students of the situation also reject the hypothesis which suggests that blacks are concentrated because of their own preferences by a process of self-segregation. There is no way to prove conclusively that this hypothesis is false because there is no place with a perfectly open housing market, with no discrimination, where one could observe how blacks located themselves given completely free choice. Most social scientists who have studied black residential patterns conclude that there is a dual housing market, one segment for whites, the other for blacks. The analysts agree that blacks have been ghettoized, excluded from free choice in the housing market.

## REFERENCES

Aldrich, Howard, and Albert J. Reiss, Jr. 1977. "Continuities in the Study of Ecological Succession: Changes in the Race Composition of Neighborhoods and Their Businesses." *American Journal of Sociology.* 8:846–866.

Burgess, Ernest W. 1925. "The Growth of the City: An Introduction to a Research Project," Ch. 2 in *The City,* (eds.) Robert E. Park and Ernest W. Burgess. Chicago: University of Chicago Press.

Chicago Commission on Race Relations. 1922. *The Negro in Chicago: A Study of Race Relations and a Race Riot.* Chicago: University of Chicago Press.

Davis, John P. 1966. *The American Negro Reference Book.* Englewood Cliffs, N.J.: Prentice-Hall.

Dollard, John. 1937. *Caste and Class in a Southern Town.* New Haven, Conn.: Yale.

Downs, Anthony. 1968. "Alternative Futures for the American Ghetto." *Daedalus.* 97:1331–1378.

Downs, Anthony. 1981. *Neighborhoods and Urban Development.* Washington: Brookings.

Drake, St. Clair, and Horace Cayton. 1962. *Black Metropolis: A Study of Negro Life in a Northern City,* rev. ed. New York: Harper & Row.

DuBois, W. E. B. 1899. *The Philadelphia Negro.* Philadelphia: University of Pennsylvania.

Duncan, Otis D., and Beverly Duncan. 1957. *The Negro Population of Chicago: A Study of Residential Succession.* Chicago: University of Chicago Press.

Edwards, Ozzie L. 1974. "Patterns of Residential Segregation within a Metropolitan Ghetto," chap. 48 in *Comparative Urban Structure: Studies in the Ecology of Cities,* (ed.) Kent Schwirian. Lexington, Mass.: Heath.

Farley, Reynolds. 1976. "The Controversy over School Busing." Paper at meeting of the American Sociological Association. New York.

Farley, Reynolds. 1978. "School Integration in the United States," pp. 15–50 in *The Demography of Racial and Ethnic Groups,* (ed.) Frank D. Bean and W. Parker Frisbie. New York: Academic.

Farley, Reynolds, Toni Richards, and Clarence Wurdock. 1980. "School Desegregation and White Flight: An Investigation of Competing Models and Their Discrepant Findings." *Sociology of Education.* 53:123–139.

Foley, Donald L. 1973. "Institutional and Contexual Factors Affecting the Housing Choices of Minority Residents," pp. 85–147 in *Segregation in Residential Areas,*

(eds.) Amos H. Hawley and Vincent P. Rock. Washington: National Academy of Sciences.
Frazier, E. Franklin. 1939. *The Negro Family in the United States*. Chicago: University of Chicago Press.
Frazier, E. Franklin. 1937/1982. "Negro Harlem: An Ecological Study," pp. 179-187 in *Urban Patterns: Studies in Human Ecology*, 2d ed., (ed.) George Thedorson. University Park,: Pennsylvania State University Press.
Frey, William H. 1979. "Central City White Flight." *American Sociological Review*. 44:425-448.
Gans, Herbert J. 1968. *People and Plans: Essays on Urban Problems and Solutions*. New York: Basic.
Guterbock, Thomas M. 1976. "The Push Hypothesis: Minority Presence, Crime, and Urban Deconcentration," in *The Changing Face of the Suburbs*, (ed.) Barry Schwartz. Chicago: University of Chicago Press.
Harrigan, Susan, and Charles W. Stevens. 1980. "Roots of a Riot." *Wall Street Journal*. May 22, 1980, p. 1.
Kain, John F. 1975. "Theories of Residential Location and Realitites of Race," chap. 6 in *Essays on Urban Spatial Structure*, (ed.) John F. Kain. Cambridge, Mass.: Ballinger.
Lake, Robert W. 1979. "Racial Transition and Black Homeownership in American Suburbs." *Annals of the American Academy of Political and Social Science*. 441:142-156.
Lieberson, Stanley. 1963. *Ethnic Patterns in American Cities*. New York: Free Press.
Liebow, Elliot. 1967. *Talley's Corner: A Study of Negro Streetcorner Men*. Boston: Little, Brown.
Light, Ivan H. 1972. *Ethnic Enterprise in America: Business and Welfare among Chinese, Japanese, and Blacks*. Berkeley, Calif.: University of California Press.
Molotch, Harvey. 1969. "Racial Integration in a Transition Community." *American Sociological Review*. 34:878-893.
Molotch, Harvey. 1972. *Managed Integration: Dilemmas of Doing Good in the City*. Berkeley: University of California Press.
Muller, Peter O. 1981. *Contemporary Suburban America*. Englewood Cliffs, N.J.: Prentice-Hall.
Myrdal, Gunnar. 1944. *An American Dilemma*. New York: Harper & Row.
*New York Times*. 1982. "Racial Violence in Boston Forcing Blacks to Move." June 2, 1982, p. 10.
Osofsky, Gilbert. 1968. *Harlem: The Making of a Ghetto*, Negro New York, 1890-1930. New York: Harper & Row.
Pearce, Diana. 1979. "Gatekeepers and Homeseekers: Institutional Factors in Racial Steering." *Social Problems*. 26:325-342.
Ploski, Harry A., and Warren Marr. 1976. *The Negro Almanac*, bicentennial edition. New York: Bellwether.
Rose, Harold M. 1976. *Black Suburbanization: Access to Improved Quality of Life or Maintenance of the Status Quo*. Cambridge, Mass.: Ballinger.

Rossell, Christine. 1978. "White Flight." *Social Policy.* 9:46–51.
Sorensen, Annemette, Karl E. Taeuber, and Leslie J. Hollingsworth, Jr. 1975. "Indexes of Racial Residential Segregation for 109 Cities in the United States, 1940–1970." *Sociological Focus.* 8:125–142.
Spain, Daphne, and Larry H. Long. 1981. "Black Movers to the Suburbs: Are They Moving to Predominantly White Neighborhoods?" *Special Demographic Analysis* CDS-80-4. Washington, D.C.: U.S. Bureau of the Census.
Spear, Allan H. 1967. *Black Chicago: The Making of a Negro Ghetto, 1890–1920.* Chicago: University of Chicago Press.
Squires, G. D., R. Dewolfe, and A. S. Dewolfe. 1979. "Urban Decline or Disinvestment: Uneven Development, Redlining and the Role of the Insurance Industry." *Social Problems.* 27:79–95.
Suttles, Gerald. 1972. *The Social Construction of Communities.* Chicago: University of Chicago Press.

Taeuber, Conrad, and Irene Taeuber. 1958. *The Changing Population of the United States.* New York: Wiley.

Taeuber, Karl, and Alma Taeuber. 1965. *Negroes in Cities: Residential Segregation and Neighborhood Change.* Chicago: Aldine.

U.S. Bureau of the Census. 1980. *Statistical Abstract of the United States; 1980.* Washington, D.C.

U.S. National Advisory Commission on Civil Disorders. 1968. *Report.* Washington: GPO.

Warren, Donald I. 1975. *Black Neighborhoods: An Assessment of Community Power.* Ann Arbor: University of Michigan Press.

Warren, Rachelle B., and Donald I. Warren. 1977. *The Neighborhood Organizer's Handbook.* Notre Dame, Ind.: University of Notre Dame Press.

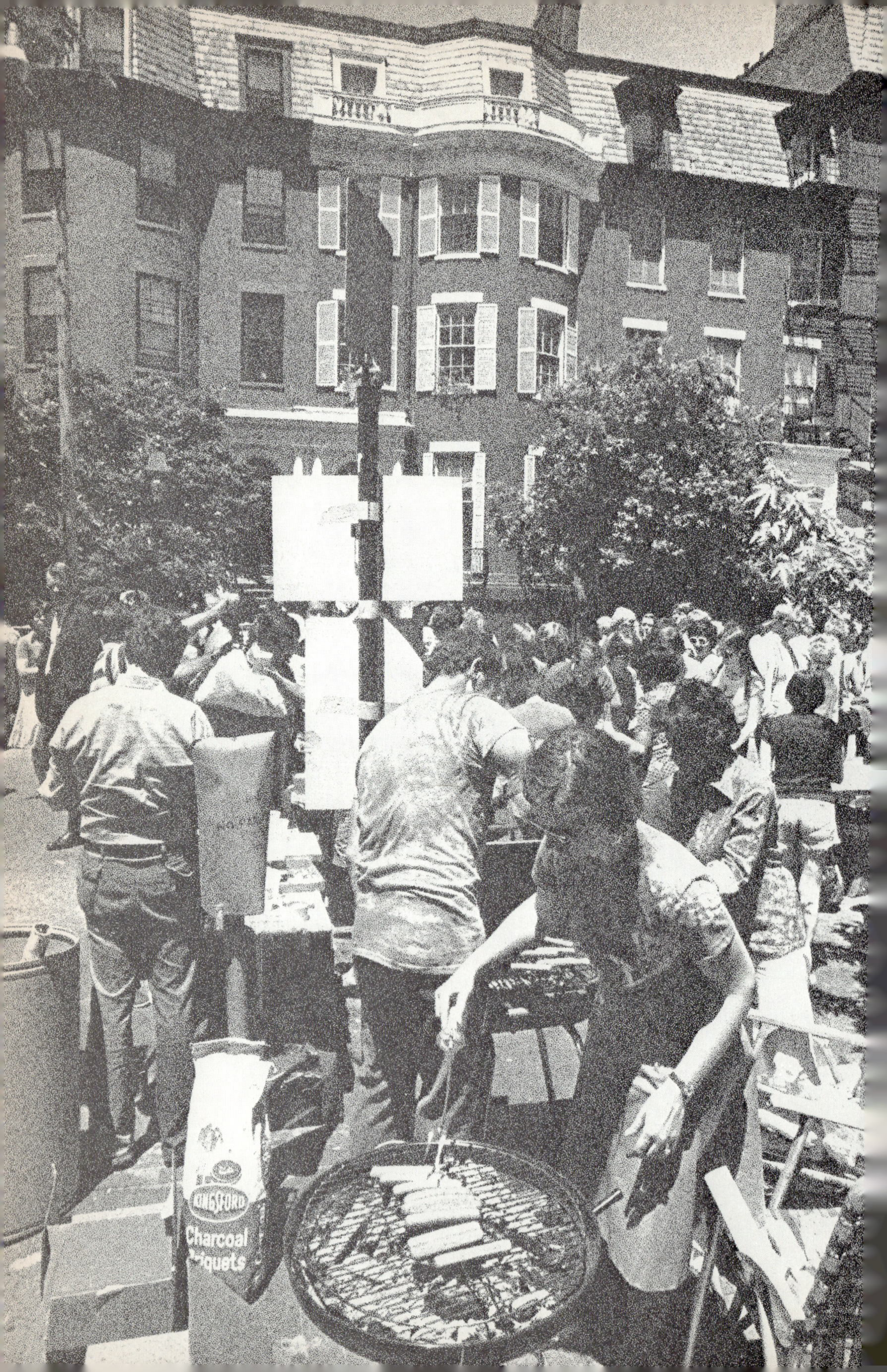
KINGSFORD
Charcoal

# CHAPTER · 9

## The Local Community

### Chapter Outline

THE DEMISE OF "PERFECT LITTLE NEIGHBORHOODS"

THE COMMUNITY OF LIMITED LIABILITY

USE AND PARTICIPATION
Local Institutions
- Voluntary associations
- The community press

Residential Use of Local Areas
- Instrumental uses
- Social psychological uses
- Changing uses

Conditions Enhancing Participation
- Homogeneity
- External threat

TYPES OF NEIGHBORHOODS
Warren and Warren's Six Types
The Urban Village: A Special Type

RESEARCH METHODS
Participant Observation
Survey Research

SUMMARY

## THE DEMISE OF "PERFECT LITTLE NEIGHBORHOODS"

Sociologists once defined "neighborhood" as a group sharing a small piece of territory and based upon primary relationships.[1] The neighborhood comprised a limited number of households that occupied a small area, were homogeneous in social characteristics—social status, ethnicity—and engaged in face-to-face interaction as well as mutual supportive activities and exchanges. The neighborhood socialized children and influenced or constrained the behavior of its members; members, in turn, identified with the neighborhood in some way. In other words, it was a closely knit little grouping of households, where the people knew each other well. This is an ideal-type definition of a kind of settlement or social group.

When sociologists began to study modern cities, they had to confront the fact that this sort of neighborhood was on the way out or already gone. The urban situation had many forces to undermine "perfect little neighborhoods," as we might call the ideal type. Four features of the metropolis prevent the existence of these perfect little neighborhoods: largeness of scale, mobility of households, modernity of transportation and communication, and dispersion of choices.

Urban scale means that the overall settlement has tens of thousands of inhabitants at the very least and may well have millions. The ideal-type neighborhood, by one calculation (Mann, 1965), could have no more than 100 households; beyond this number the inhabitants could not know each other personally or maintain other aspects of primary relationships.

Mobility also undermines the perfect little neighborhood. First, as urban society tends to foster social mobility (movement up or down in status, usually by means of occupation), households will relocate as they rise (or fall), seeking better housing or more prestigious locations. Second, the urban economy is likely to foster geographical mobility for other reasons as well. As noted in Chapter 7, the residential areas of a metropolitan area differ considerably from each other. Households are likely to move when workers take new jobs or when transitions occur in the family life cycle—after the birth of a child, a divorce, or some other crucial event (Rossi, 1955). This shifting about is antithetical to the maintenance of the primary relationships which lie at the heart of the ideal-type neighborhood. Such a neighborhood requires population stability to support trust and primary relationships. This opposition between population mobility and primary-group neighborhood was first discussed by McKenzie (1923) in a study of a neighborhood in Columbus, Ohio, and by McClenahan (1929) in her study of a middle-class Los Angeles area. The general proposition that urbanism undermines primary groups, including neighborhoods, was set forth in a more elaborate fashion by Louis Wirth (1938) in his essay, "Urbanism as a Way of Life."

The last items in the list of urban features that weaken the traditional neighborhood—transportation, communication, and dispersion—go together. Of the

---

[1] A definition like this, based upon Carpenter (1933), is discussed in Mann (1965). There are numerous sociological and geographical definitions of "neighborhood"; see Timms, pp. 7–8, and Keller, pp. 87–88, for examples.

households in metropolitan America 83 percent have at least one car, and many of the others have mobility by means of mass transportation. Similarly, 97 percent of all American households have a telephone. Thus people are not confined to their local areas to satisfy their wants or to maintain their social lives. Within a metropolitan area, an individual's significant persons and places are likely to be dispersed, not necessarily located exclusively within the local residential area.

In sum, then, these four features of modern life prevented the survival of the ideal-type neighborhood in cities and suburbs. Taking this point to an extreme, we could write off local areas as noteworthy elements of the social scene. Indeed, one urban sociologist (Wellman, 1972) published an essay entitled "Who Needs Neighborhoods?"—a question that implies the answer "No one." Another sociologist (Fischer, 1976) suggests that an urban theory, called "determinist theory," asserts city life destroys primary relationships.

But these suggestions go too far. Everyone who has been to a residential area in a city or suburb has seen local social life—basketball and baseball games, neighbors talking while fixing a car, parents and toddlers in the playground—and its facilities—schools, churches, and recreational areas. These observations imply that we need a new concept of the local area, one reflecting contemporary social life.

## THE COMMUNITY OF LIMITED LIABILITY

Recognizing that the local community has no stronghold over its members, Janowitz (1952) coined a new term, the "community of limited liability." As a metaphor, this new concept compares the residential area to the corporation, a form of business in which the partners enjoy the privilege of limited liability; that is, if something goes wrong in the enterprise, the various stockholders are protected from the liability of the whole company. In the traditional small community, each person had a total commitment, living there for a lifetime. Each person knew everyone else, and if someone got into trouble, everyone knew about it. Thus belonging to a community put the individual into a situation of total liability.

Janowitz rejected the idea that gesellschaft was the true explanation of modern urban life. This older theory said that the traditional tight little community would be shattered and that modern society would have complex, indirect social relationships. In the city, according to this theory, people would have bureaucratic and impersonal attachments. But Janowitz perceived that the metropolis still has community relationships, although of a new kind. "In varying degrees," he wrote, "the local community resident has a current psychological and social investment in his local community. In varying degrees, use of local facilities is accompanied by community orientations" (1952, p. 222). According to Janowitz, city people do not live purely by rational and instrumental actions.

Metropolitan residents are differentially involved in their local communities. Some individuals are passing through a particular community, while others stay for extended periods—as long as a lifetime. Nonetheless, each individual has the option of leaving, so liability need not be total. Furthermore, "The individual's investment is relatively small in the interactional network that constitutes the locality group, and if his losses are too great he can cut them by getting out" (Greer, 1962, p. 98). The individual may opt out of the community in either of two ways, by moving or by withdrawing from community activities (Janowitz, 1952). In general, the concept of the community of limited liability emphasizes the intentional, voluntary, and partial and differentiated involvement of urban-suburban residents in their local communities and shows that the neighborhood is becoming a more specialized, more voluntaristic, and more partial institution (Hunter & Suttles, 1972).

People vary considerably in their local community involvement; the most powerful variable affecting involvement is stage in the family life cycle. "Even among the most community-oriented 'small-town-like' areas within the metropolis, there is great variation in the importance of the local area to the individual" (Greer, 1962, p. 98). Local merchants have the greatest stake in the area; followed by home-owning residents, who also have a major investment; and, finally, by apartment-renting couples without children, who have the least investment. People in these different stages are also differentially affected by the local area. Even though households are free to leave, they cannot be totally oblivious to the community's structures; the local area may exert some constraints, especially on parents. As Greer states, "The local residential community still encompasses some very crucial structures, and therefore has a constraining force upon its members. This is especially true of those who have chosen a familistic life in the [suburbs]" (pp. 108–109).

## USE AND PARTICIPATION

### Local Institutions

Before discussing social participation in local areas, we must enumerate the facilities (in addition to housing) and institutions such areas offer. Two sociologists, Yancey and Ericksen (1979), examined 90 census tracts, city and suburban, in the Philadelphia urbanized area and categorized all their nonindustrial facilities. In the average tract the researchers found more than 100 facilities, which fell into 9 categories:

1. Schools
2. Retail stores, including small groceries
3. Bars and restaurants
4. Establishments providing personal and household services, including barber and beauty shops, auto repair and service stations, craftspersons, home services, and repair companies
5. Professional services, including drugs and medicine, banking and finance, social services, funeral services, business services, real estate, insurance, and legal services

6 Voluntary associations, including clubs
7 Government services, including police and fire stations, mass transit terminals, libraries, parks and recreation areas
8 Churches, including those with buildings and those operating out of storefronts
9 Extralocal facilities, including universities, utilities, cemeteries, and hotels

Although not every residential area has all of these, the list itemizes the sorts of facilities that can be found in local areas.

Residential areas differ in the number of facilities and in their arrangement. In general, the more people in a tract, the more facilities it has. Beyond this, older, central-city tracts differ from newer, outer-city or suburban tracts. The centrally located areas, where high proportions of individuals walk to work or use public transportation, tend to have more facilities, dispersed within the residential area. Peripheral neighborhoods, where more people drive to work, are likely to have fewer facilities, concentrated at particular locations—shopping centers or designated shopping areas.

The Philadelphia study showed that white industrial neighborhoods were the most likely to be stable, having high proportions of residents who stay for long periods of time. "Neighborhoods which are near railroads, have access to large numbers of industrial jobs, and are characterized by high proportions of industrial workers and homeowners, remain stable despite their age. Stable working-class communities have the highest levels of institutional integration, the largest number of gathering places" (Yancey & Ericksen, 1979, p. 260). Stable areas were also more likely to have retail stores.

## Voluntary associations

One of the local institutions found in Philadelphia neighborhoods and suburbs was the voluntary association. Americans are great organizers and joiners of voluntary associations—one historian called us "a nation of joiners." We tend to organize voluntary associations around all sorts of interests—from Little League baseball to the Veterans of Foreign Wars.

Voluntary associations are organizations one joins simply by choice, which distinguishes them from organizations one must join—school, business, army. Voluntary associations can also be distinguished from social networks. A network is a set of ties among individuals that is ordinarily not formalized; a voluntary association, though, is formalized, having officers, elections, bylaws, meetings, a treasury, and the like.

Many voluntary associations, such as the Little League, PTA, and church altar society, are focused upon local activities. A survey in the Detroit metropolitan area showed that the most popular types of associations were church-connected groups, followed by PTAs, sports teams, card clubs and women's or men's social clubs, and fraternal organizations or lodges. On the other hand, the least popular were political clubs and organizations (Duncan, Schuman, and Duncan, 1973).

Unlike the above-mentioned types, one type of organization is explicitly focused upon the local area and its problems—the neighborhood improvement association. The Detroit survey showed a fairly low level of participation in such organizations—about 8 percent of the people belonged. A survey in Chicago, though, showed a much higher level of participation, with more than one-quarter of the adults in local organizations (Hunter, 1974). A third survey, in Toronto, showed that about 20 percent of new homeowners, in suburban and central-city locations, joined local taxpayers' groups, but this statistic did not include renters (Michelson, 1977).

Two schools of thought exist about the importance and effectiveness of neighborhood (improvement) associations. One contends that such organizations are basically "toothless" and ineffectual. Molotch, the leading proponent of this argument, first published it after conducting a study of a section of Chicago that was undergoing racial change. He documented the attempts of certain organizations to affect the course of the change by promoting the creation of an integrated population, and he demonstrated that an almost-complete racial transition occurred despite the organizations' efforts. Molotch's interpretation was that the overall ecological forces in the city—the location of the neighborhood, the process of normal migration, and the extreme demand for housing for blacks—made it inevitable that the neighborhood would shift from white to black occupancy. The neighborhood associations might just as well have been whistling in the breeze. More generally, Molotch asserts that reports of "successful" self-help neighborhood actions are "enormously inflated in their claims." He contends, "Success is temporary, and/or limited to a few minor facets of life or (at times) the entire story is simply bogus make-believe" (1979, p. 292).

Other observers contend that there is a "neighborhood movement" of thousands of local voluntary associations which exhibit considerable vitality (Heumann, 1983; Perlman, 1978; Rosenbloom, 1981). Many of these urban organizations are working to improve housing conditions by promoting the rehabilitation of older buildings and by trying to influence banks and other financial institutions to reinvest in their areas. Many such organizations have arisen in older, working-class central-city areas, but some exist in older suburbs as well. A few of the voluntary associations are promoting the goal of racial integration, in addition to improving the housing stock. Other goals usually include improvement of schools, playgrounds, and law enforcement. In most cases, local voluntary associations are linked together into some sort of federation, sometimes under a citywide umbrella organization with staff to conduct research and fund raising. Local voluntary associations may also be linked with governmental or business organizations.

The intervention of outsiders is responsible for the formation of some of the new organizations, called "externally induced voluntary associations" by Taub et al. (1977). In restudying the Chicago district that had been examined by Molotch, they discovered a number of local organizations which had been created, directly or indirectly, by organizations outside the area. For example, the neighborhood's bank is owned by individuals who live elsewhere, but it formed an organization of locals to formulate redevelopment plans for the area. The bank also formed a "local development corporation" to deal with the Small Business Administration by borrowing from the federal agency and to make loans to local businesses. In some cases local organizations were created to comply with state or federal laws requiring citizens' committees for the execution of specific programs. For example, in order to apply for government money for a new mental health center, the district had to have a board of community residents. Taub et al. concluded that much of the impetus toward the creation of neighborhood organizations is provided by the need of large-scale organizations, such as federal agencies, to have local representatives with whom to deal. Morris Janowitz (1978) expresses this idea more elegantly: "Because of the expansion of governmental functions, including those of the welfare state, local voluntary associations become more important as mechanisms for articulating and linking the citizenry to the larger political process" (p. 271; see also Hunter & Suttles, 1972).

## The community press

The small-scale newspaper is another local institution. The city of Chicago in 1950, for example, had 82 separate local papers, each focused upon a particular district, in addition to the large-scale big-city dailies. Janowitz's classic study, *The Community Press in an Urban Setting* (1952), examined the functions of local papers. They carry advertising for local shops and services, and they also run news stories and features about local people and events. In order of prominence, the subjects emphasized in the papers were municipal services, organized religion, business enterprise, public affairs, local voluntary associations, and social and personal news. Clearly, the papers were highly localistic in their scope of interest; they avoided subjects dealing with controversy and conflict, emphasizing consensus within the area. Janowitz suggested the community press has several functions for urban life: "Community newspaper content is designed to help the individual orient himself in time and space in the local community by building and maintaining local traditions and local identifications" (p. 73). In effect, it helps people to live in the large, complex, heterogeneous metropolis by giving them the local community as an anchoring point, stressing values and interests on which there is a high level of agreement. In its localism the community press generally resembles the small-town newspaper. While no equivalent research has been done on it yet, the contemporary suburban press is coming to resemble, in scope and function, the community press examined by Janowitz. Suburbs now have numerous newspapers that carry local advertising and local news; and, in a period in which many old, established, big-city dailies are collapsing, the suburban weeklies are prospering.

    The list of local institutions in this section—schools, churches, and firehouses; stores, bars, and restaurants; voluntary associations and newspapers—tells what *is* in residential areas, but it only hints at what people *do* in their local areas. The next section discusses the ways in which city and suburban people use their local residential areas.

## Residential Use of Local Areas

Metropolitan residents use their local areas in two ways: for *instrumental* purposes and *social psychological* ones.

### Instrumental uses

The most obvious use of local areas is for residence and consumption. By definition, residential areas provide housing—good, bad, or indifferent. All sorts of daily products—foods, cosmetics, linens, newspapers, etc.—and durable goods—such as refrigerators, washers and dryers, and television receivers—are "consumed" at home, and more than 20 percent of the total national energy usage is in residential areas for heating and cooling as well as for cooking, hot water, and other amenities.[2] Personal consumption represents over 60 percent of the gross national product, and presumably much of this consumption takes place at home.[3] Almost everyone uses a residential area, with the rare exceptions of individuals without fixed residence: sailors, hoboes or "bag ladies," and persons who live in such nonresidential areas as warehouse districts (night guards, prostitutes), airports, and central business districts (people in hotels).

People also use the local facilities in residential areas. A survey in St. Louis before the period of advanced suburbanization (Foley, 1950) showed that most people shopped for groceries, went to the movies, and went to church within the confines of their local area (see Table 9-1). Attending school, for children and adolescents, was a local activity; some residents also used other local facilities such as doctors' offices. On the other hand, employment and shopping for specialized goods were extralocal. Another survey was conducted more than ten years later in Chicago (Hunter, 1974), and its results were quite similar to those from St. Louis. About three-quarters of the Chicagoans shopped for food in their local areas, but four-fifths worked in a different area. A large minority also went outside the local area for recreation.

Different categories of people tend to use, or not to use, local facilities. Stage of the life cycle makes a difference; in particular, mothers and children are heavy users of local areas. Children, of course, are limited in their mobility, but each year of age brings greater mobility. Thus the child's range of independent travel, by foot, bicycle, bus, etc., tends to increase, taking the child, by the time of adolescence, outside the neighborhood. As children's caretakers, mothers also use local facilities, especially parks and playgrounds. Older persons also tend to use local facilities, including parks, shops, medical offices, and banks; they, too, have restricted mobility, and spend a large proportion of their time close to home. Young adults without

---

[2] In 1978, U.S. total energy consumption was 78,256 trillion BTUs, of which 16,335 was residential (U.S. Bureau of the Census, 1980, p. 605).

[3] Total gross national product in 1979 was $2,368.8 billion of which 1509.8 was in personal consumption expenditures (U.S. Bureau of the Census, 1980, p. 439).

**TABLE 9-1**
**Use of Local Facilities in One Residential Area, St. Louis**

|  | Percentage distribution by location |  |  |
|---|---|---|---|
|  | Within district | Adjacent to district | Away from district |
| Food shopping | 69.3 | 26.5 | 4.2 |
| Church attendance | 77.1 | 5.2 | 17.7 |
| School attendance | 68.2 | 9.0 | 22.8 |
| Movie attendance | 58.4 | 15.6 | 26.0 |
| Miscellaneous indoor activities (association meetings, sports, etc.) | 35.5 | 9.7 | 54.8 |
| Visiting doctors' offices | 29.7 | 8.5 | 61.8 |
| Clothing, household equipment, or furniture shopping | 5.1 | 19.7 | 75.2 |
| Employment | 17.5 | 5.3 | 77.2 |
| Miscellaneous outdoor activities (sports, outings, etc.) | 10.1 | 0.4 | 89.5 |

Source: Foley, 1950.

children, on the other hand, are least likely to use the local area; they are highly mobile and, thus, tend to spend a great deal of time away from home. In addition to stage in the life cycle, socioeconomic status also makes a difference in the use of local facilities: The very poor are much more likely than prosperous people to use local facilities. This poverty-linked localism may be a function of the low levels of automobile ownership among the poor, as car owners tend not to use local facilities.

## Social psychological uses

In addition to instrumental uses, people also use their local areas for social psychological purposes, principally, neighboring and symbolic identification. (This subject is discussed further in Chapter 14, which is about social networks.)

**Neighboring** The main question here is, What sorts of social relationships exist among the residents of a locality? One stereotype says big-city residents are spatially close but socially distant—the dominant image is of people in an apartment building who may see each other in the corridor or on the elevator but fail even to say hello. But numerous studies show that this stereotype is not a true depiction of the social reality. The researchable questions here are, What sorts of social relationships exist among urbanites; how localized are they; and how much sociability is there?

"Neighboring" is a term used here to refer to all sorts of social relationships that may occur within residential areas. Originally, the concept had a rural flavor: "In essence, neighboring involves exchanges of services, information, and personal approval among those living near one another, however nearness is defined"

(Keller, 1968, p. 44). In addition to the exchange of help and advice, neighbors may engage in other social contacts, from the very casual, such as exchanging greetings, to the more familiar, such as visiting back and forth or entertaining each other in homes or apartments. At the most intimate level, neighbors may also be close friends.

**Attitudes and identification**  The second social psychological aspect of the local community refers to residents' attitudes and identifications about the place. Definitions of community often include this attitudinal aspect—people's shared feelings as an element of community, people's identification with the community, and the way in which the community influences their behavior and attitudes. In order to determine the extent to which the residents of a given locality identify with it, sociologists may ask particular survey questions. Typically, they ask how much *information* the residents have about the locality: Where are the boundaries? What is its name? The sociologist may ask how the residents *feel* about the place: Do they like the area? Would they prefer to move elsewhere? Are they satisfied with local services such as schools and police? The researcher may also ask how individuals define the place: Do they see it as a "little community within the metropolis?" Do they feel more loyalty to it than to the city in general? Urban and suburban individuals may use their local area for other purposes as well. They may use it as a sort of anchoring point, a meaningful place at human scale, that makes sense in a way in which the total metropolis does not (Janowitz, 1952). Also, individuals may use the locality for some symbolic value—to say something about their status or their special lifestyle (Duncan, 1976; Hunter, 1974; Suttles, 1972).

**Participation**  Just as surveys show different uses of local facilities (for instrumental purposes), they also indicate differential patterns of involvement in local social life. The differentials are seen most clearly in levels of participation in voluntary associations.

Table 9-2 shows that urban and suburban people are highly involved in voluntary associations and that some of these associations are locality-based. The table presents results from two surveys of metropolitan Detroit residents, taken at an interval of more than ten years (Duncan, Schuman, & Duncan, 1973). Apart from the individuals who belonged only to a labor union, about two-thirds of the adults surveyed belonged to at least one voluntary association, and most belonged to more than one. They belonged to a wide variety of organizations, from Parent Teacher Associations to the United Automobile Workers, and although the surveys did not pinpoint the locations of the associations, it is clear that some, such as the PTAs and church groups, were locality-based. PTAs were among the most popular organizations, while specific neighborhood service organizations—neighborhood clubs and community centers, as well as neighborhood improvement associations—were not among the most popular. A more recent survey, conducted in metropolitan Chicago, showed participation in neighborhood organizations at about the same level as had been found in the earlier Detroit surveys. In a middle-

**TABLE 9-2**
Association Membership by Type, Metropolitan Detroit, %

| Memberships in clubs or organizations of specified kinds | Total 1959 | Total 1971 | Men 1959 | Men 1971 | Women 1959 | Women 1971 |
|---|---|---|---|---|---|---|
| Labor unions | 28 | 27 | 47 | 45 | 9 | 12 |
| Church-connected groups | 36 | 28* | 30 | 24* | 42 | 31* |
| Fraternal organizations or lodges | 14 | 12 | 19 | 17 | 10 | 8 |
| Veteran's organizations | 6 | 5 | 9 | 11 | 3 | <1* |
| Business or civic groups | 5 | 7 | 7 | 10 | 3 | 4 |
| Parent-teacher associations | 19 | 20 | 12 | 13 | 25 | 26 |
| Neighborhood clubs or community centers | 8 | 10 | 7 | 9 | 8 | 10 |
| Organizations of people of the same nationality | 6 | 4* | 5 | 4 | 7 | 3* |
| Sport teams | 11 | 15* | 13 | 21* | 8 | 9 |
| Professional groups | 7 | 8 | 10 | 12 | 5 | 5 |
| Political clubs or organizations | 3 | 2 | 3 | 3 | 3 | 2 |
| Neighborhood improvement associations | 12 | 8* | 13 | 9* | 11 | 8 |
| Card clubs; women's or men's social clubs | 12 | 13 | 8 | 9 | 17 | 16 |
| Charitable and welfare organizations | 9 | 7 | 7 | 6 | 10 | 8 |

*Difference between years is statistically significant; other differences in the table are not.
*Source*: Duncan, Schuman, and Duncan, 1973, p. 48.

class city sample, about one-tenth of the individuals belonged, but the level of membership was higher in suburb samples, where about one-sixth were members (Choldin, 1980). Another Chicago survey found higher levels of participation than those reported in the studies cited above (Hunter, 1974). This survey showed that almost 30 percent of the adults were members of local voluntary associations, but a wider variety of organizations, for example, block clubs, were included in the tabulations. The survey also showed that different types of areas had different participation levels: The higher the socioeconomic level of the area, the higher the level of participation. Black and white areas (controlling for socioeconomic level) had equal participation levels. The higher the level of familism, the higher the level of participation.

The survey found that the characteristics of households affected their propensity to join community organizations: The longer the tenure in the area (up to six years), the higher the likelihood of joining. Age also made a difference as individuals in their thirties and forties were more likely than younger or older people to join, and parents with children at home were likely to join. Thus the characteristics affecting organizational membership are exactly the same as those affecting neighboring and local participation in general.

Returning to the Detroit surveys, we can see that participation appears to be fairly stable over time. While there were some shifts in the types of interests represented, urban and suburban adults were as likely to be members of voluntary associations in 1971 as they had been in 1959.

Participation in local activities is affected by how long the individual lives in the area. In a series of studies, Janowitz, Hunter, and Kasarda have shown that tenure influences local participation. Janowitz (1952) first showed this in his study of readership of community newspapers, in which he found that the longer an individual lived in an area, the more likely that individual was to read the local paper. Reading the paper was one way that the individual was tied into the local communications system. In a more recent study, Hunter (1974) discovered that newcomers, defined as those living in an area for less than a year, were unlikely to be involved in neighboring, unlikely to participate in local organizations, and unlikely to be hooked into local communications systems. After one year of residence, local involvement increased in a straight line, hitting a maximum for those living in the area for six years (see Figure 9-1). Additional years of residence made no difference; an individual living in the area for six years was an oldtimer. Likewise, Kasarda and Janowitz (1974), analyzing a survey of community life in England, confirmed that length of residence is positively related to local involvement and is the variable most closely related to local organizational membership.

## Changing uses

An unusual pair of surveys allows us to see how uses of local residential areas have changed in recent decades, at least in one city. In 1949 Donald Foley surveyed res-

**FIGURE 9-1**
Local involvement by tenure. Newcomers are least likely to read the local newspaper or to join a community organization. Involvement increases with additional years in the area, though. (Source: Data on newspaper readership have been recomputed from Janowitz, 1952, p. 132; data on organizational membership are from Hunter, 1974, p. 150.)

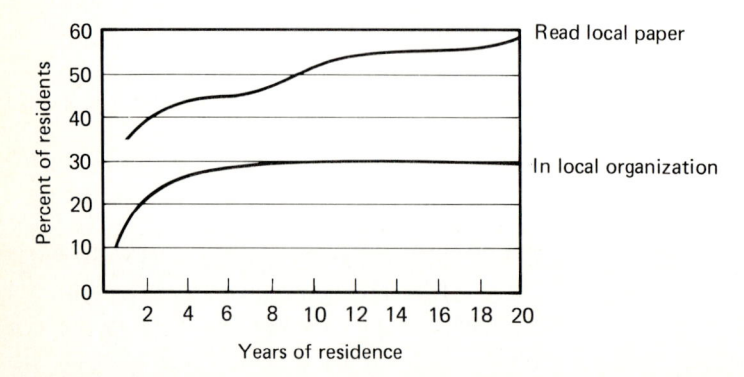

idents of three census tracts in Rochester, New York, to see how they used local facilities and what social psychological uses they made of the area.

Twenty-five years later, Albert Hunter (1975) returned to the area and repeated the same survey to see how things had changed. Some major theories (gesellschaft, and urbanism as a way of life) would have predicted that local social life should have been declining. Hunter asked the current residents how they use the local area, and then he compared their activities with those of the people who had lived there in the 1940s when the original survey had been conducted. Hunter's main conclusion, which is supported by the results presented in Tables 9-3 and 9-4, is that people in the 1970s were using the neighborhood differently from the way their predecessors had used it.

The people Hunter surveyed were using the area less for instrumental purposes and more for social psychological purposes, based on a comparison of the 1970s' and the 1940s' patterns. Specifically, Table 9-3 shows that recently people were less likely than their predecessors to shop for groceries or to go to church, to the doctor, or to the movies in the neighborhood. (Very few people worked in the area at either time.) Undoubtedly, many of the old shops and offices closed or moved away between 1949 and 1974, in line with the national trend to larger economic units. Nowadays, residents of the Rochester neighborhoods drive to a nearby suburb to go to a new, large shopping center with parking facilities. The one exception to the general pattern of results in Table 9-3 is the increase in neighborhood banking, which Hunter explained as a result of the construction of a new drive-in facility in the area. Generally, though, this local area, like many big-city neighborhoods throughout the country, is used far less in providing services than it was formerly.

**TABLE 9-3**
**Local-Facility Use at Two Points in Time**

|  | Percentage conducting this activity within five blocks of home ||
|  | Foley, 1949 (N = 437) | Hunter, 1974 (N = 154) |
| --- | --- | --- |
| Grocery shopping | 77.4 | 34.7* |
| Small purchase | 71.2 | 61.3* |
| Church | 61.5 | 51.2* |
| Movie | 49.5 | 9.1* |
| Doctor visit | 46.7 | 19.3* |
| Banking | 25.6 | 47.9* |
| Employment | 17.0 | 11.4† |

*Significant difference at .05 level between 1974 and 1949.
†No significant difference.
Source: Hunter, 1975.

**TABLE 9-4**
**Neighboring at Two Points in Time**

|  | Percentage responding "often" or "sometimes" ||
|---|---|---|
|  | Foley, 1949 (N = 446) | Hunter, 1974 (N = 154) |
| Chat with neighbors | 73.9 | 79.7† |
| Exchange favors | 58.5 | 56.5† |
| Exchange things (tools, recipes, etc) | 41.2 | 51.3* |
| Visit informally in home | 38.7 | 47.4† |
| Ask neighbors advice | 26.1 | 30.8† |
| Have picnics, parties | 17.2 | 26.0* |
| Number of neighbors chat with on block (1949: "At least half;" 1974: "All or most") | 64.1 | 43.7 |
| Location of friends (1949: "At least half live within 5 blocks;" 1974: "2 or 3 of 3 best friends live in area") | 24.4 | 34.9 |

*Significant difference at .05 level between 1974 and 1949.
†No significant difference.
Source: Hunter, 1975.

Surprisingly, Hunter found that the social psychological use of the area grew stronger. The survey's pattern of results with regard to neighboring is clear in Table 9-4. The 1974 residents were more involved with their neighbors—they were more likely to exchange things and to have social events like picnics and parties together—and they were just as likely as their predecessors to chat, visit back and forth, and the like. This, of course, contradicts the two theories that would have predicted a loss, not a gain, of neighboring.

Claude Fischer, an urban sociologist at the University of California, might contend that Hunter's findings in this Rochester neighborhood are atypical. Fischer's (1976) interpretation of recent trends is that urbanites are neighboring less and that the role of neighbor has been redefined, now including only specific locality-relevant actions. He says that essentially people living near each other become "just neighbors."

> Urbanism tends to reduce the role of neighbor toward its bare essence. That role seems to involve two essential norms or rules of behavior. The first is: Be ready to assist your neighbor at those times when physical proximity is important—either in an emergency, or when the assistance costs little and it would be silly for the other person to go long distances for it.... The second norm is simple: Don't be offensive. Good neighbors don't disturb or offend the people next door (or lower the property value of their dwelling). These are the same normative expectations generally held for any people in close physical promixity, when they are standing in line, for example, or sitting on a bus. (Fischer, 1976, p. 120)

## Conditions Enhancing Participation

### Homogeneity

Homogeneity tends to promote higher levels of participation in local activities. "Homogeneity" means that the residents of an area are alike in important social characteristics, particularly stage in the family life cycle, educational level, or ethnicity. Ethnic homogeneity in "urban villages" tends to support a high level of local involvement. The same sort of phenomenon can be seen in the "campustown" neighborhood near a large college or university. Such a residential area is likely to have a high density of people very close to each other in age, marital status, and lifestyle, giving rise to intense local participation in block parties, street dances, and the like. A research project in a housing development at the Massachusetts Institute of Technology first encountered this principle.

That study was designed to discover the effects of the housing environment on social relationships among families, and it was done in a new housing project built after World War II for married students (Festinger, Schacter, and Back, 1950). The project of small, low-rise apartment buildings and duplexes is much like dozens of others built for married students on university campuses throughout the nation. The research found an environmental effect, namely, that people tended to become friendly with others who lived near their dwelling unit. But, at about the same time, other, similar studies were conducted in public housing projects—ones with people of different races and different socioeconomic levels—which did not find that proximity led to neighboring and friendship. In combination, then, the results of these two types of studies show that proximity leads to neighboring and friendship only when the people are socially homogeneous. The reason it was so easy for the families in the MIT housing project to get together was because they had so much in common: Most of them were veterans; they were all students; their incomes were quite similar; and most of them had small children. They could take a lot for granted.

### External threat

The second factor that tends to promote involvement and participation within residential areas is an external threat. A neighborhood's residents may define any of a variety of problems as a threat, varying from a plan for widespread housing demolition for a new highway, for example, to the possibility that one or more black families will soon move into the area. Several other kinds of actions may be planned by city hall or by some municipal or other large bureaucratic organization that may spur mobilization at the neighborhood level, for example, plans to locate a drug-rehabilitation center or a halfway house for mental patients or ex-convicts in the area. Some neighborhoods have even mobilized to fight the construction of McDonald's restaurants, fearing that they would bring too much traffic, too many strangers, and too much litter to the area. Other neighborhoods have organized to fight school busing, which would bring in children from minority groups. Many

CHAPTER·9

In cities across the nation many nationalities have annual open-air celebrations in older ethnic neighborhoods, an example of which is this Portuguese festival in East Cambridge, Massachusetts. (Elizabeth Hamlin, Stock, Boston)

neighborhoods have mobilized to resist housing clearance for urban renewal or for public housing projects. Suttles' term for such efforts to resist external threats is the "defended neighborhood."

The idea is that although under ordinary circumstances an ordinary low level of neighboring and participating exists within a residential area, under the special circumstances of homogeneity or external threat, high levels of local involvement may occur.

## TYPES OF NEIGHBORHOODS

Local residential areas fall into different types, depending upon the internal way of life and the way in which they are tied to the rest of the metropolis. In Chapter 7 we saw one typology of residential areas, based upon the sociodemographic composition of each place, in social area analysis and factorial ecology. In those schemes, every census tract in a metropolitan area fell into a particular type, depending upon the sorts of individuals and households in the area. In social area analysis, for example, a tract might fall into the "white, middle-class, familistic" type, the "white, lower-class, nonfamilistic" type, or one of the other boxes in the typology. That is not the sort of typology to be presented here. The approach presented in this section puts local areas into different types, depending upon the internal social life and the external linkages. The internal social life highlights exactly those dimensions discussed above—the way people identify with their area and the extent of social involvement among the residents.

### Warren and Warren's Six Types

This typology was developed by Donald and Rachelle Warren (1977) after they studied dozens of city and suburban areas in the Detroit metropolitan area. They concluded that three dimensions differentiate residential areas and give rise to six major types of neighborhoods. In effect, the Warrens ask three questions about each residential area, and the answers to these questions determine each area's type.

**Identity**  When the Warrens examine an area, they first ask, "How much do people [here] feel they belong to a neighborhood and share a common destiny with others—a sense of consciousness about what their neighborhood is?" (Warren & Warren, 1977, pp. 94–95).

Looking at dozens of areas, they found that in some places people identify closely with their neighborhood. They feel they are a part of it, expect to stay there, and are proud of the place. Such places get a "plus" for high identity in the typological scheme shown in Box 9-1. In other places people may be quite indifferent or even negative toward their neighborhood. They may even be unaware of its name, if it has one, and they would prefer to live elsewhere. Such areas, where most people have a low level of identity, get a "minus" in the first column of Box 9-1. Identity, then, differentiates residential areas—some places have a positive sense of identity and others do not.

**Interaction** The Warrens' second question about an area is, "How often and with what number of neighbors do people visit and interact?" (p. 94). Residential areas vary greatly along this dimension—in some places no one talks with anyone else, but other places have a high degree of mutual involvement.

**Linkages** Lastly, the Warrens ask whether the area is integrated with the rest of the urban community. Does it have linkages to the rest of the metropolitan area, or is it cut off and isolated? In particular, they ask whether the neighborhood's organizations have some effective means of communication with city hall and other important institutions outside the local area. In their research, they discovered that some neighborhoods were well linked with the institutions of the wider community, while others were quite isolated, unlinked and cut off from the rest of the city.

The Warrens contend that these three dimensions—identity, interaction, and linkage—tell how the social life of the neighborhood is organized internally. "Our research shows these three factors to be among the most critical ones for understanding how neighborhoods work" (p. 95). They found that, to a considerable extent, these factors were independent of the socioeconomic level and the ethnic composition of the area's population. Thus one poor area might have a good deal of interaction, while another might have almost none at all.

Based upon these three dimensions, the Warrens defined six different types of neighborhoods, as shown in Box 9-1. For example, if the people in an area have a high degree of identity with the place, have a high level of interaction, and are effectively linked to outside institutions, their area is called an "integral" neighborhood. The other five types are similarly constructed and named.

## Urban Village: A Special Type

Another name for the "parochial" type, the "urban village" is a big-city neighborhood, housing a single dominant ethnic group, usually working class. Urban villages in many cities have withstood the pressures that work against the ideal-type neighborhood. They are usually found in central areas, and their environment is made up of relatively old buildings. Often, they are recognizable by the signs on the streets; the names in the shop and office windows—of the real estate broker, the dentist, the bakery, and, especially, the undertaker—are all likely to belong to one nationality.

The term was introduced in a book entitled *The Urban Villagers* (1962) by a sociologist-city planner, Herbert J. Gans. When the author began his research in the late 1950s, he recognized three then-popular lines of thought about urban affairs: First, central areas with small old buildings were slums; second, according to determinist theory, the neighborhood was doomed as an institution; and third, city

## BOX 9-1
## Six Types of Neighborhoods

| Type | Identity | Interaction | Linkages |
|---|---|---|---|
| **Integral** A cosmopolitan as well as a local center. Individuals are in close contact. They share many concerns. They participate in activities of the larger community. | + | + | + |
| **Parochial** A neighborhood having a strong ethnic identity or homogeneous character. Self-contained, independent of larger community. Has ways to screen out what does not conform to its own norms. | + | + | − |
| **Diffuse** Often homogeneous setting ranging from a new subdivision to an inner-city housing project. Has many things in common. However, there is no active internal life. Not tied into the larger community. Little local involvement with neighbors. | + | − | − |
| **Stepping-Stone** An active neighborhood. A game of "musical chairs." People participate in neighborhood activies *not* because they identify with the neighborhood but often to "get ahead" in a career or some other nonlocal point of destination. | − | + | + |
| **Transitory** A neighborhood where population change has been or is occurring. Often breaks up into little clusters of people—frequently "oldtimers" and newcomers are separated. Little collective action or organization takes place. | − | − | + |
| **Anomic** It's really a nonneighborhood. Highly atomized; no cohesion. Great social distance between people. No protective barriers to outside influences making it responsive to some outside change. It lacks the capacity to mobilize for common actions from within. | − | − | − |

*Source:* Warren and Warren, 1977, pp. 96–97.

## BOX 9-2
## Research Methods: Participant Observation

### Steelworkers in a Blue-Collar Community

One way to study a community is by means of participant observation. As the method's name implies, the sociologist becomes a participant in the community while simultaneously acting as a scientific observer. This fieldwork method is much like that of the anthropologist who travels to a distant island to study the way of life of a village. William Kornblum, as a young sociologist, went to study a multiethnic area on the South Side of Chicago and wrote a book about it called *Blue Collar Community* (1974). The following quotations reveal his research method as a participant observer.

> In gathering the material for this study I attempted to use whatever data and methods of analysis seemed appropriate or feasible. Among these methods were making field notes on my observations and discussions with community residents; collecting archival materials; analyzing precinct voting tallies and census tract data; interviewing community and neighborhood leaders; attending the yearly round of social and political events for all ethnic and neighborhood groups; compiling family histories; being employed for six months in one of the area's steel mills; and actively participating in most of the political campaigns described here. Like most community studies, however, this one came to depend primarily on my first-hand involvement with the people and the situations described. The process in which the student gradually becomes a participant in the milieu studied constitutes much of the substance of "field methods" in the social sciences. Issues such as "establishing rapport with respondents," "discovering" one's specific research focus, becoming aware of one's biases, and insuring the privacy of one's informants are some of the well-known methodological problems of this research style....
>
> I found a Serbian immigrant restaurant run by an enormous peasant woman and her very slight husband. Radmilla and Mike appreciated my halting attempts to converse with them in Serbo-Croatian, and they introduced me to the establishment's regulars. The majority of the patrons were Serbian immigrant men in their mid-thirties to early forties. Almost all were steelworkers. On Friday and Saturday nights they filled the restaurant to eat, drink, and dance to the popular music of contemporary Serbia.
>
> One Friday night I entered in the middle of a brawl, which I learned was the continuation of an argument started in the steel mill three blocks away. While the electric guitar and accordion ensemble played on, three or four men were shouting in Serbo-Croatian and pushing each other. At this point Radmilla, who weighed at least 250 pounds, stepped into the crowd to separate the antagonists. As she did this, a man named Stanko seized a bar stool but she pushed him away easily. Infuriated, he threw the stool at her husband, Mike, who had had just enough to drink

that he did not duck in time and was struck on the head and shoulders. In the ensuing melee I tended to the fallen Mike while Radmilla cleared the tavern and restored calm. After that evening I became a welcome friend in their tavern and I felt I had found a place where I did belong in the community. . . .

As I began hunting for an apartment, it became clear why I had chosen to study this community rather than other South Slavic neighborhoods elsewhere in the metropolitan area. South Chicago fascinated me. I had never seen such heavy industry at close range, and I was awed by the immensity of the steel mills and the complexity of the water and rail arteries which crisscrossed the area's neighborhoods. In the people's faces and in their neighborhood I saw more of the spectrum of cultural groups which had settled and built the community. . . .

I thus resolved that whatever else it accomplished my study should attempt to show what life is like in such places. It should show what political questions actually do challenge the residents, and among these would likely be the issue of working-class race relations.

In March, 1968, my wife and I moved into a tenement flat in Irondale, one of the oldest neighborhoods of first settlement in the community. . . .

When our first child was born, after a year in Irondale, we began spending a great deal of time with our Mexican neighbors because they were more likely to have young children than our somewhat older South Slavic and Italian neighbors. From them, and especially from the Mexican youth groups which hung out on our corner, I learned that there was continual conflict with the Mexicans from the Millgate and Bessemer Park neighborhoods on the other side of the community. . . .

If to every tavern clique and candy store acquaintance I had divulged my intentions to study the community, I would have probably elicited some parody of life in sociological jargon. But when I introduced myself to specific residents of the community, or whenever I interviewed someone, I attempted to explain the goals of my study as simply and consistently as I could, and the interview would generally proceed without misunderstanding of my goals.

Gradually, through these introductions and interviews, I began to become friendly with a rather large number of political activists and neighborhood leaders. After introducing myself to a local labor leader, for example, I would then find myself meeting that person during my regular round of visits to public places and community events. . . .

Also, through the normal course of life among my Mexican neighbors I had many opportunities to observe the culture and social organization of Mexican neighborhood ethnic groups. Fieldwork was becoming more than a full time occupation, and I often found myself dictating slurred field notes at 4:00 a.m. after a full day of meetings and social drinking in the area's taverns and political clubs. . . .

Soon after moving into the community I had begun a systematic effort to attend any and all public meetings in the community, to identify local leaders, and to arrange to meet with them for an introduction or a formal interview.

*Source:* Excerpts from Kornblum, 1974, pp. 229–242.

BOX 9-3
Research Methods: Survey Research

**Comparing a City Area with Two Suburbs**

The social survey is a popular research method among sociologists. The preliminary stages of a survey involve choosing a problem, focusing on particular hypotheses to be examined, and conducting a "review of the literature," in which the researcher reads publications containing research and theories about the subject. Eventually, the researcher chooses a place to study and then designs and draws a sample of individuals or households from which to collect information. The researcher must also design a data-collection "instrument" with which to collect information. In collecting the information, the researcher must employ some system of data quality control in order to ensure that the sample has been followed correctly and that the instrument has been administered consistently and accurately. Although some surveys are conducted with questionnaires which are mailed out and mailed back, researchers prefer interviews, either face to face or by phone, because mailed surveys often have low response rates that may introduce unknown biases into the data.

The following information comes from a survey that compared neighboring child-rearing practices in an "outer-city" residential area of Chicago and in two suburbs. All three areas housed middle-class whites.

**The sample**

Since the research focused upon city-suburban differences, the analysts sought to eliminate all other major variables that might be important (such as poverty, for example.) Thus the researchers chose all white middle-class areas. They wished to draw a *random sample* of households—this freed them from the suspicion that some special group of individuals had entered their sample. It also permitted them later on to analyze their results with statistical methods that demanded random samples. They drew a sample by scanning a reverse phone directory of the area. This is a book like a telephone book, except that the entries are listed in order of street address, not in alphabetical order of individuals' names. By a random process the researchers chose households from the directory and called by phone to conduct interviews. Before interviewing, though, they had to "screen" the households. Because they were sampling only women who were living with their children, they had to eliminate all older people, single males, and others who were defined out of the sample. Eventually, they had a random sample of the type of household they were studying in the three areas. And, fortunately, most people called were willing to talk with the interviewers, so the researchers ended up with a "completion rate" of 75 percent.

**The instrument**
The following is a copy of one series of questions used by the interviewers.

6. Now I'd like to ask how often you do each of the following with your neighbors.
   How often do you . . .

|   | Often | Sometimes | Seldom | Never |
|---|---|---|---|---|
| a. Chat with your neighbors? Is it | 1 | 2 | 3 | 4 |
| b. Babysit for each other? Is it | 1 | 2 | 3 | 4 |
| c. Exchange things? (like tools, recipes, etc.) | 1 | 2 | 3 | 4 |
| d. Visit each other informally? | 1 | 2 | 3 | 4 |
| e. Ask a neighbor's advice? | 1 | 2 | 3 | 4 |
| f. Have picnics or parties with neighbors? | 1 | 2 | 3 | 4 |

7. Do you currently belong to any kind of neighborhood organization such as a neighborhood improvement association or a tenant's group?
   - Yes .................. 1
   - No ................... 2

8. Do you read a local community newspaper. . .
   - Often, ............... 1
   - Sometimes, ........... 2
   - Seldom, or ........... 3
   - Never? ............... 4

9. Would you say (Bolingbrook/Hanover Park/Belmont-Cragin/your area) is mainly . . .
   - Lower class, .......... 1
   - Working class, ........ 2
   - Middle class, ......... 3
   - Upper middle class, or . 4
   - Upper class? .......... 5
   - Don't know ........... 8

*Source*: Author.

Ethnic enclaves often provide opportunities for entrepreneurship and professional practice. Depicted here is a shopping center in Miami's "Little Havana" district. (Steve Kagan)

families all wanted to live in the suburbs. With these three ideas as a background to his research, Gans began a study to understand the social dynamics within the "West End," an old area in Boston that had a reputation as a slum. He used a sociological research method known as "participant observation." He and his wife "lived in the area, and used its stores, services, institutions, and other facilities as much as possible" (Gans, 1962, p. 337). He observed public meetings in the area and "became friendly with neighbors and other West Enders, spending much time with them in social activities and conversations that provided valuable data" (p. 337). He also conducted numerous interviews "with directors, staff members, officers, and active people in settlement houses, church groups, and other voluntary associations ... also with principals, ministers, social workers, political leaders, government officials" (pp. 337–338).

Gans discovered that the Italian-Americans in the West End enjoyed a rich group life and maintained intensive family and kinship contacts, mostly within the local area. Thus, for example, adult brothers would continue to have frequent contact with each other, as would grown children with their parents, seeing each other frequently. The Italian-Americans participated in numerous localized ethnic activities. The Catholic parish was an established institution within the area, and many residents maintained ties to it. Italian shops catered to local tastes, offering the special foods that the neighbors preferred. Bars were frequented by particular groups of regulars. The residents, as a group, maintained their Italian ethnic identity in various ways, including ritual celebrations such as festivals and saints' days.

Gans arrived at two major conclusions. First, old buildings with shabby exteriors do not necessarily signify a slum. Although the buildings of the West End were old and small, they did not reveal the quality of the housing. Gans quickly learned that the residents devoted their energies to improving the interiors of the houses and apartments. Inside, the dwelling units were clean, cozy, and comfortably furnished—there was nothing remotely slummy about them. Thus, despite external appearances, the West End had a social vitality, and even its housing was acceptable to its residents. Gans's second major conclusion was that people lived in such areas by choice. Ordinarily, we think that whoever lives in a slum does so only because they have no alternatives. However, the Italian-Americans of the West End had a choice. They had regular jobs, were not in a state of poverty, and could have moved to other residential areas in Boston or even to the suburbs. Occasionally, someone from the neighborhood would move to a suburb, but West Enders thought the movers lost a great deal in the process. Disapprovingly, West Enders said that suburban people had to drive to do anything—to see someone, to go shopping, or whatever. In the West End a congruity existed between the way of life and the environment; everything was close together—residences, shops, church, etc.—and this facilitated a high-contact, closely knit way of life with localized kinship and friendship networks. The urban environment fit nicely with the way of life, and the residents appreciated this.

Urban villages can be found in large cities throughout North America. Gerald Suttles (1968) has written about another Italian-American example in the center of Chicago, a city that also has Ukranian, Polish, and other enclaves. Near the center of Toronto, the visitor may walk through Chinese, Portuguese, and other urban villages. And they exist in many other cities, from Miami with its Cubans to San Francisco with its Chinese, Russians, and others.

## SUMMARY

While the concept of neighborhood once seemed simple, the realities of metropolitan life now make it more complex. The freedom of contemporary life, supported by the automobile-freeway complex plus the telephone, liberates most individuals from the constraints of their local residential area. There are so many choices that people may or may not participate in the social life of the local area. Furthermore, social and geographical mobility means that households relocate from place to place. Not everyone is moving all the time—there are large numbers of "stayers" at any point in time—but mobility is certainly an option for many households; they need not remain in locations if they prefer to move elsewhere. These factors—transportation, communication, and potential mobility—undermined the traditional gemeinschaft neighborhood.

Nonetheless, local social life still exists in cities and suburbs, of course. Urban sociologists are now more likely to use the terms residential area, local community, or community of limited liability rather than the term neighborhood. Janowitz (1952), who introduced the concept of community of limited liability, recognized that the urban situation did not simply destroy social life; he acknowledged that city areas still had friendship and kinship networks as well as voluntary associations and even localized newspapers for particular districts. Thus social life had not been rationalized, bureaucratized, and atomized as older theories might have predicted, *but* neither was community life in the metropolis as it had been in villages and traditional neighborhoods. Janowitz recognized that local social life had become voluntary and that participation was differentiated among different segments of the population. It was voluntary to the extent that individuals could opt out simply by declining to participate or by moving away. Participation was differentiated in that some categories—children and their caretakers, for example—were highly localized, while others were quite cosmopolitan, using the local area quite minimally.

Recent views of the local community emphasize that it is used in two major ways: for instrumental and for social psychological purposes. Instrumental uses are simply housing, use of local facilities, such as schools and shops, and consumption of a variety of household goods. Social psychological uses include participation in local networks and voluntary associations—church, PTA, Little League, etc.—as well as identification and symbolic emphasis. Individuals may identify with their local area; the area may even influence their own behavior, particularly if they are socialized there—this emphasis may be manifested in local modes of dress, accents, and even levels of aspiration. Symbolically, local areas may be used for prestige enhancement or for making a statement about one's status.

Levels of involvement and participation differ across local areas. One factor which tends to promote participation is social homogeneity. A study of young graduate student families implied that similarities of occupation and stage in the family life cycle promote sociability among neighbors. Another factor which tends to promote participation—particularly political mobilization—is the presence, real or imagined, of an external threat or enemy. Occupants of a residential area who may have had very little local involvement may get together to oppose some external force. For example, residents of a local area may band together to defend their area against the threat of massive demolition for highway construction or some other form of redevelopment. Furthermore, successful organizational experiences may have lasting effects, strengthening local ties. Residents may also mobilize to oppose a governmentally imposed program such as school busing for racial integration. This sort of local-level organization is known as the defended neighborhood.

# REFERENCES

Carpenter, Niles. 1933. "Neighborhood," pp. 356-357 in *Encyclopedia of the Social Sciences,* vol. 11. New York: Macmillan.

Choldin, Harvey M. 1980. "Social Participation in Suburban Apartment Enclaves," chap. 8 in *The Consumer Experience of Housing,* (eds.) C. Ungerson and V. A. Karn. Westmead, England: Gower.

Duncan, James S., Jr. 1976. "Landscape and the Communication of Social Identity," pp. 391–404 in *The Mutual Interaction of People and Their Built Environment,* (ed.) A. Rapoport. The Hague: Mouton.

Duncan, Otis D., Howard Schuman, and Beverly Duncan. 1973. *Social Change in a Metropolitan Community.* New York: Russell Sage.

Festinger, L., S. Schacter, and K. Back. 1950. *Social Pressures in Informal Groups.* Stanford, Calif.: Stanford.

Fischer, Claude S. 1976. *The Urban Experience.* New York: Harcourt Brace Jovanovich.

Foley, Donald L. 1950. "The Use of Local Facilities in a Metropolis," *American Journal of Sociology.* 56:238–246.

Foley, Donald L. 1952. *Neighbors or Urbanites.* Rochester, N.Y.: University of Rochester.

Gans, Herbert. 1962. *The Urban Villagers.* New York: Free Press.

Greer, Scott. 1962. *The Emerging City: Myth and Reality.* New York: Free Press.

Heumann, Leonard. 1983. "The Grass Roots Response to Government Housing Intervention," chap. 23 in *Handbook of Social Interventions,* (ed.) Edward Seidman. Beverly Hills, Calif.: Sage.

Hunter, Albert. 1974. *Symbolic Communities: The Persistence and Change of Chicago's Local Communities.* Chicago: University of Chicago Press.

Hunter, Albert. 1975. "The Loss of Community: An Empirical Test through Replication." *American Sociological Review.* 40:537–553.

Hunter, Albert J., and Gerald D. Suttles. 1972. "The Expanding Community of Limited Liability," chap. 3 in *The Social Construction of Communities,* (ed.) Gerald Suttles. Chicago: University of Chicago Press.

Janowitz, Morris. 1952. *The Community Press in an Urban Setting.* Chicago: University of Chicago Press.

Janowitz, Morris. 1978. *The Last Half-Century: Societal Change and Politics in America.* Chicago: University of Chicago.

Kasarda, John D., and Morris Janowitz. 1974. "Community Attachment in Mass Society." *American Sociological Review.* 39(3):328–340.

Keller, Suzanne. 1968. *The Urban Neighborhood.* New York: Random.

Kornblum, William. 1974. *Blue Collar Community.* Chicago: University of Chicago Press.

Mann, Peter H. 1965. *An Approach to Urban Sociology.* London: Routledge.

McClenahan, Bessie A. 1929. *The Changing Urban Neighborhood.* Los Angeles: University of Southern California.

McKenzie, Roderick. 1923. *The Neighborhood: A Study of Local Life in the City of Columbus, Ohio.* Chicago: University of Chicago Press.

Michelson, W. H. 1977. *Environmental Choice, Human Behavior, and Residential Satisfaction.* New York: Oxford University Press.

Molotch, Harvey. 1972. *Managed Integration: Dilemmas of Doing Good in the City*. Berkeley: University of California Press.

Molotch, Harvey. 1979. "Capital and Neighborhood in the United States: Some Conceptual Links." *Urban Affairs Quarterly*. 14:289-312.

Perlman, Janice E. 1978. "Grass-Roots Participation: From Neighborhood to Nation," pp. 65-79 in *Citizen Participation in America*, (ed.) Stuart Langton. Lexington, Mass.: Lexington.

Rosenbloom, Robert A. 1981. "The Neighborhood Movement: Where Has It Come From? Where Is It Going?" *Journal of Voluntary Action Research*. 10:4-21.

Rossi, Peter H. 1955. *Why Families Move*. Glencoe, Ill.: Free Press.

Suttles, Gerald D. 1968. *The Social Order of the Slum*. Chicago: University of Chicago Press.

Suttles, Gerald D. 1972. *The Social Construction of Communities*. Chicago: University of Chicago Press.

Taub, R. P., G. P. Surgeon, S. Lindholm, P. B. Otti, and A. Bridges. 1977. "Urban

Voluntary Association, Locality Based and Externally Induced." *American Journal of Sociology*. 83:425–442.
Timms, D. W. G. 1971. *The Urban Mosaic: Toward a Theory of Residential Differentiation*. Cambridge: Cambridge.
U.S. Bureau of the Census. 1980. *Statistical Abstract of the United States, 1980*. Washington, D.C.
Warren, Rachelle B., and Donald I. Warren. 1977. *The Neighborhood Organizer's Handbook*. Notre Dame. Ind.: University of Notre Dame Press.
Wellman, B. 1972. "Who Needs Neighborhoods?" pp. 94–100 in *The City: Attacking Modern Myths*, (ed.) A. Powell. Toronto: McClelland and Stewart.
Wirth, Louis. 1938. "Urbanism as a Way of Life." *American Journal of Sociology*. 44:1–24.
Yancey, William L., and Eugene P. Ericksen. 1979. "The Antecendents of Community: The Economic and Institutional Structure of Urban Neighborhoods." *American Sociological Review*. 44:253–262.

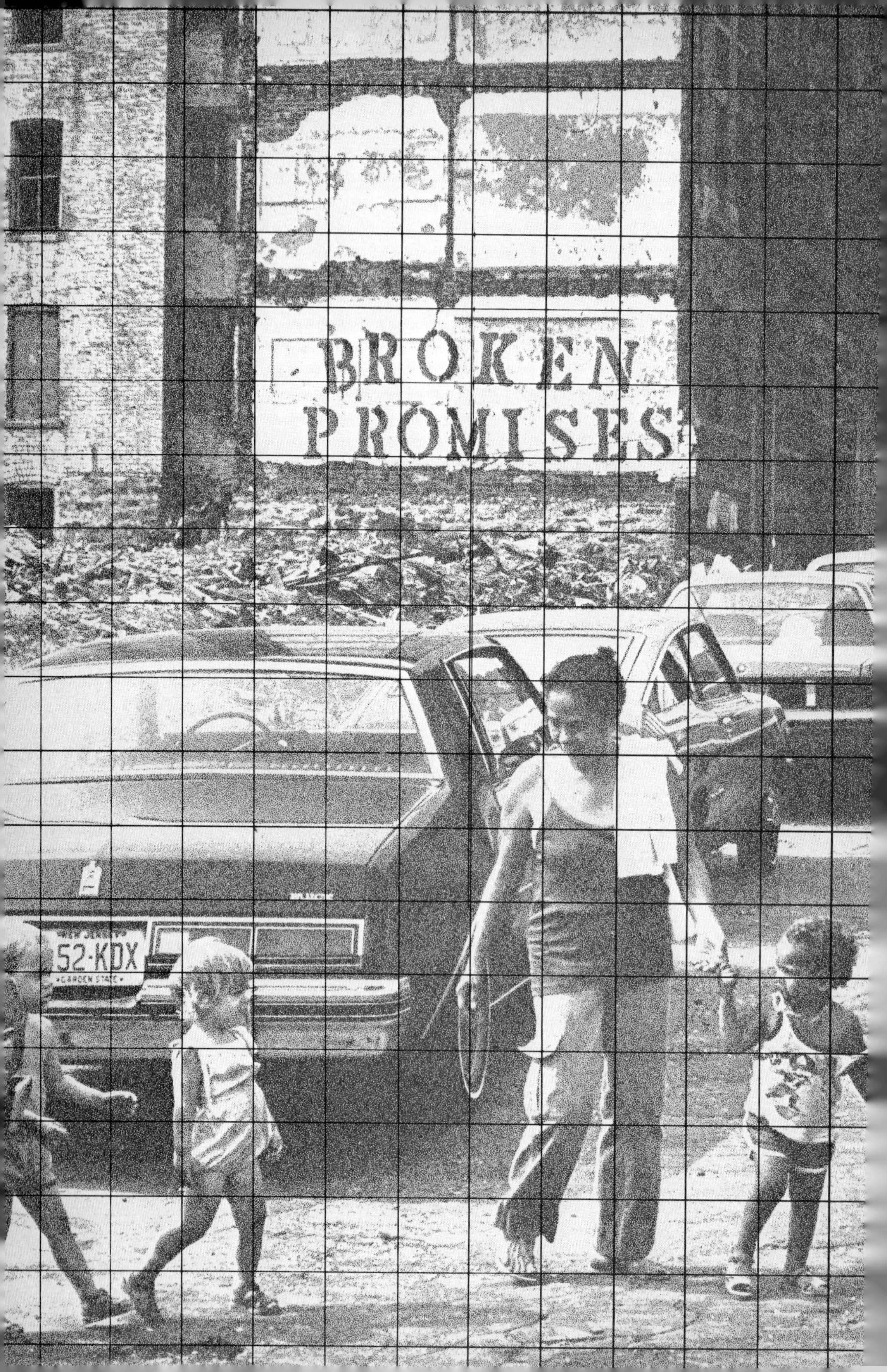
BROKEN
PROMISES
52-KDX
GARDEN STATE

# CHAPTER · 10

## Community Life: Recent Concerns

### Chapter Outline

PUBLIC OPINION ABOUT COMMUNITY LIFE

Community and Neighborhood Satisfaction
- Overall levels of satisfaction
- Factors influencing satisfaction
- Specific satisfactions and complaints

Fear of Crime
- Rising levels of fear
- Measurement and distribution of fear
- Causes of fear
- Visible signs of disorder
- Fear and community life

TWO CRITIQUES OF THE METROPOLIS

The Metropolis and Women
- Three approaches
- Specific issues

New Marxist Perspectives
- Issues and assumptions
- Neighborhood and spatial structure

SUMMARY

How do people evaluate their communities; what sorts of concerns do they express? This chapter presents concerns as they emerge in public opinion polls and in the writings of two groups challenging the status quo. The chapter starts with public opinion on the question of community satisfaction in general and then on fear of crime in particular. The next two sections discuss recent writings by two groups of sociologists: feminist scholars, who ask whether the contemporary urban and suburban communities are well arranged for women's lives, and "new Marxist" scholars, who ask whether urban sociology hasn't been misguided all along, missing the city's main facts of inequality and exploitation.

## PUBLIC OPINION ABOUT COMMUNITY LIFE

### Community and Neighborhood Satisfaction

Community satisfaction may be defined as one of a group of social indicators designed to measure the quality of life of the American people (Marans & Rodgers, 1975). Community satisfaction has been measured in a number of national and local surveys. In this section, community and neighborhood satisfaction will be discussed more or less interchangeably because analyses of surveys have shown that people's attitudes toward their neighborhoods conform very closely to their attitudes toward their communities.

### Overall levels of satisfaction

Americans express very high levels of satisfaction with their communities—study after study has shown this to be true. "Researchers in the U.S. have found that the vast majority of residents in a variety of community settings report being moderately to very satisfied with both their communities and their residential neighborhoods" (Marans & Rodgers, 1975, p. 3). After reviewing several studies, Lee and Guest (1979) wrote, "Residents have consistently and overwhelmingly responded in positive terms; favorable evaluations are normally recorded for 70 percent or more of a given sample" (p. 4). Recent surveys generate the same results. Surveying households who had moved within metropolitan Toronto, Michelson (1977) asked whether the individuals were satisfied with their new homes, locations, and neighborhoods. Both husbands and wives were positive about their new situations, over 90 percent saying they were "definitely satisfied" or "mostly satisfied" (p. 273).

Results of a large national survey (Marans & Rodgers, 1975) illustrate the high levels of community satisfaction (Table 10-1). The first column of the table shows that fewer than 1 out of 10 respondents said they were more dissatisfied than satisfied with their communities. The second column shows the same fact about respondents' satisfaction with their neighborhoods. People's most frequent response about community and neighborhood was that they were "completely satisfied." Elsewhere, the survey showed that even many of the individuals living in

**TABLE 10-1**
**Levels of Community and Neighborhood Satisfaction***

| Respondents were | With their communities, % (N = 2,153) | With their neighborhoods, % (N = 2,159) |
|---|---|---|
| 1. Completely satisfied | 38 | 46 |
| 2. | 22 | 21 |
| 3. | 15 | 13 |
| 4. Neutral | 16 | 11 |
| 5. | 5 | 4 |
| 6. | 2 | 2 |
| 7. Completely dissatisfied | 2 | 3 |
| Total | 100 | 100 |

*Respondents were handed a card with a seven-point scale and asked the following: "And what about this particular neighborhood in (name city or county)? All things considered, how satisfied or dissatisfied are you with this neighborhood as a place to live? Which number comes closest to how satisfied or dissatisfied you feel?"
Source: Marans and Rodgers, 1975, tables 7.1 and 7.12.

what are considered to be "substandard" environments report they are fairly content with their communities.

Groups differ in evaluating communities, particularly along the size-of-place dimension: the larger the place, the less likely its residents are to express satisfaction with it. Several surveys have generated this finding. Marans and Rodgers' national survey shows that central cities of large metropolitan areas have the lowest proportion of satisfied individuals, whereas small cities and towns and rural areas have the highest proportions of satisfied individuals (see Table 10-2). The larger the city, the lower the likelihood that its citizens will say their community or neighborhood is excellent. Small-town and rural residents are most likely to evaluate their communities and neighborhoods positively. Suburbanites are intermediate between small-town and big-city responses on community and neighborhood satisfaction.

## Factors influencing satisfaction

**Housing and environmental factors** Homeowners tend to be more satisfied than renters with their neighborhoods and communities, and residents of single-family houses are more satisfied than apartment dwellers (Baldassare, 1979; Lee & Guest, 1979; Michelson, 1977). More generally, Baldassare demonstrated that neighborhood density is inversely related to neighborhood satisfaction. Local facilities and upkeep also affect satisfaction; people who report that public and private facilities are conveniently located nearby tend to be satisfied with their communities. People downgrade their neighborhoods for the following reasons: too much traffic, not enough trees and clean air, crowding, ability to hear neighbors or general noise, dangerous streets, and no privacy in the yards. Maintenance of the environment

**TABLE 10-2**
**Level of Community Satisfaction for People in Communities of Different Sizes**

| Size of community* | Respondents were ||| Total | Number of respondents |
|---|---|---|---|---|---|
| | Completely satisfied, % | Satisfied, % | Neutral or dissatisfied, % | | |
| Largest cities | 20 | 38 | 42 | 100 | 226 |
| Other large cities | 29 | 32 | 39 | 100 | 239 |
| Suburbs | 36 | 41 | 23 | 100 | 455 |
| Small cities and towns | 40 | 40 | 20 | 100 | 683 |
| Rural areas | 48 | 34 | 18 | 100 | 550 |

*Communities were categorized by the degree to which they were urbanized, based on 1960 census data. The largest cities are those of the 12 largest SMSAs. Other large cities are other cities over 100,000 population. Suburbs are places with a population of less than 100,000 in the 12 largest SMSAs and rural places of less than 2,500 in all SMSAs. Small towns and cities are places with a population between 2,500 and 100,000 which are not in the 12 largest SMSAs, while rural areas contain populations of less than 2,500 and are not situated in an SMSA.

*Source:* Marans and Rodgers, 1975, table 7.7.

is "by far the most important predictor of satisfaction." This means not only how the municipality maintains the area but how neighbors keep up their houses and lots.

**Social factors** Sociodemographic differences also occur in community and neighborhood evaluation (see Table 10-3). Whites are more likely than blacks to evaluate their areas highly, and people with lower incomes and education are more likely to say they are completely satisfied.

In addition to homeownership, stage in the family life cycle and tenure make a difference. Young single persons are the least satisfied with their neighborhoods; as noted in Chapter 9, they are also the least likely to be involved. Older residents without children at home are the most satisfied. More generally, age is positively related to satisfaction. Furthermore, the proportion of survey respondents who report complete satisfaction increases as the number of years lived in the area increases. This conforms to the pattern of community involvement, which also increases over time.

The way people feel about others in the area makes a big difference. If they see the others as being friendly and similar to themselves, they are likely to be satisfied. They report greater satisfaction if they perceive an acceptable level of personal safety. Among low-income households, strong attachments to family and friends living in the area account for community satisfaction. Strong attachment to the social setting is a source of satisfaction to people in some low-income areas, especially urban villages. Even in their broader-based surveys, though, Marans and Rodgers (1975) report that assessment of neighbors, along with assessment of the

**TABLE 10-3**
Satisfaction with Macroneighborhood Expressed by Different Subgroups

| Characteristics | Completely satisfied, % | Satisfied, % | Neutral or dissatisfied, % | Total | Number of respondents |
|---|---|---|---|---|---|
| *Race* | | | | | |
| White | 49 | 33 | 18 | 100 | 1877 |
| Black | 28 | 36 | 36 | 100 | 222 |
| Other | 28 | 42 | 30 | 100 | 53 |
| *Family Income* | | | | | |
| Less than $3,000 | 49 | 29 | 22 | 100 | 291 |
| $3,000–4,999 | 48 | 30 | 22 | 100 | 287 |
| $5,000–6,999 | 42 | 32 | 26 | 100 | 268 |
| $7,000–9,999 | 44 | 33 | 23 | 100 | 366 |
| $10,000–11,999 | 46 | 38 | 16 | 100 | 272 |
| $12,000–16,999 | 46 | 38 | 16 | 100 | 320 |
| $17,000 or more | 49 | 35 | 16 | 100 | 265 |
| *Family Life Cycle* | | | | | |
| Single, age 18–29 | 22 | 41 | 37 | 100 | 167 |
| Single, age 30 or older | 37 | 40 | 23 | 100 | 93 |
| Married, no children; age 18–29 | 31 | 47 | 22 | 100 | 95 |
| Married, no children; age 30 or older | 56 | 29 | 15 | 100 | 105 |
| Married, youngest child aged 5 or younger | 36 | 38 | 26 | 100 | 436 |
| Married, youngest child aged 6–17 | 50 | 35 | 15 | 100 | 412 |
| Married, youngest child aged 18 or older | 60 | 27 | 13 | 100 | 402 |
| Separated or divorced | 40 | 31 | 29 | 100 | 179 |
| Widowed | 61 | 26 | 13 | 100 | 256 |

*Source:* Marans and Rodgers, 1975, tables 7.7 and 7.15.

upkeep of nearby houses, is the best predictor of neighborhood satisfaction (see also Baldassare, 1979; Lee & Guest, 1979).

## Specific satisfactions and complaints

Community surveys pinpoint some more specific items, going beyond the generalized evaluations. At the neighborhood level, beyond rating their areas highly, survey respondents mentioned the following:

Five out of six said the place where they live is convenient enough.
Two out of five said houses in the area were kept up very well.
One-half said they had very good neighbors.
Three out of four said they were not afraid to walk in the neighborhood at night (Marans & Rodgers, 1975).

Furthermore, people refer to a set of public services when they evaluate their communities. Their satisfaction depends upon how they see the public schools, police-community relations, and local tax rates.

**Summary**  Surveys of community and neighborhood satisfaction produce a clear pattern of results. If individuals are satisfied with their local subareas (neighborhoods), they are also satisfied with their broader communities. Rural-suburban-urban differences in satisfaction are consistent: the larger the place, the lower the level of satisfaction. Despite this, though, the vast majority of individuals report high levels of satisfaction with their communities.

Community satisfaction is one dimension of the quality of life; as such, it is a composite of how people evaluate the local environment, social life, and public services and facilities. Relevant dimensions of the local environment are housing and density, with the preference going toward single-family dwellings with substantial space between buildings. How the locality and its buildings are maintained is very important to people as they evaluate their communities. Relevant dimensions of social life are whether others are seen as friendly and as similar to oneself, and relevant dimensions of services and facilities are convenience of location and quality of schools and police-community relations.

Finally, despite the high general level of satisfaction, the surveys show some differences within the public. Blacks are less satisfied than whites; young people are less satisfied than older people; and satisfaction tends to increase as one lives longer in a particular locality. One aspect of community life that undermines satisfaction is crime and fear, another subjective social indicator.

## Fear of Crime

### Rising levels of fear

After declining for about 100 years, urban crime rates rose dramatically in the mid-1960s, resulting in rising levels of fear. City people became fearful about many situations, about walking in parks after dark, riding subways at night, passing certain buildings, and the like. Despite the rising levels of fear, which were heavily publicized in magazines and newspapers, sociologists ignored this phenomenon. Before 1978, only one article was published on the fear of crime; since then, some attention has been paid to the subject, in the form of surveys and a handful of published reports. For the purposes of urban sociology, we should consider the fear of crime, as measured, to be another social indicator representing an aspect of the quality of life in metropolitan areas.

The first central question about urban fear is whether it is caused directly or indirectly by the experience of crime. A simple approach to this question suggests that individuals who have been victims of crime should also be the most fearful and that nonvictims should be less afraid. This approach also suggests that people in the residential areas with the most crime should be more fearful than individuals living in lower-crime areas. The term "victimization" refers to the state of being made a victim of a crime; victimization surveys attempt to discover the levels of certain kinds of crimes by asking people whether crimes have been committed against them. The simple approach to the crime-fear connection, mentioned above, suggests, finally, that those categories of the population with the highest levels of victimization—age groupings, socioeconomic categories, etc.—should also have the highest levels of fear. On the other hand, though, two leading researchers on victimization, Skogan and Maxfield (1981), contend that this approach does not truly represent the genesis of fear. Arguing that the connection between fear and victimization is not necessarily direct, they hypothesize that the connection is indirect.

A related question asks which conditions of urban environment and social life are most fear-inducing. One theoretical answer to the question suggests that the public is concerned with "visible signs of disorder." Most individuals in the metropolis rarely, if ever, observe crimes in progress, but they do observe environmental conditions or other individuals whose appearance and behavior disturb them in one way or another. James Q. Wilson (1975/1977), who introduced the concept of visible signs of disorder, said that people have expectations of "fit and proper behavior" in public and semipublic places. Where these standards appear to be declining or are not maintained, people feel they are watching the disintegration of the rules that should govern public life. Wilson argued that this was a major contributor to the "sense of urban unease" which set in during the 1960s. One major study, summarized later in this section, operationalized the concept and measured public concern with it and its connection with urban fear.

The second central question about urban fear is more broad-ranging; it asks whether urban fear has become so widespread and deep that it destroys the entire possibility of community life. Wilson (1975/1977) theorized that crime and fear do have this negative effect on the city.

> Predatory crime does not merely victimize individuals, it impedes and, in the extreme case, even prevents the formation and maintenance of community. By disrupting the delicate nexus of ties, formal and informal, by which we are linked with our neighbors, crime atomizes society and makes of its members mere individual calculators estimating their own advantage, especially their own chances for survival amidst their fellows. Common undertakings become difficult, except for those motivated by a shared desire for protection. (p. 22)

This implies one effect of fear is that individuals withdraw from social interaction; they stay home more. It implies as well that they are fearful of one another, thus lacking the trust which is essential to the maintenance of community ties. This line of thought suggests our second hypothesis to be investigated: that fear tends to undermine community interaction and involvement.

## Measurement and distribution of fear

Sociological studies of urban fear are conducted by means of sample surveys. (Many vivid and useful journalistic accounts of fearful city folks also enrich our view of this problem.) The standard question that has been asked in most of the surveys is, "Is there any area right around here—that is, within a mile—where you would be afraid to walk alone at night?" Going beyond that conventional question, recent studies have included the following items:

> "When I have to be away from home for a long time, I worry that someone might try to break in."
> "I am often a little worried that I will be the victim of a crime in my neighborhood."
> "Would you say that the likelihood you will be a victim of crime in your neighborhood during the coming year is high, moderate, or low?" (Taub & Taylor, 1980, pp. 42–44).

Although this section is based upon a number of publications, it relies heavily upon one, which I shall call the "Northwestern" study (Skogan & Maxfield, 1981), that examined public opinion in three large cities—Philadelphia, Chicago, and San Francisco. Skogan and Maxfield conducted citywide surveys in each of the cities and, in addition, surveyed 10 neighborhoods more intensively. Since the federal Law Enforcement Assistance Administration had already sponsored large-scale victimization surveys in these cities, Skogan and Maxfield were able to analyze some of that agency's data to supplement their own. They also placed participant observers in the research neighborhoods to attend meetings and interview community leaders and local officials, and they systematically analyzed crime news in the newspapers of the three cities. These activities represent an elaborate multifaceted research approach to public opinion regarding crime and fear.

By and large, the public exhibits a high level of fear. People in big cities are most fearful, followed by suburban residents; the least fearful are those who live in small towns and rural areas. Table 10-4, computed from a large national survey, showed that roughly 60 percent of the population in central cities of large metropolitan areas said there was somewhere in their neighborhood where they would be afraid to walk at night. Residents of smaller cities and towns as well as of rural areas were far less likely to express this fear. In general, city size is a strong predictor of fear; the bigger the community, the higher the level of fear (Clemente & Kleiman, 1977). Among big cities, overall fear levels do not differ much (Skogan & Maxfield, 1981).

**TABLE 10-4**
**Percentage of Respondents Afraid to Walk at Night Somewhere in their Neighborhood, 1980**

| Respondents (N = 1,456) | Percentage |
|---|---|
| Central-city residents | |
|   12 largest SMSAs | 60.2 |
|   Next 88 SMSAs | 57.3 |
| Suburban residents | |
|   12 largest SMSAs | 45.3 |
|   Next 88 SMSAs | 49.4 |
| Other urban residents | 37.5 |
| Rural-nonmetropolitan residents | 30.4 |

*Source:* Author, computed from 1980 General Social Survey, conducted by National Opinion Research Center; data supplied by Interuniversity Consortium for Political and Social Research.

In regard to the more specific items, more than 40 percent of Chicagoans surveyed said they worry that their homes will be burgled when they are away; over 30 percent said they are "often a little worried" that they will be victims of crime in the neighborhood; but fewer than 10 percent said the likelihood is high that they will be victims of crime in the neighborhood during the coming year (Taub & Taylor, 1980).

The surveys reveal some differentials: single persons, the poor, blacks, and renters are more likely than others to express fear (Lee, 1983). Women are more likely than men to express it; middle-aged and elderly women, especially those living alone, in poor health, and whose dwellings had been burglarized, are more apt than other women to express fear. In sum, the fear of being victimized is especially prevalent within the most isolated and vulnerable segments of the population (Baumgart, Baumgart, & Hoyer, 1980).

The Northwestern study showed that people differentiate among crimes in their estimations of the local situation. In addition to asking about fear, the researchers asked people whether they viewed each of four kinds of crime as a problem in their residential area. With the exception of one city, people said that burglary was the worst local problem, followed by personal theft, assault by strangers, and rape (Table 10-5). (While the table apparently shows differences between cities, most of them are not statistically significant.)

## Causes of fear

The first hypothesis suggested that crime influences fear only indirectly. Skogan supports this assertion in two ways. He shows that while only a small proportion of the population is directly victimized by crime, a large proportion fears it. Furthermore, he shows that there is a lack of correspondence between victimization

**TABLE 10-5**
Crime Problems in the Neighborhood*

|  | Percentage responding "a big problem" |  |  |  |  |
|---|---|---|---|---|---|
| City | Burglary | Personal theft | Stranger assault | Rape | Number of respondents |
| City |  |  |  |  |  |
| Chicago | 20 | 25 | 10 | 7 | 390 |
| San Francisco | 20 | 17 | 8 | 6 | 446 |
| Philadelphia | 16 | 14 | 6 | 5 | 424 |
| (Significance of differences) | (.53) | (.01+) | (.27) | (.57) |  |
| Average | 19 | 18 | 8 | 6 | 1260 |

*Number of cases varies slightly from crime to crime; averages are given here.
*Source:* Skogan and Maxfield, 1981, p. 84.

differentials and fear differentials. For example, young persons are far more likely than older persons to become victims, yet the elderly are much more likely to say they are fearful. (This age difference in victimization runs counter to the impression presented in newspapers and magazines, which often run stories of predations upon elderly individuals. While these events are deplorable, they do not reflect the statistical likelihood of an older person's becoming a victim. Younger people are more likely to be out where the action is and, hence, are more exposed to the risk of victimization.) Skogan and Maxfield looked at crime rates and fear levels in 10 neighborhoods. While in most cases the residents had a fairly accurate perception of local crime levels, the researchers also found high-crime neighborhoods where the residents were either unaware of the true situation or knew and were nonetheless unafraid. On an aggregate basis in the three research cities, though, the Northwestern researchers found correlations between the perception of crime as a neighborhood problem and fear. Survey respondents who said they considered each of the four crimes as "a big problem" in their area were also likely to say "yes" to the fear question (see Table 10-6). Another writer suggested that crime is not perceived as an imminent threat to most people;" they think it must be happening somewhere else. Violent crime, in particular, is seen to be rising elsewhere, not in people's own neighborhoods, although survey respondents were likely to say that property crimes were rising locally (Garofalo & Laub, 1978). On the other hand, not everyone thinks of crime as a distant possibility. A study of black and white mothers in Philadelphia reported that many were more worried about their children's safety than they were about their own (Savitz et al., cited in Skogan & Maxfield, 1981).

Although major differences in levels of fear do not exist when comparing one big city with another, clear differences in fear do exist among neighborhoods. As Skogan and Maxfield (1981) wrote, "Both crime and disorder problems cluster together very tightly, and it is possible to fairly describe neighborhoods as troubled

**TABLE 10-6**
**Neighborhood Conditions and Fear**

| Measure of neighborhood conditions | Correlation with fear measure | Percentage responding "a big problem"* |
|---|---|---|
| *Major Crime Problems* | | |
| Burglary | .32 | 18.7 |
| Robbery/purse snatching | .46 | 18.2 |
| Stranger assault | .45 | 7.9 |
| Rape | .39 | 5.9 |
| Scale score | .43 | .... |
| *Local Social Order Problems* | | |
| Teens hanging out | .29 | 18.8 |
| Abandoned buildings | .31 | 9.2 |
| Use of drugs | .30 | 20.4 |
| Vandalism | .26 | 17.4 |
| Scale score | .26 | .... |
| *Neighborhood Conditions* | | |
| Getting worse | .28 | 26.5 |

All correlations (gamma) are significant ($p < .01$). Number of respondents varies between 1065 and 1330.
*Source:* Skogan and Maxfield, 1981, p. 113.

or not troubled, and people as in trouble or not" (p. 107). These researchers found six neighborhoods where fewer than one-third of the people said they felt unsafe, but they also found an area where more than half gave this response. Similarly, Taub and Taylor found a wide range among Chicago neighborhoods in people's expressions of fear.

## Visible signs of disorder

In addition to asking about fear and about crime as a neighborhood problem, the Northwestern researchers also measured perception of visible signs of disorder. Respondents were asked whether each of the following was a problem in their neighborhood:

1. Groups of teenagers hanging out on the streets
2. Abandoned or burned-out buildings or stores
3. People using illegal drugs
4. Vandalism—kids breaking windows or writing on walls

The researchers chose these items as indicators of apparent phenomena that could easily be defined as local problems. They consider these signs to be "early warning signals of impending danger because people have learned to associate them with things they fear" (Skogan & Maxfield, 1981, p. 92). Unsupervised teenagers are seen as potential sources of "disruption, harassment, and crime." Abandoned buildings are seen as harboring a multitude of dangerous possibilities—from housing drug dealers to attracting arsonists.

The researchers found that people were even more likely to say that these signs were big problems than to say the crimes were (Table 10-7). Furthermore, across the 10 research neighborhoods in three cities, the four specific problems were highly correlated with each other; if a person said that one of them was a problem, the person was likely to say that the others were also. Finally, a significant correlation can be seen between the perception of signs of disorder and the expression of fear. Individuals who say the symptoms of disorder are big problems are also likely to say they are afraid of crime (Table 10-6). In their study of Chicago residential areas, Taub and Taylor also found people to be concerned about visible signs of disorder. The survey asked whether respondents saw a big problem on their block with "people shouting insults; purse snatching or other street crimes; and drug users" (1980, p. 29). While there was considerable variation between neighborhoods in response to this question, about a quarter of those surveyed in three areas said public disorder is a big problem. In the other seven areas the respondents were less likely to identify this as a local problem.

### Fear and community life

**Precautionary measures** Several studies have shown that city and suburban residents have modified their behaviors in order to protect themselves from the danger of crime. "They stay off the streets at night, avoid strangers, curtail social activities, keep firearms, buy watchdogs and may even move to other neighborhoods" (Clemente & Kleiman, 1977, p. 519). As will be noted in the section in this chapter on women in the city, they tend to stop going alone into avoidable situations.

Taub and Taylor's Chicago survey revealed specific precautionary measures. About 60 percent of their respondents said they had taken general security measures, such as light timers, window bars, or new locks, to avoid crime. About 30

**TABLE 10-7**
**Disorder Problems in the Neighborhood**

|  | Percentage responding "a big problem" ||||
| --- | --- | --- | --- | --- |
|  | Teenagers | Abandoned buildings | Drug use | Vandalism |
| Chicago | 23 | 12 | 25 | 22 |
| Philadelphia | 22 | 14 | 23 | 21 |
| San Francisco | 12 | 3 | 14 | 10 |
| (Significance of differences) | (.01+) | (.01+) | (.01+) | (.01+) |
| Average, 3-city sample | 19 | 9 | 20 | 17 |

Source: Skogan and Maxfield, 1981, p. 95.

## COMMUNITY LIFE: RECENT CONCERNS

Rising levels of fear have impelled individuals, such as this woman in Flint, Michigan, to develop strategies of self protection. (Michael Hayman, Photo Researchers, Inc.)

percent said they kept a watchdog to avoid crime, and more than twenty percent said they kept a gun or some other weapon. These figures varied by race and across neighborhoods. The Northwestern researchers also probed this subject, focusing upon precautionary behavior after dark. They found that although people said they still go out at night, the most common change is to traveling by car rather than on foot. About half the individuals surveyed reported this shift. About a quarter of the respondents said that after dark they would now take an escort rather than going alone and that they would avoid certain places. The researchers wanted to discover whether city residents were carrying guns for protection after dark, but because of the illegality of this activity, the survey question was deliberately worded in a vague manner; they asked whether the respondent "takes something" along when going out after dark, and they found that about 1 in 5 answered affirmatively. One report of the Northwestern project emphasized crime as a problem of urban women; Table 10-8 shows some precautionary behaviors from that paper.

**Social effects of modified behavior** The evidence directly testing our second hypothesis is not as strong as it might be. Hypothesis two stated that rising levels of fear would undermine social connections within the community. One study

**TABLE 10-8**
Safety Precautions Taken by Urban Women, $N = 299$

| Safety precaution* | Percentage† |
|---|---|
| *50% or more of the respondents* | |
| Ask for identification from salesperson or repairperson | 50 |
| Go out with a friend or two as protection | 51 |
| Check the back seat of car for intruders before entering | 59 |
| Being alert and watchful while walking on the street | 81 |
| Deliberately leave on lights or radio when no one will be at home | 65 |
| Unlisted phone number | 57 |
| *20–50% of the respondents* | |
| Restrict going out to daytime only | 26 |
| Try to wear shoes that are easy to run in, in case of danger | 36 |
| Avoid looking people in the eye whom you don't know (on the street) | 29 |
| Avoid downtown when planning to go out at night | 24 |
| Take along something for protection, like dog or whistle, when out alone | 23 |

*These were chosen arbitrarily from a list of 42 similar items. All these practices were followed by some males as well, but their percentages are not reported here because they were based on an insufficient sample.
†Numbers represent the percentage of the sample answering "yes"; they follow this practice or "always" do this, depending upon question wording.
*Source:* Gordon et al., 1980, table 3.

shows that the individual's degree of personal integration into social networks is strongly related to the perception of human dangers in the community. Persons who were not integrated into networks were more likely than others to express concern about letting their children out of the house and felt that they were vulnerable to strangers, that they were unsafe on the street at night, and that children in the neighborhood were out of control (Hartnagel, 1979, p. 178). But these findings, while interesting, approach the hypothesis from the wrong end; they show that people without networks experience fear, but not that fear destroys networks. However, there is other evidence related to the original hypothesis.

The Northwestern study also showed that the level of social integration in neighborhoods was closely related to their crime rates (Figure 10.1). The researchers related all the research areas as to their degree of neighborhood integration, referring to the extent of residential and social ties among the residents. Areas with high degrees of neighborhood integration had high proportions of homeowners—residents with high tenure—who planned to stay there. These areas also had residents who said they felt that they were part of a neighborhood and could recognize other people in the area. When the researchers divided the areas into those in the top and the bottom half along this dimension, they found that all the places with low levels of neighborhood integration had major crime problems. And, with one exception, all the areas with high levels of neighborhood integration did not have major crime problems. \

Major crime problems

|  | Low | High |
|---|---|---|
| Neighborhood integration — Low |  | Mission<br>Lincoln Park<br>Woodlawn<br>Wicker Park |
| Neighborhood integration — High | Back-of-the-Yards<br>Logan<br>Sunset<br>West Philadelphia<br>South Philadelphia | Visitacion<br>Valley |

**FIGURE 10-1**
Neighborhood integration by crime level. These are names of neighborhoods in different cities which were in the Northwestern University survey. Integration here refers to social involvement of local residents, not to racial integration. With one exception, highly integrated neighborhoods tend to have lower crime rates, while unintegrated neighborhoods have more crime. (Source: Skogan & Maxfield, 1981, p. 106; data computed from 10 neighborhood surveys.)

The modified behaviors of urban individuals curtail their social contacts. If women are avoiding laundromats and bars, for fear of victimization, they are foregoing opportunities for social involvement. If people are less likely to go out at night and if they are more likely to drive than to walk, then they are undermining the potential sociability of neighborhood street life. As McIntire (1967) says, when people restrict their activities, social interaction is reduced. People "forego opportunities for pleasure and cultural enrichment, and they become less sociable, more suspicious" (McIntyre, 1967, quoted by Hartnagel, 1979, p. 177). Surely we are not overinterpreting the survey results on fear, concern with visible signs of disorder, and modified protective behavior by inferring that all of them tend to undermine community social life.

**Summary** Public opinion surveys show high levels of fear, highest within the big central cities, lowest in rural places, with suburbs intermediate. Within the public, there are differentials: Women are more fearful than men, elderly individuals more fearful than younger ones, and blacks more fearful than whites. Although levels of fear do not vary much from one city to another, they vary considerably among neighborhoods. In addition to fear of crime, the public opinion surveys show that people are concerned with visible signs of disorder—unacceptable phenomena in the residential area, from teenagers hanging around to abandoned buildings.

People have modified their everyday behaviors, adapting to the fear of crime. After dark they are less likely to go out alone, and when they do, they are more likely to drive than to walk. They avoid fearsome places, even such formerly innocuous ones as movie theaters and laundromats. One effect of these new attitudes and behaviors appears to be a lessening of urban sociability, more distrust of strangers, and some foregone opportunities of social interaction.

## TWO CRITIQUES OF THE METROPOLIS

### The Metropolis and Women

Women constitute a majority of the metropolitan population of the United States. In central cities, the sex ratio (the number of females per 100 males) is 115 and in suburbs it is 107. Among persons over age 65, the sex ratio is far more lopsided, at 157! Furthermore, millions of households are headed by women; 20.7 percent of central-city and 10.9 percent of suburban families are female-headed (Freeman, 1980). These figures show why women's interest in urban and suburban communities is considerable.

Nonetheless, urban sociologists have never focused upon women and their activities as a special area of concern. One scholar, Lyn Lofland (1975), has charged that this represents a blind spot in urban sociology, that research and theory have taken women for granted, and that since the community was the field of research, women—who were assumed to be carrying out a round of activities and responsibilities *at home*—were simply *there*, but not as primary subjects. Lofland offers a number of reasons for this neglect, not the least of which was the difficulty of fieldwork among women—since almost all the urban sociologists were males, they did not have legitimate entrée into the places where women spent time. Urban research usually focused upon social problems—hobbies, gangs, slums—and as women were not defined as a problem, research grants were not given to support studies of them. Lofland suggests that urban sociology will be enriched when the specific realms of women are described. She notes that there are no published studies of beauty parlors, of women and children in parks, or of coffee shops, all three being special community settings where women interact. She argues that urban sociology will become more informative and complete when such studies are done.

In the decade of the 1970s a number of social scientists began to examine explicitly women's place in the community. Their work arose in the context of feminist scholarship in the social sciences. In addition to Lofland's essay, we may cite three collections of papers on the subject: "Women and the City" (Stimpson, 1980), *New Space for Women* (Wekerle, Peterson, & Morley, 1980), and *Building for Women* (Keller, 1981). These publications reflect theoretical considerations of the subject as well as numerous studies, including surveys and analyses of census and economic data. The following section is based upon these recent essays and reports.

The feminist writers ask, essentially, whether the sociospatial arrangements of city and suburb place special burdens upon women. Is the community spatially arranged in such a way as to facilitate women's activities or, alternatively, is it arranged in ways that make these activities more burdensome than they might otherwise be?

## Three approaches

Wekerle (1980) organizes the literature on women in the urban environment under three general rubrics: (1) the dichotomy between private and public spheres of action; (2) the congruity between environment and behavior, looking at the "fit" between women's activities and the environments of home, neighborhood, and city; and (3) the question of environmental equity. Each of these highlights different aspects of the subject, but there are overlaps among them as well.

**Private and public spheres** Writers adopting this approach suggest that the situation of women in the community was produced by a historical process which divided public and private realms in modern society. Imagine a preindustrial village where women might work together, perhaps washing clothes at a pond. This sort of women's group work was eliminated in modern urban development.

> In the process of urbanization women's work was removed from the communal work spaces of the village and relegated to the private space of the individual home. The loss was significant since communications networks and political skills had developed in these communal spaces and were prevented from emerging when women's work became isolated in the home. (Boulding, cited in Wekerle, 1980, p. S190)

In the metropolis women's primary roles—mother and housekeeper—relegated them to the private realm, excluding them from the more prestigious and powerful public realm. Another author expanded this idea, identifying women's household roles as a consequence of patriarchal structure, that is, patriarchy determines women's household work, household social relations, and then the spatial structure of the community (Markusen, 1980). An American adage epitomizes the public-private concept (Hayden, 1980): "A woman's place is in the home."

**Environment-behavior congruity** Social scientists who take the second approach ask whether the physical environments of home, neighborhood, and city are well suited to women's activities. In this vein, analysts may look at physical environmental features of the community such as density, location of facilities, distance between housing units, location of workplaces, transportation systems, etc. Then they may look at family structure and activities, labor force participation, neighboring patterns, and other social relationships. Combining the two sets of observations, those on environment with those on activity patterns, they may ask whether the environment facilitates or frustrates the activities.

**Environmental equity**  Finally, the third approach suggests another set of questions. The environmental equity model focuses upon women's claimed rights to equal access to public goods and services such as transportation, housing, and social services. The following sections will highlight various studies and theories on women which may be considered within these three approaches.

## Specific issues

**Fear of crime**  As noted above, fear of crime has a larger impact upon females than upon males. A 1972 national survey showed that more than 50 percent of the women surveyed were afraid to walk in their neighborhoods at night, as compared with 20 percent of the males surveyed. Furthermore, the proportion of women reporting such fears has been rising. Margaret Gordon (1980), a member of the Northwestern University research team, focused particularly upon women, conducting almost 300 in-depth interviews to supplement the basic survey. She discovered that women in some urban districts have accurate assessments of local dangers but that women in some other places are unaware of high local crime rates. Overall, women are less likely than men to be victims of crime. Women worry more about potential problems in "avoidable situations" than in unavoidable ones. Thus Gordon reported, "Worry levels for going alone to laundromats, movies, downtown, and bars [all considered to be avoidable situations] are higher than worry levels for unavoidable situations" (p. S152). Examples of the latter are using public transportation and walking past bars, empty lots, or groups of boys.

Women respond by using more safety precautions, staying home at night, and avoiding certain parts of the city. They tend not to enter fearsome avoidable situations. "The fear of rape keeps women off the streets at night. Keeps women at home. Keeps women passive and modest for fear that they be thought provocative" (Griffin, cited in Gordon, 1980, p. S145). According to Gordon, women lose opportunities because of their fear of crime; their sociospatial range is constricted.

**Roles and locations**  A number of analysts point out the interconnections between women's roles, locational situations, and the metropolitan transportation system. "Geographers Palm and Pred were among the first to emphasize the critical connection between women's domestic roles, their travel patterns, and access to jobs, leisure activities and social services" according to Wekerle (1980, p. S206). Typically, women are responsible for child rearing and household maintenance—cooking, cleaning, etc. Increasingly, women are also members of the paid labor force, holding part- or full-time jobs.

In the first instance, then, one must look at the adequacy of contemporary residential areas for women's home activities. Comparing city and suburban areas, some social scientists have noted the dissatisfaction of suburban women with their environments, citing loneliness among homemakers. Suburbs were built deliberately at low densities. This makes contact between households difficult, except for close neighbors, unless a family owns more than one car, assuming that the first is used by a spouse to commute to work.

Lopata's (1980) analysis of urban communities concludes that the spatial arrangements of family-related facilities, combined with the absence of certain crucial facilities which would lighten women's burdens, add up to a deficient system. She writes:

> American society as a whole has not been innovative in helping women reach resources other than shopping, has not provided child-care assistance even when mothers function as consumers and definitely not to ease employment or social contact. Resources for social life and even for development of children's skills and abilities are often so located that the chauffeuring restricts the time available to a woman for many years. (Lopata, 1980, p. S169)

In a survey of homemakers, Lopata discovered that they felt "tied down" for several years. Even shopping is difficult for them, when children are along, as they must be carried, watched, and controlled. City women without cars must carry children and objects in mass transit facilities which are not designed for women needing to move children and goods.

The situation changes as women pass through the family life cycle. Young urban single women are geographically mobile within the complex of home, school, and work roles. The situation shifts radically after the birth of the first child; then the women express feelings of restriction in movement.

Older women suffer a worse set of limitations on mobility, which are exacerbated by transportation systems. Lopata's survey of widows showed that older women in the city have geographically restricted network ties and locations, staying close to home. Some are simply urban villagers, never venturing beyond their own neighborhoods. Some widows are extremely ignorant of the locations of places and ways to get about; they lack mental maps of the world beyond the confines of the neighborhood.

Women who are bringing up children without a male partner face additional problems in the communiy. These female-headed households require some special facilities and services in order to lead independent lives, according to Carol Brown (cited in Wekerle, 1980). Ironically, she observes that the type of urban residential area usually labeled as disorganized or declining by city planners is also the type most likely to provide the kinds of services that divorced mothers require: Unlike homogeneous, single-family suburban residential areas, these older city areas may have enterprises and jobs in them and are also likely to have apartment buildings, stores, public transportation, welfare services, and child care. All these are less likely to be present in or easily accessible from suburban residential areas. Brown also contends that in these older city areas there is "a greater acceptance of single-parent families and their life-styles" (cited in Wekerle, 1980, p. S2).

Women who enter the world of work also face additional problems. "Dwellings, neighborhoods, and cities designed for homebound women constrain women physically, socially, and economically. Acute frustration occurs when they defy these constraints to spend all or part of the work day in the paid labor force" (Hayden, 1980, p. S171). If a woman, particularly one without a husband, has children and works, she is constrained in job choice by the location of child care (Palm & Pred, 1974). Women's home responsibilities severely restrict the time they can spend in commuting and increase the "accessibility costs" of getting jobs and urban services (Wekerle, 1980). Indeed, in a large survey of women in the Chicago area, 85 percent said a location close to where they live was important to them in assessing the aspects of a job (Lopata, 1980).

Women's transportation situation is far different from men's. Women are less likely than men to have cars; "one study found that 70 percent of adults without access to cars are female" (Hayden, 1980, p. S175). This restricts their mobility, especially in the suburbs. Looking at automobile trips, we see that women are 50 percent more likely than men to use public transportation, both for work and for discretionary trips; fortunately, women have a more favorable attitude toward mass transit (Freeman, 1980). Elderly women and female heads of households are disproportionately represented among the metropolitan area's poorest groups; without cars, they must rely upon public transportation. Perhaps the most vivid statement about this situation is that the "daily prism" of a carless woman is shrunken, spatially compact (Palm & Pred, 1974).

**Discrimination in the housing market** Female heads of households have faced special problems in acquiring shelter, and they spend larger fractions of their incomes on housing than do male heads of households. Female-headed households are more likely to rent, to live in public housing, and to be located in central cities (Wekerle, 1980). Traditionally, the sales market for housing has been oriented to husband-wife families, particularly in banking rules and procedures for mortgages (Taub & O'Kane, 1981). Divorced and widowed women were unable to get mortgages if their incomes were based upon alimony or child support because bankers excluded these as forms of income which qualified for mortgages. In the rental market, these women have faced difficulties because many landlords and brokers discriminated against households with children. Others, like the bankers, discriminated against female tenants who were single or divorced or dependent upon public assistance, child support, or alimony for part of their income. Most states did not have laws protecting women and children from such discrimination.

Two federal laws passed in 1974 offer women some protection from these sorts of discrimination. The Equal Credit Opportunity Act helps women to qualify for financing, and amendments to the Fair Housing Act prohibit the consideration of sex as a basis for decision making in the sale or rental of housing. Other legal actions in regard to housing appear to ban the arbitrary exclusion of children in favor of demanding a reasonable basis for such exclusion.

**Summary** Returning to the three approaches to the question of women in the urban environment, we may summarize the various points. (1) With regard to the division between private and public spheres of action, it is clear that rising levels of fear of crime tend to restrict women's range of mobility. In search of safety, women are likely to stay home and forego some opportunities in the wider community which they perceive as dangerous. On a more elementary level, women's responsibilities for child rearing and household maintenance, by definition, restrict them to the private realm, while men are expected to participate primarily in the world of paid work, away from home and neighborhood. (2) Even the residential area itself is shown to have some deficiencies for daily life. Suburban life (which will be examined more thoroughly in Chapter 13) restricts women's social contacts unless they have access to a car. In the city, shops, mass transit vehicles, and other elements of the environment do not facilitate women's work, particularly when it must be done with small children in tow. (3) The question of environmental equity arises for women who head households and are disadvantaged, relative to men, in acquiring housing; who are unlikely to have cars; and who have difficulties in combining mothering and working for pay. The concerns highlighted by all three of the approaches also have considerable areas of overlap.

## New Marxist Perspectives

In addition to feminist scholars, another group of social scientists has been questioning conventional views of urban structure and process (Abu-Lughod, 1979; Guterbock, 1980). These critical theorists originated on both sides of the Atlantic, particularly in France, Great Britain, and North America. Two early and influential books inspiring this new point of view are *The Urban Question* (1972/1977; originally *La Question Urbaine*) by Manuel Castells, a Spanish sociologist who has done most of his scholarly work in France, and *Social Justice and the City* (1973) by David Harvey, an English geographer who works in the United States. Castells' work employs an explicitly Marxist framework and vocabulary—Marxist ideas have become popular among certain groups of urban economists, geographers, and sociologists.

### Issues and assumptions

Marxists reject a number of urban sociology's traditional assumptions and images. For example, human ecologists since the earliest days of the Chicago school have tended to see the social patterns of the city as a by-product of the urban land market, and they assumed that this was a free market. In it, various parties would be competing for locations and buildings, and patterns of activity and density, residential and industrial location, etc., would arise from this competition. Then social life would develop within different districts. Marxists, on the other hand, see the land market as determined by certain dominant parties, especially large banks and corporations. Locational decisions are affected by political decisions, such as mortgage policies and the placement of military installations, at the national level, and by zoning and the location of parks and amenities, at the local level. In the Marxist scheme of things political decisions are determined by dominant economic units. It should be noted, though, that Hawley, who is one of Castells' principal intellectual targets, also argues that major economic units tend to dominate community social structure (Hawley, 1971).

Marxist analysis also assumes conflict between social classes, in which the interests of workers are opposed to those of businesses, particularly large banks and corporations. The economic and political systems exploit workers by expropriating their labor and giving them no power. In feminist Marxist analysis, it is further assumed or demonstrated that males and females can be seen as being stratified such that males dominate and exploit women in a patriarchal social structure.

## Neighborhood and spatial structure

**Reproduction of labor**   From this perspective the neighborhood is seen as a place for the reproduction of labor power. This means that it is not an area in which commodities are produced but an area in which workers themselves go for rest, recreation, and sustenance when they are not engaged in productive activities. Social reproduction also involves the production of future generations of labor power. Residential activities, then, "include the direct provision of the conditions of physical and mental health, cooked meals, personal services, education, maintenance of living conditions, and child care" (Markusen, 1980, p. S25). Extending this definition, though, Molotch (1979) argues that the neighborhood is also a locale in which to exploit workers and that those who control access to the sites of reproduction have some claim on "the rewards of the exploitation process" (p. 294). Thus, even though workers receive pay for work, and capitalists receive unearned benefits from that work, capitalists also take back some of that pay in the form of rent for housing (or interest on mortgages from homebuyers).

The question of housing is important in the neighborhood context, then. Neighborhood residents are seen as exploited by owners, if they rent, as well as by banks (Stone, 1978; Susser, 1982). American households are paying increasing fractions of their incomes for housing, particularly to service mortgage debts, because interest rates rose dramatically in the decade of the 1970s (Frieden & Solomon, 1977). The practices of banks and savings and loan associations, in cooperation with the Federal Housing Authority, strongly affect the supply of housing and its cost. To be more specific, one may cite a case study of a neighborhood in New York City. The researcher, Susser (1982), contrasted the different effects of resident versus absentee landlords for the local environment. Owner-occupants in this working class–poverty area invested a great deal of their time and resources in keeping up and improving their dwellings; in contrast, absentee landlords did not maintain their buildings well. "The front doors were not locked, the stairs and bannisters were frequently in poor condition, the roofs leaked, and the heating was erratic." They put very little into maintenance and their buildings deteriorated.

Many of the absentee owners held onto their property until it could be sold or redeveloped at a profit (Susser, 1982, p. 98). In sum, Susser said that absentee landlords constituted a force toward the destruction of the neighborhood. But even without absentee landlords, a Marxist analysis would argue that the housing industry tends to exploit workers.

**Urban structure**   In a broader context, Marxist analysts recognize the inequalities among individuals and groups in the metropolis. They argue that one way in which these inequalities are expressed is through the advantages and disadvantages of different neighborhoods.

Neighborhoods may enjoy differential access to certain benefits by means of location or by power (or they may suffer from lack of access). Particular sites or neighborhoods, by their locations, may have different "externalities." A positive externality means that an individual or firm may benefit from a particular location while someone else pays for it; a negative externality means that the location has certain costs or disadvantages. "Externalities can be viewed as either costs or benefits according to whether the producer or the consumer is affected and according to the nature of the effect" (Harvey, 1970, p. 270). For example, smog is a negative externality for certain residential areas in metropolitan Los Angeles. It tends to settle in the low-lying areas in the center of the city—for them it is a negative externality. Neighborhoods in the hills surrounding the center get less of the smog—for them it is not a negative externality. Needless to say, poorer households live in the lower areas, and wealthier ones live in the hills. In metropolitan Chicago, the lakefront may be viewed as a positive externality, except where it has been developed for industry, and neighborhoods and suburbs have differential access to it by distance.

Public services and facilities may also serve as externalities to sites and neighborhoods. "The very fact of location of a public facility such as a fire station (or for that matter any public service) means that the population does not enjoy exactly homogeneous quality and quantity of fire protection as far as consumption is concerned" (Harvey, 1970, p. 273). These externalities may be seen as fringe benefits to income. Thus access to better schools or parks can be seen as part of one's income, even though it is not usually counted as income.

Various processes at the macrocommunity level and beyond may have unequal effects for classes within the metropolis. The growth of suburbs, combined with industrial development in suburbia, has had powerful effects upon the poorer classes of workers left in the city. These workers cannot afford suburban housing, and mass transportation systems are not ordinarily arranged to move people out of the city to suburban factories. This discrepancy between the location of employment opportunities and the changes in residential opportunities for poorer workers has imposed heavy accessibility costs upon the workers (Harvey, 1973). Furthermore, these costs have been imposed unequally because middle-class workers have relatively easy access to the new employment opportunities. Markusen and other writers cited in the preceding feminist section also note that women with children bear disproportionate accessibility costs if they attempt to work in the paid labor force.

Writers subscribing to this school of thought emphasize vertical linkages, which make the local community dependent upon larger, more powerful social structures. Banks have already been mentioned in the context of mortgage lending; insurance companies might be mentioned here as well. Susser, in her study of a particular New York neighborhood, described the negative effects of municipal agencies. She said the city's planning agencies were willing to transform the neighborhood into a residential area for more prosperous professional people and corporate employees, and they made the plans without the participation or consent of the area's people. She noted as well the negative effects of the welfare agency, which tended to demoralize its clients by treating them badly. Thus the community might be seen as relatively passive, while large organizations, such as the military or major steel companies, make decisions and investments having powerful local ramifications. For example, the closing of an army base or a steel mill can have earthshaking effects upon the households and labor force of a community.

**The *rentier* connection**  Molotch (1979) argues that there is a particular class, the "rentiers," which mediates the connection between large capitalists and the community. The rentier class "controls the space and/or the physical structure necessary to all aspects of capitalist production. Members of this class, the rentiers in the classic formulation, make their riches through manipulation of the sites where production occurs, where capital is circulated (e.g., banking, commerce), and where labor is reproduced (the neighborhoods)" (Molotch, 1979, p. 293). Molotch is not referring to the average real estate broker who is handling the sales of single suburban homes, though. He is writing about bigger brokers, developers, and bankers who arrange the location of industrial parks, large shopping centers, office buildings, and the like—major investments with big clients, involving employment. "Rentiers serve capitalists by finding places for production and attracting producers" (p. 294). The important thing, though, is that this investment creates positive externalities for other locations, depending upon their proximity, and this is where the rentiers collect their benefits. If they have nearby property, it is likely to increase in value.

Rentiers attempt to influence community decisions. This is why people in the real estate and building industry are often found on city councils and school and park boards. It is important for things in the community to proceed in such a way that the area is potentially attractive to additional capitalists, for example, keeping up the reputation of the schools to attract professional employees or keeping down tax rates to compete with other communities. Molotch says rentiers attempt to influence the "place-linked needs of capital," which, in turn, affect the social program of the community. The rentiers promote social conditions appropriate to capital investment, for example, property-oriented law and order and vocationally oriented and ideologically appropriate public education. Overall, the rentier's main strategy is to capture the advantages of positive externalities—to get a development into a place with or near some attraction, whether it is sunshine or a major highway intersection. One way of maintaining property rights and preventing the destruction of positive externalities is to gain legal control over them through zoning or some other device.

The neighborhood is a residual place in Molotch's scheme. Power and control are held by large corporations; the neighborhood is just an incidental place to sell things and to house people—no important actions take place there. This implies that local organizational activity is futile; therefore, Molotch contends, neighborhood self-help projects are futile. At best they may have the appearance of success, but they can never touch anything of fundamental importance.

**Criticism** To some degree, recent Marxist analyses of the metropolis may be seen as "old wine in new bottles." Many of the Marxist assertions represent the attachment of more loaded terms for conventional concepts. Thus developers and entrepreneurs become rentiers and capitalists, with more unpleasant connotations. Even before the resurgence of Marxist analysis, urban sociologists were cognizant of the role of the real estate industry in community processes (Hughes, 1931/1971; Wilhelm, 1962). And, of course, social stratification—meaning structured inequality—has always been central to sociological analysis. Nonetheless, Marxists bring different assumptions, both political and distributional, to bear upon the question of inequality. Traditional ecological writers assumed that American society operated under the terms of free competitive capitalism and that the system was fairly open, with opportunities for social mobility. Traditional urban sociologists did not assume that workers were politically impotent, but these analysts were not centrally interested in politics. They also did not assume residents did not benefit from their neighborhoods. It must be noted that traditional urban sociologists have been more committed to empirical research than the Marxist writers appear to be. Nonetheless, the Marxists remind their readers that they must not ignore urban inequalities or assume that the city is equally beneficial to all.

**Summary** The new Marxist approach instructs us not to look at the neighborhood, or even the city, by itself. It must be seen in the context of national or even supranational organizations, primarily corporations, which make investments. Neighborhood phenomena are merely by-products of decisions made for other reasons.

The neighborhood is viewed in the context of inequalities within the metropolitan community. Since there are outside advantages—positive externalities, including "natural" ones, like beaches, and manufactured ones, like schools—different locations have differential access to them. Thus inequality related to location may be considered another kind of income, beyond pay for work. Not only do different social classes have neighborhoods with different accessibility to attractions, but they have differential ability to influence decisions affecting the placement of new facilities. In particular, the rentier class influences such decisions and tends to use the results of these decisions to its own advantage.

## SUMMARY

Unlike most of the chapters in this book, the material in this chapter is evaluative, dealing with judgments of communities. Half the material represents public opinion—about satisfaction and about fear of crime—and the other half deals with recent scholarly writings from two schools of thought—feminist and Marxist. (Each section of the chapter has its own summary, above.) The section on satisfaction is mostly positive, showing that the vast majority of the public says its communities and neighborhoods are highly satisfactory. But the other three sections tend to be negative. Many city and suburban residents express considerable fear of crime. And the feminist and Marxist writers tend to be critical of the status quo; the former pinpoint those features of urban environments and social systems that put females at a disadvantage, and the latter emphasize social inequalities and exploitative relationships in the metropolis. There are some connections to be made among the facts and opinions presented in this chapter. The two quality-of-life attitudes go together—as fear increases, community satisfaction decreases. Fear of crime is connected to the feminist critique; women are more likely to express fear, and they are more likely to take precautionary measures that restrict their scope of activity. The critics argue that urban spatial structure—isolating women in residential areas—may make women more vulnerable to crime.

Perhaps the greatest contradiction in the chapter is between the high levels of community satisfaction expressed by the public at large and the Marxist contention that the workers are being exploited in the neighborhood as well as at the workplace. Perhaps a Marxist might explain this by charging that the workers fail to appreciate their true class interests or even that they have been bought off with consumer goods and deluded from seeing what is really happening. Another way of viewing the contradiction is as two opposite ways of interpreting the same facts. For example, consider the fact that tens of millions of households, living in single-family houses, owe banks large sums of money, at interest, in the form of mortgages. Stone (1978) interprets this as evidence that the bankers are exploiting the workers, even at home. Others (myself included) view this as a way in which the American system has provided an extraordinarily high level of housing to workers at all levels and has provided access to homeownership.

## REFERENCES

Abu-Lughod, Janet. 1979. "Marxist Urban Sociology." *Contemporary Sociology.* 8:192–196.

Baldassare, Mark. 1979. *Residential Crowding in Urban America.* Berkeley: University of California Press.

Baumgart, Margaret M., Richard G. Baumgart, and William J. Hoyer. 1980. "Social Factors in Fear of Crime." *Sociological Focus.* 13:55–66.

Castells, Manuel. 1972/1977. *The Urban Question: A Marxist Approach*, (trans. Alan Sheridan). Cambridge, Mass.: M.I.T.

Clemente, Frank, and Michael B. Kleiman. 1977. "Fear of Crime in the United States: A Multivariate Analysis." *Social Forces*. 56:519–531.

Freeman, Jo. 1980. "Women and Urban Policy." *Signs: Journal of Women in Culture and Society*. 5(3, Supplement):S4–S21.

Frieden, Bernard J., and Arthur P. Solomon. 1977. *The Nation's Housing: 1975 to 1985*. Cambridge, Mass. Joint Center for Urban Studies.

Garofalo, James, and John Laub. 1978. "The Fear of Crime: Broadening Our Perspective." *Victimology*. 3:242–253.

Gordon, Margaret T., Stephanie Riger, Robert K. LeBailly, and Linda Heath. 1980. "Crime, Women, and the Quality of Urban Life." *Signs: Journal of Women in Culture and Society*. 5(3, Supplement):S144–S160.

Guterbock, Thomas M. 1980. "The Political Economy of Urban Revitalization: Competing Theories." *Urban Affairs Quarterly*. 15:429–438.

Hartnagel, Timothy F. 1979. "The Perception and Fear of Crime: Implications for Neighborhood Cohesion, Social Activity, and Community Affect." *Social Forces*. 58:176–193.

Harvey, David. 1970. "Social Processes, Spatial Form and the Redistribution of Real Income in an Urban System," pp. 267–300 in *The Colston Papers*, vol. 22. London: Butterworth.

Harvey, David. 1973. *Social Justice and the City*. Baltimore, Johns Hopkins.

Hayden, Dolores. 1980. "What Would a Non-Sexist City Be Like?" *Signs: Journal of Women in Culture and Society*. 5(3, Supplement):S170–S187.

Hughes, Everett C. 1931/1971. *The Growth of an Institution: The Chicago Real Estate Board*. Chicago: Society for Social Research. Excerpted, chap. 3 in *The Social Fabric of the Metropolis: Contributions of the Chicago School of Urban Sociology*, (ed.) James F. Short, Jr. Chicago: University of Chicago Press.

Keller, Suzanne I. (ed.). 1981. *Building for Women*. Lexington, Mass.: Lexington.

Lee, Barrett A. 1981. "The Urban Unease Revisited: Perceptions of Local Safety and Neighborhood Satisfaction among Metropolitan Residents." *Social Science Quarterly*. 62:611–629.

Lee, Barrett A., and Avery M. Guest. 1979. "Subjective Evaluations of Metropolitan Neighborhood Quality." Paper presented at meeting of the American Sociological Association.

Lofland, Lyn H. 1975. "The 'Thereness' of Women: A Selective Review of Urban Sociology," chap. 5 in *Another Voice: Feminist Perspectives on Social Life and Social Science*, (eds.) Marcia Millman and Rosabeth M. Kanter. Garden City, N.Y.: Doubleday Anchor.

Lopata, Helena Z. 1980. "The Chicago Woman: A Study of Patterns of Mobility and Transportation." *Signs: Journal of Women in Culture and Society*. 5(3, Supplement):S161–S169.

Marans, Robert W., and Willard Rodgers. 1975. "Toward an Understanding of

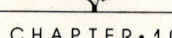

Community Satisfaction," chap. 7 in *Metropolitan America in Contemporary Perspective*, (eds.) Amos H. Hawley and Vincent P. Rock. New York: Halsted/Wiley.

Markusen, Ann R. 1980. "City Spatial Structure, Women's Household Work, and National Urban Policy." *Signs: Journal of Women in Culture and Society.* 5(3, Supplement):S23–S44.

McIntyre, J. J. 1967. "Public Attitudes towards Crime and Law Enforcement." *Annals of the American Academy of Political and Social Science.* 374:34–46.

Michelson, William. 1977. *Environmental Choice, Human Behavior, and Residential Satisfaction.* New York: Oxford University Press.

Molotch, Harvey. 1979. "Capital and Neighborhood in the United States: Some Conceptual Links." *Urban Affairs Quarterly.* 14:289–312.

Palm, Risa, and Allan Pred. 1974. "A Time-Geographic Perspective on Problems of Inequality for Women." Working paper no. 236, Institute of Urban and Regional Development, University of California, Berkeley.

Skogan, Wesley G., and Michael G. Maxfield. 1981. *Coping with Crime: Individual and Neighborhood Reactions.* Beverly Hills, Calif.: Sage.

Stimpson, Catherine R. (ed.). 1980. "Women and the American City," Special Issue of *Signs: Journal of Women in Culture and Society.* 5(3, Supplement).

Stone, Michael E. 1978. "Housing, Mortgage Lending, and the Contradictions of Capitalism," pp. 179-208 in *Marxism and the Metropolis: New Perspectives in Urban Political Economy*, (eds.) William K. Tabb and Larry Sawers. New York: Oxford University Press.

Susser, Ida. 1982. *Norman Street: Poverty and Politics in an Urban Neighborhood*, New York: Oxford University Press.

Taub, Nadine, and Geraldine E. O'Kane. 1981. "Women, the Family, and Housing: Legal Trends," chap. 10 in *Building for Women*, (ed.) S. Keller. Lexington, Mass.: Lexington.

Taub, Richard L., and D. Garth Taylor. 1980. "Crime and Urban Development." Preliminary report, Chicago, National Opinion Research Center.

Wekerle, Gerda R. 1980. "Women in the Urban Environment." *Signs: Journal of Women in Culture and Society*. 5(3, Supplement):S188-S214.

Wekerle, Gerda R., Rebecca Peterson, and David Morley. 1980. *New Space for Women*, Boulder, Colo.: Westview.

Willhelm, Sidney. 1962. *Urban Zoning and Land-Use Theory*. New York: Free Press.

Wilson, James Q. 1975/1977. *Thinking about Crime*. New York: Vintage.

CIGARS LEWIS LIQUOR
Alioto
MAYOR
KOPP
SUPERVISOR
KOPP
YES
YES
EAM

# CHAPTER · 11

## Neighborhood Change

**Chapter Outline**

STAGES OF NEIGHBORHOOD GROWTH AND DECLINE

The Neighborhood Life Cycle
- Stage 1, Rural
- Stage 2, Development in Single-Family Houses
- Stage 3, Full Occupancy
- Stage 4, Downgrading
- Stage 5, Thinning Out
- Stage 6, Renewal

Changes in Population Density
Changes in Socioeconomic Status

RESIDENTIAL SUCCESSION
　The Theory
　A Case Study

ABANDONMENT AND ARSON

"GENTRIFICATION"

MACRODEVELOPMENTS

SUMMARY

A common scene in urban novels and movies depicts a middle-aged character returning to his or her childhood neighborhood. More often than not, the neighborhood has become a slum, occupied by people of an unfamiliar nationality or color; even well-known buildings and personal landmarks are gone or have changed. This scene epitomizes the fundamental process of urban change: The parts of the community are not static; they are continuously undergoing environmental and social change.

A neighborhood may change along several dimensions: It may be growing or declining; it may be new, with construction crews scattered about building homes, schools, and other facilities, or it may be old, with crumbling curbs and sidewalks and perhaps even bands of arsonists who set fire to abandoned buildings at night. The people of an area may also change: They may move as a group, to be replaced by some new group, or if they stay, they may grow old, thereby changing the social character of the area. The very function of a part of the city may change, shifting, for example, from a neighborhood where families raise children to a place where college students and other young people reside.

## STAGES OF NEIGHBORHOOD GROWTH AND DECLINE

### The Neighborhood Life Cycle

Residential areas go through a process of growth and decline, called the "neighborhood life cycle." This process was discovered by two social scientists, Hoover and Vernon (1959), in their analysis of the New York metropolitan region in the late 1950s. They found that the age of a residential area—that is, the amount of time since it was first built—is closely related to a number of other facts about the neighborhood: the type of housing and its condition, the social class of the people, the density of occupancy, even the races and nationalities of the residents. Hoover and Vernon argued that there are young neighborhoods, middle-aged ones, and old ones. As places, the young ones are growing and the old ones are declining. It is not known yet how many years this cycle takes, but it is probably longer than fifty years and less than a hundred, with each stage probably taking between five and twenty-five years. In very old cities like London, some residential areas have buildings more than 100 years old, but they have been restored from time to time to extend their lifetimes. On the other hand, a neighborhood in which the buildings were built to last a short time (say, in a mobile-home development) would have a far shorter lifetime. The neighborhood life cycle is a metaphor that compares the residential area to a biological entity.

The human life cycle is a familiar concept, going from gestation, through infancy, childhood, adolescence, young adulthood, middle age, and old age, to death. Hoover and Vernon and others writing about neighborhood life cycles are suggesting that residential areas, like organisms, predictably pass through a series of stages. Figure 11-1 is a schematic graph showing the basic cycle.

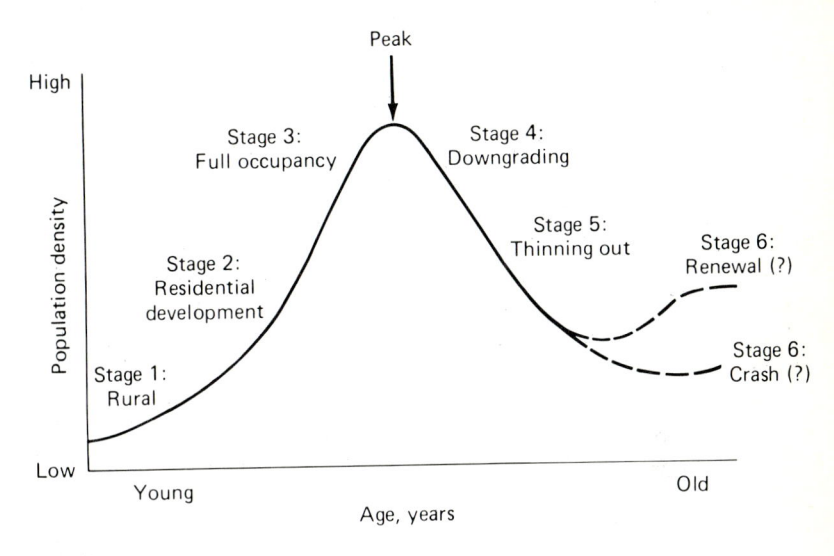

**FIGURE 11-1**
The neighborhood life cycle.

## Stage 1, Rural[1]

Before the construction of a new residential area begins, the potential for development exists in a plot of land at the edge of a built-up area. Early in the twentieth century this open land would have been adjacent to a city; more recently, it would have been at the edge of existing suburbs. This area, sometimes called the "rural-urban fringe," may simply be farmland or may comprise some mix of farms, stables, isolated factories, homesteads, junkyards, or whatever. At this point the area has a very low population density (Birch, 1971).

## Stage 2, Development in Single-Family Houses

When real estate developers and builders anticipate a demand for new housing, they begin to transform a chunk of this rural-urban fringe into a residential area. They "plat" the land into parcels suitable for single-family houses, and they invest in the infrastructure for a residential area: streets and sewers plus water and power supply. Large-scale construction of subdivisions can then take place, and numerous new houses are rapidly built (Birch, 1971; Hoover & Vernon, 1959). By the time Stage 2 is well under way, the area has many single-family homes, but some lots or bigger parcels of land remain undeveloped, still being farmed. The arrival of new

---

[1]Birch (1971) modified Hoover and Vernon's scheme by adding this stage, which necessarily precedes the construction of a residential area. I have followed his usage in renumbering the original five stages.

families calls for additional infrastructural investments in the form of new schools, shops, churches, and parks and playgrounds.

## Stage 3, Full Occupancy

Different historical periods have produced two different forms of this stage. In one form, the construction of single-family houses is followed by the addition of apartment buildings. Hoover and Vernon, who observed this development in New York neighborhoods that had emerged before 1955, called this a transitional stage in which substantial new construction still occurs, accompanied by increasing population density. New York City, however, has far more apartment housing than most other cities, and most of the neighborhoods studied by Hoover and Vernon were built before World War II. In the second, more recent, form of this stage, most urban areas have experienced a new type of development which is more suburban and never reaches high densities. In either case Stage 3 includes continued building of new residential structures to fill the open land and increased densities as all the potential land is used and the dwelling units are fully occupied. In addition, as Birch (1971) notes, "Property values and rents are close to their maximum relative to other neighborhoods in the area" (p. 80). At the end of this period, all the land has been used and most of the buildings are relatively new, so the area is still at its prime.

## Stage 4, Downgrading

Eventually, housing begins to age, rents fall, and lower-income groups begin to inhabit the dwellings (Birch, 1971). Usually, little or no new construction takes place, but population grows as the old houses and apartments are converted into numerous rooms or small apartments for rent and, thereby, are adapted to greater density use than originally designed for. (Students in many college towns will be familiar with such conversions.) Once the existing housing becomes overcrowded, population density is at its maximum, and the area is what Birch calls a "new slum" (p. 80). Other social changes occur as well; as Hoover and Vernon (1959) wrote, "The down-grading stage is often associated with the spread of districts occupied by more or less segregated ethnic and minority groups" (p. 188).

## Stage 5, Thinning Out

By this stage the area is a full-blown slum. Buildings have continued to deteriorate, and people are leaving, if they can; thus, density and dwelling occupancy are gradually reduced. Household size declines as families with children look for housing in better areas, leaving older couples behind; as immigrants prosper, and cease to double up with relatives; and as immigrants' children also move out. The population shrinkage "may also reflect merging of dwelling units, vacancy, abandonment, and demolition" (Hoover & Vernon, 1959, p. 191). Obviously, no residential construction takes place during this stage. Areas in Stage 5 are "old slums," according to Birch (1971, p. 81).

### Stage 6, Renewal

In this stage the process becomes more indeterminate. According to Birch, "The land occupied by an old slum becomes too valuable to justify its use as an old slum, and its inhabitants become too weak politically to hold on to it" (1971, p. 82). It is, after all, quite close to the CBD and has potential value because of that proximity. "Property is then reacquired, leveled or rehabilitated, and put to more efficient use, such as high-income apartments or office buildings or public housing" (p. 82). Hoover and Vernon state that the quality of housing is improved and that overall population density of the area is not changed by redevelopment. This process is considered indeterminate because it has arisen relatively recently in U.S. urban history and there are not many well-documented cases of how renewal proceeds. Furthermore, it appears that change may proceed in at least two directions. (See the sections "Abandonment and Arson" and "Gentrification," later in this chapter.)

The stages scheme does admit exceptions, of course. Hoover and Vernon comment on an area of Park Avenue that shifted from luxury apartments to office buildings as a case in which nonresidential land uses enter a residential area. In this event, the area no longer proceeds through the normal sequence of stages.

## Changes in Population Density

Avery Guest (1973), a sociologist-demographer, used an intriguing research method to examine the history of neighborhoods in one large city, Cleveland. He determined when each of the city's 221 census tracts was constructed and then grouped them into eight "cohorts" according to their ages, as shown in Table 11-1. In demography a cohort is a set of individuals with the same year of birth who are studied over time as a group; for example, a demographer might try to estimate the fertility of the cohort of females born in 1950. In the Cleveland study, Guest constructed cohorts of neighborhoods (represented by census tracts) built up at about the same time. Some of his results appear in Table 11-1, where a single column shows what happened to the population density of a cohort of census tracts over a sixty-year period. For example, by 1910 the areas built up around 1905 already housed 27.7 persons per acre; density rose considerably in these areas until the next census, in 1920, when it peaked at 36.6 persons per acre; after 1920 these areas lost population, gradually until 1960 and rapidly thereafter. Unfortunately, we have no consistent system of census tracts in the cities in the nineteenth century, so the history summarized in Table 11-1 is somewhat truncated, omitting the decades during which the oldest neighborhoods were being built.

Nonetheless, this research reveals two general points: that the residential areas have followed the neighborhood life cycle pattern and that the pattern has two

### TABLE 11-1
**Population Densities per Acre in Cohorts of Census Tracts, Cleveland, 1910–1970**

|  | \multicolumn{8}{c}{Cohort built up} |
|---|---|---|---|---|---|---|---|---|
|  | Before 1885 | By 1895 | By 1905 | By 1915 | By 1925 | By 1935 | By 1945 | After 1945 |
| 1910 | 30.6 | 32.5 | 27.7 | 10.8 | 2.8 | 0.7 | 0.5 | 0.2 |
| 1920 | 29.4 | 37.0 | 36.6 | 22.2 | 13.1 | 3.6 | 1.7 | 0.6 |
| 1930 | 22.0 | 30.0 | 34.5 | 25.0 | 22.7 | 13.7 | 7.3 | 2.6 |
| 1940 | 20.5 | 28.2 | 33.1 | 24.3 | 21.8 | 14.4 | 8.5 | 3.8 |
| 1950 | 19.3 | 27.4 | 32.8 | 24.5 | 21.3 | 15.3 | 10.7 | 6.6 |
| 1960 | 14.3 | 22.4 | 30.0 | 22.9 | 20.1 | 15.3 | 10.8 | 9.3 |
| 1970 | 8.1 | 13.7 | 22.9 | 19.9 | 19.7 | 15.0 | 10.3 | 9.0 |
| Total (N = 221) | 17 | 32 | 36 | 35 | 42 | 31 | 6 | 22 |

*Source:* Guest, 1973.

forms, the old and the new. The Cleveland study confirms Hoover and Vernon's general pattern, as density rises, peaks, and begins to decline in every cohort except the oldest one. Undoubedly, the oldest cohort, built before 1885, followed the same trajectory, but the census data capture it only in its old age, after its peak. The Cleveland statistics do not show exactly where one stage ends and another begins, but they show clearly when areas are growing and when they are losing population, or "thinning out."

The old and new patterns correspond to the times of birth and development of the residential areas, "old" meaning built and developed before 1910, and "new" meaning after 1930, roughly speaking. The main difference between old and new is in their peak densities. The old areas reached densities well over 30 persons per acre, achieved only with the construction of apartment buildings; the newer residential areas, lacking apartments, never reached equivalent density levels. The 1935 cohort peaked at 15.3 persons per acre, and the two younger cohorts peaked at far lower levels. (A "transitional" pattern is represented by the cohorts built up by 1915 and 1925.)

The different patterns of neighborhood development correspond to the dominant mode of intraurban transportation of the time. The old neighborhoods were constructed to conform with the electric streetcar system; housing was built at high densities because people had to be within walking distance of local facilities, such as shops and churches, as well. The mass diffusion of automobile ownership made all the difference. The transitional pattern arose during the early introduction of the automobile, and such neighborhoods did not attain the high densities of the earlier areas. The new pattern, though, was built during the mass diffusion of the automobile, when people could travel relatively long distances to work and even for local services. This density pattern "is indicated by a very slow rate of 'building up' [and by] relatively constant population density" (Guest, 1973, p. 61). A similar study of growth and development in Los Angeles residential areas (Duncan, Sabagh, & Van Arsdol, 1962) shows the same density patterns as the young Cleveland areas. As the main growth of Los Angeles occurred during the era of automobile transportation, these results are consistent with Guest's theory. In sum, Guest argues that the transportation system of a particular period has powerful influences on the pattern of neighborhood development, as reflected in population densities over the course of the life cycle. He notes a continually declining pattern of urban density since the early part of the century—the older neighborhoods have been thinning out for more than fifty years and the newer neighborhoods have not built up to high densities.

### Changes in Socioeconomic Status

Population density is not the only neighborhood variable that changes over time; socioeconomic status changes as well. SES tends to follow the same trajectory as density, rising in the early years and then falling. In a study of Chicago's residential areas, Hunter (1974) found that as a neighborhood began to build up, its status rose. This is because in rural Stage 1, the occupants of an area peripheral to the city are either engaged in some sort of local rural-urban-fringe occupation, such as running a garage or a kennel, or they are farmers. The newcomers able to purchase the new houses of the Stage 2 subdivisions are likely to have higher educational attainment, more income, and more prestigious occupations than the few former residents, so the status level rises measurably and continues to rise as the new population displaces the old. Eventually, though, socioeconomic status reaches a peak before density reaches its peak. If apartments are built in Stage 3, their occupants have lower incomes than the homeowners, and as the neighborhood becomes older, status falls because poorer households move in.

Even if succession does not occur rapidly in an aging neighborhood, the area falls in *relative* status (Choldin & Hanson, 1982). This is because its population is growing old and standing still in its status attributes, while other areas of the metropolitan community, especially the suburbs, are rising in status. The midtwentieth century was a period of rapidly rising educational levels and incomes, but the gains, especially in education, went to the young who settled in suburbs. Thus, because the absolute status levels of people in the old neighborhoods was fixed, they were falling behind, relative to the metropolitan population.

## RESIDENTIAL SUCCESSION

Urban sociologists often refer to the process of neighborhood change as "succession." Most frequently, this term has been used to refer to the process by which one group—usually a nationality group—replaces another in a particular neighborhood. For example, if one refers to an area and says, "Jews used to live here, but now it is the Chicano barrio (Mexican-American district)," one is referring to succession. Some urban analysts (Gist & Fava, 1974; Hawley, 1950) use the term more broadly, referring to any sort of major transition in a particular area as succession. In this broader sense, then, if a residential area is transformed into a hospital district, this is an instance of residential to nonresidential succession. In this text, for the most part, the term succession will be used in the narrower sense, referring to the process by which one set of occupants replaces another in a residential area.

## The Theory

The concept of succession was developed within the Chicago school at about the same time as the concentric circle model of the city was emerging (Burgess, 1928). Sociologists borrowed the concept from biologists, building the science of ecology, who had discovered that biotic communities change by means of a process of succession. Studying the development of lakeside sand dunes, they noted a series of stages by which the environment and its inhabitants changed. They saw that after a new dune had been formed, it had a predictable set of first occupants, particular species of grasses and insects, which were eaten by particular species of birds. Over time, the sand and soil of the dune would change, due to the influence of the plants, insects, and birds; thus, the first set of occupants would create an environment for new species of plants and animals. Once the newcomers had arrived—different plants, insects, reptiles, etc.—a succession was said to have taken place. This happened predictably through a series of successions, until a stable forest was established, several years later. By analogy, then, the urban sociologists suggested that the environment of a neighborhood was like a dune, occupied over the years by a series of different occupants through a process of succession.

Sociologically, succession was a tool to help understand the process by which different immigrant and nationality groups were moving through the city. The concept was explicated by Cressey in 1938, although it had been introduced earlier by Burgess (1928). Cressey wrote, "The common process of succession involves a cycle of invasion, conflict, recession, and reorganization.... They recur in the movement of all groups in the city" (1938/1971, p. 112). Cressey recognized that during their years in the city the immigrants had risen in socioeconomic status. Their residential choices reflected their upward mobility:

> Immigrant stocks follow a regular sequence of settlement in successive areas of increasing stability and status.... An immigrant group on its arrival settles in a compact colony in a low-rent industrial area usually located in the transitional zone near the center of the city.... These congested areas of first settlement are characterized by the perpetuation of many European cultural traits. After some years of residence in such an area, the group, as it improves its economic and social standing, moves outward to some more desirable

residential district, creating an area of second settlement. In such an area the group is not so closely concentrated physically, there is less cultural solidarity, and more American standards of living are adopted. (Cressey, 1938/1971, p. 111)

While succession is a common and natural urban process, it is not necessarily peaceful. Cressey wrote that succession begins with invasion, when a few members of an ethnic group, "who have achieved a little greater economic success than their neighbors" (p. 112), aspire to better housing in a more prestigious area and move to a different neighborhood. They are followed by larger numbers of their compatriots. "Conflict may accompany invasion," he wrote, "varying in intensity with the cultural differences and prejudices of the groups involved.... "Where marked prejudices exist and there is a fear that the invading group will cause a serious loss in real estate values, violent opposition may develop" (p. 113), even to the extent of bombing the newcomers' houses, burning crosses, or dumping garbage on their lawns. If resistance fails as often happens, recession sets in as the former dominant residents depart. They may feel the neighborhood is undesirable for them with so many members of the invading group there, or they may notice the aging of the local environment and prefer to relocate in newer areas.

Eventually, after the transition is more or less complete, the newcomers fall heir to the neighborhood; over a period of time they rebuild their institutions, reestablishing their churches, lodges, and other social organizations. Eventually, Cressey says, the newcomers become old residents, and the cycle may begin once again. Newcomers from yet another upwardly mobile group may enter the area, and the older residents or their descendants may move on to other parts of the city.

## A Case Study

Polish-Americans, the largest ethnic group in Chicago, have resided in several residential areas in that city since they first arrived (Kantowicz, 1975), and their experience represents a typical case of succession. By 1910 the city had nearly a quarter-million Polish-American residents living in five different residential areas; the cornerstone of each Polish-American settlement was a parish church with Polish-speaking priests. Kantowicz, who has studied the history of this group, remarks that it is simple to trace the dates and locations of Polish neighborhoods: "Since nearly all Polish immigrants were Catholics who, as soon as possible after their arrival, tried to organize a parish, the founding dates of Polish churches form a rough outline of the origins of Polish settlements" (p. 15). By 1888 each of the five settlements had such a church. The residential areas were not exclusively Polish, but a number of small areas, blocks, and precincts had very high Polish concentrations, some exceeding 90 percent. The largest, most highly developed area, known as "St. Stanislaus District," or "Polish Downtown," had three Polish churches, plus shops, newspapers, and fraternal organizations. By 1910 this area, comprised of tall brick tenements and "frame shacks," was very densely populated, housing 96,243 Polish-

Americans. As early as 1881 St. Stanislaus District was overly congested and unhealthful, giving the residents an impetus to seek better housing.

Before World War I, the nuclei were spread for new Polish settlements beyond the confines of the five original immigrant areas. Kantowicz states, "The Polish immigrant somehow saved a portion of each week's meager pay to buy a house or rent a more spacious flat out beyond the congestion" (1975, p. 25). St. Stanislaus District did not simply spread and expand its borders. "The greatest expansion of the Polish mass into more desirable, middle-class neighborhoods took place to the northwest, along Milwaukee Avenue, and to the southwest, along Archer Avenue. Many Poles had become acquainted with the open spaces along these streets as they rode to the two Polish cemeteries beyond the city limits" (p. 25). Kantowicz continues, "The Poles leaped over an established area of Germans and Scandinavians ... and purchased home lots about a mile and a half out from Polish Downtown" (p. 25). After about 40 families had moved to the new neighborhood, they established a parish there; later, as the area filled with their compatriots, a second parish was established. Before 1920, continuing in the same northwestern direction away from the city center, Poles began settling in two peripheral neighborhoods and established additional parishes; similar succession away from the other Polish immigrant areas took place. This case shows a single nationality group establishing a "porty-of-entry" neighborhood near the city center and subsequently moving through a series of newer, more desirable residential environments, rebuilding their institutions, in this case the church, as they went. Kantowicz's history leaves off in 1940, but succession went on after World War II, with the Polish-Americans continuing to move in the same direction, into suburbs northwest of the old neighborhoods.

**Postscript**   Although "Polish Downtown" once appeared to be a permanent fixture of Chicago's social geography, it too has undergone succession; numerous Puerto Ricans and blacks live in the area, replacing many of the Polish-Americans who have left (Kneeland, 1981). Not only have the former residents moved away, but they have taken most of their ethnic institutions, such as the newspapers and the Polish National Alliance, out of the area. What is left is an area of mixed nationalities—the older Poles who did not move, plus the newcomers—as seen on the shopping streets, which include stores with Polish names side by side with stores advertising in Spanish. As the established shops close, such as the Sajewski Music Store, once the largest Polish music specialty store in the nation, they are replaced by Latino or black small businesses. A few Polish institutions remain; the Polish Roman Catholic Union, with its Polish Museum and Library, is still there. But the process of change is epitomized by a transition nearby: A few doors from the museum there was for many years a Polish bakery; in 1980 the bakery closed, and Leon's Bar-B-Q, part of a black-owned chain of restaurants, opened a branch there. Interviewed by a newspaper reporter, the restaurant's owner said, "The Polish had [this area] pretty well locked up. Then after they could afford a little better, they moved out and we and the Spanish moved in" (Kneeland, 1981, p. A-14).

## ABANDONMENT AND ARSON

Returning to the neighborhood life cycle, we recall that the last stages of the cycle showed the area in a period of decline, perhaps leading up to a time of renewal. In recent years, though, we have seen a version of Stage 5, "thinning out," more severe than anything anticipated by Hoover and Vernon. Known as abandonment and arson, it began in older sections of many big cities in the early 1960s. As its name states, it involves the abandonment of residential structures, usually apartment buildings, and then their destruction by fire. It is a process by which, building by building, block by block, entire old residential neighborhoods have been demolished, ending up as fields of broken brick and rubble. New York City's South Bronx area is the most notorious case, having been publicized by vast amounts of newspaper, television, and even movie coverage. But there are other equally devasted areas, including Chicago's Woodlawn area and several sections of Detroit.

Steinlieb and Burchell (1974) provide an operational definition of the abandonment process as it applies to a single rented building, usually an old apartment building:

1. Owner reduces the maintenance procedures.
2. Owner stops paying taxes and allows the property to become tax delinquent.
3. Owner stops putting any money into maintenance reinvestment and allows property to fall deeper into tax delinquency.
4. Owner stops providing any vital services to the building, particularly heat and other utilities.
5. Owner arranges some legal device, a "paper sale," to avoid legal liability for the structure.

Another study is somewhat more graphic about abandoned structures. They are vacant and derelict buildings that have been vandalized—doors and windows knocked out, walls kicked in, paint sprayed mischievously on the exterior, wiring and fixtures stripped, gutters stripped—they are boarded up, and their grounds are unmaintained (Urban League study, cited in Sternlieb & Burchell, 1974).

Most social science reports on housing abandonment attempt to explain the behavior of the building owners. The type of building subject to abandonment is unattractive in the metropolitan housing market. The owner of a high-density, older, walk-up apartment building is in a poor competitive position; middle-class and working-class families have sufficient income to choose their preferred kind of housing, and they choose more modern types of accommodation. Thus the apartment building owner is holding an obsolete type of housing, and the only market for such apartments is the very poor (Moore, Livermore, & Galland, 1973). If the building is located in a city where housing codes are enforced, the owner requires a considerable rental income in order to keep the facilities up to standard. But the very poor cannot afford substantial rents, so the income is likely to be insufficient for this purpose.

A vicious cycle operates within the neighborhood. The area is likely to have increasing levels of transiency as well as violent youth gangs; thus families who can afford to leave have a strong incentive to do so. Personal insecurity is high for those who remain. The landlord is renting to tenants without steady incomes and is having trouble collecting rents regularly. Furthermore, the owner cannot obtain real estate loans through ordinary mortgage channels because the lenders perceive this type of property as a poor risk (Downs, cited in Sternlieb & Burchell, 1974).

Landlord-tenant relationships are likely to be poor, particularly if they involve white owners and black renters; there may be "racial differences generating mistrust or noncooperation" (Sternlieb & Burchell, 1974). Tenants may mistreat the building, engendering hostility from the owner. First psychologically, and then actually, the owner abandons the property.

Typically, the final abandonment occurs after the breakdown of some vital piece of mechanical equipment, usually the heating plant. If the boiler needs major repairs or replacement, the owner, recognizing that it is unprofitable to make this reinvestment, fails to fix the broken boiler, and the apartments receive no heat. At this point, some or all of the tenants may complain, unsuccessfully; then one or two families may move, leaving vacant apartments. Vagrants, gangs, or other undesirables may move into the vacant units without paying rent. This makes the regular tenants feel even more unsafe than usual; thus they have a further incentive to move. Eventually, all the old tenants vacate their apartments—the building is abandoned. The structure is then unprotected, and specialized gangs of scavengers move in to steal whatever may be valuable, such as electric and plumbing fixtures, especially copper plumbing. (Needless to say, because many elements of the abandonment-and-arson process are illegal, they are not subject to systematic research; therefore, the story must be pieced together from journalistic and anecdotal bits of information.) At this point the building has no tenants and no workable mechanical systems. The next step is fire; some arsonists will burn it, for fun or for profit. Finally, the city's building department officially condemns the structure as a public hazard and calls for its demolition. The wreckers are brought in, and all that remains is an empty lot strewn with broken bricks.

**Prevalence** Two studies attempted to document the prevalence of housing abandonment. Referring to the 1970–1971 situation, Sternlieb and Burchell reported that about 4 percent of the housing stock in Newark was in vacant and derelict buildings. An Urban League survey (cited in Sternlieb & Burchell, 1974) found that in New York City about 2 percent of the structures had been abandoned, but that in the most severely afflicted sections of Brooklyn between 6 and 10 percent had been abandoned. In St. Louis, which was declining badly at the time, the worst sections had 16 percent abandoned structures. Two deteriorating sections of Chicago had upward of 20 percent abandonment. On the other hand, of the seven cities surveyed, three—Atlanta, New Orleans, and Oakland—had no abandonment.

In a detailed study of Newark, Sternlieb and Burchell (1974) found common characteristics of neighborhoods undergoing high rates of abandonment. Areas with renters were likely to have abandonment; areas with high levels of homeownership did not have abandonment. Areas with high proportions of foreign-born residents were not likely to have abandonment; Sternlieb and Burchell surmised that immigrants are still using old neighborhoods as "staging areas." Abandonment was proceeding at high rates in areas housing blacks and Puerto Ricans and was occurring where "age succession" was taking place, that is, where elderly whites were leaving and being replaced by larger black families which were placing greater strains on the buildings. It is likely that these variables also characterize areas in other cities undergoing abandonment and arson.

## "GENTRIFICATION"

Fortunately, not all old neighborhoods are being destroyed. Another recent phenomenon is the reinvestment of private capital in city neighborhoods, one version of Stage 6, renewal.

The term "gentrification" refers to the social and environmental changeover in an old neighborhood when new residents purchase and renovate deteriorating dwellings on a noticeable scale. The term was first used several years ago in London when large numbers of young professional people—the so-called gentry—were buying and renovating small homes and row houses in several central districts. The housing had been built for middle-class families in the late nineteenth century, but the areas had aged over the decades, declining in social class (Hammett & Williams, 1980). However, they had the advantages of being close to the center of the metropolis and of having relatively small houses, and both of these features were attractive to young, urban, white-collar workers in an era without household servants. These areas became very popular among the young upper-middle class; indeed, they were transformed into fashionable districts—thus the slightly snide appelation: gentrification.

Like London, many United States cities also have old neighborhoods in which the housing is being restored by new residents. While this process became popular in the 1970s, it had been noted two decades earlier in New York City by Hoover and Vernon (1959), who mentioned it in their discussion of the renewal stage. A special sort of slum-renewal process was taking place in Greenwich Village. "Old areas of felicitous design and conveniently central location, originally high-income but deteriorated, are restored piecemeal to high-grade occupancy by extensive repair and remodeling, merger of dwelling units, and a little new construction" (Hoover & Vernon, p. 196).

Perhaps the most noticeable case, though, has been Capitol Hill, in Washington, D.C. (Gale, 1980; Randall, 1972). This area, immediately adjacent to the United States Capitol, to the east, is highly accessible to the government buildings of The

CHAPTER·11

It is very expensive to gut and "rehab" an old apartment building like this; therefore, unless this project was subsidized, the new residents are likely to be wealthier than those who used to live there. (Catherine Ursillo, Photo Researchers, Inc.)

Mall and to downtown employment centers. The Victorian and post-Victorian masonry row houses had declined for decades past their prime; by 1960 the area was occupied mostly by poor and working-class blacks, and 60 percent of the occupants were renters. The housing was old but generally sound, with scattered pockets of deterioration and dilapidation and some abandonment (Gale, 1980). Since the late 1960s, however, the area has undergone an environmental and social transformation. At first, attracted by the cheap housing and the chance for an investment which would appreciate, young people such as artists, architects, and students purchased houses and began to restore them. (Gale refers to this first group as "risk-takers.") They were followed by middle- and upper-middle-income professionals and government workers, some with children. After the gentrification, over 90 percent of the newcomers were whites; over 90 percent were college graduates; the modal age was in the early thirties; and the majority were singles or childless couples, although one-third had children. They succeeded in changing the neighborhood from a slum to a fashionable residential area, and the restored houses multiplied in value. Afterward, a survey indicated that the occupants did not intend to move, that they were satisfied with their housing, but that they were afraid of crime in the area (Gale, 1980). Gentrification rapidly spread beyond Capitol Hill to numerous other neighborhoods. According to the author of a multicity study,

"Washington has perhaps the most extensive neighborhood renewal {of any of the nation's largest cities} with several reinvestment neighborhoods almost completely surrounding the central business and government area" (Clay, 1980, p. 19).

By 1975 gentrification could be seen as a national trend, with changing neighborhoods in many cities. A survey in that year found that slightly less than half the cities had "some degree of private-market, nonsubsidized housing renovation in older, deteriorated areas" (Black, 1980, p. 7) and that this sort of development was more prevalent in larger cities. A follow-up survey four years later found that 86 percent of all cities with populations greater than 150,000 had this kind of change in progress (Black, 1980). Furthermore, this sort of redevelopment was more common in cities of the southern and notheastern regions than elsewhere in the nation. The main exceptions outside these regions are San Francisco and Seattle, which have extensive private renewal and resettlement (Clay, 1980). Another national study found that there was resettlement and private reinvestment in older neighborhoods in all 30 of the nation's largest cities (Clay, 1980).

Gentrification follows a general pattern, by type of neighborhood and by type of participant. Usually, gentrification areas are located within 2 miles of the city's central business district (Clay, 1980). Typically the areas are relatively small, covering only several city blocks, with fewer than 500 housing units, mostly single-family dwellings. The housing may be detached town houses, sometimes row houses, but almost never larger apartment buildings. Areas over 100 years old with historical significance, either local or national, or with some distinctive architectural style are ripe for this kind of redevelopment (Black, 1980; Clay, 1980). The participants are usually young white adults, single or married, without children or with small families, thus forming small households. Many are college graduates, employed as white-collar workers in business or in the professions (Black, 1980). Most purchase and renovate the houses for their own occupancy, although some cities also have speculators who buy and repair old dwellings for resale.

In addition to gentrification, a second trend in neighborhood redevelopment is occurring, also by means of private reinvestment, which receives less publicity. Clay (1980) refers to this trend as "incumbent ungrading," that is, the residents of an area improve the existing housing, and he reports that it is taking place in cities throughout the nation. Incumbent upgrading occurs in larger residential districts, unlike the more confined gentrifying areas, and while the housing is old, some from the nineteenth century, it is not as old as housing in the gentrifying areas. These neighborhoods may be variously located in cities, but they are not near mixed land uses, public housing projects, or large apartment buildings, except in Philadelphia.

Neighborhood redevelopment is not without its costs, however, and some concern has been expressed about displacement of residents by gentrification. "Displacement" refers to the fact that poorer residents lose their dwellings when they are rehabilitated; rents and house prices escalate rapidly in gentrifying areas, and the older residents, who were there for cheap housing, must leave. It is extremely difficult to measure accurately the extent of displacement, but two housing experts, Grier and Grier (1980) made rough estimates. Their definition states, "Displacement occurs when any household is forced to move from its residence by conditions which affect the dwelling or its immediate surroundings and which ... make continued occupancy by that household impossible, hazardous, or unaffordable" (p. 256). Grier and Grier acknowledge that some displacement is due to gentrification, but they estimate that it is not much (referring to the situation in the late 1970s). They say, "The numbers of households which are being directly displaced by gentrification are still small in most places—no more than 100 or 200 annually (per city), and sometimes fewer" (p. 260). In a few exceptions, though, like Washington and San Francisco, displacement is quite widespread, and Grier and Grier estimated that in those cities the numbers displaced annually are probably in the low thousands at most. Nonetheless, they conclude that even though displacement occurs in small volume, it is a problem because local public-housing authorities do not have accommodations for the displaced poor households and that, potentially, displacement is a larger problem because there may be more housing reinvestment in the future.

Journalists have publicized gentrification greatly, suggesting incorrectly that it represents a large-scale movement of the middle class back to the city. Reporting on gentrification, magazines have used such extravagant titles as "The Urban Crisis Leaves Town" and labels like "monumental renaissance." The popular press in England has promulgated the same story of gentrification's bringing suburbanites back to the city (Hammett & Williams, 1980). While it is true that gentrification is a national phenomenon, it is happening on a small scale; with few exceptions, like Washington and San Francisco, cities are likely to have only one or two areas undergoing this type of change, usually on a block-by-block basis. At the same time the urban social landscape is being "bulldozed" by much larger phenomena: continued suburbanization and "white flight," which are discussed in Chapters 8 and 12.

One analyst (Goodman, 1980) notes that the overall impact of gentrification must be small because even the cities undergoing it were losing population. "For every person who moved into a central city, two left" (Goodman, 1980, p. 14). Even Washington, D.C., which had much more gentrification than most other cities, had a 13 percent decline in population between 1970 and 1979. Goodman's research showed that between 1970 and 1978 most age groups increased their rate of migration out of cities and decreased their rate of migration into cities.

Furthermore, despite the affluence of the individuals fixing up old houses, city income leels continued to fall in the 1970s, relative to the suburbs. Long (1980) reports that in 1970, "families living in central cities had incomes that on the average were 83 percent as large as the incomes of suburban families" (p. 21). But eight years later the city families' incomes dropped to 79 percent of the suburban incomes. In Washington, despite widespread gentrification, city incomes fell relative to suburban incomes.

Both Goodman and Long assume that the journalists failed to recognize how tightly encapsulated the phenomenon is. The magazine stories showed the cities changing, when, in fact, only a few neighborhoods were being redeveloped. One political scientist coined the term "pockets of plenty" to refer to gentrified areas in otherwise poor central cities.

Clay (1980) summarizes the matter, saying, "There is no striking evidence that the trend is substantially a movement of suburban residents to central city neighborhoods. What is commonly referred to as back to the city is fundamentally a resettlement in and a renewal of older neighborhoods, mainly by middle-class people who are presently residents in the city in other neighborhoods as renters" (pp. 13-14). Hammett and Williams (1980) say exactly the same thing about gentrification in London.

## MACRODEVELOPMENTS

Changes in neighborhoods are not simply produced by local processes in small areas; they are strongly influenced by large-scale changes at the metropolitan and even the national level. Some of these macrodevelopments have been mentioned above, for example, in Guest's argument that the course of the neighborhood life cycle has been changed fundamentally by the overall shift of intraurban transportation technologies, from the electric trolley to the automobile. Housing obsolescence is also a process that is to some extent outside the control of the neighborhood. Styles and standards of housing may change in such a way as to make a neighborhood's housing unmarketable under current circumstances—old mansions may become uneconomical to operate, and apartments without elevators may be uncompetitive, for example. Also, the encroachment of nonresidential land use near a neighborhood may affect its desirability. Hawley (1950) states, "The encroachment of industry or business upon a residential area, for example, hastens, if it does not start, the obsolescence of the residential structures" (pp. 400-401). Other new facilities like expressways, airports, and hospitals may also influence the course of events in particular neighborhoods.

Growth or decline (of population as well as of economy) at the metropolitan level has a powerful effect on the course of events in individual residential areas. According to Hawley (1950), "Growth of the city constitutes the most general of disturbances" (p. 400), yielding competition for location which may release "waves of succession" across the entire city. Where the economy is expanding, builders may seek land in old neighborhoods for various nonresidential uses, including factories, warehouses, offices, etc., depending upon the situation. Hawley's argument seems most appropriate to the highly centralized mature industrial city, which had a growing CBD and growing nonresidential land uses nearby which were constantly encroaching upon neighborhoods near the center. The argument does not fit quite so closely into the highly suburbanized metropolitan situation because its growth often spreads peripherally onto adjacent rural land. But, even in the contemporary situation, old central neighborhoods may be powerfully affected by change, as exemplified by Houston, a modern boomtown.

The main influence on neighborhood change is the housing market, which can be shown to be connected to abandonment and arson as well as to gentrification. DeLeeuw, Schnare, & Struyk (1976) analyzed the relationship between the growth of housing and the growth of population in four widely diverse metropolitan areas in the 1960-1970 decade. Two areas studied—Washington, D.C., and Austin, Texas—were growing rapidly, while the others—Chicago and Pittsburgh—were not. Household and housing statistics of the four SMSAs appear in Table 11-2. Although the number of households grew much faster in Washington and Austin, builders were erecting new dwelling units in all four metropolitan areas. This disparity had major consequences for the neighborhoods of the four metropolitan areas: "In the slow growing areas ... there were substantially more new units built than new households formed and there were major declines in the number of poorest households" (deLeeuw et al., 1976, p. 129). In this situation the new housing would be occupied by the middle and upper-middle classes as well as by wealthier households, and people, in general, would be shifting to the best-available units in the market. DeLeeuw et al. note, "This process may continue until the worst quality housing is permanently vacated" (p. 129). Thus it is available for abandonment and arson. The situation in the rapidly growing communities is quite different, though. There, new construction did not keep pace with household formation, so vacancies were reduced and existing buildings were converted into more dwelling units. Having more new households than new dwelling units produced excess demand and high prices at all quality levels. The effect of this at the neighborhood level in the rapidly growing areas would be gentrification of older housing and, certainly, a demand for all the existing dwelling units. And the effect in the slow-growing cities would be abandonment and arson as surplus housing was no longer needed, even by the poor.

**TABLE 11-2**
**Indicators of Demand and Supply for Dwelling Units in Selected Metropolitan Areas**

| Indicator | Chicago | Pittsburgh | Austin | Washington |
|---|---|---|---|---|
| Percentage change, 1960-70, in number of | | | | |
|   Households | 15.0 | 6.9 | 56.5 | 52.1 |
|   Dwelling units | 15.3 | 7.0 | 53.6 | 47.1 |
| Percentage of 1970 units built 1960-70 | 1.40 | 2.11 | .83 | .72 |
| Percentage change in households 1960-70 | | | | |
| Percentage change, 1960-70, in number of households with incomes under $4,000 | −19 | −20 | −9 | −13 |

Source: U.S. Bureau of the Census, 1962, 1972 cited by de Leeuw et al., 1976, p. 129.

# NEIGHBORHOOD CHANGE

TABLE 11-3
**Households in the United States**

|  | 1970 | 1980 | Percent change |
|---|---|---|---|
| Number | 63,401,000 | 79,080,000 | +25 |
| Average size | 3.14 | 2.75 | −11 |

*Source:* 1970 data are from U.S. Bureau of the Census, 1980b, p. 45; 1980 data are from U.S. Bureau of the Census, 1980a.

In a similar vein, Clay (1980) asked, "Why is reinvestment in older neighborhoods occurring now?" and his answer emphasized demographic shifts and the housing market at the macro level. Clay notes that the children born in the 1950s, the middle of the "baby boom," came to maturity and began seeking housing in the 1970s; furthermore, continuing a long-term trend, they were forming small households at young ages (see Table 11-3). Clay suggested this large number of new entrants into the urban housing market created additional demand for housing and helped support gentrification and other forms of reinvestment.

## SUMMARY

In the various neighborhood-change processes we see the underlying urban ecology setting the conditions of social life. The neighborhood life cycle involves the interplay of environment and population: In the early decades the housing, a major part of the built environment, is under construction; its very form is strongly influenced by the technology of the period, particularly in the realm of transportation. The construction of the housing environment is tied to the demographic process of rapid growth, including an influx of young adults with children, which sets forth the conditions for the social life of the area—familistic activities along with family-oriented associational life. The housing market also determines the social-class composition of the first occupants of the new residential area.

Environmental changes continue to influence the demography and the social life of the residential area as it ages. The aging of houses affects their competitive position in the housing market; as the buildings grow older, they become less attractive to prosperous households because of simple wear and tear and, more important, because of obsolescence as newer dwellings are constructed with current designs and amenities. The neighborhood undergoes a series of successions, with decreasing social-class levels; finally, passing through the thinning-out stage, the neighborhood hits a turning point.

The area may continue to deteriorate, at worst contracting the abandonment-and-arson syndrome, or it may be renewed. Renewal may be effectuated by means of private reinvestment—gentrification or incumbent upgrading—or through government-sponsored projects, such as slum clearance and urban renewal, which are discussed in Chapter 15.

**REFERENCES**

Birch, David L. 1971. "Toward a Stage Theory of Urban Growth." *Journal of American Institute of Planners.* 37:78-87.

Black, J. Thomas. 1980. "Private-Market Housing Renovation in Central Cities: An Urban Land Institute Survey," pp. 3-12 in *Back to the City: Issues in Neighborhood Renovation,* (eds.) Shirley B. Laska and Daphne Spain. New York: Pergamon.

Burgess, Ernest W. 1928. "Residential Segregation in American Cities." *Annals of the American Academy of Political and Social Science.* 140:105-115.

Choldin, Harvey M., and Claudine Hanson. 1982. "Status Shifts within the City." *American Sociological Review.* 47:129-141.

Clay, Phillip L. 1980. "The Rediscovery of City Neighborhoods: Reinvestment by Long-Time Residents and Newcomers," pp. 13-26 in *Back to the City: Issues in Neighborhood Renovation,* (eds.) Shirley B. Laska and Daphne Spain. New York: Pergamon.

Cressey, Paul F. 1938/1971. "Population Succession in Chicago: 1989-1930," chap. 7 in *The Social Fabric of the Metropolis,* (ed.) James F. Short. Chicago: University of Chicago Press.

deLeeuw, Frank, Anne B. Schnare, and Raymond J. Struyk. 1976. "Housing," pp. 119-178 in *The Urban Predicament,* (eds.) William Gorham and Nathan Glazer. Washington: Urban Institute.

Duncan, Beverly, George Sabagh, and Maurice D. Van Arsdol. 1962. "Patterns of City Growth." *American Journal of Sociology.* 68:418-429.

Gale, Dennis E. 1980. "Neighborhood Resettlement: Washington, D.C.," pp. 95-115 in *Back to the City: Issues in Neighborhood Renovation,* (eds.) Shirley B. Laska and Daphne Spain. New York: Pergamon.

Gist, Noel P., and Sylvia F. Fava. 1974. *Urban Society,* 6th ed. New York: Crowell.

Goodman, John H., Jr. 1980. "People of the City." *American Demographics.* 2:14-17.

Grier, George, and Eunice Grier. 1980. "Urban Displacement: A Reconnaissance," pp. 252-268 in *Back to the City: Issues in Neighborhood Renovation,* (eds.) Shirley B. Laska and Daphne Spain. New York: Pergamon.

Guest, Avery M. 1973. "Urban Growth and Population Densities." *Demography.* 10:53-70.

Hammett, Christopher, and Peter R. Williams. 1980. "Social Change in London: A Study of Gentrification." *Urban Affairs Quarterly.* 15:469-487.

Hawley, Amos H. 1950. *Human Ecology: A Theory of Community Structure.* New York: Ronald.

Hoover, Edgar M., and Raymond Vernon. 1959. *Anatomy of a Metropolis.* Garden City, N.Y.: Doubleday Anchor.

Hughes, James W. 1974. "The Dynamics of Neighborhood Decline," chap. 5 in *Suburbanization Dynamics and the Future of the City*, (ed.) James W. Hughes. New Brunswick, N.J.: Center for Urban Policy Research, Rutgers University.

Hunter, Albert. 1974. "Community Change." *American Sociological Review*. 47:129–141.

Kantowicz, E. R. 1975. *Polish-American Politics in Chicago, 1888–1940*. Chicago: University of Chicago Press.

Kneeland, Douglas E. 1981. "Chicago's Milwaukee Avenue, the Polish Broadway Yields to Ethnic Changes." May 26 *New York Times*, p. A-14.

Laska, Shirley B., and Daphne Spain (eds.). 1980. *Back to the City: Issues in Neighborhood Renovation*. New York: Pergamon.

Long, Harry H. 1980. "What the Census Will Tell Us About Gentrification." *American Demographics*. 2:18–21.

Moore, Winston, Charles P. Livermore, and George F. Galland, Jr. 1973. "Woodlawn: The Zone of Destruction." *The Public Interest*. 30:41–59.

Randall, Nan. 1972. "The Hill Dwellers' Complaint." *Washington Post*, May 14, p. H-1.

Sternlieb, George, and R. W. Burchell. 1974. "Neighborhood Change and Housing Abandonment," pp. 89–124 in *Suburbanization Dynamics and the Future of the City*, (ed.) James Hughes.

U.S. Bureau of the Census. 1962. *Metropolitan Housing Characteristics*, 1960 Census of Housing. Washington, D.C.

U.S. Bureau of the Census. 1972. *Metropolitan Housing Characteristics*, 1970 Census of Housing. Washington, D.C.

U.S. Bureau of the Census. 1980. *Current Population Reports, Population Characteristics*, series P-20, no. 357. Washington, D.C. (a)

U.S. Bureau of the Census. 1980. *Statistical Abstract of the United States, 1980*. Washington, D.C.

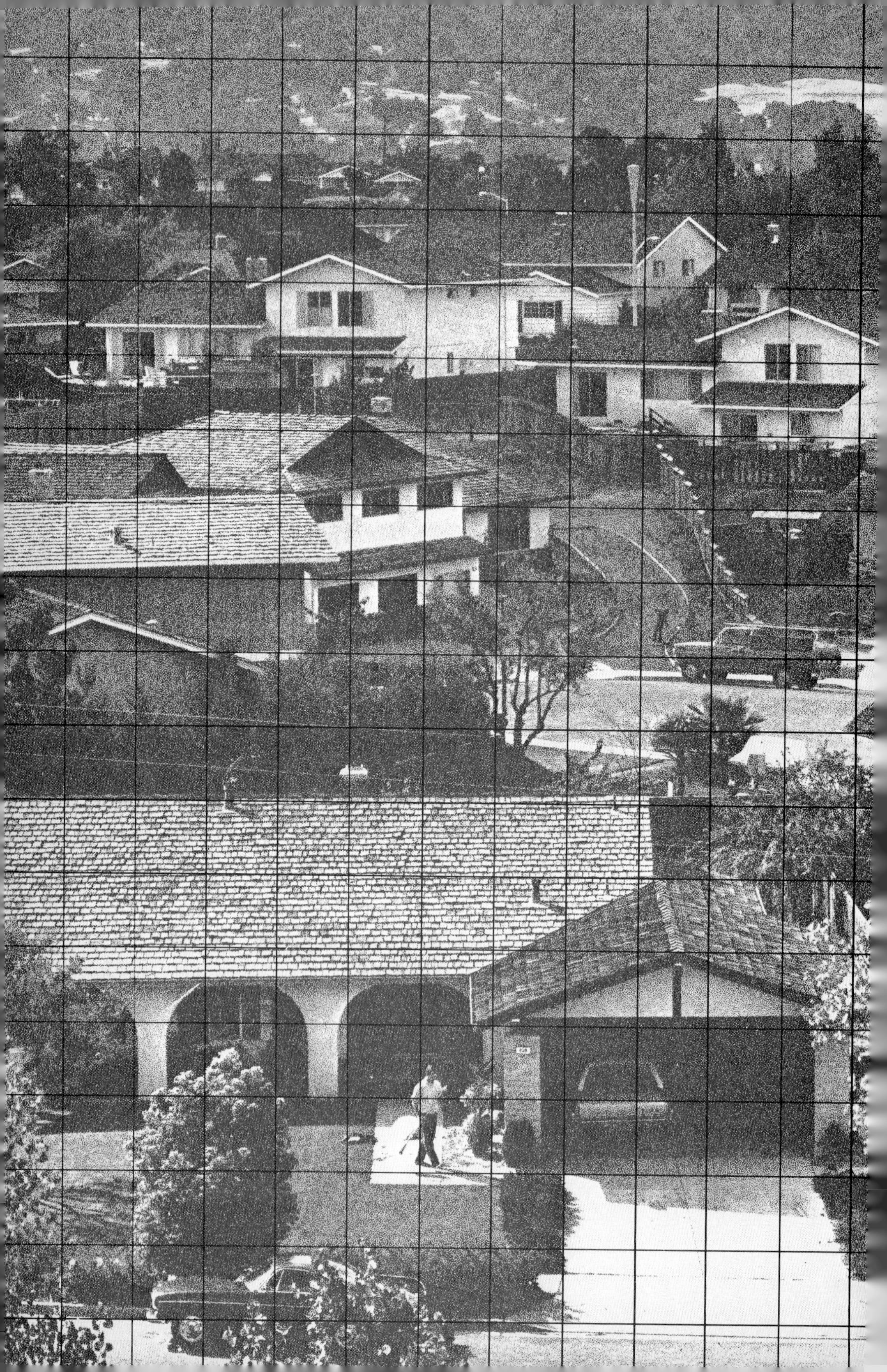

# CHAPTER · 12

# Suburbanization and the New Metropolitan Form

## Chapter Outline

INTRODUCTION
    Definitions of Suburb
    The Suburb as an American Environment
HISTORY OF SUBURBAN GROWTH
    Periods of Development
    Mass-Produced Suburbs
PEOPLE AND HOUSES
    Population Growth after 1920
    A New Metropolitan Density Pattern
THE SUBURBANIZATION OF NEARLY EVERYTHING
    Retailing
    Manufacturing, Wholesaling, and Warehousing
    Offices
    Apartment Buildings
    Entertainment and "High Culture"

DIFFERENTIATION AMONG SUBURBS
    Work and Residence
    Other Differences
- Socioeconomic status
- Proximity and age
- Race and ethnicity

CHANGE AND STABILITY
EMERGING METROPOLITAN STRUCTURE
    The Modified Multinuclear Model
- Basic concepts
- Los Angeles as the prototype

    Suburban Minicities
    Urban Realms
    An Overlay Model
SUMMARY

## INTRODUCTION

Without exaggerating, many writers have called suburbanization a fundamental shift in American society. Historian Richard Wade (1982), for example, has written, "Since 1945, suburbanization has been the most significant fact of American social and political life" (p. 20).[1] By 1970 more people lived in suburbs than in cities or rural areas. This suburban plurality grew by 1980.

But why does this matter? Perhaps suburbanization is merely an extension of conventional American urban growth; only now it has expanded beyond city limits (Banfield, 1968). Another opinion is that suburbanization is a pernicious development, threatening to undermine the American way of life. Several issues have arisen among urban researchers, such as the following: When massive suburbanization became apparent in the 1950s, critics said that suburbs were all alike and that they would homogenize the American people. Early observers said that the suburbs were simply white middle-class bedroom communities for people who worked in the cities. Other writers saw far more diversity in the suburban zone. And there has been some controversy over the permanence or fluidity of the characteristics of suburban communities, as some sociologists said that the communities were highly stable in status, while others contended that suburbs must be changing over time like other residential areas.

At first, writers tended to see the suburbs as a burden on the city. Critics contended that the educated middle class was turning its back on the city, taking away tax dollars as well as potential for leadership in solving the cities' problems. Later, writers came to take the suburbs for granted as a major segment of the metropolis which grew while the cities declined. Now there is at least one writer who contends that the suburbs are where the action is, that the suburban zone contains the real vitality of the metropolis. He is geographer Peter O. Muller, who says that the suburbs have captured *all* the key elements of the urban community (1981); the future of urban America is theirs, and therefore they deserve our most intelligent attention in attempting to understand contemporary communities.

We have two chapters about suburbs. This chapter is macroscopic and ecological. It recounts the history of American suburbs. Then it discusses the suburb as a distinctive type of settlement, its density and housing patterns, along with the technological shifts which gave rise to them. It looks at the shift of jobs from cities to suburbs; it describes the emerging metropolitan pattern after suburbanization; and it presents the pattern of socioeconomic status in the suburban zone. The next chapter comes down to the microlevel, asking whether there is a suburban way of life. Chapter 13 recounts the misconceptions of "the suburban myth" and presents sociological research findings about contemporary lifestyles.

---

[1]References for both suburban chapters are combined and appear at the end of Chapter 13.

## Definitions of Suburb

What is a suburb? The Census Bureau provides a minimal definition based upon law and demography: "A suburb is by definition an incorporated municipality within a Standard Metropolitan Statistical Area other than the central city" (cited in Lineberry, 1975, p. 3). A somewhat broader ecological definition was suggested by Downs (1973), who wrote that the term

> ...*suburbs* refers to all parts of all metropolitan areas outside of central cities. It therefore includes unincorporated areas as well as (18,000) suburban municipalities. Communities that are considered *suburbs* by this definition range in population from a few hundred to over 80,000, in land-use composition from entirely residential to almost entirely industrial with nearly all possible mixtures in between (cited in Muller, 1981, pp. 5-6).

Note that this definition says that an unincorporated built-up area near a city is a suburb too. Older definitions said that a suburb was predominantly residential and that its citizens commuted to a city to work, but suburbs should no longer be defined in this way because many are not exclusively residential and most suburbanites do not commute to the city to work.

## The Suburb as an American Environment

Beyond these bare-bones definitions we may characterize the suburb as distinctively American. From the beginning of history, urban settlements have been as dense and compact as possible. Residences and shops were squeezed together, and even when construction technology was minimal, urban structures often went up a couple of stories into the air. Furthermore, the buildings came right up to the edges of the narrow streets, maximizing intensity of land use.

The twentieth-century suburb represents an exception—the first low-density urban development. Until recently, the basic suburban unit was the single-family detached house with its own yard, preferably on a large lot. The built environment is oriented to the automobile with almost all public services distributed at driving distances from most residences—shops, offices, high schools, entertainment facilities, etc. These facilities are car-oriented with convenient parking and/or drive-through accommodations. Within the suburban zone surrounding each American city is a scattering of residences and jobs, together with shops and services, often in the form of strip commercial development. Usually, the suburban zone lacks large open or green spaces (Popenoe, 1977). Likewise, the typical suburb lacks a community focal point in the physical and social sense, except where there is a supersized shopping center.

In Europe, suburbs conform to different environmental patterns. For example, Popenoe contrasts the American suburb with its Swedish counterpart, which has low-rise apartment buildings. Swedish suburban housing has a higher density.

High-quality public transportation ties suburbs to the central city; the typical suburb is centered around an intraurban train station. Suburban residents are not dependent upon cars for daily life; they are likely to commute to the city center to work and to shop for goods not available in the local convenience shops. The Swedish suburb is compact, physically focused, and heavily endowed with public services. In Popenoe's opinion, Swedish suburbs enhance central-city areas rather than detract from them. Unfortunately, though, not all European suburbs are filled with high-rise apartment buildings and are not well-integrated with their central cities.

Special environmental, historical, and cultural factors converged to produce the American suburb. The nation has enjoyed abundant supplies of open land and wood so urban development could simply spread as populations grew. Land at the urban fringe was sufficiently cheap that individual families could afford to buy lots. Vast native forests provided so much wood that individual houses could be built relatively inexpensively. And the general affluence of the decades of the 1950s and 1960s supported large-scale home buying for all social classes except the poor. Technology also supported twentieth-century suburbanization; widespread diffusion of automobile ownership, low-cost gasoline, and the widespread telephone network also facilitated low-density, spread-out urbanism. Finally, certain facets of American culture—a preference for spaciousness and privacy combined with a desire to raise children in single-family houses—also supported the trend toward suburban living. Government policy, discussed in the next section, also supported suburban development. All these various facets of American ecology and culture combined to produce a new low-density urban form, the contemporary suburb.

## HISTORY OF SUBURBAN GROWTH

### Periods of Development

Although suburbia seemed to spring up full-blown after World War II, there have been suburbs for more than a century. Historically suburbs took different forms, depending upon the predominant technology of their times. One historical scheme (Adams, 1970, cited in Muller, 1981) divides suburban history into four periods:

1. The walking and horsecar era, pre-1850 to the late 1880s
2. The electric streetcar and railroad era, late 1880s to 1920
3. The recreational automobile era, 1920 to 1945
4. The freeway era, 1945 to the present

These correspond to equivalent periods of city development (see Chapter 4).

In the walking and horsecar era, before the 1880s, prosperous merchants and other wealthy households could maintain their distance from the lower classes by constructing walled-off areas (Muller, 1981). Some of these exclusive districts were located within the city, others out in suburbs. When walking was the dominant mode of intracity transportation, these wealthy individuals could afford to travel by carriage to the city center. At this time the city was compact, with a spatial mix of homes, shops, and workplaces.

Railroads brought a new kind of suburb, further from the city center, arranged in "strings" running along the tracks. "Morphologically, these early rail suburbs ... took the form of narrow radial corridors that contained a linear 'rosary bead' settlement pattern of discrete nodes isolated from the city as well as each other" (Muller, 1981, p. 27). Philadelphia's famous "Main Line" offers a clear example: "The area was originally developed in the 1830s as a series of commuter suburbs along the main line of the Pennsylvania Railroad"... northwest from the city. Each station formed the nucleus of a small suburb and the string became the metropolitan area's elite residential sector. It still holds that high status over a century later with such prestigious suburbs as Bryn Mawr, Villanova, and Rosemont with their estates, and hunt, cricket, and tennis clubs. (Muller, Meyer, & Cybriwsky, 1976, pp. 36-37)

Nineteenth-century railroad developers even established stations on open unsettled land at commuting distances from cities in anticipation that the stations would catalyze new suburbs. New communities did arise, typically built up within walking distance from the station and consisting of a compact residential center and a few shops. These communities were only for the affluent—residents had to be able to afford train fares to the city. These commuter settlements typically had servants' areas clustered in shacktowns or near the tracks. Like the Main Line communities, the railroad suburbs were upper-class areas, with elegant houses and estates and later developing such exclusive institutions as country clubs.

Streetcar suburbs for the new middle class arose later in the nineteenth century (Warner, 1962). These residential areas were just beyond the periphery of the city, toward the ends of the new electric trolley lines. They gave middle-class families their first opportunity to acquire the highly desired single-family detached house with a yard. Thus these areas were built up at far lower densities than the existing city's. Residents of the new suburbs depended upon the city for everything, especially work, getting only everyday goods and services locally—bread and groceries, for example (Muller, 1981). The third period, the recreational automobile era (1920-1945), merely represented continued growth of the sorts of suburbs built in the two earlier periods. The period immediately after World War II brought forth explosive suburbanization, though.

## Mass-Produced Suburbs

In the late 1940s there was enormous pent-up demand for family housing; it has been estimated that in 1947 between 2,750,000 and 4,400,000 families were living with other families and 500,000 more were occupying nonfamily or transient quarters. This was the context of massive and rapid construction of new housing (Checkoway, 1980). Traditionally, residential construction was the province of small independent builders, but a few construction companies expanded rapidly to meet the demand on a large scale. The cities themselves lacked large tracts of open space for residential development, so the developers looked to the open areas at the urban periphery. The stage was set for suburban expansion. The archetypical large-scale developer was the Levitt Company which built three whole suburbs, each called Levittown: one on New York's Long Island, one in New Jersey, and another in Pennsylvania. The Levittowns epitomized the mass-produced suburb. In a careful historical analysis, Checkoway (1980) explains how the new suburbs were made.

> What was new in the period was the ... capacity of large builders to take raw suburban land, divide it into parcels and streets, install needed services, apply mass production methods to residential construction, and sell the finished product to unprecedented numbers of consumers. ...
>
> Levitt adapted assembly line techniques to the mass production of housing. An army of trucks speeding along new-laid roads stopped and delivered neatly packaged bundles of materials at exact 100 foot intervals. Giant machines followed the trucks, digging rectangular foundations in which heating pipes were embedded.... Men, materials and machines moved past each site in teams, each performing one of 26 operations over and over again from site to site.... Materials reached the site only minutes before a team would arrive to perform its particular operation.... Levitt was less a builder, more a manufacturer of houses. (pp. 22, 26–27)

Levitt sold a good house at a cheap price and at a good profit, according to Checkoway. Large builders played a central role in postwar suburbanization; 70 percent of the houses erected in 1949 were built by 10 percent of the builders. This pattern continued as large builders accounted for 64 percent of the houses built in 1959.

In addition to the private sector's technological and organizational developments, the federal government's major programs also supported massive suburbanization. Two programs helped families purchase new houses: the Federal Housing Authority (FHA) and the Veterans Administration (VA) mortgage programs. Both programs helped families borrow money to purchase a house. The FHA program guaranteed the loans made by local banks, so if a family defaulted, the banker could rely upon the federal government to make good the loan. Under these two loan programs, couples could borrow up to 95 percent of the cost of a house and repay the loan over a long period, often twenty to thirty years. Since builders like Levitt were offering many houses in the $10,000 range, a couple with only $500 for a deposit could buy one. FHA policy discouraged loans for houses in older urban neighborhoods; the agency's guidelines clearly preferred new suburban subdivisions. Ironically, many critics of federal housing policy in the 1950s focused upon the government's central-city investments in urban renewal and public housing for the poor. But, by far, the bulk of federal effort and investment was supporting the growth of the suburbs (Checkoway, 1980; Downs, 1974). Another enormous governmental project was the Interstate Highways Act, initiated under President Eisenhower. While this public works program was mainly for constructing long-distance freeways, it was also for building their metropolitan components—expressways which connected cities with their suburban zones and beltways which facilitated travel between suburbs.

## PEOPLE AND HOUSES

### Population Growth after 1920

Since 1920 the suburban population has been increasing at a faster rate than either the city or the rural populations. Indeed, since 1950 many large cities have lost population.

Between 1950 and 1970 the suburbs were the fastest-growing segment of the U.S. population. In 1950, when the nation had about 151 million people, fewer than 1 in 7 lived in suburbs, based upon population in urbanized areas. Twenty years later the United States had over 200 million persons of whom more than 1 in 4 lived in suburbs. In two decades the suburbs added 33.6 million!

Statistics based upon the metropolitan-nonmetropolitan distinction (in Table 12-1) show which segment of the population received the nation's growth. In the twenty-year period the metropolitan and nonmetropolitan sectors both grew but the former took most of the growth. And within the metropolitan counties the great bulk of the growth was suburban. In the first decade, over 60 percent of the nation's population growth went to the suburbs, and in the second decade the suburbs took more than 70 percent (Muller, 1981, p. 4). By 1980, over 67 million Americans lived in the central cities of SMSAs, but they were outnumbered by more than 72 million individuals who lived in suburban areas (U.S. Bureau of the Census, 1982, p. 15).

A look at individual metropolitan areas gives another perspective on rapid suburban growth. Chicago, Philadelphia, and Detroit represent typical cases of large cities in the north central and mid-Atlantic regions. Taking 1920 as a peak year for these mature industrial cities, we see in Table 12-2 that the great majority lived in the cities themselves—about one-fifth of the people in metropolitan Chicago and about one-third of those in metropolitan Philadelphia lived in the suburbs. However, after 1920 the suburban proportion grew in each metropolitan area in every decade. (The only exceptions were when the city of Detroit annexed substantial amounts of territory.) Although metropolitan Chicago lagged behind somewhat, more than 40 percent of its people were suburban by 1960; in the other two metropolitan areas, this proportion exceeded 50 percent in that year. By 1970 Chicago's suburbs had more population than the city, and metropolitan Philadelphia and Detroit were on their way to becoming two-thirds suburban.

**TABLE 12-1**
Percentage Shares of Total U.S. Population Growth by Geographic Areas, 1900–1980*

| Decade | All metropolitan areas | All central cities | All suburbs | All nonmetropolitan areas |
|---|---|---|---|---|
| 1900–10 | 63.7 | 45.9 | 17.8 | 36.3 |
| 1910–20 | 76.4 | 54.7 | 21.7 | 23.6 |
| 1920–30 | 83.2 | 49.4 | 33.8 | 16.8 |
| 1930–40 | 65.9 | 27.0 | 38.9 | 34.1 |
| 1940–50 | 86.1 | 35.0 | 51.1 | 13.9 |
| 1950–60 | 84.4 | 20.1 | 64.3 | 15.6 |
| 1960–70 | 83.9 | 13.4 | 70.5 | 16.1 |
| 1970–80 | 58.5 | −1.0 | 59.5 | 41.5 |

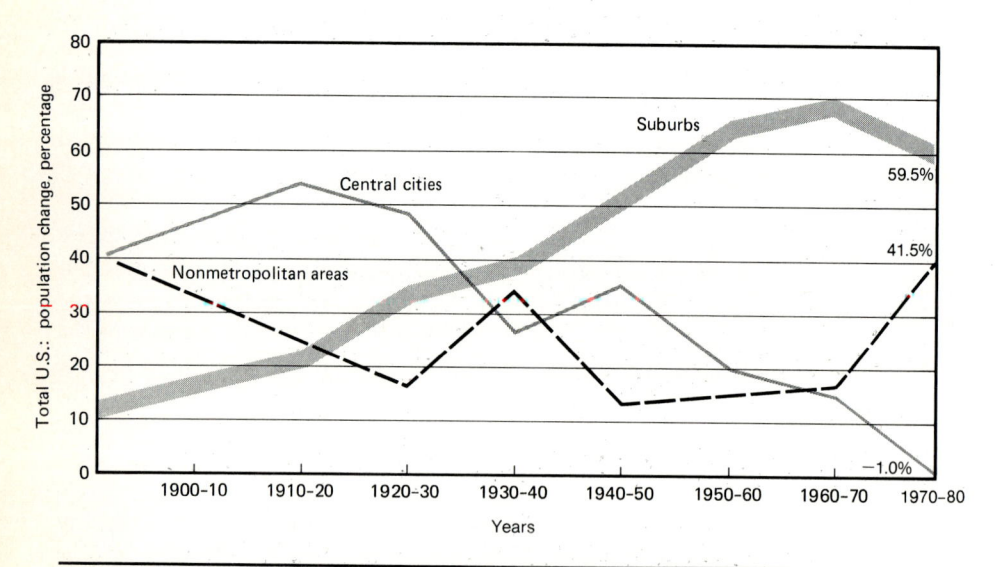

*Data for 1960–1980 based on figures for 243 areas classified as metropolitan in 1970; all other decades based on figures for 212 areas classified as metropolitan in 1960.
Source: Downs, 1973; 1980 data computed from U.S. Bureau of the Census, 1982b.

## A New Metropolitan Density Pattern

Suburbs grew faster than their central cities in every decade after 1920, but the cities were still growing. Thus, until 1940, population density at the city center was increasing, *and* new low-density population was accumulating at the spreading periphery. The classical density curve, high at the city center and diminishing toward the suburbs, was continued. Basically, the older metropolises were growing

**TABLE 12-2**
Suburban Percentage of Total SMSA Population for the 15 Largest 1980 SMSAs, 1900–1980

| Metropolis | 1900 | 1910 | 1920 | 1930 | 1940 | 1950 | 1960 | 1970 | 1980 |
|---|---|---|---|---|---|---|---|---|---|
| New York‡ | 32.2* | 32.4 | 33.8 | 36.2 | 36.1 | 38.9 | 47.3 | 51.2 | n.a. |
| Los Angeles | 44.9 | 37.4* | 36.6* | 40.7* | 42.8 | 46.5 | 53.2 | 54.9 | 55.5 |
| Chicago | 18.5 | 19.1* | 20.4 | 24.1* | 25.7 | 30.1 | 42.9 | 51.8 | 57.7 |
| Philadelphia | 31.6 | 31.7 | 32.8 | 37.8 | 39.6 | 43.6 | 53.9 | 59.6 | 64.3 |
| Detroit | 33.1* | 24.1 | 23.9* | 28.0* | 31.7 | 38.7 | 55.6 | 64.0 | 72.4 |
| San Francisco | 24.5 | 26.7 | 28.4 | 31.9 | 35.9 | 45.7 | 58.2 | 65.4 | 68.7 |
| Washington | 26.4 | 25.7 | 23.5 | 27.6 | 31.5 | 46.8 | 63.2 | 73.6 | 79.2 |
| Dallas-Fort Worth | 79.8* | 65.8* | 54.7* | 43.2* | 44.1* | 44.4* | 39.3* | 45.7* | 56.7 |
| Houston | 30.0* | 31.9* | 25.9* | 18.6* | 27.3* | 36.3* | 33.9* | 38.0* | 45.1 |
| Boston | 57.5 | 58.1 | 60.0* | 64.0 | 65.1 | 66.8 | 73.1 | 76.7 | 79.6 |
| St. Louis | 30.4 | 33.4 | 33.7 | 40.7 | 44.3 | 51.2 | 64.4 | 73.7 | 80.8 |
| Pittsburgh | 58.3* | 63.7 | 66.6* | 66.9 | 67.7 | 69.4 | 74.9 | 78.3 | 81.3 |
| Baltimore | 26.2 | 27.5 | 18.7* | 22.4* | 24.6 | 34.8 | 47.9 | 56.3 | 63.8 |
| Minneapolis–St. Paul | 20.4 | 16.9 | 15.5* | 16.6 | 19.4 | 27.6 | 46.3 | 59.0 | 69.7 |
| Atlanta | 54.7 | 43.3 | 42.4 | 41.5 | 45.9 | 54.4 | 52.1 | 69.0 | 79.1 |
| Mean for all SMSAs | 37.9 | 35.4 | 34.0 | 35.4 | 37.3 | 41.4 | 48.6 | 54.2 | 59.9 |

*First census following greater than 10 percent territorial annexation by the central city.
‡Standard Consolidated Area data.
*Source:* Based on Muller, 1981, p. 22, with additional data from U.S. Bureau of the Census, 1963, 1970, 1982a.

larger in their traditional form. The metropolises were becoming bigger in scale, more dominant over their territories, but following the conventional highly centralized form.

Recent research reveals a different timetable of suburbanization. Using a new measurement technique, Guterbock (1982) shows that the process of deconcentration generated a new metropolitan form which first became apparent in the 1950 census. Absolute deconcentration means the overall diminution of population density in the metropolitan area, including declining density in the central city itself.

Figure 12-1 illustrates the historical developments of density patterns among cohorts of metropolitan areas. In the graph each line represents a cohort of metropolitan areas of a particular age. For example, the line marked by "+" represents all the metropolitan areas started before 1870, old metropolises like New York, Philadelphia, Boston, etc. In contrast, the line marked by little squares represents young metropolitan areas started between 1940 and 1950. Guterbock's interpretation of this graph is that the old metropolises had high density, without much change, until about 1945. And the ones which began between 1920 and 1940

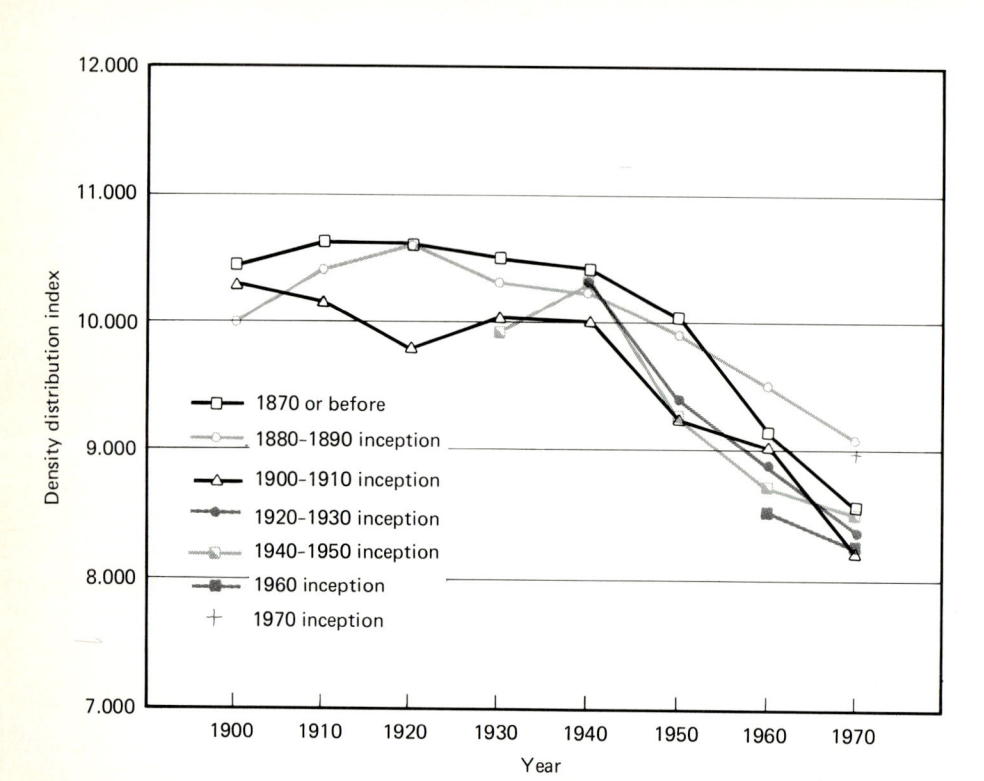

**FIGURE 12-1**
Trends in average value of the density distribution index, 1900–1970, by date of metropolitan inception. (Source: Guterbock,

started at the same high-density level. Then density in all areas, young and old, began to diminish to a new lower level.

Central-city housing was destroyed in most of the older metropolitan areas, which brought down central densities. Dwelling units were destroyed through deliberate urban renewal and slum clearance projects in which high-density, high-occupancy apartment buildings were razed and replaced by controlled-density projects. Clearance for highways plus abandonment and arson also destroyed dwellings which were not replaced. Even those central-city residential areas that suffered no demolitions and maintained full occupancy experienced falling density levels because smaller households became more popular, so buildings without vacancies still held fewer residents. Younger metropolitan areas simply continued to build at low-density levels; they expanded with more and more medium-density low-rise apartment areas in addition to low-density developments of single-family detached houses. These younger metropolitan areas never had the high-density neighborhoods of apartment buildings like those in the old cities. In summary, Guterbock says that when deconcentration occurred in the older metropolitan areas, in conjunction with slow growth, there was loss of population near the centers and absolute deconcentration overall. But the young rapidly growing cities deconcentrated because their peripheral growth was so much greater than their central growth. "The spreading-out trend is seen in all regions, and in old and new cities alike" (Guterbock, 1982, p. 16). The new metropolitan density pattern has a more even spread than that of the mature industrial city. The new pattern has a lower peak at the center and then a moderate- to low-density level throughout the metropolis, with occasional peaks.

## THE SUBURBANIZATION OF NEARLY EVERYTHING

Suburbs were once seen simply as comprising a residential zone for people who commuted to the city. In this vein, social critics anticipated that the 1950s suburban burst would just add more residential subdivisions to a sort of endless "suburban sprawl." These critics may have recognized that retail stores would suburbanize along with new housing, but it turned out that most other basic urban functions decentralized also. Factories, offices, and warehouses opened in the suburbs, bringing millions of new jobs with them. Then such traditionally urban functions as entertainment and culture moved to the suburbs. Even the apartment building finally moved out to the land of the single-family house with a yard.

### Retailing

The shopping center became part of the new automobile-based built environment; developers provided small centers for local convenience shopping—groceries, drug stores, cleaners, and the like—scattered on major streets. Large parking areas were the key feature, making the new facilities very different from traditional city shopping areas where numerous narrow store fronts were sited along streets with little or no parking. Developers soon located larger and larger shopping centers at greater intervals in the suburban zone. Eventually, they evolved into regional shopping malls, large enclosed structures including scores of specialty shops plus two or more branches of major department stores (known as "anchors"). The shopping center became a highly efficient and popular addition to the nation's system of retail distribution of consumer goods.

The optimum location for a shopping center is near a major highway which allows it to attract customers from the central city, as well as from several suburbs, and even from small towns beyond the suburban zone. Shopping centers have come to play multiple functions in community life. Most movie threaters built in the past two decades are in shopping centers. The typical shopping center includes

## CHAPTER·12

Regional shopping malls with their acres of parking, such as Fairlane Mall in Detroit's suburban zone, represent a contemporary mode of retail distribution and have emerged as present-day community centers. (Donald Dietz, Stock, Boston)

at least a couple of restaurants, and many also have "pinball arcades" with electronic games, as well as motels, banks, and other facilities. Often, the large shopping center serves as a community center—it attracts so many adults and teenagers that it is the place to see friends and acquaintances and to be seen. Many shopping center operators promote this tendency by providing rooms for community events and open space for displays, sales, etc. These operations may also hire professional entertainers—from puppet shows to wrestling bears—to give free shows in the mall, thus attracting people to the shops. In many ways, then, the shopping center functions as the community center.

Suburban shops quickly outpaced city retailers in competing for the retail dollar. At first the suburban retailers took all the growth in the metropolitan market; downtown stores did not lose dollar volume—they just stayed constant after 1950. Eventually, central-city retailing suffered an absolute decline. In Detroit, to take what may be an extreme example, downtown lost so much retail volume that major retailers like J. L. Hudson's finally closed their big main stores and continued operating exclusively in suburban shopping centers. On an aggregate level Table 12-3 shows that over a twenty-five-year period the oldest cities lost three-quarters of a million jobs in retailing while their suburbs gained well over 2 million jobs in retailing. Looking at all metropolitan areas combined, we see that while cities lost more than half a million retailing jobs, the suburbs added almost 4 million.

# SUBURBANIZATION AND THE NEW METROPOLITAN FORM

**TABLE 12-3**
Employment Changes in Central Cities and Suburban Rings (Adjusted for Annexation), 1947–1972

| Metropolitan characteristic | Number of SMSAs | Central city Mean | Central city Absolute | Suburbs Mean | Suburbs Absolute |
|---|---|---|---|---|---|
| | | Manufacturing | | | |
| **Size** | | | | | |
| Under 250,000 | 113 | 244 | 27,572 | 3,566 | 402,958 |
| 250,000–500,000 | 63 | −1,079 | −67,977 | 9,094 | 572,922 |
| 500,000–1 million | 36 | −6,289 | −226,404 | 18,872 | 679,392 |
| Over 1 million | 33 | −26,669 | −880,077 | 76,450 | 2,522,850 |
| **Inception date*** | | | | | |
| Before 1900 | 49 | −27,977 | −1,370,873 | 47,104 | 2,308,096 |
| 1900–1920 | 63 | 563 | 35,469 | 12,242 | 771,246 |
| 1920–1950 | 53 | 2,058 | 109,074 | 11,162 | 591,586 |
| After 1950 | 80 | 992 | 79,360 | 6,341 | 507,280 |
| **Region** | | | | | |
| Northeast | 42 | −18,346 | −770,532 | 16,252 | 682,584 |
| South | 98 | 3,221 | 315,658 | 11,896 | 1,165,808 |
| North central | 68 | −13,327 | −906,236 | 21,057 | 1,431,876 |
| West | 37 | 5,789 | 214,193 | 24,268 | 897,916 |
| Total | 245 | −4,681 | −1,146,845 | 17,054 | 4,178,230 |
| | | Retail | | | |
| **Size** | | | | | |
| Under 250,000 | 115 | 550 | 63,250 | 3,144 | 361,560 |
| 250,000–500,000 | 63 | 87 | 5,481 | 8,624 | 543,312 |
| 500,000–1 million | 36 | −2,225 | −80,100 | 17,961 | 646,596 |
| Over 1 million | 33 | −17,125 | −565,125 | 71,528 | 2,360,424 |
| **Inception date*** | | | | | |
| Before 1900 | 49 | −15,459 | −757,491 | 45,131 | 2,211,419 |
| 1900–1920 | 63 | 449 | 28,287 | 11,813 | 744,219 |
| 1920–1950 | 53 | 984 | 52,152 | 9,074 | 480,922 |
| After 1950 | 82 | 1,227 | 100,614 | 5,796 | 475,272 |
| **Region** | | | | | |
| Northeast | 42 | −9,098 | −382,116 | 17,522 | 735,924 |
| South | 99 | 626 | 61,974 | 12,014 | 1,189,386 |
| North central | 68 | −4,718 | −320,824 | 17,591 | 1,196,188 |
| West | 38 | 1,698 | 64,524 | 20,798 | 790,324 |
| Total | 247 | −2,334 | −576,498 | 15,837 | 3,911,739 |
| | | Wholesale | | | |
| **Size** | | | | | |
| Under 250,000 | 114 | 257 | 29,298 | 860 | 98,040 |
| 250,000–500,000 | 63 | 488 | 30,744 | 2,616 | 164,808 |
| 500,000–1 million | 36 | 184 | 6,624 | 6,970 | 250,920 |
| Over 1 million | 33 | −9,152 | −302,016 | 24,183 | 798,039 |

**TABLE 12-3**
Employment Changes in Central Cities and Suburban Rings (Adjusted for Annexation), 1947–1972 (*Continued*)

| Metropolitan characteristic | Number of SMSAs | Central city Mean | Central city Absolute | Suburbs Mean | Suburbs Absolute |
|---|---|---|---|---|---|
| Inception date* | | | | | |
| Before 1900 | 49 | −7,485 | −366,765 | 16,428 | 804,972 |
| 1900–1920 | 63 | 1,118 | 70,434 | 3,848 | 242,424 |
| 1920–1950 | 53 | 663 | 35,139 | 3,076 | 163,028 |
| After 1950 | 81 | 320 | 25,920 | 1,251 | 101,331 |
| Region | | | | | |
| Northeast | 42 | −5,236 | −219,912 | 8,007 | 336,294 |
| South | 98 | 679 | 66,524 | 4,178 | 409,444 |
| North central | 68 | −1,423 | −96,764 | 4,807 | 326,876 |
| West | 38 | 390 | 14,820 | 6,294 | 239,172 |
| Total | 246 | −956 | −235,176 | 5,332 | 1,311,672 |

*Date when city met present metropolitan criteria.
*Source:* Kasarda, 1978.

## Manufacturing, Wholesaling, and Warehousing

Just as residents and shops were decentralizing, other segments of the economy were also relocating in the suburbs. In the postwar era, companies stopped building new factories in the cities; they put them in the suburbs. Previously, central location had its advantages—proximity to railroad stations, to suppliers, and to ancillary industries; manufacturers operated effectively in multistory buildings. But when trucking displaced the railroad as the dominant mode of transportation and electricity displaced steam as a major form of energy, a new factory form arose. Manufacturers wanted single-story factories near major highways with plenty of room for employees to park their cars. The densely built city could not offer sufficiently large parcels of land, but the suburbs did. Old multistoried "loft" factory and warehouse buildings had become obsolete. Opportunities for expansion and modernization took industrialists out of the city. Furthermore, the rising fear of crime also provided an incentive for relocations. In the cities old factories were located in or near the poorer residential districts. Employers hesitated to bring employees into dangerous areas—or even to go there themselves.

Suburban manufacturing and wholesaling jobs also multiplied, as shown in Table 12-3. In the quarter-century in question, central cities lost more than 1.1 million manufacturing jobs! These same cities also lost almost a quarter-million wholesaling jobs. Simultaneously, the suburbs added more than 4.2 million jobs in manufacturing and 1.3 million in wholesaling. Not all these differences represent the actions of firms moving from cities to suburbs. New firms are always arising and old ones closing; in effect, all the new action was in the suburbs.

## Offices

Just as factories came to the suburbs, so, too, did their offices. At first suburbs just had locally oriented offices for their residents: real estate brokers, dentists, etc. Soon there were large office installations, often located near major expressways. Many large corporations moved whole divisions or even entire administrations to new suburban campuses. Like the modern factories, these had abundant employee parking, highly styled architecture and landscaped grounds, and employee amenities like cafeterias and lounges. Suburbs could compete with cities for these major offices. *The New York Times Magazine* has reported, "There are more large corporate headquarters in its suburbs than in New York City; Connecticut's Fairfield County is now second only to New York City nationally in the number of Fortune 500 corporations based there" (Kowinski, 1980, p. 19).

The suburbanization of work made an enormous impact upon commuting patterns. Originally, suburbs were conceived of as places from which people commuted to work in the city. Now that most industries have decentralized, though, workers travel from home to work without going to the city. "More than 70 percent of the suburban residents in the largest metropolitan areas work in the suburbs, too" (p. 19). A survey in New York's suburbs found that only 20 percent of the workers commuted into the central city. The rest worked in suburbs, although not necessarily in the one in which they lived (Kowinski, 1980). This is an enormously important fact: Now most people who live in suburbs do not commute to the city; they work in suburbs also.

Millions of white-collar jobs were created in suburbia as companies chose to build commodious "campuses" with parking and other amenities. Shown here is the office complex of the Martin Marietta corporation in Bethesda, Maryland. (Gwendolyn Stewart)

## Apartment Buildings

Surely the original suburban concept did not include apartment buildings—the image centered about a family in a detached house with a yard—but even the multiunit structure migrated to the suburbs. Between 1960 and 1970 the number of new dwelling units in multiunit structures (structures with two or more units) almost equaled the number of new single-family houses constructed (Zimmer, 1975). This trend continued in the next decade as well. New suburban apartment buildings were not like their traditional big-city counterparts, though. While the older ones were situated side by side along city streets, the suburban ones were built in complexes, arranged with lawns and parking areas. And while the city apartments were high-rise buildings, the suburban apartments were typically low-rise structures. Many suburban apartment complexes had additional facilities, such as swimming pools, self-service laundries, party rooms, nurseries, playgrounds, and the like, to be used by the residents in common. The complexes often had localized tenants' organizations and intensive social life (Choldin, 1980). Some projects were built exclusively for one segment of the housing market, like young singles or retired people. The increase in multiunit housing has begun to change one of the special features of American suburbanism by decreasing the proportion of homeowners and increasing the proportion of renters (Zimmer, 1975).

## Entertainment and "High Culture"

Popular culture and "high culture" are suburbanizing too. After restaurants and movie theaters, sports facilities followed suit. Traditionally, entertainment and cultural facilities were centrally located to maximize their accessibility to the whole metropolitan market and also to travelers in the CBD's hotels. The only exception might be facilities which needed considerable tracts of land, like race courses and sports fields, which were located peripherally, given the extent of the city when they were built. Recently, though, many of the new entertainment and sporting facilities are going to the suburbs. Suburbs are building civic facilities suitable for concerts. Orchestras are playing occasionally at suburban college campuses. Suburbanization has surrounded some of the older summer symphonic parks. Philanthropists are putting museums in suburbs. New convention centers and multipurpose stadiums for big-time basketball, hockey, and rock concerts are going up in some suburbs. And many major league teams are taking their games from city to suburb, or new teams start in suburban facilities. Consider for example, the football Giants, soccer Cosmos, and basketball Nets in their new stadiums in Meadowlands, New Jersey, and the former Los Angeles Rams and Angels, now in Anaheim in suburban Orange County. Not every suburb has a stadium and a concert hall; these facilities are usually located in *suburban minicities,* which are discussed later in the chapter.

**Summary** The importance of these decentralizing trends is not to be underestimated; they mean that everything the suburbanites need is present within the suburban belt. To a large extent the suburbs have become independent of their central city. Muller praises two scholars, Masotti and Hadden, for their early recognition of this independence. Masotti and Hadden referred to the "urbanization of the suburbs," defined as "the growing economic, cultural and political independence of suburbia" from the central city (cited in Muller, 1981, p. 8). Although even many suburbanites fail to recognize the new relationship between suburb and city, most of them do not commute to the city; they work in suburbia. Long ago they stopped shopping downtown and now, with the decentralization of sports and entertainment, suburbia provides for all the needs of its residents.

## DIFFERENTIATION AMONG SUBURBS

While critics once saw suburbia as a homogeneous spread of undifferentiated subdivisions, social research revealed that there is considerable variety within the suburban zone. Communities differ along several dimensions. In function, many are exclusively residential, others are mainly industrial, and still others have a combination. Some are old, others new; some are adjacent to the central city, others far from it. Some house families with young children; others house parents who have seen their children grow up and move away. Some conform to the upper-middle-class stereotype, while others are "middle middle," working class, or even poor. Suburbs even vary somewhat by ethnicity—there are suburbs with large numbers of Italian-Americans, Polish-Americans, Jews, blacks, etc.—but this subject has not yet been well researched. In sum, suburbia is a highly diversified zone, not the bland homogenized spread it was once seen to be.

### Work and Residence

Schnore, who conducted some of the earliest research on suburbanization, distinguished between suburbs which provided jobs for nonresidents and those which were primarily "dormitory towns," providing only a few jobs in small-scale retailing and services. Suburbs which provided jobs for their own residents and also for others were called "satellite cities." They were contrasted with residential suburbs, which are suppliers of labor and consumers of commodities. "Satellites are consumers of labor and suppliers of commodities" (Schnore, 1965b, p. 140). Sociologists developed a statistic called the "employment-residence ratio" to measure differences between dormitory towns and satellite cities. For each suburb, the ratio was computed by comparing the number of *workers* employed in manufacturing, retail and wholesale trade, and service jobs with the number of *residents* reporting the same types of jobs. "A high employment-residence ratio indicates that the suburb has more manufacturing, trade and service jobs than residents employed in those jobs; a low employment-residence ratio indicates a suburb that is primarily residential in function" (Stahura, 1979, p. 334). After conducting additional research, Schnore added a third type and changed the terminology.[2] "Employing" suburbs are those in which a high proportion of the workers commute in from other places; "residential" suburbs send away most of their employed residents each day to work elsewhere; and the new category is the intermediate, or "mixed," suburb, which has jobs for residents and has some inward commuting also.

In more recent research, one ecological sociologist has shown how suburbs evolve toward including more employment (Stahura, 1978). Looking at suburbs historically, he found that those which are currently employing had already had some jobs in the past. Many of the employing suburbs are fairly old, are located in the middle of the suburban zone (not adjacent to the city), and have been experiencing slow population growth. Over a thirteen-year period a number of "intermediate" suburbs added jobs and became employing communities. About half of those that started as strictly residential added jobs and became intermediate; the other half stayed residential (Stahura, 1979). The researcher, Stahura, emphasized that over time the functional role of a suburb may change.

## Other Differences

### Socioeconomic status

Although the majority are middle class, suburbs have a range of status levels. Every metropolitan area has at least one or two poor suburbs—places settled decades ago, along railroad sidings. Some housed railroad or factory workers, and these places often contained junkyards, stables, and other structures rejected by better areas. At the other end of the status continuum, of course, are the richest elite suburbs. Many of these are even "exurban," at the far edge of the suburban zone or beyond. Often these elite suburbs are zoned for very large lots, with 5- or 10-acre minimums; they have estates suitable for keeping horses. Intermediate between poor and rich suburbs are three other levels: working-class, middle-class, and upper-middle-class.

### Proximity and age

Suburbs vary by distance from the city. As in archaeology, the time of formation and growth is related to the location. The suburban zone may be conceived of as a series of rings around the city. *Adjacent* suburbs sharing a common border with the city form the inner ring. They tend to be the oldest suburbs. Beyond them

---

[2]Schnore conducted this research when it was necessary to measure the commuting at the intercounty level. More recent research has been able to examine work levels and commuting at the level of the individual suburb.

there is a gradation leading to the newest suburbs at the outermost edge of the suburban zone. The only exceptions to this tendency might be the few old elite suburbs which are also far from the city.

## Race and ethnicity

As noted in Chapter 8, blacks are following whites into the suburban zone. Black households do not scatter throughout the suburbs; they concentrate in particular locations. Like city neighborhoods, some suburbs are undergoing racial transition, becoming black suburbs. In others, particular subdivisions or sections are populated heavily or exclusively by blacks. In addition, some others are old, poor black suburbs.

Concentrations of immigrant nationality groups also occur, although they are not necessarily as clearly defined as the concentrations of blacks. In the process of neighborhood succession, each nationality usually went in one or two directions away from the city center. In the suburban era, these groups simply continued in the same direction. In Chicago, for example, Italian-Americans moved through a series of neighborhoods over the decades, always going west. Therefore, it comes as no surprise that some western suburbs have concentrations of Italian-American households. These suburbs have Catholic churches with an Italian flavor, as well as numerous Italian-oriented businesses: restaurants, bakeries, morticians, and realtors. Likewise, Polish-Americans, as their incomes and occupations improved, moved into newer neighborhoods, going toward the northwest. Now suburbs with Polish-American concentrations (plus their churches, institutions, and businesses) are to be found in the northwest sector. And the Jewish population followed the same pattern, moving north so the suburbs with Jewish concentrations are in that direction. Needless to say, there are *no* exclusively Italian-American, Polish-American, or Jewish suburbs; each community has a mix of peoples. But if you want good pasta, try Melrose Park, and if you want a good bagel, your chances are better in Lincolnwood.

Suburban ethnicity has been difficult to measure because the Census Bureau's only questions about nationality asked people if they or their parents were born in a foreign country and if so, which. By the time of heavy suburbanization, first- and second-generation immigrants were dead or dying off. Thus the decennial censuses told very little about suburban ethnicity. The 1980 census included new questions which asked individuals to say how they identified themselves ethnically. When the results from these questions are analyzed, they may show the extent and location of suburban ethnic enclaves.

## CHANGE AND STABILITY

Several studies in the late 1970s tried to determine the extent to which suburbs change over time. Two conflicting schools of thought emerged, one emphasizing the social stability of suburbs and the other contending that they change and evolve over the course of decades.

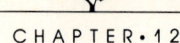

The first theory, emphasizing stability, said that a suburb's social status is more or less fixed from the start, staying constant over time (Farley, 1964; Guest, 1978). When the suburb is started, those who subdivide the land determine whether the lots are large or small and early investors set the pattern of house sizes and styles. Furthermore, the early years show who will be the first settlers. So if a suburb is first built of small houses on small lots and occupied by working-class or lower-middle-class families, such a community cannot change its status very far upward— it has neither the amenities nor the cachet for higher classes. On the other hand, a suburb of large estates which attracts the gentry from the start is unlikely to sink afterward. Farley (1964), who introduced this stability theory, correlated the socioeconomic characteristics of suburbs from 1920 to 1960 and demonstrated that a place's characteristics in the early years were likely to correlate highly with its characteristics thirty or forty years later. Many examples testify to the enduring statuses of certain suburbs, some cited already in this volume. Philadelphia's Main Line suburbs have retained their prestige for more than a century just as St. Louis's Kinloch has remained near the bottom of the status hierarchy.

Apparently, however, there is a limited amount of change among the midrange suburbs. Looking at a panel of suburbs in the New York metropolitan area (Nassau and Suffolk counties) over a ten-year period, Collver and Semyonov (1979) found some movement in income and educational status. Suburbs tended to be more stable in occupational status.

A second study of change examined suburbs in the Chicago urbanized area over a thirty-year period, from 1940 to 1970 (Choldin, Hanson, & Bohrer, 1980). This study applied an old theory to the suburbs—the neighborhood life cycle. The status of young suburbs tends to rise, apparently because of the age of the young "settlers"; a newly developing suburb may attract young families with high educational and occupational status but relatively low incomes because they are early in their professional careers. After a period of rising status, a suburb hits its peak, and thereafter it is likely to lose status, relative to other suburbs and to newly emerging suburbs.

Also emphasizing change rather than stability, Stahura has conducted research which shows increasing employment in many suburbs resulting in shifts in type. He found large numbers of suburbs increasing in their amount of local employment. Many were shifting from residential to intermediate, while others were changing from intermediate to employing. Surprisingly, suburbs throughout the status hierarchy were adding employment; socioeconomic status was not related to shifting functional role. "One possible reason," Stahura (1978) wrote, "for the lack of resistance [to local employment] may be that a substantial portion of the decentralizing employment activities are of a type which is compatible with residential uses ... e.g., central offices for industries and businesses, warehousing and distribution centers, and large retailing centers such as shopping centers" (p. 78). In other words, if developers and corporations are going to erect architecturally handsome, well-landscaped office complexes, or even factories, and if they are sufficiently segregated from residential areas, suburban citizens are unlikely to oppose them, particularly as the new establishments will absorb some of the local tax burden which otherwise would fall entirely upon the homeowners.

All the recent studies conclude that suburbia is clearly and highly stratified. Logan (1978) has proposed a theory to account for suburban stratification. He argues that wealthier suburbs are able to compete successfully for higher-status migrants, taking advantage of zoning mechanisms for excluding the poor. Such suburbs also capitalize on the communities' tax resources and social reputation to maintain their high status (Logan & Schneider, 1981). Logan contends that political, business, and industrial interests control development trends and decisions in suburbia. Their actions, in combination with ecological factors, yield a stratification of places. The dominant type of suburb has a high-status population plus an industrial-commercial base. This type of suburb establishes good municipal services and institutes restrictive zoning early in its history. It also controls bank investments in the area—thus it controls who lives there and even influences what happens nearby in the suburban zone.

In sum, the literature on stability and change shows that although some suburbs retain their socioeconomic status over long periods, there is some flux in the system. Stability theory is supported by the long-term status retention of elite and poor suburbs and by some studies of correlations between "early" and "late" statuses. Considerable change is seen in the functional roles of suburbs as more and more of them go from just residential to the intermediate or employing types. Neighborhood life cycle theory has been advanced as a way to explain change in socioeconomic status among suburbs. Logan's newer sociopolitical theory explains how top-ranking suburbs dominate the development of other communities in the vicinity within a stratification of places.

## EMERGING METROPOLITAN STRUCTURE

The concentric zones model of urban growth and form (presented in Chapter 4) was designed to explain the mature industrial city but fails to explain today's suburbanized metropolis. The real-world conditions which gave rise to Burgess's theory have changed considerably.

The concentric circles in Burgess's model all surrounded a dominant city center, but today's center is no longer dominant. Many cities' central business districts have declined severely; others are surviving; but all must compete with suburbs for office and retailing functions. The European immigrants who played a prominent role in the city of the 1920s have been succeeded by their own more assimilated children and grandchildren who have moved away from the city center. Blacks, Hispanics, and immigrants from other continents have replaced them. More broadly, the older central cities have declined in competition with the young, growing, more vigorous suburbs. Indeed, the suburban population absolutely outnumbers that of the city. What sort of sociospatial model can help explain the emerging metropolis?

As early as 1945, Harris and Ullman proposed a *multinuclear* model, which with contemporary modifications helps portray the social geography of today's metropolis. The key ideas of this model were presented in Chapter 6.[3]

## The Modified Multinuclear Model

### Basic concepts

The suburbanized metropolis is giving rise to a new model of spatial structure which builds upon older concepts and adds a couple of newer ones as well. The new model is basically an expansion of the multinuclear model, viewing the metropolis as a large agglomeration which is divided into differentiated districts which have nodal points. The concepts of zone and sector also apply to the contemporary metropolis, although the zones refer to family rather than to socioeconomic status. The suburban minicity (Muller, 1981) is a new element, though, representing a major nucleus in the suburban zone. Urban realms (Vance, 1964, 1977) is another new concept, referring to the fact that the metropolis may now be so large as to be divisible into very large areas which are somewhat separate. These ideas will be explained in the following sections, starting with a look at Los Angeles as the prototypical multinucleated metropolis.

### Los Angeles as the prototype

Los Angeles represents the prime example of multinucleation. Although Los Angeles has often been called a place without a center or an agglomeration of suburbs, it has always had a center (Banham, 1971). Situated at the intersection of main railroad lines, downtown Los Angeles had the main railroad station, city hall, office buildings, and other accoutrements of a typical big city's center. In an earlier transportation era, the intraurban street railroads converged downtown, and now the famous freeways—the Hollywood, Santa Monica, Santa Ana, San Bernardino, Harbor, Long Beach, Pomona, and Pasadena freeways—converge and form a loop around it. In addition to a CBD, Los Angeles has at least one of each of the other types of areas. The suburban San Bernardiono Valley can be classified as medium-class residential. East Los Angeles, with its Mexican barrio, and areas south of the CBD, including Watts, a black ghetto, qualify as poor residential. Beverly Hills, Bel Air, and Westwood are high-class residential. Beverly Hills, with its elite shops and office buildings, also qualifies as an outlying business district. Westwood is another

---

[3]Students should review pages 177–181 at this point.

nodal place, including the campus of the University of California at Los Angeles (UCLA). Los Angeles International Airport is a nucleus for offices and other aviation-related businesses. One heavy industrial district follows a rail-highway corridor running southeast from the center. Long Beach has another industrial district, combined with a major ocean port. Thus metropolitan Los Angeles has a number of nuclei.

## Suburban Minicities

The suburban minicity is a major new type of nucleus. According to Muller, it is a multiple-purpose center which has emerged since 1970 (Muller, 1981). (Therefore, it could not have been included in the initial multinuclear model.) A suburban minicity has a major concentration of retailing, employment, entertainment, and other activities formerly found only downtown. Increasingly, suburban minicities rival the CBDs. A typical suburban minicity has a very large regional shopping center and a good deal of additional retailing in smaller shopping complexes or in "strip" development. Ancillary to the mall will be office buildings and apartment buildings, plus hotels, restaurants, and other facilities which may accommodate visitors, conventions, and other events. Minicities also have entertainment facilities like health clubs, supper-club theaters, bowling alleys, etc. Some minicities also have other nonoffice employment.

Muller, cites King of Prussia, Pennsylvania (20 miles northwest of central Philadelphia), as a prime example (see Figure 12-2).

> At the nucleus of the complex is King of Prussia Plaza, the metropolitan area's second largest superregional shopping mall, which contains 1.8 million square feet of selling space, six major department stores ... and 200 smaller shops. Distributed about the vicinity within a 5-minute drive of the mall are dozens of highway-oriented retail facilities, including two community shopping centers; one of the region's largest industrial park complexes (over 750 acres), containing the plants and warehouses of Western Electric, GM-Chevrolet, Sears, Borg-Warner, Philco-Ford, three major pharmaceutical manufacturers, and 30 smaller companies; one of General Electric's leading research and manufacturing facilities; a variety of office parks and buildings ... the Valley Forge Music Fair, a year-round theater offering top-name entertainers weekly; five first-run cinemas; at least a dozen fine restaurants; one of the area's best-known cabarets; numerous superior quality high- and low-rise apartment complexes; and six large motor hotels. (1981, p. 163)

A minicity is always near at least one major expressway, and all the facilities are endowed with parking spaces numbered in the hundreds or thousands. Unfortunately, as Muller notes, the overall complex is almost never planned, so the different elements are designed and sited separately. There is no coordination among them; they are scattered about, the user must drive from one element to another. King of Prussia is only one example—suburban belts throughout the country have

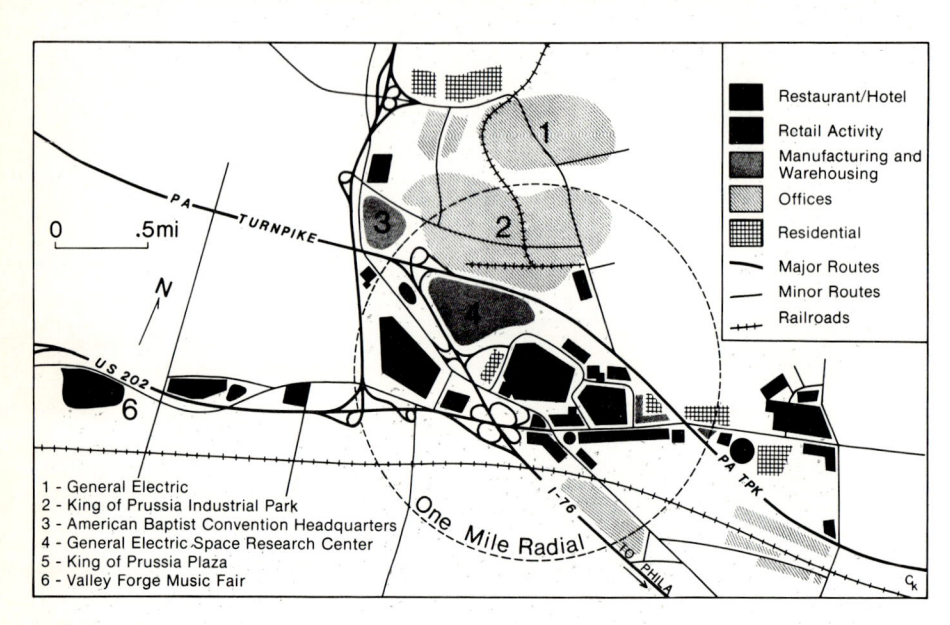

**FIGURE 12-2**
Activity areas in a suburban minicity: King of Prussia, Pennsylvania. (Source: Muller, 1982.)

minicities. Edina, in metropolitan Minneapolis, and Schaumburg, near Chicago, have many of the same elements as King of Prussia.

Suburban minicities often form around large airports. Chicago's O'Hare International is such a nucleus. Within a couple of miles' radius it has nearly 50 hotels with over 7500 guest rooms, a convention center, and a major enclosed stadium suitable for professional basketball and rock concerts (Muller, 1981). It even has what used to be part of the "zone in transition's" demimonde: strip joints and prostitution. There are other job-producing facilities in the vicinity as well: office buildings, warehousing associated with airfreight and the nearby railroad yards, and light manufacturing. With all the hotels and ancillary facilities it has become common to organize large conventions or smaller meetings at O'Hare hotels. Visitors fly in from all over the country, and they may complete their visit without getting near the center of Chicago. Dallas–Fort Worth's large, modern airport was actually planned to be the nodal point for development. It has already attracted the corporate headquarters of American Airlines and a number of other corporations (Muller, 1981).

Incorporating the suburban minicity into the multinuclear model, we have a better conception of the contemporary metropolis. Muller's model is somewhat simpler than Harris and Ullman's and he calls it the "polycentric city," but essentially it represents their multinuclear metropolis, with the addition of minicities and a new name (see Figure 12-3).

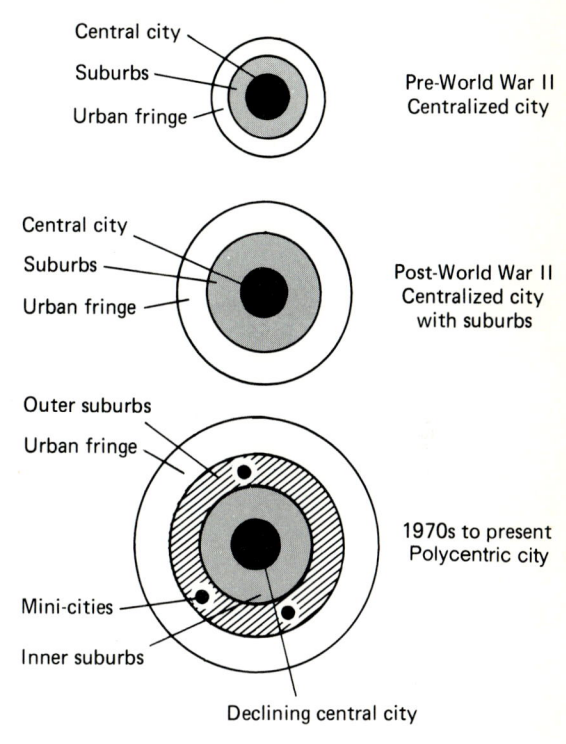

**FIGURE 12-3**
Emerging structure of the American metropolis.
(Source: Redrawn from Muller, 1982.)

## Urban Realms

The suburban belt of any large metropolis appears to be divided into realms. Even though the expressways diminish the friction of space to a large degree, people still minimize their travel costs. Thus they are likely to travel to the nearest regional shopping center rather than to one further away. Similarly, in a job search within the suburban belt they are likely to prefer a job nearer, rather than farther from, their residence. The aggregate effect of suburbanites' minimizing their travel times tends to divide the overall suburban belt into two or more realms in any large metropolitan area.

The concept of urban realm has not yet been defined precisely or operationally. An urban realm is a large "chunk" of a metropolitan area. For example, as large a metropolis as Los Angeles is considered to have six realms (see Figure 12-4). Aside from the city's CBD, each realm has at least one suburban minicity. A realm is defined by the propensity of its residents to carry out their economic activities within the realm. The division of a metropolitan area into realms is influenced by four factors: the overall physical size and terrain of the metropolitan area, its

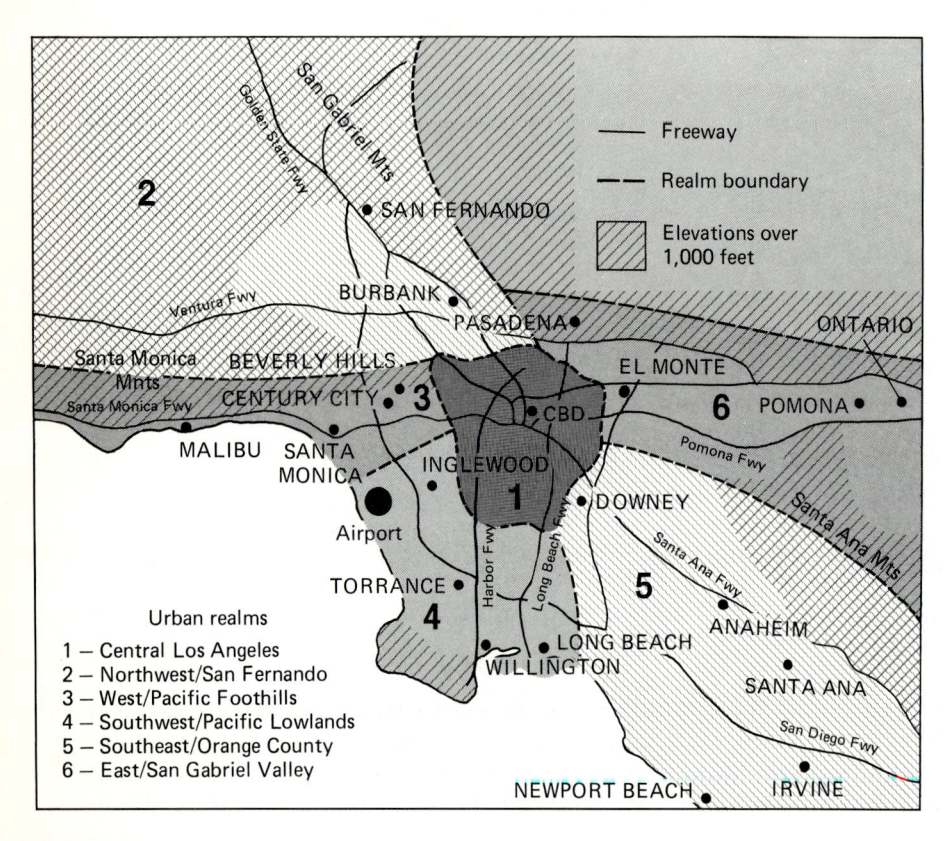

**FIGURE 12-4**
The urban realms of metropolitan Los Angeles. (Source: Redrawn from Muller, 1982.)

regional transportation network, and the internal regionalization of economic activity. The first factor suggests that the larger the metropolis, the more realms it has. The second factor suggests that particular physical features like rivers and mountains are likely to influence people's travel patterns and the division of the metropolis into smaller chunks. The third (which makes the definition somewhat circular) suggests that economic activity and travel patterns fall together and create these subsections of metropolitan areas. As Muller writes, the internal coherence of a realm "derives from its residents' utilizing economically important places within that realm rather than metropolitan-level centers outside it" (1981, p. 9). If the area is a realm, its residents are more likely to conduct their economic activities within it rather than going elsewhere. The fourth factor is the transportation system; "intrarealm ease of movement is essential, particularly toward its activity centers. Interaccessibility among suburban realms is also vital, especially circumferential links and direct airport connectors that no longer require [suburban residents] to turn to the central realm in order to reach other outlying realms and distant metropolises (Muller, 1981, p. 9).

While geographers have not yet established a precise method for dividing a metropolitan map into realms, two examples have been delineated. After studying the San Francisco Bay Area, Vance (1964, 1977) concluded that it falls into six realms. Mostly separated by bodies of water or hills, they are the city of San Francisco; eastern San Mateo County; Santa Clara Valley; eastern Marin County and adjacent parts of Sonoma County; industrial realm of Oakland and environs; and a group of valleys east of the Berkeley Hills. Similarly, Muller has divided metropolitan Los Angeles into half a dozen realms (see Figure 12-4). Vance suggests that other cities could also be divided into realms. He sees the Boston area falling into several realms: some surrounding a handful of older cities including Boston, Cambridge, and Somerville and also three major suburban areas.

## An Overlay Model

Expanded to include suburban minicities and realms, the multinuclear model begins to help us understand the structure of the contemporary metropolis. In addition, a return to the concepts of concentric zones, sectors, and segregation provides more leverage with which to comprehend the emerging metropolis.

A new model known as an "overlay" model has been proposed which integrates these three concepts. One element of the model consists of concentric zones with the CBD in the middle and the most distant suburbs at the perimeter. This is not Burgess's social-class-based model, though, it is Anderson and Egeland's (presented in Chapter 7). The zones are differentiated by household type, with the highest concentration of nonfamily households at the center and the highest concentration of families with children in the newer suburbs at the periphery. The second element of the model is sectorial, representing the distribution of socioeconomic status over space (see Figure 12-5A). As shown by Anderson and Egeland's research, this overlay conforms to the distribution in at least four SMSAs in the United States. Analysis of metropolitan Toronto shows the same overlay patterns there as well (see Figure 12-6). Toronto has small families and households in the city center with increasing familism toward the suburban periphery; thus familism is concentrically zonal. The city is divided into five socioeconomic sectors (also shown in the figure). Running east along the lakeshore is a low-status sector and a second low-status sector runs to the southwest along the lakeshore. A high-status sector runs north from the CBD. Another low-status sector runs to the northwest, a second high-status sector to the west. The overlay suggests that the city is divided into chunks differentiated by SES and familism. Adjacent to the CBD on the north, for example, there is a chunk with low SES and small households. Far to the west there is a chunk with high SES and familistic households. To complete the overlay model, several geographers add a third element: race and ethnicity.

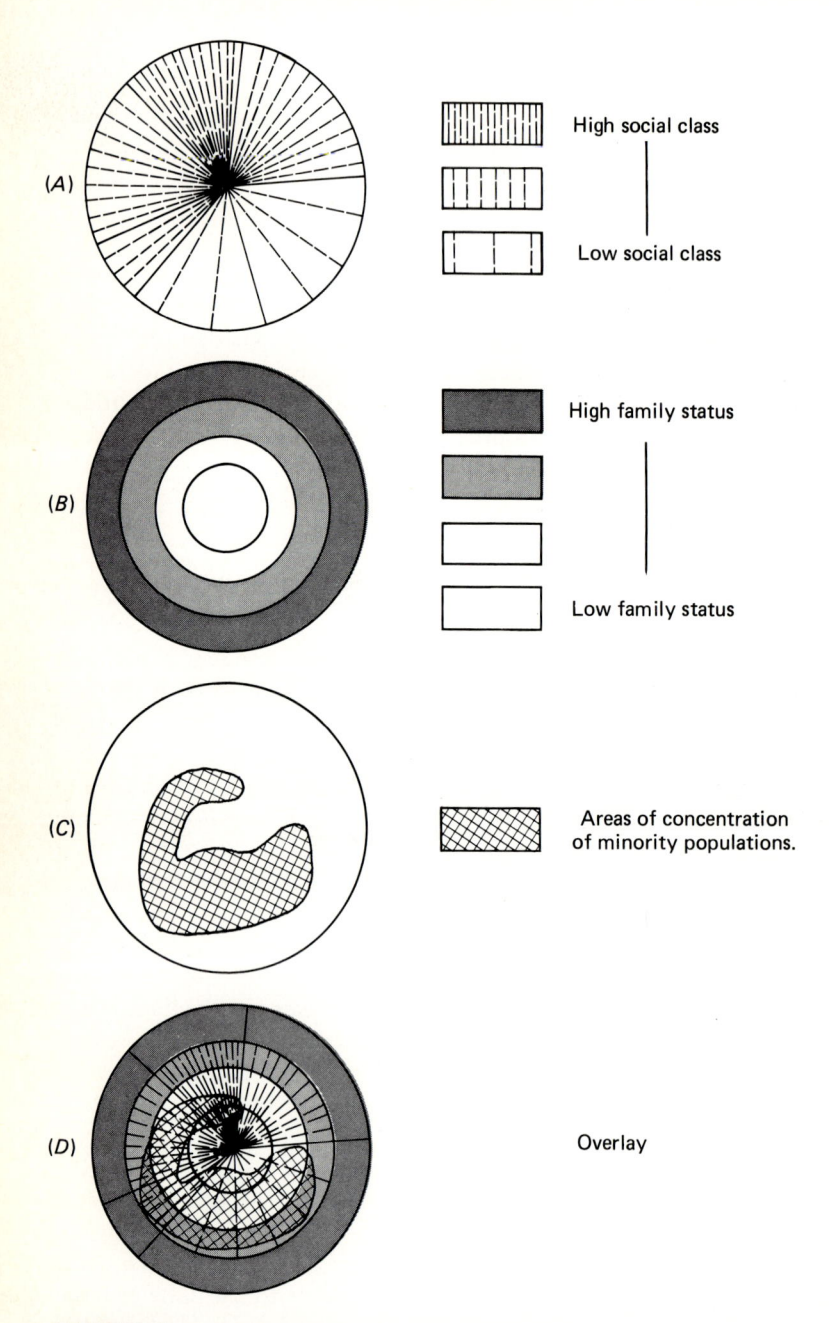

**FIGURE 12-5**
An overlay model of the metropolis. A generalized spatial arrangement of indexes of *(A)* social class, *(B)* family status, *(C)* segregation, and *(D)* an overlay of the three. (Source: Yeates and Garner, 1980, p. 267; based on Berry, 1965.)

# SUBURBANIZATION AND THE NEW METROPOLITAN FORM

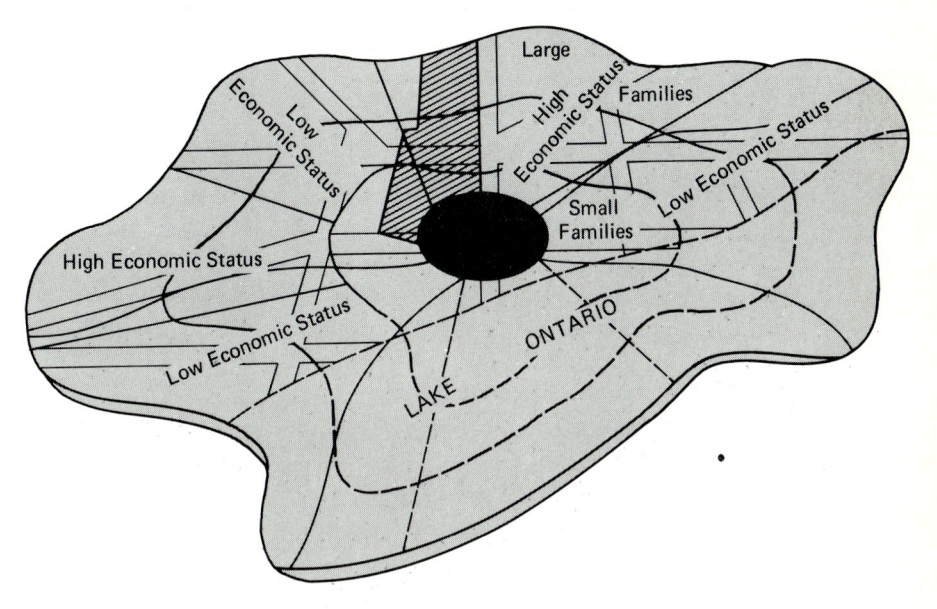

**FIGURE 12-6**
Social space in metropolitan Toronto. This is a specific example of an overlay, as shown in Figure 12-6. (Source: Yeates & Garner, 1980, p. 268; based on Murdie, 1969.)

Patterns of racial and ethnic distribution, more than those of socioeconomic or family status, tend to be products of historical accidents, so they are not located as predictably as familism and SES. When Chicago's slums were parceled out to different immigrant groups a hundred years ago, why did the Sicilians get the one near the Gold Coast while Polish immigrants got one to the northwest of the Loop? Segregated areas, such as black ghettos or Hispanic barrios, in addition to being located in happenstance fashion, may also have peculiar shapes and may overlap zonal and sectorial lines. This, too, is illustrated in the Toronto example. In this instance mapmakers show the location of Jews, one of Toronto's many ethnic groups. Note that one portion of the Jewish population lives near the CBD in a low-SES, nonfamilistic chunk of the city; presumably these are some of the older households. The rest live in the high-SES sector, in the nonfamilistic zone, or out in the familistic suburbanized area.

Building on Berry's original conception of an overlay model, geographers Yeates and Garner (1980) have diagramed the full overlay (in Figure 12-5D). Their generalized map has the initial overlay of family status and SES with an additional overlay of race and ethnicity upon it.

Ultimately, a full model of the contemporary metropolis will combine this overlay with the multinuclear, urban realms, and suburban minicities model. Imagine Figure 12-5D with two or three black dots for minicities, and you will have a sketch of the comprehensive model. A fuller elaboration of that conception will have to await further research and theorizing, though.

## SUMMARY

Suburbanization was a fundamental change in metropolitan communities after World War II. A shift so great that more people now live in suburbs than in central cities or rural areas. American suburbs represent a new form of urban development. Previous urban communities always maximized population density and intensity of land use, but suburbs, within a detached house and yard for every family, represent the first low-density urban development.

There have been four periods of suburban growth, but the greatest expansion occurred in the postwar period. In the second period, the electric streetcar and railroad era (1880s to 1920), two sorts of suburbs were established: middle-class streetcar suburbs and upper-class suburbs at railroad stations. Railroads placed stations in "strings" outside major cities, and elite suburbs formed around them. The most recent period, the freeway era, is based upon widespread automobile ownership. Suburban growth in this period was spurred by a major housing shortage in the 1940s which was alleviated by federal programs (FHA and VA) to help builders and buyers. Large builders developed systems to mass-produce suburban houses cheaply.

In recent decades all sorts of urban institutions and facilities have been established in the suburban zone in a process known as the urbanization of the suburbs. Retailing was the first, being established as soon as new subdivisions arose. Shopping centers with parking lots produced an efficient and popular form of retail distribution. Developers built larger and larger shopping centers and malls, taking all the growth in retail sales, while downtown retail areas remained constant or declined. After retailing came the suburbanization of manufacturing, wholesaling, and warehousing. None of these industries could expand in the old city environment: They needed space for single-story factories and parking lots, plus access to high-speed expressways. Even large corporate offices were built in suburbs. These developments created millions of new jobs in the suburbs, thereby changing them fundamentally. Formerly, by definition, suburbanites were assumed to commute to the city to work; now the large majority of suburbanites work in the suburban zone.

There are major differences among suburbs; they vary by proximity and age, function, socioeconomic status, and race and ethnicity. The suburban zone is divided into rings: The close-in suburbs, adjacent to the city, form one ring of the oldest communities. Farther out are the suburbs established in the 1950s, with the newest developments at the metropolitan periphery. The adjacent suburbs have older populations, while the peripheral ones have more young families. Contrary to the image of middle-class homogeneity, suburbs vary in SES; there are working-class, middle-class, and upper-class ones, with gradations in between.

# SUBURBANIZATION AND THE NEW METROPOLITAN FORM

Massive suburbanization along with changes in the cities are yielding a new macrometropolitan structure. The CBD survives, but it no longer dominates as in the mature industrial city; the new metropolis has several centers—it is multinucleated. There is a new type of center, the suburban minicity, usually consisting of a superregional shopping mall plus hotels, office buildings, condominium apartment buildings, entertainment facilities, industrial parks, etc. An emerging metropolitan model combines spatial patterns of socioeconomic status, familism, and racial and ethnic distributions. While it is far from being perfected, it will be much more complex than the concentric zones model.

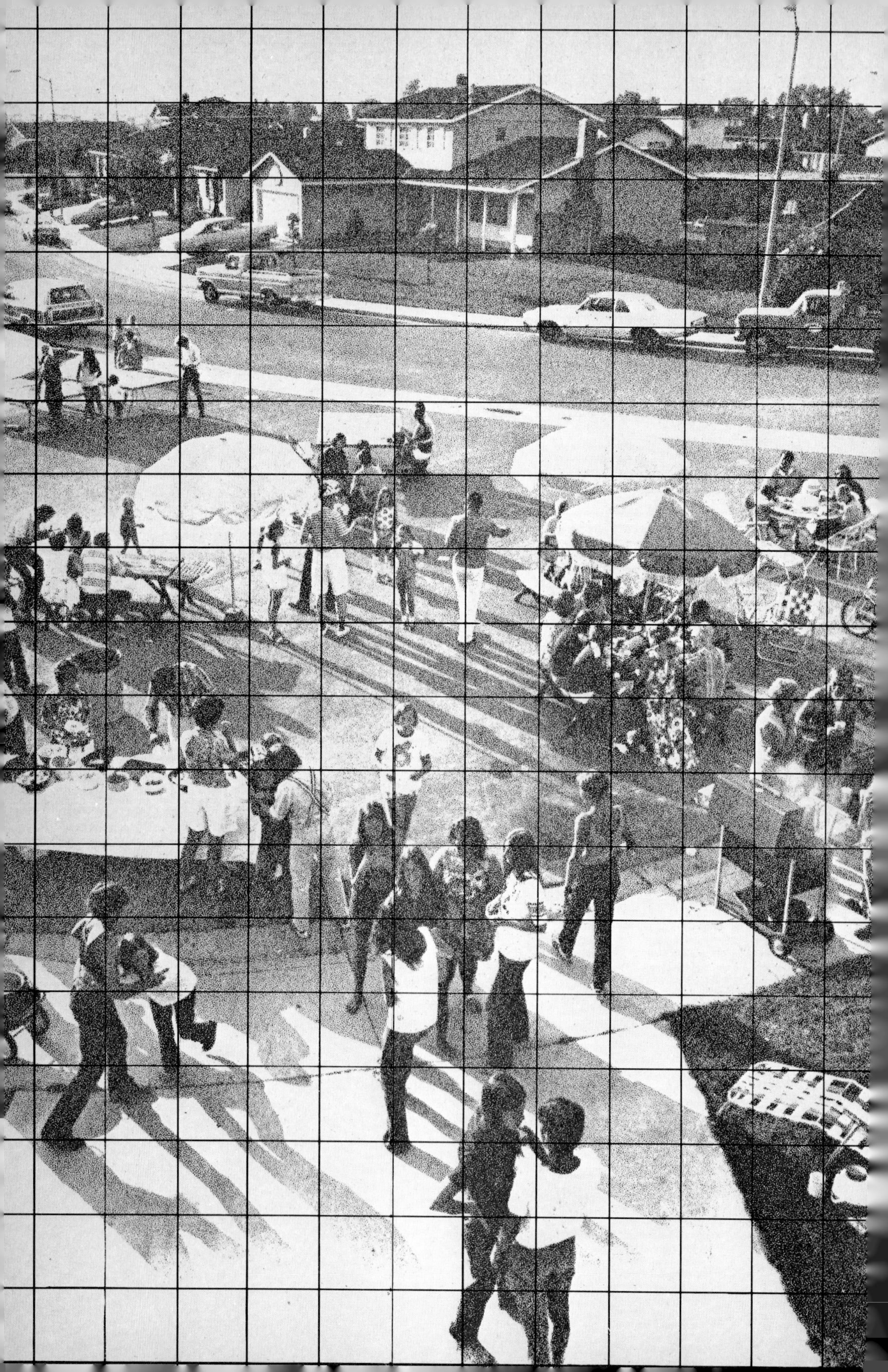

# CHAPTER · 13

## Suburban Social Life

### Chapter Outline

THE SUBURBAN MYTH
  Urban Imagery
  Images of the Suburbs
FIRST-GENERATION SOCIOLOGICAL STUDIES
  Early Research Projects
- *The Organization Man*
- *Crestwood Heights*
- Neighboring in city and suburb

  Later Studies
- *Working-Class Suburb*
- *The Levittowners*

  Summary

RECENT SUBURBAN RESEARCH
  Suburban Location: A Matter of Choice
  Suburbanism as a Way of Life
  Differences among Suburbanites
- The "characteristic Levittown household"
- Teenagers
- Feminist concerns

NEW PROBLEMS
  Aging: "The Graying of Suburbia"
  Problems and Challenges

SUMMARY

## THE SUBURBAN MYTH

### Urban Imagery

Each of us carries innumerable mental images of all sorts of things, including places and lifestyles; this is an aspect of urban social psychology. "Urban imagery" refers to the pictures we hold of particular places, sometimes in "symbolic shorthand," like having the Golden Gate Bridge stand for San Francisco or having a big apple stand for New York City. We develop such images because an individual mind cannot perceive an urban community as a whole—it is far too large, diverse, and complex. Not even one metropolis can be seen entirely, and we have already learned that hundreds of them exist. Therefore, we encapsulate them into images. In American culture, we have long maintained a generalized antiurban image, negatively evaluating cities, especially in comparison with small, rural communities, which are seen as morally and environmentally superior.

These images, made up in large part of subjective evaluative elements, are not necessarily *true* in any scientific sense. Thus it is not necessarily true that small towns are better than a metropolis. Nonetheless, urban imagery sets the conceptual field for the ways we think about communities; often, the imagery suggests the key questions of interest about communities. In recent decades, the "suburban myth" has surfaced as a dominant urban image; whether or not it is true—and the purpose of this chapter is to show that it is not—it has been very popular and has inspired much of the research about suburban social life.

### Images of the Suburbs

When massive suburbanization sprang onto the national scene, American intellectuals were fascinated, not to say revolted, by its lifestyle. Writers, from novelists to sociologists, produced a suburban myth (Berger, 1961/1971; Donaldson, 1969; Popenoe, 1977) which they promulgated in movies and novels, on television, and in weighty essays. Consider the titles of some of the novels published in the 1950s: *The Man in the Gray Flannel Suit* (1955) conjures up the image of commuting and conformity; *No Down Payment,* (1957) *The Crack in the Picture Window,* (1957) and *The Split-Level Trap* (1961) make fun of the housing and the new residential architecture of the day. The last two titles suggest something amiss in the new land. The suburban myth emphasized the similarity of housing—a standard cartoon and television joke portrayed a man lost in a subdivision, trying to find his house among all the look-alikes or entering another identical to his own. Mythmaker-critics bemoaned the bulldozing of the countryside for residential development and the mass production of similar houses. They saw ugliness in the treeless new developments and derided the suburbanites' consumption patterns in the new communities, epitomized by the barbecue grill, power lawn mower, and television set, as well as by the station wagon and martini.

The new lifestyle looked very unattractive in suburban myth. The consumption patterns and housing implied heavy conformity among suburbanites; they bought the same things and lived the same way. Critics also pointed to familism as a new way of life—suburbanites were seen as child-centered, giving up adult interests to do things for and with their children, from putting up a swing set in the backyard to supervising the ubiquitous Little League, Girl Scout, school, and PTA activities. One popular writer said America had become afflicted with "momism," a disease in which the all-powerful middle-class mother was running everybody's life. A popular periodical, *McCall's,* advertised itself as "the magazine of togetherness." The myth said suburban people were devoted to social mobility—they were on the way up and would stay in their suburb only until the male was promoted in his organization and became able to afford a higher-status suburb (or until he was transferred to a distant branch of the company, in which case the household would move to another suburb). The myth also said familism went together with a return to the church, noting that the new suburbanites were erecting record numbers of new churches in their communities. (Where else would they put them?) Finally, the suburban myth, noting the traditional republicanism in old suburbs and the heavy suburban vote for Dwight Eisenhower in the 1950 election, said suburbanism would make people become Republicans.

In sum, the suburban myth painted a nasty picture of the emerging social scene:

> The bulk of {it} ... was highly critical of suburban life. A move to the suburbs was alleged to foster overconformity, hyperactivity, anti-individualism, conservatism, momism, dullness and boredom, and status seeking, as well as a host of specified psychological and social ills including alcoholism, sexual promiscuity, and mental illness... The suburbs were portrayed as a kind of national scandal. (Popenoe, 1977, p. 3)

Perhaps the most fundamental social theme of the suburban myth was that the way of life, based upon familism, fostered a pervasive conformity which, allegedly, would produce great homogeneity.

Unfortunately, the suburban myth has shown remarkable staying power; it is still with us. For example, a popular song by Malvina Reynolds recorded by Pete Seeger refers to "little boxes made of ticky-tacky ... little boxes all the same," peopled by doctors, lawyers, and executives, whose pretty children go to summer camp and college and "all look just the same" (Reynolds, 1964, p. 28).

Furthermore, American suburbs exhibit a sense of "placelessness." The national style of residential architecture is so pervasive that one can see a California ranch house in Birmingham, Michigan, as well as in San Jose, and one can see a green-shuttered Cape Cod house in Austin, Texas, as well as in Massachusetts. Artificial plantation-style columns are as common adorning Illinois houses as Mississippi ones. Furthermore, many of the chains which build facilities in suburbs, from MacDonald's to K-Mart, use a common architectural style across the nation. And television, especially in the production of family-based situation comedies, creates generalized suburban locales, although more often than not they resemble Los Angeles.

## FIRST-GENERATION SOCIOLOGICAL STUDIES

In the 1960s sociologists began to respond to the suburban myth. Using sociological tools, they went to collect some facts from the new communities in an attempt to discover whether suburbs really made people change their ways of life. They asked, "What effects—if any—do suburbs have on their residents?" A series of research reports offered answers to this question and broadened the question as well. Three of the earliest studies, by Whyte, Seeley, and Fava, began the empirical exploration of the suburbs.

### Early Research Projects

### The Organization Man

William Whyte, a writer for *Fortune* magazine, wrote one of the most influential early studies, entitled *The Organization Man* (1956). As part of a larger inquiry into the new careers of young men who joined large national corporations after World War II, Whyte visited Park Forest, Illinois, a "typical" suburb where such individuals might live. About 30 miles south of Chicago's CBD, Park Forest was built *de novo* by a single developer; it was a fully planned community, complete with houses, apartments and townhouses, central shopping center, community facilities, etc. Whyte discovered that during the daytime, when the adult males were all working elsewhere, it became a community of women. Indeed, this fact impeded his fieldwork because gossip followed after he conducted an interview in a house or apartment. He discovered a forced sociability. In apartment and townhouse courtyards, they were expected to leave their doors open to neighbors; if another woman entered the dwelling, she was to be accepted for a period of conversation. A kaffeeklatsch took place each day, and every woman was expected to attend. Anyone violating these norms was considered to be standoffish, but a few women resented not having any rights to privacy. Whyte discovered a familistic way of life, in which the young couples devoted a great proportion of their discretionary time to activities with their children. Furthermore, although the couples had already achieved suburban residence and middle-class status, they viewed themselves as temporary residents, passing through Park Forest on their way to something better. The men expected to receive promotions or higher incomes, and they and their spouses intended to move to more prestigious suburbs. They viewed themselves as upwardly mobile.

### Crestwood Heights

*Crestwood Heights: A Study of the Culture of Suburban Life* (Seeley, Sim, & Loosely, 1956) was another influential study. Located at the outer fringes of a large Canadian city and hidden behind a pseudonym, Crestwood Heights was older and richer than Park Forest. John Seeley and a team of colleagues and assistants studied the community almost like cultural anthropologists, describing the houses, habits, and institutions of its inhabitants in minute detail. This community was filled with status-defining and status-conferring features. People needed considerable wealth to afford to live in this area, and they used the exterior and interior style of their houses to exhibit their wealth and taste; exclusive clubs in the community also conferred high status upon their members. Households in Crestwood Heights were not aiming for the next-better suburb—they had arrived. Nonetheless, newcomers engaged in considerable social climbing to join the "right" cliques and clubs. Children were carefully socialized to acceptable modes of behavior through motherly supervision, school activities, and summer camps. Altogether, Seeley et al.'s picture of this suburb shows a straightjacket of behavior conformity to a culture that emphasized materialism and status display.

### Neighboring in city and suburb

The third early study began the systematic comparison of city and suburban social life. The suburban myth implied that suburbs are really different from cities and that individuals act differently in suburbs. Fava (1959), the author of the third study, tested this idea, asking whether more neighboring occurs in suburbs, as the myth suggests. Unlike the authors of the two previously cited books, Fava did not conduct a case study of a particular suburb; she designed a sample survey to compare city with suburban life. Working in New York City's metropolitan area, she studied social life in three different sorts of areas: densely settled Manhattan, where almost everyone lives in apartment buildings; an outer-city area in the borough of Queens; and the suburbs of Nassau County. She attempted to hold constant some major social factors: race, sex, age, marital status, education, etc. In her survey she measured the amount of contact individuals had with their neighbors, and she discovered clear behavioral differences among the areas. Central-city residents were least likely to engage in neighboring; suburbanites were most likely. Central-city residents got lower neighboring scores; suburban residents got higher scores. Outer-city residents were intermediate but somewhat closer to the suburbanites. This is not to say that the city people did not engage in neighboring; most of them did, but at a lower level of intensity than the suburban individuals. Thus Fava demonstrated that there was measurably more local social life in the suburbs.

Having begun to describe something of a "suburban way of life," none of these studies determined whether suburbs have any effects on individuals. Perhaps their residents behave this way for reasons other than suburban location. The next two studies asked whether suburbs have effects on people.

## Later Studies

### Working-Class Suburb

Berger's *Working-Class Suburb* (1960/1968) explicitly tests some of the ideas in the suburban myth and in *The Organization Man*. Berger seized a research opportunity which arose when the Ford Motor Company closed an old factory and opened a new one, both located in the San Francisco Bay Area. The company closed a plant in Richmond, which Berger called a "drab industrial city," and opened a modern facility in the growing city of San Jose. Ford offered to relocate all its workers in housing near the new facility. Previously, they had lived in the old industrial community, mostly as renters, many in apartments; after the move, 99 percent became homeowners, living in "new tract suburbs which had been built not far from the plant" (Berger, 1960/1968, p. v). With a sample of 100 households, Berger took advantage of what might be called a "natural experiment." Obviously, a sociologist cannot take 100 families and move them from a city to a suburb to study the effects of the move. But when such an event actually occurred, Berger studied it as though it were an experiment. He wanted to find out whether the move to suburbia (the experimental treatment) had made a difference, and he attempted to discover the before and after situations by means of retrospective interviews conducted about two years after the move. He interviewed the families, asking about their current behaviors as well as their behaviors before the move, and then he compared the behavior in the suburb with the prior behavior to see whether the move had made a difference.

The research focused upon social mobility, politics, religion, and leisure. Quotations from Berger's report provide the gist of his findings.

> We find very little formal participation at all; 70 percent of respondents belong to no clubs, organizations, or associations at all.... (p. 59) what {do} they do with most of their spare time: they watch television.... Apparently the only TV shows which command attention of a majority are the westerns and the sports events, that is, those shows largely without middle-class content. (pp. 74–75)
>
> They do not drink martinis or wine with dinner.... One has a beer after coming home from work or on weekend summer afternoons. Beer is the "cocktail" that comes before dinner.... (p. 79)
>
> The quality of home life, then, seems to reflect few of the images of suburban life offered in the mass media. (p. 79)

Similarly, Berger discovered few changes in other aspects of the auto workers' way of life after the move to the suburbs. Unlike Whyte's organization men in Park Forest, the auto workers do not see themselves as socially mobile; they said they had reached their maximum occupational level. They did not change their political allegiances; they were Democrats when they lived in the city, and they continued to be Democrats in the new environment. Nor did they change their religious practices. A couple of changes did occur—they used their automobiles more and the women tended to become a little more involved with neighbors—but Berger discounts these as minor in comparison with the major continuities in their lifestyles.

Berger argues that *social class* makes the difference. When they lived in the city, the subjects were members of the working class. They had a particular educational background, income level, and situation within the factory and organization, and they were aware of these important facts of their lives. They had a class-based outlook on life, which affected their view of their chances for social mobility, their politics, and even their preferences in the mass media. They participated in a particular subculture, which affected the kind of family life they enjoyed, the child-rearing practices they preferred, and even the foods and beverages they chose. This subculture was theirs, deeply embedded within them. Moving from one place to another did not influence them to drop any important parts of it; they simply moved it with their furniture when they changed locations.

Berger argues further that the promoters of the suburban myth misunderstood what they perceived in places like Park Forest. He notes that the organization men were college graduates who were moving up in the middle class. The lifestyle exhibited in many of the new suburbs (a lifestyle which offended the intellectuals who promoted the myth) was simply the new middle-class lifestyle. Middle-class suburbanites' consumption habits and attitudes toward mobility and politics were just elements of a different subculture grounded in a different social-class situation, itself tied to educational background, income level, and prospects for future mobility. Furthermore, Berger argues that the suburban myth was a new version of the melting-pot image in which all Americans would be homogenized into a single national culture. By highlighting a working-class suburban way of life which was completely different from that featured in the media, Berger demonstrated the viability of heterogeneity, even in the suburbs.

## The Levittowners

Gans's volume, *The Levittowners* (1967), is a larger study than Berger's, not only looking at households before and after they moved into the suburbs but asking other questions as well. Like Berger, Gans took advantage of a research opportunity. In 1955, Levitt and Sons, Inc., the largest builder in the eastern United States, announced that it had purchased a large tract of land in New Jersey, about 17 miles from Philadelphia, and that the company planned to build a new community there with at least 12,000 houses. Gans resolved to study the emergence of a new suburb and its effects upon individuals who moved there. Levitt employed mass-production building methods, rapidly erecting a small number of different models. The resulting environment was "instant suburbia," with all the features most annoying to the critics—thousands of similar houses on treeless blocks. Gans was one of the first purchasers and lived there as a participant observer, but he also conducted surveys, collecting information about households before and after the move.

Young families from Philadelphia bought houses in Levittown; most of the men were under 40, and well over 80 percent of the households had children, mostly of elementary school ages. Most of the couples were lower-middle class, including white-collar workers such as technicians and semiprofessionals plus clerical and sales workers. Many of the blue-collar workers "were in the highest-skill, highest-status manual occupations, such as foremen, printers, electricians and plumbers" (Gans, 1967, p. 23). The newcomers said they came because they wanted better

CHAPTER · 13

In the 1950s, the Levitt Company and others mass-produced inexpensive suburban houses by the tens of thousands. They were enormously popular among young families who could buy them with small down payments and low-interest mortgages. (Allyn Baum, NYT Pictures)

housing and Levittown offered "the best house for the money." In historical context we can see that these families were formed in the wake of World War II and were caught in the urban housing shortage of the late 1940s; their children represented the beginning of the baby boom. The couples were hungry for bigger, better dwellings, and they must have been eager customers.

Unlike the auto workers, many of the individuals moving to Levittown did change their behavior: There was more joint family activity as parents spent more time with their children. The Levittowners spent considerable amounts of time working on their yards and houses and participating in backyard and community recreation. Many of the newcomers, especially females, had more contact with neighbors than they had previously had, and there was more sociability among couples. Participation in voluntary associations increased, and churchgoing increased slightly. Even some of the critics' bugaboo, conformity, was present, particularly with regard to house and lawn maintenance. Gans is quick to point out, though, that Levittowners wanted some of the conformity and tolerated what they did not want in the interest of good neighborly relations.

The fact that the Levittowners exhibited these several suburban traits did *not* mean the newcomers had been molded by the suburbs. Gans shows that the young couples who moved to Levittown had previously wanted to behave in these ways; they had wanted more interaction with neighbors. Their former environments, living in apartment buildings or doubled up with family, had frustrated their desires to lead a particular kind of family life. Rather than forcing the new suburbanites to behave in certain ways—which the mythmakers did not like—the new environment *permitted* them to behave in exactly the ways they wanted. Like Berger, Gans shows the importance of social class in affecting lifestyle, except that this second case exhibits a middle-class lifestyle. But the Levittown study shows stage in the family life cycle to be at least as important as social class. In retrospect, it hardly seems surprising that several thousand young couples with school-aged children should have exhibited a familist lifestyle. What is more surprising is that American intellectuals should have been offended by this phenomenon.

## Summary

Moving away from imagery and mythology, these five early studies began to illuminate suburban social life with empirical data. Fava's comparative survey revealed a measurable difference in local social life, with more neighboring in suburbs. Whyte's suburban description in *The Organization Man*, coupled with the description in *Crestwood Heights*, showed a distinctive lifestyle characterized by familism, materialism, and ambition. But the two studies by Berger and Gans, which considered changes before and after the individuals moved to suburbia, strongly challenge the interpretation that suburbs created the ways of life of Park Forest and Crestwood Heights. In different ways, Berger and Gans showed that social class is more important than suburban environment in generating lifestyles. Whyte and Seeley discovered a lifestyle of the college-educated middle classes, not of suburbia intrinsically. However, Berger vividly demonstrated that at least one more suburban way of life exists—that of the working class. Furthermore, Gans, in *The Levittowners*, showed that stage in the family life cycle also has a powerful effect on lifestyle, that is, young households adopt a familistic style because of their situation. They choose an environment—the single-family house with a yard—because it allows them to express the lifestyle they want. Suburbia doesn't mold them, as the suburban myth says; it permits them to live as they prefer.

## RECENT SUBURBAN RESEARCH

A handful of sociological studies conducted in the late 1970s and early 1980s continues to illuminate the issues of the earlier literature and to expand their scope to more contemporary questions.

## Suburban Location: A Matter of Choice

Gans's Levittown research showed that suburban households *chose* to be in suburbia; this theme runs through a number of other studies as well. As early as 1958, Bell hypothesized:

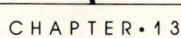

The move to the suburbs expresses an attempt to find a location in which to conduct family which is more suitable than that offered by central cities, i.e., that persons moving to suburbs are principally those who have chosen familism as an important element of their life styles (Bell, 1958, p. 231).

When asked about their locational preferences, most Americans choose not to live in big cities but prefer small towns or suburbs. However, individuals mentioning small towns want them to be located within easy driving range—say, 30 miles—of a metropolitan area, so even they want to be attached to suburbia. In choosing a suburban or small-town location, plus a single-family house with an individual yard, people express a widespread American value for privacy and space.

Michelson's (1977) recent study probed deeply into choices within a metropolitan housing market. The researcher followed couples as they shopped for housing—the market offered two kinds of dwellings, apartments and houses, and two locations, city and suburb. Before conducting the survey, Michelson noted that previous studies had said shoppers move for four reasons. Some choose a location for "status enhancement," for proximity to job location, although this reason is declining in importance. Another impetus for moving is a change in stage of the family life cycle, say, when a baby is anticipated or born. Shoppers also move if the internal space and storage capacity of a dwelling become insufficient. Finally, many shoppers move because of the broader considerations of who their neighbors would be and what they might do in the new environment. According to Bell's theory, people moved to be with greater numbers of persons who were like themselves; a process of self-selection was at work. "People would move to areas which provided the most appropriate opportunities to satisfy lifestyles they already emphasized but were not able to carry out as easily in less favorable surroundings" (Bell, cited in Michelson, 1977, p. 15).

Michelson's survey confirmed many of these hypotheses. Central-city couples with growing families chose to move to suburbs even if they had to take apartments, although they preferred to get detached houses. They said suburban neighborhoods are more suitable for raising children (Michelson, 1977). Those who were shopping for homes considered the characteristics of neighbors, as well as the status-enhancing quality of the suburban single-family home. People already living in suburbs or in the outer city chose bigger suburban homes. "The new home is a larger dwelling in a more socially acceptable neighborhood" (pp. 174–175). These houses and locations evidently held no mysteries for the shoppers, as women said they expected more housework, more entertaining, and less accessibility to shops, and recreational facilities. Later, after the households had lived in their new dwellings, the survey found that suburbanites' evaluative criteria are different from the criteria of city residents. In the suburbs, the first priority was on the house itself, followed by characteristics of neighbors, with location third; city dwellers, on the other hand, emphasized location first.

Reviewing other research on community satisfaction (from Chapter 10), we note that suburban people are much more satisfied than city people with their communities. The level of satisfaction of suburbanites is not much different from that of residents of small towns and rural areas, where satisfaction is highest. Suburban residence does not provide immunity from fear of crime, though. Suburbanites are more fearful than small-town and rural residents; indeed, the suburban level of fear is closer to the level of the city than the level of the countryside (see Table 10-4).

In sum, research on choice and satisfaction continues to disconfirm the suburban myth and to support the findings of such early studies as *The Levittowners*. Households moving to suburbs tend to do so by choice; they choose the suburb because they expect it to support their child-rearing activities. They may choose suburbia for other reasons as well, such as status enhancement. And once they reside in a suburb, they are likely to say it is a satisfactory environment (although not all residents agree, as will be noted in later sections on teenagers and feminist concerns). The theory of choice contradicts the suburban myth, though, insofar as the theory and supporting research show that people are not "zapped" by the suburb—it does not transform them. They choose the suburban location because of their stage in the family life cycle and their preferences for a familistic lifestyle.

## Suburbanism as a Way of Life

Suburban residents' social lives seem to be somewhat more localized than the lives of city people, according to a study by Fischer and Jackson (1976). These researchers analyzed the results of a national survey that included such questions as these: Do most of your friends live in the neighborhood? Is your family very interested in neighborhood problems? If you had to move from the neighborhood, would it make you unhappy? Through a comparison with central-city residents, the analysis showed that the suburban residents were more localistic. In particular, the differences emerged within the college-educated segment of the population. Among individuals who had a high school education or less, no city-suburban difference in localism existed. But among the more educated, suburban individuals were far more localistic than their city-dwelling counterparts. The study did not show a big difference in neighborhood social life of city and suburban residents, but the difference was discernible, nonetheless. The sociologists confirmed this finding with data from metropolitan Detroit as well.

A study in metropolitan Chicago also showed somewhat higher levels of neighborhood involvement in suburbs (Choldin, 1980). Like the earlier survey by Fava, in which she measured neighboring in Manhattan, Queens, and suburban Nassau County, this study compared social life in an outer-city residential area with two suburbs. The survey was restricted to middle-class housewives to eliminate social class and gender as possible factors. As shown in Table 13-1, the survey interview replicated some of the items from neighborhood surveys cited in Chapter 9. The results reveal considerable social involvement of women in outer-city and suburban areas. But the suburban women consistently participated more; they had more

**TABLE 13-1**
Local Social Involvement by Type of Community and Type of Dwelling, %

|  | Suburbs | | City | |
|---|---|---|---|---|
|  | Apartment (N = 151) | House (N = 153) | Apartment (N = 153) | House (N = 104) |
| Chat with neighbors* | 72.9 | 78.4 | 73.2 | 75.0 |
| Visit with neighbors | 61.6 | 67.7 | 43.5 | 52.9 |
| Exchange things* | 47.0 | 59.5 | 42.5 | 56.8 |
| Babysit* | 51.0 | 32.7 | 21.6 | 25.0 |
| Ask advice* | 42.4 | 40.5 | 36.8 | 35.6 |
| Have at least one friend in area | 65.3 | 67.8 | 60.5 | 54.4 |
| Picnic and party* | 39.1 | 37.9 | 24.1 | 24.0 |
| Read community paper* | 67.6 | 86.3 | 80.4 | 88.5 |
| Belong to neighborhood organization | 19.9 | 14.4 | 7.8 | 10.6 |

*Responds "often" or "sometimes."
Source: Choldin, 1980.

neighboring and more involvement in community organizations. The city area scored higher only in readership of local newspapers.

Gans (1962) had suggested that the suburbs (including the outer city areas) have produced a new form of social relationship, which he calls "quasi-primary." He says the relationship between neighbors is not fully primary—they are not that closely involved with each other. Their interaction is more intimate than a secondary contact but more guarded than a primary one. Fischer's summary of the localism question states that suburban individuals are more interested in their neighborhoods and more involved with their neighbors. Furthermore, their leisure time is more likely to be spent at home as they engage in such activities as gardening and entertaining (Fischer, 1976).

### Differences among suburbanites

Although the earlier suburban case studies implied that the people of each suburb followed its way of life, a more recent investigation highlighted differences among suburbanites. Like Gans, Popenoe (1977) studied the social life of a Levittown, although he chose the one in Pennsylvania. While Gans had observed a brand-new suburb, Popenoe encountered one which was 20 years old, populated by upper-working-class and lower-middle-class households.

To digress, the physical condition of the place is worth noting. One element of the suburban myth was that the then-new housing developments would become suburban slums after their mass-produced housing aged. This was definitely not the case in Levittown, Pennsylvania. Early landscaping paid later dividends: "What was once a raw housing development ... is now virtually a parklike setting. ... many of the Levitt streets, with their overhanging trees and abundant front-yard shrubbery, have a luxuriant facade, obscuring the fact that homes basically look alike and are for families with modest incomes ... Levittown has unquestionably grown more esthetically pleasant over the years; in no sense has it become the suburban slum that some predicted" (Popenoe, 1977, p. 115). Over the years the houses have also appreciated financially.

Popenoe employs the concept of "congruence" to deal with the social adjustment of different sorts of individuals and households to the suburban environment (Michelson, 1976). The problem is to find out whether an environment fits well with the activity patterns of the individuals who use it. In the present context, environment refers not to the outdoor environment of geomorphology, climate, and the like, but to the built environment. In studying suburbs, Popenoe looked for the fit between users and environment. He noted that Levittown worked better for some categories of households than for others.

## The "characteristic Levittown household"

Community and environment worked nicely for the most common type of household in Levittown. Having lived in the suburb for ten to twelve years, the characteristic household is composed of two married adults in their forties plus two teenagers—an older version of the original households. They are likely to have another child who has left home but lives nearby. The husband is a skilled blue-collar worker or holds a lower-middle-class job such as insurance sales; the wife is likely to work at a clerical, retail, or teaching position.

Their lifestyle centers about the home. Men work on the house or yard; women maintain the interior. Their leisure time is spent in informal family activities and in watching television (most families have two sets). Their social life is rather constricted and localistic, including one or two couples plus parents and relatives. They have barbecues in summertime and after-dinner drinks, conversation, and card games in winter. They seldom eat in restaurants or go to movies, and "almost never" go to central Philadelphia. In Popenoe's (1977) estimation, "Their life-style is not culturally rich by upper-middle-class standards, but is informal, friendly, and comfortable.... They have space for the family's needs ... most things they want are near them—work, shopping, schools, friends, and relatives" (p. 143). Dependence upon the automobile is a fully accepted part of their way of life.

Neighboring is confined within a distance of about four or five houses; Levittowners know their neighbors by name, but not beyond that distance. Typically, they do not see their neighbors socially but consider the area to be "friendly enough." Some neighbors can be counted on for help in an emergency. "In nice weather, when people are in their yards, it is common to strike up a conversation over the back fence. But the neighborhood is not as social as it once was: 'People come and go, you know, and there are so many newcomers now'" (p. 142). The characteristic Levittown family belongs to a church and often attends service on

Sunday; otherwise, though, they do not belong to any organization beyond the man's union or professional association. They express some concerns about the community: the behavior of youth and drug abuse, as well as the fact that the local environment is losing its "country" character with the growth of traffic, new stores, and business. Residents perceive that the city is coming to Levittown. Overall, though, "they are pleased to be living in Levittown and wouldn't mind living out their lives there ... they have no plans to move" (p. 143).

In contrast to the characteristic Levittown household, another type of household was quite incongruent with the local situation. Popenoe found several large working-class families who had a poor fit with the environment and social scene. These families typically have four or five children, so their little houses are overcrowded. The husband is a factory worker who works overtime to generate enough income, but the wife does not work for pay; both wife and husband have low levels of educational attainment. Their income is insufficient to maintain the consumer lifestyle of Levittown; they do not have enough money to cover repairs on household appliances, for example, or for medical emergencies. Often, the children of such families get into trouble, and the couple's marriage deteriorates while they are in their forties. According to Popenoe, their basic problem is that their housing is too small for their family, and they do not have enough money to afford the suburb's lifestyle.

## Teenagers

Not everyone finds such a high level of congruence between activities and environment as the adults of the characteristic Levittown household—teenagers and suburbs have never quite meshed. Numerous studies have noted suburbia's deficiencies for teenagers' needs; Popenoe's recent observations about Levittown, Pennsylvania, may be taken as typical. Teenagers spend a great deal of time in the local residential environment, possibly more than any other group except small children and elderly individuals. Unfortunately, in the suburb they complain of too little to do, a lack of public transportation, and the high cost of some of the recreational facilities. They say this despite the fact that, by U.S. standards, Levittown is well supplied with recreational and other public facilities—swimming pools, parks, and baseball fields—but these are used mainly by preteens. Teenagers turn to commercial facilities—bowling alleys and skating rinks, which they see as more exciting because there are people there; but they cost money, and teens cannot afford to use them frequently. Teenagers from the poorer families, in particular, cannot afford to use the commercial facilities.

In Levittown, teens "hang out" on street corners in residential areas, in parks and wooded areas adjacent to residences, at swimming pool areas when they are closed for the season, and in school parking lots, neighborhood shopping centers, and isolated snack shops. "There is no satisfactory place within the community where [they] can go to see and be seen and to watch the world go by" (Popenoe, 1977, p. 196). In a survey, half the teens said they often felt bored. They said they like the fact that the community is quiet and uncrowded and that it does not have gangs or other city problems, but they resent being dependent upon their mothers for automobile transportation. Summing it up, one teenager said, "There's not much to do here, and those things there are to do cost money; also there's no way to get to them" (cited in Popenoe, p. 159).

## Feminist concerns

As noted in Chapter 10, feminist scholars have articulated a number of complaints about women's place in urban structure. While most of their argument referred to city life, it applies at least as well to suburbia, asserting that the macrospatial pattern, with its sharp separation of work and residence, is disadvantageous to mothers who work for pay. Furthermore, the lack of mass transit and of day-care facilities makes it difficult to work and raise children. Some feminist social scientists focus their attention upon the suburban situation.

In middle-class suburbia of the 1950s, women typically stayed home as full-time homemakers. Now, as that role is more the exception than the rule, middle-class women want jobs outside the home. But, while the life of the suburban woman has changed radically, "the environment in which she exists has not" (Popenoe, 1980, p. 169). She would prefer to have her husband at home more to share domestic chores, to have an easy-to-maintain home, and to have supportive public facilities such as transportation and day-care centers.

The suburban problem hits young college-educated women particularly hard. One study showed that women did not feel restricted in movement until the birth of the first child. According to sociologist Helena Lopata (1980), who conducted a survey of women in metropolitan Chicago, "American urban, young, and single women are geographically relatively mobile within the complex of the home, school, and work roles until the birth of the first child" (p. 163). After having children, though, women feel tied down. If they move to the suburbs "for the sake of the children," their problems multiply. "The combination of mortgage, transportation costs, and the drop in income after the wife quits working pushes many Chicago area families into a curtailed social space, restricting them to informal interaction in the immediate neighborhood" (p. 163). In Levittown, young college-educated mothers were particularly frustrated by suburban life. Being tied to their small children, they depended upon the local environment for stimulation and variety in their lives, but Levittown offered little of either (Popenoe, 1977). On the other hand, according to Popenoe, their husbands had active lives outside the community, which provoked a certain amount of resentment. Reviewing the literature on women and environment, Wekerle (1980) concluded that the suburbanization of jobs and housing weighs particularly heavily on women.

Geographers Palm and Pred (1974) make perhaps the most severe indictment of suburbia as an environment for women, especially those without cars.

> It is obvious that with or without pre-school children, the carless, suburban, full-time homemaker finds herself in a position of great isolation. Her daily activity prism is restricted to those opportunities available on foot or by use of the often inconvenient or

even non-existent bus service. One cannot overdramatize the absence of opportunities in her world. Even routine shopping becomes a chore; socializing is limited to the very restricted neighborhood in which she lives ... she spends much time alone during the average weekday, and finds solace in her link to the outside world, the television set.... It is she who has the greatest number of leisure hours and yet little opportunity to invest leisure in personal fulfillment. (p. 36)

## NEW PROBLEMS

### Aging: "The Graying of Suburbia"

One thing the suburban myth and the sociological researchers agreed on was that suburbs were communities of and for young families. But now that turns out to have been a temporary situation; many of the couples who moved their families to the suburbs in the 1950s have remained in the same homes they bought then, even though their children have matured and moved away. These couples, who moved to suburbia in their thirties, are now in their sixties. Furthermore, in recent years not many of these older households were replaced by young ones. Less housing turnover has occurred than might have been anticipated—houses have appreciated beyond the reach of young couples, and many of the older couples stayed in their empty nests instead of moving to apartments. In the meantime, the inflationary decade of the 1970s was a bad time for young potential homebuyers; to the extent that they were purchasing homes, they were more likely to go to newer peripheral suburbs.

Greenwich, Connecticut, a suburb of New York City, shows a changing age distribution since 1960. In that year, after a decade of rapid growth, the largest age group was children and teens (ages 5 to 14; see Figure 13-1); a large number were in the parental generation, ages 35 to 54; and a few were in their twenties or were older individuals. Ten years after a national fall in birth rates, the proportion of small children fell and the proportion of older teens grew; that year already showed increasing proportions over age 65. By 1980 we see a new age profile, with few small children and large fractions in all adult and older categories. The third graph represents the age composition of a nongrowing population.

Other suburbs show these same trends. In the late 1970s suburban Westchester County had 18 percent of its residents over age 65, projected to reach 25 percent by 1985. In Maryland, one-third of suburban Montgomery County was over age 45 in the late 1970s (Kowinski, 1980). Gutowski and Field (1979) have called this "the graying of suburbia."

The changing age distribution can be seen in other age groups besides the elderly. One shift occurred between 1960 and 1970, when the proportion of children declined considerably. At the beginning of the decade, 32 percent of all suburbanites were under age 15; ten years later this figure dropped to 28 percent. While the proportion of children has fallen, the older age categories have increased. In addition to more elderly individuals, suburbs have growing numbers of the

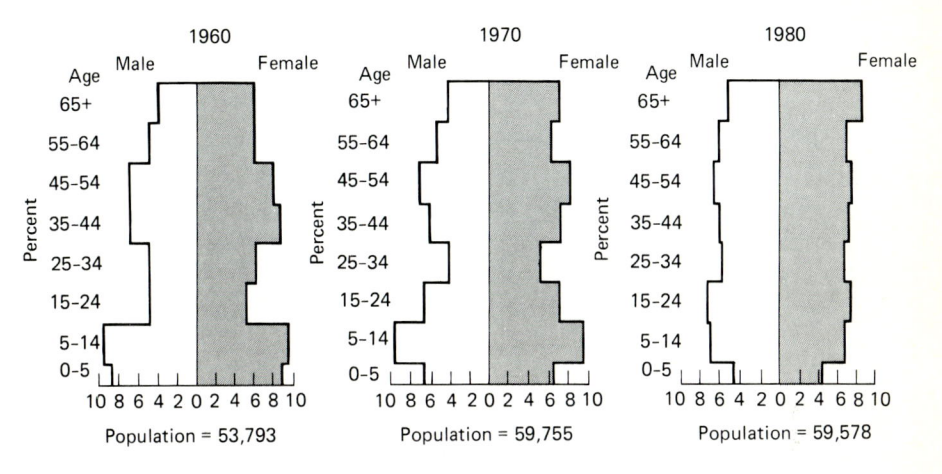

**FIGURE 13-1**
One suburb's changing age composition, Greenwich, Connecticut. (Source: Adapted from data in U.S. Bureau of the Census, 1960, p. 8-63; U.S. Bureau of the Census, 1970, p. 8-72; U.S. Bureau of the Census, 1980, p. 8-55.)

"preelderly," households with persons aged 55 to 64 (Gutowski & Field, 1979). The preelderly of the late 1970s were the couples who moved to the suburbs with their children in the 1950s.

But the graying of suburbia can be seen most directly in the increasing numbers of individuals over age 65. "Between 1970 and 1976, the number of elderly households in the suburbs rose by 31 percent, compared with 10 percent in the central cities" (Gutowski & Field, pp. ix–x). By 1980, there were 101.5 million persons aged 65 or higher in suburbs, as compared with 67.9 million in central cities (U.S. Bureau of the Census, 1982, p. 356–357). Many of the older suburban residents are homeowners, but suburbia also has substantial numbers whose incomes are at or near the poverty level.

The numbers and proportions of suburban elderly are likely to grow. Obviously, the suburban preelderly will age into the older categories, but some migration of elderly individuals from cities to suburbs will also occur. Some older individuals move to be nearer to relatives; others move because their city neighborhoods have become too fearful. Not all suburbs are aging at the same rate; suburbs that are growing overall tend to have younger populations, while older suburbs that have stopped growing are the ones with aging populations (Stahura, 1980).

These population shifts have fundamental implications for suburban social life. The suburban environment was congruent with a familistic lifestyle—houses and yards were built for young families. The buildings and yards require considerable owner maintenance, from painting to lawn mowing and leaf raking. In the automobile-oriented environment, most facilities are distant; few acquaintances are within walking distance, and few gathering places are on the block. Thus the environment may put home maintenance burdens upon individuals who cannot support them. It may be poorly suited to those older persons whose eyesight or hearing prevent them from driving, and it may keep older people away from friends or from preferred gathering places. Furthermore, suburban organizations were not designed for older individuals; they were designed for the young. Voluntary organizations and public services and facilities were youth-oriented. Adapting to an elderly population will require innovations on the parts of many suburbs.

## Problems and Challenges

While suburbia represented the major growth sector of urban American for decades, it was not without its problems. Apparently, some individuals were worried about the situation as early as 1967, because President Johnson created a Task Force on Suburban Problems which looked into "suburban sprawl" and haphazard development and even asked whether the suburbs embodied some sort of malaise. The President asked the task force to look into "the nature of the enduring economic, social, and physical problems of suburbs and of the people who live there, especially older suburbs and newer areas experiencing rapid growth" (Haar, 1974, p. xxvi). The chair of that task force later wrote that there were "widening gaps between the myths and realities of suburbia: growing crime, pollution, inadequate transportation, industrial ugliness, and rising costs of municipal services confront the suburbanite all over again with the very problems that motivated his migration from the urban core" (Haar, 1974, p. xxvi).

When the chair of the task force wrote about suburbia, he conveyed some gloomy messages:

> We have built our suburbs enthusiastically but somewhat recklessly. In the rush to provide facilities that so many citizens wanted, suburban land has been cut too fine and built up too thick, and what should have been shapely towns have grown formlessly until suburban sprawl has destroyed the sense of community as well as the sense that the citizens could control their own environment. (Haar, 1974, p. 4)

Haar was concerned about other suburban problems as well. He saw rising crime rates, including youth offenses—vandalism, illegal drug usage, and larceny—and rising rates of homicide. He wrote also about problems of the physical environment: "dirty waters, leveled hills, and built-up open spaces" (Haar, 1972, p. ii).

General problems of the 1970s were also projected to have an impact in suburbia. After the oil embargo of 1973 created severe gasoline shortages in the United States, people began to wonder whether this unique built environment which depended totally upon automobile travel would be viable in a time of greater energy efficiency. Boris Pushkarev, a prominent city planner, said, "Gasoline made this whole way of life possible. Whether and in what form this situation changes will define the future of suburbia" (cited in Kowinski, 1980, p. 19). And changes in family life, some associated with changing roles of women, suggested additional questions. "The suburbs are predicated on a way of life that is endangered in an era of two-paycheck families and frequent divorce," according to Kowinski (1980, p. 16).

In sum, while sociologists hope that the suburban myth has been laid to rest, suburbia, now a dominant feature of American society, is changing. A number of social problems have moved to the suburbs. Some writers cast a somewhat gloomy light on these developments, using such titles as *The End of Innocence* and *Suburbia: The End of the Golden Age*. One wrote, "In short, suburbia is no longer the pastoral retreat it once was, or rather, was thought to be" (Haar, 1974, p. ii).

## SUMMARY

American intellectuals responded to massive suburbanization by writing essays, novels, and movies which made fun of the new communities and their way of life. The writers created the suburban myth, which showed a new lifestyle that was middle class, child-centered, localistic, and oriented toward consumption. Within this image suburbanites exhibited great homogeneity and conformity.

Social researchers conducted several studies to discover the realities of the new communities. The earliest studies in the 1950s described middle-class residential areas and showed a good deal of familism and social mobility. A later round of studies asked whether the suburbs produce a way of life or whether other social factors may be more important. These later studies showed powerful effects on lifestyles of social class and stage in the family life cycle. One study showed that working-class households behaved in suburbia as they had in the city; the suburb's built environment had very little effect on their lifestyle, as they transported their subculture from city to suburbs. This implied that the middle-class lifestyle in many suburbs was produced by a middle-class subculture, not by the suburban environment. A second study showed that households moving to one suburb (Levittown, New Jersey) were almost all young couples with small children who were leaving city apartments or other crowded housing situations. They deliberately chose the suburban environment to be able to have more family activities. The suburb was not imposing a lifestyle on them; it was merely permitting them to express their preferred familistic lifestyle.

Recent research has shown that the suburb's built environment is more congruent with certain situations than with others. Households with married couples with nonadult children, adequate incomes, and one or two cars may be congruent with the suburb. Poorer households, though, may lack the wherewithal to maintain houses and appliances and to keep up with consumer styles. Teenagers tend to find suburbia inadequate for their needs; being too young to drive in an environment designed for cars reinforces the adolescent's dependent and possibly isolated situation. Feminist scholars also point out the suburb's drawbacks for women in the labor force. They bear the burdens of child care and household maintenance, which restrict their mobility and opportunities in the job market. Generally, the suburb makes women's social life somewhat localistic.

Suburbs have been changing in unanticipated ways. Their populations are aging from the great youth of the 1950s. Now many communities have increasing proportions of middle-aged and elderly residents. Many suburbs have passed through their phase of rapid growth and are stabilizing or even shrinking. This creates community strains regarding such controversial issues as which schools to close. Suburbs are facing many other problems as well, such as lack of coordination and planning among the multiplicity of small municipal governments; how to provide services for older people; and how to maintain an car-oriented transportation system with high-priced fuel.

## REFERENCES FOR CHAPTERS 12 AND 13

Adams, John S. 1970. "Residential Structure of Midwestern Cities." *Annals of the Association of American Geographers.* 60:37–62.

Anderson, Theodore, R., and Janice Egeland. 1961. "Spatial Aspects of Social Area Analysis." *American Sociological Review,* 26:392–399.

Banfield, Edward. 1968. "The Logic of Metropolitan Growth," chap. 2 in *The Unheavenly City,* (ed.) Edward Banfield. Boston: Little, Brown.

Banham, Reyner. 1971. *Los Angeles: The Architecture of Four Ecologies.* New York: Harper & Row.

Bell, Wendell. 1958. "Social Choice, Life Styles, and Suburban Residence," pp. 225–247 in *The Suburban Community,* (ed.) William M. Dobriner. New York: Putnam.

Berger, Bennett. 1960/1968. *Working Class Suburb.* Berkeley: University of California Press.

———. 1961/1971. "The Myth of Suburbia," pp. 143–150 in *Looking for America,* (ed.) Bennett Berger. Englewood Cliffs, N.J.: Prentice-Hall.

Berry, Brian J. L. "Internal Structure of the City." *Law and Contemporary Problems.* 30:111–119.

———, and Yehoshua Cohen. 1973. "Decentralization of Commerce and Industry: The Restructuring of Metropolitan America," pp. 431–456 in *The Urbanization of the Suburbs,* (eds.) Louis Masotti and Jeffrey Hadden. Beverly Hills, Calif.: Sage.

Checkoway, Barry. 1980. "Large Builders, Federal Housing Programmes, and Postwar Suburbanization." *International Journal of Urban and Regional Research.* 4:21–45.

Choldin, Harvey M. 1980. "Social Participation in Suburban Apartment Enclaves," chap. 8 in *The Consumer Experience of Housing,* (eds.) Clare Ungerson and Valerie Karn. Westmead, England: Gower.

———, and Claudine Hanson. 1981. "Subcommunity Change in a Changing Metropolis." *Sociological Quarterly,* 22:549–564.

———, Claudine Hanson, and Robert Bohrer. 1980. "Suburban Status Instability." *American Sociological Review.* 45:972-983.

Collver, Andrew, and Moshe Semyonov. 1979. "Suburban Change and Persistence." *American Sociological Review.* 44:480-486.

Donaldson, Scott. 1969. *The Suburban Myth.* New York: Columbia.

Downs, Anthony. 1973. *Opening Up the Suburbs: An Urban Strategy for America.* New Haven, Conn.: Yale University Press.

———. 1974. "Successes and Failures of Federal Housing Policy." *Public Interest.* 34:124-145.

Farley, Reynolds. 1964. "Suburban Persistence." *American Sociological Review.* 29:38-47.

Fava, Sylvia F. 1959. "Contrasts in Neighboring: New York City and a Suburban County," pp. 122-131 in *The Suburban Community,* (ed.) W. M. Dobriner. New York: Putnam.

Fischer, Claude S. 1976. *The Urban Experience.* New York: Harcourt Brace Jovanovich.

———, and Robert M. Jackson. 1976. "Suburbs, Networks, and Attitudes," chap. 11 in *The Changing Face of the Suburbs,* (ed.) Barry Schwartz. Chicago: University of Chicago Press.

Gans, Herbert J. 1962. "Urbanism and Suburbanism as Ways of Life: A Re-evaluation of Definitions," pp. 625-248 in *Human Behavior and Social Processes,* (ed.) Arnold M. Rose. Boston: Houghton Mifflin.

———. 1968. "The Failure of Urban Renewal: A Critique and Some Proposals," chap. 18 in *People and Plans: Essays on Urban Problems and Solutions,* (ed.) Herbert J. Gans. New York: Basic Books.

———. 1967. *The Levittowners.* New York: Random House.

Guest, Avery M. 1978. "Suburban Social Status: Persistence or Evolution?" *American Sociological Review.* 43:251-264.

Guterbock, Thomas M. 1982. "Suburbanization of American Cities in the Twentieth Century: A New Index and Another Look." Paper presented at the annual meeting of the American Sociological Association.

Gutowski, Michael, and Tracey Field. 1979. *The Graying of Suburbia.* Washington, D.C.: The Urban Institute.

Haar, Charles M. 1972. *The End of Innocence: A Suburban Reader.* Glenview, Ill.: Scott, Foresman.

———. 1974. *The President's Task Force on Suburban Problems: Final Report.* Cambridge, Mass.: Ballinger.

Harris, Chauncey, and Edward Ullman. "The Nature of Cities." *Annals of the American Academy of Political Science.* 242:7-17.

Kasarda, John D. 1976. "The Changing Occupational Structure of the American Metropolis: Apropos the Urban Problem," chap. 5 in *The Changing Face of the Suburbs,* (ed.) Barry Schwartz. Chicago: University of Chicago Press.

———. 1980. "The Implications of Contemporary Redistribution Trends for National Urban Policy." *Social Science Quarterly.* 61:373-400.

Kornblum, William, and Terry Williams. 1978. "Life Style, Leisure, and Community Life," chap. 3 in *Handbook of Contemporary Urban Life*, (ed.) David Street. San Francisco: Jossey-Bass.

Kowinski, William S. 1980. "Suburbia: End of the Golden Age." *The New York Times Magazine*. March 16: p. 16.

Lineberry, Robert L. 1975. "Suburbia and the Metropolitan Turf." *Annals of the American Academy of Political and Social Science*. 422:1-9.

Logan, John R. 1978. "Growth, Politics, and the Stratification of Places." *American Journal of Sociology*. 84:404-416.

———. 1981. "The Stratification of Metropolitan Suburbs: 1960-1970." *American Sociological Review*. 46:175-186.

Lopata, Helena Z. 1980. "The Chicago Woman: A Study of Patterns of Mobility and Transportation." *Signs: Journal of Women in Culture and Society*. 5 (3, Supplement):S161-S169.

Marshall, Harvey. 1973. "Suburban Life Styles: A Contribution to the Debate," chap. 4 in *The Urbanization of the Suburbs*, (eds.) Louis H. Masotti and Jeffrey K. Hadden. Beverly Hills, Calif.: Sage.

Michelson, William. 1976. *Man and His Urban Environment: A Sociological Approach*, 2d ed. Reading, Mass.: Addison-Wesley.

———. 1977. *Environmental Choice, Human Behavior, and Residential Satisfaction*. New York: Oxford University Press.

Muller, Peter O., Kenneth C. Meyer, and Roman A. Cybriwsky. 1976. *Philadelphia: A Study of Conflicts and Social Cleavages*. Cambridge, Mass.: Ballinger.

———. 1981. *Contemporary Suburban America*. Englewood Cliffs, N.J.: Prentice-Hall.

Palm, Risa, and Alan Pred. 1974. "A Time-Geographic Perspective on Problems of Inequality for Women." Working paper no. 236, Institute of Urban and Regional Development, University of California, Berkeley.

Popenoe, David. 1977. *The Suburban Environment: Sweden and the United States*. Chicago: University of Chicago Press.

———. 1980. "Women in the Suburban Environment: A U.S.-Sweden Comparison," chap. 7 in *New Space for Women*, (eds.) Gerda R. Wekerle, Rebecca Peterson, and David Morley. Boulder, Col.: Westview.

Reynolds, Malvina. 1964. *Little Boxes and other Handmade Songs*. New York: Oak.

Schnore, Leo F. 1965. "Satellites and Suburbs," chap. 7 in *The Urban Scene: Human Ecology and Demography*. New York: Free Press. (a)

———. 1965. "The Social and Economic Characteristics of the American Suburbs," chap. 9 in *The Urban Scene: Human Ecology and Demography*. New York: Free Press. (b)

Schwartz. Barry. 1980. "The Suburban Landscape: New Variations on an Old Theme." *Contemporary Sociology*. 9:640-650.

Seeley, John R., R. Alexander Sim, and Elizabeth W. Loosely. 1956. *Crestwood Heights: A Study of the Culture of Suburban Life*. New York: Wiley.

Stahura, John M. 1978. "The Evolution of Suburban Functional Roles." *Pacific Sociological Review*. 21:423-439.

———. 1979. "Structural Determinants of Suburban Socioeconomic Compositions." *Sociology and Social Research*. 63:328–345.

———. 1980. "Ecological Determinants of the Aging of Suburban Populations." *Sociological Quarterly*. 21:107–118.

U.S. Bureau of the Census. 1960. *Census of Population: 1960, Volume 1, Characteristics of the Population, Part 8, Connecticut*. Washington, D.C.

———. 1963. *Census of Population: 1960, Selected Area Reports: Standard Metropolitan Statistical Areas*. Washington, D.C.

———. 1970. *Census of Population: 1970, Volume 1, Characteristics of the Population, Part 8, Connecticut*. Washington, D.C.

———. 1980. *Census of Population: 1980, Volume 1, Characteristics of the Population, Connecticut* (PC80-1-B8). Washington, D.C.

———. 1982. *State and Metropolitan Area Data Book, 1982*. Washington, D.C. (a)

———. 1982. *Statistical Abstract of the United States: 1982–83*. Washington, D.C. (b)

Vance, James., Jr. 1964. *Geography and Urban Evolution in the San Francisco Bay Area*. Berkeley, Cal.: Institute of Governmental Studies, University of California.

———. 1977. *This Scene of Man: The Role and Structure of the City in the Geography of Western Civilization*. New York: Harper's.

Wade, Richard. 1982. "The Suburban Roots of the New Federalism." *New York Times Magazine*. Aug. 1, p. 20.

Warner, Sam. B., Jr. 1962. *Streetcar Suburbs: The Process of Growth in Boston, 1870–1900*. Cambridge, Mass.: Harvard.

Wekerle, Gerda R. 1980. "Women in the Urban Environment." *Signs: Journal of Women in Culture and Society*. 5 (3, Supplement):S188–S214.

Whyte, William H. 1956. *The Organization Man*. New York: Simon and Schuster.

Zimmer, Basil. 1975. "The Urban Centrifugal Drift," chap. 1 in *Metropolitan America in Contemporary Perspective*, (eds.) Amos H. Hawley and Vincent Rock. New York: Wiley.

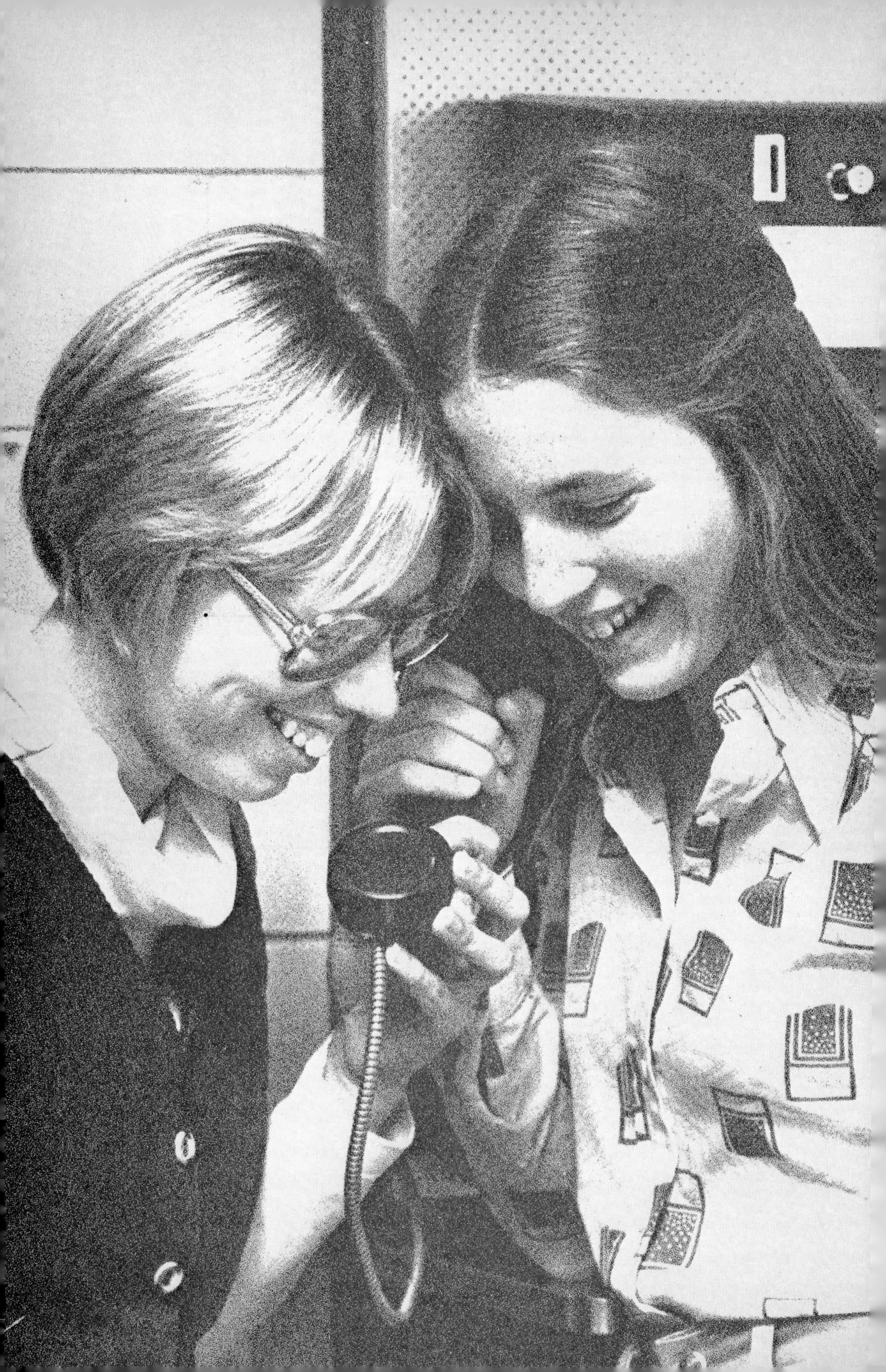

# CHAPTER • 14

## *Social Networks*

### Chapter Outline

**REDISCOVERING URBAN SOCIAL LIFE**

**TWO CASE STUDIES**
    The Intimate Ties of Toronto's East Yorkers
    Korean Immigrants in New York City

**BASIC CONCEPTS**
    Egocentric Networks
    Properties of Ties
- Multistrandedness
- Weak and strong ties
- Homogeneity and heterogeneity

    Density

**THE SMALL-WORLD PROJECT**

**FUNCTIONS OF SOCIAL NETWORKS**
    Chain Migration
    Jobs and Social Classes
    A Footnote on Gossip

**SUMMARY**

## REDISCOVERING URBAN SOCIAL LIFE

With the demise of "perfect little neighborhoods," sociologists needed a new conceptual tool to understand social life in the metropolis; they may have found such a tool in "social networks."

Before World War II, sociological theories predicted the collapse of primary-group relationships. Called "determinism" and "community lost," the theories stated that primary groupings, like family, kinship, and neighborhood, would be undermined in modern urban systems. But after the war at least three groups of researchers, working on disparate problems, revealed persistent social connections. In combination, these research findings led to the emergence of research on and theories of social networks.

In the United States, Katz and Lazarsfeld (1955) studied the effects of mass communication upon the public. Prior to their research, mass communication theory assumed a direct connection existed between the broadcaster and the listener or between the publisher and the reader; presumably, the media could directly influence the individual. This implied an atomistic public composed of isolated individuals, each being influenced by the media. Lazarsfeld and his associates (1944) conducted a series of studies to discover how people vote and how they develop their political opinions. The studies showed that individuals were heavily influenced by people close to them and were likely to vote as their parents did. Then, in a broader study of public opinion, Katz and Lazarsfeld explored people's exposure to mass media and how they chose movies, product brands, and clothing styles. The researchers discovered that communications reached people via a two-step flow. Broadcasters send messages (commercials, for example), but before these messages have their effects, they are processed locally. People develop their opinions, preferences, and choices in the context of small groups, family and kin, close friends, and coworkers. Thus the public is not atomized but consists of individuals who are linked together.

Working in England at about the same time, anthropologist Elizabeth Bott (1957) and sociologists Michael Young and Peter Willmott (1957) studied family life in highly urban settings. The sociologists found that members of London's working class were, rather than isolated, heavily involved in neighborhood and family life. Wives stayed close to their mothers, sharing tasks, and established their own homes near their parents, maintaining family connections. Bott explicitly used the term social network in explaining family life, hypothesizing that husbands and wives have different relationships depending upon their networks outside their marriages.

A third and particularly influential body of research which contributed to social network theory was a set of studies by social anthropologists in disparate communities (summarized in Hannerz, 1980). Their studies ranged from a small Norwegian farming community to an Indian town, and several were conducted in central African cities and towns.[4] Urban anthropology was a new field, the city a new setting; previously, anthropologists had studied little communities exclusively. Social relations in large multifaceted social situations could not be encapsulated as well as relations in a little village; thus the more fluid, expansive concept of a network tying people together became useful. Over the years since the late 1950s, sociologists and anthropologists, increasingly, have adopted the network concept. The concept has been particularly useful in attempting to understand how people in cities and suburbs maintain their social relationships under conditions of great physical mobility.

A social network is defined as a set of links or ties among individuals. Networks vary in several dimensions: in the number of individuals involved (networks can be large or small), in the strength of the ties, in the density of the linkages, and in other ways. The following summaries of two studies of social networks will illustrate the usefulness of the concept.

## TWO CASE STUDIES

### The Intimate Ties of Toronto's East Yorkers

An intensive study of the residents of East York, a borough of Toronto, highlights key points about social networks. Sociologist Barry Wellman (1979) and his students interviewed 845 adults in this upper-working-class, lower-middle-class, predominantly British-Canadian section of the city. The survey covered their social contacts—whom they felt closest to; where they lived; some of their social characteristics; whether they were kin, friends, or coworkers; how they kept in touch; and other aspects of social relations. The aim of the survey was to discover the nature of the social relations in a modern metropolis and to test some of the conventional theories, such as determinism and community lost. Wellman wanted to learn the geographical extent of people's contacts and how they maintained them. In each interview, the person was asked to provide detailed information about his or her six closest intimates ("the persons outside your home that you feel closest to"). The interviewer asked for characteristics of the individuals named: gender, socioeconomic status, and place of residence; for information about the relationship between the respondent and the individuals: degree of closeness, basis of the relationship (e.g., mother, coworker), frequency of contact, and kinds of assistance shared; and whether each of the six close intimates is connected with each of the others, to allow the sociologists to analyze the relationships as a network.

The survey results show that almost none of these city adults are isolated; only 2 percent reported having no one outside the home to whom they felt close, and 61 percent reported at least five intimate ties. Typically, they have ties with kin and nonkin, predominantly friends who are neither neighbors nor coworkers; the closest ties are usually with immediate kinfolk, adult children, parents, and siblings. Some people report that most of their intimate ties are with kinfolk, while others report that most are with nonkin.

**TABLE 14-1**
**Residence of Intimates by Relationship to Respondent, %**

| Residence | Child | Parent | Sibling | Other relative | Friend | Neighbor | Coworker | Total |
|---|---|---|---|---|---|---|---|---|
| Same neighborhood | 4.0 | 6.8 | 4.2 | 6.9 | 13.1 | 74.3 | 8.3 | 13.0 |
| Elsewhere in East York | 10.1 | 10.3 | 10.6 | 10.9 | 14.3 | 15.5 | 13.0 | 12.5 |
| City of Toronto | 11.5 | 27.6 | 22.0 | 22.6 | 29.9 | 4.1 | 38.4 | 24.8 |
| Elsewhere in metro Toronto | 47.6 | 14.7 | 24.8 | 29.1 | 24.3 | 4.1 | 32.9 | 25.1 |
| Outside metro Toronto | 26.9 | 40.6 | 38.3 | 30.4 | 18.4 | 2.0 | 7.4 | 24.6 |
| Number of respondents | 227 | 340 | 592 | 779 | 1,476 | 245 | 216 | 3,875 |
| % of total | 5.9 | 8.8 | 15.3 | 20.1 | 38.1 | 6.3 | 5.6 | 100.0 |

*Source:* Wellman, 1979.

Wellman discvered that the intimate ties were widely dispersed over metropolitan Toronto and beyond (see Table 14-1). Three-quarters of the intimates were located in the metropolitan area, including one-quarter in the suburbs, despite the East York location near the city center. Table 14-1 shows that the East Yorkers were unlikely to have family in the borough, parents were likely to live elsewhere in the city, but some relatives also lived in East York and in the suburbs. Despite the fact that a quarter of the intimates lived in East York (in the respondent's immediate neighborhood or elsewhere in the district), the survey clearly shows dispersion of social ties.

The researchers also explored the frequency of contact among the individuals and their means of communication; the interview asked how often people saw each other and how often they communicated by phone. Interpersonal contact and use of the phone are particularly interesting aspects of physically distant relationships. Table 14-2 shows that weekly contact in person and by phone is common even in relationships with persons living in different sections of the city or in the suburbs. The phone is a crucial device to maintain relationships dispersed over the face of the metropolitan area.

The social networks tend to be loosely knit:

The mean density of East Yorkers' intimate networks is 33%; that is, one-third of all possible intimate ties between respondents' networks are actually reported to exist. Only

**TABLE 14-2**
**Reliance on Different Modes of Contact, Controlled by Intimates' Residential Location, %**

| Mode and frequency of contact | Same neighborhood | Elsewhere in East York | City of Toronto | Elsewhere in metro Toronto | Outside metro Toronto |
|---|---|---|---|---|---|
| In person weekly or more often; telephone weekly or more often | 51.9 | 53.4 | 43.0 | 38.8 | 6.8 |
| In person weekly or more often; telephone twice per month or less | 31.5 | 15.5 | 13.1 | 11.6 | 4.8 |
| In person twice per month or less; telephone weekly or more often | 4.8 | 9.5 | 20.9 | 20.8 | 21.8 |
| In person twice per month or less; telephone twice per month or less | 11.9 | 21.5 | 23.0 | 28.8 | 66.7 |
| Total | 100.1 | 99.9 | 100.0 | 100.0 | 100.1 |
| Number of respondents | 505 | 483 | 975 | 984 | 947 |

*Residential location*

Source: Wellman, 1979.

one-fifth of the networks have a density greater than 50%, although many intimates are more weakly connected to each other. Thus, the great majority of respondents are not encapsulated within the bounds of one solitary group, but are linked through their intimates to multiple, not strongly connected, social networks. (Wellman, 1979, p. 1215)

In addition to being loosely knit, the networks are somewhat specialized in terms of what the individuals do for each other. Most people (81 percent) reported they would expect help in an emergency from someone in their networks, and 60 percent reported help is available for dealing with everyday matters; but the respondents would not expect help from a majority of their intimates, only from some.

Wellman concluded that these city people are not embedded in a tight community but live their social lives in differentiated networks. The East Yorkers are linked to various individuals who live in different residential areas, some of whom interact at work, and they maintain contact both in person and by phone, at a wide range of time intervals.

### Korean Immigrants in New York City

Illsoo Kim's (1981) participant observational study of Korean-Americans in New York City also illuminates the concept of urban networks. Noting that Koreans have been migrating to the United States since the Immigration Act of 1965, Kim examined the community life of the thousands who settled in New York. He discovered that their settlement and adjustment are in one way radically different from the pattern of the nationalities of the mass Atlantic migration which ended a half-century ago.

This key difference is what Kim calls the "nonterritorial basis" of the community. Previous immigrant groups formed enclaves, port-of-entry neighborhoods ("Little Italy," "Chinatown," etc.), where they lived together, formed ethnic institutions, and began their entry into American society. Unlike them, the Koreans are dispersed throughout the metropolitan area (Kim, 1981). They have scattered into residential areas ranging from the poverty- and crime-ridden South Bronx to affluent suburban Scarsdale; they live in lower Manhattan as well as in remote suburbs on Long Island. Most often they live in white middle-class areas in the borough of Queens, side-by-side with second- or third-generation members of older immigrant groups as well as with newer immigrants such as Cubans, Greeks, and other Asians. But nowhere do they have a single-block ethnic residential enclave. Indeed, unlike Boston's second- and third-generation Italian-Americans, who deliberately stayed in the central city in an urban village, the Koreans move to the suburbs as soon as they begin to "make it" in terms of occupation and income.

Not having their own neighborhood base, the Koreans maintain ethnic solidarity and help each other adapt by means of a highly developed set of social networks. Kim refers to one form of network as a "pseudo-extended family," which is an informal network of several nuclear families, not based on actual kinship, who

Using traditional network structures to support their entrepreneurship, the Korean-American group has rapidly entered the urban middle class. (Randy Matusow)

may act as though they were related by blood or marriage. They exchange material and emotional support and may get together on special occasions such as Christmas, New Year's Eve, and Chinese New Year's Day to eat, dance, and talk. A pseudo-extended family may be based upon residence in the same area, common occupation, or even some previous association in Korea, such as being alumni of the same school.

Another kind of social network functions as a rotating credit association (Kim, 1981), known as a "gye." In traditional Korean social structures the gye was a cooperative which pooled money and promoted mutual assistance, friendship, and goodwill. New York's immigrants have imported and adapted a form of this system. The loan gye continues as a rotating credit association, serving as a means for accumulating capital to expand common business activities and services. In addition, gyes are now used for recreational and social activities; many such networks, highly specialized in their social bases; have been established: ones composed of doctors, nurses, owners of small businesses, produce retailers, even one composed of former miners. People shift and realign their memberships; if a person moves to a different section of the metropolis, he or she may join new networks.

Most of the immigrants are Christians, and their churches are integral to their networks. The churches tend to be small, with fewer than 200 members, and like the immigrants, they are dispersed throughout the New York area. Each minister has a number of functions; serving as matchmaker, performing marriages, visiting sick members, assisting families in moving, and meeting newcomers at the airport. The minister also mediates between network members and the larger society by serving as an English-language interpreter and by making job and housing referrals. "The minister's ultimate competence is displayed in his ability to link his congregation with the dominant secular institutions of the larger society." (Kim, 1981, pp. 200–201). Other church members also serve key network roles. In every church a group of experts assumes positions of lay leadership, counseling on immigration and naturalization procedures and on employment, housing, health care, social security, and education. They help individuals operate at the interface between the immigrant network and the larger community.

Kim says no centralized metropolitan Korean-American organization or leadership has emerged, but this dense set of networks has mechanisms which hold the Korean community together. Korean newspapers in the city inform the geographically scattered immigrants of meetings and events and also try to integrate the Koreans and to generate some sort of consensus among them. Korean restaurants and churches provide space for the networks' many organizational activities. Furthermore, a good deal of overlapping occurs in memberships, because one household may be involved in several networks based upon occupation, neighborhood, home-country affiliations, etc.

This nonterritorial basis of community has two overall implications, according to Kim. Unlike previous immigrants who had geographical concentrations, Korean-Americans cannot develop political strength as a voting bloc in one precinct or ward. Also, they will not go through the process of invasion and succession, entering and leaving entire residential areas. On the other hand, they are apparently benefiting from their spatial dispersion; Korean immigrants have exhibited very rapid social mobility through retail trade and entry into the professions. Perhaps their dispersion aids their assimilation because they come into direct contact with the non-Korean community almost immediately, rather than being buffered from it by an all-Korean immigrant enclave.

## BASIC CONCEPTS

### Egocentric Networks

Network research usually looks at networks from the point of view of some specific person (ego). Figures 14-1 and 14-2 are diagrams of small, egocentric networks. In figure 14-1 the central character, ego, is shown as "x," who has seven acquaintances. In figure 14-2 the central character is ego, who is linked to seven others, but this diagram also shows the ties among ego's friends. A nonegocentric network is conceivable also, for example, all the dentists on the West Coast, but extremely large and amorphous networks are hardly researchable, so social scientists have had to

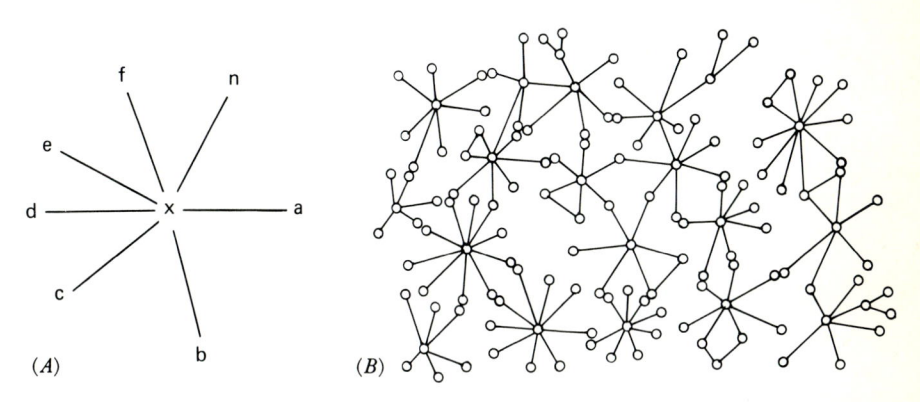

**FIGURE 14-1**
Personal networks. *(A)* Acquaintances of ego "x". *(B)* Network of acquaintances. (Source: Milgram, 1969; p. 106.)

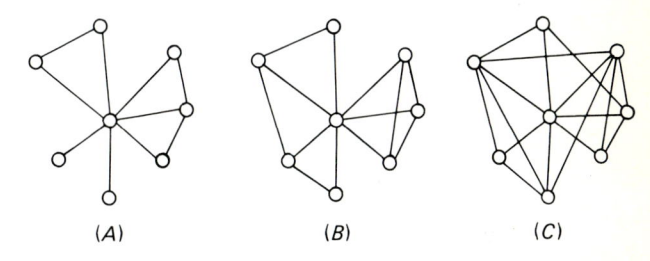

**FIGURE 14-2**
Networks of varying density. *(A)* 10 actual linkages out of 28 possible, among 8 persons; *(B)* 13 actual linkages out of 28; *(C)* 17 actual linkages out of 28.

ignore them.[1] The survey is one feasible research method in which the researcher asks a sample of individuals for information about their close acquaintances. (Wellman's, 1979, Toronto survey is one such study.) Fischer (1982) used a slightly different interview tactic in a network study. He asked each individual to name others with whom they visit, go out to dinner, ask for personal advice, borrow money in an emergency, etc. Then he asked whether these others were kinfolk, friends, coworkers, etc., and which of them knew each other. From the answers to these questions, and with help from his university's computer because there were so

---

[1]The major exception to this generalization is in the field of diffusion research. In this area, researchers attempt to discover how some technological innovation, such as a new medicine or a new agricultural invention, diffuses within a population of potential users—doctors or farmers, in these cases. Researchers inquire about interpersonal communications and linkages within large networks in diffusion studies.

# CHAPTER·14

many answers, he was able to construct individuals' social networks—but they had to be egocentric networks, because each one was built around the acquaintances of the individual who was in the sample.

Fischer's northern California survey found that the average adult is involved with about 15 to 17 others (see Figure 14-3). Despite having roughly equal numbers of social ties, rural and urban people differ in their involvements. People in towns and suburbs have somewhat more social involvement than those in a large central city and those in "semirural" areas. The smaller the community, the more likely its

**FIGURE 14-3**
Urbanism and social involvement. The rural-urban difference in total number of persons named is quite small, but rural people are more involved with kinfolk, while suburban and city people are more involved with friends and other nonkin. (Source: Fischer, 1982; p. 57.)

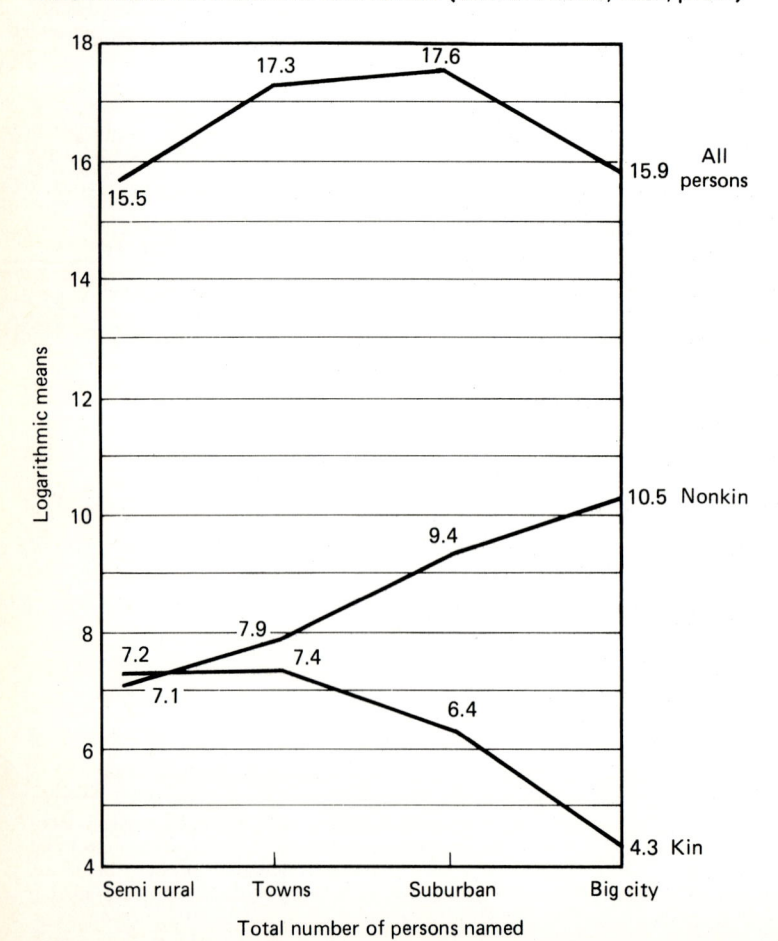

inhabitants are to be involved with kinfolk; the larger the community, the more likely its inhabitants are to be involved with nonkin—friends, coworkers, and others.

These numbers, 15 to 17, do not represent the full extent of our social contacts, which in fact is much greater. Several years ago one researcher asked a sample of men and women to keep a record of all the persons they came in contact with over the course of 100 days. On the average, they recorded roughly 500 names (Guervitch, 1961, cited in Milgram, 1969).

## Properties of Ties

There are two ways of looking at networks; we can look at the ties between pairs of individuals, or we can look at the network as a whole. Starting with the ties themselves, we will see that they vary like all human relationships. We will focus on three aspects of two-person ties.

## Multistrandedness

This concept refers to the number of ways in which two people may be involved with each other. If they have a simple, one-dimensional relationship, as between a doctor and a nurse who interact only about their work and nothing else, the tie has only one strand (work). If they work together and also share a pastime, say tennis, the tie has two strands. If they are married and have children, kinfolk, and all the other involvements of family life, the tie is multistranded.

Traditional theories of rural and urban differences, such as gemeinschaft and gesellschaft and urbanism as a way of life, state that people in small communities belong to primary groups with their all-encompassing relationships while city people are connected, if at all, by secondary segmental relationships. In the vocabulary of network analysis, those theories were saying that small-town folks shared multistranded ties and that city people, if they had ties, had single-stranded ones with people they scarcely knew. In the Northern California survey, Fischer tested these ideas too.

In order to explore multistrandedness, Fischer's interviewers asked questions about individuals' connections with others: With whom do you discuss work, hobbies, and personal problems; who helps you around the house; with whom do you go out; who would lend you money if you were in trouble? If a respondent mentioned another individual for three or more of these common activities, the researchers defined their tie as multistranded. On the average, each respondent had 2.6 multistranded ties (Fischer, 1982). Considerable differences were revealed among categories of people, though.

Metropolitan residents had just as many multistranded ties as did small-town and rural people; however, age, education, employment, and network size made a difference in multistrandedness. The major variable was age—young people were much more likely to have multistranded ties; also, individuals who were employed and those who had more education were more likely to have multistranded relationships. And people with larger networks tended to have more multistranded ties, contrary to the older theories, which said that urbanites might have more contacts, but they would be superficial. In sum, according to Fischer:

> People in the modern sectors of society—the young, educated, and urban—have, at least by this analysis, roughly as multistranded networks as their counterparts in the traditional sectors. This challenges the standard formulas. These models ought to be recast... by realizing that, when individuals gain access to more people, rather than by spreading their social life more thinly, they may actually enjoy richer social lives. (1982, p. 143)

## Weak and strong ties

Network ties differ in their strength; they may be strong or weak. "The strength of a tie is a combination of the amount of time, the emotional intensity, the intimacy (mutual confiding), and the reciprocal services which characterize the tie" (Granovetter, 1973, p. 1361). (Unfortunately, strength is not perfectly distinct from multistrandedness.) Any individual should be able to think of friends, acquaintances, and kinfolk and differentiate his or her own weak and strong ties. Most persons will find that they have many more weak ties than strong ties.

Sociologist Mark Granovetter (1973) studied the job-search process and wrote a report intriguingly named "The Strength of Weak Ties." Previous studies indicated that blue-collar workers learn about new jobs more often through personal contacts than by any other methods (such as newspaper ads and employment agencies) and that professional, technical, and managerial individuals also found employment through word of mouth. Granovetter, exploring this process further, studied a sample of professional, technical, and managerial job changers in one community and learned that most of them had found their jobs through interpersonal contacts, but the people who told them about the jobs were rarely close friends or relatives. More than 4 out of 5 of those who told them about the jobs were individuals they saw only occasionally or rarely; thus in such an important area of life as finding a job, people were benefiting from the weak ties. "In many cases, the contact was someone only marginally included in the current network of contacts, such as an old college friend or a former workmate or employer, with whom sporadic contact had been maintained. Usually such ties had not even been very strong when first forged.... Chance meetings or mutual friends operated to reactivate such ties" (Granovetter, 1973, p. 1371).

Granovetter says weak ties hold together all sorts of macrostructures in urban society; in this case, helping the economy to work by placing individuals in jobs. Weak ties bridge various cliques and diverse networks. The other side of the coin, according to Granovetter, is that structures can have too many strong ties which then make the structures ineffective. He points to the residents of Boston's "urban village" as an example (see Chapter 9). The Italian-Americans of the west end enjoyed their tightly knit family and ethnic life, but having so many strong ties, they lacked the weak ties that would have connected them to the rest of the city's political life. This made them ignorant of urban development strategy and gave them no way to articulate with other power centers in order to fight for the preservation of their neighborhood. In sum, Granovetter says weak ties are enormously important in holding urban communities together.

## Homogeneity and heterogeneity

The more similar two individuals are, the more likely they are to meet and become friends; conversely, the less similar two individuals are in social characteristics, the less likely they are to be close friends. Verbrugge (1977) calls this bias toward status similarity in adult friendships the "proximity principle." After studying friendship ties in two cities, one in the United States and one in Germany, and after studying the literature on the subject, she affirmed the principle. It holds for mating as well as for creating adult friendships.

Verbrugge's analysis showed that pairs of friends were highly likely to be similar along five variables: marital status, sex, religious preference, political preference, and employment status (whether they were working or unemployed). Five additional variables were almost as likely to show similarities within pairs of friends: occupation, nationality, age, educational prestige, and occupational prestige. In particular, pairs of "best friends" tend to be similar, more so than other close friends. In sum, the study showed that adult friendships are strongly stratified with regard to social statuses, attitudes, and demographic characteristics, and Verbrugge stated that the strong bias for similarity in age, sex, and marital status was particularly striking.

Laumann (1973) emphasized ethnic and religious similarities within friendship networks, stating, "Religious differences were found to have an especially strong impact on the form of a man's friendship networks" (p. 202). He found that Catholics and Jews were likely to have "ethnoreligiously homogeneous," interlocking networks; urban Protestants, on the other hand, were more likely to find themselves in networks which were ethnoreligiously heterogeneous and occupationally homogeneous.

## Density

The term "density" refers to the "connectedness" of the individuals within a network. Operationally defined, density is the proportion of *actually existing* relations to the relations that would exist among a given number of people if they were all directly linked to one another (Hannerz, 1980). Returning to Figure 14-2 for a hypothetical example, we see three networks, each having eight members. In the first (*a*), although everyone is tied to ego, most of the others have no links to each other; forming a low-density network. In the third (c), most of the others are linked to each other, forming a very dense network. Even in (c), though, another eleven ties are possible. The density in network (b) is intermediate between (a) and (c).

To measure a network's density, a researcher counts the number of observed ties and divides by the number of possible ones. Informally, an individual can determine the density of her or his own network, say, one composed of friends, by asking whether the friends know one another. If most of them do, the network is close-knit; if most do not, it is loose-knit.

Networks are not necessarily even in density. Imagine an individual who is a member of several networks, which extend some distance away from her or him (the individual might be at the center of Figure 14-1b, for example). This person's large network might have some cliques within it, and she or he might be a member of a group in which each of the members is directly linked with every other member. This group would be called the person's intimate or effective network, those with whom she or he interacts most intensely and regularly and who are therefore likely to come to know one another (Granovetter, 1973). Often, analyzing an ego-centered network, a researcher will find a dense cluster around ego and a gradual decline in density away from it (Hannerz, 1980).

Logically, network density is independent of the strength and multistrandedness of the ties. Nonetheless, Granovetter (1973) says one's strong ties usually form a dense network, while weak ones form a less dense network. A rural-urban difference exists here; Fischer (1982) discovered that individuals in urban communities tended to have more loose-knit networks, while rural individuals tended to have denser networks.

## THE SMALL-WORLD PROJECT

Stanley Milgram (1969), a psychologist at Harvard University, wanted to learn how much connection exists among individuals in the U.S. population—what are the links connecting seemingly distant and different people? He devised an ingenious research procedure which illuminated some basic network features. Choosing Omaha, Nebraska, because of its distance from his location in Massachusetts, Milgram attempted to find the number of intermediate individuals it would take to connect a randomly chosen person "out there" with somebody in Massachusetts. His "target person" was a stockbroker in Sharon, Massachusetts (although it could have been anyone else willing to cooperate in the research project). Milgram mailed packets to a random sample of individuals in Omaha. Each packet contained:

1. The name of the target person, as well as certain information about him. This orients the participant toward a specific individual (Milgram, 1969).
2. A set of rules for reaching the target person. Perhaps the most important rule is, "If you do not know the target person on a personal basis, do not try to contact him directly. Instead, mail this folder . . . to a personal acquaintance who

is more likely than you to know the target person ... it must be someone you know on a first-name basis" (Milgram, 1969, p. 110). This rule sets the document into motion, moving it from one participant to the next, until it is sent to someone who knows the target person and the chain is completed.
3. A roster on which the participant affixes his or her name. This tells the person who receives the letter exactly who sent it. The roster also has another practical effect; it prevents endless looping of the document through a participant who has already been an earlier link in the chain, for each participant can see the exact sequence of persons that has led up to his or her own participation.
4. A stack of fifteen business reply cards. After forwarding the document, each participant was to mail a card to the researchers at Harvard.

The main question was, How many of the documents would make it all the way to the stockbroker in Sharon, Massachusetts, and how many intermediate links would be required? Eventually, 42 documents made it all the way to the target person. The longest chain required 10 intermediaries; the shortest required 3; and the median was 5.5 intermediaries. This surprising phenomenon—that perhaps five intermediaries can connect any two individuals in an enormous nation—is why the sampling is referred to as the "small-world" project.

In effect, these jumps represent linkages between large networks or social realms. Milgram wrote, "Each of us is embedded in a potential small world structure (1969, p. 114). But he continued:

> When we state that there are only 5.5 intermediate acquaintances, this connotes a closeness between the position of the starting person and the target persons, but this is ... misleading. If two persons are 5.5 removes apart, they are far apart indeed.... We should think of the two points as being not five persons apart, but five "circles of acquaintance" apart—five "structures" apart (p. 118).

It is not that each of our acquaintances links us to the larger social world. Some acquaintances have more contacts than others; some are relatively isolated, while others have wide circles of acquaintance. Milgram's small-world research shows how connections may be made between social realms.

The small-world project carries certain implications for understanding the metropolitan community as well. One may ask how an aggregation of city and suburbs totaling hundreds of thousands or millions of people can have any unity; how can such a population be considered a community; what holds it together? If we imagine that each person is a member of one or more networks, the small-world process shows us that at least occasional linkages exist between distant networks. The importance of weak links in the job-search process also shows how widespread networks and connections between networks operate within large metropolitan populations. Both these phenomena—the small world and the strength of weak ties—show that the large community may be seen as a network of networks. (Craven & Wellman, 1973).

## FUNCTIONS OF SOCIAL NETWORKS

### Chain Migration

"Chain migration can be defined as that movement in which prospective migrants learn of opportunities, are provided with transportation, and have initial accommodation and employment arranged by means of primary social relationships with previous migrants" (MacDonald & MacDonald, cited in Tilly, 1974, p. 227). This is a familiar scenario in American history: suffering from unemployment or some other problem, a man learns of an opportunity elsewhere, perhaps from a cousin, and moves there. The cousin puts him up and helps him to find a job; the man gradually saves his earnings to send for his wife and children. Whether the migration is from Poland to Chicago or from Mississippi to Detroit, chain migration is the name for the operation of social networks in the migration process.

One study of several hundred migrants showed that nearly half (49 percent) had moved alone and the rest had moved in the company of relatives (Choldin, 1973). Even those who move alone are usually part of a migration chain, though, as they may join those who preceded them or they may be followed by others. About a quarter (24 percent) were followed by others, within two years in almost all cases, and over two-thirds of the migrants had someone waiting in the city already. Of those waiting;

44 percent were close relatives—parents, spouse, fiancé, children.
27 percent were more distant relations—aunts, uncles, cousins.
11 percent were in-laws.
17 percent were friends.

Thus kinship networks, especially close family, are the most important agency for receiving migrants, far more prevalent than any formal organization.

Social networks assist migrants by providing three kinds of help: material assistance, intermediary help, and help in making new social connections (Choldin, 1973; (see Table 14-3). In their first year in the city, most migrants received at least one kind of aid, almost always provided by members of their social networks; Table 14-3 shows that the most common kinds of help were with housing and in finding a job. Migrants were far more likely to depend upon kinfolk rather than friends and coworkers, but even friends and coworkers helped much more than agencies.

Fischer's Northern California study (1982), which examined daily life rather than migration, shows that social support is a common function of social networks. Fischer also delineates three kinds of help: *counseling,* advice and discussion regarding personal matters; *companionship,* visiting, going out, discussing hobbies; and *practical,* material assistance. His survey showed that most individuals had adequate support in all three areas. Urban residents had more counseling and companionship than those in smaller, more rural places; indeed, according to Fisher, "The small towns, not the large cities, are the places to find people without social sup-

## TABLE 14-3
### Sources of Help for Various Problems*

| | Material needs | | | | Intermediary | | | | Connect |
|---|---|---|---|---|---|---|---|---|---|
| | Hous-ing | Finan-cial | Cloth-ing | Food | Find-ing job | Met at depot | Infor-mation | Trans-por-tation | Contact other person |
| Percentage of all migrants receiving this kind of help | 64.1 | 29.3 | 18.1 | 19.8 | 50.2 | 33.4 | 36.4 | 17.8 | 14.7 |
| **Sources of help:**[a] | | | | | | | | | |
| Primary group | | | | | | | | | |
| Nuclear family | 41.9 | 49.9 | 49.4 | 36.2 | 33.8 | 48.2 | 37.4 | 38.9 | 38.5 |
| Other kinfolk | 35.6 | 29.0 | 37.3 | 33.3 | 33.0 | 34.1 | 30.6 | 29.8 | 33.5 |
| Friends, coworkers, neighbors | 18.4 | 14.9 | 5.2 | 16.3 | 26.1 | 17.1 | 29.0 | 25.4 | 27.1 |
| Private organizations | | | | | | | | | |
| Church | 0.5 | 2.4 | 2.7 | 3.8 | 0.8 | 0.4 | 0.2 | .... | 0.6 |
| Private charity organization[†] | 5.0 | 4.7 | 8.0 | 9.8 | 2.7 | 2.2 | 5.6 | 5.0 | 7.1 |
| Government and political organizations[‡] | 3.0 | 2.3 | .... | 3.7 | 6.5 | .... | 3.6 | 2.4 | .... |
| Other | 1.9 | 0.1 | .... | 0.2 | 3.4 | 1.9 | 0.9 | 0.6 | 0.2 |

*Column percentages may add to more than 100 as a respondent may have received one kind of help from more than one source.
[†]Includes settlement houses, Salvation Army, and other charities.
[‡]Includes political party help, as well as welfare and other agencies.
Source: Choldin, 1973, table 1.

port" (p. 126). The differences between places are small, and individuals are likely to find social support in their networks regardless of where they live.

During the Atlantic migration, chain migration often led to concentrations of nationalities in particular neighborhoods and occupations. One historical study looked at the experiences of Italians in New York, showing how lone males assisted male relatives and friends to immigrate. "New arrivals usually went directly to the relatives and friends who had finance their passage, and relied upon them to find their first lodgings and employment. Their guardians usually lodged them in their own quarters or found a room in the neighborhood, and found them work close by, since the 'Little Italies' were conveniently located near the principal markets of unskilled labor" (MacDonald & MacDonald, cited in Tilly, 1974, pp. 230-231). These chains of kinfolk and friends naturally went back to particular communities in the old country and brought newcomers to particular neighborhoods in American cities, sharply defining the ports of entry. Within Italian neighborhoods particular blocks were populated by people from particular towns in Italy: Calabrians on Mulberry Street were grouped according to their towns of origin, and Sicilians from the town of Cinisi concentrated in midtown Manhattan, for example. Such concentrations allowed the immigrants to preserve elements of their culture and to adapt special ways of life in the city. One problem was that most of the immigrants were new. They needed to bring over some women, but they were so poor that they also needed the women to work for pay. The tradition in Italy was that women stayed home; it was considered improper for them to be in contact with males outside the family. By having their own minineighborhood, the migrants could develop local businesses or bring work home to generate income without violating the tradition; the point-of-entry neighborhood facilitated this sort of adaptation. (It is by contrast with this historical background of ethnic neighborhood concentration that the spatial dispersion of Korean immigrants is so unusual.)

## Jobs and Social Classes

Sociologists have devoted considerable attention to the process of status attainment, asking, "What are the factors that determine where a person is located in the hierarchy of occupations?" Answers to this question have emphasized the social status of the person's father, plus the importance of educational attainment—how far an individual goes in school—in status attainment. But recent studies, including Granovetter's (1973) on weak ties, have incorporated social networks in addition to father's status and educational attainment. Lin, Vaughn, and Ensel (1981) conducted one such study.

Lin and associates consider network contacts to be *social resources*, especially if the contacts have some advantages for the job seekers. "Social resources are defined as the wealth, status, power, as well as social ties, of those persons who are directly or indirectly linked to the individual" (Lin et al., 1981, p. 1163). The researchers noted that previous studies showed weak ties tend to lead to individuals of higher status in the status hierarchy. Lin's central proposition was that social resources through networks "provide an essential transition between family background and education on the one hand and socioeconomic status achievement on the other" (p. 1163). He and his associates designed a research project to test the hypothesis that the socioeconomic status characteristics of personal contacts affect variations in the level of occupational statuses eventually attained. In their study they looked closely at how each individual found first and last jobs. Like previous researchers they found that many but not all of the persons studied used network contacts to find their jobs; the researchers focused on those cases which involved the use of network contacts.

Their data showed that an individual possesses a substantial advantage in the occupational attainment process if the person has access to and uses greater social resources; it helps to have ties to individuals with higher status than one's own. Use of social resources has its greatest impact as an individual finds the first job, but its effect persists throughout the work life. Educational attainment is fundamentally important for occupational status attainment, but beyond this, the transition from family to work is mediated by the use of social resources.

For the urban community and its stratification system, this means that social networks play a role in social mobility as well as in the maintenance of social classes. People may move upward if they get the requisite education, but they are helped measurably if they have social ties to someone with a higher status than their own. A connection exists between microsocial and macrosocial structures. At the microsocial level, individuals are involved in their intimate kinship and friendship networks; the macrosocial structure arranges the population into a set of social classes. To a large extent, an individual's network connects the individual to others of his or her own class, as indicated in the homogeneity principle. Thus, to the extent that superior social resources are necessary to achieve high status, networks tend mainly to maintain the stratification system.

## A Footnote on Gossip

The preceding sections on migration, jobs, and social classes might imply that networks function only to do the heavy jobs of a society. Not so; they function as well for little things, like choosing dresses and movies, as well as transmitting gossip. According to urban anthropologist Ulf Hannerz (1980), gossip moves through social networks, and one of its functions is to maintain the unity of groups. This applies especially to exclusive and well-bounded ones, groups like elites, professions, and minorities. Hannerz says that gossiping about people is a way of expressing and affirming norms: "Through gossip, one can bring injury to enemies and sanctions against defaulters within the group. One can also keep intruders out, as they do not have the accumulated knowledge about people and their past conduct which is the foundation of gossip as a noble art" (pp. 186-187).

Looked at this way, gossip is a means of informal social control in the context of social networks. Listening to gossip, people know what might be said about themselves if they break the rules. The rules are repeated, and they know they might be ridiculed and even reviled if they transgress them. Thus the group reaffirms the rules by repeating and emphasizing them in the form of gossip.

## SUMMARY

Social network analysis shows that urban and suburban individuals are not socially isolated; almost all of them (with the exception of perhaps 1 or 2 percent) have close social ties with others outside their homes. Furthermore, the difference between the social ties of urban and rural individuals are fewer than traditional theories would have predicted. According to Fischer, rural, urban, and suburban residents have about the same numbers of close social ties; small-town individuals have more involvement with kinfolk; while urban and suburban individuals are more involved with friends and other nonkin.

The network concept helps us to understand social life in the metropolis in the absence of perfect little neighborhoods. Most metropolitan residents have only a small fraction of their close associates in their residential neighborhood. The rest are dispersed throughout the city and suburbs; they keep in touch by means of face-to-face encounters plus telephone calls.

Between two individuals, ties within networks vary in strandedness. Close ties are multistranded; rural and urban residents have about the same numbers of multistranded ties. Close associates are likely to be homogeneous in social characteristics, particularly age, sex, and marital status.

Networks vary in density; they may be loose-knit or tight-knit. An individual's closest associates are likely to form a dense network. The networks of rural individuals are likely to be tighter than those of urban residents, but urban individuals are likely to have more social ties overall.

Social networks perform many functions:

1. They provide social support to individuals, including counseling, companionship, and practical help. Most individuals appear to have adequate supplies of all three.
2. They play an active role in migration. Most migrants participate in chain migration, which provides them with information and help. After migration, social networks provide migrants with material assistance and other forms of help.
3. In many cases, they help individuals find jobs.
4. They even transmit gossip, a device which provides informal social control.

Social networks underlie the community's social classes. Individuals' close ties tend to be with others of their own socioeconomic status. In the absence of educational attainment, this tends to restrict individuals' access to higher-status occupations. Social mobility is promoted when a person has a tie, weak or strong, to someone who can help her or him get a higher-ranking job.

Social networks play a part in tying together large populations and subsystems of the metropolis. Individuals in disparate networks may have weak ties with each other, which form bridges between different subsystems. Thus the metropolis may be seen as a network of networks.

## REFERENCES

Bott, Elizabeth. 1957. *Family and Social Network.* London: Tavistock.
Choldin, Harvey M. 1973. "Kinship Networks in the Migration Process." *International Migration Review.* 7:163–176.
Craven, Paul, and Barry Wellman. 1973. "The Network City." *Sociological Inquiry.* 43:57–88.
Fischer, Claude S. 1982. *To Dwell Among Friends: Personal Networks in Town and City.* Chicago: University of Chicago Press.
Granovetter, Mark. 1973. "The Strength of Weak Ties." *American Journal of Sociology.* 78:1360–1380.
Hannerz, Ulf. 1980. *Exploring the City: Inquiries Toward an Urban Anthropology.* New York: Columbia.
Katz, Elihu, and Paul F. Lazarsfeld. 1955. *Personal Influence.* Glencoe, Ill.: Free Press.
Kim, Illsoo. 1981. *The New Urban Immigrants: The Korean Community in New York.* Princeton, N.J.: Princeton.
Laumann, Edward O. 1973. *Bonds of Pluralism.* New York: Wiley.
Lazarsfeld, Paul F., Bernard Berelson, and Hazel Gaudet. 1944. *The People's Choice.* New York: Duell, Sloan and Pearce.
Lewis, Michael. 1978. *The Culture of Inequality.* Amherst: University of Massachusetts Press.
Lin, Nan, John C. Vaughn, and Walter M. Ensel. 1981. "Social Resources and Occupational Status Attainment." *Social Forces.* 59:1163–1181.
MacDonald, John S., and Leatrice D. MacDonald. 1964. "Chain Migration, Ethnic Neighborhood Formation, and Social Networks." *Milbank Memorial Fund Quarterly.* 42:82–97.
Milgram, Stanley. 1969. "Interdisciplinary Thinking and the Small World Problems," chap. 6 in *Interdisciplinary Relationships in the Social Sciences,* (eds.) Muzafer Sherif and Carolyn W. Sherif. Chicago: Aldine.
Stahura, John M. 1978. "The Evolution of Suburban Functional Roles." *Pacific Sociological Review.* 21(4):423.
Tilly, Charles (ed.). 1974. *An Urban World.* Boston: Little, Brown.
Verbrugge, Lois M. 1977. "The Structure of Friendship Choices." *Social Forces.* 56:577–597.
Wellman, Barry. 1979. "The Community Question: The Intimate Networks of East Yorkers." *American Journal of Sociology.* 84:1201–1231.
Young, Michael, and Peter Willmott. 1957. *Family and Kinship in East London.* London: Routledge.

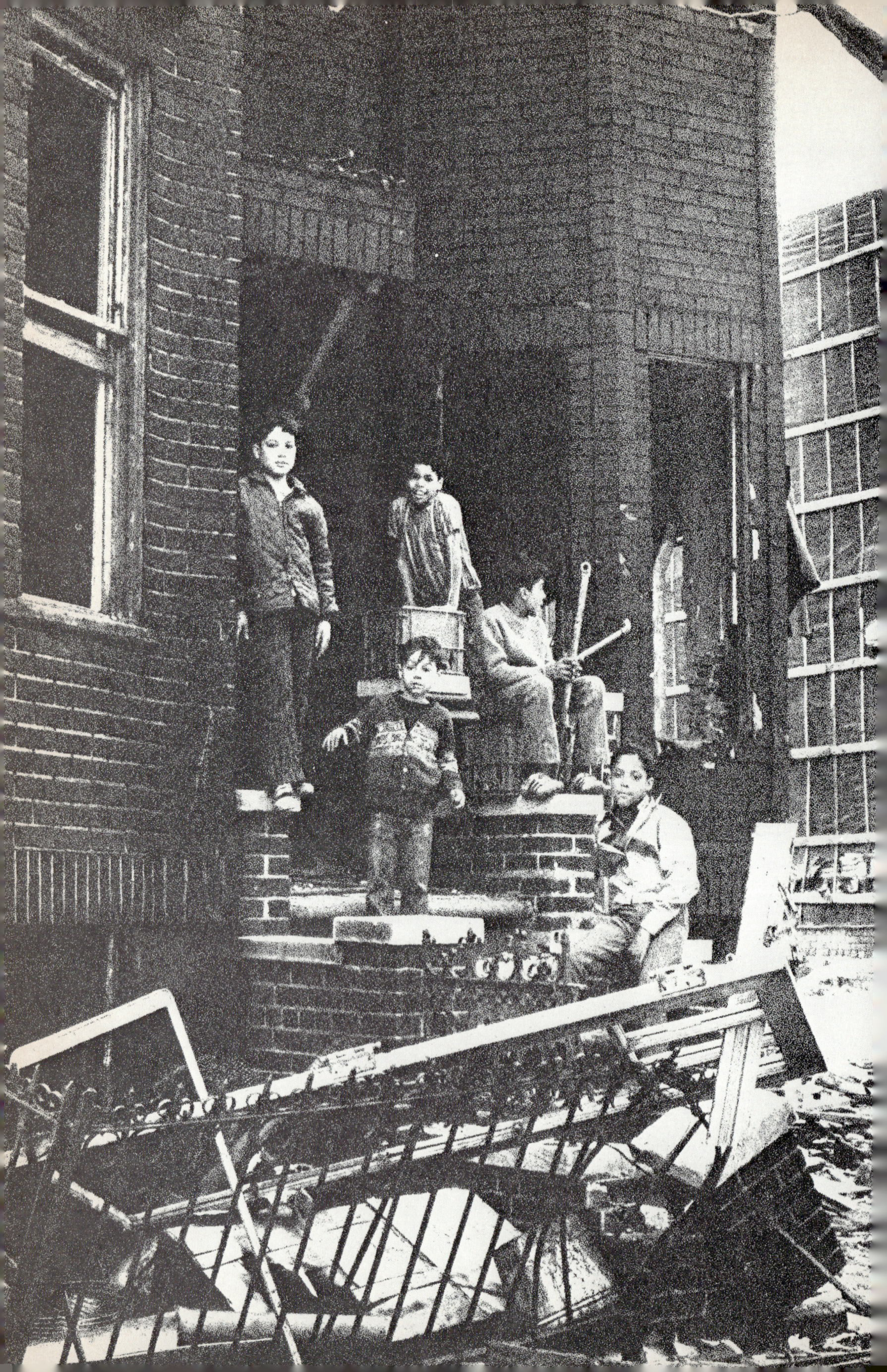

# CHAPTER • 15

# Slums: Conditions and Programs

## Chapter Outline

**BASIC CONCEPTS**
  Definition
  Location
  Poverty

**THE RESIDENTS' POINT OF VIEW**
  "Fear and the House-as-Haven"
- Nonhuman dangers
- Human dangers

  Health and Crime
- Health
- Crime
- "Urban Pathologies"

  Isolation
  Uses of the Slum

**IMMORAL LANDSCAPES**
  Red-Light Districts
  Skid Row

**SOCIETAL RESPONSES**
  Philanthropy and Regulation
  Housing Standards
  Public Housing

**FAILURES OF PUBLIC HOUSING: TWO STUDIES**
  Pruitt-Igoe: A Federal Slum
  Defensible Space: Crime and the Built Environment

**BEYOND PUBLIC HOUSING**
  Scattering the Poor
  The Experimental Housing Allowance Program
  Urban Renewal

**SUMMARY**

## BASIC CONCEPTS

Slums have been enduring features of cities since the advent of industrialism. Several sociological questions persist about slums, starting with their definition—what are their basic properties? What environmental and social properties do slums have? How are slums related to the larger metropolitan community? And, since our society has often attempted to develop policies and programs to deal with slums, sociologists ask questions about the policies as well as the slums themselves. Historically, what were the first approaches to solving the slum problem; what were their underlying premises; what were the effects? How have the approaches changed; what results have they produced? Answers to these questions form the core of Chapter 15.

The text has referred to slums at several points already. Reviewing the origins of urban sociology we noted that reformers as well as the first urban sociologists were concerned about slum conditions. Zorbaugh's classic study *The Gold Coast and the Slum* (1929) typifies these concerns. In Chapter 4 we noted that slums were a basic feature of mature industrial cities, housing the millions of immigrants who were part of the new labor force; Burgess's concentric zones model placed the slums right outside the CBD, in the zone in transition. Reviewing residential differentiation, we discovered that social area analysis divides areas into types and that cities always have some low-status areas. Studying the neighborhood life cycle, we encountered the downgrading and thinning-out stages, which correspond to the formation of new and old slums; during the latter stage a slum is likely to experience the process of abandonment and arson. Finally, studying about the black dimension and about localities, we encountered Warren and Warren's (1977) typology of neighborhoods. At least two of their types appeared to be slums, the transitory neighborhood and the anomic neighborhood, with no identity, no internal group life, and no effective linkages to the wider community. So many references to the same subject show that it is impossible to study the metropolis without considering slums. And even though the subject has been mentioned here and there, it requires a chapter to be considered more completely.

Contemporary America has a new sort of "slum problem," though, in two ways. First, the urban housing stock has improved so much that most workers occupy standard-quality houses or apartments, and second, government action to replace slums has inadvertently produced an unprecedented type of subcommunity, the public-housing project, with modern buildings but all the social pathologies of classical slums. (Public-housing projects are discussed in the second half of this chapter.)

In metropolitan areas, households, including the poor, enjoyed a substantial improvement in housing quality between 1950 and 1970. In 1950, 1 in 5 poor renters lacked hot running water and exclusive use of toilet or shower; twenty years later this proportion dropped to 1 in 12. Crowding was also cut in half for poor renters. By 1970 a discernible proportion of poor households even had air conditioners. In surveys of the poorest households in three large cities, half the respondents said the quality of their housing unit was excellent and another third said it was satisfactory (cited in deLeeuw, Schnare, & Struyk, 1976). Researchers concluded that there was "unmistakable improvement" and that "the gap between housing occupied by low-income and other households has narrowed markedly" (deLeeuw et al., 1976, p. 122). On the other hand, though, sizable numbers of poor metropolitan residents still live in substandard housing.

A survey of the housing of welfare recipients in New York City shows the sorts of dwellings occupied by the poor (Sternlieb and Indik, 1973). About 80 percent of the welfare households were in apartments, although this proportion would be lower in other cities. Some of the apartments are in "welfare buildings," in which most of the occupants are recipients. Most of the buildings are old and poorly maintained; indeed, Sternlieb saw them as essentially worn out. In another study Sternlieb (1966) studied the economies of slum housing and concluded that to some extent the "slumlord" is a mythological creature. Although Sternlieb did not say the owners of slum housing are benevolent characters, he discovered that old apartment buildings in deteriorated neighborhoods are not necessarily the best investment in the real estate industry. Operating an old apartment building is a business that is about as profitable as operating other pieces of real property; it is a business with numerous drawbacks (Sternlieb, 1966).

## Definition

The *Oxford English Dictionary* offers this old definition of "slum": "A street, alley, court, etc., situated in a crowded district of a town or city and inhabited by people of a low class or by the very poor; a number of these streets or courts forming a thickly populated neighborhood or district where the houses and the conditions of life are of a squalid and wretched character."

This description now sounds somewhat quaint; sociologist Marshall Clinard (1966) has developed a more contemporary and general concept by enumerating a series of properties of a slum.

> *Housing:* "Slums have commonly been defined as those portions of cities in which housing is crowded, neglected, deteriorated, and often obsolete" (p. 4).
> *Overcrowding and congestion:* "A slum may be an area overcrowded with buildings, buildings overcrowded with people, or both" (p. 7).
> *Neighborhood facilities:* "Poor slum housing is invariably associated with poor facilities and community services. Along with shabbiness and dilapidation, the park facilities are inadequate, the schools are of poor quality, and other public facilities are often insufficient. Streets and sidewalks often go unrepaired, and rubbish and garbage are infrequently collected" (p. 8).
> *Poor sanitation and health:* "Slums have generally been dirty and unclean places" (p. 9).
> *Deviant behavior:* "A high incidence of deviant behavior—crime, juvenile delinquency, prostitution, drunkenness, drug usage, mental disorder, suicide, ille-

gitimacy, and family maladjustment—have long been associated with slum living" (p. 9).

*Apathy and social isolation:* The rest of the community look upon the slum and its people as inferior; furthermore, the slum is isolated from the rest of the community and lacks any effective linkages with it.

## Location

Slums are usually found near city centers, where the oldest and most obsolete housing is located (deLeeuw et al., 1976). A large metropolitan area may have several slums, particularly if it incorporated preexisting industrial towns (satellite cities) into the metropolis. While the slums of northern cities are near the old center, some cities in other regions exhibit different patterns. "In some southern cities the postbellum black enclaves were on the periphery of the developed city; and in the Southwest a similar pattern, imitative of South America, developed with poor Mexicans and Indians housed outside of the main city" (deLeeuw et al., 1976, p. 156). Slums tend to expand peripherally, absorbing adjacent residential areas.

## Poverty

The slum's first and simplest function is to provide cheap housing for poor households. Table 15-1 which is based upon an analysis of "poverty areas" in 20 large

**TABLE 15-1**
**Income Distribution of Families in Entire Metropolitan Areas\* and Poverty Areas within These Metropolitan Areas in 1970, by Race†**

|  | White families | | Black families | |
|---|---|---|---|---|
| Income | Poverty areas | Entire SMSA | Poverty areas | Entire SMSA |
| Under $5,000 | .30 | .13 | .38 | .32 |
| $5,000 to $10,000 | .37 | .30 | .34 | .36 |
| Over $10,000 | .31 | .57 | .25 | .34 |

\*Metropolitan areas included are Atlanta, Baltimore, Boston, Buffalo, Chicago, Cincinnati, Cleveland, Dallas, Detroit, Houston, Los Angeles, Milwaukee, Minneapolis-St. Paul, Newark, Philadelphia, Pittsburgh, San Francisco, St. Louis, and Washington, D.C.
†Figures are the arithmetic averages of the distributions of the individual areas, and for this reason may not sum to 1.00.
*Source:* deLeeuw et al., 1976, p. 157.

metropolitan areas, clearly shows that poor households are concentrated in particular residential areas (deLeeuw et al., 1976). A poverty area was defined as a group of contiguous census tracts where the incomes of at least one-fifth of the households were below the current poverty level. Compared with the overall metropolitan areas, the low incomes of the whites and blacks in these areas is apparent. Summarizing other results of that study, deLeeuw et al. say, "On average, poverty area residents are disproportionately black (58 percent), more often live in households headed by women (nearly a third), and constitute about one-fourth of the central city population" (p. 157).

## THE RESIDENTS' POINT OF VIEW

### "Fear and the House-as-Haven"

After studying poor people for many years, sociologist Lee Rainwater (1966) wrote an essay entitled "Fear and the House-as-Haven in the Lower Class," which portrays the slum from the resident's point of view. Rainwater says that an individual's attitude toward housing and neighborhood depends upon the person's social-class position; persons in different classes make different demands upon their environments. For example, working-class and middle-class individuals may use their housing as a means to collect and exhibit certain possessions; they may use their neighborhood to show their respectability and for certain outdoor activities. They demand adequate community facilities and services. But lower-class individuals living in slums have different concerns. Confronting many dangers, they have fears, and their baseline standard for house and neighborhood is *shelter*; they need the house-as-haven to protect themselves from two types of dangers, nonhuman and human. A good way to understand Rainwater's argument is to try, mentally, to put yourself into the shoes of a poor black woman who is trying responsibly to rear small children.

### Nonhuman dangers

Rainwater begins by enumerating several physical dangers of slum environments (see Table 15-2); his list reads like the plagues on the Egyptians in the Hebrew scriptures. Each item represents an environmental danger that is much more likely to be present in a lower-class district than in any other section of the metropolis.

Slums have many environmental hazards, particularly dangerous to small children. Due to the old age of the buildings, with their obsolete, worn, and overloaded electric wiring; worn-out and unserviced heating systems; and electric room heaters; and due to uncollected trash and arson, many more fires occur in slums than in other parts of the metropolis. Roaches and rats are endemic to urban communities, more so in deteriorated old buildings and where garbage collection is insufficient. Every poor mother in a slum must worry about protecting children, particularly

**TABLE 15-2**
**Dangers in the Lower-Class Home and Environs**

| Nonhuman danger source | Human danger source |
|---|---|
| Rats and other vermin | Violence to self and possessions |
| Poisons | Assault |
| Fire and burning | Fighting and beating |
| Freezing and cold | Rape |
| Poor plumbing | Objects thrown or dropped |
| Dangerous electrical wiring | Stealing |
| Trash (broken glass, cans, etc.) | Verbal hostility, shaming, exploitation |
| Insufficiently protected heights | Own family |
| Other aspects of poorly designed or deteriorated structures (e.g., thin walls) | Neighbors |
| | Caretakers |
| | Outsiders |
| Cost of dwelling | Attractive alternatives that wean oneself or valued others away from a stable life |

Source: Rainwater, 1966.

infants. Older buildings have layers of paint which accumulated during the years when paint formulas included lead; when the thick paint chips off the wall, children may suck on the chips (strangely enough, it is supposed to taste good). Lead-based paint is poisonous and may cause mental retardation. The other nonhuman hazards in Rainwater's list are self-explanatory.

The massive Annual Housing Survey, sponsored by the U.S. Department of Housing and Urban Development and conducted by the Bureau of the Census (1982), reveals deficiencies of the worst urban housing. Statistics in Table 15-3 reflect the condition of rental units in urban parts of SMSAs, showing that

**TABLE 15-3**
**Selected Deficiencies in Urban Rental Housing, 1979**

| Deficiency | Percent of units* |
|---|---|
| Some or all wiring exposed | 3.3 |
| No working electric outlets in some rooms | 3.6 |
| Blown fuses or tripped breakers in last 3 months | 10.6 |
| Signs of water leakage from roof | 8.4 |
| Interior walls and ceilings with open cracks or holes | 11.6 |
| Interior walls and ceilings with broken plaster | 7.2 |
| Interior walls and ceilings with peeling paint | 9.5 |
| Holes in interior floors | 3.3 |
| Loose steps in common stairways | 6.5 |
| Some or all lights not working in common halls | 10.5 |

*$N$ = 19,034 households.
Source: U.S. Bureau of the Census, 1982.

although most of the units are in good condition, a discernible fraction have serious deficiencies. Since the numbers include housing units in suburbs and central cities, they probably underestimate the proportion of deficient units within central cities. (The cities' housing stock is much older than the suburbs' stock.) The survey reveals several sorts of potentially dangerous conditions in the worst rental housing: exposed wiring, overloaded circuits, peeling paint, loose steps in stairways, dark hallways, and the like.

Poor families, though, are much more likely to encounter these housing deficiencies. The same survey of three cities mentioned earlier (cited in deLeeuw et al., 1976), showed that 9 percent of the poor households lacked electric outlets in some rooms; 8 percent had exposed wiring; 11 percent had leaking roofs; and 5 percent had holes in the floors. Thus poor families were at least twice as likely as the national average to have deficient housing.

## Human dangers

As a sociologist, Rainwater emphasizes the slum's social dangers to its inhabitants. They fear fires, rats, and bad wiring, but they also fear other people. The slum's dangerous people include higher-status individuals as well as other poor persons; outsiders as well as insiders. Crime is perhaps the first of the slum's interpersonal dangers.

Although they have few possessions to offer, poor people are much more likely than wealthier individuals to become the victims of crime. In general, the level of violence is higher in slums than in other residential areas; more fights and assaults take place in slums than elsewhere. Therefore, the slum dweller's first housing need is for protection and defense.

Rainwater's list also mentions the danger of verbal hostility, meaning that the style of public interaction in the slum is likely to be rougher and more open than in other neighborhoods. He is not saying that everyone acts this way but that at least some individuals will engage in loud, insulting behavior and other verbal abuse and that our imaginary poor mother will want to avoid this behavior and to shelter her children from it.

Furthermore, external "caretakers" who work in the slums, mostly representatives of large municipal bureaucracies—teachers, welfare workers, parole officers, police officers, clinic workers—may engage in verbal or nonverbal abuse against the poor. Despite the fact that most caretakers belong to what used to be known as "the helping professions," they may behave in ways that keep the slum dwellers in their place. Many agencies have rules and procedures that are demeaning to their clients. Some employees may simply be crass; others may not appreciate cultural differences which divide some of the groups in poverty from the metropolitan majority (Gans, 1982). Whatever the reason, the caretakers can be a burden upon the slum dwellers.

"Attractive alternatives," Rainwater's last entry in Table 15-2, is perhaps the most intriguing. Slums have always housed individuals and groups who were rejected by polite society and could not live in middle-class neighborhoods: prostitutes, pimps, drug dealers, criminals, and others whose incomes come from illegal activities; slums also have teen gangs and organized crime. These groups and individuals provide the attractive alternatives; in the neighborhood they may have considerable prestige—adolescents may admire them for their cars, clothes, and other possessions. They symbolize a means to success without following the rules of teachers, preachers, and police officers—a considerable temptation. The straight slum dweller seeks refuge in a better neighborhood.

## Health and Crime

Statistical comparisons between poverty areas and the rest of the city or metropolis show that the poor mother's perspective, as presented by Rainwater, is rather accurate. This is shown in studies of health and of crime and delinquency.

### Health

Comparing 16 low-income areas of New York City with the rest of the city, public-health researchers showed that the poverty areas had substantially higher rates of infant and maternal mortality and of premature births. They also had higher rates of illegitimacy, syphilis, and tuberculosis (Ford, 1976). Results of a similar study of 19 large cities are shown in Table 15-4. Infant mortality rates, for example, are more than 50 percent higher in low-income areas than in the rest of the city. All other

**TABLE 15-4**
**Vital Statistics for an Average of 19 Large Cities of the United States, by Income Area and Color, 1969–1971**

|  | Low-income areas | | | Remainder of city | | |
|---|---|---|---|---|---|---|
|  | Total | White | All other | Total | White | All other |
| Low birth weight (2,500 grams or less) (per 100 live births) | 13.1 | 9.3 | 15.1 | 8.3 | 7.0 | 12.4 |
| Infant mortality rate (per 1,000 live births) | 30.2 | 24.2 | 33.4 | 19.7 | 17.4 | 27.0 |
| No prenatal care (per 100 live births) | 5.0 | 4.2 | 5.3 | 1.8 | 1.5 | 2.8 |
| Illegitimate births (per 100 live births) | 40.8 | 23.7 | 49.5 | 13.1 | 7.3 | 30.9 |
| Death rate from tuberculosis (per 100,000 population) | 9.5 | 8.7 | 10.0 | 3.0 | 2.8 | 4.3 |
| Death rate from violent causes (per 100,000 population) | 115.5 | 112.7 | 117.1 | 61.9 | 59.0 | 75.7 |

*Source:* Ford, 1976, p. 67.

health pathologies reported are also higher in the poor sections, for whites and nonwhites. The methodology of these studies does not permit us to determine whether the diseases were caused by poverty itself or by living in slums, but perhaps the distinction is unimportant. Clearly, the health of poor households living in poor neighborhoods is worse than that of households living elsewhere. And these poor areas are also dangerous, as reflected in the bottom row of the table, which shows that their death rate from violent causes is roughly twice as high as in other parts of the cities.

## Crime

Since the beginning of spatial analysis in urban ecology, sociologists have shown that crime and juvenile delinquency are regularly patterned over the face of the metropolis. Shaw and McKay (1942), two members of the Chicago school, discovered that juvenile delinqency was concentrated in the poorer neighborhoods near the city center and that the rates were lower toward the urban periphery. They found this pattern in several cities in addition to Chicago and their results were confirmed in Baltimore (Lander, 1954), Detroit (Bordua, 1958), and Indianapolis (Chilton, 1964). Furthermore, these ecological studies found that the neighborhood correlates of delinquency were the same characteristics that define slums: overcrowded housing; low education and income; and households composed of unrelated individuals (Wolfgang, 1970). Shaw and McKay argued that certain neighborhoods tended to produce high delinquency rates, regardless of which ethnic groups lived there at the time. Thus, as residential succession of different nationality groups occurred, a high-delinquency area would still maintain its established level.

Studies of the spatial distribution of adult crimes in general generate the same patterns as the juvenile rates. A geographical study of Minneapolis showed that several types of crimes tend to be concentrated in low-income areas. Assaults, for example, are most likely to occur in the low-income fringes of the central business district; it occurs "in or near bars and cheap rooming houses in lower class neighborhoods" (Phillips, 1974, p. 2). This study showed high rates of domestic assaults, rapes, and purse snatching. And even though the households in low-status areas do not have much wealth, they have a higher probability of being burgled than do households in other residential areas.

St. Louis's crime statistics showed patterns similar to those from Minneapolis, with several crime rates related to the social status of the neighborhood. Boggs (1965) combined an analysis of crime records with a social area analysis of the city's census tracts and found that several types of crimes were negatively correlated with the social rank factor. This meant that neighborhoods with higher status had lower crime rates; which implies that slums probably had higher rates. The types of crimes that were negatively related to socioeconomic status were residential burglary, homicide-assault, and auto theft. Forcible rape had a smaller correlation, but in the same direction. Evidently, poorer residential areas are more dangerous places than more prosperous ones. Studies of other cities show neighborhood-level correlations between crime and socioeconomic status similar to those reported by Boggs for St. Louis.

Maps of Seattle and Minneapolis (Figures 15-1 and 15-2) are typical, showing concentrations of crime in the older, deteriorated sections near the city center, with lower crime rates in nonslum districts. Analyzing crime rates in Seattle, Schmid (1960) found a pattern of regular gradients from the city center to the periphery. These gradients persisted over time for such crimes as homicide, rape, robbery, and burglary (see Figure 15-3 for Seattle's gradients).

## Urban pathologies

Analysis of Los Angeles's census tracts shows that a variety of social problems tends to cluster together spatially (Choldin, 1979). Juvenile arrests correlated with three types of adult crimes—robbery, assault, and homicide—and these rates also correlated with the rates of fires and even with low reading scores in schools. This study combined all these problems into a single index of neighborhood problems and showed that it was related to crowded housing and low socioeconomic status. Like the crime and delinquency rates of other cities, the index showed a gradient from the city center. In summary, the various ecological studies of neighborhood differences in delinquency, crime, health, and other problems show that they tend to be clustered in the poor sections near the city center—the slums.

## Isolation

Slums tend to be socially isolated from the wider community. Suttles (1968) says the wider society imposes a moral isolation upon the slum by looking down upon the slum dwellers. Residents of the slum do not necessarily conform to the outside community's moral code. Referring to one slum in Chicago, he says it has a high delinquency rate, numerous unwed mothers, several adolescent gangs, plus a reputation for having adult gangsters. Outsiders are suspicious of the low-status minority residents of the slum, who do not do well at "public relations." Furthermore, according to sociologist Michael Lewis (1978), the rest of the community derives a certain psychological payoff from the lower class because it validates their worthiness and personal success.

Slum dwellers are aware they are stigmatized by living in the slum; they know that others look down upon them (Suttles, 1968). Public-school teachers know which of their pupils are poor and which live in public-housing projects. Even the pupils' classmates know which ones are receiving subsidized lunches for poverty-level families; the children are labeled. Teachers have low performance expectations for poor children which affect the sorts of performances these children give. Furthermore, the slum dweller's isolation may be geographically real. Many poor people are relatively immobile—they do not visit other parts of the city as much as

SLUMS: CONDITIONS AND PROGRAMS

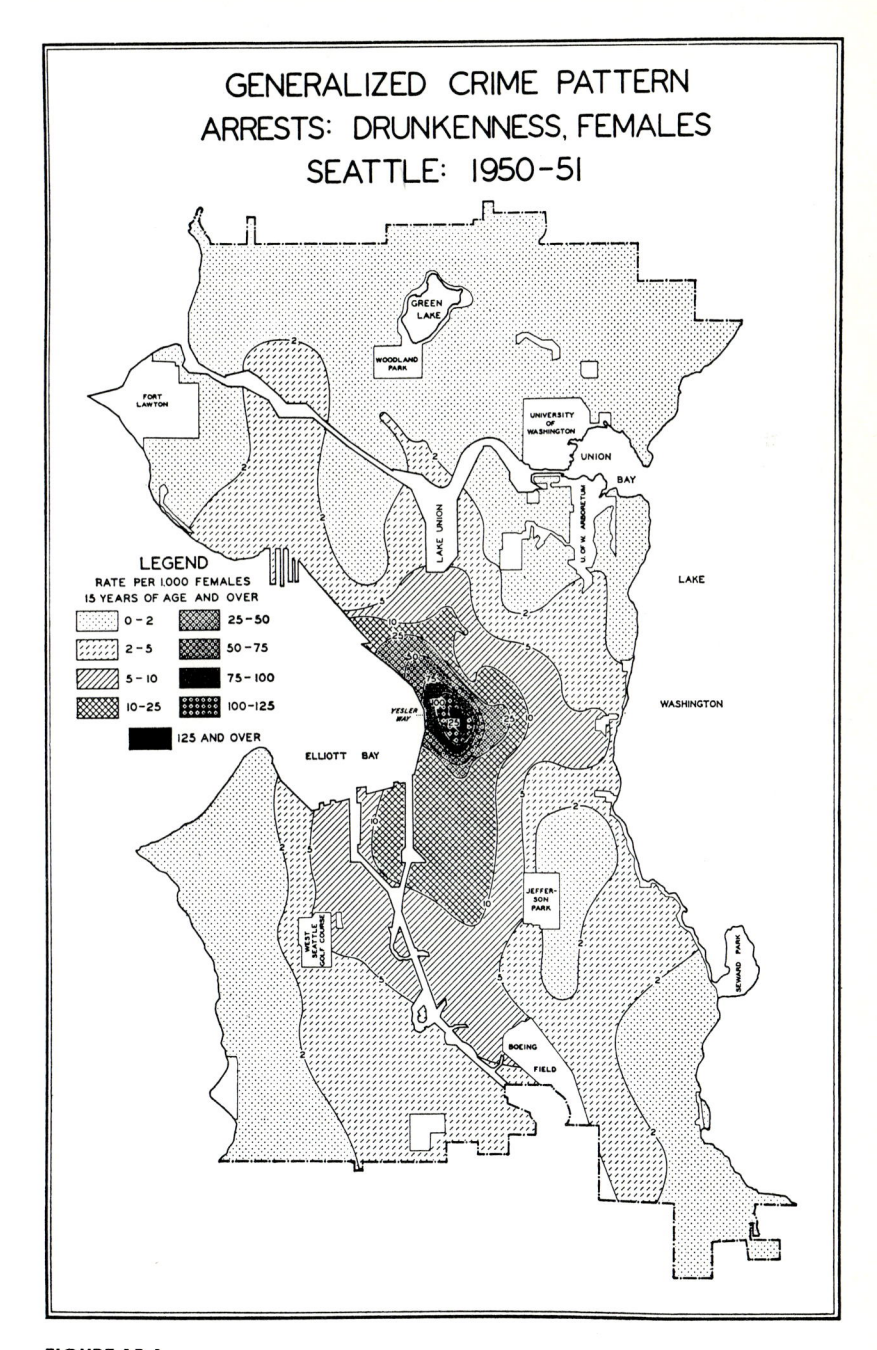

GENERALIZED CRIME PATTERN
ARRESTS: DRUNKENNESS, FEMALES
SEATTLE: 1950-51

LEGEND
RATE PER 1,000 FEMALES
15 YEARS OF AGE AND OVER
0-2
2-5
5-10
10-25
25-50
50-75
75-100
100-125
125 AND OVER

**FIGURE 15-1**
Generalized crime pattern: arrests of females for drunkenness in Seattle, 1950–1951. Schmid's research on crime rates revealed this same pattern for a number of other types of crime in the city. (Source: Schmid, 1960; figure 6.)

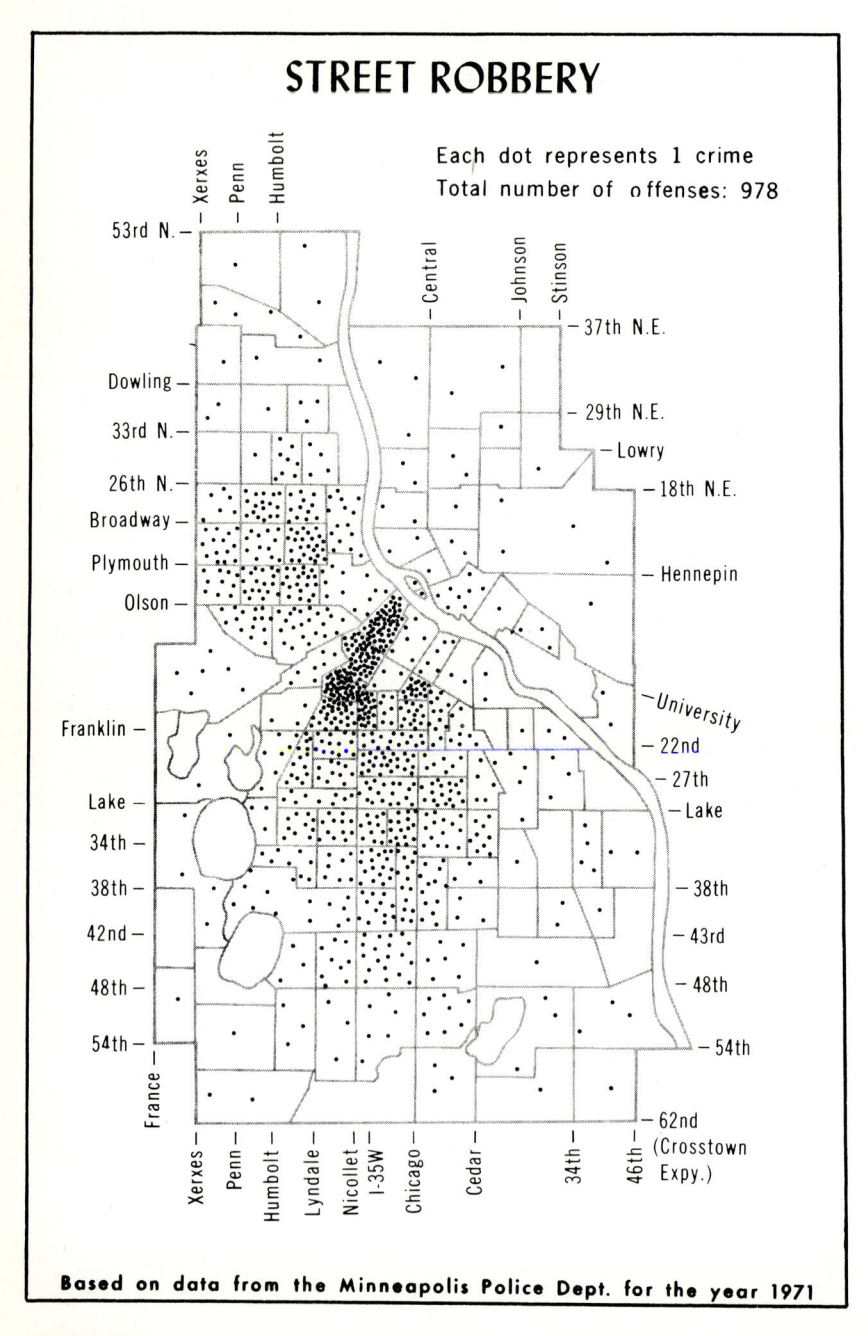

**FIGURE 15-2**
Street robberies in Minneapolis. Note the concentration at the city center. (Source: Phillips, 1972.)

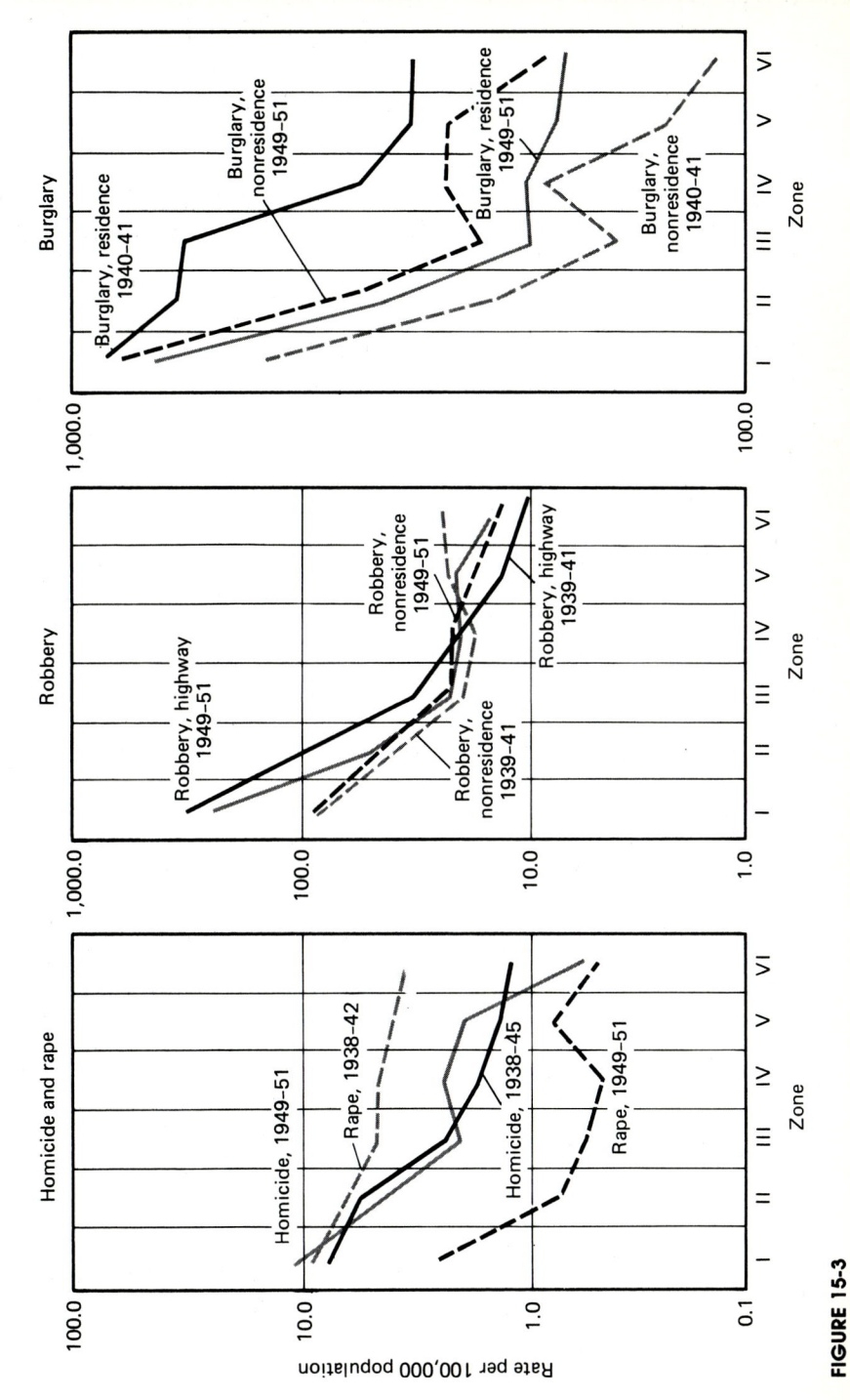

**FIGURE 15-3**
Constancy of crime gradients in Seattle. (Source: Schmid, 1960.)

others do; they are less likely to own cars; they may be ignorant of much of the rest of the metropolis and fearful of visiting unknown places. They are much more localistic than members of other classes.

Although the rest of the community looks down upon the slum as immoral and disorganized, it actually has its own codes of conduct, which may be tightly enforced. In *The Social Order of the Slum*, Suttles (1968) introduces the concept "provincial morality." During his participant observational study of a slum, Suttles discovered that the area "is intricately organized according to its own standards and the residents are fairly insistent on their demands. These demands require discipline and self-restraint in the same way as do the moral dictates of the wider community" (p. 3). Suttles explains that slum dwellers employ two strategies to ensure orderly social relations: First, they use their families as the main anchor of trust; this restricts the number of anonymous contacts they may have. Second, "slum residents can assuage at least some of their apprehensions by a close inquiry into each other's personal character and past history" (p. 8). Thus they will not rely upon formal relationships but will insist upon particularistic loyalties; this tends to form small, closely knit groups rather than widespread networks. Furthermore, kinship functions to establish further contacts and trust. "Having a brother, a cousin, or parent in another group is perhaps the most frequent reason given when a resident says, 'It's OK, they won't bother me'" (p. 229).

## Uses of the Slum

Although people often assume that slum dwellers live in a slum because they must, some of them live there by choice, because the "low-rent district" offers certain opportunities that are not present elsewhere. Furthermore, some slum dwellers are just passing through, while others may be there for a lifetime. From these two considerations, sociologist John Seeley (1959) has developed a typology of slum dwellers. Seeley's first variable is necessity versus opportunity: Some live in slums because they must, while others live there for its special or peculiar opportunities. His second variable is duration (which reflects an attitude as much as a specifiable time period): Some expect to move out of the slum when they can, while others are resigned to remaining there. Combining the variables, Seeley generates four types of slum dwellers:

Permanent necessitarians
Temporary necessitarians
Permanent opportunists
Temporary opportunists

"Permanent necessitarians" are those who have no alternatives to living in slums—the indolent, the "adjusted poor," the social outcasts. "Temporary necessitarians" may be called "the respectable poor." All their values, identifications, and associations lie outside the slum; they are unreconciled to it and would rather live elsewhere. "Permanent opportunists" are individuals who have reason to avoid middle-class residential areas, either to permit a particular lifestyle which might be rejected in such areas or to find cheap housing despite their ability to pay more for it. The three kinds of permanent opportunists are fugitives, unfindables, and the "sporting crowd." Fugitives may be avoiding the law or the credit agency; in the slum they can get anonymity and sanctuary because no one will ask too many questions. Unfindables comprise a floating population, people who live in abandoned buildings, day laborers, winos, and bag ladies. The sporting crowd, on the other hand, consists of individuals who may have ordinary jobs and incomes but who choose to live in the slum to find cheap housing which frees that portion of their income for drinking, gambling, or other amusements. Finally, "temporary opportunists" are those who see themselves as passing through the slums on their way to something better. They are usually migrants or immigrants who use the slum as a port of entry into the metropolis. They use the slum for its cheap rent, but they also get other benefits through networks within their ethnic group and through whatever ghetto institutions their group may have developed. Furthermore, the slum itself has often provided low-level economic opportunities for immigrants who have saved up to purchase its houses, small apartment buildings, or shops as first business investments. In sum, Seeley instructs us to look at the slum as a locale which may be a trap for some but which offers particular opportunities for others.

## IMMORAL LANDSCAPES

### Red-Light Districts

While they have not attracted a great deal of sociological attention, red-light districts are a persistent feature of cities (Reckless, 1933). Richard Symanski (1981), who conducted an exhaustive survey of the geographical aspect of prostitution, has introduced a new term, the "immoral landscape," to refer to areas where institutions of commercialized vice are clustered within metropolitan areas. Geographer Symanski argues that every culture defines certain activities and roles as immoral, through its laws and other evaluative codes. In the United States, where innumerable laws govern sexual behavior, soliciting for prostitution is almost everywhere defined as a crime. As such, it is rejected from "respectable" areas, and it tends to cluster in special districts. Indeed, some cities have legally defined special districts where immoral activities may occur; in the United States, the most infamous is "the Boston Combat Zone."

Prostitution is like other economic activities, according to Symanski, in that the business works more efficiently when several units are located in close proximity to each other. "Sufficient numbers are required to draw business and for an area to gain a reputation," writes Symanski. "Men see advantage in going to large prostitution districts because they provide more choice" (p. 32) and more anonymity.

The rest of the community rejects prostitution and other immoral activities. Neighbors do not want to see streetwalkers plying their trade and customers who may be drunk or rowdy; they do not want bars, customers, pimps, and vice-squad police officers in the area. The neighbors' fear of crime is not groundless. "Prostitutes engage in some crimes, primarily larceny, but mostly their image, their assumed criminality, invites other criminals to their side: con men, drug addicts who need money ... and rapists who prey on prostitutes" (p. 126). Thus, since most neighborhoods will reject prostitution, it is likely to be concentrated in places where it is tolerated or where the neighbors have insufficient influence to reject it effectively. Symanski found that prostitution is usually located in areas that house poor minorities and aged "down-and-outers"—areas with high crime rates.

Cities like Boston may officially designate areas where commercial units be located. In other cities, such units simply locate together to form an unofficial district.

Common geographical associations have been burlesque shows, peep shows, "adult" movie theaters and book stores. During the early 1970s the Times Square area between

Pornographic movie houses attract crowds near Times Square, New York's largest "immoral landscape." (Bob Combs, Rapho/Photo Researchers, Inc.)

6th and 8th Avenues and 42nd and 49th Streets had more than 25 pornographic book stores. Areas where streetwalkers solicit in New Orleans, Los Angeles and San Francisco have been invaded by alleged sex shops: rap studios encounter houses, nude painting studios, dating services. (Symanski, p. 40)

Some cities have attempted to prevent the spatial concentration of these commercial sex-related enterprises; Detroit has an "Anti-Skid Row Plan," specifying that sex-related businesses must be at least 1,000 feet apart (Symanski, p. 234), that aims to prevent the formation of clusters which could blight ordinary neighborhoods. This sort of dispersion, though, is exceptional, running counter to the tendency of like enterprises and activities to gather together.

## Skid Row

In addition to slums and red-light districts, twentieth-century cities usually have one or more skid rows, areas inhabited by homeless persons, most of whom are destitute and alcoholic. These areas are located adjacent to or near the central business district in the zone of transition; often they are near a factory or warehouse district, the waterfront, or a freight yard. Skid row provides inexpensive, substandard hotels and rooming houses, which often have cubicles, rather than full rooms, for the people to sleep in. (A cubicle is a 5- by 7-foot area, with sheet metal or thin plasterboard partitions.) Skid-row areas also provide taverns, pawnshops, and second-hand stores, as well as employment agencies for day laborers and missions which provide free meals after services (Bogue, 1963).

After conducting a survey of skid-row men in several cities, Bogue summarized their characteristics: They are homeless; they are poor; and they have acute personal problems, particularly insofar as they drink heavily and are disassociated from conventional family life. Skid-row populations include large numbers of physically disabled men and elderly men living on welfare or on small pensions, as well as destitute men without work or funds and those who are physically capable of work but who live off missions (known on skid row as "bums" and "mission stiffs"). Bogue discovered that the men lead a bleak social life; unlike typical metropolitan residents who almost all say they have close associations (as shown in Wellman's and Fischer's social network surveys), almost 40 percent of the skid-row men said they have no close friends (Bogue, p. 149). Furthermore, the men had nothing good to say about each other; they complained that men in the area drink too much, beg, are dirty, lazy, etc. Seventy percent said they dislike living on skid row; those who said they like living there gave four main reasons: the cheapness of living, proximity to employment opportunities, the people, and the hotels. On the whole, Bogue says the men of skid row find few satisfactions there. "Skid-row seems to be composed largely of discontented individuals who live in semi-isolation" (p. 169). He adds, though, that there is a minority who have friends on skid row and like living there.

A recent survey of Seattle's skid row investigated residential mobility (Lee, 1978). Skid row had two types of residents; some had spent a great portion of their life in Seattle, and others had not. A core of men had lived for several years on skid row, even in the same building, but the majority had not. Within the year of the research, over 40 percent of the men changed addresses, a much higher rate of movement than that of the general public; slightly more than half the moves made by the skid-row residents were within the same metropolitan area. Seattle skid-row residents were not pleased with their housing, offering remarks such as, "It's better than staying out on the street" and "I didn't choose to come here—it was here or a nursing home." But they also expressed a sense of powerlessness about moving to better housing. Lee states that even though they move often, they do not go through the same process of residential evaluation and decision making as does the public at large. Their residential behavior involves a good deal of unanticipated movement.

In another study, Lee (1980) reported that skid-row populations in cities across the nation are shrinking. Bogue had studied the populations of skid-row areas in 41 cities and found that their populations grew by almost 3 percent between 1940 and 1950. But, thereafter, they began a drastic decline; Lee states they lost an average of 57.6 percent between 1950 and 1970! Skid rows lost population in every region of the nation, as shown in Table 15-5. Only one city's skid row retained its population. Skid-row population loss is not just the gradual thinning out which is predicted by neighborhood-life-cycle theory—skid-row losses are far greater than those of the cities as a whole. Skid rows tend to lose more white residents than black. Since skid rows are located adjacent to downtown areas, their buildings are likely to be razed in urban renewal programs for new developments such as stadiums, hotels, civic centers, or even parking lots. When this happens, it is not known where the former denizens go, possibly to cheap housing in nearby old residential areas. Many just live on the streets in business districts, sleeping in railroad stations or outdoors in store entryways or on "heat grates" near large office buildings. Some municipalities and charities, especially the Salvation Army, operate free overnight shelters for homeless men and women. At any rate, the large, central skid row which fascinated sociologists and social reformers appears to be on the wane.

## SOCIETAL RESPONSES

Some civic leaders were concerned about slum conditions several decades before the federal government got into the act. The earliest approaches depended upon moralizing, missionizing, and philanthropy, followed by municipal regulations governing the physical qualities of residential buildings and neighborhoods. Only later, in the Great Depression of the 1930s, did the United States begin to provide governmentally supported urban housing. Then, after World War II, the federal government expanded its efforts to clear slums and to provide public housing.

**TABLE 15-5**
**Changes in Skid-Row Population Size: All Persons, Total and by Region**

| Region | 1950 median | 1960 median | 1970 median | % change, 1950–1970 | White, % change, 1950–1970 | Nonwhite, % change, 1950–1970 | Central city, % change, 1950–1970[*] |
|---|---|---|---|---|---|---|---|
| Northeast (N = 9) | 9,050 | 4,104 | 2,463 | −55.5 | −65.0 | 10.8 | −14.4 |
| North central (N = 12) | 8,589 | 5,247 | 3,316 | −61.3 | −64.9 | 7.9 | −9.5 |
| West (N = 10) | 7,282 | 5,344 | 3,298 | −58.2 | −62.3 | −26.6 | 11.6 |
| South (N = 10) | 7,003 | 3,942 | 2,601 | −54.6 | −58.2 | 27.3 | 12.8 |
| Total (N = 41) | 8,521 | 5,242 | 3,139 | −57.6 | −62.7 | 4.9 | .0 |

[*]Data are corrected for annexation, using constant 1950 central-city boundaries.
*Source:* Lee, 1980; U.S. Bureau of the Census, 1952, 1962, 1972.

## Philanthropy and Regulation

In response to the efforts of reformers like Jacob Riis, New York's upper-class citizens became concerned with the dismal conditions in the immigrants' tenements. Slum neighborhoods, with their frequent fires and epidemics, were dangerous places to live. Reformers viewed these conditions through a perspective now known as "environmental determinism," which said the physical situation causes the behavior. The basic argument was that living in the slum made people lazy, dirty, and immoral; therefore, the solution would be to get rid of the slum. The following remark illustrates environmental determinism: The adults of the neighborhood "seem inaccessible to any good influences, and it is only by removal and change of circumstances that we have much hope of seeing these barriers broken down, and a willingness manifest to listen to the truths of the Gospel." (cited in Friedman, 1968, p. 74).

One ameliorative idea was to replace the dreaded tenements with new, improved housing, called "model tenements." Such buildings were intended to be more fireproof than the existing structures, to have more stairways, as well as to provide better ventilation and sanitation. Unfortunately, the building design most widely adopted in New York City for this purpose was a poor compromise between these improved amenities and maximum profitability on the city's narrow and deep lots. The compromise was known as the "dumbbell" floor plan, which connected a front group of rooms with a rear group by a hallway. The middle of the building was indented slightly from the lot lines, providing an airshaft. Windows opened onto the air shaft as well as onto the street and rear alley. The shaft "proved to be not only inadequate for the purpose of providing light and air, but a positive hindrance to the health and comfort of tenants ... a fire hazard {and} ... a receptacle for garbage" (Lubove, 1963, p. 31). As Friedman notes, the failure of the model-tenement concept is an ironic episode in the history of housing reform.

Another ironic footnote to the effort to eliminate the slums was the concept of the "model tenant." As Friedman notes, it was difficult for the established Americans, middle-class Protestants, to understand the poor immigrants' ways of life, "hard to sympathize with the foreign ways and 'clannishness' of the poor, hard to treat with respect their Catholic and Jewish faiths" (1968, p. 73). This states the problem politely; more colloquially, the natives thought the slum dwellers were uncivilized drunks and that they lived like pigs. To remedy this, the reformers suggested that each new model tenement should have at least one household of nonimmigrant residents who would serve as model tenants; by example, these clean-living Americans could demonstrate how to live decently in the city. Needless to say, this minor effort was not an effective way to help the immigrants.

## Housing Standards

Housing reformers also attempted to solve the slum problem through legislation. Periodically during the nineteenth century, civic associations appointed commissions to study problems of sanitation or housing and recommended new municipal ordinances. Eventually, a number of cities and states enacted housing ordinances to deal with problems of light, air, ventilation, sanitation, fire protection and construction (Lubove, 1963). New York City enacted the Tenement House Law of 1867, but its provisions were weak; for example, the requirement of a fire escape could be satisfied by an inconveniently located wooden ladder. Furthermore, the city had no means by which to enforce the new standards. An 1879 law was more stringent, requiring a window in each sleeping room and prohibiting building on more than 65 percent of the area of a lot, but these rules also had loopholes and went unenforced. A later recommendation was intended to eliminate overcrowding within housing units, but it was incompatible with economic realities because immigrant families could not afford spacious accommodations and they had to take in boarders to help with the rent. Eventually, New York's Tenement House Law of 1901 specified fire-protection and sanitation standards. The law required fireproofing of halls and stairs, detailed the necessary locations and construction of fire escapes, and required the installation of a separate water closet in each apartment. In the first decade of the twentieth century, New York also began to enforce these tenement laws (although certainly not perfectly). In the ensuing decades, many other cities and states enacted similar building codes. As the level of living rose in the twentieth century, legislated housing standards were continually upgraded, requiring bigger rooms, more complete plumbing, safe electric wiring, and other amenities (American Public Health Assn., 1950; see Hole, 1965, for a study of rising housing standards in England). For several reasons, the enforcement of housing standards has always been uneven in American cities, particularly in older neighborhoods (Downs, 1981), but the laws at least define the quality of new construction.

**Public Housing**

While housing reformers succeeded in getting housing standards and regulations, they failed to get the government to provide public housing. European governments began to build and manage housing early in the twentieth century, but the United States rejected this idea as socialistic. American free-enterprise philosophy defined real estate as a basic element of the capitalistic system and ruled out governmental participation. Indeed, for most of our history, social welfare was considered to be a legitimate concern not of government but of voluntary associations and private philanthropy. The federal government first erected housing during World War I, when an urgent need existed for workers' accommodation near east coast shipyards, but after the war, the buildings were sold to private investors.

Federal policy changed fundamentally during the depression with the passage of the Housing Act of 1937, one of the later New Deal programs. The purpose of this law was to generate employment for unemployed construction workers and to provide housing for middle-class and working-class families who were experiencing hard times. The program was not targeted at the very poorest segments of the city who could not afford the project rents; slum clearance was a secondary objective of the act. The Housing Act, which was amended and expanded in 1949 and in more recent years, represents the beginning and the cornerstone of urban public housing.

A history of public housing in Chicago shows the different sorts of family housing built in three periods (Bowly, 1978). The first perod, prior to 1943, saw the construction of large housing projects in deteriorating neighborhoods. Unlike later projects, though, the early ones consisted of low-rise apartment buildings (four-story maximum), two-story row houses, or a combination of both. Conforming to the "no-frills" architectural standard of the original legislation, the projects looked somewhat regimental and offered few neighborhood amenities—a guideline aimed at preventing families from receiving deluxe accommodations at the community's expense.

The second period, from about 1947 to 1955, was a transition from the low-rise projects to the later high-rise superblocks. During the second period, Chicago's housing authority constructed various sorts of projects, some with low-rise units, but it also began to build structures up to 15 stories tall, some very large in plan. Finally, the construction of public housing went into high gear in the third period.

The high-rise years went from 1957 to 1968 and may be called "the era of the superblocks." In twelve years the housing authority built 15,591 family units, almost all in high-rise structures, "huge projects, constructed on a colossal scale with extremely low rates of site coverage by the structures and sterile landscaping treatment" (Struyk, 1980, p. 27); these projects were "massive and forbidding." Land that had formerly been divided into ordinary city blocks was consolidated through slum clearance to create the grassy areas and open space of the superblocks. These spaces soon became dangerous areas, however.

Other big-city housing authorities were also building rapidly during this period, and eventually public housing came to be a significant fraction of the rental-housing stock (see Table 15-6). By 1976, at least 5 percent of the rental housing in New York, Chicago, Detroit, Washington, St. Louis, Buffalo, and Seattle was in public projects. The percentages in Philadelphia, Baltimore, Cleveland, Boston, and Atlanta were even higher (Struyk, pp. 14–15.)

Chicago's housing authority built almost all its projects in black residential areas. City legislators from white neighborhoods rejected new projects in their areas because they could not discriminate in tenant selection (Meyerson & Banfield, 1955). A recent study of housing projects in Atlanta, Baltimore, and Detroit shows that almost all were in black areas (Struyk, 1980).

It would be an understatement to say that the public-housing program has been a disappointment to housing reformers and to liberals in general. Undoubtedly, the worst cases are the high-rise superblock projects built in the largest cities during the third period. Some observers adjudge these projects to be worse than the slums they replaced. One reporter writes of

> ...the shoddy shiftlessness, the broken windows, the missing light bulbs, the plaster cracking from the walls, the pilfered hardware, the acrid smell of sweat and cabbage, the ragged children, the plaintive women, the playgrounds that are seas of muddy clay, the

**TABLE 15-6**
**Population and Public Housing in the Largest Cities***

| Central city | 1975 population† (1,000s) | Public-housing units‡ |
|---|---|---|
| New York City | 7,481 | 116,600 |
| Chicago | 3,099 | 38,600 |
| Los Angeles | 2,727 | 8,200 |
| Philadelphia | 1,816 | 22,900 |
| Detroit | 1,335 | 10,300 |
| Houston | 1,327 | 2,600 |
| Baltimore | 852 | 16,200 |
| Dallas | 813 | 7,000 |
| San Antonio | 773 | 7,500 |
| Indianapolis | 715 | 2,600 |
| Washington, D.C. | 712 | 11,200 |
| Milwaukee | 666 | 4,400 |
| San Francisco | 664 | 7,100 |
| Memphis | 661 | 6,800 |
| Phoenix | 645 | 1,900 |
| Cleveland§ | 639 | 11,500 |
| Boston | 637 | 12,800 |
| New Orleans | 560 | 13,600 |
| Columbus, O. | 536 | 4,800 |
| Jacksonville | 535 | 3,100 |
| St. Louis | 525 | 6,700 |
| Seattle | 487 | 5,900 |
| Denver | 484 | 4,900 |
| Kansas City | 472 | 2,600 |
| Pittsburgh | 459 | 9,800 |
| Atlanta | 436 | 14,700 |
| Cincinnati | 413 | 6,800 |
| Buffalo | 407 | 4,800 |
| Minneapolis | 378 | 6,900 |

*Other large cities without conventional public housing are San Jose and San Diego.
†U.S. Bureau of the Census, 1977, *Population Reports and Estimates,* Series P-25, No. 649–698, Washington, D.C.
‡Conventional, federal public housing available for occupancy in fiscal year 1978; data from Office of Housing, U.S. Department of Housing and Urban Development.
§Authority serves all of Cuyahoga County.
*Source:* Struyk, 1980, p. 6.

bruised and battered trees, the ragged clumps of grass, the planned absence of art, beauty, or taste, the gigantic masses of brick, of concrete, of asphalt (Harrison Salisbury, cited in Struyk, 1980, p. 4)

In the same vein, according to another writer, "The wear and tear (and vandalism) from so many large, poor families jammed together has overwhelmed most public housing projects and their limited grounds" (Leonard Downey, Jr., cited in Struyk, 1980, pp. 4–5).

Some critics blame federal rental guidelines for the failure of public housing, asserting it was a mistake to concentrate so many of the poorest families together (Starr, 1971). Under the 1937 act, employed and unemployed families could live in projects, but later federal policy shifted to force lower and lower income levels. This had the effect of driving out any family that began to produce a decent income, leaving only the poorest and least successful to live together. Furthermore, public housing has evidently become an undesirable option for the eligible population and must be considered housing of last resort. Comparing the characteristics of public-housing tenants with eligible members of the population, Struyk (1980) finds that those in public housing are more likely to be black, female-headed households with three or more members and on welfare.

Other critics note the poor administration of public housing in many cities and still others point out the negative effects of the special architecture of the projects (see Defensible Space section below.)

## FAILURES OF PUBLIC HOUSING: TWO STUDIES

### Pruitt-Igoe: A Federal Slum

Before recounting the sad story of St. Louis's Pruitt-Igoe project, we can get some background from one of the first large-scale studies of the effects of public housing. Conducted by public health researchers in Baltimore, the study employed an experimental design to measure health and social consequences of a move to new housing (Wilner, Walkley, Pinkerton, & Tayback, 1962). Their study occurred from 1955 to 1958 in an early high-rise project of six 11-story buildings. The researchers studied 300 black families, examining their health and social relations when they lived in the slums and after they had moved to the project. They were compared with a control group of 300 who remained in slum housing. The analysis showed improved health, particularly for children and young adults who had less illness and fewer days of disability. Project residents said they were pleased with the apartments and their privacy and with children's play areas. Somewhat more helping took place between neighbors, but attitudes toward neighbors did not change much. Generally, a move to the project had few social effects; family life and children's school performance, as well as individual self-concept and aspirations, remained the same. Project residents soon complained about youth gangs. Thus the improved health and expressed satisfaction showed that many of the slum's nonhuman dangers were overcome by public housing, but human difficulties were largely unaffected.

Unfortunately, the Baltimore study, with its partially positive results, represents the end of an era—therafter the story of public housing, both journalistic and social scientific, is mostly bad news. The case of Pruitt-Igoe, which may be a "worst-case scenario," epitomizes what went wrong in many of the big projects in big cities.

## SLUMS: CONDITIONS AND PROGRAMS

Opened in 1954, the Pruitt-Igoe housing complex consisted of 33 buildings, each 11 stories high, with a total of 2,762 apartments (Yancey, 1971). Although it was opened as an integrated project, white renters soon abandoned the apartments to exclusively black tenancy by St. Louis's poorest households. Within five years the project became "a community scandal, both because of certain unattractive design features (for example, the elevators stop only on the fourth, seventh, and tenth floors) and because of the wide publicity given to crimes and accidents in the project" (Rainwater, 1970, p. 8). A group of sociologists and students at Washington University began to study the social life in the project, in part to understand its problems. After intensive research based upon observation and interviewing, they published their results in a book with the ironic title *Behind Ghetto Walls: Black Families in a Federal Slum* (Rainwater, 1970). The project had become so disreputable that families refused to live there; more than a quarter of the apartments stood vacant. Two-thirds of the residents were children, and more than two-thirds of the adults were females. Many of the families were dependent upon public assistance for their incomes.

To a considerable extent, but not completely, the project satisfied the shelter needs of the residents. Most residents reported that they liked their apartments, which were better than their previous dwellings. The projects eliminated some nonhuman dangers, like rats and faulty wiring, but not all; they had exposed elevator shafts, exposed steam pipes, and broken glass.

But the project failed to overcome the dangers from human sources—if anything, it produced and intensified them. In a survey conducted by Rainwater's research group, more than half the respondents said the following situations were very big problems: People throw bottles and other things out of windows; outsiders enter the project and fight, steal, and drink; children often hear bad language; children run wild and cause damage; and women aren't safe in the halls, stairways, or elevators. In Wilson's (1975/1977) terms, then, the project was filled with visible signs of disorder which had their usual effect, making people fearful. Indeed, almost all the residents (86 percent) said they would prefer to live elsewhere.

Like other city people, residents of Pruitt-Igoe were involved in social networks, but theirs were somewhat smaller and more private than usual (as compared with those studied by Fischer and Wellman). Typically, an adult would have five close associates, and on the average, one-third of them were kinfolk. "Women particularly find themselves confined to their apartments, by their responsibilities for numerous children and for keeping the house operating, and because of their suspicion of those outside ... [they] lead rather isolated lives" (Rainwater, 1970, p. 101). Public social life in the project was impossible because people were so fearful of each other. In the survey most tenants said the following were serious and frequent events: stealing, holdups, robberies, "drinking a lot and fooling around on the streets" (p. 12), alcoholism, breaking windows, teenagers cursing at adults, teenagers fighting, and "boys or girls having sexual relations with a lot of different boys or girls" (p. 12). In sum, the residents disapproved of much of their neighbors' behavior. But why the social relations in the project were so disagreeable was not simply a sociological question, and sociologists and architects alike began to ask how the physical environment itself contributed to the failure of Pruitt-Igoe.

While expressing satisfaction with their apartments, residents criticized the common areas. William Yancey (1971), a member of the Washington University research team, suggests that the public areas of the project were particularly badly designed. According to Yancey, the built environment lacked "semi-private space," areas and facilities around which neighboring relationships might develop; he says the streets and alleys of older slums used to serve this function. Furthermore, at Pruitt-Igoe he observed the degraded condition of the built environment caused by vandalism and poor maintenance: broken windows replaced by plywood; broken glass, and derelict cars. "Fences around tot lots are torn; swings, sliding boards, and merry-go-rounds are noticeably unpainted, rusted, and broken" (p. 9). The elevators smelled of urine throughout the day, he wrote.

One of Pruitt-Igoe's fundamental problems derives from the incongruity of the high-rise apartment building as an environment for child rearing, especially within the lower class. Michelson's (1970) concept of congruence suggests that built environments and activity patterns may have a potential "fit"; that is, the architectural qualities of a particular environment may promote or inhibit particular activities.

Constructed in the 1950s at the height of the federal program to provide public housing for the poor, St. Louis's Pruitt-Igoe apartments were hailed for their modern architecture. Socially, though, they rapidly degenerated into a crime-ridden, fearful environment and were demolished before standing for twenty years. (United Press International Photo)

Michelson is never an environmental determinist; he never says a particular environment will produce a particular behavior. In some real cases, though, incongruity occurs when an environment is particularly badly suited to its occupants and their needs and behaviors. Apparently, the high-rise apartment building for lower-class family life is one such incongruity. A Pruitt-Igoe resident expressed this problem herself: "Well, I don't like being upstairs like this. The problem is that I can't see the kids. They're just too far away. If one of them gets hurt, needs to go to the bathroom, or anything, it's just too far away. And you can't get outside. We don't have any porches" (cited in Yancey, 1971, p. 12). Michelson notes that mothers lose potential control of their children in the high-rise environment, whereas they might keep eye and voice contact in a lower structure. Corridors, elevators, and stairways in big buildings provide unsupervised areas where trouble can occur. More prosperous households in high-rise buildings may use them differently; the mothers are likely to have fewer children, so they can accompany them to the playground. They may hire help for housework or for child care; they may send the children to supervised programs, etc. Or they may take the most common refuge by living in a single-family detached house.

The end of the Pruitt-Igoe story is well known; the buildings were literally demolished. At first, the housing authority surmised that the original project was too densely populated and that the situation might improve if there were fewer buildings, so they razed a few of them. However, the patient did not respond to this treatment; the project failed to improve or to attract new tenants. Eventually, the authority leveled the entire project, thus ending a sorry chapter in the history of housing reform.

## Defensible Space: Crime and the Built Environment

Architect Oscar Newman (1972), also concerned with urban crime, housing projects, and the relationship between architecture and behavior, conducted an innovative study of differences in crime rates among New York City's 169 public-housing projects. The architecture of the projects varied widely; having been built in different periods, it ranged from low-rise apartments and townhouses to high-rise slabs in superblocks. The amount of crime in the projects varied; all had some crime, but some had much more than others. Since all the projects are for poor households, the research could eliminate social class or poverty as a cause of crime. The housing authority maintains its own security police which keeps records of crimes in the projects, so Newman had a rich data base to analyze. He asked whether the architectural design of a project was related to its crime level.

Newman employed ideas introduced by Jane Jacobs, an editor of an architecture magazine. Jacobs attacked prominent architectural and planning theories in her book, *The Death and Life of Great American Cities* (1961), which forms a backdrop to Newman's research. She rejected the urbanistic vision of LeCorbusier, one of the most influential architects of the twentieth century (Choldin, 1978). Enchanted with the skyscraper, LeCorbusier (1933/1967) proposed a clean, uncluttered city of the future. It would have great open spaces, dotted with crisp-looking skyscrapers for all purposes, including residence, retailing, work, education, and so on. These modern buildings would not stand side by side on streets, as in the contemporary city, though; they would be scattered in parklike environments which would be laced with high-speed highways. In a sense, the superblock was a real-world expression of LeCorbusier's concept.

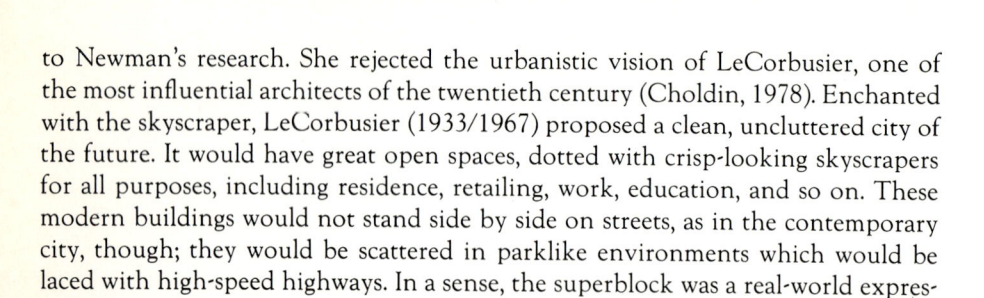

Now every large American city has superblock projects—complexes of high-rise buildings sited in open areas rather than on conventional streets. Residential superblocks in the private sector provide housing for middle- and upper-middle-class occupants; in the public sector, superblocks represent large projects for the poor. Aside from aesthetic considerations, housing reformers such as Elizabeth Wood (cited by Struyk, 1980, p. 27) advocated large projects for their effect on the slum and on the residents. Wood said public housing in the form of small apartment buildings in existing slums would fail, as the slum would overwhelm them; they would just be absorbed eventually into the texture of the slum, making no positive impact. Therefore, she advocated high-rise apartment buildings in superblocks, to be set apart from the slum and, in effect, to overwhelm it.

Jane Jacobs (1961) dismissed all such thinking as arrant nonsense, saying that the existing city could work very well, better than high rises on open sites. Advocating dense residential areas like New York's Greenwich Village, she said streets and sidewalks contribute to the community's vitality and safety. "The street has eyes," she wrote. An active sidewalk has nightlife, pedestrians, newspaper sellers, bartenders, police officers, and so on. All this activity makes the street safe because a potential purse snatcher or rapist would be deterred for fear of being observed by others.

With concepts like these, Newman asked whether housing projects' architecture and crime rates were related. His research disclosed that features of the projects' sites and their buildings were clearly related to their crime rates. Superblock projects with high-rise buildings on open sites had the highest crime rates. The high-crime building type was a high-rise slab with long "double-loaded corridors." He illustrated these points by contrasting two projects, Van Dyke and Brownsville Houses, which stand across the street from each other.

The residents of these two projects were quite similar, but Van Dyke, the high-rise project, had one and a half times as much crime as Brownsville. Both projects had large black majorities and Puerto Rican minorities, equal proportions on welfare, equal proportions of broken families, equal percentages of children, etc., so the differences in crime rates were not a function of social background. On the other hand, the built environments were different. Van Dyke had 14-story buildings (plus a few three-story structures) sited on open areas; Brownsville had a mix of six-story and three-story buildings, covering much more of the land area.

## SLUMS: CONDITIONS AND PROGRAMS

Newman stresses territoriality and visibility in explaining why some environments permit crime while others tend to suppress it. Van Dyke's open areas fostered crimes because they were a sort of "no-man's land" that strangers could use undisturbed. Residents entering their buildings at night would be unobserved and vulnerable; if a lurker waited for a victim near the mailboxes in an entryway, no one would notice. Brownsville had more of its entryways facing the street, and even in the center of the project, the entryways were arranged so that residents of lower-floor apartments could see who was near the structure and what was happening. The site's small-scale courtyards gave the residents some feeling of identity and responsibility as well as the ability to recognize strangers and criminal behavior. Newman calls this "defensible space," a built environment which tends to suppress crime.

Newman criticizes the high-rise building with double-loaded corridors as the most crime-prone type (see Figure 15-4); this structure offers innumerable opportunities for criminal behavior. Since it has four stairways from each floor, to comply with building safety codes, it offers a swift purse snatcher, mugger, rapist, or other criminal several escape routes. And since stairways and elevators have outlets to each floor, a criminal has many different places for an escape. The double-loaded corridor, by definition, has apartments on each side. The long stretch is not conducive to sociability, and since it is so accessible to strangers, residents lock their doors. They cannot exclude strangers from this semipublic area, and they have no sense of control or territoriality. Front doors of apartments in the Brownsville project, in contrast, open onto stairwells to which there is only one entrance; thus residents can recognize each other. If their children are out, they can leave their doors open but locked on a chain, so they can hear what is going on in the stairwell. Furthermore, residents learn to recognize strange and untoward noises. Because it provides a sense of territoriality, the Brownsville project has defensible space.

Sociologist Alan Booth (1981) researched Newman's defensible-space concept and, while he did not get exactly the same pattern of results, did not dismiss the idea. Booth questioned the adequacy of Newman's research procedures and the validity of his conclusions. In order to test the theory, Booth compared a sample of households which had been victimized in Omaha and Lincoln, Nebraska, with ones which had not, controlling for race, education, size of household, and age. He sent investigators to collect information about the physical characteristics of the local environment and then attempted to discover differences between the households that had and had not been victimized. The study suggests crime is more likely within apartment buildings having easy access to common areas or limited opportunity to observe what is going on. Also, outdoor areas with people present seemed to be conducive to victimization. On the other hand, the Nebraska research failed to confirm some of Newman's central hypotheses; Booth concluded, "The outdoor features of the environments studied, with minor exceptions, do not seem to facilitate or impede burglary or vandalism" (p. 557). Booth's evaluation of the defen-

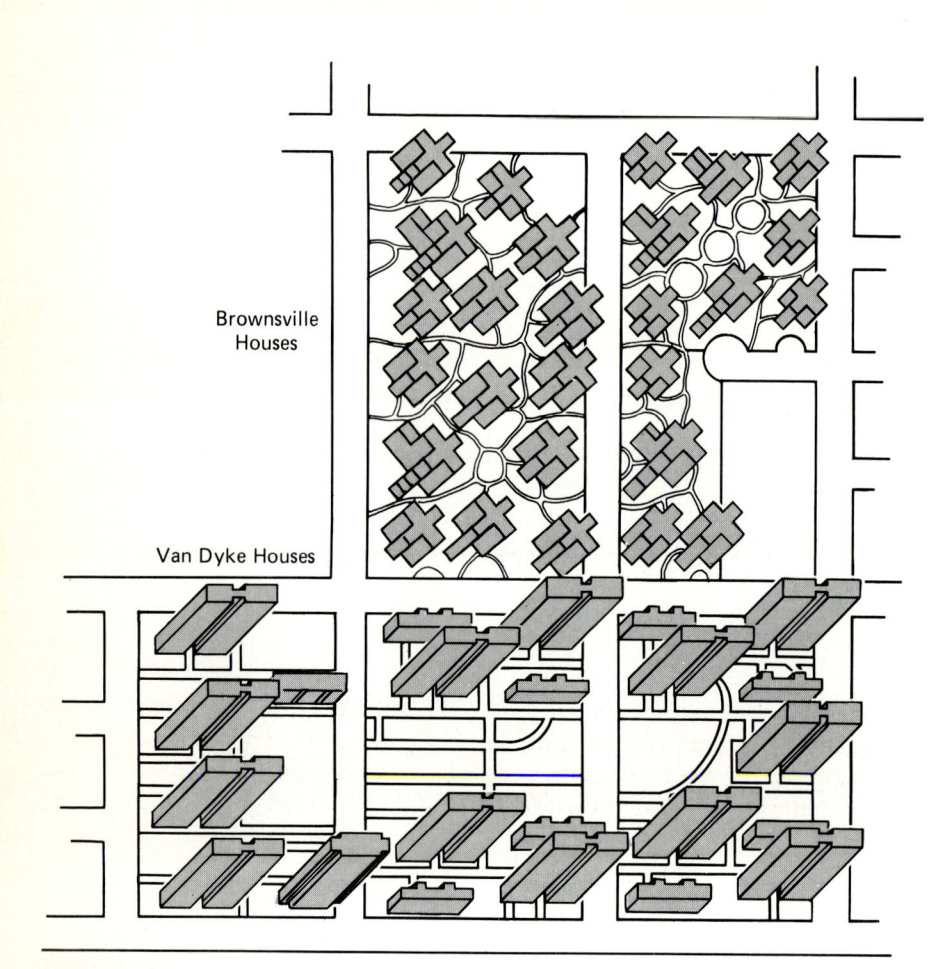

**FIGURE 15-4**
Site plan of two housing projects in New York City. Newman suggests that the open plan of Van Dyke Houses offers the maximum opportunity for crimes. The spaces between buildings belong to no one, particularly after dark. (Source: Newman, 1972.)

sible-space concept is mixed; on the one hand, he says it is a sterile idea which neglects social conditions of neighborhoods, but on the other hand, he acknowledges that it partially explained the situation in the cities he studied and says further research is needed on the subject. Overall, defensible space appears to be a provocative idea which gives an additional insight into urban processes—suggesting that we should look closely at built environments as possible influences upon crime and crime suppression—although it has not been fully researched and verified.

SLUMS: CONDITIONS AND PROGRAMS

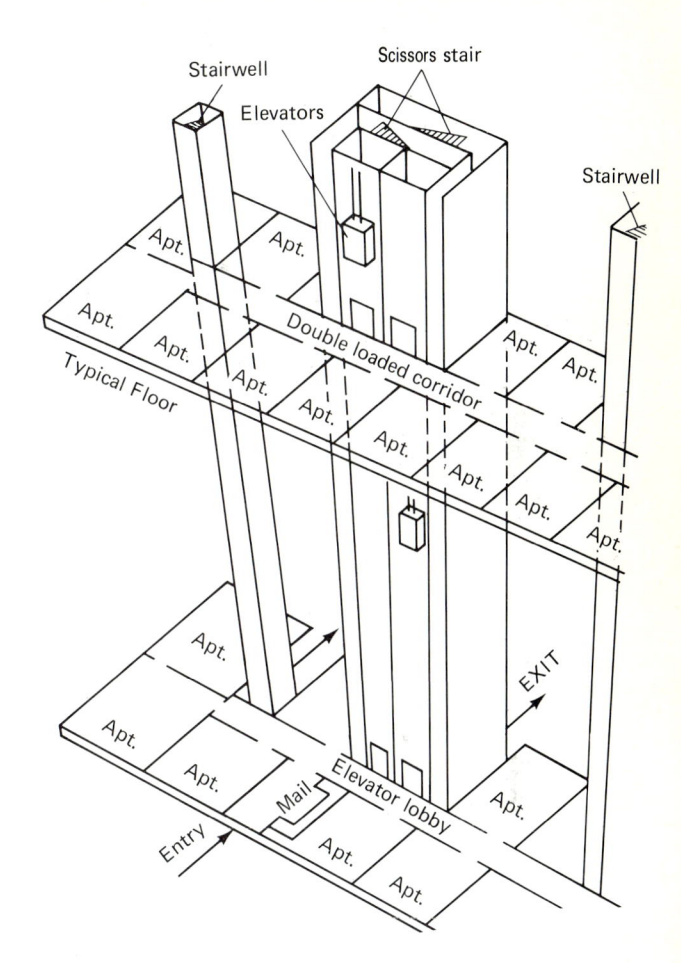

**FIGURE 15-5**
Apartment building lacking defensible space. The "x-ray" view at right reveals the circulation systems of a building with double-loaded corridors. The would-be criminal has access to many outlets via elevator or stairwell. Furthermore, the corridor itself is a sort of "no man's land." (Source: Newman, 1972.)

## BEYOND PUBLIC HOUSING

### Scattering the Poor

By the late 1960s Congress and the Department of Housing and Urban Development recognized that massive high-rise projects for poor families were a mistake, and they stopped building them. New attempts to house the urban poor went in two directions, toward building smaller structures on "scattered sites" and toward utilization of existing private dwellings by subsidizing renters. Scattered-site public housing remained a very small program due to the inefficiency of the system, in which housing authorities had to purchase many small land parcels and had to construct and administer numerous detached houses, duplexes, and small apartment buildings. Furthermore, federal policy in the 1970s emphasized rental subsidies through a program known as "Section 8." The Housing and Community Development Act of 1974 included a housing-allowance program as part of its Section 8 Lower Income Rental Assistance Program (Struyk & Bendick, 1981). This program was designed to avoid the "ghettoization" of poor minority households in housing projects, encouraging them to rent housing in the community. One part of the program was designed to encourage developers to provide new housing for low-income families. Essentially, the program said to such families, "If one-quarter of your monthly income is not enough to cover the rent for a standard-quality house or apartment, the government will pay the difference" (the difference between the rent and one-quarter of the family's income). Thus, under Section 8, families were free to shop the housing market to look for decent housing. The new-construction side of the program, which came to absorb most of the budget, said to builders, "If you build new rental units, you may rent them at fair market rates to families who are too poor to pay the rent." For each apartment and each family, the government subsidized the difference between the rent and one-quarter of the family's income. This provided an incentive to developers to build for a market that would otherwise be financially unattractive. The Section 8 program continues to the present.

## The Experimental Housing-Allowance Program

In 1970 the Department of Housing and Urban Development launched an experimental program to subsidize low-income households in the rental market. The experiment was designed to discover whether low-income households, white and minority, could improve their housing through subsidized housing vouchers. The experiment sought to discover who would join such a program; how much they would benefit; what would happen to the housing market (Would prices rise? Would owners upgrade the quality of housing?); and how much it would cost nationally. The experiment, which was divided into several sections, was run in 14 cities across the nation, involving over 30,000 households; the principal sites were Green Bay, South Bend, Phoenix, and Pittsburgh (Struyk & Bendick, 1981). It was the largest social experiment ever conducted scientifically in the United States and cost almost $160 million. Some of the principal conclusions of the experiment are the following:

> Only a minority of eligible households chose to use the vouchers. Some households chose not to participate because it would have been too difficult to

search for standard-quality housing or because they considered the benefits of the subsidy not to be worth the trouble of moving.

The principal economic effect upon participating families was to decrease the burden of rent upon their budgets, cutting it from approximately 40 to 25 percent, which allowed them to use this income for other purposes. Participants did not tend to upgrade their housing consumption greatly, although all of them had to live in or move to standard-quality housing.

Landlords repaired their units slightly to meet the program's minimum requirements for rentals. The experimental programs caused "little if any inflation in rents for recipients and no inflation at all in rents for others" (Struyk & Bendick, 1981, p. 208).

In sum, the experiment showed that housing vouchers could reduce the burden of rents for low-income households. It failed, however, to provide an incentive for the poorest families to move from the lowest-quality housing, in most cases.

## Urban Renewal

This was another major program triggered by the Housing Act of 1949 which differed from public housing in that it was aimed at preventing new slums rather than ameliorating old ones. The program flourished in the 1950s and into the mid-1960s. Urban renewal funds allowed city governments to designate certain residential areas as blighted and deteriorating areas. The federal program required the city to draw up a plan to solve the areas' problems through selective land clearance and redevelopment. The law authorized cities to acquire properties through power of eminent domain for the purpose of redevelopment, and it provided subsidies so that even after the city paid for the properties and tore them down, it could sell the lots as open land. The program also provided subsidies to relocate the households and businesses that were displaced through clearance. This aspect of urban renewal was heavily criticized because the clearance of small businesses usually destroyed them, despite the relocating allowances, which were seen as insufficient. Advocates of the poor criticized urban renewal because the cleared blighted residences had housed low-income households that were not provided for in the redevelopment plans.

Many cities used urban renewal funds for slum clearance near downtown areas where the land supported institutional development—for hospitals, university campuses, stadiums, parking garages, and civic centers. Other cities used urban renewal to redevelop neighborhoods surrounding major institutions such as hospitals and universities. In these areas, though, the new housing was uniformly priced for middle- and upper-middle-class consumers. Thus, while urban renewal may have helped recycle certain sections of the cities, it cannot be seen as a program that benefited the poor.

## SUMMARY

Cities have persistently had slums, at least since the industrial revolution; now, despite marked improvements in urban housing since 1950, American metropolitan areas still have some inferior dwelling units clustered in pockets of poverty. Contemporary definitions of slums have an environmental element—substandard housing, overcrowding, broken streets and sidewalks, visible vandalism, and uncollected trash—as well as a social element—high rates of poverty, crime and delinquency, welfare dependency, unemployment, as well as low levels of education.

Rainwater's essay on fear and the house-as-haven contains one of the major sociological theories of the slum, stating that poor individuals seek shelter from several perceived dangers, nonhuman and human. Nonhuman dangers are environmental, including fires, cold temperatures, vermin, dark areas, and the like. But the theory also enumerates the slum dwellers' fears of other persons in the neighborhood: persons who might injure them physically, verbally, or by offering illicit temptations. Gerald Suttles presents another sociological approach to the slum, emphasizing its isolation from the wider community as well as its internal coherence. Higher-status members of the wider community reject the slum, looking down upon its residents as inferior and immoral, and slum dwellers recognize they have been labeled and stigmatized. But members of the outside community do not realize the slum has its own internal moral code which may be tightly enforced among the residents. A third theoretical statement, by John Seeley, points out the different possible uses of the slum. Recognizing that many people live in the slum permanently because they cannot get out, Seeley observes that others use the place for particular purposes. For example, temporary necessitarians are simply passing through; epitomized by immigrants, these residents use the slum while they learn the city's ways and collect enough capital to move out and up in the social order. On the other hand, permanent opportunists are individuals who find particular advantages in the slum, using it either for cheap housing or to avoid the middle-class morality (as well as the law) found in other sections of the metropolis.

For well over a century urban reformers have attempted to provide better housing for the poor and to eliminate slums. During the first phase of this history, in the nineteenth century, philanthropy and civic regulation were the principal methods. Philanthropists introduced model tenements to counteract the ordinary tenements of the city. Civic leaders, after commission meetings and reports, attempted to prescribe specific standards of ventilation, fireproofing, and sanitation for urban housing, but for economic and political reasons, municipalities failed to enforce such codes. The second phase of the history started during the depression with the enactment of the Housing Act of 1937, which called for the construction of federally financed public-housing projects. After its expansion in the Housing Act of 1949, it became a program to provide apartments for the poorest urban families. With federal dollars, local housing authorities built hundreds of thousands of apartments during the ensuing decade, but in the largest cities the apartments were concentrated in very large high-rise projects that degenerated into dangerous places, federal slums. The government no longer supports construction of large projects, and recent programs seek to disperse poor households into the regular housing market to avoid "ghettoizing" them in large housing projects. The government's major attempt to disperse low-income households has been through rent subsidies.

## REFERENCES

Abrams, Charles. 1965. *The City Is the Frontier*. New York: Harper.
American Public Health Association. 1950. *Planning the Home for Occupancy*. Chicago: The Association.
Boggs, Sarah L. 1965. "Urban Crime Patterns." *American Sociological Review*. 30:899–908.
Bogue, Donald J. 1963. *Skid Row in American Cities*. Chicago: University of Chicago, Community and Family Study Center.
Booth, Alan. 1981. "The Built Environment as a Deterrent: A Re-examination of Defensible Space." *Criminology*. 18:557–570.
Bordua, David J. 1958. "Juvenile Delinquency and 'Anomie': An Attempt at Replication." *Social Problems*. 6:230–238.
Bowly, Devereux, Jr. 1978. *The Poorhouse: Subsidized Housing in Chicago, 1895–1976*. Carbondale, Ill.: Southern Illinois University Press.
Chilton, Roland J. 1964. "Continuity in Delinquency Area Research: A Comparison of Studies for Baltimore, Detroit, and Indianapolis." *American Sociological Review*. 29:71–83.
Choldin, Harvey M. 1978. "Urban Neighborhoods and Environment." *American Journal of Sociology*. 84:457–563.
———. 1979. "Crowding and Slums: A Statistical Exploration." *Research in Social Problems and Public Policy*. 1:179–194.
Clinard, Marshall. 1966. *Slums and Community Development: Experiments in Self-help*. New York: Free Press.
deLeeuw, Frank, Ann B. Schnare, and Raymond J. Struyk. 1976. "Housing," chap. 3 in *The Urban Predicament*, (eds.) William Gorham and Nathan Glazer. Washington, D.C.: Urban Institute.
Downs, Anthony. 1981. *Neighborhoods and Urban Development*. Washington, D.C.: Brookings.
Ford, Amasa B. 1976. *Urban Health in America*. New York: Oxford University Press.
Friedman, Lawrence M. 1968. *Government and Slum Housing: A Century of Frustration*. Chicago: Rand McNally.
Gans, Herbert J. 1968. "The Failure of Urban Renewal: A Critique and Some Proposals," chap. 18 in *People and Plans: Essays on Urban Problems and Solutions*, (ed.) Herbert J. Gans. New York: Basic Books.
———. 1982. *The Urban Villagers* (rev. ed.). New York: Free Press.

Greer, Scott. 1965. *Urban Renewal in American Cities*. Indianapolis: Bobbs-Merrill.
Hole, W. Vere. 1965. "Housing Standards and Social Trends." *Urban Studies.* 2:137–146.
Jacobs, Jane. 1961. *The Death and Life of Great American Cities*. New York: Vintage.
Lander, Bernard. 1954. *Towards an Understanding of Juvenile Delinquency*. New York: Columbia.
Le Corbusier. 1933/1967. *The Radiant City*. New York: Orion. (Tr. from the French.)
Lee, Barrett A. 1978. "Residential Mobility on Skid Row: Disaffiliation, Powerlessness, and Decision-Making." *Demography.* 15:285–300.
———. 1980. "The Disappearance of Skid Row: Some Ecological Evidence." *Urban Affairs Quarterly.* 16:81–107.
Lewis, Michael. 1978. *The Culture of Inequality*. Amherst: University of Massachusetts Press.
Lubove, Roy. 1963. *The Progressives and the Slums: Tenement House Reform in New York City: 1890–1917*. Pittsburgh: University of Pittsburgh Press.
Meyerson, Martin, and Edward C. Banfield. 1955. *Politics, Planning, and the Public Interest: The Case of Public Housing in Chicago*. Glencoe, Ill.: Free Press.
Michelson, William H. 1970. *Man and His Urban Environment: A Sociological Approach*. Reading, Mass.: Addison-Wesley.
Moore, William, Jr. 1969. *The Vertical Ghetto: Everyday Life in an Urban Project*. New York: Random House.
Newman, Oscar. 1972. *Defensible Space: Crime Prevention through Urban Design*. New York: Macmillan.
Phillips, Phillip D. 1972. "The Geography of Crime." Unpublished Ph.D. dissertation, University of Minnesota.
Phillips, Phillip D. 1974. "Intraurban Crime Patterns." Paper presented to a meeting of the Canadian Association of Geographers.
Rainwater, Lee. 1966. "Fear and the House-as-Haven in the Lower Class." *Journal of the American Institute of Planners.* 32:23–31.
Rainwater, Lee. 1970. *Behind Ghetto Walls: Black Families in a Federal Slum*. Chicago: Aldine.
Reckless, Walter. 1933. *Vice in Chicago*. Chicago: University of Chicago Press.
Schmid, Calvin F. 1960. "Urban Crime Areas: Part II." *American Sociological Review.* 25:655–678.
Seeley, John. 1959. "The Slum: Its Nature, Use, and Users." *Journal of the American Institute of Planners.* 25:7–14.
Starr, Roger. 1971. "Which of the Poor Shall Live in Public Housing?" *Public Interest.* 23:116–124.
Sternlieb, George. 1966. *The Tenement Landlord*. New Brunswick, N.J.: Rutgers University, Urban Studies Center.
Sternlieb, George, and Bernard P. Indik. 1973. *The Ecology of Welfare: Housing and the Welfare Crisis in New York City*. New Brunswick, N.J.: Transaction Books.

Struyk, Raymond. 1980. *A New System for Public Housing: Salvaging a National Resource*. Washington, D.C.: Urban Institute.

Struyk, Raymond J., and Marc Bendick, Jr. (eds.) 1981. *Housing Vouchers for the Poor: Lessons from a National Experiment*. Washington, D.C.: Urban Institute.

Suttles, Gerald D. 1968. *The Social Order of the Slum*. Chicago: University of Chicago Press.

Symanski, Richard. 1981. *The Immoral Landscape: Female Prostitution in Western Societies*. Toronto: Butterworth.

U.S. Bureau of the Census. 1982. "Urban and Rural Housing Characteristics." *Annual Housing Survey: 1979, Part E, Current Housing Reports*, Series H-150-79. Washington, D.C.

Warren, Rachelle B., and Donald I. Warren. 1977. *The Neighborhood Organizer's Handbook*. Notre Dame, Ind. University of Notre Dame Press.

Wilner, Daniel, R. P. Walkley, T. Pinkerton, and M. Tayback. 1962. *The Housing Environment and Family Life*. Baltimore: John Hopkins.

Wilson, James Q. 1975/1977. *Thinking about Crime*. New York: Vintage.

Wolfgang, Marvin E. 1970. "Urban Crime," pp. 270–311 in *The Metropolitan Enigma*, (ed.) James Q. Wilson. Garden City, N.Y.: Anchor.

Yancey, William L. 1971. "Architecture, Interaction, and Social Control: The Case of a Large-Scale Public Housing Project." *Environment and Behavior*. 3:3–21.

Zorbaugh, Harvey. 1929. *The Gold Coast and the Slum*. Chicago: University of Chicago Press.

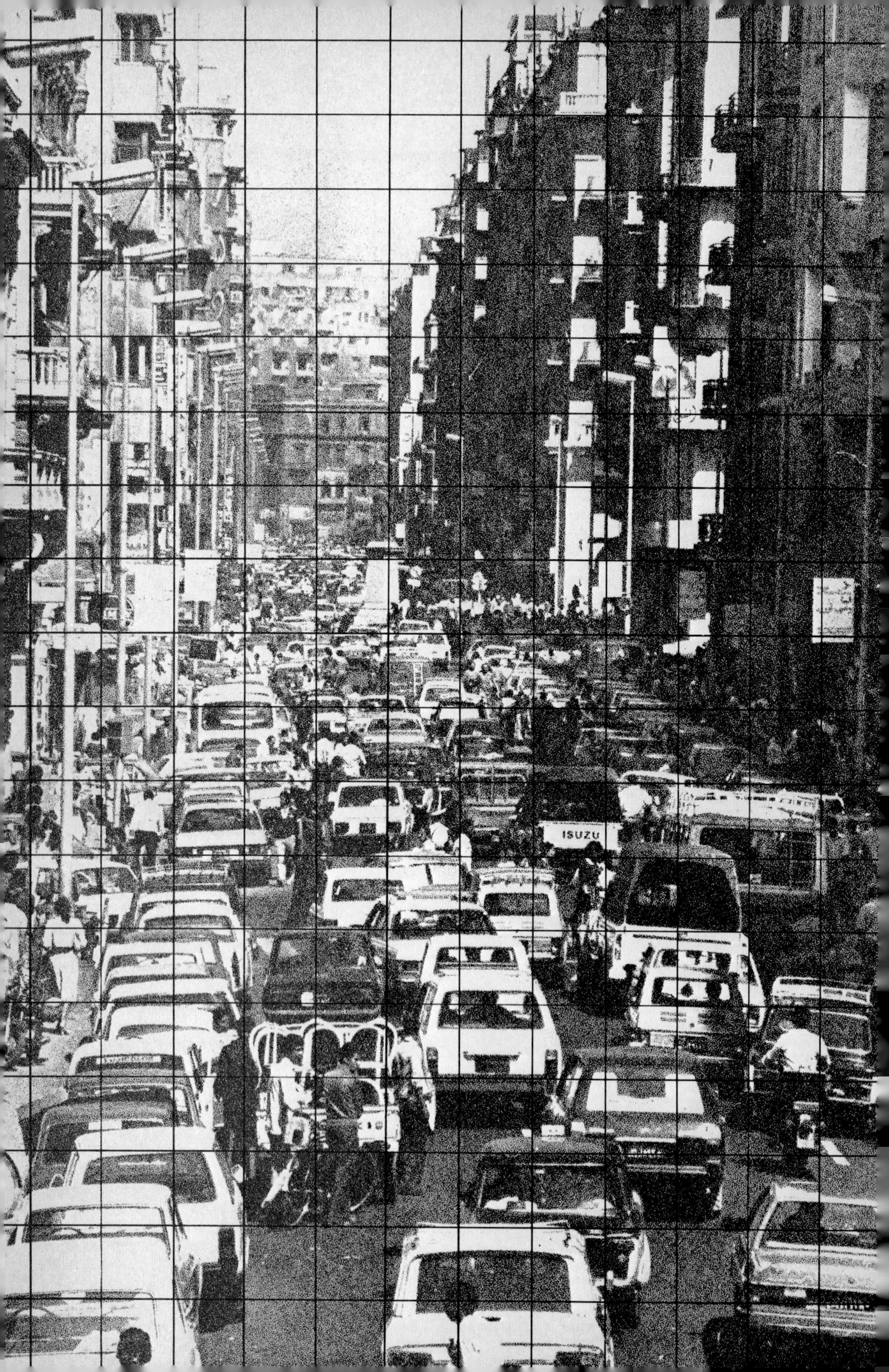
ISUZU

# CHAPTER · 16

## Third-World Urbanization

### Chapter Outline

INTRODUCTION

URBANIZATION

Developmental Sequences
- First world
- Third world
- Industrialization

Rural-Urban Migration
Examples: Two Urbanizing Nations
- India
- Mexico

THE PLACE OF CITIES IN RURAL SOCIETIES

Villages
Small Cities
The City
Linkages and Influences

DUAL CITIES

Subsistence Urbanism
- Housing and environment
- Employment

Modernizing Elites

URBAN STRUCTURE

Latin America
Dimensions of Residential Areas
- Madras, India
- Cairo, Egypt
- Calcutta, India

SUMMARY

# CHAPTER·16

## INTRODUCTION

This volume's emphasis on North American cities should not overshadow the study of urbanization and urbanism in other regions. Third-world countries have had particularly noteworthy urban developments in the twentieth century. The large majority of the world's population, the third world, is defined as those nations

**TABLE 16-1**
**Thirty Largest Agglomerations in the World, Ranked by Size, 1975 and 1990**

| Rank | 1975 | Population* | 1990, estimated | Population* |
|---|---|---|---|---|
| 1. | New York–northeastern New Jersey | 19.8 | Tokyo-Yokohama | 23.4 |
| 2. | Tokyo-Yokohama | 17.7 | Mexico City | 22.9 |
| 3. | Mexico City | 11.9 | New York–northeastern New Jersey | 21.8 |
| 4. | Shanghai | 11.6 | São Paulo | 19.9 |
| 5. | Los Angeles–Long Beach | 10.8 | Shanghai | 17.7 |
| 6. | São Paulo | 10.7 | Peking | 15.3 |
| 7. | London | 10.4 | Rio de Janeiro | 14.7 |
| 8. | Greater Buenos Aires | 9.3 | Los Angeles–Long Beach | 13.3 |
| 9. | Rhein-Ruhr | 9.3 | Greater Bombay | 12.0 |
| 10. | Paris | 9.2 | Calcutta | 11.9 |
| 11. | Rio de Janeiro | 8.9 | Seoul | 11.8 |
| 12. | Peking | 8.7 | Greater Buenos Aires | 11.4 |
| 13. | Osaka-Kobe | 8.6 | Jakarta | 11.4 |
| 14. | Chicago–northwestern Indiana | 8.1 | Paris | 10.9 |
| 15. | Calcutta | 7.8 | Osaka-Kobe | 10.7 |
| 16. | Moscow | 7.4 | Cairo-Giza-Imbaba | 10.0 |
| 17. | Greater Bombay | 7.0 | London | 10.0 |
| 18. | Seoul | 6.8 | Rhein-Ruhr | 9.3 |
| 19. | Cairo-Giza-Imbaba | 6.4 | Bogotá | 8.9 |
| 20. | Milan | 6.1 | Chicago–northwestern Indiana | 8.9 |
| 21. | Jakarta | 5.7 | Madras | 8.8 |
| 22. | Philadelphia–New Jersey | 4.8 | Manila | 8.6 |
| 23. | Detroit (Michigan) | 4.8 | Moscow | 8.5 |
| 24. | Manila | 4.5 | Teheran | 8.3 |
| 25. | Delhi | 4.4 | Istanbul | 8.3 |
| 26. | Tientsin | 4.4 | Baghdad | 8.2 |
| 27. | Teheran | 4.3 | Delhi | 8.1 |
| 28. | Leningrad | 4.2 | Karachi | 7.9 |
| 29. | Madras | 4.1 | Bangkok-Thonburi | 7.5 |
| 30. | Bogotá | 4.0 | Milan | 7.4 |

*Population in millions.
*Source:* United Nations, 1980, table 23, p. 58.

of Asia, Africa, and Latin America which are not wealthy and highly industrialized. (The "first world" consists of the wealthy industrial nations of western Europe, North America, Australia, etc. The "second world" is defined as the socialist nations allied with the Soviet Union: basically the U.S.S.R. plus the nations of eastern Europe.) Most third-world nations are poor rural societies with traditional technology and low levels of literacy. Most are now developing industry, institutions, and modern infrastructure under governmental plans and programs. Formerly, most third-world nations existed as colonies of European powers, gaining their independence in the past half-century; therefore, much of their modern urban development (as contrasted with the times when they had preindustrial cities) occurred under foreign domination or influence. Nonetheless, many third-world nations have extraordinarily rapidly growing metropolitan areas—indeed, Mexico City, Shanghai, and Bombay, with estimated 1980 populations of 15, 13.4, and 8.8 million, respectively, rate among the world's largest cities (United Nations, 1980, table 48). Table 16-1 shows that 18 of the world's largest urban agglomerations are in the third world and that majority is projected to increase in coming years.

The cities of the third world suggest several questions at the macrolevel and microlevel. As we have seen, the history of English and American cities (as well as those of other first-world regions) closely followed industrialization. But third-world cities began to grow before their societies became industrial. How and why did cities grow in those countries prior to industrialization? What was the pace of urbanization and how far has it gone? What sorts of macrourban structures emerged in these rapidly growing metropolitan areas? What sorts of amenities and institutions have arisen in the great third-world cities? At the microlevel we may ask about the nature of urbanism: What sorts of social groupings and relationships arise in these cities; how would one describe the way of life?

These questions imply a comparison with the urban sociology of American urban communities. The overall question is whether the conventional theories of urbanization, urban structure, and social life apply to third-world cities or whether social research is revealing new and different processes and forms there.

This chapter differs from the conventional treatment which usually implies that third-world cities are a disaster zone—full of wretched poverty and growing too rapidly for anyone's good. While the chapter does not neglect the deep problems and poverty of large segments of such cities, it also shows them as major centers of their societies, with important national institutions, which represent an accomplishment to their people. A Mexican social scientist, Luis Unikel (1977), reminds readers not to neglect the positive aspects of urbanization:

> The negative aspects (of urbanization), which are widely expounded through the press, publications, radio, television, include shortages in housing and municipal services, air and water pollution, congestion of traffic, emotional stress, unemployment, and marginality. Among the positive aspects, which are rarely mentioned, are the scale and external economies whch increase productivity, foster scientific, technological, and cultural

advancement, and the assimilation, though slow, of rural migrants to an urban way of life. (p. 465)

## URBANIZATION

### Developmental Sequences

#### First world

The massive growth of third-world cities followed a different series of events than that of early English and American industrial cities. The English sequence, in a nutshell, began with agricultural improvements that helped bring down mortality levels, producing surplus rural population which migrated to towns. Also, in England, the enclosure movement also pushed part of the rural population toward the urban communities. Simultaneously, the growing factory economy needed these new urban workers. To a large extent, third-world urbanization was impelled by falling mortality rates, but they occurred very differently. The introduction of the powerful insecticide DDT to eliminate malaria-transmitting mosquitoes in many tropical countries brought this epidemic disease under control and reduced death rates rapidly.

Third-world countries have experienced rapid population growth since World War II. This population explosion doubled their numbers from 1.6 billion in 1950 to 3.2 billion in 1980. In addition to the introduction of insecticides to prevent diseases, widescale innoculation against smallpox and other epidemic diseases plus the rapid diffusion of antibiotic drugs helped bring down mortality rates throughout the third world. Indeed, third-world death rates fell much faster during this period than they had in Europe during the first stage of its demographic transition. As death rates plummeted in third-world populations, though, fertility rates remained very high, as they had been in the past. Couples in these countries continued their traditional large-family childbearing patterns which, in the aggregate, continued to yield high birth rates. Thus the former balance between high mortality and high fertility became an imbalance of low mortality and high fertility. The imbalance caused unprecedented rapid growth. India, for example, already a large country in 1950 with a population exceeding 350 million, *added* more than 335 million in the next thirty years! In third-world countries, rapid population growth has occurred in both rural and urban areas, but it has certainly contributed to urbanization and the growth of cities.

In recent decades, urban populations have continued to grow in first-world countries, but more slowly than in third-world nations. Table 16-2 shows calculations and projections made by demographers at the United Nations. They show that in the "more developed regions" (first and second worlds) urban populations have been growing since 1970 at less than 2 percent per year. In western Europe the growth rate is actually less than 1 percent per year. Urban populations in third-

TABLE 16-2
Average Annual Growth Rates of Urban Areas in Major Areas and Regions, 1950–2000, %

| | 1950–1960 | 1960–1970 | 1970–1975 | 1975–1980 | 1980–1990 | 1990–2000 |
|---|---|---|---|---|---|---|
| World total | 3.35 | 2.91 | 2.84 | 2.93 | 2.93 | 2.81 |
| More developed regions | 2.44 | 2.05 | 1.75 | 1.68 | 1.50 | 1.20 |
| Less developed regions | 4.68 | 3.94 | 3.95 | 4.06 | 4.02 | 3.76 |
| Africa | 4.42 | 4.85 | 4.97 | 5.10 | 5.00 | 4.56 |
| Latin America | 4.57 | 4.21 | 4.01 | 3.86 | 3.56 | 3.06 |
| Northern America | 2.29 | 1.80 | 1.33 | 1.45 | 1.47 | 1.19 |
| East Asia | 5.46 | 3.09 | 3.06 | 3.03 | 2.82 | 2.67 |
| South Asia | 3.37 | 3.91 | 4.01 | 4.33 | 4.47 | 4.27 |
| Europe | 1.78 | 1.80 | 1.52 | 1.45 | 1.36 | 1.19 |
| Oceania | 3.00 | 2.70 | 2.67 | 2.63 | 2.37 | 1.84 |
| USSR | 3.91 | 2.75 | 2.42 | 2.23 | 1.87 | 1.35 |

Source: United Nations, 1980, table 5, p. 13.

world nations, on the other hand, are growing rapidly—at roughly 4 percent per year.

## Third world

As documented in Table 16-2, third-world populations urbanized rapidly between 1950 and 1980 and are projected to continue to do so through the end of the century. In 1950 in third-world countries about 1 person in 6 lived in an urban place, and by 1980 the urban proportion had almost doubled to 30.5 percent. The proportion urban more than doubled between 1950 and 1980 in some extremely rural regions such as China and eastern and middle Africa.

## Industrialization

In England, industry and urban population grew simultaneously. In third-world countries, though, urban populations began to grow in advance of the expansion of industry. This reversal of sequence led some social scientists to argue that the third-world countries were "overurbanized," that their urban populations were too great for their countries' economic bases. Proponents of the overurbanization thesis pointed to Asian populations, in particular. One way of looking at this concept involves the comparison of the percentage urban in a population with the proportion of its labor force in industry. The United Nations demographers looked at the ratio between urbanization and industrialization in this way for all regions of the world except China, which lacked adequate data. The researchers concluded, "The relationship between the urban and the industrial percentages is rather stable over development" (United Nations, 1980, p. 17). In other words, the ratio between percentage urban and percentage industrial is not very different in third-world nations from what it is in more developed nations. This analysis implies that the third world is not overurbanized; the authors of the United Nations report ask whether the European historical experience might simply have been an exceptional case.

## Rural-Urban Migration

During the process of urbanization, a substantial proportion of the new urban population comes from the countryside. In the third world, rural birth rates usually exceed urban ones, and rural natural increase is high. In many regions no new employment opportunities exist in agriculture. In India and Bangladesh, for example, the arable land is heavily exploited, leaving nothing for additional farmers, and the cultivated family plots are usually too small for division among a number of sons in a given family. Furthermore, the introduction of modern agricultural technology with more machines and chemicals tends to diminish the need for agricultural workers. It is not surprising then that the agricultural sector provides a strong push for migration toward cities. Not everyone is pushed out of the rural areas, though. One major difference between nineteenth-century European and American urbanization and contemporary third-world urbanization is that in the latter, *both* rural and urban populations are growing, although the urban growth is much faster than the rural (United Nations, 1980, p. 17). The United Nations study noted that a substantial fraction, perhaps one-fifth to one-half, of rural natural increase is "drained off" to cities. But the U.N. demographers emphasize that the main variable affecting rates of rural-urban migration "appears to be fairly closely related to the level and rate of economic development of a country" (p. 33). Third-world countries with higher incomes and higher economic growth rates tend to have higher migration rates to their cities. One urban attraction is that cities have higher wage levels than the rural areas.

A study comparing migrants with natives of Mexico City illuminates the relationships between migration, education, and occupational mobility. Overall, Mexico City's native-born population was more highly educated than the migrants; the natives had more schooling and were more likely to be literate. Female migrants were more likely than males to be uneducated and illiterate, reflecting a lack of educational opportunities for females in the countryside. Thus employed migrants, particularly those with agricultural backgrounds, were more likely than natives to hold jobs in "marginal occupations," which paid the legal minimum wage or less. But as migrants spend more time in the city, some experience occupational mobility, so that those with ten years or more in Mexico City are less likely than newcomers to hold marginal jobs. Natives of the city who start at low occupational levels rise further than rural migrants who start at the same level. "In contrast, migrants who enter the labor force at the skilled manual and in nonmanual occupational levels, such as skilled production workers, salesmen, and office workers, show higher upward mobility rates than the natives who entered the labor force at commensurate levels" (Unikel, 1977; p. 516). Furthermore, educated migrants had higher rates of upward mobility than educated natives. This reflects the attraction of cities to educated, ambitious young persons in the countryside. Thus, migration attracts energetic, productive individuals to urban communities.

## Examples: Two Urbanizing Nations

Brief summaries of data from two third-world nations, India and Mexico, illustrate the process and scope of urbanization.

### India

India entered the twentieth century with a very rural population, only 10.8 percent urban in 1901. Urbanization occurred over the next half-century, reflected in the 1951 census figure of 17.3 percent urban (Bose, 1977). In the two following decades, urbanization rose only slightly, to 19.9 percent. This leveling off was actually a func-

CHAPTER·16

Residential areas in third-world cities often provide water from communal taps at the street, so people have to wait in line to fill and carry heavy containers to their dwellings, as in Faridabad, India. (United Nations)

tion of rapid growth of the rural population simultaneous with rapid growth of city populations. In the decade of the 1960s, urban population grew by almost 40 percent. The country has more than 2,600 towns and cities including some of the world's largest: Calcutta, Bombay, Delhi, and Madras.

Some twentieth-century urban growth was caused by a unique historical event but most arose from rural-urban migration and from natural increase of the urban population itself. When India and Pakistan became independent from England in 1947, millions of Hindus left Pakistan to live in India. Bose estimates that these refugees added more than 6 percent to India's urban population, concentrated in cities including Calcutta, Bombay, and Delhi. There are various types of migration within India, including urban to rural as well as vice versa. Cities attract new migrants who come in search of employment opportunities; however, as Bose emphasizes, those who fail to find work encounter a "push-back" to return to the village.

Demographic projections show a continuation of massive urban growth in India. The largest cities, those exceeding 100,000 population, "have been playing an increasingly important role in the process of urbanization in India" (Bose, 1977, p. 317). In 1971, such cities had more than half the urban population, and they have been growing much faster than smaller cities. India's government makes national development plans which affect urban development to some extent. Newly established communities, including steel production cities and planned state capitals, are growing very rapidly. Being much smaller than the older metropolises, though, they do not absorb a large fraction of the new urban population. One national demographic projection shows India's overall urban population increasing from 150 million in 1981 to almost 280 million in 2001.

## Mexico

Like India's, Mexico's urban population has grown rapidly; between 1900 and 1970 it multiplied 15 times, from 1.4 million to 22 million (Unikel, 1977, p. 485). At the turn of the century it had 33 cities, and by 1970, 178. Unlike India, Mexico has had true demographic urbanization since urban growth has far exceeded rural; Mexico's percentage urban rose from 10.5 to 44.9 (see Figure 16-1). Another difference between the two countries has been that while India developed a number of

**FIGURE 16-1**
Mexico's level of urbanization, 1900–1970. (Source: Unikel, 1977, p. 489.)

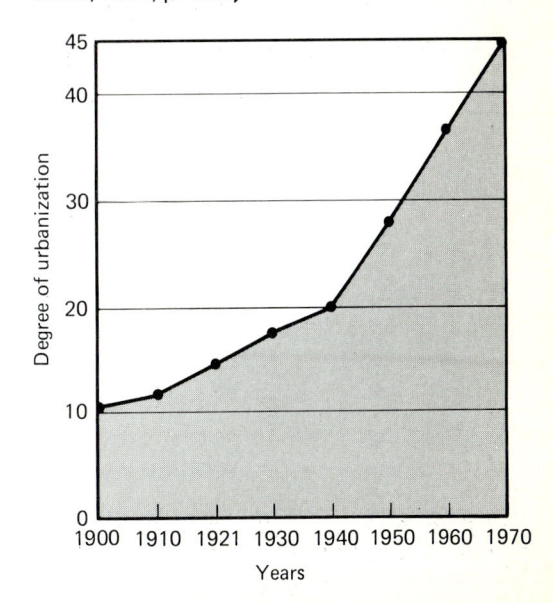

metropolitan cities, Mexico has produced one vast metropolis, Mexico City, far larger than any of the others.

According to Unikel (1977), Mexico had a low level of urbanization in 1910 but has experienced substantial urbanization in each decade since then. By 1960 Mexico's level exceeded the world average, and one projection shows an urban percentage exceeding 60 percent by 1990, which would make Mexico as urbanized as many of the first-world nations. Except for the decade of the 1930s, peasants and Indians migrated to the cities throughout the twentieth century.

The two points of view about the effects of Mexico City's large size are that some contend it is detrimental to the national society, while others maintain it is beneficial. Those who emphasize the negative aspects assert that "the Mexico City Metropolitan Area exercises an ever-increasing demand upon the country's overall resources" to support its population and its new migrants (Unikel, p. 530). On the other hand, a report of the Bank of Mexico (cited by Unikel, p. 531) suggests that "Mexico City still generates more than it consumes {and that} it has contributed to the fast development of the country" (cited in Unikel, 1977, p. 531). But this demographic and economic growth led to inequities within the nation, so that residents of the metropolitan area enjoyed far higher incomes than Mexicans in some other regions.

## THE PLACE OF CITIES IN RURAL SOCIETIES

If you have ever spoken with someone who visited a third-world city, you probably got an earful of stories about beggars, slums, congestion, and stench. Western visitors to Calcutta, to take an extreme example, will notice the pedestrian and vehicular congestion, crowded housing, people sleeping in doorways and on sidewalks, and poor women and children waiting in line with containers to get water from street faucets. Likewise, a visitor to Bogotá, Columbia, is likely to focus upon the squatter shack slums. Despite the fact that these conditions exist, it is a mistake to write off these cities, because to do so is to fail to appreciate their major institutions and the function of the cities within their societies. Since third-world societies are rural, their cities are best understood from the rural point of view. To see them in this way, we must start from the village, the kind of community in which most people reside.

### Villages

Two points from earlier chapters are relevant here. As noted in Chapter 5, almost all third-world nations are unurbanized. Thus in such countries most people live in rural areas, typically in villages. Redfield's folk-urban contrast, summarized in Chapter 1, characterized villages as small, homogeneous, and isolated. Isolation means that many rural communities have weak ties to the rest of the nation; most villagers are illiterate, so they cannot read newspapers. National governments may lack effective administrative offices in the provinces. Without electricity, villages do not have much light after dark, let alone television. The diffusion of cheap transistor radios, though, has brought mass communication to rural areas. The village mentality is likely to be traditional and localistic. Third-world cities should be seen in this village context.

## Small Cities

In contrast with rural areas, even small cities have amenities and linkages to higher-level institutions in the society; i.e., they are not so isolated. Small cities have electricity, so the streets have lights at night as well as music from phonographs and radios. Small cities have telephone and telegraph service which links them to the bigger cities. Major transport lines also provide linkages: A small city has a railroad station, access to long- and short-distance buses, truck depots, and a airline ticket office. A cinema, bookshop, and college may provide mental linkages to the broader world. Other small-city institutions include banks and government offices, including hospital, post office, police, and courts. And as noted in Chapter 5's discussion of central-place hierarchies, towns serve market functions, so they contain large marketplaces or bazaars and specialty shops of many types—hardware, pharmacy, dry goods, and others. Small cities also provide the specialized services of dentists; auto, truck, and tractor mechanics; and numerous other individuals within the community's elaborate division of labor. From the rural person's point of view, then, the small city represents a place to sell and buy things, an attraction, a center. No matter how poor or shabby it may seem to the cosmopolitan tourist, the city represents a special place in the rural context.

## The City

A metropolitan city simply expands the amenities and connections of the smaller city as well as being a center of the broader society. The big city's institutions and linkages are apparent in the built environment: Large buildings contain big banks and (corporate) offices of large enterprises (national or multinational), big hotels, theaters, monumental railroad stations, courts and governmental offices. It includes regional or central offices of organizations which had much smaller branches in the smaller cities. The metropolis also has universities and colleges plus larger bookshops and bigger, more specialized hospitals. If it is not the national capital itself, the big city has institutions which coordinate a large region and which are linked to those of the capital. Local governmental offices report to the state or regional office in the big city. Likewise, local banks are usually branches of larger banks which are centralized in metropolitan places.

## Linkages and Influences

Many of these institutions link the big city to other cities in the nation as well as to world capitals. Within the nation, the major offices—in business and government—are tied to their superior offices in the national capital. Similarly, state or regional banks report to national banks; other corporate offices are also organized this way. If the big-city banks handle foreign exchange or stocks and bonds, they will have ties to world financial exchanges and major international banks.

Many other big-city institutions have extralocal connections. Newspapers and broadcasters receive information from international wire services. University scientists read internationally distributed journals and may also publish in such outlets.

Cities have powerful effects over their hinterlands and regions economically, culturally, and politically. Hoselitz (1955) distinuished between "generative" and "parasitic" cities with regard to their extralocal economic effects: "A city will be designated as generative if its impact on economic growth is favorable, i.e., if its formation and continued existence and growth is one of the factors accountable for the economic development of the region or country in which it is located" (p. 279). In most cases, urbanization is considered to have this economic effect.

Third-world cities also have powerful effects on national culture. Teachers trained in urban colleges and universities later take new customs and ideas to their classrooms. Writers and publishers are in cities, often promulgating ideas which disrupt, modify, or transform cultural traditions. Moviemakers and mass-media broadcasters send new messages throughout the country. New products and fashions originate in cities and diffuse to towns and villages. Governments, with plans and programs to implement change, are in cities. So the third-world city must be seen as a major locus of economic, political, and social change.

## DUAL CITIES

While third-world cities contain major urban institutions, they also have enormous poverty sectors. This juxtaposition of large-scale modern institutions with the deepest poverty suggests the concept of "dual city." Third-world cities are dual insofar as they contain simultaneously the society's modernizing elite side by side with great masses of poverty-stricken households.

### Subsistence Urbanism

Subsistence urbanism means a situation "in which the ordinary citizen has only the bare necessities, and sometimes not even those, for survival in the urban environment" (Breese, 1966, p. 5). Every third-world city has a poverty district where people suffer under the conditions of subsistence urbanism.

Subsistence urbanism connotes absolute poverty, as contrasted with relative poverty. Absolute poverty means life such that one can barely survive, one lives at the edge of existence. Diet is minimal or subminimal, hardly consisting of a balanced mix of foods; individuals consume just enough to keep going, although not enough to maintain healthy resistance against disease. Housing provides minimal shelter at best; income is small and undependable; and medicine and sanitation are almost nil.

The U.S. underclass suffers from relative poverty, something very different from absolute poverty. (A few exceptions to this rule include bag ladies and homeless men, but my assertion refers, for example, to urban families living in public-housing projects and receiving Aid to Families of Dependent Children.) Relative poverty denotes the situation of the poorest class within a wealthy society's system of inequality. Liberal standards in such a society suggest that even the poorest members are entitled to certain benefits such as employment, education, decent housing, etc. The poor in the United States are only poor relative to everyone else. Their "benefits" are worse than those of the more prosperous classes who form the majority. Nonetheless, poor individuals in India, for example, would not consider a New York public-housing project—built of brick, with indoor plumbing and central heating, telephones and televisions—to represent poverty. While Americans can perceive the many social problems in such a project, it does not represent absolute poverty.

Oscar Lewis, one of the first urban anthropologists, studied poor families in several third-world countries, including Mexico, and his descriptions vividly portray subsistence urbanism (see Box 16-1).

The concept of subsistence urbanism is a counterpart to the more familiar term subsistence agriculture, a prevalent way of life in much of the third world. Rural folk in subsistence agriculture are also very poor, using very unproductive farming techniques, living at the margin of existence. Comparing rural and urban subsistence, Breese (1966) said: "This is an urbanization of very high density, of individuals living under conditions that may be even worse than the rural areas from which they have come, of not having available the kinds of work or the means of support which will permit them to do more than merely survive" (p. 5).

## Housing and environment

In subsistence urbanism, housing provides minimal shelter, often in a homemade shack. North African cities are surrounded by shack towns known as "bidonvilles," Indian cities have "bustees," and many South American cities have squatters' "favellas." In such environments residents build their own primitive shacks out of locally available cheap materials, such as mud, cardboard boxes, tin cans, tar paper, corrugated iron, wood from packing crates, and the like. Abrams (1964), an expert on housing, wrote the following scenario of how squatters built a neighborhood: "As in a military campaign, some would bivouac during the night with their stock of materials behind a newly placed billboard. Next day, the horizon would be dot-

# CHAPTER·16

> **BOX 16-1**
> **Subsistence Urbanism in Mexico City**
>
> (Located near the center of Mexico City) . . . Panaderos is a small *vecindad* consisting of a single row of twelve windowless one-room apartments which lie exposed to the view of passers-by, with no enclosing walls, no gate, and only a dirt yard. . . .
>
> Also in full view, for the use of the residents, is a large cement water trough where the women wash their dishes and laundry and bathe their children, and two broken-down toilets curtained by pieces of torn burlap and flushed by pails of water. The bare earth of the thirty-foot-wide lot is dotted with rocks and stones and forked poles that hold up the clothes lines stretched crisscross between the two neighboring buildings. Here and there, a hole dug by the children or an unexpected sewer opening, haphazardly covered by a rock, makes walking precarious.
>
> Five of the twelve dwellings have sheds or lean-tos constructed by setting up two poles and extending the kitchen roofs made of scraps of tarpaper, tin and corrugated metal, held down by stones and piled high with firewood and odds and ends. The sheds were built primarily to provide a dry, shady place to work for the artisans who live there. Two of them make tin pails, another makes toys from scrap metal and the fourth makes miniature water bottles and repairs bicycles. Piles of equipment, tin sheets, bundles of waste steel trips, wire, nails and tools, kept on old tables and benches, clutter up the space under the sheds.
>
> The other men of this *vecindad* work at various jobs; three in shoe factories, one in a belt factory and one selling newspapers. Because their earnings are small and much of it is spent on drink, every one of the wives and many of the children work to add to their income. Some of the younger women work in shops, others as ambulant peddlars, but most prefer to work at home, doing piecework, making sweets or cooked food to sell in the street nearby, dealing in old clothes, and taking in washing and ironing. The clothes lines are almost always hung with the laundry of others, providing a multicolored curtain behind which life in the *vecindad* can be conducted with a bit more sense of privacy.
>
> Many of Panaderos' 86 residents sleep on the floor, lacking beds. Many cook with kerosene or charcoal, but they do not get three meals a day regularly. They do not own knives and forks, as more prosperous people do, but eat with tortillas. They drink *pulque*

ted with new rows of hovels, to which others would be added shack by shack, until the expansion was checked by a road, by a canal, or by an owner prepared to spill blood" (p. 16). Squatters, by definition, have no legal claim to the land they occupy, so occasionally they lose their homes through government action, such as road building or other public works, or through political or aesthetic reasons. Govern-

rather than beer and buy second-hand furniture and clothing. Their only luxury possession is likely to be a radio; two individuals owned wrist watches and one household had a TV. Unlike more prosperous Mexicans, they did not have sewing machines, aluminum pots, or electric blenders.

A considerable degree of social cohesion exists in Panaderos due to kinship network ties.

Nine of the twelve households are related by kinship ties, and constitute three extended families. One mother has a married daughter in the *vecindad;* another mother has a married son and a married daughter; and a third has two married sons and one married daughter.... However, it is difficult to maintain the traditional formal respect relations between *compadres* in these crowded quarters; quarrels among the children of the *vecindad* often lead to quarrels among *compadres.* Visiting and borrowing are very frequent among the *vecindad* inhabitants who drift easily in and out of each other's rooms. There is little privacy and everyone knows each other's business. However, in some ways there is less organization here than in the Casa Grande. The Panaderos *vecindad* has no protecting patron saint, no gang of boys and girls (perhaps because it is so small), and no weekly dance.

The biological or nuclear family is the predominant type in the *vecindad.* Six of the thirteen families found in the twelve households are of the simple biological type consisting of husband, wife and children. Three apartments are occupied by widowed or abandoned women living with their grown children, and two apartments are occupied by men who have separated from their wives. In only one apartment is there a real extended family consisting of a man and his wife and their married daughter and grandchildren.

There are a total of thirteen marriages, in five of which the partners have ceased to live together. Six of the thirteen (46 per cent) were common-law marriages, five were married by both civil and church authorities, one by the church exclusively and one by civil law alone. The high proportion of 46 per cent common-law union contrasts sharply with the much lower rate of 20 per cent in the Casa Grande....

In Panaderos, the level of school attendance was 2.1 years; there was not a single primary-school graduate; 40 percent of the population was illiterate; and 46 percent of the marriages were free unions.

*Source:* Adapted from Oscar Lewis, 1958, 1961.

ment officials may fear the potential of residents of squatter neighborhoods to mobilize and form an uncontrollable movement.

Subsistence urbanism may be found in conventional buildings also. In Bombay poor families live in old tenement apartment buildings, some of which have deteriorated to the point of actual collapse (Choldin, 1978). In shacks and in buildings, there is usually one room per family, as there was in Manchester's early industrial slums. Population densities in poverty areas are usually extremely high; Cairo had an area housing 77,000 persons per square kilometer (Abu-Lughod, 1971, p. 197).

Poverty areas in third-world cities lack public and private amenities. Even the areas with regular buildings have water supplied only through public taps along the streets. To get water for home use, residents must line up with containers to fill and, even then, the water may be bacterially contaminated. Dwelling units lack toilets, so the neighbors must share public outdoor facilities. Squatter areas may also lack electricity.

One urban researcher in Mexico conducted a study of what poor migrants in a squatter neighborhood wanted from their government (Cornelius, cited in Unikel, 1977). Most of their demands referred to immediate local needs, mainly for security of land tenure. They also asked for water supply, postal service, paved streets, electricity, schools, public transportation, sewers, and garbage collection.

Apart from their potential for political unrest, squatter settlements present a major problem for third-world governments committed to improving social and economic conditions. Housing officials in such countries face a dilemma. If they choose to invest public moneys in standard-quality, modern housing projects, they cannot provide many dwelling units. Governments of these poor nations cannot afford to supply many new units, not enough to make a dent in the problem. Economic planners prefer not to allocate funds for housing because the money could be used more directly to promote economic development. The alternative to building standard-quality housing projects is to improve the conditions in the squatter shantytowns. The dilemma is that if they spend public moneys in this way, they appear to condone the illegal settlements, and even after the improvements, the neighborhoods still look unsightly, unlike new "showplace" projects. But the arguments for improving the slums are compelling. Governments can pave streets, bring running water, and install electricity. They can help the householders directly by providing subsidized loans to provide materials for proper roofs, indoor plumbing, additional rooms, etc., with the residents supplying the labor. Such programs which can rapidly assist large numbers of families are favored by many international housing experts (Abrams, 1964; Payne, 1977; Turner, 1977).

## Employment

Another fundamental problem in subsistence urbanism is the unavailability of steady work. Although most rural-urban migrants come to cities in search of work, often none is available. (This question is at the crux of the overurbanization issue.) Because of this, poor migrants work at all sorts of low-paying and undependable jobs. In Indian cities they may work as sweepers, bicycle-rickshaw pullers, or day laborers on construction projects. At worst, they may become beggars. As Breese (1966) writes, the new migrant "lacks the skills, and sometimes even the language, as well as knowledge of the ways of the city by which he can introduce himself into the more productive aspects of the urban labor market" (p. 78). Illiteracy is highly prevalent among males and females in such areas, which further limits the employment potential of the residents.

At the other extreme, third-world cities may incorporate actual villages which retain certain rural qualities. As metropolitan areas expand, outlying villages may be surrounded by urban developments. The villages become enveloped in the metropolitan fabric, much as American towns near cities were incorporated into suburban rings. In India, according to Breese (1966), some of the villagers may continue to live in the villages which may retain a rural quality; within the urbanized area, such villages offer cheap housing, marketplaces for nearby areas, and work space for services and artisans such as furniture makers.

Perhaps the ultimate question about subsistence urbanism is whether the migrants would have been better off staying at home in the rural areas. In one sense the answer is subjective, depending upon one's attitude toward the values of rural versus city life. One piece of data, though, suggests that the migrants benefit by moving to the city; a survey of migrants in Mexico City reported that after four years, 80 percent of those interviewed were satisfied with their decision to move (Unikel, 1977). After studying the question, one researcher concluded, "Undoubtedly, as bad as conditions in the cities may be {migrants} are *much better off* in the urban areas than in the countryside" (Stern, cited in Unikel, 1977, p. 530).

## Modernizing Elites

In addition to subsistence urbanism, third-world cities also have prosperous contemporary areas with modern institutions and modernizing elites. It is the juxtaposition of subsistence urbanism with modernizing elites that inspires the concept of *dual cities*. While their people share the same space and nationality, they have very little in common. Subsistence urbanites may be rural in culture, illiterate, traditional, localistic, poor. Members of the modernizing elite are cosmopolitan, educated, prosperous.

The very geography of the city sets aside a special section for the modern sector. When India was a colony, the English built a spacious, planned, modern city—New Delhi—to house the administration, leaving Delhi, the old crowded city, to the natives. In contemporary independent India, New Delhi has the modern institutions—governmental, commercial, and scientific—plus housing for people in these fields, while Delhi remains a dense, deteriorating community.

Cairo's center also has a district with elite institutions and population (Abu-Lughod, 1971). This part of the city is the most accessible to foreign visitors, having high-rise modern hotels and apartment buildings. It has department stores, "downtown" specialty shops, beauty salons, major theaters, nd exclusive clubs.

Social area analysis showed that this area had by far the highest socioeconomic-status scores. Residents of this area had the most modern lifestyle in the city: males and females were more educated, had later marriages, and lower fertility levels. Although the area once accommodated foreigners, it now houses an Egyptian elite.

CHAPTER·16

This scene of modern buildings and squatter shacks in Brasilia is not unique to Brazil. There are shantytowns in many cities, sometimes in suburban districts but also adjacent to high-quality structures. (Paul Almasy, World Health Organization)

In addition to universal literacy, and small family type, the residents have a subculture that differs radically from the culture of the majority. Women in this area deviate from traditional Muslim rules; they are educated, dress in western clothing, and engage in other contemporary practices. Although the rest of the city has a somewhat ambivalent attitude toward this district, the area also provides many service jobs for "outsiders."

Modernizing elites of such cities tend to be cosmopolitan in their modes of thought (Merton, 1957). They avail themselves of foreign magazines, newspapers and movies in addition to domestic publications and films. They are more likely to wear western clothes than native garb. Whether they are engineers, bankers, scientists, or professors, their professions require them to keep abreast of developments abroad, technological, political, etc. A vivid example of duality and cosmopolitanism occurs in Calcutta, where there is a vigorous group of moviemakers. Although most Westerners imagine that city to be a sinkhole of poverty, the epitome of subsistence, perhaps, it too has a modernizing elite with universities, advanced scientists, etc. The cinematic group there aspires to the highest aesthetic standards, making world-class films. These moviemakers are not oblivious to their environment—they make sensitive movies about Indian life—but they also follow cinematic developments in France very closely (Sinha, 1972).

## URBAN STRUCTURE

Urban sociologists and geographers have studied a number of third-world cities to discover their structure. Most commonly, the researchers have employed some modification of social area analysis or factorial ecology. They have relied upon the national censuses, analyzing small-area statistics for city wards, census tracts, or some other local division. One researcher (Weinstein, 1974) conducted a large-scale sample survey of the population of Madras, a large city in southern India, to supplement the national census.

The researchers ask, "What is the form of the city?" Usually, they take an American theoretical model as a starting point and ask whether the third-world city follows the same pattern. Thus, in the first set of studies in this literature, sociologists noticed that socioeconomic-status patterns in Latin American cities deviated from Burgess's concentric circle pattern. In the first documented Latin American cities, the highest-status neighborhoods were at the city center and the low-status areas were at the periphery (London, 1982). This was exactly counter to the concentric model, which showed a status gradient running from low to high as it moved away from the city center. This discovery of an upper-class center in Latin American cities, made initially in the 1930s, was the starting point for a series of studies on the subject.

Another fundamental question is whether the basic dimensions of spatial differentiation in third-world cities are the same as those in the industrial metropolis—that is, are the residential areas differentiated mainly by socioeconomic rank, family status, and ethnicity? The statistical techniques associated with social area analysis and factorial ecology readily allowed researchers to explore this question.

Finally, researchers have wanted to know how the third-world cities are changing. Third-world nations, also called "developing areas," are countries which have undergone enormous transitions in the twentieth century. Many have gone from colonial status to independent nationhood; they have brought industry to agricultural economies and have introduced modern bureaucratic forms of organization. They are modifying their traditional ways of life, becoming literate, and adopting modern technologies. What effects have these radical social changes had in their cities?

### Latin America

Early studies of cities in Guatemala and Mexico discovered what came to be known as a Latin American pattern of status and location. These cities were founded by the Spanish. Amato (1970) notes that they "developed for several centuries around a central plaza, the focus of the city's governmental, ecclesiastical and intellectual life" (p. 447). Imagine a green plaza surrounded by a cathedral and town hall with other major structures, such as hotels and banks, nearby. The environs of the plaza were reserved for the homes of the wealthy in these traditional Latin American cities; middle-income homes were nearby, and the poor lived in shantytowns at the urban periphery. Sjoberg (1960) contended that this form represented a case of the typical preindustrial pattern.

As Latin American cities grew and industrialized, many broke this pattern. Bruce London's (1982) review of recent studies shows pronounced changes, but they fail to converge into a new dominant pattern. As the cities grew, the urban elite was forced out of the central neighborhoods because central business districts expanded; businesses bought residential land and erected commercial buildings. This tended to undermine the upper-class ambiance of the plaza area. In a number of cases, the upper classes tended to move into one sector only, toward the urban periphery. The lower classes remained in other sectors of the periphery, but central slums also developed. This left the central city as the area of the growing middle and lower-middle strata. A study of four large South American cities reinforced this image, showing

> ...a clear shift away from traditional elite centralization toward a rather mixed pattern marked by the persistence of some elite centralization and low status decentralization, a frequently sectoral decentralization of elite groups to environmentally desirable locations, and a delayed but increasing centralization of low-status groups. (Amato, cited in London, 1982, p. 376)

Nonetheless, there are exceptions, too, so the literature does not show a uniform pattern for cities throughout the region. For example, Mexico City has adopted some features of the North American pattern, erecting new middle-income housing "on the fringes" as well as expensive suburbs further out. Perhaps the one generalization which emerges from the literature is that smaller, older cities are most likely to exhibit the plaza–upper-class centralized pattern, while larger, more industrial cities are likely to have evolved into a mixed form.

## Dimensions of Residential Areas

Before exploring the results of ecological analysis, we should note that third-world cities do not exhibit nearly the extent of separation of functions and land uses as is seen in the contemporary first-world metropolis. Many of the people who write about third-world cities, including Sjoberg, mention the low level of functional differentiation in land uses. Thus in a third-world city a given neighborhood may include houses, retail and wholesale shops, factories, and a mixture of social classes or lifestyles. Nonetheless, as the research shows, more than enough social differentiation exists to allow the careful researcher to describe the city's sections and to look for spatial patterns.

## Madras, India

Perhaps the most unusual set of findings about a third-world city appears in Weinstein's (1974) study of Madras. Weinstein found that, in general, the city did not exhibit sharp differentiation among neighborhoods, particularly with regard to family status. Relying upon his observations, he noted, "Within a radius of perhaps one or two kilometers from nearly any point in the city one can find neighborhoods encompassing the entire range of social characteristics, socioeconomic, family structural, or ethnic-group related" (p. 61). He commented on the reason for this: "We would speculate that the ecological structuring of Madras is fundamentally of a multiple nuclei form in a very special sense. It is likely that Madras ... represents an association of villages within which we might find the kinds of settlements and patterns closer to [theoretical] expectations but between which there is no clear pattern" (p. 61).

Weinstein's analysis showed that Madras's neighborhoods fail to exhibit two of the three indexes which usually appear in studies of western cities; the only one that was measurable was social rank. The distribution of residential areas did not exhibit a concentric or sectoral pattern.

Madras's social ecology has one unique feature: Neighborhoods are arranged in relation to the religious center of the city. Ecoogical studies, say, of density or socioeconomic status, usually take the CBD as a point of reference. However, in Madras the crucial center was not the CBD; it was the sacred center of the metropolis, a place which included important Hindu, Christian, and Moslem temples, that influenced the location of social groupings. Weinstein categorized the census tracts according to their composition by caste, a fundamental social differentiation in Indian society. Castes are sharply ranked from Brahmins, the highest, to Harijans (formerly called "Untouchables"), the lowest, with dozens of other castes ranked in between. Placing residential areas into five levels, by caste ranking, Weinstein found a discernible pattern in which the higher-caste groups tended to live closer to the temple center and the lower castes tended to live further away. Weinstein noted that the pattern was not ironclad but that the temple was a clear center in the metropolitan structure.

## Cairo, Egypt

Abu-Lughod's (1971) monumental study of Cairo's social ecology also revealed factors and patterns that differ from those in conventional social area analysis. Abu-Lughod reported that no clear separation existed between indicators of social rank and family cycle stage in the residential areas of that city. Studies of American cities had always shown that these were independent variables, but Abu-Lughod discovered that the main variable, which she called "style of life," combined elements of socioeconomic status, familism, and involvement in modern life. Table 16-3 shows the most important indicators of style of life.

Explaining the meaning of this variable, the researcher described areas that scored high and low. "Those portions of the city most easily identified as "modern urban" (p. 185) are the areas with high scores.

> The inhabitants ... are attired in Western clothes. Furthermore, a large majority of the men and a significant proportion of the women are ... educated, work at occupations

**TABLE 16-3**
**Most Important Indicators of Lifestyle, Cairo**

| Indicator | Correlation |
|---|---|
| Percentage of females in a census tract who are able to read | + |
| Percentage of females 16 years of age or older never married | + |
| Percentage of females enrolled in school or employed | + |
| Percentage of males in a census tract who are able to read | + |
| Fertility ratio (number of children under age 5 per 1,000 women in childbearing ages) | − |
| Average number of persons per room in census tract | − |
| Percentage of males 16 years of age or older never married | + |

*Source:* Abu-Lughod, 1971, p. 186.

> within the modern sector of the urban economy, and possess skills and/or property assuring them of a fairly adequate income.... Men and women tend to marry somewhat later than is typical in Egypt, frequently delaying marriage until the man is in his late twenties or early thirties and the woman is in the early or middle twenties. On the average, these couples tend to bear fewer children than is typical in Egypt.... The children they do have, however, are enrolled in school without question and are often kept in school to a level of education that equals if not exceeds that of the parental generation. (Abu-Lughod, 1971, pp. 185–186)

The sections of the city with low scores on the style-of-life variable form a very different picture.

> The women ... are attired in the same long black gowns, bright head kerchiefs and supplemental inky shawls that adorn their country cousins.... Only a minor percentage of [the] men can read and write, and it is a rarer handful per hundred among the women who can do even this much.... Men and women marry young, most of the men by the time they are twenty, virtually all of the girls by the age of sixteen. Early and sustained childbearing preoccupies the women, as attested by the extremely high fertility ratios in these zones.... Until recently it was a rare child who attended school, and even now with the new compulsory education laws the frequency with which girls are "overlooked" and the early ages at which most children disappear from the school system means a very low rate of school enrollment. The style of life in these quarters ... remains close to the rural model. (Abu-Lughod, 1971, pp. 186–187).

While the pattern of the city, as shown in the map of social areas, does not appear to conform to any of the classical theoretical models, it exhibits a somewhat comprehensible configuration (see Figure 16-2). The elite areas, which score high on the style of life index, are located at the center. The most traditional poverty areas, which score lowest on the index, are at what Abu-Lughod calls the "rurban periphery of the metropolis," which is more than slightly rural. Three major slum districts are near the city center, and the intermediate SES areas fan out in sectors from the center.

**FIGURE 16-2**
Contemporary Cairo's thirteen subcities, according to lifestyle factor (Abu-Lughod, 1971).

## Calcutta, India

Berry and Rees (1969) studied Calcutta, using similar statistical geographic research methods, and found some of the same results as the two previously cited studies. As in Madras and Cairo, Calcutta's residential areas are not differentiated by simple dimensions of social rank and familism. Neighborhoods differ mainly along a "land use and familism gradient," which is a complex mixture of census-based indicators. Neighborhoods near the city center have high proportions of businesses, offices, commercial establishments, and restaurants. These highly urban areas also have high proportions of employed persons and many homeless men. In contrast, peripheral areas tend to have high proportions of dwellings—mud-walled ones at that—and high proportions of females over 15 and married women. These areas appear to be similar to Cairo's somewhat rural poverty areas at the metropolitan periphery. Calcutta's structure also resembles Cairo's in the existence of a modern elite section at the center. Berry and Rees conclude, "There is thus a clear and strong land use and familism gradient in Calcutta, from commercial core to residential periphery" (p. 470). This factor is more complex, then, than the family-status dimension of neighborhoods in U.S. urban areas, which contrasts familistic areas with those housing young and old individuals. In Calcutta, this familism dimension appears to be mixed with commercial and noncommercial land uses, employment and poverty, and construction ranging from modern commercial buildings to hand-made mud dwellings.

Whereas American urban areas usually have a single stratification (social-rank) dimension, Calcutta has a complex list of several such dimensions which combine socioeconomic status with ethnicity and caste. Due to India's history of castes—which are resricted to particular occupations, such as shoemakers, goldsmiths, priests, etc.—and because many caste and nationality groups live together in particular neighborhoods, factorial ecology reflects linkages among occupation, region of origin, and caste. Thus differences between Hindu and Muslim areas appear in certain factors; occupations and incomes in others, and literacy in still others.

## SUMMARY

Cities in third-world nations have grown rapidly in recent decades. In part this urban growth represents true urbanization, because the percentage urban has risen, but in many cases the countries remain predominantly rural despite the presence of major metropolitan areas.

Urban development in the third world differs in at least two major ways from the historical experience in the now-industrial nations. Simultaneous growth of rural and urban populations is one such difference; in the United States and England rapid urban growth "drained off" some of the rural population; and eventually, rural populations shrank as urban populations grew. The other major difference is related to the first—the *sequence* of agrcultural development, industrialization, and urbanization differs somewhat in the first- and third-world experiences. In the European case, the sequence began with increases in agricultural productivity that resulted in rural population growth due to falling mortality rates. Soon thereafter, industrial development created a demand for labor in towns, which absorbed some of the population displaced from the countryside. Thereafter, industrial and urban development continued in tandem. In the third world, the sequence began with the introduction of new public health and medical technologies—DDT, innoculations, antibiotics—which quickly brought down death rates, causing rapid rural population growth and impelling migration to urban areas. Improvements in agricultural productivity and industrial development *followed* population growth. This led some social scientists to suspect that overurbanization had occurred, but recent research shows that third-world nations now conform to a worldwide relationship between urban labor force and urbanization.

Because third-world countries are so rural, their cities must be viewed in this context. Thus, although a western visitor is inclined to judge third-world cities in comparison with European or North American places, this comparison produces a distortion. It always shows the third-world city to be backward, poor, or disorganized. But such a city must be understood from the point of view of its mainly rural nation. From this point of view the metropolis, with its major structures and institutions, represents an enormous accomplishment. Fifty years ago most third-world nations were exploited colonies—illiterate, traditional, employing primitive technologies—and the modern parts of their cities were exclusively for the foreign elite. Thus it is quite an accomplishment for today's third-world nations to have large-scale institutions—whether they are post offices or airlines or universities—operated by their own people (even if foreigners complain that the institutions are not up to date).

Despite this accomplishment, the third-world metropolis invariably includes a large poverty segment, living in subsistence urbanism. This condition and way of life has been carefully described by urban anthropologists such as Oscar Lewis. Subsistence urbanism is a life of absolute poverty, "of not having available the kinds of work or the means of support which will permit them to do more than merely survive" (Breese, 1966, p. 5)). Poor families live in subminimal housing, at extremely high densities, either in shacks or in deteriorated buildings; their dwellings and neighborhoods offer few amenities. Persons in subsistence urbanism are likely to be underemployed, working at low-level jobs when they can find work.

The juxtaposition of subsistence urbanism with large-scale organizations and modernizing elites gives rise to the concept of dual cities. While the subsistence-living urbanite population is illiterate and localistic, the modernizing elite is cosmopolitan and highly educated. While subsistence urbanites live in central or peripheral slums, modernizing elites are likely to live in the modern city center or new suburbs. Members of the elite work in institutions with foreign linkages, such as government, university, or business, and they receive foreign communications in the publications they read. Thus the metropolis encompasses two radically different segments.

Studies of spatial differentiation (social area analysis and factorial ecology) reveal patterns that differ from those of American and European metropolitan areas. Far more mixing of land uses occurs in third-world cities, so residences are likely to be located near markets, shops, and other activities. The residential areas are not simply differentiated by the factors of social rank, family status, and ethnicity. Social rank and ethnicity appear to form a complex mixture, at least in India, which has vestiges of a caste system. In Egypt, the main factor appears to express the modernity of the residents of each area, varying from those who are very traditional to those who have adopted a more modernized way of life. Furthermore, third-world cities appear to have a spatial pattern that reserves the center for the upper classes. The former colonial quarters with spatious city planning, major institutional structures, etc., have become the province of the modernizing elite. Squatter slums are on the periphery, although older slums may be near the city center as well. In addition, of course, the city has a distribution of working-class and middle-class areas. At least in the largest Latin American cities, though, the upper classes are being displaced from the centers and a new suburbanized pattern may be emerging.

## REFERENCES

Abrams, Charles. 1964. *Man's Struggle for Shelter in an Urbanizing World.* Cambridge, Mass.: M.I.T.

Abu-Lughod, Janet L. 1971. *Cairo: 1001 Years of the City Victorious.* Princeton, N.J.: Princeton.

Amato, Peter W. 1970. "A Comparison: Population Densities, Land Values and Socioeconomic Class in Four Latin American Cities." *Land Economics.* 41:447–455.

Berry, Brian J. L., and Phillip Rees. 1969. "The Factorial Ecology of Calcutta." *American Journal of Sociology.* 74:445–491.

Bose, Ashish. 1977. "Urbanization in India: A Demographic Perspective," chap. 6 in *Patterns of Urbanization: Comparative Country Studies,* vol. 1, (eds.) Sidney Goldstein and David Sly. Dolhain, Belgium: Ordina.

Breese, Gerald. 1966. *Urbanization in Newly Developing Countries.* Englewood Cliffs, N.J.: Prentice-Hall.

Choldin, Harvey M., 1978. "Housing Standards Versus Ecological Forces: Regulating Population Density in Bombay," pp. 287–333 in *The Mutual Interaction of People and Their Built Environment,* (ed.) Amos Rapoport. The Hague: Mouton.

Hoselitz, Bert F. 1955. "Generative and Parasitic Cities." *Economic Development and Cultural Change.* 3:278–294.

Lewis, Oscar. 1958. "The Culture of the *Vecindad* in Mexico City: Two Case Studies," chap. 19 in *Anthropological Essays.* New York: Random House.

———. 1961. *The Children of Sanchez: Autobiography of a Mexican Family.* New York: Random House.

London, Bruce. 1982. "The Social Ecology of Latin American Cities: Recent Evidence," pp. 374–378 in *Urban Patterns: Studies in Human Ecology* (rev. ed.), (ed.) George Theodorson. University Park: Pennsylvania State University Press.

Merton, Robert K. 1957. "Patterns of Influence: Local and Cosmopolitan Influentials," chap. 12 in *Social Theory and Social Structure.* Glencoe, Ill.: Free Press.

Payne, Geoffrey K. 1977. *Urban Housing in the Third World.* London: Leonard Hill.

Sinha, Surajit (ed.). 1972. *Cultural Profile of Calcutta.* Calcutta: Indian Anthropological Society.

Sjoberg, Gideon, 1960. *The Preindustrial City: Past and Present.* Glencoe, Ill.: Free Press.

Turner, J. F. C. 1977. *Housing by People.* New York: Pantheon.

Unikel, Luis. 1977. "Urbanization in Mexico: Process, Implications, Policies, and Prospects," chap. 10 in *Patterns of Urbanization: Comparative Country Studies,* vol. 2, (eds.) Sidney Goldstein and David Sly. Dolhain, Belgium: Ordina.

United Nations, Dept. of International Economic and Social Affairs. 1980. *Patterns of Urban and Rural Population Growth.* Population Studies, no. 68. New York.

Weinstein, Jay A. 1974. *Madras: An Analysis of Urban Ecological Structure in India.* Beverly Hills, Calif.: Sage.

## ACKNOWLEDGMENTS

I am grateful to the following authors and publications for the privilege of quoting excerpts and for copying or adapting tables or figures:

B. J. L. Berry and Y. Cohen, "Decentralization of Commerce and Industry," in *The Urbanization of the Suburbs*, edited by L. Masotti and J. Hadden, copyright © 1973, by Sage Publications, by permission of Sage Publications, Inc.

E. W. Burgess, "The Growth of the City: An Introduction to a Research Project," in *The City*, edited by R. E. Park and E. W. Burgess, copyright © 1925, pp. 51–55, by permission of The University of Chicago Press.

E. W. Burgess and D. W. Bogue (eds.), *Contributions to Urban Sociology*, copyright © 1964, by permission of The University of Chicago Press.

Marshall Clinard, *Slums and Community Development: Experiments in Self-Help*, copyright © 1966, by The Free Press, reprinted by permission of Macmillan Publishing Co.

M. J. Daunton, "Towns and Economic Growth in Eighteenth-Century England," in *Towns in Societies*, edited by P. Abrams and E. A. Wrigley, copyright © 1978, by permission of Cambridge University Press.

Anthony Downs, *Opening Up the Suburbs*, copyright © 1973 by Yale University Press, reprinted by permission.

O. D. Duncan and B. Duncan, "Residential Distribution and Occupational Stratification," *American Journal of Sociology*, vol. 60, copyright © 1955, by permission of The University of Chicago Press.

Claude Fischer, *To Dwell Among Friends*, copyright © 1982, by permission of The University of Chicago Press.

Nathan Kantrowitz, *Ethnic and Racial Segregation in the New York Metropolis*, copyright © 1973, reprinted by permission of Praeger Publishers.

William Kornblum, *Blue Collar Community*, copyright © 1974, reprinted by permission of The University of Chicago Press.

Barrett Lee, "The Disappearance of Skid Row," in *Urban Affairs Quarterly*, vol. 16, copyright © 1980 by Sage Publications, by permission of Sage Publications, Inc.

R. W. Marans and W. Rodgers, "Toward an Understanding of Community Satisfaction," in *Metropolitan America in Contemporary Perspective*, edited by A. H. Hawley and V. P. Rock, copyright © 1975 by Sage Publications, by permission of Sage Publications, Inc.

Peter O. Muller, *Contemporary Suburban America*, pp. 7, 10, 163, copyright © 1981, by permission of Prentice-Hall, Inc., Englewood Cliffs, N.J.

P. H. Rees, *Residential Patterns in American Cities: 1960*, 1979, reprinted by permission of the author.

Clifford R. Shaw and Henry O. McKay, *Juvenile Delinquency and Urban Areas* (revised edition), copyright © 1942, 1969, 1972, reprinted by permission of The University of Chicago Press.

James F. Short, Jr., (ed.), *The Social Fabric of the Metropolis*, copyright © 1971, by permission of The University of Chicago Press.

W. G. Skogan and M. G. Maxfield, *Coping with Crime: Individual and Neighborhood Reactions*, copyright © 1981 by Sage Publications, by permission of Sage Publications, Inc.

Allen H. Spear, *Black Chicago: The Making of a Ghetto*, copyright © 1967, by permission of The University of Chicago Press.

G. Stevens and D. Featherman, "A Revised Socioeconomic Index of Occupational Status," in *Social Science Research*, vol. 10, copyright © 1981, by permission of Academic Press.

Donald Treiman, *Occupational Prestige in Comparative Perspective*, copyright © 1977, reprinted by permission of Academic Press, Inc.

R. B. Warren and D. I. Warren, *The Neighborhood Organizer's Handbook*, copyright © 1977, by permission of University of Notre Dame Press.

Barry Wellman, "The Community Question: The Intimate Networks of East Yorkers," *American Journal of Sociology*, vol. 84, copyright © 1979, by permission of The University of Chicago Press.

M. Yeates and B. Garner, *The North American City* (third edition), copyright © 1980, by permission of Harper & Row, Publishers, Inc.

Harvey Zorbaugh, *The Gold Coast and the Slum*, copyright © 1929, reprinted by permission of The University of Chicago Press.

*Women and the American City*, a special issue of *Signs: Journal of Women in Culture and Society*, copyright © 1980, by permission of The University of Chicago Press.

# INDEX

## NAME

Abrams, Charles, 481, 484
Abu-Lughod, Janet, 194, 321, 484–485, 489–491
Adams, John S., 356
Adams, Robert McC., 71–72, 75
Aldrich, Howard, 254–255
Alihan, Milla, 39
Amato, Peter W., 487
Anderson, Nels, 15
Anderson, Theodore R., 201, 219, 379

Back, Kurt, 285
Baldassare, Mark, 54–55, 303, 305
Banfield, Edward, 354, 452
Banham, Reyner, 114, 374
Barnum, H. G., 159–160
Baumgart, Margaret M., 309
Baumgart, Richard G., 309
Bean, Lee L., 201
Bell, Wendell, 47, 199, 201, 404
Bendick, Marc, Jr., 462–463
Berger, Bennett, 386, 389–391
Berry, Brian J. L., 39, 40, 159, 160, 165, 179, 181–183, 380–381, 491–492
Bidwell, Charles, 40
Birch, David L., 333–335

Black, J. Thomas, 345
Bleda, Sharon, 214–217
Boggs, Sarah L., 439–440
Bogue, Donald J., 148, 163, 164, 192, 447
Bohrer, Robert, 372
Booth, Alan, 55, 459
Booth, Charles, 8–11
Borchert, John, 163
Bordua, David J., 439
Bose, Ashish, 475
Bott, Elizabeth, 439
Bourne, Larry S., 139, 141–143, 159
Bowly, Devereux, Jr., 452
Boyce, Ronald R., 179
Braidwood, Robert, 71
Breese, Gerald, 480–485
Burchell, R. W., 341–343
Burgess, Ernest W., 13–15, 21–24, 39, 116–118, 192, 258, 338
Butler, Elizabeth B., 9
Byington, Margaret, 9

Cahnman, Werner J., 75, 81, 82, 89
Calhoun, John B., 54
Camilleri, Frank, 201
Carpenter, Niles, 272
Castells, Manuel, 42, 321

Cavan, Ruth S., 15
Cayton, Horace, 240
Chandler, Tertius, 80, 83
Checkoway, Barry, 358–359
Childe, V. Gordon, 68, 73, 77
Chilton, Roland J., 439
Choldin, Harvey M., 54, 126, 219, 281, 337, 368, 372, 395, 424, 440, 458, 483
Clay, Phillip L., 345, 347, 349
Clemente, Frank, 308, 312
Clinard, Marshall, 433–434
Collver, Andrew, 372
Comhaire, Jean, 75, 81, 82, 89
Condit, Carl, 113
Cordasco, Francesco, 3, 126
Cortes, Carlos E., 150
Cottrell, Fred, 43
Craven, Paul, 56, 423
Cressey, Donald, 338
Cybriwski, Roman, 58, 357

Darroch, A. G., 214
Daunton, M. J., 102, 105
Davie, Maurice, 40
Davis, John P., 251
Davis, Kingsley, 73, 79, 139
deLeeuw, Frank, 348, 433–435
Dollard, John, 230
Donaldson, Scott, 386

496

# NAME INDEX

Downs, Anthony, 57, 242, 254, 355, 359–360, 374–379, 451
Drake, St. Clair, 240
DuBois, W. E. B., 7–8, 230
Duncan, Beverly, 208–210, 212, 258, 275, 280–281, 337
Duncan, James S., Jr., 57, 280
Duncan, Otis D., 40, 41, 165, 208–210, 212, 258, 275, 280–281
Dunham, Horace, 15
Durkheim, Emile, 38, 42, 92

Eberstein, Isaac, 43
Edwards, Ozzie L., 258
Egeland, Janice A., 219, 379
Engels, Frederick, 102, 108, 110–112
Ensel, Walter M., 426
Ericksen, Eugene P., 274–275

Faris, Robert E. L., 13, 15
Farley, Reynolds, 261–262, 372
Fava, Sylvia F., 338, 389, 395
Featherman, David, 207
Fellman, Jerome, 164
Festinger, L., 285
Field, Tracey, 400–401
Firey, Walter, 40, 222–223, 225
Fischer, Claude S., 48, 50–54, 56, 59, 273, 284, 395–396, 417–420, 422–424
Fitch, John A., 9
Fitzpatrick, Joseph P., 150
Foley, Donald L., 173, 243, 244, 278, 279, 282–284
Ford, Amasa B., 438–439
Form, William H., 42
Fosdick, Raymond B., 126
Fox, Gerald, 80, 83
Frazier, E. Franklin, 230, 258
Freedman, Jonathan, 54
Freeman, Jo, 320
Freeman, John, 40
Frey, William H., 261
Frieden, Bernard, 322
Friedman, Lawrence M., 450
Frisbie, W. Parker, 43
Fustel de Coulanges, N. D., 81

Gale, Dennis E., 343–344
Galland, George F., Jr., 341

Gans, Herbert J., 42, 49, 54, 59, 254, 288–295, 391–393, 396, 437
Garner, Barry, 181, 182, 202, 380–381
Garofalo, James, 310
Getis, Arthur, 163, 164
Getis, Judith, 164
Gist, Noel, 338
Golden, Hilda H., 158, 159
Goodman, John H., Jr., 346
Gordon, Margaret T., 314, 318
Gottman, Jean, 143
Gove, Walter, 55
Granovetter, Mark, 420–422, 426
Greer, Scott, 274
Grier, Eunice, 345–346
Grier, George, 345–346
Guest, Avery M., 216–219, 302–303, 305, 335–337, 347, 372
Guterbock, Thomas, 261, 321, 361–363
Gutman, Robert, 42
Gutowski, Michael, 400–401

Haar, Charles M., 402–403
Hadden, Jeffrey K., 369
Halbwachs, Maurice, 38
Hammett, Christopher, 343, 346–347
Hammond, Mason, 71, 73, 74, 76, 77, 100, 109
Hannan, Michael T., 40
Hannerz, Ulf, 410, 421–422, 427
Hansen, Marcus L., 147
Hanson, Claudine, 337, 372
Harris, Chauncey, 171, 177, 178, 180, 181, 185, 374
Hartnagel, Timothy, 314
Harvey, David, 42, 221, 225, 321, 323
Hauser, Philip M., 150
Hawley, Amos H., 40, 42, 43, 90, 108–109, 159, 165, 172–173, 322, 338, 347
Hayden, Delores, 317
Heumann, Leonard, 276
Heyl, Barbara, 12
Hiltner, J., 220
Hole, W. Vere, 451
Hoover, Edgar M., 332–336, 343
Horwood, Edgar M., 179
Hoselitz, Bert F., 480
Hoyer, William J., 309

Hoyt, Homer, 185
Hughes, Everett C., 13, 325
Hunter, Albert, 57, 59, 173, 274, 276–278, 281–284, 337

Indik, Bernard P., 433

Jackson, Robert M., 395
Jacobs, Jane, 457–458
Janowitz, Morris, 273, 274, 277, 280, 282
Juravich, Thomas, 220

Kain, John F., 242
Kantowicz, E. R., 339–340
Kantrowitz, Nathan, 214–217
Kaplan, Charles P., 138, 139, 141, 143, 144, 150, 158
Kasarda, John, 39, 40, 43, 179, 181–183, 282, 365–366
Katz, Elihu, 410
Keller, Suzanne, 272, 280, 316
Kellogg, Paul U., 9, 12
Kim, Ilsoo, 414–416
Kleiman, Michael B., 308, 312
Kornblum, William, 290–291
Kowinski, William S., 367, 400, 403

LaGory, Mark, 220
Lake, Robert W., 264
Lander, Bernard, 439
Langer, William L., 87
Laub, James, 310
Laumann, Edward, 421
Lazarsfeld, Paul F., 410
Le Corbusier, 458
Lee, Barrett A., 302–303, 305, 309, 448–449
Lenski, Gerhard E., 43, 68
Lenski, Jean, 43, 68
Leslie, Charles M., 27
Lewis, Michael, 440
Lewis, Oscar, 481–483
Ley, David, 58
Lieberson, Stanley, 214–215, 239
Liebow, Elliot, 12, 230
Light, Ivan H., 241
Lin, Nau, 426
Lincoln, James R., 42
Lineberry, Robert, 355
Livermore, Charles P., 341
Loch, Charles S., 82
Lofland, Lyn, 92, 316

# NAME INDEX

Logan, John R., 373
London, Bruce, 487–488
Long, Larry H., 264, 347
Loo, Chalsa, 54
Loosely, Elizabeth W., 388
Lopata, Helena Z., 319, 399
Lubove, Roy, 450–451

McCague, James, 122
McClenahan, Bessie A., 272
MacDonald, John S., 424, 426
MacDonald, Leatrice D., 424, 426
McElrath, Dennis, 194
McIntyre, J. J., 315
McKay, Henry D., 20–24, 29, 193, 439
McKenzie, Roderick, 39, 42, 141, 272
McNeill, William H., 87
Madge, John, 12, 16
Mann, Peter H., 272
Manners, G., 180
Marans, Robert W., 302–306
Markusen, Ann R., 317–322
Marshall, Leon S., 101–103, 106–108, 110, 111
Marston, W. O., 214
Marx, Karl, 108
Masotti, Louis H., 369
Matras, Judah, 146
Maxfield, Michael G., 307–312, 315
Merton, Robert K., 486
Meyer, Kenneth C., 357
Meyerson, Martin, 452
Michelson, William, 42, 59, 276, 302–303, 394, 397, 456
Micklin, Michael, 40
Milgram, Stanley, 419, 422–423
Miner, Horace, 25, 27
Molotch, Harvey, 242, 253–257, 322, 324–325
Moore, Winston, 341
Morley, David, 316
Morris, R. N., 44
Muller, Peter O., 113, 264, 354–357, 359, 361, 369
Mumford, Lewis, 69, 75, 89, 90, 101, 102, 104, 108, 109, 111
Murdie, Robert A., 202, 219, 381
Myrdal, Gunnar, 230

Newman, Oscar, 457–461

Ogburn, William F., 13
O'Kane, Geraldine E., 320
Orfield, Gary, 42
Osofsky, Gilbert, 236–239

Palm, Risa, 318, 320, 399–400
Pampel, Fred, 220
Park, Robert E., 13–15, 38–39, 126, 192, 206, 220
Payne, Geoffrey K., 484
Pearce, Diana, 243
Perlman, Janice E., 276
Petersen, William, 139, 145, 147, 148
Peterson, Rebecca, 316
Phillips, Phillip D., 439, 442
Pinkerton, T., 454
Pirenne, Henri, 84
Popenoe, David, 355, 386, 396–399
Pred, Alan, 318, 320, 399–400
Preston, Richard E., 159–162
Pushkarev, Boris, 402–403

Queen, Stuart, 141

Rainwater, Lee, 435–438, 455–457
Randall, Nan, 343
Rapoport, Amos, 42
Reckless, Walter, 15, 445
Redfield, Robert, 27–29, 49
Rees, Philip H., 202–206, 209, 213, 491–492
Reimers, David M., 150
Reiss, Albert, 165, 254–255
Richards, Toni, 262
Riesman, David, 57
Riis, Jacob, 3–4, 450
Rodgers, Willard, 302–306
Roncek, Dennis, 54–55, 219
Rose, Harold M., 263
Rosenbloom, Robert A., 276
Rossell, Christine, 262
Rossi, Peter H., 272
Russell, Josiah C., 83

Sabagh, George, 337
Sandis, Eva E., 150
Schacter, Stanley, 285
Schmid, Calvin, 201, 440–441, 443
Schnare, Ann B., 348, 433–435
Schnore, Leo, 38, 40, 173, 180, 369–370

Schuman, Howard, 275, 280–281
Schwirian, Kent, 40
Seeley, John R., 126, 388–389, 444–445
Semyonov, Moshe, 372
Sharlin, Allan, 102
Shaw, Clifford, 20–24, 29, 193, 439
Shevky, Eshrev, 47, 199–201
Short, James, 12, 14, 15
Silver, Allan, 126
Sim, Alexander, 388
Simmel, Georg, 44–45, 53
Simmons, James W., 139, 141–143, 159
Sinha, Surajit, 486
Sjoberg, Gideon, 49, 67, 73, 74, 79, 488
Skogan, Wesley G., 307–312, 315
Sly, David, 43
Smith, B., 220
Solomon, Arthur P., 322
Sorensen, Annemette, 247–249
Spain, Daphne, 264
Spear, Allen H., 239–240
Squires, G. D., 243
Srole, Leo, 55–56
Stahura, John, 370, 372, 401
Starr, Roger, 454
Sternleib, George, 341–343, 433
Stevens, Gillian, 207
Stimpson, Catherine R., 316
Stone, Michael E., 322
Strauss, Anselm, 57
Struyk, Raymond J., 348, 433–435, 452–454, 459, 462–463
Susser, Ida, 322–324
Suttles, Gerald, 54, 57, 59, 223–225, 254, 259, 274, 277, 280, 287, 295, 440, 444
Symanski, Richard, 445–447

Taeuber, Alma, 230, 244–249
Taeuber, Conrad, 146, 147, 157
Taeuber, Irene, 146, 147, 157
Taeuber, Karl, 230, 244–249
Taub, Nadine, 320
Taub, Richard, 276, 277, 308–312
Tayback, M., 454
Taylor, D. Garth, 308–312
Tennant, R. J., 159, 160

# NAME INDEX

Theodorson, George A., 40
Thernstrom, Stephan, 120
Thomas, Lewis F., 141
Thomas, William I., 13, 15
Thomlinson, Ralph, 104, 145, 148
Thrasher, Frederick, 15
Tilly, Charles, 424, 426
Timms, Duncan, 192, 202, 220, 272
Tönnies, Ferdinand, 25–27, 29
Treiman, Donald, 207
Turner, J. F. C., 484
Tyack, David B., 127

Ullman, Edward L., 171, 177, 178, 180, 181, 185, 374
Unikel, Luis, 471–472, 475, 477, 478, 484–485

Vance, James E., Jr., 80, 83, 84, 87, 100, 102, 103, 109–112, 374, 379
Vaughn, John C., 426
Verbrugge, Lois M., 421

Vernon, Raymond, 332–336, 343

Wade, Richard, 354
Walkley, R. P., 454
Ward, Russell, 220
Warner, Sam B., 357
Warren, Donald I., 258–260, 287–289, 432
Warren, Rachelle B., 259, 287–289, 432
Webber, Melvin M., 56–57
Weber, Adna F., 4–7
Weber, Max, 80–83, 85, 87, 88
Weed, James A., 216–217
Weinstein, Jay, 194, 487–489
Wekerle, Gerda, 316–320, 399
Weller, Robert H., 143
Wellman, Barry, 56–57, 273, 411–414, 417, 423
Wheeler, James O., 209
White, Lucia, 57
White, Morton, 57
Whitten, Robert, 177
Whyte, William F., 12, 13
Whyte, William H., 388

Wicker, Allan W., 42
Willhelm, Sidney, 325
Williams, Marilyn, 199–201
Williams, Peter R., 343, 346–347
Willmott, Peter, 410
Wilner, Daniel, 454
Wilson, James Q., 307, 455
Wirth, Louis, 15, 44–50, 53, 59, 222, 225, 272
Wolfgang, Marvin, 439
Wrigley, E. A., 104
Wurdock, Clarence, 262

Yancy, William L., 274–275, 455–457
Yeates, Maurice, 181, 182, 202, 380–381
Young, Michael, 410

Zeisel, John, 42
Zimmer, Basil, 42, 368
Znaniecki, Florian, 15
Zorbaugh, Harvey, 15–20, 28, 29, 170, 194

# SUBJECT

Accessibility, 221
Age-sex composition, 195–196, 400–402
Aging suburban populations, 400–402
Agricultural development and urbanization, 104, 157
Agricultural revolution, 67–73
Agricultural surplus, 72
Arson, 341–343

Baltimore, Md., 454
Behavioral sink, 54
Black ghetto, 231–244
 expansion of, 252–257
 institutional development in, 238–240
 internal stratification of, 257–258
 lack of businesses in, 241
Black middle class, 234–235
Black migration, 246–250
Black suburbanization, 262–265
Blacks, 230–266
 dual housing market for, 241–243

Boston, Mass., 222–223, 294
Boston Combat Zone, 445–446
Boundary lines, enacted, 223
Built environment, 41–42

Cairo, Egypt, 489–491
Calcutta, India, 486, 491–492
Cellular city, 109, 110
Census, U.S., 41, 136–145
 census tracts to measure urban residential areas, 195–199
 history of, 136–141
Central business district (CBD), 114–119, 130, 131, 171, 179–182, 364–365
Central-place theory, 159–163
Chicago, Ill., 13–24, 116–118, 120, 124, 193, 194, 208, 212, 239–240, 339–340
 Polish-American neighborhoods in, 339–340

Chicago, Ill. (Cont.):
 South Side ghetto in, 239–240
Chicago school of urban sociology, 13–24, 29, 44, 192–194
Child labor, 102
China, 79
City, defined, 45
City walls, 74, 77, 80, 85
Cleveland, Ohio, 218, 335–337
Community of limited liability, 273–274
Community press, 277
Community satisfaction, 302–306
Commuting, 173–175, 367
Competition for space, 220–221
Concentric zones model:
 of juvenile delinquency, 21–24
 of urban growth and form, 116–120, 373
Congruence, environment-behavior, 317, 397, 456
Contrived community, 57
Cottage industry, 100

## SUBJECT INDEX

*Crestwood Heights: A Study of the Culture of Suburban Life* (Seeley, Sim, and Loosely), 388–389
Crime, 439–444, 457–461
 fear of, 306–316, 435–438
 effects of, 307, 308, 312–315, 318
Critical mass for subculture, 50–51
Crowding, 54–55
Cultural preferences, 57
Culture, 76–77

Decentralization, 354–369
Deconcentration of population, 360–363
Defended neighborhood, 285–287
Defensible space, 457–461
Demographic transition, 103, 104
Demography, 41
Density (*see* Population density)
Density distribution index, 362
Density-pathology hypothesis, 54–55
Des Moines, Iowa, 205
Detroit, Mich., 281, 364, 447
Differentiation, social, 195–199
Diffusion of innovations, 56
Displacement in neighborhood redevelopment, 345–346
Division of labor, 38
Division of work and residence, 172–173
Draft riots, New York City, 121–124

Ecological expansion, theory of, 39
Ecosystem framework, 40–44
Egypt, 79
 (*See also* Cairo, Egypt)
Elderly, the, segregation of, 219–220
Employment, suburban, 365–367
Employment-residence ratio, 369
Environment, 41–42
Environment-behavior congruence, 317, 397, 456
Ethnicity:
 segregation by, 211–217
 suburban, 371
Experimental housing-allowance program, 462–463

Factorial ecology, 199, 202–206
Factory, 100–102, 106–108, 366

Family status, familism, and factor analysis, 201–203, 205
Fear of crime, 306–316, 435–438
 effects of, 307, 308, 312–315, 318
Federal Housing Authority (FHA), 243, 358
Feminist critiques, 316–321, 399–400
Fertile Crescent, 70, 73
Folk-urban continuum, 27–29
Friction of space, 172

*Gemeinschaft and Gesellschaft* (Tönnies), 25–27, 29
Gentrification, 343, 347
Ghetto:
 black (*see* Black ghetto)
 defined, 235
 Jewish, 235
 (*See also* Segregation)
*Gold Coast and the Slum, The* (Zorbaugh), 15–20, 29, 39–40
Graffiti, 57–58
Greece, 79–82
Greenwich, Conn., 400–401
Guatemala, 79
Guilds, 87–89, 105

Harlem, history of, 236–239
Homogeneity, effects of, 285
Honolulu, Hawaii, 213
Household type, segregation by, 217–219
Housing:
 abandonment and arson, 341–343
 apartment buildings, 368
 and environmental factors, 303–304
 factory-slum complexes, 109–111
 for immigrants, 125–126
 market for (*see* Housing market)
 neighborhood life cycle and, 333–335
 public, 451–459
 quality of accommodation, 221
 single-family houses, 333–334
 standards 450–451
Housing Act of 1937, 451–452
Housing Act of 1949, 463
Housing market:
 discrimination against women in, 320

Housing market (*Cont.*):
 dual, for blacks, 241–243
 and neighborhood change, 348
Housing quality, 432, 436
Houston, Texas, 197–198
Human ecology, 37–44, 59
 criticisms of, 39–40

Imagery, urban, 386
Immigration and immigrants, 125–129, 147–150, 230–231, 338–339, 414–416, 424–426, 450
 national origins of, 147
 quota system to restrict, 148–150
Immoral landscapes, 445–448
Index of dissimilarity, 210
India:
 ancient cities of, 79
 urbanization in, 475–477 488–489
 (*See also* Calcutta, India; Madras, India)
Industrial districts, 180
Institutional districts, 183, 184
Intensity of land use, 113, 179, 180

Jewish ghetto, 235
Job search, social networks and, 420, 426–427
Juvenile delinquency, 20–24, 193

King of Prussia, Pa., 375–376
Kinship aspects of social networks, 410–415, 418, 424–427
Korean-Americans, 414–416

Land use, intensity of, 113, 179, 180
*Land Use in Central Boston* (Firey), 222
Large populations, effects of, 45–48
*Levittowners, The* (Gans), 391–393
Levittowns, 358, 391–393, 396, 399
Local facilities, use of, 278–279, 283
Locational preferences, 394
London, slums of, 8–11
Los Angeles, Calif., 114, 195–197, 199–201, 337, 374–375, 378

# SUBJECT INDEX

Madras, India, 488–489
Manchester, England, 105–112
Manufacturing, suburban, 366
Marxist urban sociology, 321–326
Mature industrial city, 98, 112–121
Medieval towns, 67, 83–90
Megalopolis, 143
Mental health, urban, 55–56
Mesopotamia, 74–77
Metropolitan models (*see* Models, metropolitan)
Metropolitan Statistical Area (MSA) 143–145
Metropolitan units, 141–145
Mexico, 79
  urbanization in, 477–478, 484
Mexico City, Mexico, 478, 482–483
Miami, Fla., 234, 294
Migration, 102, 103
  black, 246–250
  rural-urban, 474–475
  social networks and, 424–426
Military, 81, 85, 90–91
Minicities, suburban, 368, 375–377
Minneapolis–St. Paul, Minn., 204
Models, metropolitan:
  concentric zones, 21–24, 116–120, 373
  modified multinuclear, 374–377
  multinuclear, 178–179, 374
  overlay, 379–382
Modified multinuclear model of urban growth and form, 374–377
Multinuclear model of urban growth and form, 178–179, 374

Neighborhoods, 15–24, 220–224, 271–296, 411–414
  big-city (urban village), 288–295, 420–421
  boundaries of, 223
  changing uses of, 282–284
  as community of limited liability, 273–274
  crime problems and (*see* Crime)
  defined, 272–273
  density, effects of, 55
  facilities and institutions in, 274–275

Neighborhoods (*Cont.*):
  factors weakening, 272–273
  life cycle of, 332–335, 372
  "neighborhood movement" (voluntary associations), 276
  participation in, 273–289, 395–397
  racial transition in, 252–257
  redevelopment of, 343–347
  residential use of local facilities, 278–279, 283
  satisfaction with, 302–306
  social psychological uses of, 279–282
  types of, 287–289
  voluntary associations in, 275–277, 280–282
Neighboring, 279–280, 284, 389, 395–396, 411–414
Networks, social (*see* Social networks)
New York, N.Y., 116, 121–124, 236–239, 332–335, 414–416, 433, 446–447, 457–461
  slums in, 3–4, 433
Newark, N.J., 232–233, 343
Nomadism, 67–69
  fixed places, 69
Normal distribution of traits within populations, 50
Northwestern University research project, 308–315, 318
Nuclei, industrial city, 177

Occupational rankings, 207–208
Occupational segregation, 208–210
*Organization Man, The* (Whyte), 388
Overlay model of urban growth and form, 379–382

Pakistan, 79
Park Forest, Ill., 388
Participant observation (research method), 290–291
Participation in locality, 273–289, 395–397
Philadelphia, Pa., 58, 137, 357, 391
*Philadelphia Negro, The* (DuBois), 7–8
Pittsburg survey, 9–13
Police, 128, 129

Polish-American neighborhoods, 339–340
Polycentric city, 376–377
Population, natural increase in, 102, 104, 146–147
Population density, 335–337, 355, 360–363
  effects of, 46–47, 54–55, 222
  preurban, 68
Population growth, U.S., 145–146
Poverty, 124–126
Precautions against crime, 312–315, 318
Preferences, locational, 394
*Preindustrial City, The* (Sjoberg), 49
Proletariat, 108
Prostitution, 445–447
Pruitt-Igoe housing project (St. Louis, Mo.), 454–457
Public and private social worlds, 56, 317
Public housing, 451–459

Quasi-primary relationships, 49, 396

Racial segregation, levels and trends in, 245–246
  (*See also* Black ghetto)
Racial transition in neighborhoods, 252–257
Railroad suburbs, 357
Rats, crowded, experiments on, 54
Realms, urban, 377–379
Red-light districts, 445–447
Redlining, 243
Religion in urban development, 69, 75, 81, 85, 91
Residential sectors model of urban growth, 185
Restrictive covenant, 235–236
Retailing, suburban, 363–365, 375
Richmond, Va., 205
Riots, 121–124, 232–234
Rochester, N.Y., 283–284
Rome, 79–83
Rural and urban concepts, census definitions of, 139–141, 143
Rural-urban migration, 474–475

St. Louis, Mo., 454–457
San Francisco, Calif., 199–201, 243, 390

# SUBJECT INDEX

Satellite cities, 180, 369–370
Scale of analysis of urban studies, 36
Schools, 127, 128
Sector theory, 185
Sectors, residential, model of urban growth, 185
Segregation, 199, 206–224, 244–249
  of the elderly, 219–220
  by ethnicity, 211–217
  by household type, 217–219
  racial, levels and trends in, 245–246
  by socioeconomic status, 206–213
  theories of, 220–224
  (*See also* Ghetto)
Segregation index, 210–211, 244–245
Shopping malls, 363–365, 375
Skid row, 447–449
Slum:
  defined, 433–434
  and ghetto, analytical distinction between, 236
Slums, 109, 110, 124–126, 236, 295, 334–335, 432–465
  hazards in, 435–438
  health statistics for, 438
  uses of, 444–445
Small-world project, 422–423
Social area analysis, 199–202
Social construction of community, 57
Social differentiation, 195–199
Social networks, 56, 410–429
  defined, 411
  functions of, 424–426
  and job search, 420, 426–427
  kinship aspects of, 410–415, 418, 424–427
  and migration, 424–426
Social psychology, 53, 59
  of urban life, 37, 279–280, 395–400
Socioeconomic status, 199, 203, 205, 337, 370, 426
  segregation by, 206–213
Spatial differentiation, principles of, 171
Squatter settlements, 481–483
Standard Consolidated Statistical Area (SCSA), 144
Standard Metropolitan Statistical Area (SMSA), 143–145

Starfish pattern of urban development, 113, 115
Steelworkers, 290–291
Steering, 243
Stratification, 75–76, 81–83, 87–89, 108, 111, 120, 121, 221
  suburban, 373
Streetcar suburbs, 357
*Structure of the Metropolitan Community, The* (Bogue), 163–164
Subcultural theory of urbanism, 50–53, 59
Subcultures, 50–53
Subsistence urbanism, 480–483
Suburb, defined, 355
Suburban change, 372–373
Suburban employment, 365–367
Suburban ethnicity, 371
Suburban minicities, 368, 375–377
Suburban myth, 354, 386–388
Suburban stability, 372–373
Suburbanization, 354–369
  black, 262–265
Suburbs, 180, 262–265, 353–407
  aging populations of, 400–402
  history of growth of, 356–360
  manufacturing and office work in, 366, 367
  problems of, 402–403
  retailing in, 363–365, 375
  Swedish and European, comparison with U.S., 355–356
  teenagers in, 398–399
  women in, 399–400
Succession, residential, 337–340
Sumer and Sumerian cities, 74–77
Survey research methods, 292–293
Systems of cities, 158–164

Technology, 43
Teenagers, suburban, 398–399
Tenements, 3–4, 450
Third world:
  defined, 470–471
  urbanization in, 472–493
Tolerance, 56
Toronto, Canada, 302, 381, 411–414
Transportation, intraurban, 112, 113, 173
Trolley, 43, 112, 113, 130

Turf, urban, 57–58
Types (typology):
  of black neighborhoods, 258–260
  of cities, 164–165
  of neighborhoods, 287–289
  of residential areas, 200–201, 287–289

Ur, 73, 74
Urban imagery, 386
Urban life, 37, 279–280, 395–400
  social psychology of, 53, 59
Urban mental health, 55–56
Urban realms, 377–379
Urban renewal, 335, 343–347, 463
Urban revolution, 67, 73–78
Urban turf, 57–58
Urban villages, 288–295, 420–421
"Urbanism as a Way of Life" (Wirth), 44–50, 59, 222
Urbanization:
  defined, 151
  in India, 475–477, 488–489
  in Mexico, 477–478, 484
  third-world, 472–493
  U.S., 5, 150–158
  by region, 153–156
Use of local facilities, 278–279, 283

Villages:
  Neolithic, 71
  urban, 288–295, 420–421
Visible signs of disorder, 307, 311–312
Voluntary associations, 275–277, 280–282

Walls, city, 74, 77, 80, 85
Washington, D.C., 343–344
White flight, 260–262
Women:
  in cities, 316–321
  in suburbs, 399–400
Work and Residence, division of, 172–173
*Working-Class Suburb* (Berger), 389–390

Zones and zonal patterns, 116–120, 185
Zoning, 175–177

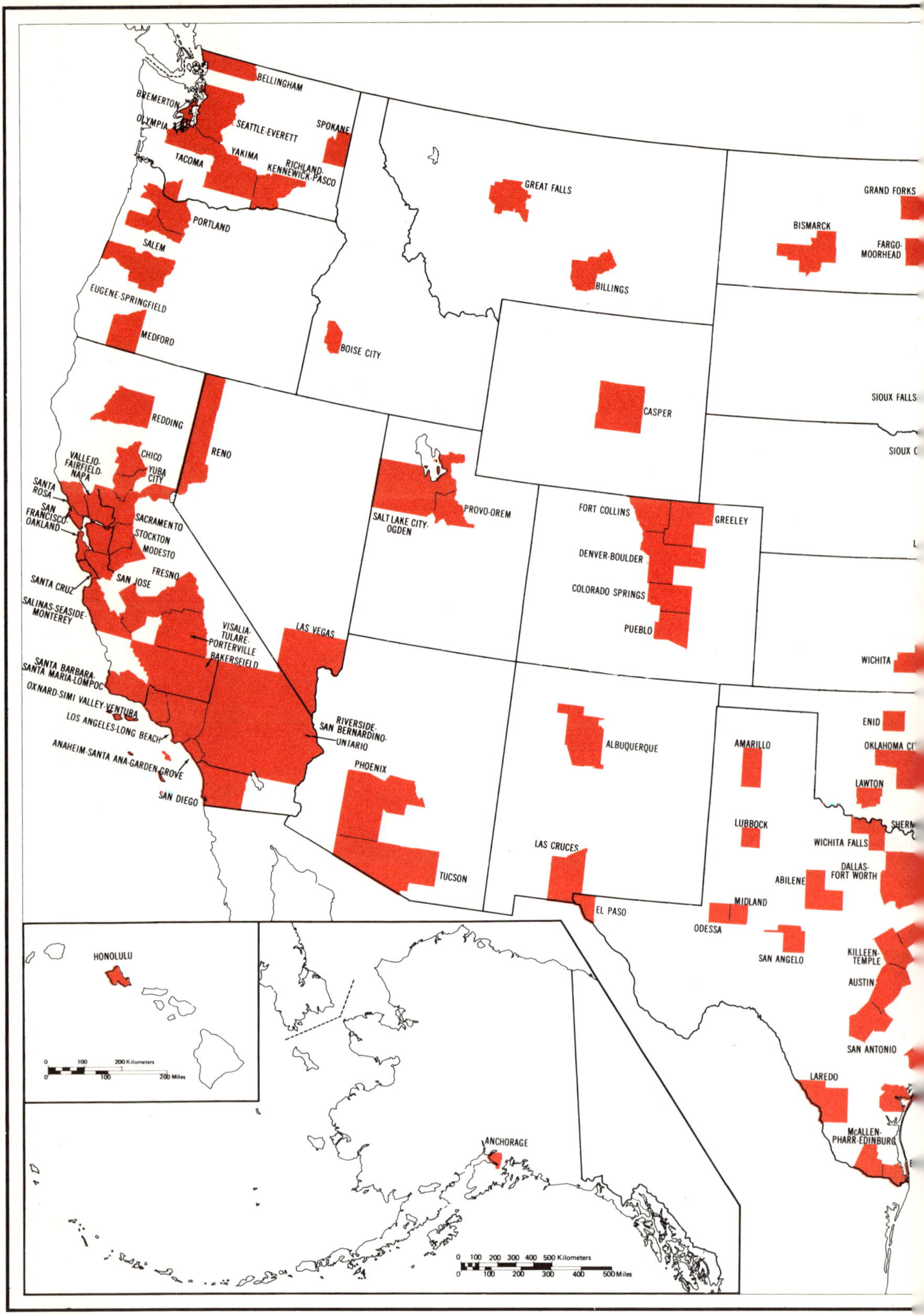
BELLINGHAM
BREMERTON
OLYMPIA
SEATTLE-EVERETT
SPOKANE
TACOMA
YAKIMA
RICHLAND-KENNEWICK-PASCO
PORTLAND
SALEM
EUGENE-SPRINGFIELD
MEDFORD
GREAT FALLS
BILLINGS
BOISE CITY
GRAND FORKS
BISMARCK
FARGO-MOORHEAD
SIOUX FALLS
CASPER
REDDING
RENO
CHICO
VALLEJO-FAIRFIELD-NAPA
YUBA CITY
SANTA ROSA
SAN FRANCISCO-OAKLAND
SACRAMENTO
STOCKTON
MODESTO
FRESNO
SAN JOSE
SANTA CRUZ
SALINAS-SEASIDE-MONTEREY
VISALIA-TULARE-PORTERVILLE
BAKERSFIELD
SANTA BARBARA-SANTA MARIA-LOMPOC
OXNARD-SIMI VALLEY-VENTURA
LOS ANGELES-LONG BEACH
ANAHEIM-SANTA ANA-GARDEN GROVE
SAN DIEGO
RIVERSIDE-SAN BERNARDINO-ONTARIO
LAS VEGAS
SALT LAKE CITY-OGDEN
PROVO-OREM
FORT COLLINS
GREELEY
DENVER-BOULDER
COLORADO SPRINGS
PUEBLO
WICHITA
PHOENIX
TUCSON
ALBUQUERQUE
LAS CRUCES
EL PASO
ENID
AMARILLO
LUBBOCK
LAWTON
WICHITA FALLS
ABILENE
DALLAS-FORT WORTH
MIDLAND
ODESSA
SAN ANGELO
KILLEEN-TEMPLE
AUSTIN
SAN ANTONIO
LAREDO
McALLEN-PHARR-EDINBURG
HONOLULU
ANCHORAGE
0 100 200 Kilometers
0 100 200 Miles
0 100 200 300 400 500 Kilometers
0 100 200 300 400 500 Miles